THE STATE OF GERMANY
The national idea in the making, unmaking and remaking of a modern nation-state

IN MEMORY OF BILL CARR
Professor William Carr, 1921–91

THE STATE
OF GERMANY

The national idea in the making, unmaking
and remaking of a modern nation-state

Edited by John Breuilly

Longman
London and New York

Longman Group UK Limited,
Longman House, Burnt Mill,
Harlow, Essex CM20 2JE, England
and Associated Companies throughout the world.

Published in the United States of America
by Longman Publishing, New York

First published 1992

British Library Cataloguing-in-Publication Data

A catalogue record for this book is
available from the British Library

ISBN 0 582 07864 4 CSD
ISBN 0 582 07865 2 PPR

Library of Congress Cataloging in Publication Data
The State of Germany: the national idea in the making, unmaking,
and remaking of a modern nation-state / edited by John Breuilly.
    p. cm.
  Includes bibliographical references and index.
  ISBN 0-582-07864-4 – ISBN 0-582-07865-2 (pbk.)
  1. Nationalism–Germany.   2. Germany–Politics and government.
I. Breuilly, John, 1946–
DD175.S85   1992
943. 08–dc20

Set by 7 in Bembo 10/12
Produced by Longman Singapore Publishers (Pte) Ltd.
Printed in Singapore

Contents

Contents

Notes on contributors

John Breuilly is Senior Lecturer in History at the University of Manchester. His publications include *Nationalism and the State* (1982); *Joachim Friedrich Martens und die Deutsche Arbeiterbewegung* (1984), and *Labour and liberalism in 19th century Europe* (1992). He is currently involved in a research project on the comparative cultural history of mid-19th-century Hamburg, Lyon and Manchester.

Michael Hughes is Senior Lecturer in History at University College of Wales, Aberystwyth. His publications include *Law and Politics in Eighteenth Century Germany* (1988), *Nationalism and Society: Germany 1800–1945* (1988), and *Early Modern Germany, 1477–1806* (1991).

James J. Sheehan is Dickason Professor in the Humanities and Professor of History at Stanford University. He is the author of *German Liberalism in the Nineteenth Century* (1978), *German History, 1770–1866* (1989), and other studies on modern German history. He is now working on the emergence of the German art museum as a social and cultural institution.

Dieter Langewiesche is Professor of Modern History at the University of Tübingen. His publications include *Liberalismus und Demokratie in Württemberg zwischen Revolution und Reichsgründung* (1974), *Liberalismus in Deutschland* (1988), and *Europa zwischen Restauration und Revolution 1815–1849* (2nd edn, 1989). Books he has edited include *Die deutsche Revolution von 1848/49* (1983), *Liberalismus im 19.Jahrhundert: Deutschland im europäischen Vergleich* (1988), and *Revolution und Krieg. Zur Dynamik historischen Wandels seit dem 18.Jahrhundert* (1989). He is currently engaged in research on Württemberg and Baden during the Third Reich.

William Carr was, until his death in June 1991, Professor Emeritus at the University of Sheffield. His publications include *Schleswig–Holstein,*

1815–1848: a study in national conflict (1963), *History of Germany 1815–1945* (1969, now in its 4th edn), *Arms, Autarky and Aggression* (1972), *Hitler: a study in personality and politics* (1978), *Poland to Pearl Harbour* (1985), and *Origins of the Wars of German Unification* (1991).

Katharine A. Lerman is Lecturer in Modern European History at St David's University College, Lampeter. Her publications include *The Chancellor as Courtier. Bernhard von Bülow and the Governance of Germany 1900–1909* (1990). She is presently working on a study of Bismarck.

William Sheridan Allen is Professor of History at the State University of New York at Buffalo. He is the author of articles on the theories of fascism and totalitarianism, the Holocaust, the German resistance to Hitler, and public opinion in the Third Reich as well as the following books: *The Nazi Seizure of Power* (1965; revised edn, 1984), and *The Infancy of Nazism* (1976).

Michael Burleigh is a Lecturer in International History at the London School of Economics and Political Science. His books include *Prussian Society and the German Order* (1984), *Germany Turns Eastwards: A Study of 'Ostforschung' in the Third Reich* (1988, 2nd edn 1990), (with Wolfgang Wipperman) *The Racial State: Germany 1933–1945* (1991). He is currently researching into the Nazi 'Euthanasia' programme and editing a *History Today* book on Nazi racial and social policy.

Peter Alter is deputy director of the German Historical Institute, London, and Professor of Modern History at the University of Cologne. His publications have been in the areas of Irish, British and German history. They include *The Reluctant Patron: Science and the State in Britain 1850–1920* (1987) and *Nationalism* (1989). He is currently writing on the *German Question and Europe*.

Mary Fulbrook is Reader in German History at University College, London. Her publications include *Piety and Politics: Religion and the rise of absolutism in England, Württemberg and Prussia* (1983), *A Concise History of Germany* (1990), *The Fontana History of Germany 1918–1990: The Divided Nation* (1991), and *The Two Germanies 1945–1990: Problems of Interpretation* (1992). She is joint editor of *German History: the Journal of the German History Society*. Her current research is into elites, dissent, and political culture in East Germany, 1945 to 1990.

Wolf D. Gruner is Professor of European History and European Studies at the University of Hamburg. He is the author of many articles on German, European and regional history and on relations between Germany and other European countries and has edited a book on *Gleichgewicht in Geschichte und Gegenwart*. His books include *Die deutsche Frage. Ein Problem der europäischen Geschichte seit 1800* (1985), *Die Rolle und Funktion von Kleinstaaten im internationalen System 1815–1914* (1985), *Bündische Formen deutscher Staatlichkeit in Geschichte und Gegenwart*, and *Deutschland mitten in Europa* (1991). He is at present writing a book on the German Confederation of 1816 to 1866.

List of abbreviations

CDU	Christlich-Demokratische Union (Christian Democratic Union)
CSU	Christlich-Soziale Union (Christian Social Union)
FDP	Freie Demokratische Partei (Free Democratic Party)
FRG	Federal Republic of Germany
GDR	German Democratic Republic
KPD	Kommunistische Partei Deutschlands (Communist Party of Germany)
NPD	Nationaldemokratische Partei Deutschlands (National Democratic Party of Germany)
NDSAP	Nationalsozialistische Deutsche Arbeiterpartei (National Socialist German Workers' Party)
SA	Sturmabteilung (Storm Troop)
SED	Sozialistische Einheitspartei (Socialist Unity Party)
SPD	Sozialdemokratische Partei Deutschlands (Social Democratic Party of Germany)

Preface

In November 1989 the Berlin Wall came down. By the end of 1990 the two German states had been reunited. Many Germans as well as non-Germans wonder what reunification means. Should one be concerned about the re-emergence of a powerful German nation-state, even if that power is based upon economic rather than military strength? Or should one consider that the changes that have taken place in Germany, in Europe, and in the world of international relations since 1945 mean that such concerns are misplaced, a product of historical preoccupations that have been rendered obsolete?

Much of this debate will focus on contemporary events and views about what is wholly new in Europe and Germany. However, it is important to question the historical perspectives that so often underlie contemporary understanding. When people refer to the 'German question', almost invariably the Germany which serves as a reference point is the unitary nation-state which existed between 1871 and 1945. How one understands the 'question' is then linked to one's view of that nation-state – its internal character, its foreign policy, and its own changing history. However, this perspective is misleading. It excludes the other 'Germanies' of the modern period – the Germany of the Holy Roman Empire, of the Napoleonic period, of the post-1815 Confederation, of the German National Assembly in 1848–9. It often neglects the point that before 1871, between 1871 and 1945, and after 1945 there was never a single, indeed often not even a dominant, idea of what Germany was or should be. Rather there were different, changing and conflicting views. Finally, the perspective can often assume some simple and direct connection between what Germans thought Germany should be like, and what in practice happened in Germany. Yet it may be that the actual nation-state of 1871 or 1919 or 1933 (and 1990?) did not express any 'idea' of Germany at all.

The purpose of this book is to recover something of the plurality, changeability and contingency of the idea of Germany. Most of the chapters – those by Hughes, Sheehan, Carr, Lerman, Burleigh, Fulbrook and Gruner – began life as talks in a series I organised in the academic year 1989–90 under the title of 'The Making and Unmaking of a Nation-State'. I asked each speaker to consider two particular questions. First, for the period and subject under consideration, what was meant by ideas such as German, Germany and nationality? Second, what, if any, were the political consequences of such ideas?

The idea for the series was conceived in the academic session 1988–89 and the speakers and topics fixed upon by the spring of 1989. Only during the course of the talks did the dramatic changes take place in Eastern Europe which led rapidly to German reunification. What had begun as primarily a question of historical understanding suddenly acquired a contemporary significance. It seemed to me that there was a very special merit in turning the talks into a book. There was a danger after November 1989, and especially after unification in 1990, that the flood of books and articles on the German question would be fixated on the present situation. Historical interpretation, insofar as it was introduced into the discussion, would run the danger of being too strictly subordinated to very immediate concerns. The theme of these talks was clearly central to any historical perspective on contemporary German events, but having been worked out before November 1989 had a valuable distance from those events.

There were omissions in the original series of talks which needed to be addressed in the book. The chapters start in the late eighteenth century, when ideas of political reform in 'Germany' were gathering pace. There was, however, a large chronological jump from James Sheehan's study of Napoleonic Germany to William Carr's consideration of German unification under Bismarck. Something on the national question in 1848 was needed, and Dieter Langewiesche agreed to write a chapter on this subject.

Michael Burleigh's fascinating study of a particular branch of academic study – the study of Eastern Europe – casts new light on continuities of national thinking from Weimar, through the Third Reich, to post-1945 Germany. However, it needed to be complemented by a study of the fate of nationalism under the Third Reich in more general terms, and this is undertaken by William Allen. Mary Fulbrook considers the ideas of nationality in the two Germanies which emerged out of the ruins of 1945 and Wolf Gruner looks at the place of Germany in contemporary Europe against a broad historical perspective. However, neither of them had much opportunity to consider the nature and importance of ideas of German nationality in immediate post-1945 Germany. Peter Alter has done this.

Other chronological omissions remain: on the restoration period 1815–48, on the character of Bismarckian Germany between 1871 and 1890, and on the Weimar Republic. However, it is not possible to include everything in a single book. Furthermore, the chapters on the preceding and succeeding periods cast light on these phases. In my Introduction I also try to trace broad continuities and changes for the whole time span covered by this book, and in particular to make points about these relatively neglected periods. Finally, in the Conclusion, in a necessarily speculative way, I turn to the prospects for a united Germany in the immediate future.

What is important is that the general reader, as well as specialists who focus on only one small part of modern German history, should be able to get from this book a sense of the varying, conflicting, changing meanings of terms like Germany, German and nation and an appreciation of the complicated and often surprising connections between such terms and the actual political history of modern Germany.

I would like to thank the contributors to this book. They all coped very well with their editor. I am happy to acknowledge the support of the Department of History at Manchester University which provided some financial support for the original series of talks. Above all, I wish to thank the Goethe Institut in Manchester, and especially its Director, Gerhard Murjahn. For a number of years the Institut has generously supported series of talks on modern German history. Without the Institut there would have been no talks and, therefore, no book. I would like also to thank Ian Kershaw for his advice on the Introduction and Conclusion.

William Carr sent me the final version of his chapter just a couple of weeks before his death on 20 June 1991, aged 70. His loss will be felt greatly by historians of modern Germany. His books, ranging from specialist studies to a very successful textbook on nineteenth- and twentieth-century Germany, have been a major contribution to our understanding of modern German history. He was also a wise and considerate friend of younger historians. This book is dedicated to his memory.

John Breuilly
Manchester
August 1991

CHAPTER ONE
The national idea in modern German history

John Breuilly

I

The history of Germany between 1871 and 1945 has been the subject of intensive study and strong, often violent disagreement. Could unification have taken place in some other way? Could the new nation-state have developed different political structures and pursued other foreign policies? How much of the responsibility for the world wars lay with those outside Germany? Should Hitler and National Socialism be understood as exclusively German phenomena – the culmination of a peculiar national history – or as an extreme version of a politics which could also be found in other parts of Europe? Those are questions which an interested reader can pursue in many other books (see Further Reading). This book has a rather different, though closely related theme: the character of the national idea in German history and its political significance.

Before this theme can be approached properly it is necessary to put aside certain ways in which modern history, especially German history, is commonly understood. The unitary nation-state of 1871–1945 serves as the reference point for our understanding of all modern German history. More generally, the unitary nation-state is commonly regarded, whether for good or bad, as the 'normal' political unit of the modern period. The history of modern Europe is seen as the history of the rise of the nation-state. Older political units were destroyed through this process – both small polities such as city-states, bishoprics, archbishoprics and petty princedoms, and also the large multi-national dynasties. Germany is one example of this process. The Holy Roman Empire, made up of these kinds of political units, was destroyed with the rise of the territorial state, and eventually the most powerful of those states – Prussia – eliminated the remaining small states and expelled the multi-national Habsburg dynasty from Germany in order to construct a nation-state.

That process is one side of the equation – namely the destruction of other kinds of states. The other side of the equation is what makes the new state a *nation*-state. This is generally assumed to be a sense of national identity within the population of the new state. A history of the creation of Germany is, therefore, a history both of the way in which Prussia constructed a new state and of the development and growth of a sense of national identity, most strongly expressed in the form of nationalism. The historians who celebrated the story of unification, known as the *kleindeutsch* (little German, meaning a Germany under Prussian leadership which excluded Austria) or Borussian or Prussian school of history, saw that story in terms of the convergence and eventual joining together of Prussian state power and German national feeling. It is most evident in the unfinished history of nineteenth-century Germany written by Heinrich von Treitschke.[1] In that study chapters alternate between Prussian-centred political history and German-centred cultural history.

This story can also be seen as one specific variant on a general theme in modern history. Many historians begin their narratives of the formation of this or that nation-state by looking at the origins of a sense of national identity and the construction of early nationalist movements, and then go on to connect that to the formation of new states. Conversely, the ways in which the German case is understood have shaped general views of nationalism and state formation. In his influential book *Nationalism* Kedourie starts with the striking sentence:

> Nationalism is a doctrine invented in Europe at the beginning of the nineteenth century.[2]

Germany serves as a major example for Kedourie's argument. In that argument, the history of the formation of a nation-state is the history of how nationalism moves from being a doctrine at the political margins to becoming the central ideology of the modern state. So general views of nationalism and understandings of the history of German nationalism are inextricably linked. It is necessary, therefore, to look critically not only at specific interpretations of German nationalism but also at ways of approaching the subject of modern nationalism generally.

It is easier to criticise the view that the formation of the German nation-state was inevitable, the German variant of a modern pattern, than to replace it. Many criticisms are no more than variations upon that view, arguing for example that the Prusso-German state could

1. H. von Treitschke, *Deutsche Geschichte im 19. Jahrhundert*, 5 vols, (Leipzig, 1879–94; Königstein, 1981). There is a seven-volume English translation (London, 1915–19).
2. E. Kedourie, *Nationalism* (London, 1971), p. 9.

have evolved in a liberal direction or that there is no essential continuity between the national ideas that prevailed in imperial Germany,
in the Weimar Republic and in the Third Reich. However, the unitary nation-state still serves as the reference point, only it is now associated with different views about its character or potential. Sometimes
one teleology replaces another. Thus those historians who look back
to the 'federalism' of the Holy Roman Empire and the German Confederation to find models for how contemporary Germany (and Europe) might evolve; or who focus on the German National Assembly
of 1848–9 and the Weimar Republic in order to locate a liberal and
parliamentary tradition, can be as guilty of a selective distortion of
German history as those who take the unitary, illiberal and expansionist qualities of the German nation-state as its 'essential' features. In this
introduction I wish to question this search for an 'essential' Germany,
by showing how changeable and contingent were ideas of German
nationality. Having argued that, however, I will go on to connect the
argument to broader interpretations of nationalism in order to show
that one does not have then to go to the opposite extreme of seeing
German nationalism and the formation of a German nation-state as
historical accidents, whether lucky or unlucky.

II

> There must be some special magic in this word 'German'. One can see
> that each person calls 'German' whatever it suits him and whatever assists
> his party standpoint. Thus the use of the word changes according to
> requirements.[3]

So opined Bismarck in 1864, shortly after coming to power as minister-president of Prussia. He was as guilty of this charge as anyone.

The chapter by Michael Hughes demonstrates a variety of meanings
for terms such as German and Germany in the last decades of the Holy
Roman Empire. For some the terms were deliberately emptied of political content. The passage from Schiller which is quoted by Hughes

---

3. A Bismarck speech of 22 January 1864 before the Prussian *Landtag*. Quoted in
W. Mommsen, *Stein, Ranke, Bismarck: ein Beitrag zur politischen und sozialen Bewegung*
(Munich, 1954), p. 187. For the full text see *Bismarck: Werke in Auswahl: Vol. 3* (Stutt-
gart, 1965), pp. 231–8 (231). *My translation*.

sees in political power a snare and delusion, insisting rather that German greatness be sought outside, even against the world of politics. Even that has to be treated with some scepticism, however, as Schiller expressed this sentiment when French power was already penetrating the German lands. 'Cultural' greatness could perhaps serve as a compensation for political quiescence. What is more, Schiller expressed a form of cultural elitism. Although Schiller, Goethe and others used German as the vehicle for expressing their ideas, their elevated notion of art disabled them from becoming truly popular figures in their own time. Their transformation into literary giants who prepared Germany culturally for a later stage of political greatness was a posthumous construction.

Hughes focuses upon those who sought political reform within the Holy Roman Empire. The great problem here is that the Holy Roman Empire, though clearly 'German' in some sense, appears wholly unfitted politically as a vehicle for nation-state formation, whereas the territorial states of the time, so clearly the political model for the later nation-state, possessed little of that 'German' quality. Hughes shows that we must not measure the Holy Roman Empire against a model of the territorial state into which all sovereignty is concentrated. Nevertheless, he also rightly warns us against the recent trend to argue that the Holy Roman Empire really was capable of reform. With the rejuvenation of French power after 1789 it became increasingly apparent that the sovereign territorial state, resting on some kind of popular legitimacy, would destroy all other kinds of states. It was in the Napoleonic period, which witnessed the destruction of the Holy Roman Empire, that ideas of the sovereign territorial state with clear frontiers and a constitutional relationship to its subjects took hold in the German lands.

This might suggest that the political ideas Hughes discusses had no significance. They were part of the vocabulary of an obsolete and failed political structure. Dalberg, for example, who is considered as a would-be imperial reformer in the 1780s by Hughes, clearly fails when he seeks, by means of collaboration with Napoleon, to continue with a programme of German political reform. Yet one needs to appreciate that Dalberg remained politically significant. Men who had learned their politics in the Holy Roman Empire were involved in drawing up various schemes for the organisation of Germany which were discussed with increased vigour as the defeat of Napoleon moved from the realm of fantasy to that of possibility and then to that of fact. Rather than see German nationalism at this time as an anticipation of a later German nation-state or as one way of expressing some 'essential' German idea, we should therefore regard it as one aspect of a political culture which was fast becoming obsolete.

The reason it was becoming obsolete was because the most important political developments went on at the level of the territorial state, as Sheehan makes abundantly clear in his chapter. The term 'patriot', both in and beyond the German lands, principally meant reformers who wished to create some popular legitimacy for their particular state. Thus it makes sense to call Montgelas a Bavarian patriot, or Stein and Hardenberg Prussian patriots. As Sheehan also makes clear, the reform programmes of these patriots were motivated by the need to strengthen states which had been desperately weakened by French successes. That applied to 'collaborator' states such as Bavaria, Baden and Württemberg which had won new territory as much as it did to 'resister' states such as Austria and Prussia which had lost territory. Indeed, it is the distinction between reforming patriots and their conservative opponents which is more important than that between those who would work with or fight against Napoleon. Most Prussian reformers, for example, saw no alternative to collaboration with Napoleon until the failure of the Russian campaign at the end of 1812. Even Baron Stein, revered as a German patriot who fought unremittingly against Napoleon, helped administer those parts of Hannover Napoleon gave to Prussia in 1805 and spent a large part of his time as Prussian first minister in 1807–8 negotiating a peace settlement with France.

Sheehan focuses on the reforming process within the territorial states which came to dominate the German lands after 1806. Here I would just draw attention to the marginal role any notion of *German* patriotism played during those years. First, there were the nationalist intellectuals. These picked up on the ideas of the German cultural elitists such as Schiller. They also drew upon Herder who had argued that each nation, identified largely by its language, had a unique character and value. Perhaps the best known is Fichte who, in his lectures of 1808, *Addresses to the German Nation*, developed this Herderian notion, arguing that the language needed to be preserved in all its purity and that there should be an organised programme of education to make Germans aware of their national character. Berlin was still occupied by French troops at this stage and the French censor considered it advisable to allow Fichte to lecture, in part because a programme of educational and cultural renewal presented no threat to the French, unlike any advocacy of guerrilla warfare or popular insurrection. Prussia remained almost wholly quiescent under French control, in marked contrast to countries such as Spain and Russia.

There were other German patriots who were closer to political power than these intellectuals and who advocated more immediate resistance. The best known of these is Baron Stein. An imperial knight who had been 'abolished' by Napoleon's reforms, he had also been a long-serving official in the Prussian service. He had risen to ministerial status in the unreformed administration before 1806 and began to counsel reform only in the months immediately following the military defeats of October 1806. These limited reform proposals, and especially the violent manner in which he pressed them upon the king, led to his dismissal for 'insolence' in January 1807. He retired to Nassau where he wrote a famous reform memorandum, the Nassau Denkschrift. This over-praised document focused upon civil reform designed to increase civic participation and reduce government expenditure, but ignored entirely the pressing problems of military expenditure and relations with France. He was appointed chief minister in October 1807 and served for almost exactly a year before being dismissed on Napoleon's insistence.

There was Stein, the patriotic reformer dedicated to strengthening the Prussian state and realistically negotiating with France. There was also the Stein who dreamed of a rising against the French, inspired by the Spanish insurrection of 1808. After his dismissal Stein resided in Austria and advised the government there which declared war on France in 1809. In the propaganda build-up to this war, in which the Austrian government hoped to obtain support from other parts of Germany whose governments were allied with Napoleon, sentiments of German patriotism were invoked. Incidentally, Herder's idea of connecting German patriotism to 'folk' culture had more impact in the Austrian court, where the Empress and others wore 'peasant' costumes at balls, than it did in Berlin which was still much influenced by the Francophile contempt in which Frederick II had held most things German. Thus German patriotism had different meanings at this time, and it is misleading to make much of any particular connection to Prussia.

The war proved short and disastrous for Austria. It brought Metternich to power in Vienna with a policy which insisted on collaboration with Napoleon, a repudiation of patriotic state reform, and an intense suspicion of German national sentiments or ideas of appealing to popular forces beyond the control of the existing government. Stein now removed himself to Russia. As Franco-Russian relations deteriorated after 1810, so Stein became an adviser to Tsar Alexander. In 1812 he was joined by patriots from Prussia who could not accept the military alliance their king had made with Napoleon. Stein was charged with the task of administering occupied areas in Germany after the failure of Napoleon's Russian campaign and the advance of Russian soldiers into central Europe.

It does make sense, therefore, to call Stein a German patriot and, furthermore, one who had considerable political influence. But what kind of patriot was he and what kind of influence did he possess?

In a famous letter of 1812 Stein expressed his patriotic sentiments.

> I have only one fatherland, and that is Germany, and because according to the old constitution I belong to that and not simply to any part of that fatherland, so am I committed to the whole fatherland and not to any one part of it. To me the dynasties at this moment of great developments are a matter of complete indifference. My wish is that Germany will be great and strong, in order that it win back its standing and independence and nationality and assert itself in its position between France and Russia.[4]

The passage repays close attention. At first glance, one might see Stein as being animated by traditional imperial patriotism of the kind analysed by Hughes. The reference to the 'old constitution', his own status as a deposed imperial knight, his intense hatred for the French satellite states which were created out of the destruction of the Holy Roman Empire: all seem to bear this out. But there are contrary indications. Stein was himself one of these collaborators in 1803–6 as Prussia also profited from the destruction of the Holy Roman Empire. One must remember that the letter which is quoted was to Graf Münster, a representative of the old Hannoverian interest, and Münster wished to be assured that Stein no longer served Prussia, a regional rival that might stand in the way of a Hannoverian restoration or that he was too closely tied to Russian interests which had, after all, in 1807 largely confirmed Napoleon's position in Germany.[5] Above all, it was the very exclusion of Stein from state power which led him to German patriotism. The Napoleonic satellite states, Prussia and Austria had all failed – Germany became a substitute idea.

It is also clear that Stein recognised that simple imperial restoration would not suffice; the old Holy Roman Empire was too weak a structure to assert itself between France and Russia. Equally, he was not thinking in terms of the construction of any kind of unitary national state. There is little evidence that Stein saw any close connection be-

---

4. Stein to Graf Münster, quoted in G. Ritter, *Stein: eine politische Biographie* (Stuttgart, 1981), p. 408. For the full text of the letter see *Freiherr vom Stein: Briefe und amtliche Schriften*, vol. 3 (Stuttgart, 1961), pp. 817–18. My translation.

5. Indeed, this is made clear in the opening of the letter which is usually omitted from quotations in secondary sources. What is more, suspicion of Stein's Russian connections and of his lack of concern with specifically Prussian interests created hostility between Stein and Prussian patriots such as Yorck in 1813–14.

tween language and 'cultural' nationality on the one hand, and citizenship and political loyalty on the other. He defended the inclusion of Poles in the Prussian state on the grounds that the Hohenzollern dynasty could rule in a way that would satisfy both German and Polish speakers. From 1814 when a post-war settlement had to be considered, his main concern seems to have been with the way in which Prussia and Austria as the major (but not the only) German powers could cooperate with one another and the remainder of the German lands to prevent a power vacuum developing.

Arguably this was precisely what was aimed at in the 1814–15 peace settlement, and in particular in the form of the German Confederation. Stein objected to the way in which the Napoleonic creations such as Baden and Bavaria were preserved, but the general idea behind the Confederation fitted in with many of his patriotic ideas.

One can draw a number of conclusions from this. First, German patriotism was marginal in the Napoleonic period. At a popular level loyalties to confession, region, narrow self-interest, and traditional rulers prevented any conception of German identity playing a significant role. Indeed, it was only where such loyalties were even stronger – as in Spain and Russia – that a kind of populist resistance to Napoleon developed. However, it would be quite misleading to see this as having anything in common with modern nationalism, although nationalist myth-makers recruit such resistances to their cause. For modern patriotism, in which state and nation are connected by ideas of culture and constitutionality, one has to turn to France and England at this time. As yet modern political movements in Germany were starting to develop only within the newly forming territorial states formed out of the destruction of the old Germany. At that political level it was the battles between reformers and conservatives within the modernising territorial states which mattered most. German ideas could be used in those battles and in the conflict with Napoleon, but they could be used by Austrians as well as Prussians. Ideas of cultural nationality could also be used by other states, without any implication of a related political programme. In 1808 the Bavarian government invited Goethe to draw up a German *Volksbuch*, intended to make clear the cultural glories of Germany. Goethe declined the invitation, but what is interesting is that the government asked him, seeing no conflict between such an enterprise and the attempt to build up the Bavarian state, a Napoleonic creation and ally. Genuine German patriotism tended to be disassociated from the centres of political power and sometimes took a cultural form which actually implied political quiescence. Where, as with Stein, it had a political focus, it was fluid, changing according to circumstances, and rarely, if ever, thinking about state reform in unitary and national terms.

It is from this perspective that it is valuable to look at the German Confederation established in 1814–15. The Confederation has generally had a bad press. For those historians who look to some long-standing German tradition of 'federalism', it is far inferior to the Holy Roman Empire. It did not last nearly as long. It could appear the instrument of Austria and Prussia, unable to provide liberties and protections for the less powerful as had been – sometimes – the case in the old Empire. For those historians who look forward to modern statehood – unitary, national, rooted in popular sovereignty – the Confederation appears equally deficient.

Neither of these models could have been achieved in 1814–15. The catastrophic failure of the old empire, the destruction of the many small states in the south and west, including the temporal power of the Catholic Church, ruled out restoration. Austria and Prussia, both anxious to check the power of the other, were compelled instead to work with the medium-sized states which Napoleon had created. There were exceptions. The 'pure' satellite states of Westphalia and Berg, ruled by relatives or cronies of Napoleon, were abolished; the British interest required the restoration of Hannover; the need to compensate Prussia in Germany for loss of Polish territory, combined with the failure of Saxony to abandon Napoleon before the Battle of Leipzig in October 1813, led to the transfer of northern Saxony to Prussia. But the major Napoleonic creations in southern Germany – Baden, Bavaria and Württemberg – ruled by native German princes, were preserved.

Precisely the same forces prevented anything other than a confederal arrangement. Hardly anyone with political power thought of, let alone wanted, a unitary nation-state or modern constitutional arrangements. It would have raised institutional and boundary questions which many statesmen would not have understood, let alone answered. Neither, however, did they think purely in terms of a system of totally independent states in the German lands. The failure of the Confederation to develop powerful confederal institutions has led historians to underestimate the 'restoration' intentions at work in 1814–15. Statesmen then did not think, as we do, of states as territorially compact concentrates of sovereignty. Their political culture was of the kind described by Michael Hughes. Notions such as a confederal army, confederal courts, constitutional 'harmonisation' in which central governments would be reined in by estate assemblies, and the retention of special political privileges by some of the casualties of the

Napoleonic transformation, such as the imperial knights – all made sense within this political culture. They also made sense to those who were concerned that lack of coordination between the German states could create a dangerous power vacuum, and that vesting too much power into the hands of central government, even if this took the form of bureaucracy commanded by monarchy, might promote some of the levelling purposes of the French Revolution.

Many of these intentions came to nought. The individual states did increasingly become the centres of power. This was most obvious in the way the Confederation came to be used by Austria and Prussia as an instrument for interference in the affairs of other states. But, less obviously, the fact that Austria and Prussia *had* to interfere in this way, through the use of political power rather than by means of constitutional conventions as in the old Empire, also showed that these other states were strengthening their central institutions. Finally, Austro-Prussian conflict on such matters as a confederal army prevented any practical achievements. The fact that the institutions which created this territorial state-power were bureaucratic rather than parliamentary has often meant that historians whose criteria of modernity are liberal as well as national have failed to see the modernising character of the Confederation and its individual members.

The changes introduced in 1814–15 altered the political meaning of the idea of German nationality. Older political idioms drawing upon imperial traditions, sometimes newly flavoured with romantic or Catholic ingredients, came to seem more and more irrelevant, taking on an increasingly precious and reactionary character. Individual states, especially the Bavarian monarchy, promoted values of cultural Germandom, but did not see this as in any way charged with political implications that would threaten them.

Where German nationality did take on a new political significance was in relation to the development of modern state power. In a positive way, above all in Prussia, German nationality could be seen as an ally to state interest. Prussia had become a much more 'German' power in 1814–15 – losing Polish territories, acquiring new lands in central and western Germany, and facing the problem of a territorial division between her two western provinces and the rest of the state. Austria, by contrast, had opted in 1814–15 to exercise her influence in Germany by 'indirect' means and had made her major territorial gains elsewhere.

The national idea was also taken up by some opposed to modernising but illiberal states. Liberal opponents of many of the smaller princes, for example, found that they were blocked as much by Confederal

interference as by their own ruler. This led them towards a programme of national as well as state reform and also encouraged contacts between like- minded opponents in the various states. Increased
literacy, the growth of a 'public opinion' which modernising states
inadvertently created even as they also practised censorship, the multi-
plication of contacts across regions and states – all this gave a cultural
underpinning to elite liberal nationalism.

There were other kinds of oppositions. For example, the construction of larger states created religious minorities. Rhenish Catholics had
become an important minority within Prussia, adding their numbers to
those of Catholic Germans in provinces such as Silesia; Protestants in
Franconia and in the Palatinate constituted a large minority in Bavaria.
To the old conflicts between the confessions were added new conflicts
as a modernising, increasingly secular state sought powers in such areas
as education and marriage. Very often such minorities saw in more
powerful national institutions a means of reducing the interference of
the individual state. The same was true of artisans and peasants, vil-
lagers and townspeople, who rejected many of the innovations imposed upon them from the state capital.

This made the national idea a widespread, even a popular one by
1848, yet an idea which was unclear and to which people subscribed
for diverse and even contradictory reasons. Dieter Langewiesche shows
in his chapter how many of the illusions associated with the idea of
nationality were exposed in 1848–9, and how the 'springtime of nations' turned into a winter of discontent and national conflict. At the
same time, the German National Assembly clearly steered the national
idea in a liberal and modernist direction. It became increasingly clear
that a national state would have to be a sovereign and territorial state;
plans for some other way of sharing power were discredited. That in
turn meant that clear views were required as to the institutional features and boundaries of such a state. It also became clear in 1848–9
that Austria as a multi-national dynasty could never accept such a state.
However, it was not clear that Prussia, a dual nationality dynasty,
could be much more positive.

Thus a convergence between liberal nationalism and the Prussian
state was by no means inevitable. Clearly, however, 1848–9 had made
any other possible convergence between state power and nationality
unrealistic. The advocates of *Realpolitik* who argued the national role
of Prussia did so, therefore, by bolstering the negative point that no
other solution was possible with the argument that 'progress', understood as a kind of unstoppable historical force, would compel a convergence between Prussian power and German nationality. Many

liberal nationalists, both within and outside Prussia, did not believe that Prussia could play a positive role in creating a nation-state until she herself liberalised, and saw such liberalisation coming about as a consequence of economic and social progress. Many conservative Prussians also believed that a national Prussia would also be a liberal Prussia, and therefore opposed any abandonment of the dualist partnership with Austria.

The way in which Bismarck managed to overcome this political division is described by William Carr in his chapter and need not be considered further here. I would only add that a unique feature of Bismarck's thinking was that he accepted much of the case put forward by the liberal *Realpolitiker*. If and when Prussia 'went forth'[6] into Germany she would eventually have to concede constitutionalism and cooperate with progressive social and economic interests. However, he believed also that this could be done on terms which would preserve much of the old order, though conservatism would have to re-found itself in modern conditions.

What is also clear from Carr's chapter is how risky was Bismarck's course and how easily it might have failed. Neither the arguments of inevitability nor of Bismarck's diplomatic genius should obscure that basic point. Furthermore, there was no groundswell of national feeling in 1866–7 to support Bismarck. What also needs to be stressed is that the achievements of 1866–7 could, from a 'national' perspective, be better described as a *division* rather than a unification. The Confederation was destroyed; Austria was excluded from contacts with other German states; the south German states were tied militarily and economically to Prussia but struggled against further political connections; and in northern Germany a 'greater Prussia' was created as most of the new territories were annexed as new provinces. No wonder many nationalists opposed what Bismarck had done.

The 'completion' of unity in 1870–1 stands in a complicated relationship to what had been created in 1866–7. On the one hand, the Second Empire was more German and less Prussian. The war of 1870–1 had been one between nations, unlike the 'civil war' of 1866. The south German states were not annexed to Prussia but preserved, and this required the creation of more powerful 'German' institutions through which they could be connected to Prussia. However, the state was accordingly less unitary than the greater Prussia of 1867, its 'constitution' taking the form of a treaty between states rather than formu-

6. Frederick Willian IV in March 1848 had declared that Prussia would 'go forth' into Germany.

lating the desired relationship between a state and its citizens. Consequently the federalism of the Second Empire took the form of tolerating different kinds of governments, rather than devolving power from the centre on a uniform basis.

As a consequence, a major tension within the new state concerned how far the national idea should be associated with reform and change designed to create a more unitary and uniform state and society. The problem for those conservatives at the centre of power was that their desire to defend the status quo conflicted with the need to undertake reform in order to preserve or enhance the power of the new state. The national idea was taken up by reformers to justify the erosion of state rights, and the concentration of greater powers into national institutions. National liberals were the principal spokesmen for such a programme, but their arguments could also be taken up by radicals and even socialists who could see in this a way of undermining a state-based conservatism. However, precisely this kind of pressure could force national liberals into an increasingly illiberal definition of their programme – for example, deprecating parliament as a cockpit of factions which would undermine national unity. By the 1880s the national idea had been shorn of much of its liberal, reformist character and was used instead as a call to the defence of existing institutions, above all the army and the monarchy. New institutions, for example the navy, were supported only where their authoritarian character ensured they would not fall prey to 'factions', that is the popular parties which opposed the liberals. Indeed, it would not be going too far to say that national arguments in defence of the status quo had increasingly become the central component of national liberal as well as conservative ideology. This could obscure the national commitment of their political opponents.

National institutions acquired greater powers thereafter not so much because this was seen as ideologically desirable by those in power, but rather because it was a practical necessity. Innovations in such fields as welfare and warfare (health insurance, navy-building) could be undertaken only by the central state, and so new agencies had to be set up to carry out these tasks. As Kathy Lerman makes clear in her chapter on Chancellor Bülow, this presented insoluble problems to a conservative who both took up the national idea as a rallying cry and as a programme of military and colonial assertion, and yet at the same time tried to practise a 'do-nothing' conservatism.

The result was incoherence. One can see this at the level of national symbols. The symbols of the nineteenth-century nationalist movement – the colours of black–red–gold, a unitary constitution, a national hymn or anthem: this all came into conflict with the federalist, state-rights, monarchist traditions which the German Empire tried to preserve. The result was a flag which uneasily combined German with Prussian colours, the lack of an official national anthem until 1922, and a 'pragmatic' constitution which was placed over the constitutions of individual states, was never revised, and which could not, therefore, take proper account of the increasing power of national institutions.

Yet that increased power had to find some expression in political consciousness. Political regionalism declined in the Second Empire. By 1914 political opposition, be it Catholic or socialist or radical, was largely focused on Berlin and organised by nationwide bodies. Participation in the state increased – measured by voting, membership of political parties and other organisations, those affected by national welfare and educational policies, or those serving in the armed forces. More generally, industrial and urban growth, and mass literacy had created a sphere of public opinion which governments could not ignore. Many of these new participants did not like the way national institutions functioned. By 1912 most voters voted for parties opposed to existing arrangements. Specifically nationalist policies on such matters as colonies and navy-building were as vehemently opposed as they were supported. Right-wing nationalism was itself riven by the tensions between energetic and populist imperialism and defence of the status quo.

Nevertheless, the mere existence of Germany as a powerful and in many respects successful state transformed the scope and character of the national idea. There were two aspects to this. First, at the institutional level it was clear by 1914 that political habits had been created by people who had known nothing other than the Second Empire. Arguably 'political identity' should be understood as the assumptions which accompany such political habits, rather than a separate set of reflections which are deliberately communicated to the population. Second, it was in the last decades before 1914 that a genuinely industrial society was created and which made possible, in a linguistically and ethnically fairly homogeneous society, the development of 'standard national culture'.[7]

As a consequence, by 1914 few German speakers in the German Empire thought of Germany as anything other than the territory of that Empire, and of themselves as anything other than national members of that state. This was the basis of a latent sense of national identity which extended beneath the level of everyday political conflict. The extent of this was made clear in August 1914 when Germans of

7. See E. Gellner, *Nations and Nationalism* (Oxford, 1983) for this idea and how it is connected to industrialism.

all political persuasions rallied to the country. Although many of the internal political divisions had re-emerged by 1918, at the same time the war constituted a national experience far beyond any earlier event.

The problem was how to give this strong sense of national identity political expression after the war. The images of the Weimar Republic are so frequently those of division and weakness, that it is necessary to emphasise the strengths and agreements which were also important. The Weimar Republic was, by twentieth-century standards, a more 'national' state than the Second Empire. It was federalist, granting large powers to the constituent states. However, this was constitutional federalism which devolved that power in a systematic and uniform way, quite unlike the federalism of the Second Empire. Sovereignty now resided with an elected parliament, a national institution in a way in which the Hohenzollern monarchy never had been. There was an official national anthem and the adoption of the black-red-gold national colours.[8] Although some writers have seen Weimar continuing traditions of federalism from earlier centuries, I would rather stress that this was in many ways the first unitary nation-state in German history.

Furthermore, there was a significant, if limited and often implicit political consensus. Few wished to return to the monarchical order. The Second Empire, by losing the war, had discredited itself. Few accepted the justice of the Versailles peace settlement – the difference was rather between those who believed there was no choice but to accept the settlement and then to seek gradual revision and those who advocated rejection of the settlement. William Allen in his chapter draws attention to the widespread acceptance of the nation-state and national identity, even extending to the German Communist Party. What is more, one must bear in mind how Weimar survived major crises – the immediate post-war turmoil, the multiple crises of 1923, and for nearly four years the greatest depression known to modern capitalism, although of course that ultimately was the major cause of the downfall of the republic. Its institutions survived longer than those of liberal democracy in post-war Italy. Its fate was not exceptional: east of the Rhine, only one liberal democracy created at the Versailles settlement still survived by 1938 – namely Czechoslovakia. The 'failure' of Weimar has to be put in that perspective.

All that said, it is also clear that Weimar suffered from grave weak-

8. Furthermore, the declaration of the national colours is presented as an end in itself at the beginning of the constitution (Article 3). In the constitution of 1871 the adoption of the colours black-white-red are presented as a technical consequence of having a 'German' navy and merchant marine, coming in Article 55 in a section on shipping and navigation.

nesses. Many could not accept its legitimacy, viewing it as the product of defeat, the work of those who had collaborated with Germany's wartime enemies. The range and depth of political divisions made it impossible to create stable parliamentary government in which power alternated between parties or groups of parties which all accepted the constitution. Much power remained out of the control of public authorities – in the hands of big business, the army, the bureaucracy, and these groups in turn felt no commitment to the republic. Few accepted the boundaries of the state as final and legitimate, although the extent as well as the character of boundary revision was a matter of dispute. So although a territorial, sovereign national state, the territory, the sovereign institutions, and even the claim to patriotism were all matters of bitter dispute.

What this meant was that in times of crisis the national idea – an idea which was almost universally accepted in some form or another – could be turned into a weapon against government and parliament. The national idea meant unity whereas parliament meant division; it meant strength whereas the republic was weak. How it came about that Hitler and the National Socialist movement were best able to exploit the national idea in these ways is something which cannot be considered here. It is a complex story on which there is a mass of literature. (See Further Reading.) I would stress only two points. First, Hitler's success was predicated on the basis of a near universal acceptance of the nation-state as the political norm, coupled with a widespread rejection of the Weimar Republic as the legitimate form of that nation-state. Second, for most Germans the attraction of Hitler lay in the novel and energetic way in which he subscribed to that national consensus. It was not the specifically Nazi components of his ideology (anti-Semitism, race-centred nationalism, the drive for living space in the east) which appealed so much as the belief that he and his party had a better chance than most (and at least deserved an opportunity) of creating strong government which would tackle the problems besetting Germany.

The problem for the historian of the national idea in the Third Reich is, therefore, to relate this 'mainstream' nationalism (which itself had conservative, liberal and radical variants) to the specifically Nazi components of nationalism. In a particularly illuminating way this is what Michael Burleigh does, showing how right-wing nationalists of Weimar could, through a combination of ideological shifts and opportunist adjustments, make the transition to Nazi ideas of blood and race. This is important for the light it casts upon the relationship between more traditional forms of nationalism and the radical nationalism of National Socialism.

How far most Germans ever came to accept distinctively national socialist ideas is a difficult and contentious subject. Clearly foreign policy successes which did not merely undo Versailles but went further (e.g. the Anschluß with Austria) could evoke some popular response. This might be taken to mean that for many Germans the idea of Germany extended beyond the Germany of 1871, let alone that of 1919. On the other hand, it might be taken to mean that the citizens of a country which identify with it as their nation will normally accept increases in its power and territory if these do not appear to involve great sacrifice on their part. Indeed, William Allen goes further and argues that the fear that such sacrifices might be called for far outweighed pleasure in the triumphs.

I think one has to make some distinctions between these various phases of foreign policy and domestic responses. The Austrian enthusiasm for the Anschluß, for example, should be regarded less as the expression of a long-standing desire to be a part of Germany than as another bitter response to the defeat of 1914–18 and the internal crises which beset Austria in the 1930s. After all, the pan-German movement of Schönerer before 1914 had never commanded widespread support. The anti-Semitism of Austria in 1938 could in turn be linked to the feelings of crisis in the country. Certainly it was far stronger in Vienna than in Berlin. It was, after all, in Vienna that Hitler had learnt his anti-Semitism. Very different appears to be the response of Reich Germans, who were much cooler towards the union and took much less active a role in anti-Semitic actions.[9] This has an important implication. 'National' identity was bound up with political habits and institutions: Reich Germans had a different identity from Austrian Germans. The experience of war and defeat rapidly undermined Austrian enthusiasm for membership of a greater Germany. Yet it would be superficial to say that Austrians then conveniently 'forgot' that enthusiasm; their political traditions and experiences did indeed make them very different kinds of Germans from those who had grown up in the Reich. How a separate national identity was, on that basis, developed after 1945 is beyond the scope of this book.[10]

Again, one has to be discriminating about the popular response to other foreign policy achievements. The repudiation of Versailles (its

9. William Allen argues this very strongly. So far as 'Crystal Night' in 1938 is concerned, it seems to me that much of the distaste was for the lawless and violent nature of anti-Semitic action, rather than a principled antipathy to anti-Semitism as such.

10. See Robert Knight's contribution to 'Panel Discussion: Responses to the Question – "What has been the driving force behind German unifications and reunifications – cultural identity, power politics, or economic necessity?" ' *German History: Journal of the German History Society.* 9/2 (1991), pp 158–63

arms limitations, the demilitarised Rhineland) would naturally evoke widespread support because there had been a national consensus opposing Versailles. Nevertheless, this was always tinged by fear of war. I would not go quite as far as William Allen in depicting popular opinion as negative in response to the defeat of Poland in 1939 and France in 1940, but it appears to be the case that it was *after* the victory, and partly in response to the ease of such victories, that enthusiasm was expressed. Again, most Germans in principle had no objection to defeating Russia, but insofar as one can judge from the very guarded responses people offered in public, there was a feeling that it was unwise to embark on war on a second front. And as soon as the war clearly started to go wrong, certainly from the time when the defeat at Stalingrad had become common knowledge, the popularity of Hitler and the regime sank quickly. How far and how quickly this led to anti-nationalism along the lines argued by William Allen, or rather to a return to a more moderate and traditional nationalism, is a matter for debate.

It is also difficult to ascertain the extent to which the Third Reich actually did succeed in overcoming the internal divisions which beset the Weimar Republic. The regime preached the message of 'national community' (*Volksgemeinschaft*) and abolished many of the bodies which institutionalised internal conflict (parliament, trade unions, a free press), replacing them with institutions supposed to express national unity. How far that also abolished identification with 'sub-communities', and how far the new institutions actually managed to nurture a new sense of national identity is more debatable.[11] The key argument in William Allen's chapter is that the actual nationalist actions of the Third Reich not only went against 'mainstream' currents of national thinking, but also had the effect of gradually destroying all forms of nationalism. The assertion of national power brought with it war and defeat and occupation; the persecution of internal 'enemies' brought with it state terrorism and the destruction of the rule of law and the fear that you might be next on the list; the policy of a *Volksgemeinschaft* failed in fact to eliminate social divisions and was often seen as an opportunity for corrupt Nazis to enrich themselves. More generally one might argue that the descent into cultural barbarism undermined a sense of national identity which was based upon Germany's cultural as well as political and economic achievements.

Arguably there were also positive responses to some of these

11. Allen used the notion of 'subcommunities' in an essay comparing Italian fascism and National Socialism when in opposition. W.S. Allen, 'The appeal of fascism and the problem of national disintegration', in H. Turner (ed.) *Reappraisals of Fascism* (New York, 1975).

measures – for example, conventional middle-class values could support measures against the left, against trade unions, and against ethnic and other minorities, though naturally there would be an equally negative response from the working class, the left, liberals, and many committed Christians. Furthermore, responses could vary over time. Many Germans after 1945 recalled the years 1933 to 1939 as the best of their lives and replied affirmatively to the statement that Hitler would have been one of the greatest Germans but for the war. There are, of course, problems in interpreting such testimony, but it does point to a nuanced picture. Generally, however, the scholarly consensus has come to stress the failings rather than the successes of *Volksgemeinschaft* ideologies and policies in the Third Reich.

The year 1945 was as close as is possible in a modern society to a new beginning. Clearly Germans had to bring to their new situation some sense of what they were as Germans. As Peter Alter makes clear, physical survival was the overwhelming preoccupation and most Germans had little time to concern themselves with the issue of 'national' survival. Partly this was because the extremely harsh situation left little time for any other concerns. But partly it relates to William Allen's point that Hitler had discredited *every* kind of national sentiment.

The Allies were not committed to a division of Germany, once Austria had been restored and boundary changes made to take account of the interests of states such as Poland and Czechoslovakia. Partition emerged more as a consequence of the new Cold War divisions than as a deliberate policy to keep Germany weak. As Mary Fulbrook makes clear, it was in committing themselves to one or other side in that Cold War, that the political elites of West and East Germany came to construct new states. Only gradually, and in the case of the German Democratic Republic (GDR) somewhat later, did the states which developed out of this *de facto* partition seek national legitimacy. It was the commitment to the 'West' or to the 'East', and incorporation within an international bloc which mattered most. Any idea of national legitimacy was subordinated to that broader commitment. Adenauer's fear that a united Germany might lead the Federal Republic to abandon that Western orientation led him to look with grave suspicion on most ideas of reunification. German conservatives in the Federal Republic sought to combine the cultivation of a sense of national identity with this clear Western commitment.

By the 1960s opinion polls showed that in the Federal Republic a generation which had grown up since the war had little regard for national unity and regarded the GDR as a foreign place. Indeed, the increasingly strident manner in which conservatives talked of the need to create a sense of 'national identity' by the 1980s points to the decline of such a sense, replaced rather with a commitment to the institutions of the successful Federal Republic and integration into broader western institutions.

Mary Fulbrook also argues that similar developments were taking place in the GDR, though of course the lack of political freedom, of opinion polls and electoral contests between independent political parties makes it much more difficult to demonstrate. Certainly it would appear to be the case that any lack of 'legitimacy' (and the events of 1989–90 surely demonstrate how far the GDR regime lacked such legitimacy) was *not* related to a sense that the country was deficient as a *national* state. Indeed, the cultivation of national history from the 1970s points to the fact that the regime actually felt it necessary to try to manufacture support in that area. This policy failed along with the rest of its policies. More to the point – the sheer existence of a stable system for forty years was bound to shape the values, attitudes and habits of those who had never lived under any other system (even if they could imagine what that might be like).

By 1989 very few Germans in either state regarded national unification as an important, or likely prospect. Unification came about less as a result of a strong commitment to the idea of a united Germany than because of the power vacuum created by the collapse of communist power in East Germany. The role of 'nationalism' in 1989 was important – both in the sense of the commitment of the Federal Republic to the ideal of unification (a commitment which Chancellor Kohl then proceeded to act upon in a very decisive way) and of the desire of most East Germans to gain access to the West through unification. But its importance was principally in conditioning responses to a crisis that originated for other reasons. Furthermore, its own ambiguities are now becoming increasingly apparent. I will take up these points at greater length in the Conclusion.

That is why the creation of a reunified Germany can so easily coexist with a sincere commitment to European federalism and even to a disavowal of international power politics. (One thinks of the criticisms of Germany for not being prepared to act like a 'real' power during the Gulf War, and the rather feeble argument that the Basic Law of 1949 forbade Germany from acting any differently.) The case for linking German unification with European integration, and for stressing the complementarity of national and European identities, is strongly put by Wolf Gruner in his chapter. This case is not merely to check foreign fears or nationalist tendencies, but rather expresses the way political values have developed in Germany since 1945.

In 1871, 1919 and 1945 changes in the borders and institutions of Germany were associated with war. In 1933 and the years up to 1939 they were associated with the rise of an extremist nationalist movement to power and the use of state violence both at home and abroad. In 1989–90 change came about peacefully, guided by moderate political forces. The national idea, having entrenched itself as a 'natural' identity since 1871, was essential to that change. East Germans could only look to West Germany as the state they wished to join on the grounds of common nationality; no other East European state has such an opportunity open to it (though Jews can look to Israel as their true home). West Germans felt a moral obligation to the commitment to reunification enshrined in the Basic Law of 1949 and adhered to in all subsequent diplomatic undertakings, again because of this assumption of a common national identity.

That 'natural' sense of national identity goes back to the 'mainstream' national sentiment established between about 1890 and 1933. Before then any sense of national identity was usually confined to minorities and had varying political, often anti-political characteristics. That mainstream national sense was destroyed as an active political sentiment between 1933 and 1945 and has only played a part in the transformation of 1989–90 because of crises caused by many other factors.

III

Thus the meanings to be attributed to such terms as German, nationality and nation-state have varied greatly in content and significance between the late eighteenth century and today. One also has to view these meanings against a broader background. National histories tend to take the nation for granted. Historians are often suspicious of general theories, preferring to look at the 'facts' before them and on that basis telling a story 'in its own terms'. Without considering the general problems with this view, it is clear that the emergence of national consciousness and the formation of nation-states are general features of modern history. So it is worth asking if the case of Germany is but a specific variant of a general theme.

The general theme is the convergence of nationality and state to form nation-states. One obvious way of explaining this convergence is to see one of these as cause and the other as effect. Nationalist historians see the history of nation-state formation in terms of the rise of national awareness among both elites and at a popular level. Politics eventually has to follow the pressure of this sense of national identity and so nation-states are formed. Other historians have seen nationalism as little more than an ideological fig-leaf used by states and other interests to justify the expansion of their power both to their subjects and to outsiders.

Such accounts are unsatisfactory. It is clear that a unified Germany was created long before nationalism was a strong and active political sentiment, certainly before it was a widespread and popular feeling. Equally, however, it is clear that Bismarck would not have appealed to the idea of Germany unless in his view it had possessed some independent political significance.

The idea of a 'convergence' between national feeling and the Prussian state is also deeply flawed. I have already argued that the idea of German nationality had many, changing and often conflicting meanings, so it can hardly be seen as a constant or growing element which at some point 'combines' with state power. Furthermore, this idea of changing meanings can also be applied to the idea of the Prussian state. Prussia constantly changed her territories, her institutions and her relationships with her subjects and other states. What is more, the very idea of what it meant for a state to expand her power and territory changed. When Frederick the Great annexed new territories after a successful war, he did not invoke the idea of Germany or issue a constitution. Instead, for example in the case of Silesia, he agreed to respect the customs and traditions of the new acquisition provided its inhabitants transferred their allegiance to him. The policy of creating uniform institutions was first pursued, rather fitfully, in post–1815 Prussia. The decision to take this further and to extend it to constitutional as well as administrative arrangements came only in 1848. It is not a coincidence either that the description of Prussia as *a* state was only first officially used in its first constitution, that of December 1848. By 1866 it had become 'obvious' that Prussia could legitimise the extension of her power in Germany, power acquired in the first instance through war, only by constructing a constitutional state. Clearly a modern notion of the Prussian state needs to be related to a modern notion of German nationality. In order to do this we need to return to the era of the French Revolution and Napoleon.

The Revolution, especially with the outbreak of war between France and much of the rest of Europe in 1792, transformed and brought together the ideas of state and nation. The state was no longer understood as a dynastic construct, legitimised by tradition, its mission as guardian of the Christian faith and protector of the customs and laws of its subjects. Even before 1789 this understanding had been questioned by those who saw the monarch as a secular and reforming figure, the purpose of whose rule was to maintain and increase the happiness of his subjects. However, the break of 1789–92 made the shift to a new understanding quite clear.

The state was now an instrument, not in itself a sacred institution. But whose instrument? It was the instrument of its subjects. To effect this change, those subjects had to become citizens. Citizens were equals; therefore the distinctions of privilege had to be abolished. In principle this was a project which did not ask questions about the language or customs or history of the subject-citizen. In practice, in the midst of war against other states as well as against internal rebellions, the successive governments of France fused the idea of nation as the body of the citizens with the idea of the nation as the French.

This affected other parts of Europe in various ways. In part it stimulated a similar sort of patriotic resistance. However, without the prior internal changes of the kind that had taken place in France, this was of limited importance. Usually what is regarded as 'nationalism' turns out on closer inspection to be either the response of marginal elites – as in Germany – or a populism stimulated by very traditional institutions and sentiments – as in Spain.

At the level of individual states it produced patriots, who recognised the need to reform governments and their relations to their subjects in order to survive, whether as collaborators or opponents of Napoleon. What is important is that this reform process did not come to an end in 1814–15, even if the explicitly political, liberal side of it was severely set back. With the growth of market economies, of a more complex civil society which could not be simply ignored or controlled by governments, there also developed an enlarged sphere of 'public opinion'.

In these circumstances the idea of 'Germany' could acquire new significance in a variety of ways. First, in terms of the balance of power, it was clearly necessary to try to ensure that the German lands did not once again lapse into so decentralised and weak a situation as to create a power vacuum. Austro-Prussian dualism, rather than the realisation of federalist principles laid down in 1814–15, served this purpose. Once the principal rivalry came to be that *between* Austria and Prussia, clearly the working definition of Germany provided by their dualism would no longer suffice. Both states would then appeal to alternative notions of Germany to justify their own policies.

Second, and this relates to general views of nationalism, changes in the relationship between state and society conferred a new significance upon ideas of 'political identity'. The secular, territorial state made larger claims upon its subjects and yet, with the development of market economies, an enlarged public opinion, and a greater and more diverse subject population, there was a decline in the controls associated with churches, nobilities, guilds and monarchies – that is a society based upon a web of privileges. This was why states considered it so necessary to issue constitutions, to build up a favourable public image. It was necessary to find new, 'public' ways of controlling subjects and eliciting their cooperation and support. As we have seen in the case of the Bavarian monarchy, part of such an enterprise could consist of cultivating notions of German cultural nationality.

There was a long-standing sense of such notions, seen in the use of words such as '*deutsch*' and '*Germania*'. Generally, however, such terms had had little direct political significance before the late eighteenth century. Now both governments and oppositions to governments began to invest them with political significance. The idea of politics being about *representation* – of classes, of citizens, of the general interest – constantly pressed those active in politics to say *who* they represented. To refer to the sentiments, language, traditions, customs – in short, the *culture* – of those who were ruled, was one, increasingly important way of answering this question.

What is more, 'culture' in this sense acquired an increasing autonomy. The growth of communications, the increased importance of schooling, the need to find common terms to address larger audiences for newspapers and journals and books – all this enhanced the role of teachers, journalists and authors. They operated these specialised cultural institutions through the medium of language, and so the idea of nationality as cultural and a matter of language became more significant. This was not peculiar to Germany and considerations of these kinds have been central to some general interpretations of the development of modern national consciousness.[12]

One should not take the argument too far. As 1848–9 revealed, the idea of German nationality was still politically fluid and could lead to conflict, and was also something which had not really penetrated much below elite level. Nevertheless, those elites mattered. When the Prussian government came to pursue a policy of confrontation with Austria within Germany, it had to take account of those elites.

Bismarck did not really do much in this way before 1866. Until then his policy was largely one of Prussian aggrandisement and he

---

12. See, above all, Gellner, *Nations and Nationalism*; and B. Anderson, *Imagined Communities: Reflections on the Origins and Spread of Nationalism* (London, 1983).

ignored, even opposed, the liberal sentiments which dominated nationalism. Part of his genius, however, consisted in his recognition that the enlarged Prussian state needed the cooperation of the 'political nation', and this could be obtained only by constitutionalism and the acceptance of many liberal policies. State-formation under modern conditions, even if achieved by means of successful war in the first instance, could no longer take the traditional form of adding to the property of the monarch.

Placing unification, therefore, within a broader context of the development of the modern territorial state, a market economy, and an increasingly autonomous culture, enables us both to understand the German case better and to relate it to general approaches to the rise of the nation-state.

In the early years of the Second Empire there was little in the way of a 'national consensus'. Regional, political and religious differences still mattered more to most Germans than did the nationality they had in common. For many, a German nation-state could not be regarded as complete if it excluded Austria. For others, the central role of the authoritarian Hohenzollern monarchy led them to reject the idea of the new state as a German and national one.

Nevertheless, the 'nation-state' itself can extend and consolidate this sense of national identity. Given that most of the inhabitants of the new state were native speakers of German; that participation in government did increase; that national institutions touched people's lives in more and more ways; and that generally the power and prosperity of the country increased between 1871 and 1914 – given all that, it is no wonder that the Second Empire established itself, territorially if not institutionally, as the normal idea of Germany. Again, historians of other 'nation-states' in western and central Europe have argued that the creation of national consensus and identity at a popular level first became significant only in the three or four decades before the First World War.

I would argue that the idea of Germany which was formed in those decades has continued to be the 'normal' idea of Germany. In the optimistic period at the beginning of the First World War, politicians on the right could lay claim to an expanded view of Germany; as they were to do again in their critique of Versailles; and also in the Third Reich. Many Austrians welcomed the 'return' to Germany in 1938, and Reich Germans accepted that and other additions to Germany's territory and power. But these were exceptional sentiments and periods, soon undermined by defeat. In any case, the desire to exercise control over other peoples does not display any peculiarly German nationalist sentiment: it is quite clear that the British or the French were not averse to imperial power. What has endured, however, is the sense that the two German states (but not Austria) really do share a common national identity. That has often been a rather latent sense, not one which informed practical politics for much of the period between 1945 and 1989 and which did not set itself against broader forms of internationalism or increased acceptance of one's own 'partial' German state as legitimate and complete.

A sense of nationality, therefore, is very closely bound up with the fortunes of the modern territorial state. In the cases not only of Germany, but also of Britain and France, it was arguably in the period 1890–1914 that such a sense was created at a mass level. That did not, of course, preclude bitter divisions, but such divisions tended to be about the form rather than the fact of the nation-state. Furthermore, the simultaneous development of such national sentiments in other states worked in a mutually reinforcing way.

However, the bitter divisions within post-1919 Germany made it difficult, then impossible, to find political institutions which could command a national consensus. The politicians of Weimar tried to embody the idea of a nation-state in political institutions, but they were rejected. The Third Reich took flight from institutional solutions into the idea of the 'leader' state and imperialist expansion. The politicians of the immediate post-war years were preoccupied with adjusting to the pressures exerted by their former enemies, leading to division as those enemies themselves came into conflict and treated their sphere of Germany as a client. The success of the Federal Republic of Germany from the 1950s finally provided an alternative and stable political identity to that of *kleindeutsch* Germany, despite the efforts of some to maintain a commitment to that latter Germany. As with the Second Empire, a key element in this achievement has been simple survival and economic growth. But unlike the Second Empire, it has also been the product of a democratic constitution which has positively integrated most citizens into the institutions of the state. That success story not only made West Germans uninterested in 'old-style' nationalism, but also turned their state and society into a beacon of hope for the inhabitants of East Germany. For much of the post-war period, hope has taken the form of escape to the west or aid from the west. The German Democratic Republic did undoubtedly create a stable political structure and addressed some of the issues of 'political integration'. It did not survive merely by coercion. Nevertheless, it did not have the strength that a democratic constitution and a high standard of living created in West Germany. Moreover, the mere fact that East Germans could look to West Germany as a model weakened the GDR. It was the bankruptcy and collapse of the German Democratic Republic that brought about reunification rather than any strong commitment to an earlier model of Germany. Once again, one has to see the idea of nationality as important, but not all-important and also as taking a different form in this situation from the forms it had taken in earlier decisive moments of state-formation in Germany.

Obviously, the making, unmaking and remaking of a German nation-state is a unique history. Something of that history will be considered in the chapters in this book. Yet at the same time it is one 'national' history among many, and needs to be seen in that context. It also has to be seen as one element within a broader process of modernisation.

SUGGESTIONS FOR FURTHER READING

The best general survey of nineteenth- and twentieth-century German history is W. Carr, *A History of Germany 1815–1945* (1st edn., 1969), now due to come out in a fourth edition extended to take account of the events of 1989–90. Generally on the role of nationalism and of national identity in German history see M. Hughes, *Nationalism and Society: Germany 1800–1945* (London, 1988); and the interesting, though in my view misleading, argument presented in H. James, *A German Identity 1770–1990* (London, 1989).

More detailed for the earlier part of the period is J. Sheehan, *German History 1770–1866* (Oxford, 1990). We lack anything really up-to-date in English for the 1866–1900 period. Interesting is H.-U. Wehler, *The German Empire 1871–1918* (Leamington Spa, 1985) but this is a translation of a book which first appeared in 1973. Wehler's approach, treating the new nation-state as in some ways defective, has been criticised in D. Blackbourn and G. Eley, *The Peculiarities of German History* (Oxford, 1984). Generally for post-1900 German history see V. Berghahn, *Modern Germany: Society, Economy and Politics in the Twentieth Century* (Cambridge, 1987, 2nd edn.).

Weimar Germany, its collapse and the Third Reich have generated an enormous historical literature. On Weimar and its collapse see now I. Kershaw (ed.) *Weimar: Why did German Democracy Fail?* (London, 1990). For problems of interpreting the Third Reich see I. Kershaw,

The Nazi Dictatorship: Problems and Perspectives of Interpretation (London, 1989, 2nd edn.). Alter and Fulbrook provide guidance to further reading on post-1945 Germany.

For a general treatment of nationalism I would refer to J. Breuilly, *Nationalism and the State* (Manchester, 1985) which includes a treatment of nationalism in the periods of German unification and of National Socialism. Other general works I have found illuminating are E. Gellner, *Nations and Nationalism* (Oxford, 1983); B. Anderson, *Imagined Communities: Reflections on the Origins and Spread of Nationalism* (London, 1983); and A.D. Smith, *National Identity* (London, 1991).

CHAPTER TWO

Fiat justitia, pereat Germania? The imperial supreme jurisdiction and imperial reform in the later Holy Roman Empire

Michael Hughes

The recent reopening of the 'German question', with the rapid achievement of reunification, accelerating progress towards European political union, and the 'historians' dispute' (*Historikerstreit*) has revived debates about German identity, different forms of national unity and Germany's place in Europe. No new conclusions have been reached but a lot of old questions have been re-asked in stimulating ways. The 'nation-state' of 1871–1945 is no longer the only model of Germany available, although it has proved remarkably resilient. This led, for example, to a long neglect by German historians of the tradition of federalism and its equation with particularism and reaction. Loose federative political structures like the Holy Roman Empire and *Mitteleuropa* are again interesting. After a decade of concentration on Germany's recent past, the focus of historical attention has widened, with growing attention on the pre-unification period and even the later Holy Roman Empire.[1]

Historical judgements of the Holy Roman Empire have in the past too often been based on inappropriate or anachronistic models. Its image has also changed with the prevailing political climate. The concentration of many German historians on the process of state creation (*Staatsbildung*) has also distorted the picture. The growth of the individual German states interfered with the growth of the Empire as a state, while the fact that the Empire and its institutions continued to

---

1. R.A. Fletcher, 'History from below comes to Germany: the new history movement in the Federal Republic of Germany', *Journal of Modern History*, 60 (1988), pp. 557–68; G. Strauss, 'The Holy Roman Empire revisited', *Central European History*, 11 (1978), pp. 290–301.

exercise functions of government prevented the states possessing total and undivided sovereignty. Dismissive views of it were common in the later nineteenth century, after the unification of 1871, portrayed in nationalist historiography as the end of German weakness symbolised by the Old Reich.

In recent years the view of the later Holy Roman Empire among historians has changed and become much more positive. The Reich is no longer just a *Doktorfrage* but is becoming a very popular choice of subject for a *Doktorarbeit*. The latest substantial textbooks on the later Empire reflect this new approach.[2] Perhaps the pendulum has swung too far; there is some danger now of a new form of anachronism, a new *Reichsromantik* or *Reichspathos*, with the Holy Roman Empire being portrayed as a combination of the European Court of Human Rights, the United Nations and the European Community. The fact that the Empire was, at least in part, devoted to peace, freedom and justice derived as much from external factors as from a conscious choice of its inhabitants. This idealisation of the old Reich is itself part of the 'new nationalism' seen recently in Germany. What the new work has clearly shown is that the imperial institutions, traditionally written off as moribund, were active long after 1648. In recent years there has been a minor boom in studies of one of these, the imperial cameral court (*Reichskammergericht*).[3]

Though pre-modern in essence, the Reich did show evidence of growth, vitality and progress and can no longer be seen as a nation in aspic. The looseness of the German constitution provided opportunities for a great variety of different evolutions and there was nothing inevitable about developments. The post-1648 German political system was a mixture of different features, the geological record of successive accretions: the relics of a unitary German monarchy, important survivals of a feudal political structure, the skeletal remains of an aristocratic limited monarchy and distinct traces of federal elements. Tension between the old *Lehensordnung* (the feudal bond between lord and vassal) and the evolving federative structure continued to affect the Empire until its end. The relative weight of imperial power, or its substantial vestiges, the *Reservatrechte* (the residual powers that remained with imperial institutions) and the 'liberty', or power, of the Estates of the Empire changed with the political situation inside and outside

2. H. Schilling, *Höfe und Allianzen: Deutschland 1648–1763* (Berlin, 1989) and H. Möller, *Fürstenstaat oder Bürgernation: Deutschland 1763–1815* (Berlin, 1989) emphasise the need to appreciate the *Rechts- Freiheits- und Friedenstraditionen* which the Empire embodied, even if its form was bizarre to modern eyes.

3. V.Preß, *Das Reichskammergericht in der deutschen Geschichte* (Wetzlar, 1987).

Germany. The first was strengthened by Austrian influence in the Reich, the attachment of the small states to the Emperor and patriotic enthusiasm, especially in war and most especially after victories; the second was fuelled by *raison d'état*, the need for self-help and disillusionment with the Empire (*Reichsmüdigkeit*).

This chapter, originally delivered as a talk in a series entitled *The Making and Unmaking of a Nation-State*, deals with one aspect of the development of German national sentiment in the eighteenth century. It will focus upon imperial consciousness (*der Reichsgedanke*), in particular upon support for the system of superior imperial or federal jurisdiction, exercised after 1497 through the two courts of the Empire, the *Reichskammergericht* and the *Reichshofrat*. The title chosen, 'Let there be justice, even if Germany perishes!', was the motto for Germany suggested by the young Hegel in his 1802 draft *The German Constitution* (*Die Verfassung des Deutschen Reiches*), in which he wrote of Germany as a shadow state, a state of the imagination, which existed only in its rights, laws and judicial system.[4] Other commentators were less pessimistic. The notion of a Reich of the spirit – the idea that Germans, because of their intellectual and cultural superiority, did not need a political framework – is familiar. It was expressed by Schiller in the often-quoted statement of 1804:

> The German Empire and the German nation are two different things. The glory of the Germans has never been based upon the power of its princes. Separated from the political sphere, Germans have established their own values. Political defeats could not undermine those values.[5]

This chapter will argue that, in a similar way, the survival of imperial jurisdiction, symbolised in the proverb *Reichsrecht bricht Landesrecht* – imperial law takes precedence over state law – represented a kind of Reich of the law, the Reich as a *Justizstaat* , abstract but nonetheless important. This jurisdiction enjoyed support from an important section of German intellectual opinion *and* a much wider public opinion from the fifteenth century until the end of the Empire in 1806 and even after 1806. Furthermore, a revitalisation of imperial jurisdiction was one of the aims of the movements for reform of the constitution of the Empire from the fifteenth century to the eighteenth century,

---

4. The draft was not published until 1893: G.W.F. Hegel, *Politische Schriften*, vol. 1 (Frankfurt, 1966), pp. 29ff. It is analysed in S. Avineri, *Hegel's Theory of the Modern State* (London, 1972), and there is a translation in T.M. Knox (ed.) *Hegel's Political Writings* (Oxford, 1964).

5. Quoted in T. Schieder, 'Friedrich der Große – eine Integrationsfigur des deutschen Nationalbewußtseins im 18. Jahrhundert', in O. Dann, (ed.) *Nationalismus und sozialer Wandel* (Munich, 1986), pp. 113–27.

known as *Reichsreform*. Its main manifestations were found in the writings known collectively as *Reichspublizistik*.[6] *Reichspublizistik* was not 'publicity' but the study of German public law (*Staatsrecht*), the nature of political authority and the distribution of power in the Empire. Knowledge of imperial law and history continued to be seen as important; academic lawyers were often employed as diplomats, administrators and advisers by governments, and university law faculties were often approached by governments for their opinions on unclear legal points. The importance of the debate among theorists and writers in forming public opinion was shown by the great importance the Emperor and the German princes attached to having in their employment writers of legal and historical polemics, versed in the law and constitution of the Empire. A new four-year training course for administrators instituted in 1780 at Vienna included in its curriculum German legal history, German constitutional law and imperial law. The university at Göttingen, the best university in eighteenth-century Germany, was a major centre for their study.[7]

The *Reichspublizistik* had two main aspects: analysis of the nature of the imperial constitution and proposals for its improvement and change. It was produced from the fifteenth to the early nineteenth century, with marked clusterings in the late fifteenth and early sixteenth centuries, the years after 1648 and in the last decades of the eighteenth century. There was a lively debate on the imperial constitution and attempts to find a new intellectual basis for what, during centuries of development when different forces had pulled it in contradictory directions, had developed into an exotic hybrid. The debate still goes on. At the twenty-eighth annual congress of German historians at Cologne in April 1970 there was a lively discussion of the question 'What was the Reich?'. Professor Wandruszka reached the interesting conclusion that it was 'a possibility'.

Speculation about the German constitution and its improvement seemed to become particularly intense in periods of instability, war or post-war adjustment. For example, the religious troubles of the 1530s produced a lively debate on the issue of the German states' right of resistance against the Emperor, which expanded into considerations of the nature of the imperial constitution. The periods after the religious peace of 1555 and the Thirty Years' War saw similar peaks. The

6. The Max Planck Institute in Göttingen has a collection of over 10,000 items of *Reichspublizistik*. The best survey in English is H. Gross, *Empire and Sovereignty: A History of the Public Law Literature in the Holy Roman Empire 1559–1804* (London and Chicago, 1973; repr. 1975).

7. C.E. McClelland, *State, Society and University in Germany 1700–1914* (Cambridge, 1980), pp. 43ff.

treaties of Westphalia included provisions for major changes in the imperial constitution but these were not put into effect. After 1648 friction between the Emperor and the princes, between princes and their subjects and between factions in the free cities all increased. The relationship between the confessions was still uncertain and the smaller states in particular were aware of their vulnerability. All this contributed to a lively interest in the nature of the Reich. Polemicists, often sponsored by the German governments, especially the Protestants, mobilised arguments drawn from history, political theory and law to attack or defend the position of the Emperor, the Electors, the princes and the free cities. Opponents of imperial authority usually had as their target not the existence of the Empire but the supposed ambition of the Emperor to subvert the constitution and establish a despotism.

Reform proposals formed the other main aspect of *Reichspublizistik*. The most common recipe to deal with the problems of the German constitution was a decisive recognition of the federal nature of the Empire and its institutional expression. In spite of their obvious weaknesses, objections to their mode of operation and campaigns by the German princes to restrict their competence in support of claims that their governmental functions (*Landeshoheit*) should include total judicial sovereignty,[8] the function of the imperial courts in resolving conflicts betwen governments and between rulers and subjects was seen by commentators as one of the best aspects of the Reich constitution. The *Landfrieden*, the acceptance that peace should be the normal condition of society and that disputes should be resolved by judicial means, became increasingly important in the fifteenth century. Banning all measures of violent self-help, the *Fehde*, the private war fought under *Faustrecht* (the 'right of the fist') and laying down what could and could not be properly undertaken by individuals and governments in pursuit of their rights, the peace was an essential guarantee of order in a very complex political, religious, economic and social structure. By implication, an imperial supreme tribunal was an essential corollary of it. At first only geographically and chronologically limited *Landfrieden* were enacted and the activity of the king's supreme court was intermittent. A peace covering the whole Empire (*Reichslandfrieden*) was first proclaimed at the Mainz *Reichstag* in 1235 and a temporary one-year *Landfrieden* was issued in 1467, involving an absolute ban on *Faustrecht*. There was an aulic tribunal (*Hofgericht*) attached to the royal court, though it is not clear how wide was its competence or how

8. M. Hughes, *Law and Politics in 18th-Century Germany* (Woodbridge, 1988), pp. 44ff.

consistent its activity. The same is true of the short-lived cameral court (*Kammergericht*) in the court of Frederick III.

More consistent progress was made in the last decades of the fifteenth century. There was near unanimity in the reform literature of the time on the need for a revival of imperial authority in the Reich, in particular the establishment of effective imperial jurisdiction with a permanent court in a fixed location in the Empire. The diets of 1486 and 1487 refused to provide the Emperor with the financial help he requested in order to compel him to agree to the establishment of a permanent court. The first universal permanent general peace for the whole Empire was proclaimed at the Worms diet in 1495 and the first permanent imperial court, the imperial chamber court (*Reichskammergericht*), was set up to administer it in the same year, to be followed two years later by the imperial aulic council (*Reichshofrat*). The establishment of the Circles and the Ordinance of Execution of 1555 completed the structure.

The conviction that an effective imperial jurisdiction was beneficial to Germany was not restricted to academic and political opinion, but was deeply rooted in popular feeling. Images of the Hohenstaufens Frederick I and Frederick II as powerful rulers and of the Interregnum of 1250 to 1275 as the anarchic 'terrible time without an Emperor' were sharply etched in popular memory. Enhanced imperial jurisdiction figured in many of the millenarian and apocalyptic works of the late fifteenth and early sixteenth centuries, such as the anonymous *Reformation Kaiser Sigismunds* and *Reformation Kaiser Friedrichs II* (attributed to the named Emperors and dated 1435 and 1441 but in reality written in the early 1520s) and the *Book of the Hundred Chapters*. The notion of the Emperor as a judicial *deus ex machina* was a common feature, seen for example in the Kyffhäuser legend of the sleeping Emperor waiting to return to save Germany. Such ideas also became prominent during the peasant risings of the late fifteenth and early sixteenth centuries. The peasant 'parliament' at Heilbronn in 1525 considered a plan put foward by the former Mainz official Friedrich Weigandt for a fundamental reform involving the Emperor taking back to himself all his lost powers and establishing a centralised state with a hierarchy of imperial courts.

In the seventeenth century such plans were put forward, among others, by Pufendorf, Hippolitus a Lapide and Leibniz. Many of these schemes shared common features, a standing imperial executive, a permanent treasury and a standing army, as well as a German national law code. These would unify Germany and enable her to fulfil her function as a barrier against the establishment of the French universal monarchy which threatened the whole of Europe. Leibniz called for the codification of all imperial law in a new *Codex Leopoldinus*. Even the extreme anti-imperialist Hippolitus a Lapide's plan for a conversion of the Reich into a princely republic contained a proposal for a tribunal to deal with disputes between the princes who were to share sovereignty in it.

The period after the Seven Years' War saw another peak in the output of *Reichsreform* literature. The war intensified the debate on government, administration, the law and constitutions, as had the Thirty Years' War. Like that war it was in some respects a German civil war: during it the army of the Empire was mobilised and defeated by Prussia. It involved a suspension of the imperial constitution, threw into stark relief the problem of the relationship between the two German great powers and the rest of the Empire, and threatened to re-open old political and religious divisions. During the war Prussia's anti-Habsburg propaganda raked up all the old charges that Austria aimed at establishing a Catholic absolutist despotism in Germany and religious friction continued to trouble the *Reichstag* after 1763. It added to Germany's identity problems: many Germans admired Frederick II while realising that his actions threatened the stability of the Empire. There was a rash of works on what it meant to be German in the 1760s.[9] The war showed up the inadequacies of existing administrative systems and produced a vigorous reform effort in individual German states, large and small, reinforced by economic problems experienced after the war in some states where the stability of the coinage had been undermined and inflation was high. As a result of these and other factors the whole relationship of the state and society came under examination.[10]

The war also roused expectations of change; a period of instability, which had lasted since 1740, seemed to have come to an end in 1763. Strangely for the 'Age of Reason' there was in the 1760s a millenarian atmosphere in some quarters with predictions of a coming great spiritual revolution, the greatest overturning since the Reformation, which would sweep away ignorance and allow a victory of Reason. The war was followed by a pause in the struggle between Prussia and Austria,

9. W. Sheldon, 'Patriotismus bei Justus Möser', in R. Vierhaus (ed.) *Deutsche patriotische und gemeinnützige Gesellschaften* (Munich, 1980), pp. 31–49, especially p. 31.

10. E. Weis, 'Absolute Monarchie und Reform in Deutschland des späten 18. und des frühen 19. Jahrhunderts', in F. Kopitzsch (ed.) *Aufklärung, Absolutismus und Bürgertum in Deutschland* (Munich, 1976), pp. 192–219; K. Epstein, *The Genesis of German Conservatism* (Princeton, NJ, 1966), pp. 237ff; G. Parry, 'Enlightened government and its critics in 18th century Germany', *Historical Journal*, 6 (1963), pp. 178–92.

which was to become serious again only in the late 1770s as a result of Joseph II's policies. The year 1764 saw the election and coronation of Joseph as king of the Romans, that is automatic successor as Emperor to his father Francis I, whose failing health was the main reason for the election. This event, attended by considerable pomp and ceremonial, was widely seen as a new beginning for the Reich and a symbol of its new unity. Joseph was the first king or Emperor elected by all the electors without dissent and no new restrictions were placed on him in his capitulation of election. These facts were commented on by contemporaries as an optimistic sign for the future.

The optimism was soon disappointed. The Reich faced a number of new problems and old ones soon reappeared. For example, religious conversions meant that in 1763 there were seven Catholic and only two Protestant electors and there was a continuing pressure from some of the princes for a reduction in the dominant position of the electors. Joseph's attitude to the Reich was practical, unsentimental and insensitive. He paid lip-service to the imperial idea: in April 1787 he wrote to the coadjutor of Mainz, Dalberg, assuring him of his concern for the 'general welfare of Germany, our common fatherland . . . because I love it and am proud to be a German', but his marginal comments on memoranda on reform of the Empire written by Dalberg in 1787 included: 'I don't understand what this idiocy is all about' and 'This is pure fantasy'.[11] Joseph viewed the Empire as a source of possible advantage to Austria and little more. Long-standing Habsburg ambitions to acquire Bavaria in exchange for more remote territories were revived. Reform of the Catholic Church in Austria was undertaken, which involved infringements on the rights of German prelates. In the 1780s Joseph tried to revive lapsed imperial rights of presentation to benefices in imperial abbeys and foundations, of which there were almost 300 in the Reich, using the aulic council for this purpose. This did nothing to add to the Emperor's popularity in the German Catholic Church. Joseph also proposed a reform of the imperial courts, ignoring the rights of the princes in this matter. The reform was suspected to be a cover for attempts to ensure that the verdicts of the *Reichshofrat* were more uniformly in Austria's political interest and the suspicion was well-founded.

Such actions raised questions about the role of the Emperor. One expression of growing disquiet was a revival of the notion of *Drittes Deutschland*, the Third Germany, also known as trialism, the idea that the states which made up Germany without Austria and Prussia should

11. Quoted by R. Vierhaus ' "Patriotismus" – Begriff und Realität einer moralisch-politischen Haltung', in Vierhaus (ed.) op.cit., p. 15.

come together to defend their independence against the two German great powers. National feeling also expressed itself in calls for a strengthening of the Reich against the larger states, especially Prussia and Austria, which seemed ready to sacrifice the smaller states for their own narrow interests. The partition of Poland was seen as a dreadful warning of what could happen in the Reich. This was the origin of the *Fürstenbund* (League of Princes) of 1785, itself a symptom of a growing constitutional crisis. It began as a movement among some of the medium-sized princes to build a union of Third Germany and it was only later taken over by Prussia for its own ends, when its original purpose was abandoned. Its stated aim was to preserve the status quo in the German constitution and Article 4 of its Act of Association committed its members to seek a reform of the imperial supreme courts and to defend them against imperial encroachments. The establishment of the *Fürstenbund* added to the constitutional debates and new questions were asked about the relationship of the Emperor to the Empire. Disenchantment with the situation was typified in an anonymous pamphlet of 1787, which asked *Warum soll Deutschland einen Kaiser haben?* (*Does Germany need an Emperor?*) and concluded that the office was now redundant as the whole Empire was against the tide of the times.

Such a view was unusual. Politically informed Germans looking at their country in the later eighteenth century found much to bemoan but also much to praise. Some reacted with resignation, others with a desire to change things; very few thought in terms of sweeping away the Reich and replacing it with something else. For one thing, it was difficult to define acceptable alternatives. For most commentators the Holy Roman Empire was the ideal German community, in spite of its obvious flaws. There was a widespread view that Germans were singularly fortunate in the constitution of their country, which allowed a wide measure of freedom to the individual states and to individual Germans, while protecting certain basic rights against encroachments. Imperial law guaranteed to all subjects freedom to practise one of three legal religions somewhere in the Empire, freedom of movement within the Empire to all who were not *glebae ascriptus* (those tied to the soil under tenancies which placed legal restrictions upon them), the right to inherit property anywhere in the Empire, the right to justice in properly conducted courts and the right to security of person and property under the law. Already in the second half of the eighteenth century the modern notion of freedom as something to be enjoyed by the individual was beginning to grow up alongside the older tradition of liberties as privileges possessed by particular groups; in the eyes of many commentators the imperial constitution was flexible enough to accommodate and protect both.[12]

As a result there was a widespread belief that any political arrangement for the German nation must combine unity and diversity in correctly balanced proportions. There was also a conviction that the end of the Empire would be a catastrophe and real fears of a great cataclysm (*Umwälzung*) if the structure of the imperial constitution was disturbed. The preservation of the Empire as a loose framework was held to be in the interest of Europe and the individual German states. At the same time the old medieval universalist view, which had seen the Reich as the leading state of Christendom and the Emperor as its secular head, was passing away and was being replaced by a new universalism more in tune with the enlightened spirit of the age, a combination of patriotism and cosmopolitanism which saw the advancement of Germany as beneficial to the whole of humanity.[13]

There are, of course, inherent difficulties in assessing how representative or influential the views of a small educated elite were and how far they were in advance of political and social realities and how far lagging behind them. German public opinion was real in the late eighteenth century though far from united; a distinction must be drawn between the views of the educated, a small group in which there were widely differing opinions, and those of the mass of the people whose horizons were narrow and to whom the idea of Germany was very remote. That said, there is growing agreement that German national sentiment existed as a growing force in the later eighteenth century.

A recent important study of the French Revolution[14] has drawn attention to the great intensity and mobilising power of a new form of patriotism which emerged in France after the Seven Years' War. This produced a new concept of citizenship which took precedence over regional, class or group loyalties, taught that all patriotic citizens had a duty to involve themselves in state affairs and began to break down the walls between the state and private spheres so typical of the *ancien régime*. While various factors produced a more restrained situation in Germany, it is clear that something similar existed there in the later

12. For a basic introduction to the increasing importance of a concept of the individual see K. Epstein, *The Genesis of German Conservatism* (Princeton, NJ, 1966), pp. 29ff; and for a fuller treatment, M. Berman, *The Politics of Authenticity* (London, 1971).

13. Vierhaus, 'Deutschland im 18. Jahrhundert: soziales Gefüge, politische Verfassung, geistige Bewegung', in F. Kopitzsch (ed), *Aufklärung, Absolutismus und Bürgertum in Deutschland* (Munich, 1976), pp. 173–91, especially pp. 176–7. See also F. Meinecke, *Cosmopolitanism and the National State* (Princeton, NJ, 1970).

14. S. Schama, *Citizens* (London, 1989).

eighteenth century. Although it was still very much a minority move-ment, the numbers of those who saw themselves as patriots or *Vater-landsfreunde* were increasing. Access to university education and the emergence of the concept of the all-round education (*Bildung*) con-tributed to growing pride in middle-class achievement. Another factor was the rise of an all-German middle class, a group of mobile, edu-cated and professional people, including academics, students, officials, officers, diplomats, musicians and projectors[15] whose links with their *enges Vaterland* (narrow fatherland) weakened as they moved around the Reich[16]. The press, though censored in many states and small, was expanding, particularly the periodical press, and this acted as a unifying force, as did the expanding network of clubs, reading circles and Ma-sonic lodges.[17] One feature of all this was a growing knowledge of and interest in the history of Germany and a better appreciation of how it had developed to its present 'monstrous' state.

The concept of the good citizen or patriot was political, social and moral: he was seen as having a duty to act as a model in his personal life, to involve himself in *die gemeine Sache* (the general or common interest) and to work for the common good of the fatherland, rising above the narrow class, occupational, religious or regional group to which he belonged. F.C. Moser defined a patriot as follows:

> A true patriot is . . . a godly, honest, steady, patient, courageous and wise
> man, with a thorough knowledge of the laws and the constitution, of the
> causes of prosperity and defects in his fatherland, which he uses to find
> the best help and the most enduring improvements. He seeks this at all
> times, motivated by a true love of mankind, without consideration of
> party or person, or serving his own interests.[18]

15. 'Projectors': people who went round hawking wonderful projects to solve, usually at a stroke, the economic problems of a state. Some were alchemists, some were of the John Law type. The term (in German *Projector* or *Projektmacher*) was widely used in the seventeenth and eighteenth centuries.

16. W. Ruppert, *Bürgerlicher Wandel* (Frankfurt and New York, 1981), pp. 137f., 185f. U.A.J. Becher, *Politische Gesellschaft: Studien zur Genese bürgerlicher Öffentlichkeit in Deutschland* (Göttingen, 1980), pp. 216–18. H. West, 'Göttingen and Weimar', *Central European History*, 11 (1978), pp. 150–61, has material on the growing recognition of the importance of travel and mobility.

17. Möller, op.cit., pp. 496ff; R. Vierhaus, 'Deutschland im 18 Jahrhundert'; in R.Vierhaus (ed.) *Deutsche patriotische und gemeinnützige Gesellschaften* (Munich, 1980), pp. 187–8; J. Van Horn Melton, 'From enlightenment to revolution', *Central European History*, 12 (1979), pp. 103–23, especially p. 11 on the massive expansion in the output of periodicals after the Seven Years' War. The largest 'political' journal, Schlözer's *Statsanzeigen*, printed about 4,500 copies.

18. Quoted by N. Hammerstein, 'Das politische Denken Friedrich Carl von Mosers', *Historische Zeitschrift*, 212 (1971), pp. 316–38 (332). There is some material on the Patriots in M. Lindemann, *Patriots and Paupers: Hamburg, 1712–1830* (Oxford & New York, 1990), pp. 5ff.

The Patriot movement represented a kind of political 'third way' between the corporative state of Estates, regarded as reactionary, and the enlightened absolute monarchy, and a middle culture between the Frenchified courts and nobility and the traditional regional *altständisch* (old estate or corporate) culture. It was based on the involvement of the people, by which was understood the middle classes, in the state and in that lay the roots of popular sovereignty, democracy and modern nationalism.

In Germany the issue was complicated by the fact that every German had two states, the territorial state and the Reich. 'Fatherland' could mean either of these or the German nation as an abstract cultural entity without borders. German patriotism was therefore innately ambivalent; it could lead to support for the untrammelled freedom of the individual states (*Staatssouveränität*) to liberate the reforming urges of progressive rulers, or for a revitalisation of the imperial constitution as a barrier against the despotism of an unenlightened prince.

A majority of the German Patriots accepted that the essence of a good political system was one in which the only limits on freedom were those made necessary by the common good and in which there was some mechanism to restrain or moderate the exercise of power. This could include enlightened public opinion, written constitutions or law codes, creating the state based on law (*Rechtsstaat*), intermediate powers, such as parliamentary institutions, or the imperial laws and tribunals.

The Empire was far from ideal as a political organisation, but it was held to be capable of reform which would bring it closer to such an ideal. There was also a general acceptance that the Empire had ceased to be a unitary monarchical state in anything but a symbolic sense and had evolved into a federative state. To enable it to exercise its vestigial state-like functions the Reich needed appropriate federal institutions, including a high court to act as an ultimate tribunal of appeal, to set standards of law and to arbitrate in disputes. Although it had ceased to be a power structure, it was still an organisation based on law, a structure capable of preserving peace and order. The principles implicit in absolutism, *la loi c'est moi, le droit c'est moi*, the unfettered right of the ruler to legislate, did not apply in the Holy Roman Empire. There rulers were held to be restrained by godly law, natural law, the fundamental laws of their state and the laws of the Empire. Imperial jurisdiction represented an independent judicature in the terms of Montesquieu's division of powers. The governments of the German states were subject to restraints on their freedom of action which were universally knowable in the form of imperial law. The behaviour of governments was itself subject to external standards of what was right, including minimum standards in the dispensing of justice. In all such matters the imperial courts exercised a supervisory, interpretative and enforcing role.

All these factors contributed to a wave of *Reichsreform* literature of enormous proportions in the later eighteenth century. The overwhelming bulk of the output was quite impractical and Utopian and much was anonymous or by obscure authors. It was produced by academics, *literati*, administrators of states large and small, historians and journalists. The authors, in a manner typical of the time, often combined academic and official functions.[19] Catalogues of names are tedious but examples will illustrate the wide interest in the German constitution and the great variety of the reform schemes put forward. These included a general secularisation, the elimination of the small states, trialism, institutional reform, the establishment of a genuinely representative *Reichstag* and a strengthening of imperial jurisdiction.

There was no unity among the advocates of *Reichsreform* though there are dangers in exaggerating the differences between them and in assigning the various publicists to hermetically self-contained categories. Interestingly, all shades of opinion saw something positive in the constitution of the Empire, at least as the framework for a political renewal of Germany. The reform movement had 'enlightened' and 'traditionalist' schools within it. Some like J.J. Moser were conservatives or legal positivists, concerned primarily with describing the German constitution and law as they had developed historically over centuries.[20] They were not concerned with measuring the constitution against some abstract rational model and their remedy for the obvious problems was a universal observance of imperial law as it stood rather than reform of it. Moser and others assigned to the constitutional law of the Empire the function assigned by Bodin and Hobbes to the sovereign, to act as an impartial agent for the maintenance of peace in a society threatened by internal dissolution. Justus Möser, another kind of 'traditionalist', was a powerful defender of the rights of Estates and corporations and strongly supported the Empire as guarantor of those rights.[21]

19. U.A.J. Becher, *Politische Gesellschaft*, op.cit., pp. 12–15.

20. Mack Walker, *Johann Jakob Moser* (Chapel Hill, NC, 1981).

21. Some notion of his assessment of success of the *Reichsreform* movement can be seen in the title of one of his works: *Ein sehr großer Vorschlag, der nicht ausgeführt werden wird* (*A very ambitious proposal which will not be put into practice*). J.B. Knudsen, *Justus Möser and the German Enlightenment* (Cambridge, 1986), includes (pp. 99ff) material on imperial reform literature.

The reform schemes put forward by J.J. Moser's son, Friedrich Karl Moser, in the 1750s and 1760s, in a number of pamphlets and books, especially his anonymously published *Von dem deutschen Nationalgeist* (*On the German National Spirit*) (1765) and *Patriotische Briefe* (*Patriotic Letters*) are better known. Moser, like his father, was a practical administrator and politician, as well as an academic commentator. He was chief minister of Hesse-Darmstadt and a member of the imperial aulic council in the years 1767 to 1770 and 1780 to 1798. He saw the revival of the court as the starting-point in his scheme for a patriotic revival of Germany.

Other writers were more progressive. Karl Friedrich Häberlin (1756–1808), an academic lawyer, a practitioner in the *Reichskammergericht* and a diplomat in the service of Brunswick, was a leading advocate of *Reichsreform*. He regarded the imperial courts as the last barrier against despotic government and praised the imperial system for giving Germans a measure of freedom and security, the like of which was enjoyed only by the English. A.L. von Schlözer, one of the fathers of German liberalism, was a pioneer of political journalism in Germany as well as an academic historian and his journal *Staatsanzeigen* had the largest circulation of any such publication in Germany. Otto Heinrich Freiherr von Gemmingen (1755–1836), a diplomat, playwright and author, while Badenese envoy in Vienna, published a pamphlet *Ich bin ein Deutscher und will ein Deutscher bleiben* (*I am German and wish to remain German*). Wilhelm Ludwig Wekhrlin (1739–92) was a bold and active journalist of advanced views and publisher of a number of magazines, the most famous of which was *Das graue Ungeheuer* (*The Grey Monster*). In November 1783 Wilhelm von Edelsheim, chief minister of Baden, put forward a scheme for a union of the Third Germany, excluding the two great powers, plus an institutional reform of the Reich. One of the best-known advocates of *Reichsrefor* including a thoroughgoing modernisation of the judicial system, was Karl Theodor von Dalberg, the last elector of Mainz.[22] Other examples were Johann H.G. von Justi, a Prussian officer, professor of *Cameralwissenschaft* (the 'science of administration') in Vienna and supervisor of the Prussian glass and steel works, Wiguläus F.A. Kreitmayr, chancellor of Bavaria in the 1760s and a noted commentator on imperial law, and Gerlach

---

22. After 1803 von Dalberg played an important role in the reorganisation of Germany by the French, with whom he cooperated willingly. He probably believed it would be possible to enlist Napoleon as a genuine protector of German interests, to retain something of the imperial constitution and to defend the smaller states. He was mistaken on every count. Neither Napoleon nor the larger German rulers intended the League of the Rhine to be a genuine union.

A. von Münchhausen, prime minister of Hannover and a prominent legal and constitutional theorist.

Support for a powerful federal jurisdiction reappeared during the troubled last years of the Reich and after its end in 1806.[23] There is still dispute among historians whether the French period, 1792 to 1814, saw a rapid modernisation, the catching-up of a Germany previously sunk in lethargy and stagnation, or brought to an end an established process of political change.[24] During it major steps were taken to turn Germany into a confederation of sovereign states. Mediatisation swept away hundreds of 'sovereign' entities. Many of the German states began substantial internal reform and this often involved a sustained assault on the rights of privileged corporations, which had earlier looked to the imperial courts to preserve their position. For such groups the virtues of the mediating and conserving imperial structure became more obvious when it had disappeared.

Napoleon originally planned to establish a federal supreme court in the Confederation of the Rhine (*Rheinbund*) established in July 1806. A draft constitution was drawn up in February 1806 but this did not come into effect. The powerful member states were unhappy about any diminution of their sovereignty.

Attempts were made to resurrect something of the institutional framework of the Holy Roman Empire during the negotiations at the Vienna Congress in 1814 and 1815 and there was a lively debate on the advantages and disadvantages of the old imperial constitution. There were many calls, especially from the mediatised and smaller states, for the restoration of the office of Emperor hereditary in the house of Austria and for a revival of at least the legal protective framework of the Empire in the form of the supreme court. Twenty-nine governments, later joined by five more, argued that they were not bound by the Treaty of Paris, under which a Germanic confederation was to be established, not having been signatories to it, and that, in calling for the restoration of a modernised Empire, they spoke for the majority of Germans. This early plea for national self-determination was not to come to anything, mainly because of the unwillingness of

23. See the list of reform proposals in H. Schulz for the period 1797 to 1806 in his 1926 Gießen dissertation *Vorschläge zur Reichsreform in der Publizistik von 1800–1806*. See also R. Berney, 'Reichstradition und Nationalstaatsgedanke (1789–1815)', *Historische Zeitschrift*, 140 (1929), pp. 57–86; and W. Mommsen, 'Zur Bedeutung des Reichsgedankens', *Historische Zeitschrift*, 174 (1952), pp. 385–415.

24. R. Vierhaus, 'Politisches Bewußtsein in Deutschland vor 1789', *Der Staat*, 6 (1967), pp. 175–96. See also H.-U. Wehler, *Deutsche Gesellschaftsgeschichte: vol. I. 1700–1815* (Munich,1987).

the larger states to tolerate anything which infringed their sovereignty, but it was the subject of lively discussion.[25] Prussian draft constitutions for the Confederation, W. von Humboldt's *Denkschrift über die deutsche Verfassung* (*Memorandum on the German constitution*) (1813) and Hardenberg's draft of 13 September 1814, contained provision for a federal court to act as a tribunal of first instance in disputes between member states. Under another article subjects were to be allowed access to this court under certain circumstances.

There was a skeletal superior jurisdiction in the 1815 Confederation but it did not develop. The built-in anomaly between the claims of the member states to total sovereignty and the *Bund*'s powers of supervision and intervention was never resolved.[26] There was no supreme court in the Confederation though it was laid down in the Act of Association that each member state had to have a proper independent judicial system with three separate instances and Article 53 of the Vienna Final Act gave the *Bund* limited rights of intervention to deal with differences between member states and in defence of subjects' rights.

In addition, the Federal Diet did, on occasion, operate as an informal judicial tribunal, reproducing some of the functions of the old imperial courts. This quasi-judicial authority was possible under Article 13 of the Act of Confederation, which laid down that all member states had to have constitutions based on Estates. The restoration of Estates constitutions was to lead to political battles in a number of states, as the nobility and other privileged groups tried to use this as a means of undoing modernisation measures, for example the abolition of privileges, carried through during the Napoleonic period. In 1816 the liberal Grand Duke of Saxe-Weimar asked the Federal Assembly to guarantee the constitution he had just negotiated with his subjects and specifically requested it to enforce verdicts of the Saxe-Weimar supreme court against grand-ducal officials if the Estates brought successful cases against them and a future Grand-Duke refused to carry out the verdict. In spite of considerable opposition from Metternich the Diet agreed to this. During the debate the representative of the Saxon

25. H. Ullmann, 'Zur Entstehung der Kaisernote der 29 Kleinstaaten vom 16.November 1814', *Historische Zeitschrift*, 116 (1916), pp. 459–83; H. Durchardt, 'Reichsritterschaft und Reichskammergericht', *Zeitschrift für historische Forschung*, 5 (1978), pp. 315–37 (especially p. 337); and H.R. Feller, *Die Bedeutung des Reichs und seiner Verfassung für die mittelbaren Untertanen und die Landstände im Jahrhundert nach dem Westfälischen Frieden* (Marburg dissertation, 1953), p. 180, note 78. Generally for diplomacy in 1814–15 see E.E. Kraehe, *Metternich's German Policy* 2 vols (Princeton, NJ, 1963–84), vol.2.

26. F. Hartung, *Deutsche Verfassungsgeschichte*, pp. 176–77. See now D. Grimm, *Deutsche Verfassungsgeschichte 1776–1866* (Frankfurt, 1988), pp. 65–68.

states said that it was necessary to avoid the impression that the only aim of the Confederation was to secure the sovereign rights of the states while denying subjects the rights they had enjoyed, as least in theory, under the previous imperial constitution. The Federal Assembly also involved itself in constitutional disputes in Württemberg (1817) and Lippe-Detmold (1819–1838), in the latter case establishing a mediation commission, but it refused attempts by representatives of more liberal governments to make it a general constitutional court of appeal. During the French period constitutions had become firmly established as part of the German political scene and there had been a clear change of attitude on how the exercise of power was to be restrained. The nineteenth century liberal notion of the *Rechtsstaat* as a guarantee against abuses of government power found its strongest expression in Germany in the idea of an independent judicial system and the right to impeach ministers, rather than other barriers against tyranny, such as the division of powers or a right of resistance deriving from an implied contract. But Rotteck and Welcker's *Staatslexikon* (1845–8) praised the imperial courts as ornaments of the old imperial system and expressed the view that their revival would be greeted with enthusiasm in the Germany of the 1840s. The 1848 German constitution proposed in §125 a *Reichsgericht* as a supreme court of cassation and a constitutional court.[27]

Some historians argue that imperial jurisdiction had a negative side: the availability of litigation to subjects suffering oppression weakened the Germans' self-help instincts and strengthened their tendency to look for help and reform from above. Some see the existence of the imperial courts as a barrier to modernisation; by defending the Estates, based as they were on corporate liberties and privileges, they prevented the introduction of reforms like equality before the law and the abolition of tax exemptions.[28] It is possible to exaggerate the immobility of the Empire and the glacial nature of change in it. The basic concern of the imperial courts was indeed to maintain the legal status quo, to preserve existing rights against encroachment, but they did, for example, intervene actively in constitutional disputes in a number of states and free cities to protect the subject or to mediate new constitutions. They did not act simply to preserve the power of traditional elites; their main function was the maintenance of public order and

27. See E. Hucko (ed.) *The Democratic Tradition: Four German Constitutions* (Leamington Spa, 1987), pp. 102–4.

28. G. Strauss, 'The Holy Roman Empire Revisited', p. 292; the Empire was " a structure that guaranteed status, privilege and property by acting as a barrier against change."

observance of the law. In his 1802 draft on the German constitution Hegel recognised this in his description of the German Reich as 'a system of the most comprehensive justice' ('*ein System der durchgeführtesten Gerechtigkeit*').

SUGGESTIONS FOR FURTHER READING

K. O. v. Aretin, *Heiliges Römisches Reich 1776 bis 1806: Reichsverfassung und Staatssouveranität*, 2 vols (Wiesbaden, 1967).

T.C.W. Blanning, *Reform and Revolution in Mainz* (Cambridge, 1974).

J. Gagliardo, *Reich and Nation: The Holy Roman Empire as Idea and as Reality 1763–1806* (Bloomington, Ind. and London, 1980).

H. Gross, *Empire and Sovereignty: A History of the Public Law Literature in the Holy Roman Empire* (Chicago and London, 1973).

M. Hughes, *Law and Politics in Eighteenth-Century Germany* (Woodbridge, 1988).

Journal of Modern History, 58 (1961), Supplement, 'Politics and Society in the Holy Roman Empire 1500–1806'.

H. Möller, *Fürstenstaat oder Bürgernation: Deutschland 1763–1815* (Berlin, 1989).

B. Roeck, *Reichssytem und Reichsherkommen. Die Diskussion über die Staatlichkeit des Reiches in der politischen Publizistik des 17. und 18. Jahrhunderts* (Stuttgart, 1984).

H. Schilling, *Höfe und Allianzen: Deutschland 1648–1763* (Berlin, 1989)

H. Schulz, *Vorschläge zur Reichsreform in der Publizistik von 1800–1806* (Diss., University of Gießen, 1926).

J.J. Sheehan, *German History 1770–1866* (Oxford, 1989).

G. Strauss, 'The Holy Roman Empire revisited', *Central European History*, 11 (1978), pp. 290–301.

J.A. Vann, *The Swabian Kreis: Institutional Growth in the Holy Roman Empire 1648–1715* (Brussels, 1975).

J.A. Vann and S. Rowan (eds) *The Old Reich* (Brussels, 1974).

M. Walker, *Johann Jakob Moser and the Holy Roman Empire of the German Nation* (Chapel Hill, NC, 1980).

CHAPTER THREE

State and nationality in the Napoleonic period

James J. Sheehan

In order to establish its identity, every nation must seek to create a national history. As official versions of the nation's origins, these histories forge a nation's links to its past, provide justifications for its present, and establish guidelines for its future. Because national histories tell the story of how a nation had to become what it is, they are all both deterministic and teleological. However many distractions and defeats a nation might suffer on its path to nationhood, the path itself was set, the national journey planned, the final destination unavoidable. Of course there are often those who attempt to delay the nation's formation: foreign enemies, who are frightened or envious of the nation's power, and – even worse – domestic opponents, who cannot or will not accept the nation's true destiny. Characteristically, national histories describe how the representatives of true nationhood eventually triumph over their foes at home and abroad in a struggle that continues to resonate in the contemporary political world, where international enmity and internal discontents still test the nation's resolve.

Germany is the *locus classicus* of national history. Nowhere else in Europe were historians so deeply engaged in the political process of nation-building, nowhere was history a more powerful weapon in the battle for national identity, and nowhere did an official version of the national past triumph so completely over its rivals. By the middle decades of the nineteenth century, the advocates of a Prussian-led German nation-state had begun to formulate an account of the German past that bolstered Prussia's claims. After 1866, when Prussia's military victories opened the way for her political hegemony, this account became – and in many ways remains – 'German history'. Central to this account is a dual process of self-awareness: it is essentially the story of how the German folk became aware of their identity as Germans and of how the Prussian state became aware of its mission to create a German nation-state. Bismarck, the architect of German national unification, brought these two stories together in a series of military and political triumphs. The result was the Germany that had to be, the Germany created between 1866 and 1871.[1]

In this version of the national past, the revolutionary period has an especially important part. In 1842–3 Johann Gustav Droysen, one of the founders of the Prussian (or *kleindeutsch*) school of German history, interrupted his work on the Hellenistic period to deliver a series of lectures on what he called 'the age of the wars of liberation', which were published three years later. Although Droysen discussed developments from 1770 to 1815, the culmination of his story was those 'unforgettable years . . . in which for the first time in centuries, the German *Volk*, together and with a deep sense of unity, struggled and won'. But for Droysen, and for the generations who followed him, the wars of liberation involved not only a mobilization of the *Volk*, but also a recognition on the part of the Prussian state that it had a historic mission to fulfil. 'From then on,' Droysen wrote, 'it belonged to the true character of the state to be national, and to the true character of the *Volk* to have a state'.[2]

In this chapter I offer a critique of this traditional view of state and nation in the revolutionary period. I shall argue that the most important impact of the French conquest was not on German national identity, but rather on the politics of the various states, that among the German states the Prussian experience was not exceptional, but rather part of a larger pattern of reform and reorganization, and finally, that the impact of nationalism during the so-called 'wars of liberation' was limited to a small minority of Germans, especially German intellectuals, whose memoirs and historical accounts helped to create a mythic image of the national past.

STATES AND REVOLUTION

The period with which we are concerned was one of the most turbulent in modern European history. Between the storming of the Bastille

1. For more on these issues, see J. Sheehan, 'What is German history? Reflections on the role of the nation in German history and historiography', *Journal of Modern History*, 53/1 (1981), pp 1–23, W. Hardtwig, 'Von Preussens Aufgabe in Deutschland zu Deutschlands Aufgabe in der Welt', *Historische Zeitschrift*, 231/2 (1980), pp. 265–324, and the essays in O. Büsch and J. Sheehan (eds) *Die Rolle der Nation in der Deutschen Geschichte und Gegenwart* (Berlin, 1985).

2. Droysen, *Vorlesungen über das Zeitalter der Freiheitskriege* (Gotha, 1886, 2nd edn.), vol. 1, p. 3 and vol. 2, p. 457.

in 1789 and Napoleon's final defeat at Waterloo in 1815, war and rebellion raged across the continent, sometimes spilling over into Europe's colonial extensions. Ancient institutions crumbled, kings toppled from their thrones, territories changed hands with bewildering speed. From the Iberian peninsula to the heart of imperial Russia, statesmen struggled to survive while ordinary men and women felt the power of political change and paid the price for political conflict. Like the years between 1914 and 1945, the only other modern period with which it might be compared, the revolutionary era was characterized by a reciprocally reinforcing collapse of both the domestic and international orders. Within France itself, the war that began in the spring of 1792 'revolutionized the revolution' as the new government desperately sought to mobilize the nation's social and political energies, first just to survive, then to sustain an ever-widening circle of conquest. At the same time, the victorious French armies brought revolutionary change with them, to the lands annexed to France, to the satellite states established along France's frontiers, and, most important of all, to those states that tried to imitate French methods in order to stop French expansion. As a result of almost a quarter of a century of continued upheaval, the style, scope and stakes of politics were permanently transformed.[3]

This transformation was particularly significant for the history of German Europe, that diverse and politically fragmented collection of states, independent cities and semi-sovereign territories, which in 1789 was still loosely knit together by the Holy Roman Empire. Almost from the start, the reverberations within France were felt by the old-fashioned regimes along the Empire's western border. In 1792 and 1793 French forces conquered, were driven from, and finally reconquered German territory on both sides of the Rhine. By the end of the decade, the revolutionary armies, now under the inspired military leadership of Napoleon Bonaparte, had pushed deep into German Europe. After a series of stunning victories against the major German states, Napoleon established a system of allies and satellites in order to provide a buffer between France and potential enemies in the east. In 1806 he collected these polities in the Rhenish Confederation, a French-sponsored league that replaced the old Empire, which passed virtually unmourned from the historical stage. But because they were never enough to satisfy his apparently insatiable lust for power and

---

3. On the relationship between domestic change and international conflict, see T.C.W. Blanning, *The Origins of the French Revolution Wars* (London and New York, 1986) and G. Best, *War and Society in Revolutionary Europe* (New York and Oxford, 1986).

glory, Napoleon's conquests did not bring stability. Finally, after his disastrous defeat in Russia in 1812, his former allies edged away and his old enemies recovered their will to resist him. In October 1813 a multi-national force defeated Napoleon at Leipzig and within a few months, his domination over central Europe was broken. But long after the Emperor himself had reached his final exile, the effects of his rule remained.

Although the geographical shape and political order of almost every German state changed between 1789 and 1815, the intensity of change varied: it was greatest in the areas on the west bank of the Rhine that were directly annexed by France, weakest in a few of the middle-sized northern and central states that somehow managed to stay out of the path of the French juggernaut. But with few exceptions, every German polity had to bear the extraordinary costs of war – costs that were hardly less punishing for France's supposed allies than for her would-be antagonists. Moreover, many states had to come to terms with a radical redefinition of their territorial identity: at one time or another, almost 60 per cent of the German population changed rulers in this period. Taken together, the fiscal burdens of war and the political task of state building required that governments find new ways to mobilize the social, economic and spiritual resources of their populations. Whether they wanted to or not, German statesmen had to follow the French example: We must create, the Prussian reformer Hardenberg wrote,

> a revolution in the positive sense . . . to be made not through violent impulses from below or outside, but through the wisdom of the government . . . Democratic principles in a monarchical government – that seems to me to be the appropriate form for the spirit of our age.[4]

Among the most durable political creations of the revolutionary era were the so-called *Mittelstaaten*, the medium-sized states in south-western Germany that Napoleon assembled from the scattered fragments of the old Empire. In the following brief summary of German politics, I shall concentrate on the most important of these states – Baden, Württemberg and Bavaria – whose development I shall then compare with the situation in Prussia.

Napoleon's decision to establish the *Mittelstaaten* was dictated by French national interests: the Emperor wanted a band of states large enough to stabilize his eastern frontier, but not powerful enough to challenge France. With this in mind, he provided cooperative dynasties

---

4. P. Thielen, *Karl August von Hardenberg, 1750–1822* (Cologne and Berlin, 1967), p. 207.

with former free cities, ecclesiastical principalities, and other minor imperial territories. Relatively speaking, the biggest beneficiary from this apparent largesse was the Margrave of Baden-Durlach, who, in addition to becoming a Grand Duke, greatly expanded his modest holdings with the former bishoprics of Constance, Basel, Strassburg and Speyer, as well as part of the Palatinate, including the cities of Mannheim and Heidelberg. The Duke of Württemberg received a royal title as well as substantial territories. The Elector of Bavaria, also a newly minted king, now ruled over the most important of the new states, which comprised the rich lands once held by bishops and independent city-states.

Of course polities had always grown and declined, added territories after victory, lost them after defeats. In the past, however, when a territory changed hands it was often simply grafted on to its new owner, usually joined through dynastic ties and military force; only gradually, if at all, were these new lands fused with the conqueror's social and political order. Such an arrangement could not work in the revolutionary period. In the first place, in the course of the eighteenth century statesmen had developed a new sense of what states should be like: no longer just conglomerates of varied pieces, states should have unified laws and common institutions, through which they could be uniformly governed and centrally controlled. Moreover – and more important than these still largely theoretical aspirations – the old methods simply could not have worked given the scale of state-building the new governments faced. In a state like Baden, for example, which had to absorb extensive new possessions with diverse institutions and loyalties, conglomeration would have produced chaos. And chaos was just what the French patrons of the new states wanted to avoid. Instead they wanted stability and support – money, resources and manpower to feed the limitless appetites of the imperial war machine. To provide these things, the governments of the *Mittelstaaten* had to organize and control their recent acquisitions.

Except in Württemberg, where King Frederick played an important political role, the direction of reform in the *Mittelstaaten* was in the hands of civil servants, who used the special opportunities offered by the revolution to impose their own vision on their states. Most of these men had held important positions under the old regime; many, such as Count Montgelas in Bavaria or Karl von Hardenberg in Prussia, came from aristocratic families with European connections. Not surprisingly, the reformers' first task was to create a well-ordered and responsive administrative apparatus. Everywhere the jumble of overlapping jurisdictions that had limited the effectiveness of pre-revolutionary bureaucracies was replaced by ministries with well-defined responsibilities for particular governmental functions. At the same time, lines of command between the central government and the localities were sharpened, new administrative districts were created, and the relationship between state authority and traditional institutions was clarified. Several states also instituted new regulations governing the recruitment, promotion and conduct of state employees, who were thereby protected from unwarranted interference by the monarch. In effect, the new administrative arrangements increased civil servants' power over their societies as well as over their own institutions.

Reform also involved social emancipation. This meant the removal of traditional restraints on people's mobility, property and labour. For instance, guilds lost most of their power to limit the number of those who could practise a particular trade; cities lost the right to control who could reside within their walls. Jews, whose ability to work and live where they wished was tightly restrained, were given greater – but by no means total – social and economic freedom. Peasants were freed from many of their dues and services that tied them to their landlords. All in all, emancipation was supposed to release the productive forces in society and thereby encourage economic growth and social progress. But at the same time, it cleared the institutional ground between the individual and the state by cutting away that web of traditional bodies that had once surrounded – and sometimes protected – most Germans. In this sense, emancipation was closely tied to the growth of bureaucratic power, indeed the two were different sides of the same historical movement.

We can see the connection between bureaucratization and emancipation in the constitutions that were introduced into most of the *Mittelstaaten* in the final stages of the reform era. On the one hand, these constitutions set legal limits on governmental power and provided guarantees for individuals' civil rights. On the other hand, however, they also affirmed the central importance of the civil servant for the political and social order. Constitution and administration – *Verfassung* and *Verwaltung* – were not opposing developments, but integral parts of the process of state-building: Baden, for instance, had both the strongest constitution and the most firmly entrenched bureaucracy of any German state.

While the French victories were creating the newly enlarged states of the south and west, the kingdom of Prussia had remained on the sidelines. From 1795, when Prussia had signed a peace treaty with the French in order to concentrate on getting its share of the disintegrating Polish state, until 1806, the Prussian government had tried to pursue a policy of self-serving neutrality. During this period, some progressive elements within the civil service had tried to press for reform, but their efforts were frustrated by the indecisiveness of the king and the power of the old elites at court, in the army, and in local government. But in Prussia, as in the *Mittelstaaten*, foreign affairs created the possibility for domestic reform: in 1806, King Frederick William allowed himself to be drawn into a war with Napoleon at a most inopportune moment. The result was the twin military disasters of Jena and Auerstädt and the dismemberment of the kingdom. There seemed good reason to believe that Prussia's long and difficult climb to great power status had come to end.

In the period of crisis that followed defeat, the Prussian reformers got their chance. Led first by Baron vom Stein, then by Hardenberg, a new government introduced many of the same measures that were being adopted throughout the German lands. The bureaucracy was reconstituted, ministries formed, local administration redesigned. Serfdom, which was more onerous in Prussia's eastern provinces than in most of the southern and western states, was abolished. The authority of the guilds and local communities – weaker to begin with than in many states – was further limited. Moreover, the king, prompted by his reform-minded advisers, promised that he would grant his subjects a constitution that would guarantee their basic rights and introduce representative institutions.

Both the origins and structure of the Prussian reforms strongly resembled developments in the *Mittelstaaten*: in all of these states, external pressures were decisive; in all of them, civil servants played key roles and administrative reform had a special place; everywhere, emancipatory measures struck down traditional privileges and encouraged mobility and growth. There was not, as Prussia's scholarly admirers once argued, anything inauthentic about the changes introduced in the south and west, nor was there anything unique about the process in Prussia. If anything, the Prussian reforms were more limited in scope and qualified in accomplishment than their counterparts in Bavaria, Baden or Württemberg. In large measure this was because Prussia, unlike these smaller states, was able to rebuild its army and regain a place among the major powers: on the basis of these foreign political achievements, the king recovered the will and the ability to set limits on reform, broke his promise of a constitution, and reinstated some of the privileges of the old elites. Ironically, the same foreign political successes that opened the way to reaction after 1815, later became the basis for Prussia's claim to leadership of the German national movement.

STATES AND THE NATION

Before following the second strand of our story during the Napoleonic period, it is necessary to say a few words about the *nation* as a historical category. In the national histories that I mentioned at the beginning of this chapter, the existence of the nation is assumed. National histories show how people become conscious of the nationality they already possess, how states realize their national mission, how nation-states take their true form. Not surprisingly, the language of national history is filled with organic imagery: nationalism has deep 'roots' in the past, ideas provide the 'seeds' of nationhood, nations 'grow' and 'mature'. The message of these metaphors is clear: nationality is an essential element of human identity, nations are the most important focus for public loyalties, the nation-state is the most natural unit of political organization. In fact, when seen against the broad sweep of European history, all of these propositions are dubious: the triumph of nationalism and the nation-state was short-lived and incomplete, the always problematic product of a particular set of historical circumstances. Of course for centuries people had thought of themselves as French, or German, or English, but these national identities were almost always less important than their religion, region, immediate community and kin. For most of Europe's past, therefore, nationality ranked fairly low among people's various loyalties and a fusion of national identity and political organization would have seemed neither necessary nor possible.[5]

During the eighteenth century some Germans became aware of their nationality's importance. To an intellectual like J.G. Herder, for example, all authentic cultures had a national base: a people's art and literature drew its strength and character from the language, mores and past experiences of the collectivity that Herder called the *Volk*. At a time when Germans were creating a national literature, this insistence on the cultural nationality seemed to make a great deal of sense. Moreover, to educated men and women – the readers and writers who made this national literature possible – German culture, that is *their* culture, seemed clearly superior to the Frenchified culture of the aristocracy and courts. German national consciousness, therefore, was

5. Among the many theoretical works on nationalism, I find those by Ernest Gellner especially useful: see his *Nations and Nationalism* (Ithaca, NY, and London, 1983). See also J. Breuilly's broadly based and carefully argued insistence on the centrality of politics for understanding nations and nationalism: *Nationalism and the State* (Manchester, 1982).

inseparable from a cultural struggle against foreign and especially against French influences. But virtually no one believed that this cultural struggle had to do with politics as we understand it. Nationality had little or nothing to do with states.

After their initial enthusiasm for the French Revolution had passed, most German intellectuals viewed what was happening west of the Rhine in terms of this cultural antagonism between Germans and Frenchmen. Now, however, the enemy was not a superficial and materialistic court culture, but a shallow and mechanistic rationalism that threatened deeper, more authentic German values.

We can see this shift with particular clarity in the career of Joseph Görres. Born in 1776, Görres grew up in Koblenz where he witnessed the upheavals following the French invasion. Originally, Görres viewed the invaders as the instruments of enlightenment ideals and historical progress; in 1798 he laid his essay on 'Universal Peace' at 'the altar of the fatherland', by which he meant the French republic. But when he went to Paris a year later, he was shocked by what he found. The French, he discovered, might be quicker and wittier than the Germans, but they were also unreliable and shallow; the Germans were slow, but persistent and deep. Eventually he recognized that the divisions between the two nations were profound; France was his fatherland no longer.[6]

At first, Görres's hostility towards the French had no political implications. But in late 1812 and 1813, as Napoleon's military fortunes began to decline, Görres began to talk about a national uprising against the tyrant, an uprising that would be 'the destiny of the species for many generations'. Soon he became a leading ideologist for the 'war of liberation', whose sacred mission he celebrated in an influential journal, *Der Rheinische Merkur*. Together with a number of other prominent intellectuals who were inspired by this last great struggle against the French, Görres now argued that national culture had to have a political basis: the identity of the *Volk* and their lands, he believed, required common institutions and a common constitution. Although these advocates of a united Germany were often uncertain about its precise shape and divided about what kind of institutions it should have, they did see − as a thinker like Herder had not − that nationality was a political as well as a cultural phenomenon.

The nationalist intellectuals' prominence was greatly enhanced by their relationship with the political leaders of the anti-French campaign. In the course of 1813 and 1814, Görres and other self-ap-

6. On Görres's development, see Sheehan, *German History, 1770–1866* (Oxford, 1989), pp. 374ff.

pointed spokesmen for the *Volk* were taken up by the leaders of Russia and Prussia, who subsidized their publications and apparently endorsed their ideas. Although national historians have made a great deal of this cooperation, it is important to bear in mind how very brief and instrumental it was. Understandably enough, Napoleon's enemies recognized the potential advantage of having public support for their efforts. Moreover, they wanted to put pressure on those German princes still allied to France by threatening to mobilize their populations against them. Nevertheless, as soon they could, most governments withdrew their always tentative endorsement of national enthusiasms. With Napoleon safely out of the way, Görres, for example, found himself without official support. Before long, the authorities closed his journal, censored his writings, and eventually forced him into exile.

It is also important not to lose sight of the fact that the popular appeal of nationalist propaganda was very limited. Even among intellectuals, the group most susceptible to nationalist feelings, there were many who looked upon the war with hostility and suspicion. Goethe, for example, never approved of patriotic posturing, while the philosopher Hegel retained his admiration for Napoleon until the very end. There were, to be sure, a number of young people who donned what they regarded as authentic Germanic outfits and performed gymnastics under the leadership of *Turnvater* Jahn on Berlin's Hasenheide. Some students rushed to the colours in 1813 and fought valiantly in Freiherr von Lützow's Free Corps. Theodor Körner, a young poet who died while serving with Lützow, left behind some stirring verses celebrating the joys of comradeship and the thrill of combat:

> As brothers we are all together
> Which makes our courage grow,
> Joined by language's holy bond,
> By one God and one Fatherland,
> Faithful, German blood.

But patriotic youngsters like Körner were a small minority in 1813 – even, as it turns out, among Lützow's volunteers, who were mainly craftsmen and labourers, not the idealistic students whose legendary exploits have been celebrated again and again in the histories of national liberation.[7]

We have no way of knowing how deeply nationalist feelings pene-

7. H. Zimmer, *Auf dem Altar des Vaterlandes: Religion und Patriotismus in der deutschen Kriegslyrik des 19. Jahrhunderts* (Frankfurt, 1971), p. 35. On the social composition of the Free Corps, see the data gathered by R. Ibbeken, *Preussen, 1807–1813* (Cologne and Berlin, 1970).

trated into German society. There is some evidence that most people remained unmoved by the struggle against France, probably because they were preoccupied, as they had every reason to be, with the harsh necessities of everyday life. The strongest opposition to France seems to have been caused less by the new national ideals than by more traditional sources of antagonism: the opposition of devout Christians towards French religious policies, the hostility of those who suffered from French taxes or economic competition, the resentment of tightly knit communities towards strangers. Significantly, the only popular German rising against France (which in fact began as a rebellion against another German state) took place in the Tyrol, a region that was socially and culturally far removed from national ideology. Overall, therefore, the role of the *Volk* in their own liberation was limited. Napoleon was defeated and driven out of German Europe by an alliance of states, whose regular armies defeated him in the field. The victors at Waterloo were those dogged defenders of the old regime, the Duke of Wellington and General von Blücher.

By forcing it into the mould of national history, conventional historiography has not only distorted the details but also obscured the real significance of the revolutionary period for German developments. This significance had less do with creating the national future than with destroying the past: by sweeping away the Holy Roman Empire, most of the free imperial cities, the lands of the imperial nobility, the ecclesiastical principalities, and scores of other small polities, the forces of war and revolution cleared the social and political landscape of a thicket of traditional institutions that had ordered German public life for centuries. The immediate beneficiaries of this process were the states. Their triumph was, first of all, a matter of political geography; from the hundreds of entities that were scattered across German Europe in 1789, only about two dozen remained, the most prominent and important of which were those medium-sized states whose imprint has still not totally disappeared from the political map. But as important as the states' geographical pre-eminence was the triumph of the principles upon which state power rested, the principles of political sovereignty, integration and cohesion. From this perspective, we can see the revolutionary era as the culmination of the bureaucratic state's prolonged struggle against traditional limitations on its power.

But is it unreasonable to ask if this triumph is not itself part of the nation-building process? After all, wasn't the map of central Europe in 1815 one step closer to national unification than the kaleidoscopic landscape of the old Empire? The answer is yes, but only if the maps are set within the narrative frame of national history. Outside this frame, it is equally possible to argue that the *Mittelstaaten* formed after 1800 were impediments to nation-building since they were surely more willing and better able to defend their independence than most of the territories they absorbed.

But in two important ways the revolutionary period did help prepare the way for German unification under Prussian leadership.

First, Prussia emerged from this period substantially strengthened, in part by the reforms introduced in her political and military institutions, but much more by the addition of new territories in the west. The possession of substantial parts of the Rhineland and Westphalia provided the Hohenzollern with a bridge of influence across north-central Europe. Furthermore, the acquisition of the rich resources of the Ruhr (whose potential was unrecognized in 1815) helped provide the basis for Prussia's industrial and military power in the second half of the century. The coal and iron of the Ruhr had much more to do with the settlement of the German question in 1866 than the nationalist rhetoric of patriotic intellectuals and the youthful enthusiasm of the student volunteers. Ironically, the loss of a great deal of Polish territory in the east, against which Prussia had protested so vigorously in 1815, also enhanced her potential as a leader of the national cause.

Second, the story of the revolutionary period took on a significance of its own, important less for what happened than for what people thought had happened. In memoirs, history books, novels, and paintings, the 'wars of liberation' were shaped to fit an unfolding narrative of nation-building, in which the *Volk*'s historic rising became at once prologue and precondition of the nation's ultimate triumph. And like all authentic national myths, this saga was written and rewritten to fit the needs of different historical moments, from the early days of Bismarck's Reich, when Treitschke celebrated the reformers in his great history of the nineteenth century, to the closing days of Hitler's, when Goebbels tried to inspire patriotic fervor with a film about the heroic defence of Kolberg against the French. As historians, it is our task to view the myths of national history with critical detachment without ever losing sight of their power and persistence.[8]

8. The most suggestive work in English on the evolution of national myths is by George Mosse. See especially his *The Nationalization of the Masses* (New York, 1975). The most recent treatment of these issues is M. Hughes, *Nationalism and Society: Germany, 1800–1945* (London, 1988).

SUGGESTIONS FOR FURTHER READING

A complete guide to documents and source materials can be found in
K. Müller (ed.) *Absolutismus und Zeitalter der französischen Revolution
(1715–1815)* (Darmstadt, 1982). Among the recent works in German
the best are T. Nipperdey's *Deutsche Geschichte, 1800–1866: Bürgerwelt
und starker Staat* (Munich, 1983) and H. U. Wehler's *Deutsche Gesellschaftsgeschichte*, vols 1 and 2 (Munich, 1987). Wehler's extensive foot-
notes cite the most important literature, with particular emphasis on
social and economic developments.

The most complete treatment of the period in English is J. Sheehan, *German History, 1770–1866* (Oxford, 1989). On the revolution's
impact in particular regions, see T.C.W. Blanning's *The French Revolution in Germany: Occupation and Resistance in the Rhineland, 1792–1802*
(Oxford, 1983) and M. Walker, *German Home Towns: Community,
State, General Estate, 1648–1871* (Ithaca, NY, 1971). Three older
works are still useful for the evolution of political ideas: E.N. Anderson, *Nationalism and the Cultural Crisis in Prussia, 1806–1815* (New
York, 1939), R. Aris, *History of Political Thought in Germany from 1789
to 1815* (London, 1936) and G.P. Gooch, *Germany and the French Revolution* (London, 1920).

CHAPTER FOUR

Germany and the national question in 1848

Dieter Langewiesche

THE GERMAN CONFEDERATION AS A MULTI-NATIONAL LEAGUE OF STATES

No German national state was established in the territorial reordering of Europe which took place at the Congress of Vienna. The German Confederation which in 1815 replaced the Holy Roman Empire of the German nation was a league of states. Its establishment may have dashed the national hopes of many Germans but it fulfilled the wishes of European monarchs for a new international system in which no one state was dominant. The German Confederation was a mixture of the weaknesses and strengths which existed in central Europe. It bound forty-one states together so loosely that there was never any chance that they could pursue a common and active foreign policy. At the same time its existence acted as a constraint upon Russian or French attempts to achieve predominance in Europe.

The Confederation appeared unlikely to provide the basis of any moves towards a national state for a number of reasons. First, three foreign monarchs were connected to the Confederation through personal union: the English King as king of Hannover (until 1837); the Danish king as Duke of Holstein and Lauenburg (until 1864); and the King of the Netherlands as Grand Duke of Luxemburg and, from 1837, Duke of Limburg (until 1867). Second, Austria especially, but also Prussia, the two leading powers within the Confederation, were semi-detached members. The Prussian provinces of West and East Prussia, as well as its possession, the Grand Duchy of Posen, were not included within the Confederation. Austria, the old German imperial power, was a multi-national monarchy. Its Polish, Hungarian and Italian possessions also were not included in the Confederation. However, in those territories that were included, there lived nearly 6 million people of non-German nationality – Czechs and Slovenes,

Poles and Croats and Magyars, as well as more than 400,000 Italians. In various parts of the Habsburg monarchy which did belong to the Confederation, non-Germans predominated, as in Bohemia, Moravia, Silesia, Carinthia, Gorizia and Trieste. There were more Poles than Germans in the Grand Duchy of Posen as well. Thus within the Confederation and the closely connected Habsburg dynasty there lived just about every European nationality which did not yet possess its own nation-state. The Confederation was in danger of being plunged into nationality conflicts as soon as nationalism began to develop among these stateless nations. Every attempt to turn the Confederation into a German national-state must conflict with the interests of other nationalities, and every attempt by any of those nationalities to establish their own states must end up clashing with the German national movement. When revolution broke out in 1848 these latent problems were brought out into the open.

THE DREAM OF THE 'SPRINGTIME OF PEOPLES' AND ITS EARLY END

In 1848, for the first and last time a revolution covered the greater part of the continent – from France over the German and Italian states, throughout the territories of the Habsburg dynasty into Moldavia and Wallachia, Balkan possessions of the Ottoman Empire. Other states did not go unscathed. Reforms were speeded up in the Scandinavian countries, Belgium, the Netherlands and Switzerland. There were attempts at uprisings in Ireland, Spain, Greece and even in England. These all failed as did hope of radical change in Russia. This was a truly European revolution, but one which was to turn the various nations against one another.

The revolution began in February and March accompanied by the hope that this would see the 'springtime of the peoples', as this dream was called by contemporaries. It was a dream of a Europe in which the brotherhood of peoples would replace the self-seeking diplomacy of the old powers, inaugurating an era of a peaceful Europe made up of nations with equal rights organised into democratic states. Many writings, speeches and images testified to this belief that men stood on the edge of a new age, an age of independent and democratic nations.

The dream soon melted away. The idea of the nation did indeed come to be the strongest tie holding men together within the revolutionary movements, men who pursued very different goals within their different societies. But this same powerful ideal also led nations and nationalities against each other and into alliances which contradicted their democratic and liberal objectives. This was a general phenomenon: there was nothing special about the German national movement in this regard.

HALYCON DAYS OF REVOLUTION IN THE HABSBURG DYNASTY

We can begin our tour of the European nationality conflicts which undermined the attempt to establish a German national state with the observations of a shrewd contemporary who himself experienced and suffered through the dramatic evolution from solidarity to conflict. The report was that of a student from Cernowice, the largest town in Bohemia, who was living in Vienna, perhaps the best vantage point from which to see these changes. The Habsburg dynasty was more affected than any other state by the claims to equal treatment made by the various nationalities and Vienna was the dynasty's seismographic centre. When a constitution was promised, the student wrote to his parents in Cernowice in mid-April 1848 that

> the most touching scenes took place. While mounted soldiers, greeted everywhere with applause, rode through the city announcing the news, one could see Poles and Germans, Italians and Bohemians, Hungarians and Tyroleans link arms and solemnly promise to reject every kind of national hatred. Citizens embraced students with tears of joy. One cannot describe how happy people were. In the evening there was a procession. The National Guard marched from the university along the street to the castle carrying before them a picture of the Emperor. Cries of 'Long live his Majesty!' continued through the whole night.[1]

These happy days of revolutionary harmony did not last long. Only three months later, in July, the same witness, a committed democrat, member of the Academic Legion (an independent part of the National Guard made up of students) which had played a key role in the early

1. P. Frank-Döfering, *Die Donner der Revolution über Wien: Ein Student aus Czernowitz erlebt 1848* (Vienna, 1988), p. 41.

stages of the revolution, described very different scenes when writing to his father. When the Hungarians 'praise their nobility', the Germans react with contempt.

> For isn't it the case, dear father, that the Hungarians never loved our Emperor as we German Bukowiner [inhabitants of the Duchy of Bukovina] do. It seems very odd to me the way in which the entire Italian contingent within the student body gradually no longer take up their posts, and there is a rumour that they have gone to help the Piedmontese. Now they fight against the dynasty and one hears that they would like to press on into the Tyrol.

Just as he wrote, another student burst into his room and jubilantly announced:

> the great victory of our general Radetzsky in Italy [the battle of Custozza on 25 July in which the Piedmontese army was defeated] . . . That removes the danger from the south to our country for the time being. But it brings with it a strange feeling when one thinks back to just a few months ago to the sense of brotherhood and the promises that were made of lasting friendship. That had a very short life. Now everyone has gone to the other extreme. It seems that those scenes, which I saw with my own eyes, have disappeared in the gunpowder smoke of the battlefield. Isn't it often the case, dear father, that one man's freedom leads to the oppression of another? Thus the cause in Italy is about the freedom of Italians but it also threatens us Germans in the Tyrol. Such questions of politics and philosophy drive one to despair. What appears good in philosophy, can be cruelly disfigured in the vicious world of politics.[2]

This student saw the nationality conflict from the perspective of some-one who had hoped to see the creation of a democratised dynasty under German leadership. If he had had better contacts with the dif-ferent non-German nationalities in Vienna he would have been able to recognise, even at the beginning of the revolution, that the dream of a 'springtime of peoples' could become a nightmare of nationalities. That could be seen more clearly and earlier in Vienna than anywhere else. By the end of March delegations of all the Slav nations – Slovaks, Serbians, Croatians, Czechs, Poles – appeared in Vienna to put their demands to the central government. They held festivals of brother-hood in Vienna. On one occasion 3,000 people took part. A partici-pant reported:

> a national celebration of a like never before experienced. Slavs demonstrated harmony and mutual respect. Harmony, the lack of which

2. Ibid., pp. 104–5.

has always been our great weakness and the cause of all our unhappiness, is now becoming a reality.[3]

This hope for harmony among the Slav nations was also soon dashed. There was only negative unity – against German demands such as the claims made by the German National Assembly to Bohemia, Moravia and Habsburg Silesia and against the Magyar claims to domination in transleithelan Hungary. That was the limit of practical agreement of Austro-Slavism which sought national autonomy against the larger and more powerful Germans and the Magyars and also against the ideas of Russian Pan-Slavism. In view of the threats from the Germans and Magyars the aim of Austro-Slavism in 1848 was not only to preserve the multi-national Habsburg dynasty, but also to reform it in order to create and protect rights of national self-determination. One might understand this as a rather modern idea, anticipating some of the projects of European integration of our own time which envisage autonomous nations under a supra-national umbrella. However, this would be misleading. The national movements in 1848, in the Habsburg Empire as elsewhere, sought to wrest freedom in both their internal and external affairs from the control of those who had held power over them. However, when these movements came into conflict with one another, they did not hesitate to form alliances with the old power-holders. Precisely because they could not resolve conflicts between themselves, these movements looked to the idea of a monarchical authority to do that for them. The illusion that it would be possible to use the old dynastic power structure to promote the cause of national liberation can be observed in all the areas where in 1848 national issues reached a crisis.

ILLUSIONS OF POWER IN FRANKFURT

In the German National Assembly meeting in Frankfurt there was an alarming expression of imperial wishes. Deputies talked of German hegemony from the North Sea and the Baltic to the Adriatic and the Black Sea. Money was collected in all German states for a navy which would project German strength into the wider world. This extravagant

3. Cited in R.G. Plaschka, *Nationalismus, Staatsgewalt, Widerstand: Aspekte nationaler und sozialer Entwicklung in Ostmittel - und Südosteuropa* (Munich, 1985), p. 154.

nationalism found support on the left as well as the right. Deputies looked to the past to justify visions of great power. Varnhagen von Ense appreciated acutely the problems of justifying the boundaries of a German nation state in historical terms:

> A union of Germans, unity for Germany – for some time these words have sounded sweet to the lovers of the nation. Unfortunately the actual issue is difficult, and we never seem to be able to pin it down. It is hard to determine precisely what nationality means because it has changed constantly from the earliest times. Franks and Anglo-Saxons left their homes, mixed with other nationalities, and in this way achieved greatness and freedom. Lombards and Vandals similarly lost their distinctive nationality when they moved to distant lands. Switzerland broke away from Germany, Slav Bohemia and Gallic Belgium joined Germany, and Alsace and Lorraine were given up. How can we decide what we should claim for Germany? There is no satisfactory solution to be had to this mixture of nationalities. We should be satisfied if we come even close to such a solution. In any case, nationality is not the sole, not even the most important basis on which to form states. Shared laws and freedoms are undoubtedly much more important than ethnic ties, especially when these ties have been broken and obscured.[4]

Eventually the majority of the National Assembly came round to this sensible point of view. Imperial rhetoric was confined to the domain of wishful thinking which the euphoria of revolution had spawned. It would, therefore, be unfair to judge the National Assembly of 1848–49 only by that rhetoric. Nevertheless, the assembly was no more prepared voluntarily to abandon national claims than any other nationality which sought a nation-state in those years.

VAIN HOPES FOR THE RESTORATION OF POLAND

How quickly oaths of solidarity between nations could turn into national rivalries is shown in the abortive attempts to create a Polish state. Since the failure of the Polish rising of 1831 the aim of Polish restoration had been taken up by all European freedom movements. Even within the German Confederation there were set up Polish associations which offered financial and moral support to Polish refugees.

4. V. von Ense, *Kommentare zum Zeitgeschehen. Publizistik, Briefe, Dokumente 1813–1858*, ed. W. Greiling (Leipzig, 1984), p. 172.

In March 1848 it appeared that revolution had once again placed the restoration of Poland on the agenda. The new Prussian government declared its support for 'national reorganisation' in the Grand Duchy of Posen, which had a Polish majority. The foreign minister von Arnim hoped for French help against Russia in order to restore Poland. This policy failed, partly because the French government and the Prussian king both rejected it, but also because the German and Polish national movements came into conflict with one another as soon as they moved from the pre-revolutionary expression of sentiments to concrete political action. It proved impossible to divide Posen into a German and a Polish area in a way which would satisfy everyone. Poles and Germans were geographically too mixed. There would have been harsh decisions whatever decisions had been taken. What was actually decided was particularly harsh for the Poles. The German National Assembly, in conjunction with the Prussian government, shifted the demarcation line to such an extent that there were more Poles living in the German territory which was intended to form part of the German nation-state than there were living in the Polish residue of Posen. Even this residue would remain under Prussian government if the Prussian National Assembly could have its way. So the German and Prussian National Assemblies, along with the Prussian government, had united together against the policy of restoring a Polish state. Against that united front the Polish national movement had no chance. Its militia was inferior to the Prussian army. It could expect no help from the major powers. In the great debate on Poland in July 1848 some left-wing members of the German National Assembly did try once more to press back German claims in favour of Polish ones. However, this attempt to restore some balance between the nations was voted down by 341 to 31.[5]

GERMAN–CZECH CONFLICTS

Another source of tension which the German national movement could not avoid was to be found in the Habsburg regions of Bohemia,

5. The parliamentary debates on the national problems are described in detail in G. Wollstein, *Das 'Großdeutschland' der Paulskirche: Nationale Ziele in der bürgerlichen Revolution von 1848/49* (Düsseldorf, 1977). A short but well-informed survey is provided by H.H. Brandt, 'The revolution of 1848 and the problem of central European nationalities', in H. Schulze (ed.) *National-Building in Central Europe* (Leamington Spa, 1987).

Moravia and Silesia. These belonged to the German Confederation but only a minority of the population were German. Only some of those Germans took part in the elections to the German National Assembly. The Czechs, and Poles in Silesia, boycotted the elections. There were, however, important differences between the three areas. In Bohemia a strong Czech movement had already emerged with the aim of bringing the three areas under a single political authority with a high degree of autonomy, although within a continuing Habsburg dynasty. This plan not only was resisted by the Germans of the whole region (about 2.4 million) but also was rejected by parliaments in Moravia and Silesia.

There was a lively debate in the German National Assembly on the subject of Bohemia where about 1.7 million Germans lived alongside some 2.6 million Czechs. No one was prepared to admit the option of giving up the territory, but equally there was no majority support for the view that German claims should be defended by war if necessary. The issue of whether to compromise did not divide Germans along left and right lines. The majority of the assembly were more reticent on this issue than they were on those of Posen or Schleswig. They did not offer any territorial concessions, but they did, almost unanimously, declare the need to provide guarantees of the rights of national minorities. Otherwise they left the problem to the Habsburg monarchy. It came up with a military 'solution'.

At the beginning of June 1848 a Slav congress met in Prague, intended as a public reply to the German National Assembly. However, the united front of Slavs which was desired did not come about. The problems and interests of the various Slav nations diverged too much from one another. The Czech national movement reached its climax with the congress, but also started now to go into decline. The Prague insurrection, which followed in the middle of June, had devastating consequences. First, it revealed the social divisions within the Czech camp and had the effect of pushing the political spokesmen of the movement rightwards. Second, the Germans of Bohemia, Moravia and Silesia now began to organise themselves as a political force. Third, the repression of the insurrection by Habsburg soldiers under the command of Prince Windischgrätz showed that the old order had recovered some of its power. What is more, in using that power it received support from other nationalities, in particular the Germans and the Magyars. Of those Germans who expressed their views on the subject, only a very few regarded the defeat of the Czech insurgents as a victory for the counter-revolution rather than for German interests. Varnhagen von Ense was one of that minority. Immediately after the events in Prague he wrote:

Regrettably many Germans have allowed their sense of nationality to
make them arrogant and unjust. They raise themselves above the Slavs and
blindly deny them the rights of freedom and independence. But what is
the situation of the Germans? Can we be so confident about our own
affairs?...I consider this failure to acknowledge the rights of other
nationalities as a threat to our own rights . . .In any case, in Prague it was
not the cause of the Germans which triumphed over that of the Czechs,
but rather it was military power which struck down citizens.[6]

Generally those who subscribed to the German cause, whether they
lived in Vienna, Prague or Berlin saw the matter differently. The
Bohemian Germans regarded the Prague insurrection primarily as an
anti-German protest. Some sent votes of thanks to Windischgrätz. It
was this man, a symbol of reaction, who was raised up to the status of
the saviour of Germans in Bohemia. Furthermore, the Prague insurrection had a European significance. For the first time in 1848 the
superior power of regular soldiers was made clear. The myth of the
barricade which had begun in Paris in February was now destroyed by
soldiers' guns: first in Prague, then more spectacularly in Paris later in
June; and again in Vienna in October. Only where the revolutionary
national movement had formed its own army or could get support
from some of the existing troops was there effective resistance to the
old elites who were quickly regaining confidence. This happened to a
degree in Italy and above all in Hungary. By contrast the German
revolutionary movement depended upon Prussian or Austrian soldiers
to enforce its national claims against other nationalities. Only a few
recognised that such national victories strengthened the counter-revolution. This was what happened in Italy.

ITALY AND THE GERMAN NATIONAL MOVEMENT

Until 1848 a liberal Italian nation-state had been one of the aims of
the German national and liberal movement. The aim was not given up
during 1848, but there was unwillingness to give up German claims to
those parts of northern Italy which belonged to the German Confederation. The German National Assembly declared, specifically in relation to the Tyrol, that 'no portion of sacred German soil can be

6. V. von Ense, op.cit., pp. 169f.

surrendered'.[7] Against this the Italians demanded the immediate separation of the Italian lands of Trient and Roveroto from the German Tyrol. A majority of the German National Assembly rejected this demand, although there was a clear language boundary which could have been drawn. At most the assembly was prepared to offer legal guarantees to national minorities. The assembly did not wish to surrender Trieste, where 8,000 Germans lived among 44,000 Italians and 25,000 Slovenes. In its debate on Italy in August the assembly left it to the German national government (the provisional authority created by the assembly with the Habsburg Archduke John at its head) to negotiate with the Austrian government on the matter. It was obvious to everyone what this would involve. By this time Austria had already embarked upon military action against the Italian movement, having its first significant success at the battle of Custozza on 25 July. As with Windischgrätz in Prague, now was Radetzsky celebrated as a defender of German interests. That was clear from the letters of the student in Vienna already quoted. It is also clear from many newspaper articles. The *Grenzboten*, still worth reading as a source of revolutionary opinion, declared that 'it would require rather more than cosmopolitan self-denial to resist celebrating the brilliance and courage of the Austrian army'. It added that 'it will do us no harm, if foreigners learn to respect our weapons as well as the humanism of our extreme left-wing philosophers'.[8] Admittedly the German National Assembly avoided making decisions about the Italian question, but its sentiments were made clear in the speeches of many deputies. Like a magnet, the future German nation-state should draw other nations to it. From this perspective they wished to avoid any weakening of the Habsburg Empire because they saw it as a German power – led by Germans politically, shaped by German culture, a part of German history, and a German outpost in Italy and the multi-national region of south-east Europe.

7. Cited in Wollstein, op.cit., p. 228. See especially P. Burian, *Die Nationalitäten in 'Cisleithanien' und das Wahlrecht der Märzrevolution 1848/49: Zur Problematik des Parlamentarismus im alten österreich* (Graz and Cologne, 1962), pp. 161–74.

8. *Die Grenzboten* 7/3 (1848), p. 279. For reports on articles in various German newspapers, see Wollstein, op.cit., pp. 238ff.

THE SCHLESWIG-HOLSTEIN CONFLICT: EUROPEAN AND GERMAN TURNING POINT

The conflict between Denmark and the German nation in the duchies of Schleswig and Holstein has a unique character among the nationality problems of 1848. No other conflict aroused such emotions among Germans as this one; no other conflict brought a general European war so close; and no other conflict made as clear as this one the interaction between national and revolutionary developments.

The upsurge of the German national movement in the 1840s was closely linked to the disputes between Germans and Danes over Schleswig. Should Schleswig be incorporated into Denmark, should it retain its traditional ties to Holstein which was part of the German Confederation, or should it be brought itself into the Confederation? These were the questions. The answer of the German national movement was clear: the two duchies must remain indivisible and must be German. The Danish minority in Schleswig must accept that. When the Danish government decided on 22 March 1848 to incorporate Schleswig into the Danish state, the Germans immediately began to resist the decision. They set up a provisional government which was recognised by the *Bundestag*, the supreme body within the German Confederation. Schleswig participated in the elections to the German national assembly although not part of the Confederation. Prussian soldiers occupied Schleswig at the request of the provisional government and with the approval of the Confederation. When, thanks to British mediation, Prussian troops were pulled back to southern Schleswig, there was a storm of protest and indignation throughout Germany. Hardly anyone disassociated themselves from this feeling. Even Varnhagen von Ense, who counselled moderation in all other disputes in order to balance and reconcile other nations, had no doubts on this question. 'Our war against Denmark is a just war' and 'opinion in England' was 'quite unfairly' 'very much against us'.[9]

The German National Assembly declared that the Schleswig-Holstein question had become a matter of national honour. But it had also become a problem for European diplomacy and a question of power within Germany.

For the European powers a German national state represented a challenge, a threat to the balance of power which had been restored following Napoleon's defeat. Nevertheless, historical research has

---

9. V. von Ense, op.cit., p. 163.

shown that the powers had not deliberately opposed German unity. France played only a subordinate role in European questions in 1848. Even in the Schleswig-Holstein dispute she was fairly marginal so far as Britain and Russia were concerned. The Russian Czar rejected all revolutions but was only likely to intervene if and when the revolution overturned a German prince – which did not happen; or if it forcibly took over foreign territory – which did seem likely in Schleswig. The British attitude was less clear cut. The British government was not prepared to put any military obstacles in the way of a German nation-state provided it did not expand the territory of Germany.[10] The British even launched an initiative to divide Schleswig along a language boundary but this was rejected by both the Danes and the Germans. Both did so on the basis not of national self-determination but in order to retain lands which both claimed by historical right. Denmark was the weaker militarily but it had a strong diplomatic position. It was defending what it already possessed, while it was the Germans who wished to expand. What is more, they wished to expand into a key strategic area, the 'Bosphorus of the North'. This was something neither Britain nor Russia could permit. Their pressure forced Prussia to conclude an armistice at Malmö on 26 August 1848. In effect that meant giving up German claims. Germans were outraged, and the National Assembly rejected the armistice. The assembly wanted the Prussian army to enforce the national claim upon Schleswig even at risk of a European war. Only the refusal of the Prussian king prevented that policy being adopted.

The majority of the German National Assembly came to terms with this 'capitulation' by Prussia. Yet the German national movement, especially its left wing, felt itself betrayed. The left preached the idea of achieving German freedom, both within and internationally, by means of a national war. The republicans took this idea up particularly vociferously and pushed it to extremes. They could see that to accept the Malmö armistice meant not only to give way to international pressure but also to concede the impotence of the revolution and its newly created institutions against the old order within Germany. Everyone could now see that without the Prussian army the German national assembly and government could achieve nothing. The nation and its

10. See two recent studies with extensive bibliography: G. Heydemann, 'The "Crazy Year" 1848: The revolution in Germany and Palmerston's policy', in Schulze (ed.) op. cit., pp. 167–82, and K. Bourne, 'Nationsbildung und britische Politik: Das Kabinett zwischen 1846 und 1852', in A.M. Birke and G. Heydemann (eds) *Die Herausforderung des europäischen Staatensystems: Nationale Ideologie und Imperialismus* (Göttingen and Zürich, 1989), pp. 96–118.

new institutions had brandished the sword, but the Prussian king retained a firm control over it. Many now recognised what Varnhagen von Ense expressed forcefully:

> The Danish war and the armistice are clear humiliations for us, a slap in the face for the arrogant loudmouths who wanted to make out that a nation that is yet to be born was a conquering nation.[11]

Power lay with the Prussian military which stood behind the Prussian king. Recognising the Malmö armistice, which the Prussian king had agreed without consulting the National Assembly, meant placing the fate of the new nation-state in the hands of a king, indeed a king who was soon to reject with contempt the imperial title that that assembly was to offer him. Thus as early as August 1848 the German national revolution had lost the leader to which it looked. Without this leader it was not possible for the National Assembly and the revolutionary movement to complete the task of internal political reform which it had set itself. The subsequent acceptance of the armistice meant placing the German national revolution into the hands of the Prussian king. The left did not wish that. Therefore they had to insist on a continuation of the war. They also hoped that a national war would set off a new wave of revolutions. In Germany they would be able to sweep away the monarchies, and in Europe bring the nations together in a war against Tsarist Russia, the bastion of reaction. The alternatives were seen as either ending the Danish war and avoiding the threat of European war or renewing revolution in Germany and Europe. The German national movement showed its capacity to compromise by backing down on its national claims and coming to terms with the decision in favour of peace.

National German historiography has always portrayed this decision as a betrayal of the national cause. 'Left' historians have seen it as a betrayal of the revolution. The culmination of this nationalist tradition can be seen in the historiography of the German Democratic Republic where publications right up to the end of that state displayed no appreciation of the dilemma which confronted nationalists at the time: defence of the revolution against the resurgent old elites of Germany or preservation of peace with Britain, Russia, and possibly also France.

11. V. von Ense, op.cit., p. 183.

CONCEPTIONS OF THE NATION-STATE IN GERMANY

It was only in France that revolution in 1848 replaced monarchy with a republic. (The cases of Rome and Venice are rather more limited in scope and importance.) Everywhere else the revolution stopped at the foot of the throne. This meant in Germany that a national state could be established only as a federation with a monarchical head. The demand for a unitary republic which a section of extreme left-wing opinion pressed stood no chance, not least because it went against a federal tradition. The two risings in Baden in 1848 in support of a republic did not find popular support anywhere in Germany, indicating that a 'silent majority' were opposed to the idea of a republican nation-state. Furthermore, there was no political centre in Germany comparable to Paris, London or Brussels. The German National Assembly was a focus for national politics but it was rivalled by the Prussian National Assembly in Berlin and the Austrian *Reichstag* in Vienna. The other German states also had their own parliaments, often newly elected, and their governments included men out of the pre-1848 liberal opposition. This influx of new men worked to strengthen the capacity of the various states to resist any unitary tendencies. New princes did come to the throne in Bavaria and Austria, but this worked to stabilise government and dynasty. Consequently there was no question of establishing a centralised state along French lines. Furthermore, if monarchy survived in the individual states, then any national state that was created would also have to have a monarchical head. The self-esteem, power and standing of the German princes meant it was unthinkable that they might accept the leadership of an elected President.

The head of any future national state, rather like the Emperor drawn from the Habsburg line in the Holy Roman Empire, would need to be a considerable ruler in his own right. Once again Varnhagen von Ense was perceptive:

> The power of the Imperial Administrator [*Reichsverweser*] has no foundation, just as with some earlier Emperors who had no great dynastic standing. Such Emperors came to depend upon the Empire for support, which meant they could do little of value for the Empire.[12]

The Austrian Archduke Johann, whom the German National Assembly had named as provisional Imperial Administrator on 29 June 1848, was popularly known as 'Johann the Landless'.

12. Ibid., p. 175

The soldiers he uses to enforce his decisions are lent to him and can always be recalled; the money he needs for his government comes in the form of grants which can be cut off any day. His ministers, even the civil servants who apply his laws, are on temporary loan. [The] newly created imperial power [had] no roots.

Von Ense concluded that such an imperial role needed, as a matter of urgency, to be filled by a ruler of a strong state who could overcome 'the lack of power in German unity'.[13]

For von Ense there was only one possible candidate for this role: the King of Prussia. Admittedly he misjudged Frederick William IV, wrongly believing that the king was prepared to do a deal with democratic forces in Prussia and Germany.[14] He did recognise that Austria could not take the leadership role in Germany. A whole series of problems stood in the way.

The current fragmentation of Austria, the wars which beset her non-German lands, the uncertain future which she faces, [above all the fact that] Slavs and other non-German peoples make up a majority of her inhabitants.[15]

The German National Assembly and the national movement throughout Germany debated these problems at length and in detail. There appeared to be two possibilities: a greater German (*großdeutsch*) or a smaller German (*kleindeutsch*) nation-state. The *großdeutsch* solution entailed dividing the Habsburg territories into a German and a non-German part, these joined together merely by a personal union. Only the German portion would belong to the new nation-state. Such a nation-state would have had generally the same territories as the German Confederation, perhaps with some losses in the south and southeast borderlands where the majority of inhabitants were non-German. Given the territorial continuity with the Confederation, such a nation-state could have been fitted into the European arrangements worked out in 1814–15. That would mean that this solution might be acceptable to the other European powers. However, it would mean the division of the Habsburg dynasty. We can only speculate what that would have meant both for Austria and Europe. Perhaps it would have divided power between Germans and Hungarians in a way reminiscent of what happened within the Habsburg dynasty in 1867 in reaction to the emergence of the *kleindeutsch* solution. Perhaps it would have led

13. Ibid., pp. 176f.
14. W. Bußmann, *Zwischen Preußen und Deutschland: Friedrich Wilhelm IV – Eine Biographie* (Berlin, 1990).
15. V. von Ense, op.cit., p. 177

to the emergence of nation-states along the lines of what was to happen after the First World War.

The majority of the National Assembly and of the national movement wanted to see the *großdeutsch* nation-state. There were a variety of motives. Some saw it in terms of the German imperial tradition. Many Catholics were concerned that without Austria, a German state would be dominated by Protestantism. South German democrats and liberals feared a Prussianised Germany. Some considered that the individual states would have real autonomy in a greater Germany, whereas the removal of Austria would tip the balance too much towards the one major state of Prussia and undermine any genuine federalism.

The *großdeutsch* solution required Austrian agreement, whether voluntary or compelled. However, by October at the latest when imperial troops regained control of Vienna, the counter-revolution was firmly entrenched. The old elites who had regained power rejected any proposal to divide the monarchy and were prepared to risk war to avoid that happening. Opinion outside Austria was not prepared to go that far. Given that, a bare majority of the National Assembly decided on 27 and 28 March 1849 in favour of the *kleindeutsch* nation-state and offered the Emperorship of Germany to the King of Prussia. Most of those who supported this did so only because they could see no way forward without excluding Austria. Many hoped that at least a Habsburg Empire dominated by Germans would be a natural ally of the German state.

No one can know if the Habsburg Emperor would have been prepared to accept this exclusion of Austria without a war. He was never put to the test because the Prussian king sharply rejected the crown offered to him by the National Assembly. This was just a matter of Frederick William's own inclination and will. He was also rejecting the idea of parliamentary monarchy which the imperial constitution laid down not only for the nation-state but also for all the member states. He was rejecting, therefore, not only the imperial title, but also the constitutional control of the crown and its essential support, the royal army. In this Frederick was at one with the Habsburg Emperor and his decision also secured the loyalty of the old elites.

The refusal of the King of Prussia to become head of a German nation-state completely undermined the work of the National Assembly. It wanted to bring about political revolution in Germany, but only by means of reform. The whole strategy of the assembly was based upon securing agreements with the various German princes and their governments. When the Prussian king refused his agreement, then the National Assembly and most of the national movement gave up their constitutional projects. They were not prepared to use force to try to take the matter any further. Some have condemned this as a betrayal of the revolution. But such a judgement fails to understand the basic character of the German revolution of 1848–9. Only a minority of the national movement wanted a radical break with the past which included the monarchy. Most of the rest of the national movement also wanted a democratised Germany. When the reform alliance with the Prussian monarchy broke down, it destroyed the basis of the German national revolution. Within the national movement there was a very great diversity of conflicting views about the political and social character which a future Germany should have. These disagreements were held in check only by a common wish for a German national state. Once the reform strategy had failed in 1849, the national movement broke up into its conflicting elements. The last phase of the revolution confirmed what had long been obvious. There was a majority within the population for creating a nation-state in agreement with the monarchies, but not for a national revolution opposed to the monarchies. One major reason was the fear that a political and national revolution which was not held in check within the monarchical framework might turn into a social revolution.

In addition to the *großdeutsch* and *kleindeutsch* ideas which were discussed within the National Assembly and the national movement, there were further proposals made by the Austrian and Prussian governments which were intended both to end but also to continue the revolution. These alternatives brought the two German powers in conflict with the National Assembly and each other.[16] Both alternatives would have altered the constitutional work of the National Assembly in a conservative direction. However, the Prussian plan was closer to that of the National Assembly and did at least aim to establish a national state. Prussia proposed the creation of a *kleindeutsch* and federal state with a common constitution and an elected parliament and linked to Austria within a broader Confederation. Basically Prussia offered Germans and the German princes a conservative version of the nation-state which the National Assembly had proposed. The Prussian plan failed because some of the German princes rejected it, and above all because it encountered fierce opposition from Austria. Austria was able to use the renewal of crisis in Schleswig-Holstein in 1849–50 to isolate Prussia internationally. With the possibility of war in which Russia would take Austria's side, Prussia gave up its German plans in November 1850.

16. See especially A. Doering-Manteuffel, 'Der Ornungszwang des Staatensystems: zu den Mitteleuropa-Konzeptionen in der österreich-preußischen Rivalität 1849–1851', in A.M. Birke and G. Heydemann (eds), op.cit., pp. 119–40.

Austria's German policy also failed. In 1849 the Austrian minister-president, Prince Schwarzenberg, had demanded the incorporation of the entire empire within the new German state. This would have meant the creation of an empire with 70 million people, bringing together central Europe, northern Italy and much of south-east Europe within one giant federal state. It would have destroyed the territorial arrangements worked out in 1814-15 and upset the balance of power. Consequently the British and French governments, along with the Russian Tsar, worked to persuade Austria to give up this idea. The plan would probably have failed because of resistance from German princes, but pressure from the European powers ensured that it was given up before that issue arose.

A *kleindeutsch* Germany with a monarchical head would not have encountered such opposition from the other powers. Probably they would not have rejected a *großdeutsch* Germany either, although they would not have welcomed this because it would have weakened the stabilising role of the Habsburg dynasty in the multi-national regions of central and south-east Europe. But a federal state which combined a greater Germany with a greater Austria was completely unacceptable. What the other powers most preferred was the restoration of the old order. This was what happened at the Dresden Conference of May 1851. Given the absence of any other practical options, the German Confederation was restored by all the German states. That brought to an end the governmental sequel to the 1848 revolution. But it did not end the demands for a German nation-state: 1848 had made clear that the smaller Germany was the most acceptable option. In this sense the experience of 1848 prepared the ground for the foundation of a smaller Germany between 1866 and 1871, although of course it did not make that foundation inevitable.

INTERNATIONALISM OF THE GREAT POWERS – RIVALRY OF NATIONS

The revolution began with the dream of a 'springtime of peoples'; it ended with the reality of counter-revolutionary solidarity among states. It was not the nationalists who had managed to work together, but rather the Great Powers. Despite their own mutual rivalries and political values, the major powers had made common cause against the revolution. France, the motherland of revolution, did not try to export her revolution or even provide military support, as in Belgium in 1830, for a new nation–state borne out of revolution. Indeed, France helped in the repression of the revolutionary Roman Republic.

Prussia took on that repressive role in Germany. In July 1849 she used military force to crush the revolution in Saxony, Baden and the Palatinate. Russia, the bulwark of reaction which had not been directly affected by revolution in 1848, provided military assistance to Austria in August 1849 to crush the Hungarian Revolution. With that achieved Austria was able to go on to compel Venetia to surrender. That brought the revolution in Italy to an end and also left Austria free to turn back to German affairs and to oppose the Prussian *kleindeutsch* policy. Even Britain, a model for many European liberals, both by diplomatic means and by a very clear policy of non–intervention, helped Austria to defend her position in Italy and Hungary.

Great Power internationalism faced only two opponents. There was an insignificant pacifist movement which reached across national boundaries. There was also some ineffective cooperation among a few revolutionaries who vainly hoped to spark off internationalist activity among various nationalities. Instead, nationalism led to nationality conflicts. National movements were prepared to cooperate with counter-revolution in order to advance their interests against those of other nations. This was a general pattern in 1848, not something confined to Germany. Probably little fundamental would have been been different if the revolutionary movements of Germany and Hungary had been able to cooperate. Many had hoped that such an alliance might have broken the international solidarity of counter-revolution. Perhaps the German revolution might have developed in a different way if the Hungarian army had obstructed the repression of revolution in Vienna in October 1848. However, that would not have solved the great problem of conflicting national claims. Neither the German nor the Hungarian national movements showed any willingness to make concessions to other nationalities. A successful alliance between the German and Hungarian national movements would not have been enough to sustain a 'springtime of peoples' in Europe.

SUGGESTIONS FOR FURTHER READING

The best general treatment of 1848 in Germany is W. Siemann, *Die deutsche Revolution von 1848/1849* (Frankfurt am Main, 1985). There are good shorter general accounts in T. Nipperdey, *Deutsche Geschichte 1800–1866* (Munich, 1983), and J. Sheehan, *German History 1770– 1866* (Oxford, 1990).

For a survey of the revolution in Europe generally see P.N. Stearns, *The Revolutions of 1848* (London, 1974); for shorter studies see R. Price, *The Revolutions of 1848* (London, 1988), and D. Langewiesche, *Europa zwischen Restauration und Revolution 1815–1849* (Munich, 1989).

Specifically on the national problems see H. Lutz, *Zwischen Habsburg und Preußen. Deutschland 1815–1866* (Berlin, 1985); H. Schulze (ed.) *Nation-Building in Central Europe* (Leamington Spa, Hamburg and New York, 1987); A. Sked, *The Decline and Fall of the Habsburg Empire* (London, 1989); H. Rumpler (ed.) *Deutscher Bund und deutsche Frage 1815–1866* (Vienna and Munich, 1990).

On the national debates in the German National Assembly there is the detailed, somewhat descriptive account by G. Wollstein, *Das 'Großdeutschland' der Paulskirche: Nationale Ziele in der bürgerlichen Revolution 1848/49* (Düsseldorf, 1977); shorter and analytical is Wollstein, 'Mitteleuropa und Großdeutschland – Visionen der Revolution 1848/49', in *Die deutsche Revolution von 1848/49*, D. Langewiesche (ed.) (Darmstadt, 1983), pp. 237–57.

CHAPTER FIVE
The unification of Germany

William Carr

Until the winter of 1989–90 the division of Germany into two sovereign states, the legacy of the first Cold War in the late 1940s, seemed an immutable feature of the international landscape, unlikely to be altered in our lifetime. Since November 1989 the situation has been utterly transformed in a bewildering succession of dramatic events: the breaching of the Berlin Wall; the fall of Erich Honecker; the abandonment by the Socialist Unity Party of its monopoly of power; the holding in March 1990 of the first free elections since 1933 – which though massively influenced by West German parties reduced the Communists to a small and discredited rump in the new *Volkskammer*; monetary union between the two Germanies in July; formal union between them in October; and all-German elections in December. In one tumultuous year the forty-year division of Germany had been overcome.

The jubilant scenes as the Berlin Wall was torn down and the enthusiastic declarations of leading political figures in both states testify to the desire of ordinary Germans for reunification of their country, even if the initial euphoria was subsequently diminished by growing awareness of the heavy financial costs and general consequences of the marriage between two disparate social and economic systems. Similarly in the 1860s the desire of the articulate sections of the German public for a united nation played an immensely important role in the final outcome. Nevertheless, it would be a misunderstanding of a complex historical process to imagine that national feeling was the principal factor bringing about the creation of the German Reich in 1871 any more than it has been in the reunification of the two Germanies in 1989–90. In recent months a number of factors have come together to transform the shape of Europe: the changes in the Soviet Union associated with Mikhail Gorbachev; the peaceful revolutions taking place in central and eastern Europe (with the tragic exceptions of Romania and civil war in Yugoslavia) as the Russians relaxed their grip over these countries; the desire both in Washington and Moscow to reduce the crippling burden of armaments for sound economic reasons; and, in consequence, the diminishing military importance of a divided Germany as a strategic buffer between the rival NATO and Warsaw Pact alliances. Similarly in the middle of the nineteenth century several developments interacted to make the unification of Germany possible. While no one would dispute that the role of Otto von Bismarck was of crucial importance in the creation of the German Reich, we should remember that

> men make their own history . . . they do not make it just as they please, but under circumstances directly encountered, given and transmitted from the past.[1]

Bismarck's personality and policies constitute one, but only one, of the determinants of unification which will be analysed in this chapter.

We commence with the power-political contest between Austria and Prussia. Their rivalry in its modern form originated in the mid-eighteenth century when Frederick the Great attacked Silesia in 1740. Only after two long wars did he finally secure it for Prussia in 1763. Thirty years later the French Revolution rocked thrones to their foundations all over Europe, compelling rulers to remember that what they had in common was more important than their power struggles, at least for the time being. Consequently Austria and Prussia joined with the other Great Powers gathered together at the Congress of Vienna after the final defeat of Napoleon to draw up a peace settlement to protect Europe against future French aggression. Barriers were erected to contain the French. In the north the former Austrian Netherlands were joined to Holland; in the south-east the Austrians were given the provinces of Lombardy and Venetia in northern Italy; and in the west the bulk of the Napoleonic creation, the Kingdom of Westphalia, was handed over to Prussia to compensate her for the loss of territory to Russia. This territorial acquisition shifted the centre of gravity of Prussia westwards towards the Rhine and away from the Polish territories which had been her primary interest in the past. During the Vormärz period (the term literally means 'pre-March', i.e. the period in German history before March 1848) it seemed unlikely that Prussia would be called upon to fulfil her obligation to defend the Rhineland. The Restoration governments of Louis XVIII and Charles X were not disposed to cause trouble in central Europe. Nor was the July Monarchy; the war scare of 1840 was no more than a brief aberration. And had it

---

1. Karl Marx, *The Eighteenth Brumaire of Louis Napoleon* (Moscow, 1954), p. 10.

come to war, Prussia could have relied on Austrian help against the common danger despite the failure to resolve the vexed question of control of the federal forces in wartime which Prussia saw as her right, a claim resisted by the Austrians. At the same time, the fact that West-phalia was separated from the core land of Brandenburg-Prussia by 20 kilometres at the narrowest and 200 at the widest points encouraged the Prussians to try and extend their influence over the small interven-ing territories, northwards over the North German plain (the Kingdom of Hannover) and southwards (Electoral Hesse and Nassau) roughly down to the line of the river Main. Given the prevailing philosophy of the day, any large state would have had the same objective. Prussia with her militaristic structure and expansionist history was more likely than most to succeed.

Any change in the balance of power in favour of Prussia would inevitably affect the position of Austria. In the past our image of Aus-trian policy has been deeply coloured by the works of *kleindeutsch* (lite-rally 'little German', i.e. those committed to a Germany which excluded Austria) historians such as von Droysen and von Treitschke who wrote as enthusiastic supporters of Protestant Prussia, the victor of 1866 and 1870. For these historians Austria was an 'unGerman', 'reac-tionary' and Catholic power whose multi-national empire drew her inexorably towards south-eastern Europe and away from Germany, but whose stubborn refusal to recognise the logic of her position retarded unification under the Hohenzollerns. However, seen from the perspec-tive of the Ballhausplatz (the seat of the Austrian foreign ministry in Vienna) Austria also had a 'mission' as legitimate as that of Prussia. For centuries the defender of Catholicism against the Turk, Austria now thought of herself as the pivotal power holding a precarious balance in Europe between Orthodox Russia in the east and 'godless' France in the west. To fulfil this European mission the Austrians believed it es-sential to maintain their presence in the German Confederation (the loose association of states created in 1815) where they exerted much influence over the medium and small states. If the balance of power was upset in Germany, the corollary was an upset in the balance of European power totally unacceptable to Austria. From the days of Metternich to those of Rechberg (Austrian foreign minister from 1855 to 1859) she was willing to recognise a degree of Prussian influence north of the River Main. What she would never do was abandon her position of primacy at Frankfurt where her representative presided over the deliberations of the Federal Diet. However, the maintenance of her position in Germany against Prussia, in northern Italy against France, and in south-eastern Europe against Russia required a considerable military effort which strained her resources to breaking-point on several occasions. Paradoxically enough the Achilles heel of financial instability was an added reason why dualism was mandatory for Austria. However much she suspected Prussian intentions, Austria realised that only by cooperation with the heirs of Frederick the Great could Prussia be held in check and the strain on Austrian resources correspondingly reduced.

To pursue a dualistic policy proved increasingly difficult after the 1848–9 revolution. Though Frederick William IV had rejected the crown of a *Kleindeutschland* offered him by the Frankfurt Parliament, he was enough of a Hohenzollern to want it if the German princes could be persuaded to offer it to him on a plate. The Erfurt Union (Prussia's diplomatic version of *Kleindeutschland* in 1849–50) failed because Prince Schwarzenberg, Francis Joseph's new chief minister, took up the challenge, refusing to be driven out of the Confederation. War was avoided in 1850 when Prussia backed away and the old political structures were restored. Suspicion of Prussian policy remained very much alive in the minds of policy-makers in Vienna while in Berlin the king and his ministers continued to resent the 'humiliation' of 1850. While this did not preclude superficial cooperation between the two great German powers to preserve the conservative order of society against the threat which the forces of liberalism and nationalism were thought to present to it, nevertheless the episode of the Erfurt Union served as a warning to the Austrians of what Prussia might well repeat if the international situation deteriorated.

The tranformation of the international scene after the Crimean War is a second general factor without which unification would not have occurred when it did or in the form that it did. The old solidarity of the conservative powers, linchpin of international order since 1815, was fatally disrupted by the war in the Crimea. While Britain and France fought Russia, Austria remained neutral but pursued an intricate policy of armed mediation which alienated Russia from her. To protect her growing strategic and commercial interests in south-eastern Europe Austria forced Russia out of the Danubian principalities of Moldavia and Wallachia and, to add insult to injury, supported Anglo-French proposals to end the war.

Another destabilising factor weakening Austria's position still further was the accession to power of Louis Napoleon. Although the new dictator did not abandon traditional French objectives such as the acquisition of France's 'natural frontiers', his avowed commitment to the overthrow of the settlement of 1815 introduced an unsettling element into international affairs. His belief in the principle of nationality (though not to the point of endangering French interests) posed a general threat to Austria, his uncle's old enemy, and a particular threat in northern Italy where the Austrian presence was a major obstacle to Italian unification under Piedmontese leadership. When war broke out in Italy in 1859 Austria fought alone against France and Piedmont. Russia had no especial interest in western Europe and none in supporting Austria, while Prussia equivocated, attempting to drive a hard bargain over command of the federal forces before she would come to Austria's assistance.

Austrian defeat in Italy and the constitutional changes she was obliged to set in motion in her empire made dualism more necessary than ever for Austrian survival as a European great power. Cooperation with Prussia was, however, more difficult than ever because the changing international scene from the mid-1850s had affected Prussian objectives in Germany. The growing belief in Berlin that Prussia could not rely on the support of most German states or on Austria in the event of a war in the west, coupled with the threat France was now thought to present to the Rhineland, convinced the policy-makers in Berlin that Prussia required a stronger power base to defend herself against France. What the frontiers of the Prussian state should be was indicated by Bismarck, then ambassador in St Petersburg; writing to the Prussian foreign minister in 1859 he urged the latter to seize the opportunity presented by the Italian war:

the present situation has put the winning card in our hands again provided we allow Austria to become deeply involved in the war with France and then march southwards with our entire army carrying frontier posts in our big packs (*Tornistor*). We can plant them either on the Bodensee or as far south as Protestantism is the dominant faith.[2]

At this time the Prussian government was, as we have seen, torn between self-interest, a sense of loyalty to Austria and distaste for revolutionary politics, and did not heed Bismarck's (unsolicited) advice. Three years later, when Bismarck was in charge of Prussian policy, the likelihood that she would act solely in accordance with her power interests was greatly increased. If she chose to do so, the constellation of forces would be in her favour. Russia would not come automatically to Austria's assistance. And by astute diplomacy it might be possible to neutralise France and thus to isolate Austria. That the object of war was not national unification but the creation of a Great Prussian state is evident from Prussian behaviour in 1866. The legiti-

2. Bismarck, *Die gesammelten Werke* (Berlin, 1923–35), 14, no. 724, Bismarck to Gustav von Alvensleben, 23 April–5May 1859.

mate rights of several rulers north of the river Main were brushed aside by the victorious Prussians; Schleswig-Holstein, the Kingdom of Hannover, Electoral Hesse, Nassau and the city of Frankfurt were annexed outright, creating a solid power base down to the river Main.

The creation of *Kleindeutschland* would not have been possible without the reformed Prussian army. The Erfurt Union failed not only because the romantic conservatism of Frederick William IV held him back at the last minute from war but also because it was recognised in Berlin that Prussia was not strong enough to fight the Austrians. Regent William, who became king in 1861, is often depicted as the compliant associate of his servant Bismarck. In fact the king was one of the makers of *Kleindeutschland* in his own right. A professional soldier by training, he was greatly concerned by the sorry state of affairs revealed during the 1859 crisis when Prussia mobilised several army corps (though with no clear political objective). He determined to reform Prussia's armed forces to enable her to play a role in German affairs commensurate with her military traditions. On his initiative and in the teeth of opposition from the liberal-controlled lower house, the *Landtag*, the army was doubled in size from 50,000 to 110,000 men with greatly augmented reserves. Of course, Prussian liberals were as anxious as conservatives to see Prussia playing an active role in Germany. What they objected to was an increased period of service with the regular army and in particular the demotion of the *Landwehr*, the territorial element in the army introduced by the Prussian reformers in an attempt to break away from the *Kadavergehorsamkeit* (literally the obedience of corpses) of the old Frederician army. But General von Roon, like his royal master, wanted a strongly disciplined fighting force not subject to any civilian influence. This was not only for possible use against other states, but also because conservatives always had an enemy within in mind; an obedient army completely under royal control might be needed to put down uprisings at home which they supposed would result from the spread of liberalism and socialism.

This modernised army under its able chief of staff, Count von Moltke, proved itself at the battle of Königgrätz in June 1866. Not that there was anything inevitable about the Prussian victory. Moltke's controversial encirclement and annihilation strategy did not succeed completely; the bulk of the Austrian army managed to withdraw south of the Danube; and had General Benedek, the Austrian commander, seized his opportunity to attack the first Prussian army, the course of history might have been different. As always, the side making the fewest mistakes won the day. All the same it remains true to say that without the army reforms initiated by Regent William and carried out by war minister Roon and Moltke, Prussia would not have been in a position to risk war with any hope of success.

Before military history staged a welcome come-back in recent years many historians laid heavy emphasis on the economic dimension of the German problem and in particular on the role of the German Customs Union (the *Zollverein*) in bringing about a measure of economic unification; Germany, as John Maynard Keynes suggested, was united 'more by coal and iron than by blood and iron'. Again, one is reminded that the *kleindeutsch* historians depicted the *Zollverein* as a first step on the road to political unification.

Recent research suggests that it was not so simple as that. It is frankly most difficult to assess the extent to which commerce was stimulated by the *Zollverein*. No doubt a larger market did prove beneficial to some enterprises but it has to be remembered that economic growth was influenced by improvements in communications, especially the spread of railways. Furthermore, doubt has been cast on the entire concept of a 'unified' market requiring only a political roof to crown the edifice. Industrialisation, which dated back to the eighteenth century, affected only some German regions where natural resources and skills favoured development. The key to understanding the growth of the *Zollverein* lies not in economics but in finance. The rulers of the medium and small states joined the *Zollverein* to obtain sources of revenue to finance the modernisation many of them undertook in the early nineteenth century, sources which had the additional advantage of being outside the control of local *Landtage*. Hence, despite deep suspicion of Prussia's predatory intentions, Bavaria, Württemberg and Baden renewed the customs treaties in 1852 and again in 1864. Of course, Prussia had an economic whip-hand because of her growing industrial potential in the late 1850s and early 1860s and through control of key communications arteries along the Rhine, Elbe and Oder. But while it is true to say that the *Zollverein* is 'better seen in the context of the individual states' struggle for financial solvency and economic consolidation',[3] Prussian statesmen were well aware of its political significance. Finance minister Friedrich von Motz, under whose energetic leadership the Prussian Customs Union was extended in the late 1820s, admitted that

> the more natural the attachment to a customs and commercial system is . . . the more intimate and deep will be the attachment of those states to some political system.[4]

3. J. Sheehan, *German History 1770–1866* (Oxford, 1990), p. 434.
4. Quoted in H.-W. Hahn, *Geschichte des deutschen Zollvereins* (Göttingen, 1984), p. 56.

And Prussian foreign minister Count Christian Bernstorff remarked after Prussia concluded her first major extra-territorial treaty with Hesse-Darmstadt that, however one-sided the agreement (which made generous concessions to that state), it would 'place Prussia in a position to exert its influence over the [smaller states] in the most equitable manner'.[5] In other words, financial inducements were consciously employed to further the strategic objectives of linking up the western with the eastern territories.

The *Zollverein* did not lead inevitably to the creation of a Prussian-dominated *kleindeutsch* state; as a former US President once remarked: it takes a lot of effort by a lot of people before any development moves into that assured category. Still, one should not go too far in the opposite direction. Recent historical work on the *Zollverein* makes the valid point that, although it did not make unification along *kleindeutsch* lines inevitable, growing economic ties did at least prevent any attempt at a federal solution to the German problem.[6] This was because Austrian and Prussian economic interests were increasingly divergent in the 1860s.

Through an accident of geography Prussia, the most populous state in the Confederation (Austria had a larger total population than Prussia but fewer inhabitants within the part of the state belonging to the Confederation), was well endowed with the raw materials of the first Industrial Revolution: coal, iron and zinc. And as agrarian reform encouraged the movement of poor peasants away from the countryside and the handicraft industry was declining, Prussia possessed an abundant labour reservoir to man her industrial system. In addition the low tariff policy of the *Zollverein* was beneficial to some manufacturers as well as to Prussian landowners (for whose profit the policy was primarily devised).

It would be quite wrong to suppose that the Industrial Revolution did not come to the Habsburg dominions. It is, however, true to say that industrialisation took place at a much slower pace and that it was impeded by Austrian bureaucracy. Prussian officials pursued policies conducive to industrial growth; they actively promoted free-trade ideas; and they helped remove feudal restrictions in the countryside, thereby facilitating the emergence of efficient estates devoted to large-

5. Quoted in L.J. Baack, *Christian Bernstorff and Prussia: Diplomacy and Reform Conservatism 1818–1832* (New Brunswick, NJ, 1980), p. 125.
6. See, for example, Hans Werner Hahn, 'Mitteleuropaïsche oder Kleindeutsche Wirtschaftsordnung in der Epoche des Deutschen Bundes,' in H. Rumpler (ed.), *Deutscher Bund und deutsche frage 1815–1866* (Vienna and Munich, 1990), pp. 186–214.

scale production. Austrian bureaucrats did much less to free the Habsburg Empire from the grip of feudalism. True, customs barriers between Austria and Hungary were removed in 1850; the next year prohibitive tariffs on foreign imports were abolished and the number of tariffs was cut by almost 50 per cent. A significant expansion of the railway system improved communications; in 1859 trades and professions were freed from all restrictions; and in the countryside the abolition of the *robot* (compulsory labour services) was completed. Though tariff reductions did give an impetus to development, the pace slackened after the depression of 1857 which severely affected Austria. Coal and textile manufacturers were able to veto further tariff reform. The basic problem was caused by high production costs; the inaccessibility of raw materials and transportation problems obliged manufacturers to demand higher protection against foreign competition. So although there was an increase in trade with the rest of Germany in the 1850s, much more trade was carried on inside the Habsburg dominions than with the rest of the world. And, once again, the most serious brake on Austrian progress was chronic insolvency from 1811 onwards. The national debt actually trebled between 1848 and 1866; armed mediation during the Crimean War gravely strained Austria's finances, while the 1859 war brought them virtually to the point of collapse. Only through massive loans (which were then not available for investment) did Austria stagger on. Between 1860 and 1866 she was spending 40 per cent of her state receipts on her army and navy.

Finally, we turn to a consideration of the ideological forces of nationalism and political Catholicism, each of which in its own way contributed to the emergence of a *kleindeutsch* state.

A rough-and-ready definition of nationalism might be the belief that a people bound by a common language or common traditions has a right to set up its own state in which all the citizens – no longer objects to be exploited by tyrannical rulers – participate actively in political life through representative institutions. This definition fits the circumstances of countries such as Britain, Spain and France tolerably well, for in these cases geography has been a major determinant of frontiers. But the ethnic and cultural mixture in central Europe made it extraordinarily difficult until well into the twentieth-century to decide what frontiers a German nation-state should possess.

Three 'national' solutions of the German problem were on offer in the mid-nineteenth century. First there was the *kleindeutsch* state which amounted to Prussian domination of Germany and the complete exclusion of Austria from the German state. Second, there was the *großdeutsch* (greater Germany) idea, the essence of which was the maintenance of the traditional ties with Austria which the vast majority of Germans were reluctant to sever. Third, there was the idea of *Mitteleuropa*, the middle European state, an Austrian scheme whereby the whole of the Habsburg dominions would be included in a huge common market stretching from the Baltic to the Black Sea. Not one of these solutions was national in the modern sense of including only German speakers under one national roof. The *kleindeutsch* state of 1871 included Poles in Posen, Danes in north Schleswig, and French people in Alsace-Lorraine, while it excluded German-speaking Austrians. *Großdeutschland* would have included not only German-speaking Austrians, but also Czechs in Bohemia, Italians in Trieste and Slovenes in Carinthia. *Mitteleuropa* would certainly have included all German speakers but also Czechs, Slovaks, Magyars, Ruthenes, Romanians, Serbs and Croats in one huge racial conglomeration run by the Habsburgs. It should be remembered that political activists at that time applied a quite different yardstick to determine nationality. If the language spoken by the upper classes – the officials, pastors and professors – was German, as it was in large areas of central and eastern Europe, then the area was deemed 'German'. While most Germans had no wish to prevent local populations speaking their Polish, Czech or Danish, nevertheless educated Germans regarded these languages as inferior cultural media.

Clearly the Reich of 1871 which *kleindeutsch* historians lauded as the inevitable outcome of a long historical process was in reality a truncated 'national' state which had ruptured the natural connection with Austria. For that reason among others the German question remained on the agenda long after 1871. After the First World War Poles, Danes and French parted company with imperial Germany. But the Weimar Republic, though a more German state, still excluded the Austrians now reduced to a shadow of their former glory. *Ein Volk, ein Reich, ein Führer* was one of the slogans which helped put the Nazis into power. Hitler's annexation of Austria in 1938 made the Republic a more German state. But the incorporation of Czechoslovakia in 1939 made it a less national state as Hitler's imperialist ambitions rapidly unfolded. After the defeat in the Second World War, because the victorious powers could not decide on the shape and political future of a German state, occupation zones were turned into separate states for the next forty years, dividing the people still further.

If the *kleindeutsches Reich* was not a national state, how did it come to be widely accepted as such in educated circles? The answer lies in part in the more effective propagation of their views by the advocates of *Kleindeutschland*.

Mitteleuropa and *Großdeutschland* had their supporters and their organisations such as the German Reform Society (*Deutsche Reformverein*). But they possessed nothing comparable with the propaganda machine created by the *kleindeutsch* advocates. As industrialisation spread inside the *Zollverein*, a thrusting entrepreneurial and professional class emerged organised through local chambers of commerce and in professional bodies. For economic and national reasons many of them became staunch supporters of unification. Increasingly irritated by restrictions on their economic activities outside Prussia, they persuaded themselves that nothing but benefit would flow from the creation of a German Empire based on the area of the *Zollverein*. In 1858 the Congress of German Economists was founded, attracting to its meetings civil servants, journalists and academics as well as merchants, financiers and industrialists. Their aim was promotion of tariff reform and removal of all restrictive legislation. In 1860 the German Jurists Congress was founded to advance reform of the legal system. In 1861 the German Commercial Association was founded to agitate for a reformed commercial code. Out of the inaugural meeting of the latter came initiatives which led to the creation of the National Society. This body, which took its name from the Italian society which harnessed middle-class opinion behind Cavour, was established to coordinate national liberal political activity. Significantly radicals as well as moderates joined the National Society. Never numbering more than 25,000 members, this society played a crucial role in the creation of a steamhead of opinion principally in northern and central Germany favourable to the establishment of a *kleindeutsch* state. While it enjoyed some lower middle-class support, the upper-class leadership never sought to recruit a mass membership, not only because of fear of popular action likely to erode their own privileged position, but also because they supposed governments would yield to the power of liberal arguments.

National sentiment and economic calculation worked hand in hand. Virulent outbursts of anti-French feeling in 1813 and again in 1840 had not permanently affected relations with their French neighbours, as witness the friendly greetings exchanged in 1848 between the Frankfurt Parliament and the French National Assembly. The year 1859 was, however, a turning-point in Franco-German relations. The French attack on Austria in northern Italy where the first Napoleon had won his spurs aroused excited comment in Germany. While liberals were sympathetic to Italy's struggle for independence, many feared that if France was victorious Napoleon would attempt to seize the so-called 'natural' frontier in the Rhineland. Anti-French feeling quickly manifested itself in the press and at popular festivals, scientific congresses and in *Landtage* all over Germany. The nationalist agitation reached a high point in November with the centenary celebrations of Friedrich Schiller's birth. This time anti-French feeling did not die down. It received a fresh impetus in the spring of 1860 when Napoleon acquired Savoy and Nice from Piedmont as the price of French intervention in northern Italy. All shades of German opinion, liberal and conservative, were united in the belief that an attack in the west was imminent. For the first time demands were heard for the annexation of Alsace and Lorraine to safeguard Germany's frontiers against French aggression.

Anti-French feeling remained a permanent feature of Franco-German relations throughout the 1860s, and strengthened the demand for a strong Reich led by Prussia, the guardian of the Rhineland. Nationalist organisations such as the German Sharpshooters League (*Deutsche Schützenbund*) founded in 1861 and the German Glee Singers League (*Deutsche Sängerbund*) in 1862 institutionalised this intense nationalism. It was kept alive at popular festivals organised by these bodies which attracted thousands of spectators from the broad middle classes. Even wider circles of the population were influenced by popular anti-French literature circulating in the 1860s.

All these organisations, from the Congress of German Economists to the Sharpshooters' League, helped create a climate of opinion favourable to unification. Interlocking directorates and overlapping membership bound the organisers close together. 'The same liberals', remarks one authority, 'who supported the Progressive Party joined the *Nationalverein*, attended the sessions of the Congress of German Economists and addressed the meetings of the gymnasts and sharpshooters'.[7] While it would be quite misleading to imagine that national liberalism altered the thrust of Prussian policy, it is true to say that this steamhead of opinion for a *kleindeutsch Reich* dovetailed neatly into the expansionist designs of that state.

The second ideology, political Catholicism, which emerged as a formidable force at the close of the 1860s, may seem at first sight more likely to retard than advance the creation of a united Germany. That depends to some extent on the feasibility of the *großdeutsch* solution supported (if only nominally) by many Catholics who were opposed to Prussia on religious as well as on political grounds.

In recent years a school of revisionist historians has taken up the

---

7. T. Hamerow, *The Social Foundations of German Unification 1858–1871: Ideas and Institutions* (Princeton, NJ, 1969), p. 358.

cudgels on behalf of the Confederation. Revisionists quote with approval the remarks of a contemporary observer in 1866 who believed that the Confederation was

> the last statesmanlike concept of European diplomacy . . . not only did Germany live at peace with its neighbours; it acted as a brake on any European state which desired to breach the peace of the world. The only error . . . was that it assumed all the members possessed moral stature . . . Prussia had made it clear for a long time that she would not bow to majority decisions. On the day she said that openly the Confederation was smothered to death.[8]

These historians go on to point out, rightly, that far from being the culmination of an inevitable historical development, the Reich of 1871 was the product of a civil war which set German against German, dividing not uniting them. Moreover, where the old Confederation had kept the peace for fifty years, the new Reich plunged Europe into a disastrous war within thirty-four years. Twenty-five years later the same militaristic elements went to war once more, this time to leave Germany more divided than ever before.

It seems unlikely that the Confederation could have been reorganised on federal lines maintaining the Austrian connection and combining maximum freedom for its members with a stronger central authority than the Federal Diet. First, its reputation had sunk so low in the esteem of most liberals – because of its failure to tackle pressing problems and its close association with reactionary measures – that it is difficult to envisage its transformation into a forward looking national state. This was reinforced by the conservative policies pursued by states such as Bavaria and Württemberg, in particular their opposition to a directly elected national parliament. Second, while the Third Germany could preserve its independence by playing Austria and Prussia off against each another (as they had done between 1848 and 1852), as long as Austria preferred dualism the reform schemes of these states (however impracticable) could never be realised. Indeed, as some of them appreciated, a stronger Confederation would not be in Austrian interests because it would inevitably weaken the ties with her non-German possessions. Finally, the rivalries between the states forming the Third Germany militated against close cooperation which might have enabled them to exert some influence. Economically Saxony and Württemberg looked to the *Zollverein* whereas Bavaria was attracted by the markets of the Danubian basin, while politically the attempts of

---

8. Quoted in H.-U. Wehler, *Das deutsche Kaiserreich 1871–1918* (Göttingen, 1980), p. 160.

the latter to become the predominant state in south Germany aroused the suspicions of her neighbours. For all these reasons hopes of a re-formed Confederation maintaining the link with Austria were unrealis-tic from the start.

On the other hand, the strength of political Catholicism on the eve of the war of 1870 may well have exerted some influence on Prussian policy and thus on the creation of *Kleindeutschland*. That was because the democratic connotations of political Catholicism posed a threat not only to the established order of things in south Germany but also by implication to monarchical power everywhere.

Political Catholicism originated with the reaction of the Catholic Church to the attempts of liberal movements to reduce her monopoly of power in education and over matrimony. As the Church had emerged from the trauma of the French Revolution a more Rome-oriented body, so successive pontiffs adopted an increasingly intransi-gent attitude towards the modern world. In the old Confederation there were 23 million Catholics and 20 million Protestants. Once Aus-tria's 12 million Catholics were excluded Protestants were in a ma-jority. The Catholic feelings of vulnerability coincided with dislike of Prussian domination of the North German Confederation. The ruth-less treatment of defeated states, disregard of dynastic rights and the minimal concessions Bismarck made to liberalism confirmed south Germans in their opposition to eventual union with the north. It was the merger of opposition to Prussia with opposition to liberal attempts to introduce secular education and civil marriage which produced the phenomenon of political Catholicism. In France and Belgium attempts by the state to control the Church led to the emergence of liberal Catholic movements which broke completely the close association of state and Church (throne and altar) characteristic of Catholicism for centuries. In Germany Catholics were much less affected by liberal currents. What the Church authorities borrowed from liberal Catholi-cism were the techniques of mass political participation to underpin their campaign against liberalism.

After the expulsion of Austria from Germany the four southern states remained in a no-man's land sandwiched between victorious Prussia, defeated Austria and a France determined to prevent further extensions of Prussian power. But despite the conclusion of defens-ive/offensive treaties with the southern states (entered into because they were conscious of their vulnerability to French attack) it was by no means obvious that the south would gradually be absorbed into the Prussian sphere of influence as Bismarck seems initially to have thought likely. Elections to the new Customs Parliament in 1868 disappointed him. The campaign slogan 'From Customs Parliament to Union Parliament' indicated what national liberals hoped would result from the elections. In fact anti-Prussian and anti-Protestant sentiments carried the day. Forty-nine opponents of union were returned to the Berlin parliament and only thirty-six unionists. The message was clear: while the southern states valued the economic advantages which the *Zollverein* brought to them, deep hostility to Prussian militarism remained the dominant theme.

The important point to bear in mind is that anti-Prussianism was growing stronger, not weaker, by 1870. In Württemberg where the government had not harassed Catholics, nevertheless the Greater German Party for which most Catholics voted cooperated with the People's Party in opposing increased taxation to meet the costs of military reorganisation consequent upon the conclusion of its defensive and offensive treaties with Prussia. In March 1870 the two parties which had a majority in the *Landtag* introduced a motion to cut expenditure and reduce the period of service with the colours – a feature arousing much popular discontent. The government, fearing new elections, postponed a decision until the autumn. Although it attempted to conciliate the opposition in the high summer by offering slight cuts in military expenditure and a reduction in the period of service, it was by no means certain that this would have resolved the crisis. The government was determined to make no new concessions while the opposition was assured of support from grass-roots organisations pledged to a taxation boycott.

In Baden and Bavaria where governments had attempted to curtail Church activities, parties hostile to Prussia had been founded. The Catholic People's Party founded in Heidelberg in 1869 demanded freedom for the Church to manage her own affairs, unification on a federal basis with the inclusion of Austria in a German Reich, and the introduction of universal suffrage. The last demand was significant; it had dawned on Catholic politicians that a broad franchise would, with the help of the rural clergy, enable them to mobilise the masses and swamp the urban basis of political liberalism. But it was in Bavaria that political Catholicism became a major force in response to government attempts to reduce Church control over schools. In the winter of 1868–9 the Bavarian People's Party or Patriotic Party was founded. It won an overall majority in the chamber in May 1869, and despite intense government pressure maintained its hold after elections in October. In February 1870 the crisis deepened when both houses of the *Landtag* carried a no-confidence motion which eventually forced the Hohenloe ministry, which was favourable to union with the north, to resign. Subsequently the lower house proposed cuts in the military budget and a reduction in the period of service with the colours. In July the new minister-president and the finance minister declared these proposals totally unacceptable, making a head-on collision between government and opposition inevitable.

The outbreak of the Franco-Prussian War and the outburst of patriotic feeling which swept through the south has obscured the fact that the two largest states in the area were gripped by a political crisis much more serious than the one facing Prussia in the first half of the 1860s. Opinion had been mobilised and polarised in both states. On one side crown, military and civil service were defending privileged positions against determined opponents with grass-roots support such as the Prussian liberals had never sought in their struggle with the Prussian crown.

It would be going much too far to suggest that Bismarck plunged the North German Confederation into war in 1870 merely to divert attention from a serious internal threat to the stability of the conservative order of things. However, we know that he was concerned about the deteriorating situation. The British ambassador reported in February 1870 that Bismarck had said that in the event of serious complications in Bavaria the Prussian army would march into that state at once. And in March after the fall of Hohenloe it was rumoured in Berlin that three army corps had been designated for use in Bavaria and Württemberg.

At the same time Bismarck was worried about the situation facing him in Prussia. National Liberals were becoming increasingly restive as evidence mounted of deepening southern opposition to final unification. In February Eduard Lasker, the liberal leader, attempted to force the pace with a motion asking the *Reichstag* to recognise the national aspirations of Baden (which had a pro-Prussian government) and help it join the north. Behind this lay the hope that the other southern states would follow suit, making the creation of *Kleindeutschland* an accomplished fact. If France chose to fight over this issue, well and good. Patriotic feeling would then drive the south into the northern camp. Bismarck opposed the motion, having no desire to allow the National Liberals to dictate the course of events. Yet he needed their political support more than ever before. For without it the government could not secure favourable majorities in the forthcoming *Landtag* and *Reichstag* elections, it was extremely doubtful whether the Iron Budget would be renewed, i.e. the arrangement entered into in 1867 whereby military expenditure was outside *Reichstag* control for the next four years. Furthermore, the price of agreement might well be some movement towards responsible government, for frustrated National Liberals were turning more and more to constitutional issues, encouraged to some extent by the establishment of the liberal Empire in France in January 1870. But Bismarck was adamantly opposed to further political concessions. That he was on the look-out for some way out of the impasse by reviving the flagging national issue is suggested by his determined attempt in the spring of 1870 to obtain an imperial title for King William – with no success, for neither Württemberg nor Bavaria were eager to confer such an honour on a Hohenzollern. Therefore it seems not unreasonable to suppose that National Liberal reactions to deadlock over final unification combined with serious political unrest in south Germany – for which the growth of political Catholicism was largely responsible – may well have played a part in the decision to go to war in 1870.

These reflections lead naturally to a consideration of the Bismarck factor. The qualities and objectives of this extraordinarily talented statesman have been aptly summarised by a recent writer:

> The Minister-Presidency of Prussia was not his objective but only a means to a higher goal. The issue for him was the territorial expansion and consolidation of Prussia in a revolutionary Europe, a path he was convinced could only be traversed by establishing Prussian hegemony in Europe at the expense of Austria but in conformity with the interests of the other European powers. The means were revolutionary, the goal conservative . . . Add to this his tendency to extremes, his eagerness at moments of tension to go to the limits, his towering ability to juggle with several balls at once, to oversee a situation in all its complexity, to separate tactical means from strategic goals but nevertheless to keep both in view, finally the tendency – which bordered on self-destruction – to go *va banque* when a situation reached crisis point – in all this lay his superiority over his opponents at home and abroad.[9]

Hagen Schulze quite rightly emphasises the particularist character of Bismarck's policy. Significantly his hero was Frederick the Great and his yardstick for measuring the worth of a Hohenzollern was simply whether the ruler had acquired territory for his kingdom. All his life Bismarck remained a servant of his king (provided he got his way); and all his life his objective remained the creation of a Great Prussian state stretching from the Rhine to the Oder and from the Baltic Sea

9. H. Schulze, *Der Weg zum Nationalstaat: Die deutsche Nationalbewegung vom 18. Jahrhundert bis zur Reichsgründung* (Munich, 1985), pp. 113–14. The book by Schulze referred to here has now appeared in an English translation. The details are as follows: H. Schulze, *The Course of German Nationalism: from Frederick The Great to Bismarck, 1763–1867* (Cambridge, 1991).

to Lake Constance. That this would involve war with Austria was a near certainty in his view:

> The only parade ground for our policy is Germany [he wrote in 1853] . . . and it is precisely this that Austria believes she needs as a matter of urgency; there is no room for both [of us] . . . we take the breath away from each other's mouths; one of us must yield or be forced to do so by the other.[10]

While Bismarck was never a nationalist in the liberal sense which implied popular participation in the affairs of state, nevertheless the authoritarian Prussian state was perfectly compatible with the conservative philosophy of nationalism. This postulated the existence of several German states, each a manifestation of the *Volksgeist* (spirit of the people) and each with the right to an independent political existence. Prussian expansionism at the expense of smaller states could, therefore, be clothed in nationalist garb of a sort. This was what Bismarck meant when he declared in 1858 that there was 'nothing more German than Prussian particularism properly understood'.[11] Furthermore, the coincidence of the power drive of the Prussian state with the liberal demand for a *kleindeutsch* state was a bonus mark for Bismarck, prompting the frank remark years later after the Reich of 1871 had come into being that

> whether one considered the main issue from the Borussian angle to be the leading role of Prussia or from the national angle to be the unification of Germany, both objectives coincide.[12]

Much has been written about Bismarck's extraordinary diplomatic expertise exemplified above all in his handling of the Schleswig-Holstein crisis. One of the keys to this, as to all his skilful diplomatic operations, lay in an acute awareness of the intimate and ever-changing relationship between domestic policy and international affairs. But whereas conservatives believed that the stability of the established order at home depended on stability abroad, and National Liberals that disorder abroad would bring about political change at home, Bismarck saw another possibility: stability of the monarchical order at home combined with disturbance of the balance of power abroad. 'Great crises', as he commented years before, 'represent the weather that is conducive to Prussia's growth if we use them without fear and perhaps

---

10. Bismarck, *Die gesammelten Werke*, 14, no. 1,480, Bismarck to Leopold von Gerlach, 19–20 December 1853.
11. Ibid., vol. 2, no. 343, 'Einige Bemerkungen über Preußens Stellung im Bunde' (March, 1858), p. 317.
12. Ibid., vol. 15, p. 198.

very ruthlessly'.[13] In exploiting favourable situations he displayed an acute sense of timing, an understanding of the relationship between means and ends, and an ability to keep several options open to the last possible minute.

When the male line of the Danish royal house died out in November 1863 the German liberals demanded immediate occupation of the duchies and the recognition of Duke Friedrich as ruler of an independent Schleswig-Holstein, this in defiance of the Treaty of London in which the Great Powers recognised Prince Christian as lawful successor to the Danish throne and to the duchies. Bismarck had two objections to this: first, the creation of another small state in north Germany controlling the mouth of the Elbe was not in Prussian strategic interests; and second, it would give an enormous impetus to liberalism certain to weaken the power of monarchy everywhere – or so conservatives thought for they grossly over-estimated the revolutionary potential of liberalism. While resolutely refusing to be stampeded by German liberals into precipitate action against Denmark, Bismarck was able to some extent to deflect their wrath yet not antagonise the Great Powers: Prussia, with Austrian support, occupied Schleswig to compel the Danes to abide by promises made to the German powers in 1851–2 but broken by the virtual annexation of Schleswig in March 1863. Securing the cooperation of Austria was less of a diplomatic masterstroke than is often supposed: Austria dared not assume the leadership of a national crusade; she could only hope that by working with Prussia she could contain that restless power and keep it on a conservative keel. Bismarck was careful to reassure the great powers that Austria and Prussia recognised King Christian and were concerned only to make him keep the Danish promises. But, of course, Bismarck calculated that Denmark had no time to comply with the ultimatum. And once in possession of the duchies he calculated that the situation could then be moulded in Prussian interests. By the end of 1863 he favoured the annexation of the duchies to round off Prussian territory in north Germany.

The flexibility of his diplomacy was evident at the London Conference in the summer of 1864 when the Great Powers attempted to revolve the dispute in the spirit of the old Concert of Europe. Bismarck did not rely on Prussian military strength alone to rule out any restoration of the status quo – he was able to point to the explosive state of German public opinion (which now expected the creation of an independent Schleswig-Holstein in the very near future) to demon-

---

13. Ibid., vol. 1, no. 473, Bismarck to Baron von Manteuffel, 15 February 1854.

strate how impossible that would be. The dangerous option of an independent state – which he reluctantly supported – was scotched because the Danes would not abandon their compatriots in North
Schleswig. Partition – which Bismarck would have accepted to be rid
of the North Schleswig Danes – was unacceptable to Denmark. Thus
the Conference collapsed, the war continued and Austria and Prussia
ended up in possession of the duchies. Denmark's mistaken policy,
Austria's willingness to work with Prussia, the wish of Britain, France
and Russia to avoid conflict and the military power of Prussia, all
contributed to a favourable situation which Bismarck could not have
created but which a less able practitioner of the diplomatic arts might
not have been able to exploit so successfully.

The 'revolutionary means' in Bismarckian diplomacy to which
Schulze refers is exemplified in his handling of France. In the conservative circles in which Bismarck grew up it was axiomatic to suppose
that the forces of revolution could be held at bay only if the three
great conservative powers stood shoulder to shoulder as they did in the
days of Metternich. The rise to power of Napoleon III aroused in
conservatives the sort of alarm and foreboding which Hitler's appointment as Chancellor did in the 1930s. Only by keeping Napoleon in
diplomatic purdah could a *bouleversement* of the international status quo
be prevented. Bismarck, second to none in his defence of the class
interests of the Junkers, showed a deeper appreciation of the nature of
the Napoleonic regime than most of his conservative contemporaries.
Ideologies come and go, so that a country's 'interests' or what the
rulers think these 'interests' are, are a better guide to policy. Napoleon
was unlikely to launch a revolutionary 'war of liberation' but was
more likely to exploit situations to advance French interests. That
thought transformed an ideological pariah into a possible ally for Prussia. And, as relations with Austria rapidly deteriorated after 1864, the
cornerstone of Bismarck's diplomacy was the attempt to neutralise
France during what he was convinced would be an inevitable conflict
with Austria for mastery in Germany.

It was essential to keep the floating mine away from the Prussian
ship by reassuring Napoleon – as Bismarck did at the Biarritz meeting
in October 1864 – that any agreement Prussia made with Austria such
as the Gastein Convention (which divided the duchies between the
two German powers) was of a purely temporary nature. For any suggestion that Prussia would help Austria retain Venetia would alarm
Napoleon (one of whose objectives was to acquire the province for
Italy) and would encourage him to negotiate with Austria, offering her
assistance against Prussia in return for Venetia.

At Biarritz Bismarck dropped vague hints of compensation for France should Prussia become master of Germany. Arguably Napoleon proved too slippery a character even for Bismarck. In the spring of 1866 with a German war a certainty, Bismarck's attempts to obtain specific promises of neutrality from France failed. Napoleon was determined to keep a free hand to intervene at a crucial moment in what contemporaries thought would be a long war. Consequently the war of 1866 was a high-risk operation for Prussia against whom the vast majority of states were ranged. No one foresaw the dramatic victory at Königgrätz which decided the outcome in a few weeks. Bismarck was well aware of the *va banque* nature of the decision to fight. Talking to the British ambassador hours before the ultimatum to the neighbouring states expired he remarked that:

> If we are beaten, I shall not return here. I shall fall in the last charge. One can but die once; and if we are beaten it is better to die.[14]

Bismarck was, in fact, much more the inveterate gambler running great risks than the accomplished crystal-gazer of popular legend who planned wars with foresight and deliberation and with absolute confidence that Prussia would win.

Though very much a man of the eighteenth century in his whole-hearted commitment to the aggrandisement of the state he served, Bismarck was very much a man of the new century in his quick appreciation of the growing importance of public opinion. True, he was scathing in his comments on 'German public opinion': 'our growth in power', he remarked to an erring diplomat, 'cannot issue forth from legislative chambers or from the press but from Great Power politics carried on by force of arms'.[15] Nevertheless, he made considerable efforts to try to manipulate *kleindeutsch* opinion in Prussian interests. He founded a new press organ, intervened frequently to correct articles and tried through his contact men to influence the foreign press. His efforts were largely wasted because of his blatant illiberalism. To push the army reforms through the *Landtag* in the teeth of liberal opposition he persecuted his opponents, censored the press and even removed the immunity of deputies in a determined attempt to smash them politically. No rapprochement with liberalism was possible as long as the constitutional crisis continued in Prussia.

When schemes for the reform of the Confederation were circulating in the early 1860s Bismarck's 'revolutionary' proposal for a directly

14. Lord Augustus Loftus, *Diplomatic Reminiscences* (London, 1984), vol. 1, p. 60.
15. Bismarck, *Die gesammelten Werke*, vol. 14/2, no. 999, Bismarck to Robert von Goltz, 24 December 1863.

elected German parliament was dismissed on all sides. Conservatives were horrified that one of their number could flirt with the revolution and liberals rejected it as a desperate ploy by an old reactionary for whom time was running out. Both were wrong. Bismarck realised from his observation of Napoleonic France that universal male suffrage could benefit the conservative interest in the countryside; the rural vote mobilised by landowners could, in the absence of a secret ballot, swamp urban liberals whose mistrust of the masses robbed them of a long-term political future. But that lay in the future – on the eve of war opinion was solidly against Bismarck.

If liberals, especially in Prussia, were better disposed towards Bismarck after 1866 that was not because the minimal concessions made to liberal opinion in the constitution of the North German Confederation satisfied them, but simply that the completion of the *kleindeutsch* state seemed imminent. And it was widely supposed that when the four southern states joined in Bismarck would not be able to resist pressure for fully responsible government. To further concessions he was, however, adamantly opposed, both as a champion of monarchical prerogative and also because of the need to reassure the south German governments that entry into the Confederation at some future date would not threaten their conservative regimes. It has been suggested earlier that concern about the domestic situation in Prussia, coupled with the rising tide of radicalism in the south, may have been significant factors influencing the decision to go to war in 1870.

That war was not fought primarily to complete the unification of Germany on *kleindeutsch* lines. Although Bismarck was very ready to orchestrate national resentment against French demands for territorial compensation during the Luxemburg crisis, he had not the slightest intention of waging a national war in 1867 to unify Germany; while National Liberals would have supported war with enthusiasm, the southern governments might well have refused to come to Prussia's aid under the terms of the defensive and offensive treaties. When war did come in 1870 Bismarck ensured that the threat from France – real or supposed – lay at the centre of the dispute over the Hohenzollern candidacy. He calculated quite correctly that fear of 'French aggression' would spark off a wave of anti-French feeling sweeping the southern governments into war.

That war would be the likely outcome of the candidacy Bismarck must have known from the spring of 1870 onwards. How the situation would unfold he cannot possibly have known. But just as the Danes played into his hands by their (understandable) intransigence in the winter of 1863–4, so did France in 1870. After the withdrawal of the candidacy – a victory for France and a severe blow to Bismarck – they demanded a promise from the King of Prussia that the candidacy would never be renewed. The king's firm (but courteous) refusal was depicted by Bismarck in the celebrated Ems telegram and in the circular to German embassies abroad as an indignant rebuff to an insufferably rude ambassador who persisted with his impertinent demand. The intention was to arouse German national feeling on a point of honour and to provoke the sensitive French – deeply worried about their loss of influence over German affairs – into a declaration of war. Thus Bismarck succeeded in locating the causes of the war in unreasonable French demands, not in German pressure to complete the *kleindeutsch* state. These circumstances ensured that when the southern governments did negotiate entry into the new German Reich Bismarck – not the National Liberals – was in control of the situation. Nor did he neglect the international perspective. By shifting responsibility for the war on to French shoulders Bismarck effectively tied the hands of the great powers. Only later in the century did the alteration in the balance of power consequent upon the creation of the Reich in 1871 become a matter of concern to them.

SUGGESTIONS FOR FURTHER READING

W. Carr, *The Wars of German Unification* (London, 1991).

L. Gall, *Bismarck: The White Revolutionary*, 2 vols (London, 1986).

M. Hughes, *Nationalism and Society: Germany 1800–1945* (London, 1988).

H. Schulze, *The Course of German Nationalism: From Frederick the Great to Bismarck, 1763–1867* (Cambridge, 1991).

O. Pflanze, *Bismarck and the Development of Germany: The Period of Unification 1815–1871* (Princeton, 1990) 2nd edn .

J. Sheehan, *German History 1770–1866* (Oxford, 1990).

CHAPTER SIX

Bismarck's heir: Chancellor Bernhard von Bülow and the national idea 1890–1918

Katharine A. Lerman

On 30 March 1909 Bernhard von Bülow, the fourth Reich Chancellor of imperial Germany, stood up to defend his record in the German *Reichstag*. Chancellor speeches were major events in public life before the First World War and Bülow was renowned for the brilliancy of his verbal swordsmanship. He gave a bravura performance in which he stressed his lifelong commitment to the national idea and his role as custodian of the national interest. 'In nearly forty years of service', he declared,

> in often difficult, often very difficult circumstances, I have proved my
> loyalty to King and Fatherland, Kaiser and Reich. In foreign as in
> domestic policy I have never known any guiding star save the good
> [*Wohl*] of the monarchy, the good of the country, reasons of state
> [*Staatsraison*], the national idea and the Kaiser idea, which for me are
> indissolubly linked.[1]

Bülow's words, however, had a hollow ring to them in March 1909 for it was common knowledge that he had lost the confidence of Kaiser Wilhelm II as a result of his handling of the *Daily Telegraph* affair the previous November. In addition, as early as August 1908, Bülow had recognised that the government might be 'heading for a fiasco' with its Reich financial reform and that while its failure 'would give me *une très belle sortie* . . . for our country, its domestic well-being and its external prestige, it would be a blow from which it would be difficult to recover.'[2] In March 1909 one of his closest advisers told

---

1. Bülow's parliamentary speeches can be found in the *Stenographische Berichte* of the *Reichstag* and Prussian *Landtag* (Berlin, 1897–1909), and also in J. Penzler (ed.) *Fürst Bülows Reden*, vol. 1 (1897–1903), vol. 2 (1903–6) and H. Hötzsch (ed.) vol. 3 (1907–9) (Berlin, 1907–9).

2. Zentrales Staatsarchiv (ZSA) Potsdam, Hammann Papers, 14, Bülow to Hammann, 3 August 1908 and 14 August 1908.

him that the fundamental problem with the reform was the lack of clarity over the government's aims. Without the will to resolve the issue, Bülow faced certain parliamentary defeat. By May Bülow was already preparing his next and final speech for the *Reichstag* which he knew would be his 'swan-song' and which he delivered on 16 June. Concerned not to appear irritated, annoyed, piqued, depressed or sorry for himself, he told his chancellery chief, 'At this of all times I must appear superior, distinguished and self-assured, as a *statesman*'.[3] Eight days after his speech the *Reichstag* rejected the inheritance tax and Bülow left Berlin for Kiel to secure the Kaiser's agreement to his resignation.

Throughout his career Bülow repeatedly maintained that he was motivated solely by the national interest. He believed he was emulating imperial Germany's first Chancellor, Otto von Bismarck, when he subscribed to the view that patriotism was the highest morality in politics and that everything else should be subordinate to the *salus publicae*. Historians' verdicts on Bülow's nine-year chancellorship, however, have generally been harsh, and the fourth Chancellor has traditionally been seen as a man who squandered Bismarck's legacy and irreparably damaged the public interest. While several historians have discerned some reformist potential in German domestic politics during his chancellorship, especially during the period of the so-called Bülow Bloc parliamentary coalition of 1907–9, it is rare to come across the view that Bülow was 'far more weighty and courageous a statesman than his historical reputation would allow'.[4] The marked deterioration in Germany's diplomatic position and the bitter antagonisms which were evident in German domestic politics by 1909 appear to speak for themselves. As Johannes Haller, who wrote one of the first historical assessments of the Bülow years, concluded:

> In the Bülow era glossing things over and hushing things up, cover-ups and cooking the books were elevated into a system. If we suffered a set-back, it was made into a success, and even if the failure was all too evident, in the given circumstances it had still to be a welcome result. The Chancellor, unsurpassed in the art of just about 'arranging' things yet again and sorting out even the most muddled situation, really accustomed the nation to locking the stable door only after yet another horse had bolted. Thus arose that atmosphere of comfortable optimism and sweet self-deception in which vigorous political thinking was lulled to sleep

3. Bundesarchiv (BA) Koblenz, Loebell Papers, 6, Bülow to Loebell, Whit Monday 1909.
4. T. Cole, 'Kaiser versus Chancellor: the crisis of Bülow's chancellorship 1905–6', in R.J. Evans (ed.) *Society and Politics in Wilhelmine Germany* (London, 1978), p. 41.

[*einschließ*], the feeling of responsibility became numb, the ability to [make] a free, personal decision was suffocated by shallow smooth-talking, until the great mass of the nation, half-dreaming, ultimately stumbled towards its fate, a host of blindmen with a blind leader at their head, [staggering] towards the abyss.[5]

How was it that a man who was so conscious of his role in history as Bismarck's heir, and so insistent about his commitment and devotion to the new German nation-state, could attract such condemnation? This chapter will explore Bülow's conception of the national idea, his contribution to German foreign and domestic policy between 1897 (when he became state secretary of the Foreign Office) and 1909, and how his emphasis on the national idea came to hinder rather than facilitate the emergence of a patriotic consensus in Germany before the First World War.

BÜLOW'S CONCEPTION OF THE NATIONAL IDEA

Bernhard von Bülow liked to be compared with Otto von Bismarck. The wars of unification were the most formative experience in his adolescence and he never spoke of what Bismarck had achieved without reverence and awe. Moreover, throughout his life he insisted on his personal and political loyalty to his predecessor, whom he had met for the first time as a young boy. His father, Bernhard Ernst von Bülow, was state secretary of the Foreign Office under Bismarck in the 1870s, and Bülow himself spent seventeen years in the German Diplomatic Service under Bismarck's watchful eye. Herbert von Bismarck, the Chancellor's son, complimented him in 1885 on being 'really the only one of all our diplomats who lets himself be impregnated with the political ideas of my father.'[6] When Bülow became Chancellor in 1900, he was widely regarded as a worthy successor to Bismarck and one of the most intelligent and talented men in the German ruling elite. Selected by Kaiser Wilhelm II as early as 1895 to be 'his Bismarck',[7] Bülow deliberately fostered an image of himself as

5. J. Haller, *Die Aera Bülow: Eine historisch-politische Studie* (Stuttgart and Berlin, 1922), pp. 148–9.
6. W. Bussmann (ed.) *Graf Herbert von Bismarck: Aus seiner politischen Privatkorrespondenz* (Göttingen, 1964), Bülow to Herbert Bismarck, 31 October 1885, p. 331.
7. See J.C.G. Röhl, *Germany Without Bismarck: The Crisis of Government in the Second Reich, 1890–1900* (London, 1967), p. 158.

the legitimate and deserving heir of the first Chancellor. His parliamentary speeches and public pronouncements, his private letters and memoranda, his book, *Deutsche Politik* (Berlin 1916), and the four volumes of his posthumously published memoirs, all contain appeals to Bismarck's memory, attempts to place and justify his own political actions within the Bismarckian tradition, and evidence of a self-conscious desire to go down in history as a man who consolidated and built upon Bismarck's legacy.

Bülow's relationship to Bismarck was a paradoxical one and there is abundant evidence that he did not fully understand Bismarck. But it is impossible to discuss his political ideas without reference to Bismarck for, in the late 1880s and early 1890s, Bülow developed a concept of 'the national idea' which reflected both his recognition of Bismarck's achievement in unifying Germany around Prussia and his perception of the weaknesses inherent in the Bismarckian Empire, particularly as manifested after Bismarck's dismissal in 1890. In addition Bülow inherited a 'method' from Bismarck, for he saw the first Chancellor as a statesman and *Realpolitiker* who had no fixed principles or beliefs in politics but, rather, swam with the current and achieved what he could for the nation. Finally, he came to appreciate the function Bismarck fulfilled as a symbol of German unity and power. This not only encouraged Bülow as Chancellor to promote 'the Bismarck myth' and his own role (unlike his two predecessors) as Bismarck's real epigonus, but also it led to a lifelong confusion in Bülow's mind of appearances with reality. As a diplomat observing events in Germany from St Petersburg in the 1880s, he believed that Russia's fear of Germany was significantly increased after the Reich Chancellor made a 'colossal speech'; and he wrote that the 'unqualified machinations' against Bismarck after the death of Kaiser Wilhelm I in 1888 'shattered . . . respect and confidence in Germany, that is, the foundations of our power position and of world peace.'[8] In his memoirs Bülow stated revealingly that the Germans were disliked, even before Bismarck made German power an object of envy, because 'we underestimated the value of forms, of appearances and, as the Greek philosopher demonstrated long ago, mankind judges by appearances and not by the reality of things.'[9] As Chancellor, Bülow consciously attached supreme importance to the politics of prestige. How his policies were seen became more important than what they achieved.

8. Bussmann, *Bismarck*, Bülow to Herbert Bismarck, 12 February 1888, p. 508 and 13 April 1888, p. 513.

9. B. von Bülow, *Denkwürdigkeiten*, 4 vols. (Berlin, 1930–1), vol 1, p. 27.

Bülow borrowed his concept of the national idea from the German historian, Heinrich von Treitschke, and in his memoirs he claimed that Treitschke's *German History* and Bismarck's speeches constituted the basis of his political thought and feelings. Nevertheless Treitschke's influence on Bülow should not be exaggerated. Bülow admitted when he first read Treitschke that he found some passages offensive, and as Chancellor he did not hesitate to criticise Treitschke's views. In urging the benefits of a heightened national consciousness, Bülow drew on his experience of the summer of 1866 and his participation as a volunteer in the Franco-Prussian War. He was completely out of sympathy with those Prussian conservatives who complained about the 'dilution' of Prussia in 1866 and with constitutional liberals who rejected the authoritarian structure of the new Reich. Rather he revelled in the nationalist euphoria. As he wrote later in *Deutsche Politik*, Bismarck had achieved in one decade what had been mismanaged and neglected for centuries.

It was after Bismarck's dismissal that Bülow began to refer to the national idea in his correspondence, and it was clearly in part a device to enable him to come to terms with the departure of the great man. As Bülow emancipated himself personally and politically from the influence of the Bismarck family in the 1890s, he sought to separate Bismarck from his achievement and transferred his loyalty to the new Kaiser. 'The Bismarckian epoch belongs now to history', he wrote to his friend Karl von Lindenau three weeks after Bismarck's resignation.

> Its fruits must be ripened and in my opinion that is only possible by working together, united and devoted, under the Kaiser and for the Kaiser, in whom I have confidence because I believe that there is much of significance in him.[10]

A year later he told another close friend, Philipp zu Eulenburg-Hertefeld, that he would have preferred it if Bismarck had remained in office but they now had to demonstrate that the Reich could be ruled without him. Even the greatest individuals were transitory phenomena. 'The idea, the national idea, is above all change and has to be helped to victory *à tout prix et quoiqu'il arrive* [at any price and whatever happens]. There is no salvation except through this formula.'[11] Bülow's successful elevation of the national idea above all other considerations was indicated in 1897, shortly before his appointment as state secretary of the Foreign Office, when he wrote in a personal memorandum that

10. BA Koblenz, Bülow Papers, 99, Bülow to Lindenau, 9 April 1890.

11. J.C.G. Röhl (ed.) *Philipp Eulenburgs politische Korrespondenz*, 3 vols (Boppard am Rhein, 1976–83), vol. 1, Bülow to Eulenburg, 28 May 1891, p. 685.

he wished Bismarck would die soon as he only made the task of governing more difficult.

Given the political instability which ensued after Bismarck's dismissal, the urgency of a solution to the Empire's domestic problems and Bülow's own role in the intrigues to restore stability by increasing the power and prestige of the monarchy and (not least) securing his own appointment as Wilhelm II's Chancellor, it is perhaps not surprising that Bülow's private correspondence in the 1890s was preoccupied with the internal weaknesses of the Empire – the problems of confessional disunity, particularism and class conflict, the constitutional clash between monarchical authority and the pretensions of a democratically elected *Reichstag*, and the potential dangers, as well as strengths, inherent in Kaiser Wilhelm II's personality. Moreover, Bülow drew on his knowledge and understanding of German history, and he attributed German disunity in the past more to internal divisions between Germans than to the hostility or manipulations of foreign powers. Again and again the national idea was offered by Bülow as the panacea for these problems. Concerned about the *Reichsverdrossenheit* (weariness with the Reich) in the south German states, Bülow pointed out to Philipp Eulenburg that the population in the south had been particularist, ultramontane, *großdeutsch*, and even in favour of the Napoleonic Confederation of the Rhine, but had never supported the Hohenzollerns. Germany's entire internal and external future, he wrote in 1895, depended on the progressive strengthening of the ties between the south German states and the Reich, the nurturing of the national idea. Without the national idea, the Prussian monarchy, too, would be like 'a mill-wheel without water'. Prussia's fortunes were now inseparably linked to those of the Reich and any weakening of the Reich idea would be a step on the road to disaster. And of all Bismarck's policies as Chancellor Bülow was most critical of the *Kulturkampf* which had undermined national unity by setting Protestants against Catholics, Germans against Germans. The Catholic Centre Party, Bülow maintained in 1892, represented the old Germany which had fought in the Thirty Years' War under the imperial Habsburg flag and which had to be merged with the Hohenzollern Reich if the latter's unity and future were to be secure. Bülow's emphasis on the national idea was his response to the deep pessimism about the political situation which pervaded all levels of the German ruling elite by the middle of the 1890s. He believed that the monarchy could be popularised by strengthening the bonds between the imperial crown and the nation and rallying all nationally minded elements behind it. This in turn could be achieved by banging the national drum and creating a closed phalanx of conservative, liberal and Catholic support in opposition to the unpatriotic socialists.

Bülow's prolific correspondence before 1897 reveals an acute awareness of the divisions between Germans, the new and unfinished nature of the Bismarckian Empire, and the overriding need for consolidation which could come only through 'constantly striving forwards' and creating national feeling. Indeed, Bülow's political ideas and observations, as well as the importance he attached to the national idea, are ultimately intelligible only within the context of the continuing struggle for national unification. Even before Bismarck's resignation Bülow wrote:

> The German, who is still in many ways lacking the excitable national pride and the schooled sense of political advantage of other peoples, abandons himself all too easily to self-opinionated defiance and naive doctrinairism when the sky appears to him [to be] completely cloudless. Despite the best prospects of peace, our domestic and foreign policy should be geared to [the possibility] that the end of the century could easily bring us the decisive struggle for the monarchical nation-state.[12]

While Bülow repeatedly urged that the conduct of policy had to be calm, cautious and consistent, he always returned to the benefits of a heightened national consciousness and the integrative potential of German nationalism. In 1890 he insisted that everything, including domestic policies, had to be subordinated to Germany's unity and position as a European power. But the 'social imperialist' hue to much of what Bülow wrote in the 1890s – the idea that an ambitious foreign policy would divert attention away from problems at home – is unmistakable, as is the sense in which the promotion of national feeling became an end in itself. 'I am putting the main emphasis on foreign policy', Bülow wrote after moving into the Wilhelmstrasse in 1897. 'Only a successful foreign policy can help to reconcile, pacify, rally, unite.'[13]

BÜLOW'S ROLE IN GERMAN FOREIGN POLICY

At first glance Bülow's stress on his Bismarckian credentials and his custodianship of Bismarck's inheritance appear particularly incongruous

12. Ibid., Bülow to Eulenburg, 2 March 1890, p. 471.
13. Röhl, *Germany Without Bismarck*, p. 252. For a now classic social imperialist interpretation of German policy before 1914, see H.-U. Wehler, *The German Empire 1871–1918* (Leamington Spa, 1985).

in the light of his contribution to German foreign policy between 1897 and 1909. For, with the exception of Kaiser Wilhelm II, no other individual came to symbolise more the overweening arrogance, aggressive insecurity and deluded optimism which characterised German *Weltpolitik* before the First World War. His appointment as state secretary of the Foreign Office in 1897 coincided with Germany's embarkation on an ambitious programme of naval expansion and popular imperialism which promised to break through the confines of Bismarckian diplomacy and underline the claims of a new nation-state to world power status. It was Bülow who told a rapturous *Reichstag* in December 1897 that the times when the German people had left the earth and sea to their neighbours were over and that Germany, too, demanded her 'place in the sun'. Well before his resignation in 1909, his mere continuance in office was construed as a major obstacle to any improvement in Anglo-German relations. 'The road which Germany took in 1897 led to diplomatic isolation, war, military defeat and the collapse of the monarchy' was John Röhl's judgement of the significance of the ministerial changes of 1897.[14] Far from consolidating Bismarck's legacy, Bülow's conduct of German foreign policy precipitated the destruction of the Bismarckian Empire and the demise of the Prussian monarchy which that Empire had been designed to safeguard.

What is equally curious, however, especially when he knew he was destined for high political office several years before 1897, is the complete absence of any discussion of *Weltpolitik*, the need to acquire colonies or Germany's 'world historical' task in Bülow's correspondence before 1897. Bülow wrote extensively about Germany's historical and political development, but it is clear that he saw Germany's international position in traditional, conservative and continental European terms. In the 1890s his reflections on German foreign policy hinged upon such issues as the reliability of Germany's alliance partners, the security of the Empire within the European state system and the danger of a hostile coalition directed against Germany. Commenting on Germany's problems from abroad, Bülow appeared to take little cognizance of the economic shift that was taking place in Germany in the 1890s and how Germany's rapidly growing population, burgeoning industry and expanding commerce and trade were creating new imperialist pressures. Indeed, in 1890 he still assessed the internal strength of the Empire exclusively in military and moral terms. Finally, although he was in favour of annexations during the First World War and convinced once war broke out that France had to be destroyed

14. Röhl, *Germany Without Bismarck*, p. 277.

economically, there is no mention in his correspondence before 1897 of the need for territorial adjustments in Germany's favour or any specific foreign policy aims. Nor is there any evidence before his meeting with the Kaiser and Tirpitz in June 1897 that he believed that Germany needed a huge battlefleet.

What emerges from Bülow's correspondence before 1897 is, rather, a commitment to the political boundaries of the Bismarckian nation-state within Europe and a sometimes naive optimism and faith in its future. Unlike the Pan-German nationalists whose wild ambitions and expansionist ideals he later attacked in the *Reichstag*, he had a political, not an ethnic concept of the nation. Far from dreaming of the inclusion of Austrian Germans in a future Greater German Reich, he was concerned with the internal balance and cohesion of the Empire, as well as the ascendancy of Prussia, and he clearly viewed the prospect of a greater number of Catholics or new national minorities with alarm. As with Bismarck, Bülow saw language and culture as legitimising a political entity which had primarily served to secure the position of Prussia. He thus found it perfectly acceptable that the new German nation-state excluded Germans but included the formerly French provinces of Alsace and Lorraine, as well as substantial numbers of Poles and Danes. While Germany's relationship with Austria was complicated by considerations of language, culture and religious confession, Bülow regarded the Dual Monarchy essentially as a foreign power to be mistrusted. He was convinced that there could be no return to the situation before 1866 when Austria and Prussia had struggled for control over German affairs; nor could there be a return, after the incorporation of the south German states into the Empire in 1871, to a Prussia or north Germany confined to the frontiers of the Rhine and Main. Prussia's future was inseparably linked to the Reich, and Bülow appeared wedded to the territorial status quo.

Of course these observations are in no sense intended to conceal that there was a broadly aggressive thrust in Bülow's political outlook before 1897. 'I believe in the rising star of the German nation', he wrote to Philipp Eulenburg in 1887,[15] and on several occasions he maintained that, provided Germany kept up her defences, she could await 'elemental events' or 'the decisive struggles of the future' with equanimity. Bülow had a simplistic, Social Darwinist view of international relations according to which youthful and vigorous nations emerged victorious from their struggles against the sick and dying. International diplomacy was analagous to a battlefield or a chessboard on

---

15. Röhl, *Eulenburg*, vol. 1, Bülow to Eulenburg, 25 December 1887, p. 258.

which one made one's moves and played to win. There was also a certain rigidity in his thought. Like Friedrich von Holstein (the influential counsellor in the Foreign Office) and others in the 1890s, he over-estimated the conflict of interest between Russia and Britain, and believed that if Germany kept free from trouble and made no precipitate moves or commitments, she could reap the whirlwind that would eventually come. He did not share Bismarck's interest in the ascendancy of Germany within a stable Europe but, rather, believed Germany would profit from the conflicts of others. 'The sharper the antagonism between Russia and England, the better for us', he wrote in 1895.[16] But the key point here is that he believed time was on Germany's side and he had certainly not formulated any clear foreign policy goals. Convinced of the cultural superiority of the German nation and confident in Germany's strength, his ideas certainly did not exclude the possibility of an eventual war against Britain, but he generally inclined towards the more complacent outlook of *tout arrive à qui sait attendre* (everything comes to him who waits).

It is frequently assumed that Bülow was in full control of German foreign policy from his installation as foreign secretary in 1897 and that *Weltpolitik* was his policy. Unlike his predecessor, Adolf Marschall von Bieberstein, Bülow was a professional diplomat who was seen as having expertise in this area; his first speech in the *Reichstag* in December 1897 heralded what appeared to be a fundamental reorientation in German foreign policy; moreover, it was clear that the official responsibility of the Reich Chancellor, Chlodwig zu Hohenlohe-Schillingsfürst, for the conduct of foreign policy became purely nominal between 1897 and 1900 and that Bülow was 'the real Minister of Foreign Affairs'.[17] When Bülow became Chancellor in October 1900 the basic continuity of German foreign policy was unaffected. Oswald von Richthofen, who was under state secretary in the Foreign Office between 1897 and 1900, became Bülow's successor as foreign secretary, but there was no question that he remained Bülow's deputy.

Nevertheless, attempts by historians to show that Bülow not only managed the day-to-day conduct of German foreign policy but also had a 'grand design' or 'world power concept' which he pursued consistently from 1897 have generally been difficult to substantiate and ultimately unconvincing. There is no evidence of a grandiose foreign policy concept in Bülow's thought before 1897 and, even allowing for the rather lame argument that he could not reveal the full scope of his

16. Ibid., vol. 2, Bülow to Eulenburg, 28 September 1895, p. 1552.

17. Haus-, Hof- und Staatsarchiv Wien, PA III, 151, Szögyényi to Goluchowski, 9 April 1898.

intentions for understandable diplomatic reasons, the official documen-
tation for such a thesis remains poor after 1897. As Peter Winzen has
acknowledged, if one leaves aside the issue of *Weltpolitik* and colonial
acquisitions, Bülow's approach to foreign policy issues was remarkably
consistent. From the middle of the 1890s Bülow (and Holstein) advocated a policy of cautious reserve in international relations, believing
that Germany should not lean too heavily towards either the Franco-
Russian combination or Britain and that she would thereby profit
from the conflict of interest between them. This 'free hand' policy was
entirely compatible with the building of the navy from 1898. Finally,
if Bülow did have a grand design or *Weltmachtkonzept* when he took
over the conduct of German foreign policy in 1897, its underlying
assumptions (for example, the expectation that Britain would remain
isolated and on relatively good terms with Germany) were question-
nable by 1902 at the latest, but Bülow continued to be responsible for
German foreign policy until his resignation in 1909.

All the available evidence suggests that, far from developing his own
grand design or world power concept, Bülow 'inherited' his foreign
policy in 1897. Once he was initiated in June 1897 into plans hatched
by the Kaiser and Alfred von Tirpitz to embark on an ambitious naval
armaments programme, he did not make a 'decisive breakthrough
from a continental to a world political concept'[18] but, rather, agreed
to conduct German foreign policy in accordance with the needs of the
navy. Bülow freely admitted that he was assigned his foreign policy
task in 1897. In 1912 he wrote:

> The task I was set when the conduct of foreign affairs was assigned to me
> on 26 June 1897 on the *Hohenzollern* was to make possible our transition
> to *Weltpolitik* (trade, shipping, overseas interests, the consequences of the
> huge development of our industry, our increasing prosperity, the increase
> in our population) and above all the building of the German navy,
> without clashing with England, for whom we were in no way a match at
> sea, but preserving German dignity and our position on the continent.[19]

He did not himself integrate the naval programme into a comprehensive strategy aimed at world power. He agreed to subordinate
considerations of diplomacy to the requirements of naval armaments.
Bülow already knew well that 'the value of a person for H.M. depends
on his willingness or usefulness to cooperate directly or indirectly in

18. Winzen, 'Prince Bülow's *Weltmachtpolitik*', in *Australian Journal of Politics and
History*, 22 (1976), p. 232.
19. ZSA Potsdam, Rath Papers, 9, Bülow to Rath, 12 February 1912. Bülow gives
the same version of events in his memoirs and in *Deutsche Politik*.

increasing our supply of ships'.[20] Moreover, he believed in swimming with the current: not only was *Weltpolitik* already a fashionable word by 1897 but also the Kaiser made his famous *Weltreich* speech in January 1896. In his correspondence with the Kaiser after 1897 Bülow always referred to the fact that he was implementing Wilhelm's great plans and pursuing his aims. There is no conclusive evidence that behind the well-worn formula of *Weltpolitik* Bülow had any grandiose *Weltmachtkonzept* of his own which he sought to put into effect.

Bülow was prepared to play a specific and subordinate role in a military monarchy. He unfailingly supported Tirpitz, the state secretary of the Reich Navy Office, and never questioned naval or military demands. In 1906, when Tirpitz's resignation appeared a real possibility, he wanted to avoid everything which looked as if he might be withdrawing his support from the state secretary, 'especially as he is now finally beginning to have the confidence in me to which I indeed have a claim after supporting him constantly for seven years and which is also in H.M.'s interest.'[21] He wanted Tirpitz to have no doubts about how sincerely and seriously he wanted him to remain in office. Bülow never interfered in naval matters; he had only a very superficial grasp of the technical details of the naval legislation, and he never questioned the wisdom of the naval programme until his position was irreparably weakened in 1908. At the same time the coordination between the Foreign Office and those responsible for naval and military matters was clearly inadequate during his chancellorship, although this also reflected structural deficiencies in the Bismarckian constitution. During the Russo-Japanese War vital information about the condition of the Russian fleet never reached the Foreign Office and never entered into the calculations of Bülow and his subordinates. Similarly, the Chancellor and Foreign Office were informed only very belatedly in February 1905 about an operations plan, already approved by the Kaiser in December 1904, to invade Denmark and seize vital Danish waterways as a preliminary to a war against Britain. Bülow expressed no objections to the plan (and nor did he raise diplomatic objections to the notorious Schlieffen Plan) but was merely concerned that it should be kept secret. The 'incalculable catastrophes' if the information became known clearly weighed more heavily on the Chancellor than the consequences of such an invasion.[22] The whole areas of naval ar-

20. N. Rich and M.H. Fisher (eds) *The Holstein Papers*, 4 vols (Cambridge, 1955–63), vol. 4, Holstein to Bülow, 17 February 1897.
21. PA Bonn, IA Deutschland, 122, no. 9, Bd. III, Bülow to Hammann, 7 July 1906.
22. See J. Steinberg, 'Germany and the Russo-German War', *American Historical Review*, 75 (1970), esp. pp. 1,970 and 1,978–9.

maments and military and naval planning were effectively 'off-limits' for the Chancellor. Bülow believed it was consistent with his patriotism and his loyalty to the monarchy not to make any objections to the demands of the generals and admirals.

With such crucial areas of decision-making beyond his control, the Chancellor's 'responsibility for the conduct of His Majesty's foreign policy' must necessarily be qualified and questioned. In addition Bülow's style of foreign policy management throws into doubt whether he was capable of pursuing a consistent strategy or *Weltmachtkonzept*. As soon as he became Chancellor in 1900 he informed the Foreign Office that, since he was intending to devote his attention to domestic policy and his relations with the Kaiser, beyond continuing to sign important political instructions and telegrams, he wanted to be shown only matters 'of real personal significance for me'.[23] Bülow delegated major aspects of German foreign policy to his subordinates, especially Holstein, Richthofen and later Alfred von Kiderlen-Wächter, who all complained they were overburdened with work. His sudden interventions, which, as during the First Moroccan Crisis, were often prompted by his concern to maintain the Kaiser's confidence, contributed to the notorious 'zig-zag course' of German foreign policy between 1900 and 1909 which baffled even German ambassadors. In addition, after Richthofen's death and Holstein's resignation in 1906, Bülow found that he could trust neither the new state secretary, Heinrich von Tschirschky und Bögendorff, nor the latter's successor in 1907, Wilhelm von Schön, both of whom were personally chosen by the Kaiser. Tschirschky criticised the Chancellor's lack of activity and wrote to a friend in 1907 that even Otto Hammann, Bülow's Press Chief and one of his closest advisers, 'asked me recently whether I really knew what B[ülow] did all day.'[24] While the novelty of Bülow's ostensibly relaxed style of leadership was appreciated in the Foreign Office when he took over in 1897, the virtually anarchic conditions which prevailed by 1908 could barely be concealed. It was Bülow's negligent behaviour, in passing on the text of the Kaiser's interview to the Foreign Office without reading it himself and without giving his subordinates adequate instructions, which precipitated the *Daily Telegraph* affair of November 1908, though he chose to blame the Foreign

23. PA Bonn, IA Deutschland, 122, no. 13, Bd. I, Bülow to Foreign Office, 19 October 1900.
24. A. Monts, *Erinnerungen und Gedanken des Botschafters Anton Graf Monts*, ed. K. Nowak and F. Thimme (Berlin, 1932), Tschirschky to Monts, 23 May 1907 (P.S. of 25 May), p. 451.

Office. Kiderlen-Wächter, who was summoned to the Foreign Office
to take charge of the Bosnian Crisis and to deputise for the distraught
state secretary, was appalled at the conditions he found there, complained that Bülow did not bother at all about foreign policy, and
resigned himself to having to do everything on his own. Bülow, he
acknowledged privately, was a greater *Schweinehund* than he had ever
imagined. He was lazy and superficial, and acted only when his position with the Kaiser was at stake.[25]

Bülow never abandoned his conviction that the best foreign policy
was a pragmatic one and that there was no room for any kind of
formulae in diplomacy. He believed that he could rely on his own
diplomatic instincts and proven experience to manage affairs successfully and that he would reach the right decision almost intuitively. His
interventions in foreign policy frequently bear the hallmarks of hasty
improvisation and indecision (as evidenced, for example, in the negotiations for a Russian alliance in 1904–5 and his inability to decide
whether the Björkö Treaty corresponded to Germany's real interests)
and historians have searched futilely among the Foreign Office records
for evidence of mature consideration on Bülow's part. While he may
have believed that he was being 'frightfully clever and Bismarckian'
(Jonathan Steinberg) in pursuing a cautious and pragmatic policy
which involved no firm commitments, he also of course really had no
option after the passage of the navy laws of 1898 and 1900 but to
approach foreign policy like 'the caterpillar before it has grown butterfly wings'.[26]

The confusion which surrounds 'Bülow's foreign policy' between
1897 and 1909 arises primarily from the gulf which separated his
rhetoric from reality. For while Tirpitz, Holstein and possibly even the
Kaiser may have had a clear sense of what they hoped to achieve,
Bülow was willing to be the front-man for the policies (or, in the case
of the Kaiser, the emotional needs) of others. Bülow was prepared to
pursue an empty prestige imperialism which sacrificed genuine German interests to the desire for a propaganda victory at home. His
parliamentary speeches and press propaganda in 1901–2 confirm the
impression that he preferred to antagonise Britain than alienate an An-
glophobic German public. In early 1906 Bülow accepted that Ger-

25. See E. Jäckh (ed.) *Kiderlen-Wächter der Staatsmann und Mensch: Briefwechsel und
Nachlass*, 2 vols (Berlin and Leipzig, 1924), vol. 2, esp. pp. 12–18 and 100; F. Thimme
(ed.) *Front Wider Bülow* (Munich, 1931), p. 56.
26. BA Koblenz, Richthofen Papers, 5, Bülow to Richthofen, 26 July 1899. See
also P. Kennedy, *The Rise of the Anglo-German Antagonism 1860–1914* (London, 1980),
p. 239.

many's Moroccan initiative had led to isolation and defeat at the international conference in Algeciras, and he was concerned only that this
was not how the conference was perceived at home. 'After agreement
has been reached', he told Hammann in March 1906, 'the impression
must be aroused that from the beginning I had in mind a definite goal
– and indeed achieved exactly that – which, however, could not be
revealed immediately.'[27] Bülow's presentation of the results of the
Moroccan Crisis as a success for Germany was later described by Friedrich Wilhelm von Loebell, the Head of Reich Chancellery, as his
'greatest rhetorical achievement'.[28] Nevertheless Bülow's concern to
depict all foreign policy initiatives in this way reflects a deep insecurity
about the extent of national consciousness in Germany. It also suggests
a fundamental insecurity and self-consciousness in his own identity as
Reich Chancellor of a new and dynamic European power. As he told
Loebell in October 1908, when requesting him to draft a short speech
on the Bosnian Crisis:

> I believe it will have a good effect! It demonstrates that the Reich
> Chancellor is on the alert. It corresponds to what the Ministers in
> England, France [and] Italy have done. The longer I am Reich
> Chancellor, the more I see it is above all a question of the Chancellor
> holding his ground [*sich behauptet*], standing in the foreground and not
> letting himself be effaced.[29]

BÜLOW'S APPROACH TO DOMESTIC POLITICS

The relationship between foreign and domestic policy during Bülow's
Chancellorship is a complex one which cannot be reduced to any
simple formula. Bülow himself believed that the energies of the nation
should be harnessed to serve the maintenance of its position in the
world. But he also saw a nation's position in the world as dependent
on the degree of national feeling and solidarity among its people. In
1905 he told the German ambassador in Washington that 'for the
power position of a state neither the population figure nor the unity of

27. ZSA Potsdam, Hammann Papers, 11, Bülow to Hammann, 18 March 1906.
28. BA Koblenz, Loebell Papers, 27, unpublished memoirs, p. 77.
29. ZSA Potsdam, Reichskanzlei, 798/2, Bülow to Loebell, 10 October 1908.

language is decisive, but the agreement or divergence of national aspirations and goals.'[30] Bülow had a keen appreciation of the functional uses of nationalism, and, as we have seen, he hoped to exploit foreign policy successes to overcome divisions and promote social cohesion at home. He also consciously used foreign policy issues to distract attention from domestic problems, and he deliberately accentuated his role as the leader of German foreign policy when he needed to bolster his personal position and prestige. An unambiguously aggressive foreign policy between 1897 and 1909 was incompatible with the Tirpitz Plan which required a period of international stability and calm while the navy was being built. *Weltpolitik*, as officially propounded by Bülow, was deliberately vague, and frequently appeared to mean no more than the peaceful cultivation of Germany's overseas interests without endangering the security or future of the nation. Bülow variously sought to arouse national feeling, safeguard the fleet, reassure Germany's neighbours and satisfy domestic opinion. Finally, there was less homogeneity of outlook within the German ruling elite than is often assumed, and Woodruff D. Smith has recently indicated that German *Weltpolitik* (in a broadly imperialist sense) was not only tailored to the requirements of mass consumption, but also resulted from efforts to create consensus within the ruling elite itself.[31] When Bülow became Chancellor in 1900 and assumed responsibility for German domestic policy, he was determined to counteract the divisions and centrifugal tendencies within the executive and present the government as united around national issues. Since German foreign policy was an important element in this, Bülow's ultimate inability to impose unity on the conduct of foreign policy and the failures in German foreign policy from 1905–6, not only undermined the Chancellor's wider popularity and prestige, but also had a highly detrimental effect on his position within the executive.

The essence of Bülow's approach to domestic politics from 1900 was his desire to rally a broad range of support for the government and the monarchy. This not only entailed bringing together all nationally minded elements in the *Reichstag*, including the Catholic Centre Party, but also encouraged him to begin his chancellorship by touring the south German states and reassuring their governments of his commitment to the Bismarckian federal constitution. Bülow hoped to rally support for the government by pursuing a calm, consistent domestic

30. T. Schieder, *Das Deutsche Kaiserreich als Nationalstaat* (Cologne and Opladen, 1961), p. 92.
31. W. D. Smith, *The Ideological Origins of Nazi Imperialism* (Oxford, 1986), p. 6.

policy which gave priority to national issues and sought to avoid any kind of domestic confrontation or crisis. He told the Prussian Ministry of State in October 1900 that the best way to avert domestic conflict was to reduce the quantity of legislation to the absolute minimum. The less the political parties had to do, the less they would have to fight over.

This highly conservative approach to domestic politics was not very realistic or practical at a time when enormous strains were being placed upon traditional social and political structures as a result of rapid economic change and an intensive naval armaments programme. In addition, Bülow inherited a number of thorny domestic issues in 1900, notably the conflict in the Prussian *Landtag* over government plans to extend the canal system and the need to revise Germany's tariff and commercial policy, which could not long be deferred. But, after witnessing the divisive course of German domestic politics in the 1890s, Bülow's instinct was always to withdraw or postpone contentious issues if at all possible. He preferred to close the Prussian *Landtag* in May 1901 rather than suffer a defeat over the Canal Bill and be pushed into a dissolution. In 1902 he also wanted to postpone a resolution of the tariff issue since he feared a government defeat. Later in his chancellorship he deferred the reorganisation of the Reich's finances until it was a matter of the utmost urgency.

When domestic issues could not be avoided Bülow sought to turn them into 'life and death questions' for the Reich. The tariff, the reorganization of the colonial administration and the Reich financial reform were whipped up by the Foreign Office Press Bureau into vital national issues which had to be resolved in accordance with the government's wishes if the security and future of the nation were not to be endangered. If the Social Democratic Party's (SPD) obstruction of the tariff succeeded, Bülow told his Press Chief in 1902, this would signify 'the greatest danger for peace, order, economic prosperity [and] constitutional institutions'.[32] He acknowledged that the longstanding dispute over the succession to the small principality of Lippe-Detmold was originally of little significance; but in 1904, when the death of the Regent renewed the crisis and Bülow wanted to enhance his personal role in achieving a settlement, he was prepared to argue that it threatened 'the foundations of the Reich'.[33] The Reich's financial preparedness was as important as its military preparedness, he insisted in the

---

32. ZSA Potsdam, Hammann Papers, 7, Bülow to Hammann, (17 October 1902).
33. PA Bonn, IA Deutschland, 122, no. 1a secr., Bd. 2, Bülow to Foreign Office (Posadowsky), 14 October 1904.

Reichstag on 19 November 1908, and failure to bring the financial reform to a successful conclusion would irreparably damage Germany's prestige abroad and strength at home.

Bülow's parliamentary speeches before 1909 consistently called for the nation's representatives to transcend their party differences and focus exclusively on what was good for the nation as a whole. While this salutation sometimes paid off, it reflected a fundamental naivety about the sources of political and ideological conflict. In *Deutsche Politik* Bülow wrote dismissively of the political parties which could not unite to resolve 'essentially unimportant questions of legislation' and which fought out 'slight differences of opinion on details of financial, social or industrial policy, with such acrimony as if the weal and woe of the Empire depended on them.' The varied life of a nation could not be 'stretched or squeezed to fit a programme or a political principle'.[34] But, even when the political parties were convinced of the national importance of a Bill (as they were with respect to the financial reform in 1908–9), this did not necessarily help them to agree on the substantial questions of detail. Patriotism could not bridge the divisions between the 'bourgeois' parties when they were intent on defending their sectional interests. For all his pragmatism and concern to find 'the middle way', Bülow further confounded the problem of building such a consensus because he clearly did not have a personal position on many issues of domestic policy, frequently had only limited contact with the relevant state secretaries, and was inclined to tack with the wind in consultations with parliamentary deputies. Throughout his chancellorship he was primarily concerned about the level and range of support for an initiative in the parliaments and whether it had the backing of the Kaiser. During the first eighteen months of the Bülow Bloc, the nature of the conservative–liberal coalition was allowed to determine what legislation was introduced into the *Reichstag*.

The one major initiative in domestic policy to which Bülow committed himself wholeheartedly as Chancellor was the Germanisation of Prussia's Polish provinces. This policy, which culminated in the Expropriation Law of 1908, had the support of the Kaiser, and Bülow believed he was continuing along the path which Bismarck had set. Bülow professed sympathy for the tragic course of Polish history and he recognised that there was little danger by 1900 that the Prussian Poles would receive any foreign backing for their aspirations to na-

34. B. von Bülow, *Deutsche Politik* (Berlin, 1916) pp. 184–5. Earlier version translated into English as *Imperial Germany* (London, 1914). See p. 117.

tional independence. The issue for Bülow was whether the Eastern Marches would be German or Polish. If the German Empire wanted to retain Posen and West Prussia, it was imperative that Germans settled in these areas, that the 'right compound' was applied to 'the national cell tissue' in good time. German colonisation of the Polish provinces was a 'national duty' and Bülow maintained his policy confirmed the nation's belief in the power of its national culture.

Bülow's concern about social and political divisions and his overriding desire to avoid domestic crises reflected his conviction that the national idea, the degree of national consciousness and purpose, was paramount in internal affairs. The intensity of national feeling was the most important quality in a political party, and it was the internationalism of the SPD, not least its apparent willingness to see Alsace and Lorraine returned to France, which Bülow saw as the major gulf separating it from the other parties. But Bülow's fear of domestic conflict also stemmed from his anxiety that a domestic crisis might lead to the internal disintegration of the Reich. In a political system which gave enormous power to the Kaiser and permitted the *Reichstag* no effective control over the executive, there was no satisfactory mechanism for the resolution of class tensions.

In the 1890s Bülow had been concerned to avoid civil conflict arising from a clash between the Kaiser and the *Reichstag* or from conservative pressure to launch a preventive strike against the socialists. Although the Kaiser expressed his hope in 1895 that Bülow as Chancellor would help him to 'clean up this rubbish heap of parliamentarism and the party system at home',[35] Bülow himself warned against a *Staatsstreich*, the violent overthrow of the Bismarckian constitution and the disenfranchisement of the working class. Rejecting Bismarckian methods of repression and exceptional laws as inappropriate after 1890, he argued that it was better to rely on the healing powers of time and nature than to resort to medicine or drastic operations on the body politic. Bülow remained convinced that the German people were too law-abiding to approve of a *Staatsstreich*, and that the disunity of the bourgeois parties had contributed significantly to the growth of the SPD. If the socialists were isolated by rallying the liberal middle classes and the Catholics behind the government, wooing the working class with material benefits and banging the national drum, they could then be left to die a slow death. He was later to see the patriotic attitude of the SPD in 1914 as vindicating his views.

Whenever the pressure increased for more drastic action against the

---

35. Röhl, *Germany Without Bismarck*, p. 158.

socialists, as after the SPD's electoral gains in 1903, Bülow worried about the 'incalculable consequences' of a domestic conflict. In December 1906 he was prepared to dissolve the *Reichstag* over a national issue and launch a nationalist election campaign against the SPD and Catholic Centre only because he knew that he would otherwise be ousted from office. The campaign itself was a highly risky undertaking and, since the Centre actually gained seats in the elections of 1907, it was only a qualified success. Moreover, in excluding the Centre from the bourgeois coalition against the socialists, Bülow embarked on a course which contradicted the domestic strategy he had urged since the 1890s. He was merely fortunate that the elections signified a defeat for the SPD and thus alleviated conservative pressure for more extreme, unconstitutional action in the last years of his chancellorship.

The government's apparent victory in the elections of 1907 and the inclusion of left liberals in the Bülow Bloc did not, however, open the way to progressive reform. From the 1890s Bülow and his friend, Philipp Eulenburg, had been determined to find a 'third way' between the twin perils of reaction and revolution, and Bülow's conception of 'personal rule in the good sense', with the Kaiser exercising his power constitutionally through loyal advisers, was seen as the best way of maintaining the delicate constitutional balance in imperial Germany while satisfying the Kaiser's pretensions to autocratic rule. In 1897 when he moved to Berlin, Bülow described the cultivation of his relationship with the Kaiser as his 'main task' and he wrote that if he did not keep in close contact with the monarch constantly 'the *status quo*, which was welded together with difficulty, will fall apart at the seams'.[36] This seemed the best way to obviate the need for extreme solutions to the political problems of the Empire, but it also ruled out the possibility of reform. The most flattering interpretation of Bülow's commitment to maintain the constitutional status quo is that he hoped to 'help Germany over' the difficult reign of Kaiser Wilhelm II, but this seriously underestimates his personal ambition.

In his memoirs, written after the collapse of the monarchy, Bülow claimed that Bismarck had given too much power to the Kaiser and that after 1890 Germany should have evolved in the direction of parliamentary government. He also claimed that he himself had tried to give Germany greater parliamentary freedom through his Bülow Bloc experiment between 1907 and 1909. But this was a myth which he himself debunked in *Deutsche Politik*.

The statement uttered from time to time that my idea was to change the

36. BA Koblenz, Bülow Papers, 99, Bülow to Lindenau, 20 November 1897.

distribution of power between the Crown and the Parliament in favour of the latter, that is, to introduce parliamentary government in the West European sense of the words, belongs to the thickly populated realm of fables. In my eyes the dividing line between the rights of the Crown and of Parliament were immutably fixed.[37]

Quite apart from his professions of royalism, Bülow consistently rejected parliamentarism as unsuited to the German character. The slow-witted Germans would not tolerate all the chopping and changing; a serious and cautious people, they would find the unavoidable fluctuations frivolous or become immersed in doctrinaire disputes. But above all Bülow believed that the introduction of a parliamentary system would destroy the unity of the nation. In 1894 he maintained that if Kaiser Friedrich III had lived long enough to inaugurate parliamentary government in Prussia, 'Prussia would today be a kind of Belgium or Baden if it still existed at all.'[38] On another occasion he declared that if the German nation-state adopted parliamentarism, it would suffer the same fate as the Polish Commonwealth, dissolve internally and end up being partitioned. In Bülow's opinion the Prussian monarchy, the army and the civil service were all more representative of the true interests of the German people than the *Reichstag*.

Bülow's record between 1900 and 1905 (when his position was strongest), his attitude to Prussian suffrage reform (which he wanted tied to a reform of the *Reichstag* suffrage) and his handling of the *Daily Telegraph* affair (when he failed to secure constitutional guarantees from the Kaiser) all indicate further that he was in no sense a reformer. While he toyed with ideas of constitutional reform, such as the introduction of Reich Ministries, as a method of bolstering his position in 1906, he rejected the options once it became clear that his own freedom of manoeuvre would be curtailed. Bülow's concept of the national idea essentially committed him to the political and constitutional status quo. As he wrote to Loebell in 1912, he had 'tried to maintain the existing order of things north of the Rhine and east of the Elbe' not merely because he was a Prussian conservative through and through but above all because he was convinced that 'Prussian values [*Preußentum*], Army and agriculture are the firmest foundations of Germany's power position, our unity and our future.'[39]

The wide gulf which separated Bülow's public rhetoric from the reality of his position and role became as evident in his management of domestic policy as it was with respect to German foreign policy.

37. Bülow, *Deutsche Politik*, p. 340 (English edn, p. 277).
38. Röhl, *Eulenburg*, vol. 2, Bülow to Eulenburg, 15 December 1894, p. 1431.
39. BA Koblenz, Loebell Papers, 7, Bülow to Loebell, 10 February 1911.

While the Chancellor talked and wrote about politicising the nation, reviving the bureaucracy, adapting to the modern world and recognising the forces of change, his conception of how this might be done was essentially circumscribed and narrow. Even in the 1890s Bülow not only equated the national interest with the interests of the Kaiser and government but also identified the interests of the monarchy with his own political career. During his chancellorship he increasingly equated the national interest with his own political survival and reputation. His press directives reveal how, while publicly urging the nation to focus on the big national tasks, he himself became preoccupied with the minutiae of selling his public image. Bülow wanted to be perceived as King Karl in Ludwig Uhland's poem who steered the ship of state into safe harbour. By 1909 his overriding concern was to draw attention to his own services in preserving the security, dignity and interests of the nation.

Yet by 1909 Bülow's harping on the national interest had helped to destroy any semblance of patriotic consensus in Germany. The government was thoroughly demoralised and there was evidence of a creeping fatalism and pessimism in both political and military circles in Berlin. The federal states resented the humiliating role they had been assigned in the resolution of such vital 'national' issues as the tariff and financial reform. There was widespread public disgust at the system of rule and the image of the regime was tarnished after a series of diplomatic failures, political crises and homosexuality scandals. Bülow's willingness to swim with the current and his apparent reluctance to defend the Kaiser during the *Daily Telegraph* affair of November 1908 had helped to alienate the government's traditional supporters on the right, many of whom were already chafing over their pairing with the liberals in the *Reichstag*. Moreover, the Chancellor's repeated exhortations to be guided solely by the national interest, while at the same time apparently espousing a policy of 'drift' in domestic affairs and leading Germany into diplomatic isolation, had contributed to the fragmentation and radicalisation of the political right. Bülow, who had sought to stifle the embryonic 'national opposition' from 1900 by heaping scorn on the 'beer-hall politics' of the Pan-German League and publicly staking his claim to be the sole custodian and interpreter of the Bismarck myth, was confronted by a nationalist offensive which directly

40. See especially R. Chickering, *We Men Who Feel Most German: A Cultural Study of the Pan-German League, 1886–1914* (Boston, Mass, 1984), pp. 63–9, 213–23, 253–62; G. Eley, 'Some thoughts on the nationalist pressure groups in imperial Germany', in P. Kennedy and A. Nicholls (eds) *Nationalist and Racialist Movements in Britain and Germany before 1914* (London, 1981), pp. 40–67.

attacked his conception of the national idea.[40] Bülow's chancellorship ensured that the competence of Germany's rulers could be credibly challenged in the name of patriotism. Far from promoting social cohesion and what Bülow called a healthy national egoism, *Weltpolitik* and domestic stagnation exacerbated the divisions within German society. The failure to spread the financial burden of the naval armaments programme more equitably demonstrated conclusively that his conception of the national idea was no substitute for domestic political consensus.

Although Bülow's political views must be located within the broad tradition of German conservatism, his personal background and political mentality cannot be seen as very typical or representative of the German ruling elite before 1914. While he came from a privileged and aristocratic north German family with a long tradition of service to the state, he was born a Dane, married an Italian Catholic and chose to live abroad during his long retirement, as he had done for much of his life before 1897. While extolling the national idea and the superiority of German culture, he clearly took pride in his cosmopolitanism and cultivated a suave, urbane manner which was attractive not least to Kaiser Wilhelm II because it contrasted with the traditionally rather dull and dour exterior of the Prussian bureaucrat. His insistence on his loyalty to the Prussian monarchy and the traditional pillars of the Prussian state was couched in unfamiliar, modern and progressive language which easily made him suspect to many conservatives in Berlin. While he acknowledged that German unification had been achieved by men of conservative political persuasion, he also recognised that the national idea had been born in liberal circles.

Bülow, like many of his generation, was in a sense a victim of the struggle for national unification. Intoxicated by Prussian successes in the 1860s but highly conscious of the imperfections, the unfinished nature of the Bismarckian Reich, he believed that the only way to hold it together was through the manufacture of national feeling. Convinced of Germany's peculiar path to nationhood and that Bismarck was 'only conceivable on German soil, only completely comprehensible to the German', Bülow compared Bismarck to a mirror in which the nation could see itself reflected.[41] The dominance of this single image came to prevent him from appreciating the multifarious layers of German identity.

Yet ultimately even his professed love for all things German can appear spurious and insincere. Again and again, Bülow chastised the

---

41. Penzler, *Reden*, vol. 1, Bülow's speech of 16 June 1901 at unveiling of Begas's memorial statue in Berlin, pp. 225.

Germans in the *Reichstag* for being dogmatic, self-opinionated, doctrinaire, unpolitical, unpatriotic, slow-witted and plodding. In 1902 he complained about 'a lack of patriotism and political stupidity such as can only be found unfortunately in our country'.[42] In his memoirs his description of the Kaiserin as 'typically German' is almost insulting as he compares her irreproachable and dutiful nature to the soulfulness, zest, toughness, coquetry, passion and charm of foreign women.[43] Somehow one has the impression that, for Bülow as for Hitler after him, the German people could not quite live up to his expectations.

The journalist Theodor Wolff later wrote of Bülow that 'his feeling for a few persons closely related to him was the only warm feeling in him, the only one that did not merely flicker on the surface and evaporate in fine phrases'.[44] When Bülow left office in July 1909 there were few to express regret about his departure. A vain, superficial and ultimately rather lonely figure, he sought refuge in Italy but never gave up his hope of being recalled to office until the last year of the war. Devastated by Germany's defeat and scathing about Weimar democracy, Bülow took some comfort from Hindenburg's election as President in 1925 and Stresemann's conduct of foreign policy. He died at the age of 80 in October 1929, convinced that better days would come for the German people when they were once again infused with national feeling.

SUGGESTIONS FOR FURTHER READING

B. von Bülow, *Memoirs*, 4 vols (London, 1931–2).

B. von Bülow, *Imperial Germany* (London, 1914).

R. Chickering, *We Men Who Feel Most German: A Cultural Study of the Pan-German League, 1886–1914* (Boston, Mass, 1984).

G. Eley, *Reshaping the Right: Radical Nationalism and Political Change after Bismarck* (London and New Haven, Conn, 1980).

R. J. Evans (ed.) *Society and Politics in Wilhelmine Germany* (London, 1978).

42. ZSA Potsdam, Hammann Papers, 7, Bülow to Hammann, 19 July 1902.
43. Bülow, *Denkwurdigkeiten*, vol. 1, p. 263.
44. T. Wolff, *Through Two Decades* (London, 1936), p. 10.

I. Geiss, *German Foreign Policy 1871–1914* (London, 1976).

P. Kennedy, *The Rise of the Anglo-German Antagonism 1860–1914* (London, 1980).

P. Kennedy, and A. Nicholls (eds) *Nationalist and Racialist Movements in Britain and Germany before 1914* (London, 1981).

K. A. Lerman, *The Chancellor as Courtier: Bernhard von Bülow and the Governance of Germany, 1900–1909* (Cambridge, 1990).

N. Rich, *Friedrich von Holstein: Politics and Diplomacy in the Era of Bismarck and Wilhelm II*, 2 vols (Cambridge, 1965).

J. C. G. Röhl, *Germany Without Bismarck: The Crisis of Government in the Second Reich, 1890–1900* (London, 1967).

J. C. G. Röhl and N. Sombart (eds) *Kaiser Wilhelm II: New Interpretations* (Cambridge, 1982).

W. D. Smith, *The Ideological Origins of Nazi Imperialism* (Oxford, 1986).

B. Vogel, *Deutsche Rußlandpolitik: Das Scheitern der deutschen Weltpolitik unter Bülow 1900–1906* (Düsseldorf, 1973).

H.-U. Wehler, *The German Empire 1871–1918* (Leamington Spa, 1985).

P. Winzen, *Bülows Weltmachtkonzept: Untersuchungen zur Frühphase seiner Außenpolitik 1897–1901* (Boppardamam Rhein, 1977)

P. Winzen, 'Prince Bülow's *Weltmachtpolitik*', *Australian Journal of Politics and History*, 22 (1976).

CHAPTER SEVEN

Scholarship, state and nation, 1918–45

Michael Burleigh

In Germany, separate academic studies of Russia and Eastern Europe at the nation's universities commenced in the decade before the First World War.[1] Government needed expertise especially on Russia, and the demand was met by the exiled Baltic German publicist Schiemann, and his talented protégé, the historian Otto Hoetzsch, who became the first incumbents of chairs in multi-disciplinary Russian and East European studies.[2] During the First World War, military and industrial interests assisted in the foundation at Breslau and Königsberg of institutes devoted to East European studies, and the more thorough economic exploitation of that region. The radically altered circumstances of the Weimar Republic saw a fresh wave of institutional expansion, with new centres of expertise in Berlin, Danzig, Leipzig and Munich. Here, however, the emphasis was upon the provision of a scientific basis for revisionist territorial claims against the post-Versailles successor states to the east of Germany.[3]

Following a temporary lull in public activity due to the exigencies of the Hitler–Pilsudski Pact, *Ostforschung* – or research on the East – as this congeries of disciplines had come to be known, thenceforth enjoyed boom conditions. A new series of institutes was established in

1. For the early history of the discipline see H. Giertz, 'Das Berliner Seminar für osteuropaische Geschichte und Landeskunde', *Jahrbuch für die Geschichte der USSR und der volksdemokratischen Länder Europas* (1967), 10, pp. 184–5; M. Hellman, 'Zur Lage der historischen Erforschung des ostlichen Europa in der Bundesrepublik Deutschland', in F. Wagner (ed.) *Jahrbuch der historischen Forschung* (Stuttgart, 1980), pp. 14–16, and G. Camphausen, *Die wissenschaftliche historische Russlandforschung im Dritten Reich 1933–1945* (Frankfurt am Main, 1990).

2. Biographies include K. Meyer, *Theodor Schiemann als politische Publizist* (Frankfurt am Main, 1956), G. Voigt, *Otto Hoetzsch, 1876–1946* (East Berlin, 1978), and U. Liszkowski, *Osteuropaforschung und Politik: Ein Beitrag zum historischpolitischen Denken und Wirken von Otto Hoetzsch*, 2 vols (Berlin, 1988).

3. M. Burleigh, *Germany Turns Eastwards: A Study of Ostforschung in the Third Reich* (Cambridge, 1990, 2nd edn.) pp. 22ff.

Cracow, Poznan and Prague, while individual *Ostforscher* entered the service of the most notorious agencies of a barbaric regime.[4] After 1945, the staff in lightly sanitised versions of these institutes lent their collective expertise to the refashioned animosities of the Cold War. The immediacy of the Communist threat in the Soviet-occupied Zone, and the tragedy experienced by millions of ethnic German refugees, also offset the need to confront the part played by an entire academic discipline under the Nazi regime. Finally, to close the vicious circle, the claims made by these West German institutes, not to speak of the integrationary requirements of the SED and other Eastern European Communist regimes, resulted in the creation there of departments and institutes, whose purpose was to monitor 'imperialist *Ostforschung*' as the scientific face of West German or NATO 'revanchism'.[5]

This barest of outlines of the institutional history of *Ostforschung* already suggests a high level of political responsiveness on the part of the people who persistently subscribed to the usual canons of scholarly objectivity. The prodigious archival and published legacy enables us to ask and answer a number of questions about the relationship between professional experts and the state; about the degree of permeability evinced by mainstream conservative nationalism under the impact of *völkisch* and scientific racism; and finally, concerning the continuities and discontinuities of nationalist thought and practice between Weimar, the Third Reich and the Federal Republic.

The overwhelming majority of the scholars discussed in what follows operated with a mind set on 'the East' which was heavily influenced by centuries of Prussian-German contacts with Poland and Russia, as well as by the state of contemporary relations. Broadly speaking the received picture consisted of a mix of negative and positive elements. The Germans were 'bearers of culture' to the Slavs. The latter had arrived in the region posterior to the former. Their backwardness was epitomised by the mismanaged political economy of Poland and the tottering political structures of Tsarist Russia. Metaphorically, this backwardness was often expressed through the notion of a 'cultural gradient' declining from the 'civilised' West towards the

---

4. The most recent studies of these institutes in occupied Poland are C. Klessman, *Die Selbstbehauptung eine Nation* (Düsseldorf, 1971), S. Gaweda, *Die Jagiellonische Universität in der Zeit der faschistischen Okkupation 1939–1945* (Jena, 1981), and B. Piotrowski, *W sluzbie rasizmu i bezprawia: 'Uniwersytet Rzeszy' w Poznaniu (1941–1945)* (Poznan, 1984).

5. Burleigh, *Germany Turns Eastwards,* pp. 300ff. See also H. Elsner, 'Abteilung für Geschichte der imperialistischen Ostforschung', in M. Hellman (ed.) *Osteuropa in der historischen Forschung der DDR* (Düsseldorf, 1972), vol. 1, pp. 123–31.

'uncivilised' East. The German mission to bring civilisation and order to the Slavs was gradually given a biological accent in the form of the slogan '*Drang nach Osten*', whereby the Germans were somehow compelled to venture eastwards. Since by the late nineteenth century this notion was wildly at variance with a general demographic drift westwards, the perception grew that the Germans were holding back an uncontrollable Slavic flood or wave. The East as a literary and historical construct was thus simultaneously a land of opportunity and demographic menace, notions which have endured to the present time.[6]

If for much of the late nineteenth century these ideas lent a crude legitimacy to Prussian-German rule in partitioned Poland, during the Weimar Republic they were employed to justify German claims to lost territories. Archaeologists, historians, philologists and geographers provided the scientific armaments for their government's claims to parts of Poland and Czechoslovakia, while government rewarded them by licensing and financing institutional expansion. This relationship became both closer and released from any ethical or professional constraints.

From the 1920s academic studies were used to substantiate revisionist territorial claims in the East. Much of this work reflected racist modes of thought, although the provenance of the racism was usually cultural-historical rather than seriological. The facts of post-war political frontiers, which of course were not the single handiwork of the victors at Versailles, were systematically undermined through *parti pris* interpretations of history, or by the application of dubious geographical concepts. Scholars, such as Wilhelm Volz, working under the aegis of the Leipzig *Stiftung für Volks- und Kulturbodenforschung* maintained that in addition to the territories more or less densely settled by Germans there was a further area, in which, regardless of mere numbers, their cultural influence was allegedly paramount.[7] The layout of villages, the contours of fields, the style of brickwork, and the contrast between 'order' and 'chaos' would be the criteria for where political frontiers ought to run. However, it is important to stress the differences between this cultural chauvinism, and more specifically National Socialist modes of thinking. What would the latter have made of Volz's assertion that 'Race does not decide ethnicity . . . rather will and consciousness of nationality'?[8] The historians devoted a great deal of sterile

6. On these concepts, see W. Wippermann, *Der 'Deutsche Drang nach Osten': Ideologie und Wirklichkeit eines politischen Schlagwortes* (Darmstadt, 1989).

7. See A. Penck, 'Deutscher Volks- und Kulturboden', in K.C. von Loesch (ed.) *Volk unter Völkern* (Breslau, 1926), pp. 62–73.

8. W. Volz (ed.) *Der ostdeutschen Volksboden: Aufsätze zu den Fragen des Ostens* (Breslau, 1926), pp. 5–6.

assiduity to questions such as: who settled the contested regions first, or who had made the greatest contribution to their culture? They trawled deep in time to establish a continuous German presence before and after the Slav migrations; and recent history to stress the artificiality and transience of the Polish nation-state in contrast to the dynamic, state-forming, capacities of the Germans and their rulers. This last concern also involved giving generous attention to a series of submerged nationalities, such as the Kashubians and Pomeranians, as a means of further subverting the legitimacy of the Polish nation-state.[9]

All of these tendencies were well represented in a collective volume edited by Karl Brandi and Albert Brackmann, entitled *Deutschland und Polen*, which appeared in August 1933. Brackmann's own contribution can be said to exemplify the culturally argued chauvinism which permeates the book:

> While the Slav peoples of Europe, including the Russians, still lay in a deep intellectual slumber, the monk Widukind wrote his Saxon history in the monastery of Corvey on the Weser, the nun Hroswitha in the abbey of Gandersheim her song to Otto the Great and her classical dramas, and in Magdeburg Bruno of Querfurt his life of St Adalbert and bishop Thietmar his chronicle . . . Where then could one find in Poland cultural centres like Corvey or Gandersheim or Magdeburg – not to speak of the centres of ancient civilisation on the Rhine? Gnesen and Posen were settlements of the most primitive type.[10]

Some of the contributions also reveal a casual reliance upon biology as a causal agency, with 'Nordic blood' accounting for resistance which the Saxons met from other Slavs, or the wholly anachronistic use of contemporary geopolitical concepts, not to speak of the language of late-nineteenth-century nationalism. Thus Max Hein could write:

> As in the year 1000 it was again the Germans . . . who sought to realise the christianisation and germanisation of the Prussians and their addition to the German Lebensraum and to the German, and at the same time West European, sphere of civilisation. The Prussian venture of the Teutonic Order is, on the one hand, the fulfilment of a great German cultural mission in the East, and on the other, the expansion of the all too narrow Lebensraum in the old Reich.[11]

Deutschland und Polen was one of the earliest products of the increasingly close relationship between certain scholars and government agen-

9. Burleigh, *Germany Turns Eastwards*, pp. 30–1; 60–1; 117–31.

10. A. Brackmann, 'Die politische Entwicklung Osteuropas vom 10–15 Jahrhundert', in Brackmann (ed.) *Deutschland und Polen. Beiträge zu ihren geschichtlichen Beziehungen* (Munich 1933), p. 30.

11. M. Hein, 'Ostpreussen', *Deutschland und Polen*, p. 126.

cies. The book was heavily subsidised by the latter and, via Brackmann the editor, the contributions were cut to suit the dictates of the current political line.[12] This process had begun as early as 1931, when interested government departments expressly decided to license Brackmann's personal institutional ambitions on the grounds that this 'had the advantage that the work can be carried out under a certain political control'.[13] The line between scholarship and government was drawn a year later by the Social Democratic minister-president of Prussia, Otto Braun: 'scholarship can supply the politicians with the material from which they can draw their conclusions'.[14]

The end product of this collaboration was a Berlin-based research institute, the *Publikationstelle* or 'PuSte', and half a dozen multi-disciplinary regional research associations to which every prominent scholar in the field was attached. Collectively, these bodies had the following functions: the coordination of scholarship in the Reich dealing with the East; subsidising of scholarship conducted by ethnic Germans in Eastern Europe, and the maintenance of contacts between them and their colleagues in the Reich; the monitoring and translation of hostile scholarship; the political vetting of applications to use German archives; and finally, the censorship and control of German scholars studying ethnic minorities in the Reich, lest they inadvertently cast doubt on the ethnic homogeneity of Germany.

The principal beneficiaries of the governmental largesse channelled through these organisations were ethnic German scholars living and working in Eastern Europe. In the case of the North East German Research Association (NODFG), two eager young scholars, Walter Kuhn and Kurt Lück, were kept afloat through the good offices of Brackmann and government money.[15] Both were obsessively interested in the history and current circumstances of German ethnic minorities in Poland and the western Ukraine, with Lück shoring up one such community through the foundation of a rural credit agency.[16] While Kuhn was primarily involved in the application of biological concepts to explain the expansion and contraction of these settlements,

12. For the details see Burleigh, *Germany Turns Eastwards,* especially pp. 61–8.
13. BA (Koblenz), R421/1812, 'Vermerk über die kommissarische Beratung am 11 Dezember 1931 betreffend wissenschaftliche Ostmarkenforschung', Reich Ministry of the Interior to State Secretary in the Reichskanzlei.
14. BA (Koblenz), R431/1812, 'Protokoll über die Besprechung im grossen Sitzungssaal des Preussischen Staatsministeriums in Sachen der Ostmarkenforschung am 24.2.32', p. 215.
15. For the financial arrangements see for example, BA (Koblenz) R153/1309, 'Vorschläge über Beihilfen', pp. 5–6.
16. See H. von Rosen, *Wolhynienfahrt 1926* (Siefgen, 1982), p. 64 for Lück's work on behalf of the ethnic German peasants.

Lück graduated from mindlessly cataloguing the contribution of German civilisation to the Poles,[17] to 'modernistic' ventures into the analysis of ethnic stereotypes. Vast quantities of literary, oral and visual evidence from 'below' were deployed in the interests of proving the permanency of Polish-German nationality conflicts, and hence, as a way of depicting German aggression as essentially reactive and self-defensive.[18] Other scholarship to benefit from this academic version of *'Osthilfe'*, included Peter Heinz Seraphim's studies of the 'economic danger that lies in the existence of . . . Jewish population groups for these people and states', investigations designed to establish 'which possibilities exist for the solution of the eastern Jewish problem'.[19] In the late 1930s Seraphim converted these studies into a racist version of developmental economics, with the Jews as the obstacle to rural Eastern Europe's route to 'modernity'.[20]

The corollary of promoting studies of ethnic Germandom, or on the allegedly deleterious influence of Jews on the economies of Eastern Europe, was tight control over studies of Slavic ethnic minorities within Germany. This control ranged from withholding research funds from younger scholars working on ostensibly innocuous aspects of the history and culture of Lusatian Sorbs,[21] to interference with the publications of distinguished professors of Slavic philology, notwithstanding assurances that they 'not only served the truth but . . . also worked throughout as a German Slavist'.[22] Government-inspired interference further encompassed such semantic issues as the substitution of the word 'resettlement' for 'colonisation' in descriptions of the German presence in the East.[23] Such

---

17. K. Lück, *Deutsche Aufbaukräfte in der Entwicklung Polens* (Plauen, 1934).

18. K. Lück, *Der Mythos vom Deutschen in der polnischen Volksüberlieferung und Literatur* (Leipzig, 1943, 2nd edn). This insidious line of argument has been present in some of the work which sparked off the West German 'Historikerstreit'. See R.J. Evans, *In Hitler's Shadow* (London, 1989), especially p. 56.

19. BA (Koblenz), R153/98 P. H. Seraphim, 'Bericht über den Entwurf einer Arbeit Das Judentum im osteuropaischen Raum', 9 January 1936.

20. P.H. Seraphim, 'Das ostjüdische Ghetto', *Jomsburg, 1 (1937)*, pp. 439–65; Seraphim, 'Die Judenfrage im General-gouvernement als Bevölkerungsproblem' *Die Burg* 1 (1940), pp. 57–62. On Seraphim see G.F. Volkmer, 'Die deutsche Forschung zu Osteuropa und zum osteuropäischen Judentum in den Jahren 1933 bis 1945', H.J. Torke (ed.) *Forschungen zur osteuropäischen Geschichte*, vol. 42 (Berlin, 1989) pp. 148ff.

21. See for example BA (Koblenz), R153/1263 Wolfgang Kohte to the Deutsche Forschungsgemeinschaft 21 August 1937 concerning a grant application by Dr Paul Wirth.

22. BA (Koblenz), R153/1258 Professor Reinhold Trautmann to Albert Brackmann, 13 April 1939.

23. Geheimes Staatsarchiv (West Berlin) Rep. 92, *Nachlass* Brackmann, no. 82, Brackmann to Klante 21 June 1937 and Brackmann to Aubin 21 June 1937, relaying the information that the Ministry of the Interior wanted the word 'colonisation' avoided at all costs.

interventions seriously annoyed committed Nazi historians like Hans Mortensen, who indignantly complained 'I, for my part, would never publish or make known anything that would damage Germany or the German people, even if it was the scholarly truth'.[24] Censorship ventured into the absurd when, for example, Emil Meynen's *Deutschland und Deutsches Reich* was banned in 1936 because his claim that Germany encompassed German-speaking areas such as Alsace-Lorraine or Switzerland was regarded as diplomatically inopportune at that moment in time. The question inevitably arose, not least in Meynen's mind, 'how can we sing the national anthem: '*Von der Etsch bis an den Belt*'?[25]

Since individual words were subjected to the quickly changing exigencies of high politics, how did political change affect such fundamental conceptual components of historical writing as the state, and how responsive were these scholars to the rise of that Nazi universal form of scientific explanation, namely biological racism? Historians of academic life in Nazi Germany writing immediately after the war, for example Max Weinreich, would have regarded the contention that Nazism had had a 'progressive' impact on the historical and social sciences, as the triumph of a small academic truth over the large fact of German academia's dismal descent into illiberalism.[26] This post-war consensus is no longer universal. One minor by-product of the search for Nazism's intended or inadvertent 'modernising' effects on German society, has been the argument that certain allegedly 'progressive' developments in modern German social history owed as much to the mould-breaking of the indigenous Right, as to the influences of American and French sociology. Who needs Braudel or Bloch when one already has Otto Brunner?[27] In the case of Ostforschung, it is claimed that the multi-disciplinary, regional rather than national, and socially extensive nature of the subject, anticipated many of the prac-

24. BA (Koblenz), R153/627 Mortensen to Brackmann 15 January 1938.

25. For the details of this anecdote see M. Rössler, '*Wissenschaft und Lebensraum*': *Geographische Ostforschung im Nationalsozialismus* (Berlin, 1990), pp. 67–9.

26. M. Weinreich, *Hitler's Professors: The Part of Scholarship in Germany's Crimes against the Jewish People* (New York, 1946).

27. This question was first formulated by C. Klessmann in his 'Osteuropaforschung und Lebensraumpolitik im Dritten Reich', P. Lundgreen (ed.) *Wissenschaft im Dritten Reich* (Frankfurt am Main, 1985), p. 353. Since then the question has exercised the minds of a number of North American and German academics. See J. van Horn Melton 'From folk history to structural history: Otto Brunner and the radical conservative roots of German social history' (unpublished manuscript, 1989), and W. Schulze, *Deutsche Geschichtswissenschaft nach 1945* (Munich, 1989) for examples. For a critique of the 'modernisation' thesis in general see M. Burleigh and W. Wippermann, *The Racial State: Germany 1933–1945* (Cambridge, 1991).

tices of a modern social history, whose intellectual ancestry has conventionally been traced from either external influences, or the subterranean stream of the German historical Left. This is certainly how some of the *Ostforscher* regarded matters at the time. Thus, in 1937 the Breslau historian Hermann Aubin argued that the territorial losses after the First World War had forced historians to abandon the limitations imposed by 'dynastic-territorial historiography'. The 'tearing asunder' of 'German *Lebensraum*' after 1918 led historians to abandon history based on the nation-state in favour of ethnological and cultural-geographic concepts which in turn made the present political frontiers seem epiphenomenal and hence revocable.[28] This brand of regionally focused 'total' history would in turn serve to mobilise popular consciousness of the *Volk*'s potential horizons. This conceptual shift was made explicit by Erich Keyser in an article published in 1933:

> Historians in the nineteenth century forgot that a substantial part of the *Volk* were not comprised within the borders of Germany, but like the Austrian or Baltic Germans were foreigners in their own states . . . The *Volk* is more than the nation; it comprises the totality of those who shaped by blood, soil, and culture, are the real subjects of history. The nation, on the other hand, is purely a political entity . . . In this regard nineteenth-century historical writing, quite apart from its liberalism, differed from ethnic history in that it was predicated solely on the state rather than on the *Volk* . . . The national idea is directed towards the state, while the idea of the *Volk* transcends the state and its borders.[29]

Although it is, of course, debatable whether in the *longue durée*, a concern with ordinary people, or indeed, inter-disciplinary or regional studies actually represent an advance over other more traditional forms of historical inquiry – a point often made by the Left as well as by the self-appointed guardians of academic orthodoxy on the Right – none of these historiographical issues should obscure the fact that in Germany, the 'progressive' methods were accompanied by a reliance upon race as a causal agent, and served political ends which moved smoothly from revisionism to murderous racial imperialism. By 1942, for example, Erich Keyser was crediting *Ostforschung* with a role in proving that 'the German East, from the Elbe to the Gulf of Finland, from

28. H. Aubin, 'Zur Erforschung der deutschen Ostbewegung', F. Petri (ed.) *Grundlagen und Perspektiven geschichtlicher Kulturraumforschung und Kulturmorphologie* (Bonn, 1965), pp. 108–9; Klessman, 'Osteuropaforschung und Lebensraumpolitik', pp. 372–3; Burleigh, *Germany Turns Eastwards,* pp. 304ff.

29. E. Keyser, 'Die völkische Geschichtsschreibung', *Preussische Jahrbücher* 234 (1933), pp. 5–6.

the Inn to the Black Sea, deserves to be the unitary *Lebensraum* of the German people'.[30]

If it is essential to counter attempts to restore the work of Aubin, Brunner and the rest to its 'rightful' place within a 'modernist' story of historiography, through the omission of any reference to their use of *völkisch* racism, so one should be equally careful, in the interests of both accuracy and fairness, to establish the thin line separating them from full-blown scientific racists. In the case of some of the *Ostforscher* mentioned above this can be done by examining their relationship with the Leipzig-based anthropologist Otto Reche, the driving force behind the Society for Blood Group Research, the North East German Research Association's expert on racial questions, and an adviser to the Hereditary Health courts.[31]

Although already elderly by the outbreak of the Second World War, Reche spotted a role for himself as a scientific adviser to government agencies concerned with the occupied eastern territories. In late September 1939 he began bombarding Brackmann with unsolicited schemes for the ethnic rearranging of the conquered areas, schemes which Brackmann then relayed to both the Ministry of the Interior and then the SS.[32] Working on the principle that 'we need Raum but no Polish lice in our fur', Reche made the following stark suggestions:

> The newly acquired land must be made empty of all foreign ethnic elements; all foreign races, foreign peoples are to be resettled . . . The present inhabitants of the newly ceded areas are racially, and therefore in character, talents and capabilities too, for the most part totally useless. Above all the *c.* two million Jews and Jewish hybrids must be pushed out as soon as possible. . . . The emigrant Poles can take their moveable goods – in so far as this does not prejudice the interests of the German state – with them; one may proceed less charitably with the Jews.[33]

Having drawn a blank with the Ministry of the Interior, which was preoccupied with economic questions, Brackmann helped Reche find the right address, namely the Race and Resettlement Office of the SS. Reche's memoranda went to SS-*Gruppenführer* Günther Pancke, and

---

30. E. Keyser, 'Die Erforschung der Bevölkerungsgeschichte des deutschen Ostens', in H. Aubin, O. Brunner, W. Kohte and J. Papritz (eds) *Deutsche Ostforschung. Ergebnisse und Aufgaben seit dem erstern Weltkrieg* (Liepzig, 1942), p. 91.

31. Burleigh, *Germany Turns Eastwards*, p. 127.

32. BA (Koblenz), R153/288 Brackmann to Essen (RMdI) 28 September 1939; Brackmann to Reche 1 November 1939.

33. BA (Koblenz), R153/288, O. Reche, 'Leitsätze zur bevölkerungspolitischen Sicherung des deutschen Ostens', 24 September 1939, pp. 1–6.

via him to the *Reichsführer*-SS.[34] Having established the connection, Reche proceeded to volunteer his thoughts on the racial quality of prospective German settlers in the East; on the need for the creation of a 'warrior nobility' consisting of SS veterans; and on the practicalities of fingerprinting 'Jews and other scoundrels'.[35]

Reche in turn figured as one of the contributors selected by Aubin, Otto Brunner and Wolfgang Kohte for the massive Brackmann *Festschrift*. Although Aubin personally solicited Reche's chapter, he began to have serious reservations once the finished typescript appeared on his desk. By the third page, Aubin was reduced to scribbling 'again pure fantasy' in the margins.[36] The final version, which Aubin saw fit to publish, had two related agendas. An historical part, designed to demonstrate that residual barbarian Germans had 'enslaved' the incoming Slavs, but had then interbred with them in the way of Germans in East Africa with the Hottentots(!), and a contemporary investigation of the questions 'what have we before us of racial value?' and how was one to establish the necessary 'biological boundaries against elements that are racially far apart from us?'[37] Brackmann's response to this extraordinary venture into biological ahistoricity was that it would be 'an extraordinarily important foundation for all other works in the field of German ethnic research'.[38]

Although Aubin and Brackmann were aware of the dangers for conventional scholarship latent in the studies of men like Reche, they were also tantalised by political power, regardless of who happened to exercise it, and desirous of the ultimate validation their society could confer, namely recognition of their work's relevance. Confronted by a regime which awarded no prizes for intellectual inquiry *per se*, they desperately stressed the applied nature of what they were doing, and its relevance to policy measures of the present. It is important to stress that the scholars themselves took this particular initiative, for example with Aubin announcing in September 1939: 'We must make use of our experience, which we have developed over many long years of effort. Scholarship cannot simply wait until it is called upon, but must make itself heard'.[39]

34. Berlin Document Center (Reche file), Pancke to Reche 8 November 1939, etc.

35. BDC (Reche file) Reche to Pancke 14 November 1939 and 18 November 1939 enclosing 'Entwurf für einen bevölkerungsstatistischen Fragebogen'.

36. BA (Koblenz), R153/1049, Aubin to Papritz, 12 November 1941 with notes on Reche's contribution.

37. O. Reche, 'Stärke und Herkunft des Anteils nordischer Rasse bei den Westslawen', Aubin *et al.* (ed.) *Deutsche Ostforschung*, vol. 1 p. 88.

38. BA (Koblenz), R153/1050 Brackmann to Otto Reche 10 July 1942.

39. BA (Koblenz), R153/291 Aubin to Brackmann 18 September 1939.

Many members of this branch of the academic profession slid into progressively collusive relationships with the operative agencies of the Nazi regime. There is no evidence whatsoever that they had any scruples in dealing with policemen, thugs and murderers. Aubin, Brackmann and their staff quickly made their talents known to Governor-General Hans Frank in occupied Cracow, with a view to exerting a decisive influence upon the construction of a German system of higher education and research in place of a once thriving Polish academic culture which Frank and his associates had destroyed.[40] Aubin lectured before Frank in a university whose professors were in concentration camps, and Brackmann tried to secure an influence over Frank's pet project, the *Institut für deutsche Ostarbeit* in Cracow. Although his influence was short-circuited by more skilled operators on the ground, he and his colleagues elsewhere continued to have scholarly contacts with an institution which represented the apogee of scholarship fully instrumentalised in the service of political power. As experts on ethnic questions, and as firm believers in the policy of separating different ethnic groups, the *Ostforscher* were also involved in the creation of new boundaries, and its corollary, the physical relocation of whole populations. For many of them, this was – and in some cases remains – a matter of firm conviction.[41] As early as September 1939, groups of *Ostforscher* in Breslau and Berlin were working on ways of consolidating the German populations in areas mainly inhabited by Poles, which included the expropriation of the property of the alleged political activists and the deportation of post-First World War migrants.[42] From the winter of 1940, Walter Kuhn and Kurt Lück, by now an SS-*Haupsturmführer*, were active in repatriating Volhynian Germans, who themselves were racially 'screened', to villages from which the indigenous Polish inhabitants had been forcibly deported to the *Generalgouvernement*.[43] Lück was also heavily involved in the deliberate falsification of atrocity stories concerning Polish attacks on ethnic Germans in the wake of the September 1939 invasion, stories which were intended to legitimise systematic and massive brutalities carried out by the Germans against Poles and Jews in the name of racial purity.[44] Finally, Brackmann's staff were responsible for sup-

40. Burleigh, *Germany Turns Eastwards*, pp. 257ff.

41. Ibid. pp. 157–8. Interview with Dr J. Papritz in Marburg on 11 August 1986.

42. BA (Koblenz) R153/291 Wolfgang Kohte to the President of the Reich Statistical Office 3 October 1939, see also the paper 'Bevölkerungsfragen im Polen', 1 November 1939.

43. See BA R57/1836 Prof. W. Kuhn to the Chef der Sicherheitspolizei und des SD-Einwandererzentrale Nord–Ost 'Lodsch' 22 January 1940 and BDC file Kurt Lück.

44. K. Lück, *Marsch der Deutschen in Polen. Deutsche Volksgenossen im ehemaligen Polen berichten über Erlebnisse in den Septembertagen 1939* (Berlin, 1940).

plying the Gestapo and SS agencies with cartographical and statistical data on the 'Jewish Question', materials which were intended to give racial policy greater efficacy and precision.[45]

This spiral of collusion continued following the German invasion of the USSR; the *Publikationsstelle* continued to channel detailed economic and ethnological information to a host of government agencies, while assisting in the systematic plundering of Russian academic institutions. Beyond making off with entire libraries and archives, some of the *Publikationsstelle* staff were seconded to SS departments, where plans were being laid for the racial, economic and political refashioning of the entire eastern region. Specifically, one of Brackmann's cartographers worked for Professor Konrad Meyer's SS planning bureau, the agency responsible for the infamous *'Generalplan Ost'*.[46] Under the terms of this plan millions of Germans would be gradually settled in a network of towns and defensive villages; the indigenous population having been literally decimated or deported. Even the landscape itself was to have been altered, with hills, trees and prefabricated villages, so that the 'German man can feel at home'.[47] These connections suggest that the *Ostforscher* had moved very far from the idea of the classical nation-state: in theory and in practice.

After 1945, most of the surviving *Ostforscher* passed smoothly back into West, and sometimes, East German academic life. In a political climate which did not ask many questions, they were successful in weaving their specific concerns into the refashioned animosities of the developing Cold War. It seems likely that this was done with the blessing of various Western intelligence agencies who began tapping the wisdom of the *Ostforscher* shortly after the war. Copies of the old institutes and new journals were accompanied by a number of familiar academic reappointments.[48] However, during the 1970s, and probably under the impact of détente, their influence slipped from having one of their number in Adanauer's cabinet, to being the scientific flank of an expellee lobby to which politicians nodded, but increasingly did not bow. Territorial claims based on the presence of substantial ethnic

---

45. BA (Koblenz R153/286 RSHA to the PuSte on 2 November 1939 acknowledging 'Anteil der jüdischen Bevölkerung an der Gesamtbevölkerung der polnischen Haupt-und Kreisstädte und sonstigen Städten über 10,000 Einwohner innerhalb des deutschen Interessengebietes'.

46. Burleigh, *Germany Turns Eastwards*, pp. 163–4. See also M. Burleigh, 'Die Stunde der Experten', in M. Rössler and S. Schleiermacher (eds) *Der 'Generalplan Ost': Aspekte der nationalsozialistischen Planungs- und Vernichtungspolitik* (Nordlingen, 1991), pp. 93ff.

47. Rössler, *'Wissenschaft und Lebensraum'*, pp. 181–2.

48. Burleigh, *Germany Turns Eastwards*, pp. 300ff.

minorities have been marginalised by the realities of late-twentieth-century diplomacy, by the migration of ethnic Germans to the Federal Republic, and by the resurgence of a nation-state whose vocation is economic prosperity and the absorption of the economically prostrate former GDR rather than the achievement of a greater territorial extent. Although the post-war continuities are considerably fainter than those linking the conservative nationalism of the Weimar period with the racial imperialism of the Third Reich, on a psychological level some would maintain that there are still outstanding problems. While a united German state will probably remain inward looking for the immediate future, there are vestiges of an older sense of a German civilising mission, bringing 'order' to the 'chaos' of Eastern Europe, in the words and actions of some of the entrepreneurial and bureaucratic *Macher* heading eastwards to Leipzig or Dresden. There does not seem to be much talk of what the people there can contribute to the emergent state in the way of recompense.

SUGGESTIONS FOR FURTHER READING

M. Burleigh, *Germany Turns Eastwards: A Study of 'Ostforschung' in the Third Reich* (Cambridge University Press, 1988; 2nd edn. 1990); M. Burleigh and W. Wippermann, *The Racial State: Germany 1933–1945* (Cambridge University Press, 1991); G. Camphausen, *Die wissenschaftliche historische Russlandforschung in Dritten Reich 1933–1945* (Frankfurt am Main, 1990); G. F. Volkmer 'Die deutsche Forschung zum osteuropäischen Judentum 1933–1945', in H.-J. Torke (ed.) *Forschungen zur osteuropäischen Geschichte* (Berlin, 1989) vol. 42.

CHAPTER EIGHT

The collapse of nationalism in Nazi Germany

William Sheridan Allen

The career of Adolf Hitler abounds in ironies. He rode to power on a promise to unite all Germans, to make them respected and powerful, and to build a permanent bulwark against international Communism. After a dozen years of rule he left Germany divided and weak, a people morally discredited and the object of near universal suspicion and contempt, and he brought the Soviets into Berlin for the next two generations. But the greatest irony is that Hitler achieved supreme leadership by appealing to nationalism; he was widely viewed as 'Germany's greatest nationalist'; yet his Third Reich permanently damaged the German popular faith in nationalism. How and why that happened is the topic of this chapter.

My analysis will require at least some theoretical assertions, inevitably controversial in view of the expanding debate over the nature and role of modern nationalism.[1] I will argue that there are different types of nationalism,that Hitler and his most fanatical followers used a vocabulary of nationalism common to most types but with a content not shared by most of his supporters, that major aspects of the nationalist programme became malfunctional when Hitler carried them out, and that during the Third Reich the different types of nationalism that had helped bring Hitler to power were re-evaluated after he turned them into policy. Because Germans who had applauded the verbiage of nationalism found its actualisation threatening, they rejected nationalism. What was once seen as a unitary phenomenon splintered completely. Above all I will argue that nationalism in Germany became discredited because its effects no longer served its supposed purposes. Instead of enhancing security and well-being, nationalism as practised by Hitler

---

1. For an analysis of general theories see J. Breuilly, *Nationalism and the State* (New York, 1982), pp. 18–36, 365–73. My approach to nationalist functions is much narrower than his, though I certainly second his argument that for Germany nationalism produced a 'pseudo-solution' (pp. 349f). Further evaluations of theory are in M. Hughes, *Nationalism and Society: Germany 1800–1945* (London, 1988), pp. 1–23.

became a threat to personal security and so it lost its appeal to most Germans. What survived the Third Reich was a public attitude quite different from the sentiments represented by Nazi extremists.

I

Prior to the Third Reich, in the Kaiser's time and even more so in the years of the Weimar Republic, nationalistic sentiments became increasingly pervasive throughout Germany. By the eve of the First World War, German nationalism in one or another form had become almost universally prevalent, especially within the middle classes and the political Right. Then it deepened: as happened in virtually all combattant countries, the First World War intensified nationalist fervour in Germany. What had once seemed to many as just a trick of the 'establishment' was now perceived, through the passions of total war, as a pre-requisite for surviving a life-and-death struggle. The sufferings of the First World War certainly left most Germans opposed to any renewed armed conflict, a view that was to continue throughout the Third Reich. Yet the wartime commitment to the nation persisted after the fighting stopped and remained almost as intense during the 1920s as it had been during the actual war years.

Germany's defeat and its extended post-war national humiliation were widely assumed, in the Weimar era, to be both an instance of foreigners exploiting Germany and the reasons for the many social and economic ills that beset the Weimar Republic. This causal linkage even applied to events that were, at the most, only lightly connected with the Armistice of 1918 or the Treaty of Versailles: hyperinflation, the structural unemployment of the 'rationalisation era', the agricultural crisis, the political and sexual turmoil of the 'flapper years', the Great Depression. Yet all were blamed, by right-wing orators, on Germany's international weakness. With Germany effectively disarmed, manifestly defenceless against foreign incursions, saddled with emotional burdens of war guilt, and supposedly crushed by reparations debts, national solidarity seemed wholly defensive in nature. Even the Left expressed this attitude. It was the Social Democratic leader Philip Scheidemann who said: 'Any hand must wither that puts itself and us in these chains' (by signing the Treaty of Versailles).[2] Socialists excori-

2. D. Lehnert, 'The SPD in German politics and society', in R. Fletcher (ed.) *Bernstein to Brandt: A Short History of German Social Democracy* (London, 1987), p. 115.

ated the Right for 'hurrah patriotism', i.e. for insincere patriotism, rather than for nationalism *per se*.[3] Even the Communists used the vocabulary of nationalism, arguing that only a Soviet Germany could adequately defend the country. As for the many parties of the moderate and extreme Right, nationalism became more than ever the standard language of their political appeals, even if various leaders and constituents understood the common vocabulary differently.

This was at least partly because, as had been true even in the nineteenth century, nationalism served different functions for different groups. It also had differing qualities. For almost all Germans there was a real sense of pride in the achievements of their united nation and its culture. Germany had blossomed in science, technology, social welfare, urban administration, music, education, trade and manufacture. Consequently there was much to be proud of. National pride also enhanced personal self-esteem for those who needed that; at the very least it provided everyone with a sense of identity. Few Germans, even if they disliked some aspects of their country, wanted to feel shame over their identification with Germany, or at least with German culture.[4] Providing identity and pride was perhaps the most modest function of nationalism and also the most widespread.

For others, however, nationalism had more specifically goal-directed and less lofty uses. Ever since Bismarck discovered how politically beneficial an appeal to nationalistic sentiments could be, German conservatives used nationalism as a ploy to disarm their foes and to win broad electoral support. In time some conservatives came to believe their own rhetoric, but there also remained an element of the cynicism and insincerity that Bismarck had displayed. Certainly there were very few conservatives who were willing to sacrifice their own self-interest for the good of the nation (in fact most of them thought that the two things were one and the same). By the 1920s the tradition was well established in Germany that nationalism was, among other things, a potent weapon against the Left. It is worth remembering that in Kaiser Wilhelm's time the Socialists were excoriated as *vaterlandslose Gesellen* ('the unpatriotic guys').

Nationalism also had a social function. For the middle classes of Germany, aspiring to escape a status that left them permanently ranked below the aristocracy regardless of their achievements, but also at risk

3. W. S. Allen, *The Nazi Seizure of Power: The Experience of a Single German Town 1922–1945* (New York, 1984, rev. edn), p. 43.

4. As a Marxist, then a Zionist, Hannah Arendt criticised almost everything in the country of her birth, but still identified with the German language: E. Young-Bruehl, *Hannah Arendt: For Love of the World* (New Haven, Conn, 1982), p. 199.

of sliding into the proletariat, nationalism meant a claim to social upgrading and social security. From the time of the French Revolution of 1789, nationalism has carried revolutionary implications by elevating group allegiance over individual self-interest. Customarily the nation has been portrayed as a sort of family: *la patrie, das Vaterland*. Consequently nationalism has a potential for social equalisation, all members of the family having theoretically the same claims to its protection and the same status. Social distinctions based on birth or wealth may thus be challenged on the grounds that common nationality should override them. Status, say many nationalists, should be based on the value of an individual's contributions to the nation's needs.

Down to Hitler's time Germany showed extraordinary status-consciousness: foreigners found few things more absurd than the German quest for and insistent use of titles as appendages to their names. One of the handiest things about the social levelling functions of nationalism was that it could change the status of members of the middle class without also demanding any equalisation of income or property. Unlike socialism, nationalism did not threaten to obliterate objective class differences. It was also morally gratifying because it appealed to the very edifying concept of *noblesse oblige*. The middle and upper classes should respect workers out of a sense of duty. Whatever other functions nationalism performed for the German middle classes, it certainly supplied them with an attractive social ideology.

Apart from its political and class functions, nationalism could also provide psychological protection against the threat of change. It is an ideology that insists that the inherited qualities of the nation are unique and precious and therefore must be preserved against internal as well as external threats. By exalting the value of individual identification with the nation and by demanding national cohesion, it concentrates collective hostility against anyone who might deny the supreme importance of the nation as a group. Therefore it can be used to justify intolerance, the repression of dissidents, the persecution of minorities, and the enforcement of conformity. In times of upheaval, such as the first third of the twentieth century clearly were for Germany, large numbers of people – regardless of their social or political adherence – may focus their anxieties upon others who are different. The 'other' may seem a threat because of his otherness. It is convenient to claim that people who are different threaten the cohesion of the national community. While such scapegoating will not cure the basic problem of existential insecurity, it has the psychological advantage of providing a clear target for otherwise shapeless anxieties. Further, if persecuting minorities is done in the name of the national collectivity, that not only provides the anxious individual with potential allies but also lends some respectability to what would otherwise be considered unjustifiable attitudes.[5]

This list of functions performed by nationalism in Germany before the advent of the Third Reich is brief and incomplete, yet even so it is enough to indicate that German nationalism had many different qualities and attracted people for quite divergent reasons.[6] As has been found in other countries too, there are many kinds of nationalists – some good, some bad, some indifferent.[7]

Note also that the above set of functions performed by nationalism consists of items really related to domestic needs. None of them links directly to what was to be Hitler's actual programme: war, imperialism and genocide. At the moment of his triumphant accession to the leadership of Germany in 1933, Hitler began the process of dissolving the apparent common bond of the disparate nationalists (by carrying out *his*, not *their* programme) so that their actual differences about nationalism could become apparent to them.

In the period when Nazism was gaining enough mass backing to put Hitler into office as Reich Chancellor, Hitler appealed to Germans by focusing on all the functions of nationalism described above. He promised to unify the Germans and thereby strengthen the country so that it would no longer be exploited by foreigners. He evoked pride in Germany's achievements and called the Germans a *Herrenvolk*. He was adamantly opposed to 'Marxists' and proposed to stamp out the SPD and KPD and to convert the workers to nationalism. (This, incidentally, was probably what won him the most votes.) He offered a new national community, the attractive *Volksgemeinschaft* that would elevate all patriotic Germans into a common status as 'racial comrades'. And he threatened to crack down on all forms of deviation: sexual, artistic, ideological.

These promises, delivered with enough vagueness so that each group could believe that Nazism was chiefly pursuing that group's own goals, were directly attuned to the functions nationalism was presumed to provide. That, plus the disintegration of Weimar democracy and the vast pool of 'protest votes' available, won the NDSAP about two-fifths of the electorate in free elections.[8] It made the cre-

5. I owe much of this analysis to my colleague at SUNY/Buffalo, Dr. Norman Solkoff, Distinguished Professor of Psychology.

6. Hughes, op.cit., pp. 3–5, 15–17, 122, 194f.

7. This point is more fully developed by N. Davies, *God's Playground: A History of Poland*, vol. 2: *1795 to the Present* (New York, 1984), pp. 9–13.

8. I have analysed this more extensively in 'The Nazi rise to power: a comprehensible catastrophe', in C.S. Maier *et al* (eds) *The Rise of the Nazi Regime: Historical Reassessments* (Boulder, Col, 1986), pp. 9–18.

ation of the Third Reich possible. But it was also to provide a perversion of what Germans really wanted.

II

From the start of his rule, Hitler tried to make nationalism perform its expected function, as he had promised. The results, however, were not what Germans had expected. During the period of the Nazi 'seizure of power' (the first six months of the Third Reich, conveniently marked off by the law of 14 July, 1933, that made the NDSAP Germany's only legal party) and the consolidation of the regime (conveniently marked by Hitler's purge of the Stormtroopers and his assumption of Hindenburg's powers, both in the summer of 1934), Hitler most definitely carried out one of his campaign promises. He destroyed the trade unions plus the Social Democratic and Communist organisations.

Ian Kershaw has argued that this above all was a widely applauded policy,[9] though it was obviously unpopular among that third of the country who were adherents of these working-class organisations. In any case, for those to whom nationalism was primarily a weapon against the Left, Hitler's attack on 'Marxism' fulfilled long-held desires. Yet many were also appalled by the Stormtrooper thuggery that accompanied the destruction of the Left. Such concerns were both allayed and heightened by the lawless violence used against the *SA* in June 1934. The 'execution' without trial of Ernst Roehm and hundreds of others meant than any German could be subjected to the same fate. Thus the price paid for the entire policy was the elimination of the *Rechtsstaat*: official lawlessness and state terrorism became evident to all.[10]

Since the rule of law had been one of the great achievements of the German nation, dating back to the reign of Frederick the Great, even ardent nationalists were very uneasy over this aspect of the Nazi dicta-

9. See I. Kershaw, *Popular Opinion and Political Dissent in the Third Reich: Bavaria 1933–1945* (Oxford, 1983) and *The Hitler Myth: Image and Reality in the Third Reich* (Oxford, 1987).

10. That non-politically motivated denunciations and Gestapo actions based on them became customary is shown in R. Gellately, *The Gestapo and German Society: Enforcing Racial Policy 1933–1945* (Oxford, 1990), Ch. 5 and *passim*.

torship. Worse still: by carrying out the anti-Marxist desires of conservative Germans, Hitler showed that a curse can be attached to the fulfillment of wishes. Beyond that, once the Left had been smashed, did one really continue to need the Nazis? The question was both pertinent and irrelevant since the dictatorship was, by 1934, unchallengeable.

Before Hitler's shattering of the organised working-class movements, many Germans had perceived them as a threat to their security. After it their lives were insecure in different and more immediate ways. This same pattern was to be followed in most of the other features of the Third Reich. In other words, originally appealing expectations of nationalism were shown to be malfunctional.

A second example consists of the problematical assumption of the post-First World War years that a united Germany could successfully overcome the consequences of Germany's defeat in 1918. Of course many of the punitive provisions of the Treaty of Versailles had already been negotiated away by the Weimar Republic. Reparations payments ended with the 'Hoover Moratorium' of 1931. Hitler promised to reverse the defeat of 1918 and from 1933–39 he did that and more. That was, on one level, undoubtedly gratifying to Germans who had been upset by losing the First World War. On the other hand, very few Germans wanted to go to war again, the memory of what war had cost being far too fresh. Therefore Hitler's aggressive foreign policy frightened his countrymen. By the summer of 1934 both the Gestapo's 'morale reports' and the reports of the Social Democratic underground used the same term to describe the noticeably evident fear of war among the population: *Kriegspsychose* ('war psychosis'). From then on each of Hitler's serial coups produced an ever-growing public anxiety.[11] That he succeeded repeatedly in getting his way without war until September 1939 did not cause popular exultation over national triumphs so much as bewildered relief that disaster had once again been avoided.

During such moments as the confrontation with Czechoslovakia and the Western democracies over the Sudetenland in September 1938, the public was not gripped by war fever but by numb fear. Eyewitness accounts from Berlin on the occasion of a military parade at the height of the Sudetenland crisis describe Germans watching it in stony silence, 'the most striking demonstration against war I've ever seen' (William Shirer).[12] When the Second World War actually broke

11. M.G. Steinert, *Hitler's War and the Germans: Public Mood and Attitude during the Second World War* (Athens, Ohio, 1977), pp. 7f and *passim*.

12. W.L. Shirer, *Berlin Diary: The Journal of a Foreign Correspondent 1934–1941* (New York, 1979), pp. 142f "Sept. 28, 1938".

out in 1939, foreign newsmen reported Germans to be stunned and gloomy, but jubilant when a false rumour of peace was circulated a month later.[13] Not even the *Wehrmacht's* stunning victories over the French and British in 1940 proved reassuring, let alone an occasion for celebration. When the news of the German army's capture of Paris hit Berlin, its citizens responded with indifference.[14]

As Hitler's war turned catastrophic, with defeat, retreat, massive casualties, and constant bombing of the Reich, Germans learned the lesson of how dangerous aggressive nationalism could be. What national solidarity there was in the face of catastrophe was forced on Germans by circumstances: the beleaguered country had become, in contemporary language, a 'community of fate'. But that is a far cry from eagerness to fight or to risk all on behalf of the nation's gain.

In sum: during the 1920s many Germans believed that their lives would be bettered if Germany became strong enough to prevent foreign domination. As Hitler achieved and exceeded that goal, most Germans became fearful of his recklessness, which could endanger their lives. When war did come, they experienced directly how destructive and dangerous radical nationalism could be. This was not what they had hoped for when they had applauded diatribes against 'the fetters of Versailles'. The vocabulary of defensive nationalism remained a staple of Nazi propaganda. The reality of agressive nationalism undercut the original function of protecting the people.

Even the most popular of Nazi concepts, the socially homogenising 'folk community', fell prey to a similar cleavage between expectation and actualisation. Hitler and many Nazis sincerely tried to introduce new standards of status, not least because they felt contempt for the old order and saw it as a threat to any war effort. At the beginning of the Third Reich there was widespread enthusiasm among middle-class Germans for the 'idealism' of patriotic solidarity. Workers, however, never bought it. They viewed the entire programme as a corrupt sham and their non-cooperation was a big problem for the regime.[15] The material side of this 'social revolution' was rapidly undermined by Germany's rearmament, while specific groups, such as farmers, became bitter over the inadequacy of Nazi policies.[16]

13. Ibid., pp. 191, 201, also 205, 207f. See also J.W. Grigg's recollections, UPI dispatch, 2 September 1979.

14. Shirer, op.cit., pp. 395, 403f.

15. Analysed and documented in T.W. Mason, *Arbeiterklasse und Volksgemeinschaft: Dokument und Materialien zur deutschen Arbeiterpolitik 1936–1939* (Opladen, 1975). An English translation is supposed to be published in the near future.

16. D. Schoenbaum, *Hitler's Social Revolution: Class and Status in Nazi Germany 1933–1939* (New York, 1968).

Even the erstwhile enthusiasts became appalled by the incredible corruption perpetrated by Nazis who were supposed to implement 'folk community' programmes, like Labour Front leader Robert Ley.[17] One constantly repeated Nazi slogan was *Gemeinnutz vor Eigennutz* (the 'collective benefit precedes the individual's'). But it was common knowledge that Nazi leaders were determined to gain and defend their own power, at the expense of each other, even to the detriment of their common cause. What Germans concluded, obviously, was that their leaders were hypocrites. Furthermore, Germans grew to resent the regimentation imposed upon them by local party leaders – the 'little Führers' – trying to implement 'folk community' policies.[18] Ultimately the 'folk community' meant little more than the Nazi Block Warden exacting contributions from each household for 'Winter Aid', which funds, most Germans believed, were corruptly appropriated by Nazi bigwigs for their self-enrichment. What most ordinary Germans got out from the 'folk community' was a lot of propaganda.

Also the persecution of dissidents and minorities failed to end psychological insecurity, as had been expected, because it became too widespread and violent. Conservative Germans applauded the Gestapo's putting 'Marxists', homosexuals and Jehovah's Witnesses into concentration camps, but began to grow nervous over the violence against Germany's Jews.[19] The single most widespread cause of public disaffection from Nazi actions came on the occasion of the *Kristallnacht* pogrom in November 1938.[20] Shame and concern over this disgraceful incident carried over into the war years, where many Germans believed that their cities were targeted for Allied bombing according to whether or not a synagogue had been burned in their town on *Kristallnacht*. As the news of the Holocaust gradually became whispered about at home, usually because of reports by soldiers on leave from the Eastern Front, Germans were increasingly ashamed. For example, most of those in the 20 July 1944 plot felt driven to resist Hitler primarily because of his crimes against the Jews.[21] The same was true of the student dissidents in the 'White Rose' organisation.[22]

17. R. Smelser, *Robert Ley: Hitler's Labour Front Leader* (Oxford, 1988).
18. The resentments are discussed in Kershaw, *Hitler Myth*.
19. The extent of public complaint is detailed in K.A. Schleunes, *The Twisted Road to Auschwitz: Nazi Policy towards German Jews 1933–1939* (Urbana, Ill, 1990, expanded edn).
20. I analysed this in 'The German popular response to *Kristallnacht*: value hierarchies vs. propaganda', in L.H. Letgers (ed.) *Western Society after the Holocaust* (Boulder, Col, 1983), pp. 69–82 and 98–108.
21. P. Hoffmann, *The History of the German Resistance 1933–1945* (Cambridge, Mass, 1977) and *German Resistance to Hitler* (Cambridge, Mass, 1988).
22. I. Jens (ed.) *At the Heart of the White Rose: Letters and Diaries of Hans and Sophie Scholl* (New York, 1987).

Ultimately everyone was potentially threatened by Nazi assaults against anyone who was 'different'. By the end of the Third Reich the SS was seriously considering the mass extermination of all 'ugly' people.[23] Hardly any Germans knew about that, but most came to know about the Nazi attempt to murder all mentally retarded or congenitally ill Germans. By September 1939 one could also be beheaded for listening to the wrong radio station. The persecution of 'others' had come to exemplify the French proverb: 'In eating, the appetite increases.'

Since all the above malfunctions of nationalism were heavily promoted by Nazi propaganda which was so incessant and pervasive in the Third Reich, why was it not successful? It was, to the extent that it reinforced the Nazi leaders in their convictions, confused and isolated individuals, and convinced even those who did not believe it that everyone else was believing it. But Nazi propaganda could not reverse previously held convictions. No propaganda can. Beyond that, Germans had become highly sensitised to and quite sceptical of any propaganda as a result of the feverish politics of the Weimar era.[24] That they came to disbelieve their own government is evidenced by the fact that almost all Germans listened to the BBC during the Second World War. They literally risked their necks for accurate information.

But the primary reason for the failure of Nazi propaganda was that when it conflicted with reality, as discovered through experience, reality won. A major instance of this was that despite a constant propaganda campaign by Goebbels from 1942 to the end of the war, to persuade all Germans that they would win the war if they never surrendered, almost all Germans did surrender when their home towns were approached by Allied armies.[25] Of those who did not, the usual reason was that they were forced to continue fighting, not that they had been convinced to do so by the propaganda.

Finally, one should note that the very structure of the Nazi dictatorship undercut nationalism. As a form of self-identification, nationalism cannot be imposed. It has to be felt and believed by an individual. But the Third Reich discouraged voluntary commitment in all regards because it was determined to regiment its own people. The incessant controls, the herding of people into compelled demonstrations of en-

23. R. Hilberg, *The Destruction of the European Jew* (New York, 1979), p. 642ff.

24. W. S. Allen (ed. and trans.) *The Infancy of Nazism: The Memoirs of Ex-Gauleiter Albert Krebs 1923–1933* (New York, 1976), p. 81.

25. J. Stephenson, '"Resistance" to "No Surrender": Popular Disobedience in Württemurg in 1945', in F.R. Nicosia and L.D. Stokes (eds) *Germans against Nazism: Nonconformity, Opposition and Resistance in the Third Reich* (Oxford, 1990), pp. 351–67.

thusiasm, the coerced conformity, all had the effect of treating the people as objects: the *Herrenvolk* as serfs. In response, even once willing enthusiasts became passive, bored, resentful, apathetic, withdrawn.[26] Ultimately very few Germans volunteered for any aspect of their nation's needs because almost all Germans had come to expect their rulers to tell them what they had to do. Under the stress of the Second World War, Germans became chiefly concerned with their own and their family's survival. This privatisation was the antithesis of nationalism. Or to put it another way, Hitler had finally created the conditions wherein nationalism no longer made any sense.

III

The death and destruction of the Second World War ended almost all nationalistic sentiments in Germany, especially the most radical ones. But some survived even Hitler. He had taken nationalism to the extreme limits and had thereby discredited it, disillusioning his one-time followers. It was not simply that nationalism had been shown to be life-threatening rather than life-enhancing. On top of that direct experience came the post-war evidence of the crimes committed in Germany's name. It was overwhelming and undeniable and Germans realised that they had partaken of a moral, rather than just a physical, catastrophe. Some argued that Hitler was an aberration and that Germans could retrieve their self-esteem by returning to the good parts of their national heritage.[27] West German political leaders have consistently and freely voted for reparations to the victims of Nazism and to the state of Israel, in the clear conviction that atonement can pave the way for renewed pride in Germany. Officially and privately Germans have extolled their martyred countrymen who resisted Hitler, especially those who, like the 20 July 1944 conspirators, had explicitly claimed to be risking their lives in order to restore Germany's national honour.

So the nationalism of pride and self-identification survived Nazism, though that pride was often for aspects of Germany that Hitler hated. Though nothing done by the Treaty of Versailles matched the break-up of the Reich into two separate and antagonistic states, such as pre-

26. Allen, *Seizure*, pp. 282–92: 'Life in the Third Reich'.
27. F. Meinecke, *The German Catastrophe* (New York, 1947).

vailed from 1949 to 1989, there was nothing during those years comparable to the nationalistic outrage of the 1920s. Since 1945 calls for the reunification of the fatherland were generally ritualistic. A substantial number of West Germans grew comfortable with Willy Brandt's formula: 'One nation; two states'. During and since the reunification of the two Germanies, the predominant emotion in West Germany was not nationalistic exaltation, but pragmatic concern about how much this new unity was going to cost. Some leading intellectuals, such as Günter Grass and Hans-Ulrich Wehler, publicly opposed the whole idea of a united Germany.[28]

One post-Hitlerian surprise was the adoption of some nationalistic attitudes by the SPD, beginning already in 1945. But that stance stemmed at least partly from deliberate calculation: the Social Democrats wanted to avoid being outflanked by nationalists ever again. None of their leaders ever indulged in radical rhetoric. They simply insisted that foreign exploitation was as repugnant as the domestic variety and that democracy required self-determination. And by the 1960s the Social Democratic nationalism was as muted as their erstwhile 'Marxism' had become. That was at least partly because even mild nationalistic appeals did not win them many votes. Germans were too cool towards the whole notion of the nation.[29]

Almost all this change in the nature and extent of German national sentiments is largely a legacy of the Third Reich. The most nationalistic government the world has known left its people very doubtful about anything other than an understandable and rational acceptance of the indisputable fact that they were Germans: a self-identification that, like the heritage of most nations, involves both pride and shame.

SUGGESTIONS FOR FURTHER READING

W. S. Allen, *The Nazi Seizure of Power: the Experience of a Single German Town, 1922–1945* (rev. ed., London, 1989).

R. Bessel (ed.) *Life in the Third Reich* (Oxford, 1987).

B. Engelmann, *In Hitler's Germany: Everyday Life in the Third Reich* (New York, 1986).

28. G. Grass, *Two States – One Nation?* (New York, 1990).
29. Hughes, *Nationalism and Society*, p. 226 and *passim*.

R. Gellately, *The Gestapo and Germany Society: Enforcing Racial Policy, 1933–1945* (Oxford, 1990).

S. A. Gordon, *Hitler, Germans, and the 'Jewish Question'* (Princeton, New Jersey, 1983).

R. Grunberger, *The 12-year Reich: A Social History of Nazi Germany, 1933–1945* (New York, 1971).

P. Hoffmann, *German Resistance to Hitler* (Cambridge, Mass., 1988).

M. Hughes, *Nationalism and Society: Germany 1800–1945* (London, 1988).

I. Kershaw, *The 'Hitler Myth': Image and Reality in the Third Reich* (Oxford, 1987).

I. Kershaw, *Popular Opinion and Political Dissent in the Third Reich: Bavaria 1933–1945* (Oxford, 1983).

D. Peukert & J. Reulecke (eds) *Die Reihen fast geschlossen: Beiträge zur Geschichte des Alltags unterm Nationalsozialismus* (Wuppertal, 1981).

D. Schoenbaum, *Hitler's Social Revolution: Class and Status in Nazi Germany, 1933–1939* (New York, 1966).

M. Steinert, *Hitler's War and the Germans: Public Mood and Attitude during the Second World War* (Athens, Ohio, 1977).

CHAPTER NINE

Nationalism and German politics after 1945

Peter Alter

April 1945 was the cruellest month. Hitler's Third Reich, the scourge of Europe for twelve long years, was at last finished, politically and militarily as well as morally. Most German cities lay in ruins, devastated by bombs, shelling and fire. Millions of refugees and 'displaced persons' were on the move. As the Allied forces liberated German-occupied Europe and directed their offensive towards the centre of the Reich the concentration camps revealed horrors which were beyond human imagination and comprehension. The collapse of the National Socialist dictatorship was accompanied by the dissolution of the German state. After Germany's unconditional surrender on 8 May 1945 the country was occupied by the four victorious powers. The traditional territorial organisation of the Germans had come to an end. Total war was followed by total defeat – and the defeat of 1945 was incomparably more far-reaching and final than that of 1918, affecting people's lives more directly. In 1918 the horrors of war had remained largely on battlefields abroad; in 1945 they were brought to German soil proper. It seemed to be *finis Germaniae*.

The unconditional surrender of May 1945 brought an era of German history to a close. It was a turning-point of the most fundamental kind. The enormity of what had happened and the task of rebuilding Germany led contemporaries to speak of a *Stunde Null* (hour zero) – appropriately at the time, although years later it became apparent that no comprehensive new start had actually taken place in Germany in 1945. But most Germans felt that after the end of the Nazi dictatorship a break with basic traditions of their history was necessary, and the will to make this break was there. These traditions included thinking in militarist and nationalist categories, which was now held responsible for developments that had led to the establishment of the Nazi regime in Germany in 1933, and to the unleashing of the Second World War in 1939. German policy, the deluded activities of the Nazis, who were responsible for the war and the Holocaust, had perverted the national idea. Thus it was only natural that in 1945 nationalism was often linked with National Socialism as a criminal ideology, and that the Germans had grave doubts about the nation and the national state. As principles of state organisation, it seemed, they had run their course.

The momentous change in the thinking of the Germans which will be outlined here was rooted in the experience of National Socialism and the Second World War. The direct confrontation with a ruthless dictatorship, with crime and destruction had an impact on the German mentality which is still visible today. In the West German state on the territory of the former Reich, the Federal Republic of Germany, the national state and a national consciousness were no longer the highest values; freedom, peace and tolerance now ranked above them. The conviction that national egoism and rivalry between states did not provide an adequate basis for the coexistence of the European peoples had gained ground. In the mid-1960s the philosopher Karl Jaspers published a political polemic, *What is becoming of the Federal Republic?*, in which he expressed dismay about the political consciousness of the West Germans:

> It has been said that there is a *vacuum* in our political consciousness. It is true that we do not yet have our hearts in a political objective, nor do we have a feeling of standing on ground that we have created ourselves. . . The vacuum will not be filled by a national consciousness. That is either missing, or it is an artificial one.[1]

Even when the unification of the two states which were successors to the eclipsed German Third Reich was on the international agenda in 1989–90 the West German people were reluctant to accept the rhetoric of nation, and many in fact distrusted and rejected it. In the summer of 1990 the Munich historian Thomas Nipperdey observed that rejecting the nation was 'something specifically German'. He warned his readers against the 'fatal inclination'

> to impose our non-national-consciousness on other oh-so-backward peoples. It seems that the world is once again to be saved by the most progressive, a better, post-national entity, and one feels the arrogance of the seemingly so noble rejection of the national. We should not feel superior.[2]

1. K. Jaspers, *Wohin treibt die Bundesrepublik? Tatsachen, Gefahren, Chancen* (Munich, 1966, repr. 1988), pp. 177–8. For their generous advice and help I am very grateful to my colleagues Angela Davies, Eva A. Mayring and Lothar Kettenacker.

2. T. Nipperdey, 'Die Deutschen wollen und dürfen eine Nation sein', *Frankfurter Allgemeine*, 13 July 1990, p. 10. Almost a year after unification the Berlin writer Peter Schneider wrote: 'Faced with unification, West German society turns out to be morally and intellectually unprepared for the challenge. The problem is precisely *not* the new German nationalism some people fear but the almost total lack of it. In the ruins of the National Socialist megalomania, West Germans fell back on a very convenient credo: I only believe what I see (in the till)' (*Time*, 1 July 1991, p. 40).

I

The rejection of the nation and its elevation into an absolute value after the *Wertzusammenbruch* (collapse of all values) at the end of the war, the turning away from the idea of the national state as the value central to all politics, grew out of the experience of the 'German catastrophe'.[3] In defeated and occupied Germany, therefore, the process of settling accounts with the past from the start also concentrated on nationalism and its consequences for German history. 'Nationalism', now frequently equated with National Socialism, acquired unequivocally negative connotations. As a polemical term and a term of political demarcation, it has retained these to the present day in Germany. Nationalism was seen as the opposite of devoted patriotism, which does not necessarily relate to the nation, and permits competing loyalties to exist. Nationalism was considered the antithesis of free democracy and a 'healthy' national consciousness, whatever these terms might mean. The public debate after 1945, however, took place within a very small circle. The participants were leading intellectuals, who had either opposed the Nazi regime or had survived the dictatorship abroad in forced or voluntary emigration. The debate did not widen and enter party politics until the 1950s, when political and economic conditions in West Germany had settled.

In 1945 and immediately thereafter, the mass of the German population was, of course, preoccupied almost exclusively with simply surviving. Its attitude towards political issues therefore tended to be one of apathy and indifference.[4] Many people believed that in the foreseeable future the occupying powers would take over politics, operating over the heads of the Germans. It is, unfortunately, not possible to make more precise statements about the level of awareness among the German people, their political attitudes and their political thinking in the early post-war period due to lack of information. However, there is much to suggest that the idea that the German population harboured a powerful but unexpressed potential for resentment and nationalist feeling in 1945 and thereafter is incorrect. Even the millions of refugees, brutally expelled from eastern Germany and other parts of central, eastern and south-eastern Europe, seem not to have provided a

3. F. Meinecke, *The German Catastrophe: Reflections and Recollections* (Cambridge, Mass., 1950). The German edition was published in 1946.
4. B. Marshall, 'German reactions to military defeat, 1945–1947: the British view', in V.R. Berghahn and M. Kitchen (eds) *Germany in the Age of Total War* (London, 1981), pp. 218–39.

breeding ground for surviving or new nationalisms, as some contemporaries predicted. Militant political revisionism and right-wing nationalism were never to play more than a marginal and, apart from occasional flowerings, rapidly diminishing role in the politics of the Federal Republic after its founding in 1949.

There is evidence to suggest that nationalism was already being firmly condemned a few weeks before Germany's surrender to the Allies. When the Thuringian concentration camp, Buchenwald, near Weimar, was liberated by American troops in April 1945, a number of former inmates, all supporters of democratic socialism, drew up a list of demands and ideas which were to guide Germany's new politics. Some of these ideas found their way into Allied occupation policy, and also into the programmes of the newly established German parties. The Buchenwald Manifesto of 13 April 1945, 'For Peace, Freedom, Socialism', was an ambitious and pioneering attempt 'to rescue Germany from this historically unprecedented collapse and to secure for it again the respect and trust of the council of nations', by opening up a perspective for the future. It contains statements about Germany's future domestic and foreign policy. In foreign policy, the manifesto calls for all forms of nationalism to be abandoned. The authors advocate the creation of a 'European-wide awareness'. They continue: 'To achieve this we need a new spirit. It is to be embodied by a new type of German – that of the German European. Nobody can re-educate us, if we do not do it ourselves in freedom.' As the first concrete steps on this long path the Manifesto recommended that Germany should come to an understanding with its direct neighbours in the east and west, Poland and France, and cooperate with them. It also suggested that 'Germany should enter the Anglo-Saxon cultural area'. The authors of the Manifesto combined this suggestion with the wish that their country be accepted into 'the international organisation for peace and security as soon as possible'. In other words, they wanted Germany to become a member of the United Nations, which was then in the process of being set up.[5]

The language of the Buchenwald Manifesto was rather vague and general, but its authors made sufficiently clear the direction in which they wanted Germany to go. The dissolving of a traditional national consciousness in a European consciousness which the Manifesto demanded was also put forward at the same time by the liberal economist, Wilhelm Röpke, as the objective of all German policy in the

---

5. The Buchenwald Manifesto is printed in M. Overesch, *Deutschland 1945–1949: Vorgeschichte und Gründung der Bundesrepublik. Ein Leitfaden in Darstellung und Dokumenten* (Königstein, 1979), pp. 171–6.

new Germany. A German by birth, Professor Röpke had emigrated in 1933 and had been teaching in Geneva since 1937. His book, *The German Question,* was published in Switzerland in the spring of 1945. Two years later, a third edition had to be printed. The book was translated into English, French and Italian. Its arguments and demands captured the contemporary imagination.

The influence of Röpke's work on the German public and on German politicians in the post-war period cannot be overemphasised. According to the historian Hans-Peter Schwarz, it was 'the most consistent and well-founded blueprint for German politics' in the German language in existence at the end of the war.[6] In it, Röpke diagnosed the Germans, and at the same time prescribed a therapy for all their ills and troubles. He believed that the Germans were now ripe for a moral revolution. In his opinion, the fact that it had not happened in 1918 was a disaster. At the end of the First World War,

> the poison of nationalism was not got rid of, but under the influence of defeat, collapse, and economic and social upheavals, was only propagated further. The very serious readiness for a searching self-examination that existed after November, 1918, was quickly dissipated and reduced to impotence in face of the opposite determination to return all the more defiantly to the old spirit.[7]

The Germans had paid the penalty in 1933 and 1945. In 1933, 'with the Third Reich, the German Reich founded by Bismarck came to its end'.[8] Twelve years later, the Germans suffered

> the complete bankruptcy of a spirit, a policy, a type of patriotism and of collective morality, which the Nazis had utilized in order to carry matters to the uttermost extreme. In blind obstinacy the wrong path was pursued to the end, until the leaders themselves saw no way out except through taking their own lives. The people, as such, will not commit suicide, but will turn back provided that they are shown a way back.[9]

Röpke recommended a threefold revolution for the Germans: political (decentralisation), economic (liberalism) and moral. 'The solution of the German question', Röpke went on,

> contained in this threefold revolution is the only one that holds out the promise of real permanence. It permits the fulfilment of all just and reasonable claims from the victors for the future security of Europe in face of Germany [*sic*]; and at the same time it is the solution which every

6. H.-P. Schwarz, *Die Ära Adenauer* (Stuttgart, 1981), p. 393.
7. W. Röpke, *The German Question* (London, 1946), p. 180.
8. Ibid., p. 188.
9. Ibid., p. 184.

German patriot with clear vision and goodwill must desire for his homeland, once he has himself recognized the nature of the German question. Germany had become a danger to her neighbours because she had become infected with a grave malady. It is therefore the common interest of victors and vanquished that she should at last be thoroughly cured.[10]

Röpke drew the general conclusion that

only if the Germans are cured of regimentation and proletarianization will they really turn away for good from the narcotics of nationalism and totalitarianism, and recoil in disgust from every sort of political mass-hysteria.[11]

Another great liberal of the post-war period agreed with Röpke's assessment and his prediction about the difficulty of Germany's path back into the community of nations. Theodor Heuss, who had been a member of the *Reichstag* in Berlin until 1933 and was elected the first President of the Federal Republic in 1949, condemned the nationalist excesses of Germany's most recent past no less firmly. Like Röpke, he recommended a fundamental purification. 'For twelve years we were in the hell of history', Heuss said in March 1946 in a lecture he gave in destroyed Berlin.

For a long time we will be in the purgatory of purification. And then Paradise? No, Paradise exists only in utopian novels…We shall be happy without Paradise if only we get back to the firm ground of a free life. We should receive this in the name of democracy…When it comes to democracy, the Germans have to go right back to the beginning and learn to spell the word, even if they call themselves democrats today. They are in the ghastly position of having no word that denotes what the English call 'fairness'.[12]

At the same time Alexander Abusch, a Communist journalist and later Minister for Culture in the GDR, who had left the country during the Nazi period, made a similar complaint: 'Many Germans discovered patriotism, belatedly and incorrectly, as an extreme form of supernationalism.'[13] And, like Röpke and Heuss, he believed that a 'moral renewal of the German people' was inevitable:

Under the curious conditions of long-term occupation by the armies of

10. Ibid., p. 194.
11. Ibid., p. 193.
12. T. Heuss, 'Um Deutschlands Zukunft', in Heuss, *Aufzeichnungen 1945–1947* (Tübingen, 1966), pp. 206–7.
13. A. Abusch, *Der Irrweg einer Nation: Ein Beitrag zum Verständnis deutscher Geschichte* (Berlin, 1946), p. 184.

the United Nations,[14] the German nation must renew itself, its leaders as well as the rank-and-file. This means that it must translate the most urgent lessons of its history into new action, and at last complete the democratic revolution of 1848 and 1918 in one step.[15]

Historians also had their say in this debate about German nationalism, German faults and guilt. Friedrich Meinecke, the doyen of German historians and 84 years old at the time, concluded his famous book of 1946 on *The German Catastrophe* with a chapter on 'roads to survival'. Meinecke, who saw nationalism that was becoming amoral as the 'immediate prelude to Hitlerism',[16] accepted that 'the work of Bismarck's era has been destroyed through our own fault'.[17] Nevertheless, he claimed, 'even a partitioned Germany robbed of her national political existence, which is our lot today, ought to remember with sorrowful mourning the unity and strength that she previously enjoyed.'[18] In terms of foreign relations Meinecke could conceive of Germany 'only as a member of a future federation, voluntarily concluded, of the central and west European states'.[19] He suggested that in order to be prepared for this the Germans needed to 'work under the auspices of humanity for the purification and intensification of our moral existence'.[20] Even a scholar as wise and perceptive as Meinecke, however, could suggest only in extremely vague terms what this purification and intensification actually involved. 'The areas in which we must spiritually establish ourselves again are marked out for us. These areas are the religion and the culture of the German people.'[21] Meinecke made a special plea for contemplation of the 'sacred heritage of the Goethe period'.[22] He wanted to see every German town and larger village possess 'in the future a community of like-minded friends of culture', for which he suggested the name *Goethegemeinden* (Goethe Communities).[23]

The 'roads to survival' which Meinecke pointed out reveal his idealism, but also show that he was out of touch with real life. They testify to his helplessness in the face of what had happened, the de-

---

14. United Nations was the term for the wartime coalition from January 1942.
15. Abusch, *Der Irrweg*, p. 268.
16. Meinecke, *The German Catastrophe*, p. 24.
17. Ibid., p. 115.
18. Ibid., pp. 108–9.
19. Ibid., p. 110.
20. Ibid., p. 112.
21. Ibid.
22. Ibid., p. 9.
23. Ibid., p. 120.

pressing present, and the overwhelming tasks of the immediate future. More pragmatic men such as Meinecke's colleague at the University of Freiburg, Gerhard Ritter, and the journalist Ernst Friedlaender, both of whom tended towards the liberal conservative camp, also spoke of the spiritual renewal of Germany. But when it came to condemning thinking in national categories, they were more restrained. During the war Ritter had been close to the resistance around Carl Goerdeler, the Lord Mayor of Leipzig, and he became a leading historian in the early years of the Federal Republic. As early as 1946 he expressed the opinion that a people 'which on principle dispenses with "national consciousness" loses itself. This makes it morally worse, not better.'[24] Retaining national values, however, for him was not the same thing as giving up the idea of 'educating German young people and Germans in general to strive for world peace and greater, democratic freedom'.[25]

Ernst Friedlaender, who had spent many years abroad, had worked as a leader-writer for the new weekly, *Die Zeit,* since 1946. Early in 1947 he called for a thorough debate on national thinking, which he wanted to distinguish from *nationalist* thinking. 'We have every reason', he wrote in *Die Zeit*

> to come to some decision concerning the terms 'nationalism' and 'nationalist'. Since Germany's surrender the public meaning of these words has become exclusively and solely derogatory. Before the surrender, for twelve years the same words had had an unquestionably positive meaning in official propaganda. This is part of the absolutely necessary process of reassessing values that is in progress in Germany. But what is at issue here is less the words than the values.[26]

His quarrel was not with the liberal nationalism of the early nineteenth century, but with 'imperialist nationalism' of a later age. This variant of nationalism, according to Friedlaender, was

> unscrupulous national egoism that, as the example of Nazism has shown, can lead to unprecedented crimes, can precipitate a world war. This nationalism has lost the moderation which grants all peoples an *equal* right to existence, to freedom and dignity.

In Friedlaender's opinion, 'justified anti-nationalism' must not be allowed to

---

24. Gerhard Ritter to Erwin Eckert, 8 July 1946, in K. Schwabe and R. Reichardt (eds) *Gerhard Ritter: Ein politischer Historiker in seinen Briefen* (Boppard, 1984), p. 414.

25. Gerhard Ritter to Hellmuth Ritter, 23 June 1947, in ibid., p. 430.

26. E. Friedlaender, 'Nationalismus, 6 February 1947', in N. Frei and F. Friedlaender (eds) *Ernst Friedlaender: Klärung für Deutschland: Leitartikel in der ZEIT 1946–1950* (Munich and Vienna, 1982), p. 35.

become an anti-nationalism that attacks the nation and the people instead
of nationalism. And that is why it is absolutely necessary to draw a clear,
universally comprehensible dividing line between the 'national' and the
nationalistic, which allows us to say yes to the one, and no to the other.
Without it, we are groping in the dark, not only with respect to our
thinking and values, but also in our practical politics.[27]

Friedlaender's conclusion was a plea for the 'national', or, as it was
often put later, for a 'healthy' national consciousness:

> Today, in any case, when the subject of debate is nationalism as it relates
> to the politics of power, which can clearly be distinguished from the
> 'national' without any risk to the spiritual health of the people, there is no
> cause to throw the national overboard. We have no reason to agree with
> a minority among us which, tormented by national fear of itself and
> national self-hatred, would prefer to let Germany disappear, which would
> agree to Germany being divided up for the benefit of all its
> neighbours...After all, it is neither good nor healthy if in our present state
> of emergency organisation we are to be 'undernourished' in terms not
> only of physiological, but also of national calories. For this, too, produces
> symptoms of deficiency. These can give rise to mental cramps, which are
> the opposite of the re-education we are working for.[28]

This determined and positive but differentiated attitude towards nationalism made Friedlaender almost an outsider in post-war Germany.

As far as I can see, contemporaries' assessments of nationalism and
national thinking have not moderated over time. In his book on the
German question published in 1948 Gerhard Ritter reflected upon
'German neo-nationalism'.[29] He used the same long chapter, almost
unchanged, in the revised second edition of the book, which appeared
in 1962.[30] In this chapter Ritter continued the story of German nationalism into the time of the Weimar Republic. In 1948, however,
he had avoided discussing the problem of nationalism in post-war Germany. But at that time his judgement on nationalism was unequivocal.
Nationalism, wrote Ritter,

> is never and nowhere the expression of a peaceful and secure national
> consciousness. On the contrary, it arises out of a national consciousness
> that is touchy, somehow startled, and driven to worry or indignation. The

27. Ibid., p. 36.
28. Ibid., p. 37.
29. G. Ritter, *Europa und die deutsche Frage: Betrachtungen über die geschichtliche Eigenart des deutschen Staatsdenkens* (Munich, 1948), pp. 55–150.
30. Ritter, *Das deutsche Problem: Grundfragen deutschen Staatslebens gestern und heute* (Munich, 1962), pp. 55–146.

more shrilly it expresses itself, the more likely it is that in the final analysis there is an inner insecurity behind it.[31]

In both editions of his book Ritter defines nationalism as 'a political national consciousness, exaggerated in its bias, and raised to the level of presumption'.[32] But we have already suggested that Ritter's attitude towards nationalism was fundamentally ambivalent. In his expanded 'conclusion' of 1962, he writes: 'Because it was misused for the most dreadful acts of violence, nationalism has rightly fallen into disrepute.' He then continues:

> But was it not also the symptom of a strong, unbroken vitality? If this desire for recognition had been directed towards sensible goals, it need not have had a destructive effect.[33]

Among the early Federal Republic's leading politicians, the Christian Democratic (CDU) Chancellor, Konrad Adenauer, often addressed the problem of nationalism. In most cases, official visits to other European countries provided the occasion for his comments. Thus early in 1949 in Berne, Adenauer expressed the opinion that there were only relatively few 'supporters of nationalism of the type propagated by Hitler' in Germany. However, he believed that a reawakening of national feeling was noticeable in the western half of the divided country. On this occasion Adenauer used the same argument which Gerhard Ritter had put forward in 1946:[34] 'One can only welcome the reawakening of a healthy national feeling that does not stray from the right paths, for a people that no longer possesses a national feeling has lost itself.'[35] One year later, when the political status of the Saar district was at issue,[36] Adenauer feared the revival of nationalist movements among the German people.[37] When 'one section of the Germans' resisted the Schuman Plan which was to be the first important step towards closer economic union in Europe Adenauer interpreted this in 1951 as evidence of the difficulty 'of liberating this section of the Germans from the nationalistic thinking they have so far

31. Ritter, *Europa und die deutsche Frage*, pp. 55–6.
32. Ibid., p. 55.
33. Ritter, 'Schlußbetrachtung: Hitler und das Deutschland von heute', in Ritter, *Das deutsche Problem*, p. 204.
34. See above, p. 161.
35. Speech in Berne, 23 March 1949, in K. Adenauer, *Erinnerungen 1945–1953*, vol. 1 (Stuttgart, 1965, 2nd edn, 1973), p. 188.
36. The Saar district was occupied by the French who gave it a special status within their zone of occupation. French policy aimed at separating it from the rest of Germany.
37. Adenauer, *Erinnerungen*, vol. 1, p. 307.
38. Ibid., p. 467.

been pursuing'.[38] In the same year, 1951, he declared on a visit to London that 'the overwhelming majority of the German people have outgrown nationalism'.[39] In his memoirs Adenauer unequivocally called nationalism the 'cancerous sore of Europe',[40] and in April 1958 he described himself to a high-ranking Soviet visitor as 'a pronounced opponent of nationalism'.[41] In 1955 he agreed with the President of the European Union that the Germans had to come to see the desired reunification of their country as a pan-European and not as a national problem. A German 'nationalism of reunification' would result in the political isolation of Germany in Europe.[42]

Adenauer, an opponent of Hitler and co-founder of the conservative CDU, was only too well aware that any signs of a new German nationalism would cause deep anxiety abroad. Nationalist movements in the new Federal Republic, which was more or less the creation of the Western powers, would be observed with suspicion, and impede the consolidation of the young state. It is true that after 1945 the German policy of the Allies, and their public opinion at home, long reflected a deep mistrust of Germany. A memorandum which the British foreign secretary Anthony Eden transmitted to his colleagues in the War Cabinet at the beginning of 1945 is entirely typical of the attitude of the Allies. In this 'study of the German mentality and its possible development in the future',[43] the danger of a revival of National Socialism after the foreseeable defeat of Germany was rated as slight – unlike the threat of a continuing German nationalism. 'It would be superficial to regard Hitlerism as likely to remain a menace of the same order as German nationalism and German militarism. These two evils may unite again under a new totalitarian cloak.'[44] The memorandum continued on a warning note:

> The mere resentment of defeat and disarmament, quite apart from the final political, economic and territorial settlement imposed upon her, will be enough no doubt to inflame nationalist and militarist feelings in Germany... It is, however, a fact, simple and unoriginal but inescapable, that Germany's mental reaction to defeat will be determined, in the long run, not by the mere fact of defeat, but by the settlement it leads to. It will be determined most of all by the territorial settlement, and by such

39. Ibid., p. 501.
40. Ibid., p. 425.
41. Adenauer, *Erinnerungen 1955–1959*, vol. 3 (Stuttgart, 1967), p. 383.
42. Ibid., p. 252.
43. Thus Anthony Eden in his introductory remark (Public Record Office, London, FO 371/46791/C 150, W. P. (45) 18: German Reactions to Defeat, p. 1).
44. Ibid., p. 5.

possible accompanying burdens as the wholesale transfer of populations from ceded areas.

The memorandum argued that Germany's territorial losses and the accompanying expulsions of Germans from the areas where they had lived for centuries would place a heavy burden on any post-war European order from the start.

> To exacerbate Germany's feelings of nationalism and militarism by inflicting on her very extensive territorial losses, which she will regard as unjust and intolerable and to which she will never become resigned, would gravely diminish any hope there may be that Germany might eventually become reconciled to the settlement of Europe, and cooperate in its maintenance.[45]

Sir Robert Vansittart's well-known view that there was a deep-seated flaw in the German 'national character' seems to have been widely held right across the political spectrum in wartime Britain and immediately after the close of hostilities in the European theatre of war.[46] It undoubtedly influenced much of Britain's policy-making towards occupied Germany and may help to explain British mistrust of early anti-fascist and democratic associations in post-war Germany. Any political activities by Germans encountered the British suspicion that under the guise of 'democratic' groupings some potent nationalist movement might re-emerge and threaten the security of the occupying forces.[47] As the Labour leader and future British prime minister, Clement   Attlee, put it rather simplistically in the summer of 1944:

> It was an illusion to imagine that there was a normal Germany to which one could return. There had been no normal Germany for fifty years or more, except one governed by a centralised and militaristic machine.[48]

The historian A.J.P. Taylor was only expressing the mood of the time when he drew the following rather sweeping conclusion in his widely read book, published in July 1945, *The Course of German History*:

---

45. Ibid., p. 6.
46. A.M. Birke, 'Geschichtsauffassung und Deutschlandbild im Foreign Office Research Department', in B. J. Wendt (ed.) *Das britische Deutschlandbild im Wandel des 19. und 20. Jahrhunderts* (Bochum, 1984), pp. 171–97. H. Fromm, *Deutschland in der öffentlichen Kriegszieldiskussion Großbritanniens 1939–1945* (Frankfurt and Berne, 1982).
47. See A. Glees, *Exile Politics during the Second World War: The German Social Democrats in Britain* (Oxford, 1982), esp. pp. 124–44. F. Pingel, 'Verborgener Nazismus unter demokratischem Gewand? – Ein Beitrag zum Deutschlandbild im Wandel (Britische Besatzungszone 1945/46)', in Wendt (ed.) *Das britische Deutschlandbild*, pp. 198–218.
48. Quoted in L. Kettenacker, 'Großbritannien und die zukünftige Kontrolle Deutschlands', in J. Foschepoth and R. Steininger (eds) *Die britische Deutschland- und Besatzungspolitik 1945–1949* (Paderborn, 1985), p. 37.

The history of the Germans is a history of extremes. It contains everything except moderation, and in the course of a thousand years the Germans have experienced everything except normality...One looks in vain in their history for a *juste milieu,* for common sense – the two qualities which have distinguished France and England. Nothing is normal in German history except violent oscillations.[49]

Thus it is hardly surprising that as an occupying power, Britain, for example, closely observed real or alleged manifestations of nationalism in post-war Germany. The mood of the German people and their political attitudes were attentively monitored. But on the whole, the information about nationalist activities which the Public Opinion Research Office collected, or which is contained in consular reports to the Military Government in Germany, is of limited use. It is impressionistic and often highly speculative, and suggests that there was no question of a survival or revival of German nationalism after the surrender. The Allies' fears in this respect, therefore, were exaggerated, perhaps even unfounded.

For example, a British intelligence report from Berlin, dated July 1945, contains the following statement:

The prevalent mental attitude, where it is not one of dumb indifference, is one of complete cynicism. They [the Germans] have learnt at last how disastrously wrong their own propaganda was.[50]

Three months later, little had changed in the attitude of the German people. 'With regard to politics', we read in a report from the end of October 1945,

there is still a general apathy among the mass of Germans. All four parties are by way of starting new drives to combat this, but they all admit that they have so far not touched the great masses of the nation.[51]

The Allies had expected that in occupying Germany they would have to contend with far more hostile acts by Germans against the occupying forces than in fact occurred. But at the end of 1945 the situation was summed up thus: 'We could not expect the Germans to be so

49. A.J.P. Taylor, *The Course of German History: A Survey of the Development of German History since 1815* (repr. London, 1976), p. 1.

50. Public Record Office, London [=PRO], FO 1005/1706: HQ British Troops Berlin, Intelligence Summary no. 1, 8 July 1945.

51. PRO, FO 1005/1727: HQ British Troops Berlin, Political Intelligence Report no. 15, 27 October 1945. The report refers to the newly founded political parties: the Social Democrats, the Liberals, the Christian Democrats and the Communists.

devoid of national feeling as to accept being occupied with com-
placency or even with resignation.'[52] The shock of Germany's collapse
and fear of an uncertain future together had the effect of paralysing the
German population.

Occasionally opinion polls, an instrument for the analysis of political
attitudes hitherto unknown in Germany and imported by the Anglo-
Saxon occupiers, produced unsettling results. In the summer of 1947 a
sample of 350 people in Hamburg was asked: 'Has the dictatorial
method of Government advantages over a democratic form?' More
than half of the people asked (57.5 per cent) replied in the affirmative,
with 19.1 per cent of the sample justifying their reply by saying that in
the present crisis, strict organisation and planning were necessary.[53] In
September of the same year, a British poll of 6,000 Germans of both
sexes produced a result which, from the point of view of the occupying powers, was even more depressing. The survey asked whether
National Socialism was a bad idea, or a good idea badly carried out,
with the result that about 50 per cent of those interviewed thought
that Nazism was a good idea badly carried out.[54]

The reliability and value of such opinion polls may be questioned,
especially as other observations from the British side contradict their
findings. Thus, for example, a consular report from Bremen sent to
the Political Division of the Military Government at the end of 1948
suggests that

> the Germans are beginning to gain confidence at least in their local
> democratic institutions…and feel that democracy cannot be imposed by
> dictatorial methods. It would be a mistake, even a contradiction to
> describe this tendency as nationalistic, though in an entirely different sense
> nationalism has always been strong in Bremen, and has been more vocal
> of late amongst the Right Wing parties…The press and responsible
> opinion has uttered frequent warning against nationalist temptations and
> there has been more than a hint that not only the USSR but even the
> Western allies…may have encouraged nationalist manifestations in support
> of their Machiavellian ends.[55]

52. PRO, FO 1005/1700: CCG (BE), Intelligence Review no. 1, 12 December
1945.

53. PRO, FO 1014/190: CCG (BE), Reaction Report for June 1947 from Information Control Hamburg.

54. PRO, FO 1056/130: Morale Report no. 111A. See also an American report of
September 1946 in A.J. Merritt and R.L. Merritt (eds) *Public Opinion in Occupied Germany: The OMGUS Surveys, 1945–1949* (Urbana, Ill., 1970), pp. 103–6.

55. PRO, FO 1049/1782: Political and General Report on Land Bremen for December Quarter 1948 to CCG (BE) Political Division, Berlin, p. 3.

However, just a few weeks later, a morale report by the Public Opinion Research Office pointed out that

> increasing anti-British sentiments and a revival of German nationalist feeling are reported on all sides, perhaps because it has become fashionable to recognize these symptoms which have, in fact, always been there. Such sentiments are now expressed with increasing confidence.[56]

II

How could the danger of a revival of aggressive nationalism in Germany be banished? How could a 'post-national' Germany be created – a Germany that, after the dreadful events of the period from 1933 to 1945, wanted to be accepted back into the family of nations? Looking back, the Bavarian politician Franz Josef Strauß, who was highly influential in shaping the history of the Federal Republic from the start, wrote: 'In 1945 and later...we asked ourselves: what is to happen now? Does this Germany have a future at all?'[57] The philosopher Karl Jaspers later reminded his readers of the major task which the Germans had faced after the end of the Third Reich:

> From 1945 the question was: will a German state now be born out of a change in political consciousness among statesmen and population? Or will it be an external order, without a source in the hearts and minds of the people, without a new political mentality?[58]

Many answers were given to this question in the immediate post-war period, especially by those Germans who gradually assumed political responsibility and, under the supervision of the occupying powers, attempted to lay the foundations for a democratic society in Germany. Although these answers differed in detail, they can in fact be reduced to a few guidelines which were intended to shape the future Germany. All sides in the Western zones, politicians as well as journalists, agreed that the unity of the German state should be preserved, that a federal constitution should be the objective, and that Germany's internal order should be based on the values of Western democracy. In its relations with its western neighbours Germany should aim for closer economic

56. PRO, FO 1056/131: CCG (BE), Public Opinion Research Office, German Morale Report no. 29, 1–31 January 1949, p. 1.
57. F. J. Strauß, *Die Erinnerungen* (Berlin, 1989), p. 60.
58. Jaspers, *Wohin treibt die Bundesrepublik?*, p. 67.

and political co-operation. In fact, these ideas had long been discussed by the Anglo-Saxon powers. They were now accepted in more or less modified form by the Germans. For example, the British Foreign Office memorandum of early 1945 cited above had predicted a revival of particularist feelings, which favoured a federal structure for Germany. It had also mentioned the incorporation of Germany into a new European order.[59]

The ideas put forward by the Americans and the British, later joined, only reluctantly, by the French, fell on fertile soil among the Germans after the surrender, if only because they seemed to point a way to the future and to provide a guarantee against the return of nationalism. The 'right to unity', much cited in internal German debates after 1945, was explicitly described as a desire that had nothing to do with nationalism, but a great deal to do with human rights. 'I reject any suggestion that this legal claim is nationalistic', wrote the journalist Ernst Friedlaender in 1947. 'Nationalism is nothing but unjustified national egoism. Someone who has been robbed and does not relinquish his property is no more an egoist than we are nationalists because we do not give up the right to our homeland.'[60] In his memoirs, the liberal politician Reinhold Maier reported on the beginnings of political life in Württemberg, in which he was actively involved. He remembered that some of his speeches had been received in silence. 'But when I came to the part about the German fatherland, the faces of my listeners lightened for a minute, and their workmen's hands relaxed into softer or louder applause.'[61]

Although Maier was very much a regional politician, he still clung to German unity. At the same time, however, he advocated a federal Germany, in which 'powerful *Bundesländer* would be members of a united Germany'.[62] Wilhelm Röpke wanted to go further than Maier. He suggested that the rebuilding of the state in Germany should be preceded by decentralisation, to be achieved by the dissolution of the Bismarckian Empire and the weakening of Prussia. He called for the buried tradition of the old German states to be resuscitated:

> That means that the Rhineland, Westphalia, Hanover, Hesse,
> Schleswig-Holstein, and the rest, must acquire the rank of independent

59. PRO, FO 371/46791/C 150, W.P. (45) 18: German Reactions to Defeat, p. 2 and p. 6.

60. E. Friedlaender, 'Der deutsche Standpunkt, 27 February 1947,' in Frei and Friedlaender (eds) *Ernst Friedlaender*, p. 98.

61. R. Maier, *Ein Grundstein wird gelegt. Die Jahre 1945–1947* (Tübingen, 1964), pp. 212–13.

62. Ibid., p. 162.

German States...This is the very cure that corresponds to our detailed diagnosis of the German malady. Germany must regain her character of a 'nation of nations', and return to the good traditions from which, three generations ago, she departed to her undoing.[63]

Germany's recovery, he claimed, depended essentially

on this *Einheitsdeutscher* – who is simply the *Bismarckdeutscher* with his dangerous mentality – giving place once more to the true type of the Bavarian, Hanoverian, Rhinelander, or Württemberger.[64]

Röpke believed that conditions in Germany favoured confederalism, for

Munich, thank Heaven, is still Bavarian, Hamburg is still itself, Cologne is still Rhenish, and we can only congratulate ourselves if they are determined to remain so.[65]

In Röpke's view the aim of Germany's political transformation was 'the constitution of a genuine German *confederation*'.[66]

Unlike Röpke, however, the new political parties in their first statements unequivocally advocated a federal rather than a confederal structure for the new German state. The platform of the Christian Democratic Party in the Rhineland and in Westphalia, published in September 1945, states simply: 'The form of state appropriate to the German people is the *Reich* as a federal state.'[67] In 1946 the Bavarian Christian-Social Union called for a political structure of Germany 'on a federal basis'.[68] The Social Democrats wanted the same thing:

The German republic of the future should be built on *Länder*, which do not see their highest purpose in their own existence, but which regard themselves only as the building blocks of a higher national order.[69]

The Liberals, finally, in February 1946 were working with guidelines which stated:

This state is to be built upon the broadest foundations, starting from the bottom. At the lowest level the *Gemeinden* are to administer their own affairs independently; above them the *Kreise* should do the same; and, at a

63. Röpke, *The German Question*, p. 186.
64. Ibid., p. 190.
65. Ibid.
66. Ibid., p. 207.
67. Printed in T. Stammen (ed.) *Einigkeit und Recht und Freiheit: Westdeutsche Innenpolitik 1945–1955* (Munich, 1965), p. 87.
68 Ibid., p. 99. See also Strauß, *Erinnerungen*, p. 100.
69. Political Guidelines of the SPD, May 1946, in Stammen (ed.) *Einigkeit*, p. 124. Also C. Schmid, *Erinnerungen* (Berne, 1979), p. 293.

higher level, the *Länder*. The limits of autonomy are to be set by the *Reich*. The *Reich* alone directs and makes policy.[70]

In March 1946 Reinhold Maier, who in the meantime had become minister president of Württemberg-Baden, explained: 'We know what we are aiming for – namely, a federation with considerable powers for the centre, but without an emasculation of the *Länder*.[71] Attempts by conservative circles in Bavaria to turn their *Land* into an autonomous state and to return to a constitutional monarchy under the House of Wittelsbach remained a rather curious episode without wider significance.[72] Opinion polls conducted in 1947 and 1948 revealed that the overwhelming majority of Germans in the Western occupation zones wanted a unified state on a federal basis.[73]

Just as they agreed on the organisation of Germany as a federal state, the major parties and their leading representatives were also largely unanimous on Germany's commitment to Europe after 1945. It is well known that for Konrad Adenauer, Germany's integration into the West was the highest priority. After his first visit to Bonn in November 1949, the US secretary of state Dean Acheson summed up his impressions of Adenauer thus:

> I was struck by the imagination and wisdom of his approach. His great concern was to integrate Germany completely into Western Europe. Indeed, he gave this end priority over reunification of unhappily divided Germany.[74]

Four years earlier, in October 1945, Adenauer had already spoken out in favour of creating a German federal state to consist of the Western occupation zones. The economy of the West German area, he suggested, should be closely linked with those of France and Belgium, 'in order to create common economic interests'.[75] Adenauer also wanted the Netherlands, Luxemburg, and if possible, Britain, to be involved in this association.[76] Thus the origins of the later European Coal and

70. Stammen (ed.) *Einigkeit*, p. 108.
71. Quoted in K.-J. Matz, *Reinhold Maier (1889–1971: Eine politische Biographie* (Düsseldorf, 1989), p. 309.
72. See Walter Dorn's notes of February 1946: W. Dorn, *Inspektionsreisen in der US-Zone: Notizen, Denkschriften und Erinnerungen aus dem Nachlaß*, ed. L. Niethammer (Stuttgart, 1973). Also Strauß, *Erinnerungen*, pp. 99–100.
73. E. Noelle and E.P. Neumann, *Jahrbuch der öffentlichen Meinung 1947–1955* (Allensbach, 1975 3rd edn), p. 145.
74. D. Acheson, *Present at the Creation: My Years in the State Department* (London, 1969), p. 340.
75. Adenauer, *Erinnerungen 1945–1953*, vol. 1, p. 35.
76. Enclosure with a letter by Adenauer to the Lord Mayor of Duisburg, 31 October 1945, in H.P. Mensing (ed.) *Adenauer: Briefe 1945–1947* (Berlin, 1983), p. 130.

Steel Community and the European Common Market, which Adenauer was to help found, are already visible here in 1945.

The leader of the other major party in post-war Germany, Kurt Schumacher of the SPD, also strongly supported German integration into Europe. The SPD's programme of 5 October 1945, which was largely composed by Schumacher, states that the SPD

> is aware that in order to achieve vital European economic unity both Germany and the world need to create adequate political forms. As Montesquieu once said: 'Europe is simply a nation which is made up of several nations.'[77]

In June 1946 Schumacher wrote:

> Social democracy does not want a new, integral Germany as a new nationalism. It wants to see Germany as part of a new European confederation from the start…Today something that has always been true has become clear, namely that national and international are not opposites…The greatest enemy of the nation is not the international idea, but nationalism.[78]

A few weeks previously Schumacher had stated:

> A new Germany must not be a nationalistic Germany. It must fit into the framework of European needs right from the start. As far as we are concerned, we Germans are prepared to give up several potential aspects of future sovereignty in favour of this new Europe. But we ask the same of the other European countries.[79]

As a public opinion poll held by the British Military Government in April 1948, for example, showed, the German people strongly supported a policy of European integration.[80]

III

The rejection of national categories by most Germans after the turning-point of 1945, the distance they wanted to keep to such matters

77. Stammen (ed.) *Einigkeit*, p. 117.

78. K. Schumacher, 'Die Sozialdemokratie im Kampf (June 1946)', in Schumacher, *Nach dem Zusammenbruch. Gedanken über Demokratie und Sozialismus* (Hamburg, 1948), p. 162.

79. Schumacher, 'Deutschland braucht den Sozialismus (March 1946)', in ibid., pp. 133–4.

80. PRO, FO 1012/818, CCG (BE), Public Opinion Research Office, Information and Statistics, Report no. 7: German Views on Marshall Plan, United Nations, Western Union and Bizonia, 23 June 1948, p. 1.

and the aversion they felt for them are vividly reflected in their attitudes towards national symbols. The choice of a 'national anthem' after the establishment of the Federal Republic is a graphic example. The bitter realisation that their national feelings had been misused by a criminal regime profoundly affected the national consciousness of the Germans. After 1945 they could no longer have a naive national feeling such as that which had been characteristic of the nineteenth century. An uncomplicated relationship with nationalism was no longer possible for them. It has recently been claimed that the lack of a well-developed German national feeling is 'an anomaly requiring explanation' in a European context.[81] Undoubtedly, recent German history and the thorough discreditation of national values since the collapse of the Third Reich provide some of the explanation.

Insecurity about national symbols, discontinuities in their use, and doubts about their general validity are, in fact, nothing new in the history of Germany since the creation of a national state in 1871.[82] After the experience of National Socialism, however, the national symbols which had been in general use until then had become almost devoid of any meaning. The creation of new symbols and their acceptance by the German people was therefore a protracted process. When the Federal Republic of Germany was founded in 1949, agreement was most easily reached about a flag for the new state. Without a great deal of discussion in the Parliamentary Council, the black, red and gold flag of the 1848–9 revolution and the Weimar Republic was accepted as the *Bundesflagge* (Art. 22 of the Basic Law). In October 1949 the constitution of the other German state created out of the ruins of the Third Reich declared that black, red and gold were also the 'colours of the German Democratic Republic'. Since the wars of liberation against Napoleon in the early nineteenth century these colours had symbolised the democratic tradition in German history.

The choice of a national anthem for the Federal Republic, a tradition which the politicians wanted to retain, proved to be much more difficult.[83] In the process, the fact that the German state had not had an official national anthem at all until 1922 was forgotten. After Bismarck established the Reich the main contenders were 'The Watch on

81. Thus H. Mommsen, 'Nationalismus und Nationalstaatsgedanke in Deutschland', *Journal Geschichte* 6 (1990), p. 47.

82. See the pioneering study by T. Schieder, *Das Deutsche Kaiserreich von 1871 als Nationalstaat* (Cologne and Opladen, 1961). Also E. Fehrenbach, 'Über die Bedeutung der politischen Symbole im Nationalstaat', *Historische Zeitschrift* 213 (1971), pp. 296–357.

83. For the long debate on a German national day see H. Hattenhauer, *Deutsche Nationalsymbole: Zeichen und Bedeutung* (Munich, 1984), pp. 129–35.

the Rhine' ('*Die Wacht am Rhein*'), and the Prussian royal anthem, which had been adopted as the imperial anthem, '*Heil Dir im Siegerkranz*', sung to the same tune as 'God save the Queen'. Not until the end of the nineteenth century did Hoffmann von Fallersleben's 'Song of Germany', set to a melody by Joseph Haydn, become popular.[84] And not until 1922, that is under the Weimar Republic, was the 'Song of Germany' (*Deutschlandlied*) declared the official German national anthem by the President of the Reich, Friedrich Ebert.[85] During the Third Reich, it was largely discredited by the fact that it was mostly sung together with the *Horst-Wessel-Lied*, the party song of the National Socialists. In the Control Council Law no. 154 of July 1945 the Allies prohibited the singing not only of Nazi songs but also of 'German anthems' in general, in order 'to prevent...the continuation and revival of military instruction'.[86]

At the end of 1949, as Allied policy for Germany changed, this prohibition was lifted and discussion of the problem of a German national anthem began almost immediately in the new Federal Republic. After all, it was argued, the Federal Republic was one state among other states, all of which clung to their national symbols, and the new German state could not simply ignore that. In September 1951 an opinion poll was held in the Federal Republic of Germany, and 73 per cent of those asked were in favour of the reintroduction of the 'Song of Germany' as a national anthem; 30 per cent of them voted for the third verse, which begins with the lines 'Unity and Right and Freedom/For the German Fatherland', whereas only 25 per cent favoured the better-known first verse ('*Deutschland, Deutschland über alles*').[87] Only a year earlier there had been a scandal when Adenauer, the Federal Chancellor, had called for the third verse of the 'Song of Germany' to be sung at the end of a large political meeting in Berlin.

84. Schieder, *Das Deutsche Kaiserreich, p. 75.*

85. H. Tümmler, '*Deutschland, Deutschland über alles*': Zur Geschichte und Problematik unserer Nationalhymne (Cologne and Vienna, 1979). Hattenhauer, *Nationalsymbole*, pp. 59–61. U. Mader, 'Wie das "Deutschlandlied" 1922 Nationalhymne wurde', *Zeitschrift für Geschichtswissenschaft* 38 (1990), pp. 1,088–100. According to Mader the British government played a role when the decision on the German national anthem was made. In June 1920 it had asked the German government 'what the German national anthem was at the present time'. The foreign minister Walter Simons suggested in the *Reichstag* 'to give a simple and honest answer to the British government: at the moment the German people has no national anthem'. He then gave a number of reasons to explain this curious fact (p. 1,091).

86. See O. Busch, *125 Jahre – 'Deutschland, Deutschland über alles'* (Munich, 1967), p. 26.

87. Noelle and Neumann, *Jahrbuch,* p. 159.

On that occasion the Western Commandants in Berlin had pointedly remained seated, while prominent Social Democratic politicians had left the assembly hall.[88] In the public debate of 1951 and 1952, a national anthem was often declared superfluous, and frequent calls were made for it to be replaced by a supranational European anthem.[89] The Federal President at the time, Theodor Heuss, publicly declared himself against using even the third verse of the old 'Song of Germany' as a national anthem because in his opinion 'the profound turning-point in the history of our people and our state calls for new symbols'. He wanted to avoid restoring nineteenth-century political ideas and movements.[90]

But from 1950 on it was clear that the majority of the West German people saw the third verse of the 'Song of Germany' as their national anthem.[91] Theodor Heuss's attempts to popularise a completely new German anthem had had little success. Against this background Konrad Adenauer finally prevailed against Heuss's misgivings. As the result of an exchange of correspondence between Adenauer and Heuss in April and May 1952, published in the Federal Government's official Bulletin, the third verse of the 'Song of Germany' was accepted as the national anthem of the Federal Republic of Germany. Some contemporaries saw this – perhaps correctly – as the symptom of an unintended, and fundamentally undesired, national restoration. But the rather bureaucratic and unsentimental way in which a decision had been arrived at about the necessity for, and opportunity to introduce, an official national anthem, can equally be seen as something else. It can be seen as a symptom of the political culture and mentality of a German people that had emerged, purified, from the excesses of nationalism.

SUGGESTIONS FOR FURTHER READING

M. Balfour, *West Germany: A Contemporary History* (London, 1982).
D. Botting, *In the Ruins of the Reich* (London, 1985).

88. M. Overesch, 'Grenzen der Erneuerung: Die bundesdeutsche Nationalhymne', *Journal Geschichte* 1 (1988), p. 12. Tümmler, '*Deutschland*', p. 17.

89. Overesch, 'Grenzen der Erneuerung', p. 14.

90. Heuss to Adenauer, 2 May 1952, in *Bulletin des Presse- und Informationsamtes der Bundesregierung* 51/6 May 1952, p. 537.

91. Overesch, 'Grenzen der Erneuerung', pp. 16–17.

R. Dahrendorf, *Society and Democracy in Germany* (London, 1968).

R. Ebsworth, *Restoring Democracy in Germany: The British Contribution* (London, 1960).

A. Hearnden (ed.) *The British in Germany: Educational Reconstruction after 1945* (London, 1978).

L.E. Jones and K. Jarausch (eds) *In Search of a Liberal Germany: Studies in the History of German Liberalism from 1789 to the Present* (New York, Oxford and Munich, 1990).

A. Mann, *Comeback: Germany 1945-1952* (London, 1980).

B. Marshall, *The Origins of Post-War German Politics* (London, 1988).

T. Sharp, *The Wartime Alliance and the Zonal Division of Germany* (Oxford, 1975).

I.D. Turner (ed.) *Reconstruction in Post-War Germany: British Occupation Policy and the Western Zones, 1945–1955* (Oxford, 1989).

H.A. Turner, *The Two Germanies since 1945* (New Haven, Conn., 1987)

R. Willett, *The Americanisation of Germany, 1945–1949* (London, 1989).

CHAPTER TEN

Nation, state and political culture in divided Germany 1945–90

Mary Fulbrook

The excesses of German nationalism under Adolf Hitler achieved the destruction of the German Reich: the severance of the recently united Austria (since 1938), the loss of eastern territories of Prussia to Poland and the Soviet Union, and the division of what remained into two separate states, divided from one another by an almost impermeable 'Iron Curtain' which also served to divide the post-war world. With the expulsion of millions of ethnic Germans from their former homes in the east, and the imposition of radically new political systems and ideologies in the newly created states, the chances for the long-term success of post-war arrangements might at first sight have seemed slim. Yet for over forty years the reduction and division of Germany appeared to have provided the basis for an almost unprecedented period of political stability in central Europe: surviving longer than the Weimar Republic and the Third Reich put together, the two Germanies developed into model instances of their respective socio-political types. It took major upheavals originating elsewhere in the eastern Europe of the later 1980s to inaugurate a revolution in East Germany which finally brought down the Communist regime and placed the issue of German unity back on the serious political agenda in 1989–90.

What role did perceptions or new definitions of national identity play in the political dynamics of the two Germanies? How far did the imposition of new political forms actually serve to transform patterns of political culture among Germans, East and West? And what have been the implications of changing patterns of political culture for the relative stability of the two Germanies over forty years, and for the dramatic developments of 1989–90, which have, with astonishing speed, sealed the effective end of the post-war period?

'NATIONAL IDENTITIES' IN A DIVIDED NATION

The issue of identity has plagued post-war Germans, East and West. Neither state, at the time of foundation, was considered to be permanent; there was therefore the outstanding question of the survival of a transcending German nation, which would ultimately at some time be reunified. On the other hand, both states – perhaps the West more than the East – did in fact demote national unity in favour of integration and stabilisation in their respective blocs. Thus new forms of 'national myth' had to be developed, which both retained the links with the past – representing the present as the only legitimate successor state – and yet defined the particular part of the divided present in distinctive terms, to legitimise the partial state as representative of the whole. This process was further confused by issues concerning the immediate Nazi past: the explanation of its location in the longer sweep of German history, the degrees of responsibility and guilt for the Holocaust, the extent to which the successor states had made clean breaks with the discredited past, or were burdened by continuities or inadequate overcoming and mastering of the past. To some extent, both Germanies had difficulty with developing new forms of national pride precisely because of the Third Reich, and sought different paths of escape from this problem: whether through attempted submersion of German nationalism in wider western European integration (in the West), or by historical simplification and disavowal of responsibility (in the East).

Such processes of attempted legitimation and self-definition took place under very different political constraints and within different social and intellectual contexts in each of the two Germanies. In the German Democratic Republic (GDR), views of the past and present were very much state-sponsored (or at least self- and state-censored) varying with the degrees of relative liberalisation at different times in the GDR's history. In the Federal Republic of Germany (FRG), debate has been much freer, a greater diversity of views more evident, and questions of national identity have been hotly contested political terrain.

In the FRG, during the 1950s there was a degree of 'collective amnesia', combined with widespread efforts to escape a compromised past by seeking submergence in a transcendent, European identity. From the early 1960s interpretations of German history took on a particularly heated and political significance. From the Fischer controversy over German responsibility for the First World War onwards, the West German historical profession has been characterised by considerable diversity and sharply stated differences of approach. 'New orthodoxies' in such fields as social history, the history of everyday life, and feminist history have arisen to challenge previously dominant approaches. There has also been a proliferation of interest in regional and local history, which has spread beyond the bounds of the historical profession as lay members of history workshops have explored forgotten aspects of the immediate environment.

The political significance of historical interpretations in West Germany was revealed to an extraordinary degree in the so-called *Historikerstreit* (dispute among the historians) of the mid- and later 1980s. Simplifying what has been an extremely muddy debate, characterised by vitriolic accusations, misquotations and misrepresentations, one may broadly summarise the essential underlying thrust as follows. A number of largely conservative historians sought to relativise the crimes of the Nazi past by attempting to locate them within a wider context. In part this was a context of comparison with other evils, arguing that as Germans were not uniquely evil, therefore they had no need to be uniquely ashamed of their national identity. In part, Nazi acts were seen as responses to the crimes of others, as in Ernst Nolte's arguments linking Hitler's policies to Stalin's crimes. In response, a range of critics of this new conservative revisionism sought to show how little supporting evidence there was for many of the (frequently rather vaguely phrased) hypotheses, and also what were the political and moral implications of these new ways of whitewashing, justifying or relativising the past.[1] There was a close connection between this debate – carried out not only in learned journals and books, but also in the national press and public debate – and the new conservatism of West Germany under Chancellor Kohl, given heightened significance in the run-up to the 1987 elections. We shall turn to the question of the impact or popular importance of national identity in a moment.

In rather different ways, the role of history and historical consciousness had political significance in the GDR too. In particular, a twofold process can be observed in the period after *Ostpolitik* (the policy of seeking agreements with the GDR and other Eastern European states pursued by the FRG). On the one hand, there was a conscious effort

---

1. For balanced introductions to the debates in English see R.J. Evans, *In Hitler's Shadow: West German Historians and the Attempt to Escape from the Nazi Past* (London, 1989); C. Maier, *The Unmasterable Past: History, Holocaust and German National Identity* (Cambridge, Mass, 1988); and the section on the *Historikerstreit* in *German History*, 6/1 (1988). For a flavour of biased political diatribe masquerading as 'academic' argument, from a right-wing point of view, see D. Bark and D. Gress, *A History of West Germany*, vol. 2, *Democracy and its Discontents* (Oxford, 1989), pp. 415–44.

in the early years of the Honecker regime to establish a form of cultural *Abgrenzung* (demarcation), separating a distinctive GDR identity from the wider German identity which would underline common links with the West. This was essentially an attempt at a psychological and cultural distancing from the West at a time when physical contacts and communications between the two states had been made easier. Thus, in the 1974 revision of the GDR constitution, references to 'German' were replaced wherever possible by 'GDR'. (Some curious anomalies were allowed to remain, such as the rather startling *Deutsche Reichsbahn* on the somewhat geriatric East German trains.) On the other hand, particularly from the late 1970s and early 1980s, there was a marked change in official GDR views of German history. The *whole* of German history was now terrain to be appropriated by the GDR, with a distinction being made between 'traditions' and 'historical legacies' or 'inheritances' (*Tradition* and *Erbe*), such that only certain aspects were viewed as 'progressive' and to be built upon. The resurrection or re-evaluation of previously demoted historical figures – Luther, Frederick the Great, Bismarck – and of phases and elements of German history (notably that of Prussia), provided evidence of a new attempt to anchor the German people in a form of nationalist legitimacy or pride in their national identity. This carried with it the risk of emphasising a common German-ness with the West – particularly when parallel exhibitions and celebrations (for example, of Berlin and of Luther) were mounted in competition over common anniversaries.[2]

Officially in the 1950s and 1960s both states were formally committed to reunification. The FRG, in the Hallstein Doctrine, refused even to recognise the legitimacy of a separate state in what it continued to call 'the Zone'. After *Ostpolitik* there was essentially agreement to differ. The GDR adopted a class theory of the nation which argued for the development of two different nations in the two Germanies, while the FRG view was that there were 'two German states in one German nation'. Notwithstanding official views, it is clear that the relationship between the two Germanies was quite distinctive. The GDR recognised the value and importance of its special relationship with its richer twin, despite its assertions of separateness, while the FRG increasingly paid only (rather embarrassed) lip-service to the notion of re-unification. Nor were the dynamics of the relationship between the two Germanies always just a mirror of those between the two super-powers, as the rapprochement between the two Germanies

2. I have discussed these issues at greater length in M. Fulbrook, 'From *Volksgemeinschaft* to divided nation', *Historical Research* 62/148 (1989), pp. 193–213, where further references can be obtained.

in the early to mid-1980s at a time of increased tension between the two super-powers illustrates. Whatever the debates over partial identities, some concept of a wider whole and common bonds remained clearly alive – even with Erich Honecker when he returned in 1987 to visit his homeland in the Saar.

Thus in neither Germany, it may be suggested, was there an entirely successful resolution of the problem of promoting a partial national identity as well as sustaining wider notions of being 'German'. Let us now turn to the issue of whether, in practice, the two Germanies had in fact been developing rather distinctive profiles of popular political culture, whatever the official views of national identity.

DIVERGING PATTERNS OF POLITICAL CULTURE

More important than official views or public debates in shaping popular patterns of political orientation have been the actual political structures of the two Germanies in the period 1949 to 1989. Living in different environments, subjected to different pressures and constraints, perceiving different opportunities and harbouring different aspirations, people in the two Germanies *did* in fact develop rather different sorts of political culture in the period up to 1989. There might be some common German identity in theory; but in practice, what one can observe is an actual growing apart, which, if the division had been sustained for another couple of generations, might have made the two Germanies as 'foreign' to each other, or as convinced of their differentness and separate identities, as – over a very long historical period – do the German-speaking Swiss, or, over a more recent historical period, the Austrians. Not only outward appearances, so noticeable in November 1989 as East Germans streamed across to stare in amazement at the consumer goods of the West after the opening of the Berlin Wall (BMWs and Mercedes versus Trabants and Wartburgs, fashionable affluence versus blue jeans and denim or black leather jackets), but also modes of behaviour, attitudes, patterns of 'being-in-the-world', developed in different ways in the two Germanies.

Such differences are extraordinarily difficult to define, to identify and to explain. Here only a preliminary periodisation and characterisation can be suggested. Clearly, there is not even a simple, homogenous base-line from which the development of the differences

can be traced. In what were the Soviet and Western Zones of occupied Germany after the defeat of the Third Reich, there were a wide
range of political and cultural traditions and attitudes. These were further complicated by post-war population movements, and by the coming to terms with new post-war conditions. Whatever the degree to
which German society had or had not been permeated by any 'Nazi'
ideology (itself a difficult question to answer), it is clear that there was
only a minority of die-hard Nazis after 1945.[3] While a minority of
democratic Germans were politically active in the occupation period –
contributing to the foundation or resurrection of German political parties, the re-emergence of intellectual and cultural life – probably the
most prevalent preoccupation of a majority of Germans at this time
was sheer material survival, amid the ruins and rubble. (This view is
borne out by Peter Alter's chapter in this book.) A very widespread
attitude was a determination to keep out of politics, for fear of 'getting
one's fingers burnt'.[4]

After the foundation of the two Germanies, developing differences
can be observed. In the West, attitudes more favourable to democracy
correlated with the economic successes of Adenauer's Germany. While in
the mid-1950s, many Germans still assented to authoritarian, monarchist
and even pro-Hitler statements in opinion surveys (such as agreeing with
the assertion that Hitler would have been one of the greatest statesmen
ever, had it not been for the war), by the early 1960s more democratic
sentiments were expressed by greater proportions of the population. Political scientists at this time suggested there was an increasing pragmatic
support for democracy, with a sense – in contrast to the association of
economic chaos with democracy in the Weimar Republic – that now the
'system worked'. The later 1960s were characterised by increased polarisation of varieties of political culture, with hostility between an emerging
new left and what were viewed as materialistic, bourgeois *Spießbürger* who
refused to come to terms with the Nazi past. The importance of gener-
ational conflict, which in Germany took on a particularly acute and

3. On popular opinion in the Third Reich, see the by now classic studies by I.
Kershaw, *Popular Opinion and Political Dissent in the Third Reich* (Oxford, 1983) and *The
'Hitler Myth': Image and Reality in the Third Reich* (Oxford, 1987). For the immediate
post-war period see Chapter 9 by Peter Alter in this volume.
4. There is as yet no full account of the transformation of popular political opinions
after the war. These comments are based on a reading of the reports of the Military
Government (such as the OMGUS attitude surveys), the post-war press (such as the
Süddeutsche Zeitung, one of the first German newspapers to be licensed in the American
zone, the early editions of which provide interesting insights into the attempted reconstruction of democracy) and of a range of auto-biographical material located in the
Institut für Zeitgeschichte, Munich.

pointed form in confronting 'the sins of the fathers', should not be under-estimated. This polarisation in many ways continued through the 1970s and 1980s. However, extremist views – left and right – were held only by minority groups (even if these minorities committed acts of terrorism or staged demonstrations and agitated in ways affecting large numbers of people). The broadest spectrum was encompassed by citizens assenting to the procedures of parliamentary democracy, with a marked development of citizen participation in democratic processes compared with earlier decades.[5]

The pattern of development was different in the GDR. In the 1950s there were many who, in grumbling fashion, either tried to come to terms with their new circumstances or left for the economically more attractive West. Among the politically active, those whose commitments were at odds with the new hard-line Marxist-Leninist orthodoxy of SED leader Walter Ulbricht were systematically purged: already in the merger of the KPD and SPD to form the SED in 1946, then again after the SED became a 'party of a new type' (following Moscow) in 1948; then after the uprising of June 1953, and again in 1956 and 1958 there were purges of those whose more humanistic approaches (for a 'Third Way' form of democratic socialism, for example) were not in line with Ulbricht's fairly Stalinist views. In the 1960s, some political scientists – notably P.C. Ludz – perceived the development of more positive appoaches to the regime. Particularly under the New Economic System (1963–70), and with the new status accorded to technical experts, there was, on this view, the development of a more career-oriented achievement society, in which people sought to make the best of a seemingly unalterable situation. The building of the Berlin Wall, closing the last means of exit to the West, in 1961, obviously also contributed to this reorientation. While the economy was recentralised under Honecker from 1971, the focus on consumer satisfaction and the improvement of living conditions through social policy measures (for example, on housing, or maternity provisions), as well as the increased ease of contacts with the West after *Ostpolitik*, contributed to a continuation of this process of learning to live with the regime. Dissenting intellectuals, such as Havemann and Bahro, were relative easily isolated (through house arrest or exile

5. For a lucid summary of such developments see D. P. Conradt, *The German Polity* (London, 1986, 3rd edn); for earlier analyses, S. Verba, 'Germany: the remaking of political culture', in L. Pye and S. Verba, *Political Culture and Political Development* (Princeton, NJ, 1965). For intriguing details of opinions and attitudes on different issues over the years, see the volumes edited by E. Noelle and E.P. Neumann, *Jahrbücher der öffentlichen Meinung* (Allensbach: Verlag für Demoskopie, series).

to the West) and did not gain mass followings. Even the widespread protests about the expulsion of the subversive singer Wolf Biermann in 1976 had as a consequence little more than increased disaffection (and loss of party membership) for many writers, with increased numbers choosing to leave for the West in the later 1970s.[6]

What was particularly interesting about developments in the GDR was the formation of what Günter Gaus called a 'niche society', a retreatist culture characterised by a double life: conformity in public, authenticity in private. This retreatism was in many ways similar to the adaptations to living with an intolerant and intrusive regime which many people developed in Nazi Germany.[7] Clearly there were many differences between the degrees and modes of intolerance of the Third Reich and the GDR, as well as their intrinsic aims and ideals. The GDR was obviously far more humanitarian in at least some of its aspirations – towards emancipation and equality – even if in practice this seemed, under the circumstances of bureaucratic state socialism, to have entailed an unacceptable repression of liberty. Leaving aside these wider questions, what is of interest here is that the retreatist mode of political orientation actually helped to stabilise the East German regime over twenty-five years or so (from the early 1960s to the mid-1980s). Combined with the relative isolation of dissent – and the ease of exporting awkward individuals to the West – the prevalence of the retreatist mode, in combination with at least a minimum of material satisfaction, resulted in a degree of domestic political stability.

From the late 1970s, and especially from the mid-1980s, qualitatively new forms of political orientation developed, in ways which have yet to be fully explored by western analysts. An important turning-point came with the Church–state agreement of 1978, in which the role of the Church as the only autonomous social institution in the GDR was officially recognised. It now became possible, under the wing of the Church, for wide-ranging discussions to take place about alternatives to the prevailing orthodox views. In the early 1980s, the Protestant churches became important as an umbrella for the emergence and development of unofficial peace initiatives, which differed from the official, state-sponsored peace movement in that they op-

6. See for example P.C. Ludz, *The German Democratic Republic from the Sixties to the Seventies* (Harvard Centre for International Affairs, Occasional Paper no. 26, November 1970); R. Woods, *Opposition in the GDR under Honecker, 1971–1985* (London, 1986).

7. G. Gaus, *Wo Deutschland liegt* (Munich, 1986). I have developed at greater length a theory of the relationship between intrusive states and retreatist forms of political culture in my article 'The state and the transformation of political legitimacy in East and West Germany since 1945', *Comparative Studies in Society and History*, 29/2 (1987), pp. 211–44.

posed Warsaw Pact as well as NATO nuclear missiles. From the mid-1980s, these dissenting groups proliferated in two important respects. They became more numerous, and began to organise outside the protective framework of the Church, and they began to deal, in a specialised fashion, with an increasing range of issues, concerning themselves not only with peace, but also with human rights and environmental questions. These groups formed the background to the emergence, in the late summer of 1989, of new parties and organisations – notably the New Forum – which, for the first time in the history of East German dissent, sought official status and concerned themselves with the whole gamut of problems with which governments have to deal, including the reorganisation of the economy and the political system itself. On the evidence of some of these activists, who had been brought up in the authoritarian system designed to produce conformists, it was extremely difficult to learn how to be democratic, to speak and debate freely, to tolerate differences of opinion, and to pressurise for change in a peaceful manner. The role of the Protestant churches should not be underestimated in helping to shape the distinctive characteristics of secular dissent in the late 1980s.[8]

While recognising the crucial importance of such developments, it must be observed that such activities and orientations were characteristic of only a minority of East Germans. Private grumbling combined with public conformity remained the most predominant political orientation for most, even in the summer of 1989. We shall come back to developments in the revolutionary autumn in a moment.

THE IMPLICATIONS OF NATIONAL IDENTITY AND POLITICAL CULTURE FOR REGIME STABILITY AND CHANGE

Patterns of popular political culture are but one element among many in explaining stability and change in different types of regime. Popular support for a regime may not be as central to stability in practice as is often assumed. Political passivity and indifference may be as important

8. These developments have yet to be fully explored. My comments here are based on discussions with some of those involved, both among East German dissenters and Westerners who worked with them.

in making certain developments possible, as opposition may be in deflecting other developments. There is as yet no definitive interpretation of either the causes or consequences of patterns of political culture: frequently, cultural elements are taken as givens in any historical explanation. Here, some suggestions may be made concerning the location of the developments sketched above in a wider framework for interpreting the dynamics of the two Germanies in the various stages of their history.

Division and consolidation of the new regimes

First of all, it can be suggested that notions of a German nation transcending the divided states played very little role in political developments – and particularly the consolidation of division – in the early period. Even before the foundation of the two states, German politicians in the Soviet and Western Zones were cooperating with their respective occupying powers in the processes of socio-economic separation and eventually political division. (A particular example might be the Munich conference of German *Land* Prime Ministers in June 1947, when there was clearly no will to reach agreement among the Germans, or to compromise to a greater degree in the interests of unity than the respective occupying powers were prepared to do.) In the early 1950s Adenauer's determined policies of western integration took precedence over any prospect of unity, even when reunification was quite possibly negotiable in the spring of 1952. Although Adenauer's actions were certainly in line with the policies of the Western Allies, they were not determined by the latter; it was his own decision – supported by the Americans and British – not to take Stalin's first note seriously.[9] In June 1953 the West Germans were content merely to observe the East German uprising, rather than intervene to aid their East German brethren: again, stabilisation of the status quo was preferred to any riskier strategy. The same might be said of the Berlin crisis at the time of the building of the Berlin Wall in August 1961. National unity was effectively jettisoned by the West German political leadership in favour of the benefits brought by stability, economic growth, and incorporation in the western part of a divided world. In the East, it might be said that there was less leeway for independent

9. See particularly R. Steininger, 'Germany after 1945: divided and integrated or united and neutral?', *German History* 7/1 (1989), pp. 5–18, for a discussion of early 'missed opportunities'.

decision-making on the foreign policy front: East German Communists were clearly more at the behest of Moscow than West German politicians were of the Western powers. Nevertheless, given the fact that East German Communist leaders would certainly lose their own political position of dominance in a united Germany, they had very little reason to be interested in the effective dissolution of their state in a united democratic Germany.

Nor, it might be suggested, did popular notions of national identity, or patterns of political orientation to the new regimes, play much of a role in their initial rather successful consolidation. Sheer growing affluence in the period of the 'economic miracle' played the greatest role in bringing West Germans around to supporting the idea of democracy in principle. Other factors too were important in the early phase of West German democracy. These included Adenauer's policy of incorporating former Nazis – including many in high places – in the new regime, thus avoiding a potential breeding ground of serious opposition. Anti-Communism in the era of the Cold War was also a useful transitional ideology. The reconstruction of western Europe more broadly – in the context of the Marshall Plan, the birth of the European Economic Community, and the security framework of NATO – also served to integrate and stabilise the new West Germany in a new international framework. These 'external' factors, along with the material successes of the early years as well as the at least pragmatic commitment of various economic, intellectual and moral elites to West German democracy (in sharp contrast to elite attacks on Weimar democracy), together help explain the early consolidation of the new regime in the West.

While East Germany certainly did not experience the spectacular economic successes of the West – and indeed suffered considerably, from reparations, from reorientation towards a less developed set of economies in Eastern Europe, and from the loss of skilled labour in the flood of refugees to the West in the 1950s – it too experienced a certain qualified consolidation in the early period. Most notably, Ulbricht, whose position up to 1953 had been by no means unassailable, was able to confirm his own hold on power and remove those who held less hard-line views from positions of influence in the SED. The relative discipline and uniformity of official views in the SED proved to be a major factor in its subsequent hold on power over the next three decades. More important than any assent to the new East German regime on the part of the masses were at this time the threat of coercion, the difficulty of alternative options, the amnesty for former small Nazis, and the still possible escape route to the West – as well as the hope that the division was impermanent, and would not long remain. From August 1961, the option of attempted escape was too risky for all but a handful.

The 'established' phase

One could perhaps denote the period from the early 1960s to the late 1980s as the 'established' phase in the history of divided Germany. During this period, the prospect of reunification appeared increasingly remote, the nature of a divided post-war world, under the respective spheres of influence of the two super-powers, increasingly 'normal'. Division appeared to have given Germans a stability never achieved in a united German nation-state; and, in the longest period of peace experienced in Europe in the twentieth century, division seemed to many (particularly West Germans!) an acceptable price to pay. Neither Germany was without domestic tensions; yet each, in different ways, appeared to be a system intrinsically capable of reproduction and development, rather than one which – like the Third Reich – was inherently destructive and self-destructive, or building up internal tensions inevitably leading to a revolutionary conflagration. Given the ultimate demise of the GDR with the revolution of 1989 this point is worth reiterating: had it not been for wider changes in the Eastern European context, the collapse of the East German Communist state from internal tensions alone would have been exceedingly unlikely.

West German democracy was not without its difficulties during this period. Right-wing extremism was constantly viewed with anxiety, from the *Land* electoral successes of the NPD in the later 1960s to the rise of the Republicans and their local election triumphs in Berlin and Frankfurt in 1989. Racism, largely directed against the foreign worker (*Gastarbeiter*) population, provoked concern. The terrorism of the Red Army Faction was a continuing, at times major, if intermittent, problem from the early 1970s. State measures to deal with extremism, encroaching arguably on to the legitimate bounds of democratic debate (such as the *Berufsverbot* implied by the 1972 Decree Concerning Radicals whereby political considerations would influence appointments in the public service sector), contributed to the polarisation between Left and Right (and to some extent between younger and older generations) evident from the late 1960s. The rise of citizens' initiatives and pressure group politics – over environmental and peace questions, and particular local issues – as well as the challenge mounted to established political parties by the emergence of the Greens on to the national political scene, have been viewed by some as thorns in the flesh of 'sensible' democracy.[10] The established political parties suffered from scandals (such as the Flick affair) and accusations of bribery and corruption (for example, in the bitterly contested and narrow votes ratifying Brandt's *Ostpolitik*, and in the related 1972 election campaign). Perhaps a less obviously problematic, but in some ways serious, aspect of the functioning of West German democracy was the role of the chameleon FDP, rarely gaining over one in ten votes (and sometimes little over the one in twenty necessary to gain representation in the Bundestag) but able nearly always to determine the balance of power and political complexion of the government. On each occasion where there was a major change at national level – 1966, 1969, 1982 – it was the FDP which determined the switch.

More broadly – as adumbrated above in connection with views of its past – West Germany continued to suffer from a perceived identity crisis: not only the contested question of 'coming to terms with the past' (particularly the Nazi past), but also the question of its role in the present, was problematic. This was summed up in the phrase, coined already in the 1960s, of being an 'economic giant but a political dwarf'; it was also connected with certain difficulties in Germany's relationship particularly with its erstwhile enemy and victor, then saviour and protector, the USA. To some extent, influential elements in the FRG sought to overcome both aspects of the problem by reasserting pride in being German while at the same time attempting to subsume West German identity in a wider, and increasingly integrated, European identity. (This focus on European integration continued to be put forward as the supposed solution to fears of a resurgent greater German nationalism with the events of 1989–90.) If one wants a key clue to West Germany's stability in the 'established' phase, however, it can still be summarised in two words: economic performance. Clearly this is not the place to embark on a major review of West German history in this period, but it may be said briefly that West Germany rode the economic troubles of the 1970s and 1980s remarkably smoothly (in contrast, for example, to a declining Britain); and that without the continued and widespread affluence of West Germans, their political history would probably have been very different.

How does one explain the rather different – but in many respects more surprising – relative political stability of the GDR in the quarter-

10. Evaluations of later West German democracy differ remarkably: for contrasting views, see Conradt, op.cit., and Bark and Gress, op.cit.

century from the early 1960s to the later 1980s? It seems to me that four factors in East German regime stability are of major importance; and that, again perhaps oddly, issues of national identity and popular political orientation in the end played a greater role in the demise of this non-democratic state than they did in any political developments in its democratic twin in the West.

The key factors explaining both the relatively long-lived stability of the GDR and also in the end – in their transformation – its final collapse, have to do with the international situation; the cohesion of elites; the incorporation and defusing of dissent; and the (minimal) satisfaction of material needs. Here, we shall deal with the established phase; the next section will consider the end of the post-war era and the revolution of 1989.

While the Cold War continued, the Soviet Union could never contemplate a serious breaking of ranks among Warsaw Pact countries, and would intervene to suppress any domestic developments which seemed to threaten Soviet interests. This is the key difference between all earlier unsuccessful uprisings in Eastern European countries (1953, 1956, 1968, 1980–81) and the revolutions of 1989. The existence of Communist regimes in Eastern Europe was, at the most basic level, predicated on the latent or manifest coercion of the Soviet Union.

Second, if one turns to domestic features contributing to regime stability, a key factor has to do with elites. The political elite, the SED, was for a long time a more disciplined and at least publicly united party than were other Eastern European Communist parties at certain times (the Czechs in 1968 under Dubcek, the Poles in 1980–81 when faced with the challenge of Solidarity). This East German Communist authoritarianism and discipline clearly require further exploration. Other elite groups were, for a series of different reasons, in large measure either coopted (the technical intelligentsia) or their challenge as potential counter-elites deflected (for example, the cultural intelligentsia). A partial exception became the Protestant churches, a question to which we shall return.

Third – and related to the cohesion or cooption of elites – an important factor in the relative lack of domestic sources of political instability in the GDR from the early 1960s to the mid-1980s was the fact that dissent was relatively successfully incorporated, defused – or exiled to the West. Alone among East European states, the GDR had a western twin which automatically recognised rights of citizenship for those who had fled or been exiled from the East. This proved a useful safety valve from the point of view of the East German regime: dissenting groups lost their articulate and active leaders, or critical writers tired of censorship and self-censorship left to become submerged in the wider seas of intellectual dissent in the West. Even with the emergence of the unofficial peace initiatives in the early 1980s, members of the Protestant church leadership – concerned to protect the delicate balance of Church–state relations, and to pressurise gradually for change – to some degree stepped in to moderate the actions of dissenters and to contain oppositional activity within certain bounds (as in, for example, the ending of the 'Swords into ploughshares' armband campaign).[11]

Finally, there is the issue of East German economic performance. Quite obviously, East Germans were aware of the enormously greater affluence of West Germans, and this was a potent and particular source of grievance – again, in contrast to places like Poland or Hungary, which did not have a living example of what they might have experienced had political conditions been different. On the other hand, however, the East German economy had the best performance among Eastern Bloc countries, and although choice was severely limited and quality low by Western standards, there was not actual *want* or acute food shortages, as in Poland at different times. For all its shortcomings and inefficiencies (not to mention low health and safety standards and high levels of pollution), the East German economy did actually work – until its collapse with the opening of the borders in 1989. Thus, for the East German masses, there was not the basis for food riots – which, in Poland at different times, combined with the dissent of the intellectuals to produce more revolutionary domestic situations. While the external and elite elements in the situation appeared unassailable – while the USSR controlled its empire, and the domination of the SED was asserted with confidence – material dissatisfaction alone would not suffice to produce a revolutionary situation. The masses might grumble; but they would not rise in a hopeless revolt simply because the choice in East German greengrocers was between cabbages and more cabbages, while West Germans ate bananas, peaches and grapes.

---

11. For the view of the Church as a moderating or stabilising influence in the early 1980s, see M. Fulbrook, 'Co-option and commitment: aspects of the relations between church and state in the GDR', *Social History* 12 (1987), pp. 73–91. Clearly things changed somewhat in the later 1980s when the delicate balance of the earlier 1980s was changed with the proliferation of dissenting groups outside the Church, the diversification of opinion within the Church – and within the SED – and with a changed external context (with hopes for reforms along Gorbachev's lines).

The 1989 revolution

From the mid-1980s all the four factors just identified began to change, in different ways. Most important for bringing about changes in the German situation were the changes in Soviet policy under Gorbachev. With domestic economic and political difficulties, and the introduction and promotion of reforms which had reverberations for democratising and liberalising currents in other Eastern European states, Gorbachev presided over the new non-interventionism in Eastern Europe. In Soviet spokesman Gennady Gerasimov's disarming phrase, the new approach to Eastern Europe was characterised by the 'Sinatra doctrine' of 'letting them do it their way'. This was the essential precondition for the fundamental political changes which took place in Poland, and particularly Hungary – where the dismantling of the Iron Curtain between Hungary and Austria provided the location for the refugee crisis of the summer of 1989. The flood of East German refugees over this border to the West was the precipitating factor in the East German domestic political crisis, which, it may be added already, would not have advanced very far if the USSR had not permitted it to continue and, indeed, encouraged change.

Second, there was the crisis among the East German domestic elites. Already from the mid-1980s, the SED had been losing its monolithic profile. This partly had to do with the fact that Honecker was ageing, and there was a succession question in the air; this was overlain by the context of discussions of *glasnost* and *perestroika*. Thus while many pointed to Egon Krenz as the likely crown prince, *aficionados* mentioned the name of an obscure, but more liberal, potential leader of the SED waiting in the provincial wings: Hans Modrow. The resistance of the old-guard leadership to the Soviet reforms had fostered more open debates and shifting of positions – and less disciplined conformity in the certainties of the party line – among the wider SED membership, with greater differences emerging between grass-roots and activists, between local and central leaderships, than had been seen since the 1950s. These uncertainties were to play a key role in the way the peaceful revolution was to unfold.

Third, given the new and more hopeful conditions, dissent had been proliferating and emerging into organised opposition already over some years before 1989. From the mid-1980s onwards, groups had been organising *outside* the bounds of the Church, discussing human rights and environmental issues as well as peace initiatives. These took advantage of the situation of regime crisis in the late summer of 1989 to argue for the need for change *within* the GDR, to transform it into a place were people would want to stay and work for a better future.

Finally, there is the issue of mass discontent. Clearly this was the major factor behind the refugee crisis: people wanted to cross while the going was good, abandoning home and possessions in search of better conditions in the West. But it was not the *cause* of the revolution, first, in that it was a *result* of the wider changes in Eastern Europe (and specifically, the dismantling of the Iron Curtain on the Austro-Hungarian border), and second, in that the masses played a minimal role in the very early phases of the actual revolution in East Germany itself. It was brave and committed dissenters who dared to march around Leipzig in the early days, before the turning-point of 9 October when the use of force to suppress the revolution was officially renounced. The details of this turning-point are themselves interesting: it was a local decision, not even ratified by local party leaders, which in the course of the evening received backing from Berlin (in the person of Krenz) which determined the calling-off of the troops. Once it was clear – a rather faltering process, with different patterns in different localities – that demonstrating would not result in mass bloodshed, more and more people came out on the streets to proclaim '*Wir sind das Volk*' ('We are the people').

If ever a 'GDR national identity' existed (though not the one for which the regime had been striving for over forty years), it was between 9 October and 9 November 1989. For a month, a tremulous solidarity of a wondering people forced concession after concession from a regime which attempted to salvage what it could from the situation by a 'last revolution from above'. The final concession – when it was clearly no longer possible to try to imprison the entire East German population under a form of national house arrest – proved the undoing both of the Communist regime and the fragile and short-lived GDR national identity. The opening of the Berlin Wall on 9 November was equivalent to the opening of floodgates; and with the westwards stampede, the East German economy and state entered the chaotic period of effective collapse. The simple replacement of one word in the slogans of the autumn symbolised the deflection of the revolution: '*Wir sind das Volk*' became '*Wir sind ein Volk*'. A transcending national identity was claimed, to preside over the abandonment of the past and to express the desperate hope to acquire overnight the life-style of the West. It was, essentially, the vote for the Deutschmark, as fast as possible, which then determined the right-wing outcome of the March 1990 elections.

The end of a divided nation

What did the dramatic developments of 1989–90 reveal about the national identity or diverging identities of the Germans in the two Germanies? The picture is a complex and multi-faceted one. In the first place – as at all times in German history – there was no one uncontested conception of what made up a 'German national identity'. This has been, perhaps, the sole consistent feature of the changing history of Germans in central Europe since the beginnings of notions of the German nation in the early Middle Ages, and is traced in the various other chapters in this book. So the difficulties in redefining a united Germany's role in the radically changed conditions of late twentieth-century Europe, after the end of the Cold War, are but a new variant on an old, ever-changing theme.

What are the distinctive features of this new stage of an old problem? The importance of being German – if one can put it that way – for many Germans in 1989–90 lay in the economic strength of the FRG. Notwithstanding the emotions aroused among the West as well as East German people by the breaching of the Berlin Wall, and the long-standing obligations, officially recognised and adhered to, on the part of the West German leaders towards the East Germans, as well as the continuing ties of family and friendship between East and West, the degree of divergence between the two Germanies during forty years of separation should not be underestimated.

In all manner of spheres, assumptions and orientations to life were revealed as being different in East and West: many aspects are only surfacing to consciousness with the realisation of changes occurring or likely to occur with unification. For example, the taken-for-granted reliance on generous maternity provisions and almost universally available child-care facilities for East German mothers, who assume that it is abnormal *not* to work, stands in some contrast to the patchy, largely private nature of West German provision for pre-school children and the rather different considerations concerning the combination of work and family in the West. Whatever one's views on the 'double burden' rather than 'emancipation' of women in East Germany (where the traditional division of labour in the household remained largely resistant to social policies affecting the non-private sphere), there was clearly a considerable divergence of attitudes on the gender front. More diffuse and difficult to specify are differences in what one might call degrees of individualism. By and large, East Germans did *not* have to take autonomous decisions, or be aggressive, competitive and thrusting on the market-place; they *did* have to learn to obey and carry out decisions taken above. Adapting to the conditions of market capitalism – with not only the benefits of affluence when all goes well, but also the risks of unemployment, homelessness and squalor amid plenty – would clearly prove to be problematic for many. Learning to think independently, and have the courage to articulate one's own view even when contradicted by others – and often to agree amicably to differ – would also be something of a problem for those affected by East German authoritarian education and socialisation processes. Although in the winter of 1989–90, on experiencing for themselves the apparent consumers' paradise of the West, many East Germans felt bitterly that they had lost or wasted forty years, and would now have to jettison overnight all the sacrifices of the past which had in the end been for nothing, others felt that under an effective West German takeover much of value in GDR life would be lost. This was particularly felt among those – many of them Christians – who had spearheaded the early stages of the peaceful revolution of the autumn, hoping to be able to build a 'Third Way' form of democratic, humanistic socialism. To collapse into crass materialism appeared to these a profoundly depressing denouement to the revolution.

In other respects, currents previously suppressed now found a – not always welcome – voice. This was true of right-wing extremism in the GDR, fomented to some extent by West German Republicans in the winter of 1989–90, although it had existed before. Anti-Semitic acts such as the desecration of Jewish graves (including those of Helene Weigel and her non-Jewish husband, Bertolt Brecht), as well as racist attacks on foreigners in the GDR, increased after the relaxing of police control and political repression of such acts. Problematic, too, would be a 'coming-to-terms', under democratic auspices and conditions of free debate, not only with the previously inadequately confronted Nazi past, but also the compromises and complicities of life in the Stasi-state. 'De-stasification' was already beginning to take on parallels with the denazification of the post-war period; and the grumbles were being heard again of the *Bonzen* (roughly, bigwigs) remaining in position, benefiting from new circumstances as they had from the old. A post-revolutionary period of uncertainty and insecurity was beginning to pave the way for a new wave – a double wave – of coming to terms with two sets of compromised pasts.

Developments in West Germany were in some respects simpler; but West Germany did not remain intrinsically unaffected by the East German changes. There, too, new currents arose or were made manifest by the changing situation. There were new social prejudices in a period of increased pressure on housing and jobs, when the West German economic miracle appeared threatened by the incorporation of growing numbers of emigrating East Germans, or by the rises in taxes and interest rates to accommodate the merger of the two economies. Moreover, uncertainties on the role – and even the boundaries, while Kohl played to the far-right gallery in prevaricating on Poland's western border – of the new united Germany allowed the reassertion of revisionist voices which not so long before had seemed essentially anachronistic. To a much greater degree than in the East, young West Germans had taken little interest in their twin state, and many had barely regarded it as much more than an entity related only by the dimmest of historical ties. (There was scarcely the same acute thirst among Westerners to travel to, and experience the deprivations of, the East as there was among young East Germans to make the opposite journey to the West. Nor were many, if any, young West Germans tempted to watch the monotonous fare of East German television night after night, in the same way as East Germans avidly watched the Western media.) While the victory in the East German national elections of the political forces supported by the West German conservative parties ensured that West German political and economic arrangements would in the main be taken over to a new Germany, that new united Germany would still be a different entity than the partial state, the Federal Republic had been; and West Germans would have to accommodate themselves and adapt to the new circumstances, although in different ways and from different base-lines than their Eastern brethren.

CONCLUSIONS

For four decades, the democratic and Communist states established in the western and eastern parts of a divided nation were more successful – in their own, rather different terms – than were their historical predecessors, from imperial Germany through the Weimar Republic to the Third Reich. This success is perhaps particularly surprising for two reasons: first, neither state was an intrinsically 'legitimate' nation-state, but rather an impermanent entity in a divided nation; and second, the new political forms which were imposed did not, at least initially, represent the outcome of indigenous political orientations. It has often been said that a major problem of the Weimar Republic was that it was a 'Republic without republicans'. Even more might such a comment be made about the two post-war German states at the time of their foundation: a Communist state with precious few Communists, and a democratic state with probably less than a majority of democrats in any deep-rooted sense.

Neither state succeeded entirely in finding a satisfactory solution to the problem of 'national identity', whether at an all-German level or at the level of the partial state. All-German notions played little role in the early stages of division and consolidation of the two states. With *Ostpolitik*, West German aid to East Germany – in recognition of its common bonds with East German citizens and desire to improve their material and human circumstances – paradoxically helped to sustain division through bolstering the East German regime. That does not mean that the GDR would have collapsed earlier without such aid. Material distress alone does not lead to revolution and the crucial external preconditions for such revolution were absent until the late 1980s.

At the level of partial 'national identities', the attempted construction of different East and West German identities must also be viewed with some qualification. Official propagations of a 'GDR national identity' were probably never swallowed wholesale by more than a minority of the population, although this might – had 1989 not intervened – have changed eventually with the passage of generations. There were certain bases for (limited) pride in the GDR's modest economic achievements compared to its Eastern European neighbours, and these comparisons might have displaced those made with the richer West Germany if the division of Europe had continued – but this is to speculate. In the West at least a number of highly articulate intellectuals continued to suffer from explicit identity crises, and attempts to proclaim any universally valid notion of national identity remained intrinsically contentious and politically divisive.

Despite all this, however, the two Germanies *did* begin to develop distinctively different profiles or patterns of political orientation. In the West, a combination of external factors and domestic economic success contributed to the early establishment of democracy. As a *result* – not a precondition – of the consolidation of democratic political structures, more democratic forms of political orientation spread among greater proportions of the populace. A predominance of monarchist and authoritarian sympathies prevalent in the 1950s gave way to pragmatic assent to democracy by the early 1960s; by the late 1960s, this had become support for democracy in principle. Once the transformation of most West Germans from 'fair-weather' to 'principled' democrats had taken place, the economic and political troubles of the 1970s (economic recession, oil crises, terrorism) could more easily be weathered. By the 1980s, there were widespread moves for more participatory, and not purely representative, democracy, which arose at a time of new challenges on the international military and environmental fronts. With the passage of generations, and the changing of issues, the West Germans of the late 1980s were not the same sorts of people as those of the 1940s, whatever the mythology of popular folklore among Germany's former enemies, such as Britain, which began to be expressed over the issue of German unity in the winter of 1989–90.

In the East, a combination of coercion and attempted indoctrination were important in the early phase of establishment. From 1961, a widespread retreatism into a 'niche society', combined with the isolation, defusing or exiling of dissent, for two decades or more contributed to the maintenance of a modicum of domestic stability. In the 1980s dissenting voices developed into more active, organised opposition groups. Interestingly, the early stages of the 1989 revolution revealed just what new forms of political culture had emerged among a minority in the GDR: that minority, typified by New Forum in the early autumn, that was in favour of a form of democratic socialism rather than capitalist democracy as in the West. In the event, when the majority – who had until 1989 led quiet political lives in the retreatist mode – took the opportunity to go West (both before and even more after the opening of the Berlin Wall), the economic collapse of the GDR took away the material conditions for any such experiment in democratic socialism to be attempted.

It was the Cold War which divided Germany; it was the end of the Cold War which removed the conditions sustaining division. Within each of the two Germanies, it was the support or co-option, in different ways, of a range of elite groups which determined the relative domestic stability of each partial state over the forty years of division. When a regime crisis, in the context of changed external circumstances, precipitated the loss of elite control in East Germany, then active opposition could take advantage of the situation to initiate major forces for change. Finally, with the emergence of the masses on to the political scene – expressing the simple desire for a better standard of living and an end to repression – the final basis for the existence of a separate East German state was removed.

While the parameters of the current situation are relatively clear, there are still many uncertainties on the form, social and economic profile, and particularly military alliance of any future united Germany.

We may end with a few wider ruminations. In a very simple sense, a 'German nation-state' has never really existed, given the complicated ethnic boundaries of central Europe and the existence of German minorities outside wherever 'Germany' happened to be at any given time, while non-German groups lived within 'Germany'. So in some respects the unification of Germany is simply another variant of the centuries-old game of redrawing the boundaries of 'Germany' in central Europe and redefining – or constructing – an identity for what lay inside.

There are nevertheless some interesting new features to the current situation. These have to do with the changed structural location of the state in the late twentieth-century with respect to both supra-national and sub-national levels. There is, on the one hand, the set of movements 'upwards', integrating European states into wider economic and political decision-making networks – most notably, with the moves for enhanced significance for the European Community and wider European integration. On the other hand, there is a simultaneous set of movements in almost the opposite direction: the resurgence of local nationalisms in multi-national states (such as in the former USSR) or of regional and local identities in nation-states. *Heimat* and local particularism are attaining new significance in a period of trans- or supra-national entities. Clearly, with the ending of the Cold War and the collapse of the Soviet Empire in Eastern Europe, the 1990s constitute a major historical watershed. The era of European nation-states which began in the early nineteenth century may be nearing a significant end. The task of the historian is to explain the past, not predict the future; but no doubt the land in the centre of Europe will continue to play a central role in European history. Perhaps Germans' difficulties with concepts of national identity, and the arguable irrelevance of these concepts to patterns of political stability and change, represent a helpful corrective to the virulent consequences of earlier views of the role of the German nation.

SUGGESTIONS FOR FURTHER READING

See the following for introductions to the history of the two Germanies:

M. Balfour, *West Germany: An Introductory History* (London, 1982).

V. Berghahn, *Modern Germany* (Cambridge, 1987, 2nd edn).

D. Childs, *The GDR: Moscow's German Ally* (London, 1983).

M. McCauley, *The GDR since 1945* (London, 1983).

G. Smith, W. Paterson and P. Merkl (eds), *Developments in West German Politics* (London, 1989).

H.A. Turner, *The Two Germanies since 1945* (New Haven, Conn, 1987).

My own views are developed at greater length in M. Fulbrook, *Germany 1918–1990: The Divided Nation* (London, 1991).

CHAPTER ELEVEN

Germany in Europe: the German question as burden and as opportunity

Wolf Gruner

PRELIMINARY REMARKS

'In the year 1990 the future of Europe appears more open than at any time since the end of the Second World War.'[1]

So began the new book on Germany and her neighbours by the former Chancellor of the Federal Republic of Germany, Helmut Schmidt. This is an appropriate judgement of the historical crossroads at which we now find ourselves, bringing with it both risks and opportunities.

In the 1990s one can envisage two possible lines of development. In the first the changes in Eastern Europe could lead to the re-emergence of nationalism and of a Europe of nation-states in a new form. This development would stop or at least delay the policies of European integration being pursued in Western Europe. In the second the democratisation of Eastern Europe, the introduction of market economies, and the reunification of Germany could all promote the integration process by locking Germany more closely into a network of European connections, and thereby accelerating and even completing the tasks of integration. European states would give up or at least reduce their political freedom in favour of a pan-European structure. At the end of this path there would come a day of the kind described by Lothar Späth in his recent book *1992: The Dream of Europe*:

Church bells peal throughout Europe. They ring in the new millennium *and* a new epoch in European history. In the park in front of the European Parliament in Strasbourg people sing and dance and celebrate. They link arms and wave European flags. The treaties setting up a United

1. H. Schmidt, *Die Deutschen und ihre Nachbarn* (Berlin, 1990), p. 12.

States of Europe (Vereinigten Staaten von Europa; Les Etats Unis de l'Europe) come into force on 1 January 2000. There is a ceremony in which the first European President, the former Prime Minister of Luxemburg (until 31 December 1999) is sworn in by the President of the European Parliament.[2]

The unity of Europe which had broken apart in the medieval period is restored on a new basis which transcends the nation–state. The centuries-old dream of unifying Europe, of the creation of a single European nation, has become a reality.

Most Germans wish to see this second path followed, the one that leads to European unity.

However, we are not nearly there. The path to a United States of Europe, to a European federal state will be steep and stony, but nevertheless it could be travelled. Germany, reunited on 3 October 1990, must play the leading role in this process, and not only for historic reasons. The authors of the Basic Law, the constitution of the Federal Republic, set out the moral obligation.

> The German People…animated by the resolve to preserve their national and political unity and to serve the peace of the world as an equal partner in a united Europe…have enacted…this Basic Law.[3]

The creation of a united Europe remains after German reunification a constitutional commitment, only now it applies to *all* Germans. In the treaty establishing German unity there is a reference to the obligation '…by means of German unity to contribute to the unification of Europe and the creation of a peaceful order in Europe'.[4] A united Germany should be an integral part of this greater Europe, a pillar in the new European building. Germany will take its place in the common European home to which medieval popes swore allegiance.

The chances of European unity are not too bad because Europeans have little choice but to follow this path and to persevere in it despite all the dangers. However, there are many basic problems which will have to be confronted.

1. What would be the constitutional forms of a new European polity: a federal state, a federation of states, a Europe of sovereign states, or of groups of such states, a Europe of nations or a Europe of regions?

---

2. L. Späth, *1992: Der Traum von Europa* (Stuttgart, 1989), pp. 9–24. This is not a quotation but a summary of the points made by Späth in this part of his book.

3. *The Basic Law for the Federal Republic of Germany*, 23 May 1949, Preamble.

4. *Vertrag zwischen der Bundesrepublik Deutschland und der Deutschen Demokratischen Republik über die Herstellung der Einheit Deutschlands: Einigungsvertrag*, dated 31 August 1990, Presse und Informationsamt der Bundesregierung, *Bulletin* no. 104 (6 September 1990), pp. 877–1,120 (877).

2. Can the peoples of Europe free themselves of the burdens of the past and bring the process of European integration to its conclusion? Is it true that one can find no historical justification for such integration because the history of Europe reveals inveterate hostility to integration?[5]
3. The German question has always been a European question, since long before 1939 and at least since the eighteenth century. Will reunification settle that question once and for all or will it for both historical and new reasons turn out to be an obstacle in the way of European unification?
4. Which role can and should the new German state play in Europe?
5. How European is our thinking and feeling? Are convinced Germans also committed Europeans? Or are they rational Europeans, Europeans by default because lacking in national identity? Do Germans lack a sense of Europe as a cultural and spiritual reality, not just as the consequence of successful political and economic integration?

These are the questions and problems which press upon us. As an historian it is not possible to invent a formula for German and European unity. It is possible, however, to sketch out the German dimensions of European history and the European dimensions of German history and to bring to light ideas about a common Europe which have been concealed under the categories imposed by the nation-state. This will be both necessary and valuable in the promotion of a European historical perspective and an understanding of what Europe means. Historical knowledge is an important element in forming the 'future of history' (Sheehan). Sheehan suggested that it was time to put aside the idea that the foundation of a united Germany in 1871 was somehow the central event in modern German history. Rather one should

> acknowledge that the present period has a legitimacy of its own, a legitimacy which comes not from its relationship to the old Reich, but from its place within a broader and deeper historical tradition. The German present is not a postscript to the imperial past; it is a new chapter in a much older story.[6]

Recovering a sense of the fullness of German history beyond its relationship to the founding of modern Germany brings home to us such issues as the federal tradition in German statehood and how this fitted into a broader European setting, it leads us to question that idea of a continuity which runs from Arminius through Luther, Frederick the Great and Bismarck to Hitler, and enables us to re-evaluate German history.

5. See R.W Foerster, *Europa: Geschichte einer politischen Idee* (Munich, 1967), p. 156.
6. J. Sheehan, 'What is German history?', *Journal of Modern History* 53 (1981), pp. 1–23 (23). See now Sheehan, *German History 1770–1866* (Oxford, 1990).

What Sheehan says about Geman history can also be said about European history. The European present also has to be linked to a re-evaluated European history. It cannot be reduced to the links between the nation-states; it must be seen as something more than the sum of these national histories. We should seek to go beyond such propaganda. If we take off our national spectacles, be they tinted German, Czech, British, Russian, French, Dutch, Polish, Italian or Hungarian, new perspectives open up to us which can help us move beyond the nation-state, can promote new ideas and can bring us closer to the goal of European unity in all its complexity. There needs to be a concern with 'Europe as reality and as task'[7] in order to link past, present and future.

In what follows I wish to select three elements from European history. Closer consideration of these elements can help us understand the situation in which Europe and Germany find themselves now.

1. The first element is the tension between the national and the European idea since the breakdown of the unity of Christendom.
2. The second element is the European dimension of the German question, or the German problem as it has often been termed by Germany's neighbours. The German problem has been and remains of great concern to those neighbours.
3. The third element is to consider the issues of European unity and the German question in relation to the process of western integration since 1945.

I will conclude with a consideration of what it will mean for Europe, for states both inside and outside the EC, and for the European unity process now that a united Germany is a member of the EC.

THE IDEAS OF THE NATION-STATE AND OF EUROPEAN UNITY

Geographically the core area of Europe is fairly clearly defined. This allows, despite the variety of landscapes and of national, cultural, linguistic, religious and political histories, a certain element of unity to

7. *Europa als Wirklichkeit und Aufgabe* is the title of a reader intended for the final class of primary school in Hamburg from the year 1954. The book contains documents concerned with European history and culture.

persist.[8] This sense of common European links and traditions which developed over centuries was obscured in the period in which the nation-state and national attitudes came to be dominant. This has also affected historical study which

> came to be placed clearly and completely within the framework of the nation and of the national homeland, rather like a child put into a tight jacket in order to prevent freedom of movement.[9]

A survey of lecture courses given at German and other European universities, as well as the history curricula of schools, makes it clear that this tight jacket is still worn. The central point of reference is national and generally the history of the nation dominates. This is an obstacle to the promotion of any sense of historical community at a European level. If we wish to develop a European identity, without denying the significance of the regional and the national, then we must try to develop European perspectives.[10] We need to explore the reasons for the development of nationalism and the nation-state in Europe and also see how the idea of Europe has evolved along with that development.

One feature of modern European history is the close connections between the formation of the nation-state, the principle of sovereignty, the concern with security and the concept of a balance of power. These in turn are related to a certain idea of Europe. At first there seems to be no connection between that idea and the concept of the balance of power. Yet that concept, especially in terms of a European balance of power implies an understanding of the ties that bind the continent together.[11]

One can find the origins of the ideas of both the nation-state and of Europe in the medieval period. The sharpening conflict between Empire and Papacy for pre-eminence in Christendom destroyed the unity and universalism of the Christian West. Christendom had embraced equally all the various European lands. The dynastic nation-state idea contributed to its disintegration. Special interests displaced unity. Tensions between the territories of the various European peoples took on increasingly a dynastic-national character. That in turn promoted a

---

8. See D. Hay, *Europe: The Emergence of an Idea* (Edinburgh, 1967, 2nd edn); O. Halecki, *The Limits and Divisions of European History*, (London, 1950); P. Wolff, *The Awakening of Europe* (Harmondsworth, 1987).

9. Leonard Reinisch, in his preface to Reinisch (ed.) *Die Europäer und ihre Geschichte. Epochen und Gestalten im Urteil der Nationen* (Munich, 1961), p. vi.

10. S. de Madariaga, *Portrait of Europe* (London, 1952), preface.

11. Cf. W. Gruner, 'Deutschland und das europäische Gleichgewicht seit dem 18 Jahrhundert', in Gruner, *Gleichgewicht in Geschichte und Gegenwart* (Hamburg, 1989), pp. 60–133.

desire to win back the lost unity. With the emergence of nation-states from the early modern period and their dogmatic insistence on the need for national sovereignty, such a European idea seemed increasingly utopian and idealistic.

There is not space here to consider in detail the tension between the European and the nation-state ideas.[12] My main concern is to indicate that early plans for the restoration of European unity – and until the eighteenth century Christendom was the central point of reference in such plans – contain elements which continue to figure in plans for European Union in the twentieth century. Thinkers with whom such ideas are associated include Dante Aligheri, Pierre du Bois and Georg von Podiebrad, and in the seventeenth and eighteenth centuries, Emeric Crucé, the Duke of Sully and the Abbot de St Pierre.[13]

Podiebrad's *Treaty for a League of States* (*Vertrag zu einem Staatenbund*) (dated 1462/63) takes as its point of departure the emergence of nations within Europe. His plan failed, but it influenced later plans. The members of the league should accept a limitation upon the sovereignty of the individual states, decisions taken by a majority of states, a court of arbitration, a Supreme Court, a league army and executive authority.

There were various motives behind attempts at European unity since the fifteenth century apart from the wish to overcome national barriers. We encounter such plans especially at times of political and economic crisis. They are frequently presented as a way of ensuring perpetual peace and contributing towards prosperity. The authors of such plans came from widely differing backgrounds. It is often difficult to establish their contemporary and later significance. As with the national movements from the late eighteenth century they increasingly recruited from intellectual and political-social elites who were involved in politics. However, unlike the national movements of the nineteenth century, the European movement did not acquire a popular basis.

In its early stages the nation-state was seen in dynastic terms, but this changed with the French Revolution, which also spread the national idea throughout Europe. Into the twentieth century nationalism, the nation-state, and the national character of politics have come to shape an increasingly wider and international political order.[14] The

12. See W. Gruner, 'Probleme und Aspekte der europäischen Einigung bis zu den Römischen Verträgen', in A. Schomaker *et al.* (eds) *Pläydoyer für Europa. Beiträge zur Europäischen Einigung* (Hamburg, 1989), pp. 11–62.

13. Cf. F.H. Hinsley, *Power and the Pursuit of Peace* (Cambridge, 1967).

14. This conjunction of nationalism with increasing international ties led Theodor Schieder to refer to the nineteenth century as an 'age of antinomies'. T. Schieder, 'Europa im Zeitalter der Nationalstaaten und Europäische Weltpolitik'. bis zum Ersten Weltkrieg', in *Handbuch der Europäischen Geschichte*, vol. 6 (Stuttgart, 1968), pp. 3ff.

idea that the nation–state was the only thinkable way in which a world of nations could be organised became a dominating dogma. Plans for European unity, grounded in motives other than that of power politics, were disparaged as utopian.

Despite their differences one can see common elements in the various ideas about European unity, even if combined in different ways. The intellectual forerunners go back to the fifteenth century, but they have been forgotten by historians in the grip of a national approach towards the past. Among these elements there are recurrent references to certain institutions which also appear in ideas about European Union today. These include European assemblies, a council of states, a parliament, courts, an army, and an agency to enforce compliance with a European treaty upon offending states. Almost all these plans have a federalist character which is situated somewhere between the notions of a league of states and a federal state. In addition to the various institutions which have been constructed since the European Community for Coal and Steel in 1952, these constitutional proposals for some kind of United States of Europe can provide us with some guidance. Germans can also usefully draw upon their own federalist tradition. After the Second World War Paul Claudel saw in partitioned Germany a way 'to bring together rather than to divide the peoples of Europe'.[15] Germany lies at the centre of Europe and its geography makes it a central focus of European concerns. How Germany is organised politically is crucial to any European order, especially since the political nation, described by Ortega y Gasset as 'the obstacle to any creative historical movement'[16] has been at the centre of German political action. The relationship of Germany to Europe has been an important component, both in the past and today, of the German question.

15. Paul Claudel, quoted in R. Weizsäcker, 'Die Deutschen und ihre Identität', talk given on 8 June 1985 in Düsseldorf to the twenty-first assembly of the Evangelical Church, Presse und Informationsamt der Bundesregierung, *Bulletin*, 64 (12) June 1985, pp. 537–44 (544).

16. J. Ortega y Gasset, *Der Aufstand der Massen* (orig. 1930; Reinbek bei Hamburg, 1961), p. 136.

THE HISTORICAL AND EUROPEAN DIMENSIONS OF THE GERMAN QUESTION

The Germans, now once again in a single state, have an important role to play in the process of European unification. Germany is made up of what was the most Eastern part of Western Europe and the most western part of eastern Europe. Germany has no great power profile which could stand in the way of pragmatic policy-making. This provides Germany with a 'second chance' to shape the European order in the twentieth century.[17] Much depends upon whether the emphasis is upon a German Europe or a European Germany. The first would involve a renewed drive for hegemony over the rest of Europe. Some of Germany's neighbours have expressed anxiety that this could be the direction taken by the reunified Germany. To avoid these anxieties, and the dangers associated with such a direction, it is the second policy which must be pursued. To achieve this we must aim to be Europeans, though without ceasing to be Germans, and also Rhinelanders, Bavarians, Saxons, Mecklenburgers, and so on. How is this to be done?

Partly it requires historical understanding. Such understanding is important to any sense of identity. The President of the Federal Republic, Richard von Weizsäcker, has stressed this in various speeches to his countrymen in recent years:

> If a people do not know how they stand in relation to their past, then it is easy for them to be led astray in the present, for they have an identity problem.[18]

Perhaps this is why so much has been written and said recently about the question of identity in Germany. Germans cannot escape from their history; the burden of that history remains with them today.

The German question has always had a European dimension and has never been only a German concern. Following the creation of an atomic balance of power between the super-powers by the end of the 1950s and then the erection of the Berlin Wall, the German question no longer seemed as important as before. It seemed that the construction of two Germanies, especially when the Federal Republic signed treaties both with the German Democratic Republic and other Eastern European states, had settled the German question for the foreseeable

17. The point was made by the historian Fritz Stern, who also pointed out that Germany wasted her first chance, and history does not normally provide second ones.
18. Weizsäcker, op. cit., p. 539.

future. The German question did surface again with the conflicts arising out of the NATO 'double-track' decision[19] and the discussions
about neutralism which that decision stimulated. However, although
this created some anxieties, both within Germany and among her
neighbours, it did not really call into question the stability of the two-
Germany arrangement. For younger people in the Federal Republic
the German question seemed dead. Even on the eve of the events
which would lead to the collapse of the German Democratic Republic
there was talk of altering the references in the Basic Law to German
unity. The GDR was regarded as a foreign and distant land. Eastern
Europe was ignored. The term 'Germany' came to mean 'West Germany', and 'Europe' meant 'Western Europe'. Germans had come to
forget the close links there were and always will be between the German problem and the process of European unification.

The long-serving Italian ambassador to the Federal Republic of
Germany said the following in a talk given in 1986:

> The European solution of the German question, indeed the European
> vision of those who founded the Federal Republic, began with a lesson
> that was drawn from German history. This was to see the European idea
> as a negation of that German history. The Europe of the future would be
> an 'answer' to history. But one must move towards new and positive
> decisions if the mistakes of the past are to be avoided and a universal and
> eternal peace secured.[20]

Another Italian, the journalist Luigi Barzini, also considered this question:

> The unification of Europe without Germany would be impossible and
> pointless, but with Germany would entail the acceptance, for all members,
> of the German problem.[21]

He concluded that the issue of European unity must wait until the
German question had been solved.

> One must be content with what there is, for the time being anyway. The
> future is in the laps of the gods. It will probably be decided, once again,
> by Germany's decisions. And Germany is, as it always was, a mutable,

---

19. The term used to describe the policy of installing intermediate-range nuclear
missiles in Western Europe, including the Federal Republic of Germany, while continuing to negotiate on arms control agreements with the USSR.
20. L.V.G. Ferraris, 'Betrachtungen zur deutschen Geschichte', talk given on 2 October 1986 in Berlin, MS, p. 15.
21. L. Barzini, *The Europeans* (Harmondsworth, 1983), p. 266.

Proteus-like, unpredictable country, particularly dangerous when it is unhappy.[22]

What is it that gives the German question such priority? To understand this one needs some definition of the term 'German question', though this has varied greatly from one observer to another.[23] There are at least two levels on which to approach the subject: a national-German and a European–international one. Both have a strong historical dimension which one can see determining policy-making in the Second World War and which continues to influence policy-making today.

This became vividly apparent in the political reactions and public comment which accompanied the process of German reunification in 1989–90. Statements by various European politicians and newspaper cartoons bear witness to this. Germany's neighbours have very mixed feelings about the end of German partition.

In the winter of 1990 the *Los Angeles Times* and the *Economist* commissioned a poll of opinions among Germany's neighbours concerning reunification. The headline for the article describing the findings of the poll was 'They like it and they fear it'.[24] There was joy at the way in which the citizens of the GDR had thrown off Communist rule in a peaceful revolution coupled with anxiety and insecurity triggered by the spectacle of popular support for reunification among Germans.

Historically the European–international dimension has also played an important part in the German question, and this cannot be neglected in the present situation. Kurt Schuemacher's insistence that 'one could not see the German question only from a German angle... that there was no German question which was not simultaneously a European question', is a view that has long been accepted.[25]

To make progress we need to introduce further differentiation. In terms of period there are shifts in the nature of the German problem from the Peace of Westphalia of 1648, since the French Revolution, and since the Second World War. One also needs to distinguish between themes of power politics, security interests, European unity, political ideologies, and the principle of the self-determination of peoples.

The different perspective of Germans and their neighbours can be seen in the way Germans use the term 'German question' whereas

22. Ibid., p. 267 (concluding sentence of the book).
23. For different ways of defining the question see W.D. Gruner, *Die deutsche Frage: Ein Problem der europäischen Geschichte seit 1800* (Munich, 1985), p. 15ff.
24. *The Economist*, 27 January 1990, pp. 29f.
25. K. Schuemacher, *Reden – Schriften – Korrespondenzen 1945–1952* (Bonn and Berlin, 1985), p. 382.

their neighbours prefer the term 'German problem'. They are aware of the problems raised since the middle of the nineteenth century in central Europe, problems which sometimes Germans seem to have forgotten. These problems were of European significance up to 1914 and came to take on an even broader, global importance after 1918.

There are six levels on which one can approach this problem: the geographical situation of Germany in the centre of Europe; the economic, political and military potential of Germany; the population question; the political and constitutional arrangements of Germany; the issue of security and balance of power in Europe; the image of Germany. It is impossible to consider these in detail in a short essay.[26] Here I will focus upon the last issue – the image of Germany. In many ways this connects the other elements. It is a certain image of Germany which unsettles some of Germany's neighbours. Apart from support for national self-determination for Germans there is the fear that the old German Adam will re-emerge.

One can see this in the interview with the British minister Nicholas Ridley that was published in the *Spectator*, in which questions such as whether Germany was planning to take over Europe or to establish a 'Deutschmark Zone' were raised, and which led to his resignation.[27] One can also see it in the leaking of a Chequers memorandum of 25 March 1990 from Margaret Thatcher's private secretary, Charles Powell. In *The Times* the Irish historian and journalist Conor Cruse O'Brien warned of a

> pan-German entity, commanding the full allegiance of German
> nationalists, and constituting a focus for national pride... In the new
> proud, united Germany, the nationalists will proclaim the Fourth Reich,
> for while the term *Reich* is associated with victory and periods of German
> ascendancy, that of *Republik* is associated with defeat and the ascendancy
> of alien values. I would expect a reunited Germany to bring back the
> black-white-red flag of the Hohenzollerns, and possibly a Hohenzollern
> Kaiser to go with it.[28]

26. Gruner, op.cit., pp. 11ff; Gruner, *Bündische Formen der Staatlichkeit in Geschichte und Gegenwart* (Duderstadt, 1990), pp. 29ff.

27. 'Saying the unsayable', *Spectator*, 14 July 1990, p. 8.

28. Conor Cruse O'Brien, 'Beware a Reich resurgent', *The Times*, 31 October 1989, p. 18. A version of this article, which appeared in German translation in *Die Welt* on 4 November 1989 under the title 'Wenn Nationalisten das Vierte Reich ausrufen', left out the last sentence quoted above, though without indicating the omission. O'Brien was mistaken about the question of flags. The flag of Prussia used to be black and white. Red and white were the colours of the old Empire. The flag of imperial Germany was a combination of both. Thus the national colours of Germany before 1918 were black, white and red.

There was a similar argument by the Spaniard Heleno Saña who lives in Germany and experienced as a child the attacks by the German air squadron 'Legion Condor'. For him

> the Germans are again on the march. Suddenly their restless activity threatens the status quo in Europe. We non–Germans must be ready for a new Teutonic offensive. Certainly this time it will not take the form of tanks and artillery fire, but ultimately the aim is the same: to expand the power of the Germans at the cost of smaller and economically weaker countries.[29]

Saña believes that the coming down of the Berlin Wall removed the restraints upon Germany. He was disturbed by the 'sight of the masses'. He saw this

> demonstration of mass exhibitionism which Europe has seldom experienced since the end of the war. And it will not be the last one. Bear in mind that these are not any crowds, but crowds of a special quality, made-in-Germany crowds, more gifted than just about any other to act and react as a mass, always ready to organise, to shout, to wave flags and posters, to shout slogans, to follow orders blindly, to march forward and to attack. In the future Europe must reckon with such a crowd, for it is already on the march in the Fourth Reich.[30]

These expressions could be easily multiplied from the last twenty years. They show how a certain image of Germany shapes people's views about how the peoples of Europe can live together. We cannot really reduce our picture of others to just a few key words, but it is what happens. We must also remember that such national stereotypes, particularly images of the alien, have a functional role to play.

This image of Germany has changed historically. Until the mid-nineteenth century the dominant image of the German lands (rather than Germany) was quite positive. The emphasis was upon the romantic, emotional German who loved singing and drinking and who, with his rich cultural and religious traditions, had made a major contribution to European culture. However, from the time of the foundation of the Second Empire in 1870–72 the picture began to change in negative ways. Thus the Frenchman Paul de Saint-Victor wrote in 1870:

> We do not go any more into the idyllic German forests. His *vergiss-mein-nicht* (forget-me-nots) are spattered with blood.[31]

29. H. Saña, *Das Vierte Reich: Deutschlands später Sieg* (Hamburg, 1990), p. 22.
30. Ibid., p. 25.
31. P. de Saint-Victor, *Barbares et Bandites* (Paris, 1971). The German term for forget-me-nots is used in the French original.

The assertion of a British journalist in January 1871 that 'Politically, Prussia is a camp and the Prussian a conscript'[32] indicated another shift of image. Since the late eighteenth century Prussia had been seen as a combination of militarism and effective bureaucracy. Now the image was reduced to that of militarism. Then the image of Prussia was projected upon the image of Germany. This negative image was promoted in the years up to the First World War. With the help of propaganda this image was more firmly established during the First World War. That image of Wilhelmine Germany persists to this day.

Germans themselves contributed to this picture in various ways, through historical writing, speeches, the over-bearing, often aggressive nationalism of the Wilhelmine period, and general boastfulness, as evidenced in statements such as the following.

> [The Germans are]...the people of art and science.... the bearers of human culture....We are the first of all nations, by virtue of our spiritual power, our knowledge, our ability.[33]

> [The Germans regard themselves] as the most gifted cultural nation in the world.[34]

The experience of National Socialist Germany could only seem to confirm this negative image of the German character.

The British historian A.J.P. Taylor expressed the views of many when he gave vent to his mistrust of this German character in a book written in 1944 (first published in 1945), which is still used in the teaching of history:

> The history of the Germans is a history of extremes. It contains everything except moderation, and in the course of a thousand years the Germans have experienced everything except normality. They have dominated Europe, and they have been the helpless victims of the domination of others; they have enjoyed liberties unparalleled in Europe and they have fallen victim to despotism equally without parallel; they have produced the most transcendental philosophers, the most spiritual musicians, and the most ruthless and unscrupulous politicians. 'German' has meant at one moment a being so sentimental, so trusting, so pious, as to be too good for this world; and at another a being so brutal, so unprincipled, so degraded, as to be not fit to live. Both descriptions are true: both types of Germans have existed not only at the same epoch, but

32. F. Harrison, 'Bismarckism: or, the policy of blood and iron', *Fortnightly Review*, December 1870, pp 631–49 (641).

33. O. Klopp, *Die deutsche Nation und der rechte deutsche Kaiser* (Freiburg i.Br., 1862), p. 47.

34. A.B. (anon), *Die deutsche Frage* (Hamburg, 1859), p. 30.

in the same person. Only the normal person, not particularly good, not
particularly bad, healthy, sane, moderate – he has never set his stamp on
German history. Geographically the people of the centre, the Germans
have never found a middle way of life, either in their thought or least of
all in their politics.[35]

One could find many similar estimations from the period of the Second World War in British, French and American archives, in pamphlets and publications of all kinds. More positive, discriminating and
well-meant critical judgements are rare, although among those with
power and in the media there always could be found some voices who
condemned this wholesale indictment of the whole German people.

One critic of this dominant image of the Germans thought it
possible 'that the Germans have been saddled by a divine Providence
with a double dose of original sin'. He complained that in this image
one always encounters Fichte and Hegel, never Kant and Humboldt.
A scientific method which could provide reliable evidence on what
was typical for a people needed to be developed. Until then it must
remain open whether

> Fichte's nationalism and Hegel's aggressiveness are more typically German
> than Kant's belief in a firm international order and Humboldt's belief in
> the state as the servant rather than the master of its citizens.[36]

A passage from a British memorandum written almost exactly forty-
five years before the meeting of the 'experts' at Chequers very clearly
reflects the widespread view of Germans which even today a democratic Germany must confront. Here the view was expressed that National Socialism was

> just an extreme manifestation of the German character. [The German
> submissiveness and 'double personality'] causes the transfer of allegiance
> from the discarded leader to the conqueror, with admiration for his power
> and success. The German therefore now obeys the conqueror and will do
> so as long as the latter acts in the way the German is accustomed to. He
> becomes most humble, submissive, indifferent and apathetic, and is quite
> content to see his country occupied... he is prepared to leave everything
> to the occupying powers; it is the job of the conquerors to run Germany
> and to solve her problems, he has no ideas on the subject and no
> contribution to make; all he wants is order, work and bread. But if the
> conqueror in turn fails and does not make good his promises... the
> German will in time turn away from the conqueror, and will again listen

35. A.J.P. Taylor, *The Course of German History* (orig. 1945; London, 1971), p. 1.
36. J.C. Maxwell Garnett and H.F. Koeppler, *A Lasting Peace with Some Chapters on
the Basis of German Co-operation* (London and New York, 1940), p. 279.

to some new self-proclaimed saviour of the German Volk and will follow him as before.[37]

Even when recent polls of neighbouring countries have shown, with the exception of Poland, support for German reunification, nevertheless one also encounters this image of the 'ugly' (*häßlich*) German. This is especially true at times of crisis. I can only list some of the crises since 1945 which have brought these opinions back to the surface.

The conflicts in the 1950s concerning German rearmament; the treaties with East European countries; the first meeting between Willy Brandt and Stolph in Erfurt in 1970; the increased cooperation between the Federal Republic and the GDR; the debates on the 'double-track' decision of NATO and the discussions of neutralism; the emergence of the Greens and the Republikaner as political forces; and finally the dynamic and momentum of the reunification process, coupled with a fear of Germany going it alone.

Concern at developments since November 1989 was aroused both by the speed at which events have moved and also by the way in which Germans have gone about reunification. For example, an adviser on foreign affairs to the former French prime minister Chirac remarked critically in an article in *Newsweek* that

> the Germans these days resent any restraint from outside. Understandably they feel that the German unification process is *their* business, as Chancellor Kohl's 10-point plan made clear. They feel that they do not have to consult anybody, nor give any additional 'conditions' or 'guarantees' to anyone....I am also disturbed by mounting evidence of a new German assertiveness – some say outright arrogance – which translates at times into a neglect of others' legitimate concerns.[38]

There were fears that the romantic Germans, wanderers within the world, could also explore new options which would take Germany out of the Western alliance – a new Rapallo, or Tauroggen, or Hitler–Stalin pact.

This image of Germany also plays a part in the approach to security questions. It is reasoned from historical experience that a single and powerful Germany placed in the centre of Europe automatically will be a security risk, and that Germany will not be bound by treaties and agreements if these do not suit her interests. The view was expressed

37. Public Record Office London (PRO), FO 371/16864, *The German Character*, 1 March 1945.

38. Pierre Lellouche, 'Frenchmen and Germans: the relationship between the two allies is turning increasingly sour at the very time it is needed most', *Newsweek*, 12 February 1990, p. 4.

in a British memorandum drawn up shortly after the outbreak of the Second World War.

> Germany has shown that if she is sufficiently strong, no treaties or undertakings will deter her from taking by force anything that she may happen to want. Therefore security in Europe is only possible if Germany is not strong enough to act in this way.[39]

This belief played a central role in post-war policy towards Germany and Europe. It was felt that even the dismemberment of Prussia (not the whole of Germany) and the construction of a federal state, although creating a better foundation for a stable and functioning democracy in Germany, would not offer a lasting security to Germany's neighbours.[40] Only with the partition of Germany in 1948–9, a policy which it had been difficult for the Allies to pursue openly or explicitly, did a satisfactory solution seem to have been found. Each of the states could become a 'star pupil' within their respective blocs. Reunification was promised, but one hoped that the promise would never be put into practice. Until 9 November 1989 the watchword was 'Security before the right of self-determination'.

THE GERMAN QUESTION AND EUROPEAN WEST INTEGRATION

In post–war discussions of European questions the term 'integration' became a key idea. It represented a political conception which bound together an image of Germany with views about how to handle security questions, and how the German state should be organised. In relation to Germany integration could be seen negatively, in terms of containing West Germany, or positively, in terms of admitting West Germany as a equal in a community of states.

One can see this from a particular example. From the late 1940s the tensions between the two power blocs led to the idea of rearming West Germany. There was opposition to this not only from within Germany but also from Germany's neighbours, who feared that rearmament would also strengthen West German economically and help lay the basis for a renewed phase of aggression.

39. PRO, FO 371/24370, 'Postwar Security', 12 March 1940.
40. Cf. PRO, FO 371/39080, 'Confederation, Federation and Decentralisation of the German State, and the Dismemberment of Prussia', November 1944.

In connection with the tying in of West Germany to a more tightly organised community of West European states, there were disagreements about the form of economic, political and military integration. The possibility of German reunification constantly played a role in these disagreements. The plan of the French prime minister Pleven in 1950 to establish a European army, the treaties for a European Defence Community, and the question of West Germany's entry into NATO all set off heated debates over the issue of military integration between the Federal Republic and her neighbours. One can see this in the responses of two of Germany's smaller neighbours, Belgium and Denmark, both of which had been occupied by Germany during the Second World War.

In November 1951 the party congress of the Belgian socialists supported the idea of a European army but, by a large majority, opposed the rearmament of West Germany. The fear was that in the event of German reunification the defence forces of the remainder of Western Europe would be too weak. German rearmarment posed a threat to democracy and world peace. Some of the speakers in the debate recalled the Nazi–Soviet pact of 1939, the Treaty of Rapallo, the Convention of Tauroggen, and warned against over-hasty moves towards European unity. The potential German threat meant that there should be no move towards European Federation which did not include Britain. Only a few delegates, like Paul Henri Spaack, saw in the formation of a European Federation an opportunity to solve the German question. In relation to Germany he advocated a policy of 'bold trust' (*Politik des kühnen Vertrauens*), that is taking Germany in as an equal member of such a federation. If this did not happen, but instead the fears of revanchism determined policy, then the West would repeat the mistakes it had made after 1918. The West had denied to a friendly, democratic Weimar Republic what it later gave to Hitler.

Spaack saw the only way forward in the full integration of West Germany into a European Federation. Only this could overcome the anxiety of the German threat. Without Germany Spaack believed there was no chance of a strong Europe developing which could assert itself as an equal partner against the two super-powers. Furthermore, Spaack, as a citizen of a small country, was convinced that the age of the sovereign nation-state in Europe was coming to an end.

Around the same time there was also a debate on security matters in the Danish parliament, the *Folketing*. Fears were expressed about the dangers that Europe and the world might face if democracy were to fail in a rearmed Germany and the military were to take power. It would be preferable to neutralise Germany and to control the German problem in this way. The Danish foreign minister argued against the view that an unarmed, neutral Germany would contribute towards security, peace and a reduction of tension in Europe. On the contrary, a country with 60 million people at the heart of Europe which had become a military vacuum would be a threat to peace.

The debates since the 1950s on security arrangements which would bind a reunited Germany into a European order have been constantly accompanied by the theme of neutralism and neutrality. Even during the Second World War the question of the political organisation of Germany was connected to the task of reducing the German threat to security. Although it is the case that today the majority of Germans have no desire to see a strong, centralised German state, it is necessary for Germans to appreciate these fears of a reunited Germany on the part of her neighbours. For them the unitary German state makes possible the concentration of all the resources of Germany into one pair of hands, as it did in the Wilhelmine period and under Hitler. What is more, a 'Fourth Reich' would be economically much more powerful than its predecessors.

It also should be borne in mind that most other European states have little experience of a federal state system. The point is often forgotten or neglected that federalism has been the traditional form of German state organisation rather than the unitary, unified state. German statehood has developed historically and in the present within a tension between the centralised state and the federal principle. Examples of the latter are the Hansa-Bund, the Holy Roman Empire of the German Nation, the German Confederation of 1815, its successor the North German Confederation, and the Federal Republic. The idea of the normal German state as the Prusso-German power state has pushed these other traditions into the background.

German historical writing, following upon a national movement oriented towards a unitary and powerful nation-state and rejecting federalist ideas, has helped contribute to the contemporary European image of what German unity might mean. A federalist state permits an evolutionary development which mixes together different kinds of statehood. It allows of formations from confederations to leagues of states to a federal state with numerous intermediate stages. This process can be halted or broken at any time. In the development towards a united state of Europe Germans can use their federal historical tradition to good effect and can link it to the West European unifying developments and institutions since 1945. German deputies, for example, were involved in the working out of constitutional proposals for the European Parliament and some submitted their own constitutional schemes.

With Altiero Spinelli as its secretary (Spinelli had already outlined proposals for a European Federation during the Second World War) the Institutional Committee (established 1981) of the first directly elected European Parliament, submitted in 1984 a draft treaty for a European Union. This was accepted by the Parliament on 14 February 1984. This envisaged a two-chamber system within a federal state structure, and aimed for a balance of institutions which does not yet exist. Since then German deputies have outlined proposals for European Union which draw more strongly upon the constitutional model of the Federal Republic of Germany.

Will German unification, welcomed by the European Parliament, accelerate the process of European unification? Will it turn the constitutional ideas of the European Parliament more quickly into reality?

A UNITED GERMANY AS PART OF A UNITED STATES OF EUROPE

In this section I wish to see what credible arguments one can put forward about the role of a united Germany in Europe. It is my view that most Germans see the future in European rather than German terms. 'From Germany to Europe' is the one sensible maxim of German policy, not the resurrection of older plans, such as those developed during the Second World War, of a united Europe organised through German power.

The changes in Eastern Europe and the dissolution of the two political blocs have ended the unnatural divisions of both Germany and Europe. They open up new perspectives for a unification of the continent based on what has already happened in Western Europe. They also demand new pan-European thinking, a vision of Europe, the use of the imagination. Those who work for a united Europe must always remember that they are a link in a tradition which goes back a long way and which in this century is associated with names such as Briand, Stresemann, Churchill, Monnet and Spinelli. These men 'provide us with examples that it is not pointless to try to work out a new conception of the future of Europe'.[41]

41. H. Schmidt, op.cit., pp. 562f.

There are, in my view, two key guidelines for the path to a European nation. Already in 1930 Ortega y Gasset wrote that

> Nationalisms are dead-ends... They lead nowhere. Only the decision to make one nation out of the various groups of people in the world can reinvigorate Europe. Our continent will win back its self-belief and, as a consequence of setting itself a great task, put its own house in order.[42]

The experiences of the Second World War turned Jean Monnet into a convinced European and architect of the Iron and Steel Community. When the European Community was established he wrote

> The 'Common Market' is not a static creation; it is a new and dynamic phase in the development of our civilisation. The essential characteristic of this new phase is that nations have now begun to accept that their problems are joint problems and cannot be settled by national measures only.[43]

However, the Europe of nation-states has not yet been superseded. The process of European integration has stagnated. In the light of this, Monnet, in his memoirs, insisted on the need to push on unceasingly for a United States of Europe. There was no alternative. This was a path on which there could be no turning back.

> As our provinces learnt yesterday, so must our nations learn today, to live together under common rules and under common, freely devised institutions, if they wish to make progress and master their own fate. The sovereign nations of the past are no longer the units within which the problems of the present can be solved. And the community [that is the EC] is only one stage on the path to a form of world organisation in the future.[44]

Today we need new concepts for the building of the common house of Europe, for the future organisational forms of Europe, which go beyond fine speeches without serious commitment.

For example, Poland, Hungary and Czechoslovakia already formally meet the requirements set out by the draft treaty of the European Parliament for membership of a European Union. They are no longer 'peoples' democracies' but have turned themselves into pluralist democracies along Western lines which form governments by means of democratic and free elections. This also fulfils a central requirement for membership of the EC. Article 2 of the draft treaty on European Union declares:

42. Gasset, op.cit., p. 136.
43. J. Monnet, 'Introduction', in R. Mayne (ed.) *The Community of Europe: Past, Present and Future* (New York, 1963), p. 5.
44. J. Monnet, *Erinnerungen eines Europäpers* (Munich, 1980), p. 662.

Every democratic European state can apply for membership of the Union.[45]

However, an immediate entry of these states, even if formally justified, given the simultaneous intensification of efforts at political integration in Western Europe can serve the interests neither of Western Europe nor of the aspirants of Eastern Europe. The new Europe must leave open a place for the USSR in the European house. Besides the EC states, the states of east-central and south-eastern Europe and the USSR, there are states which do not belong to the military alliances, for example the EFTA member states, the European signatories to the Conference on Security and Cooperation in Europe, and those states which are merely members of the Council of Europe. All these states and groups of states must find a place in the Europe of the future. The Council of Europe, which since 1949 has stimulated changes in the political landscape of Western Europe, can play an important part in the changes within Europe. In a transitional phase the Council of Europe and its institutions could serve as a way of tying together all European states and groups of states.

On the basis of geography and its special European position Germany, deliberately but not arrogantly, must take on a constructive and creative responsibility for the growing together of Europe, though without presenting itself as the 'master' of this process. If Germany is to do this, to take the second chance in the twentieth century in a European sense, and not, as an anxious Europe fears, to reverse a lost war by other means into a victory, with Germany the master from Atlantic to Pacific, then it must act for a Europe beyond that of nation-states. Germans must renounce state egoism and attempts at hegemony. They must oppose the nationalist rhetoric of a minority and demonstrate that a democratic Germany will also be a European Germany. Germany, once more a sovereign state since 3 October 1990, must take up once again its centuries-long tradition of European peacemaker. If a united Europe is to develop, Germany must place its potential in the service of the common European interest. Other Europeans hope that this will furnish a welcome and reconciling conclusion to the German question.

The path to a united Europe, as for a united Germany, will take the federalist form. The discussions in the nineteenth century and after 1945 of a German constitution with 'narrower' and 'wider' federations can be

---

45. 'Entwurf eines Vertrages zur Gründung der Europäischen Union', printed in R. Bieber and J. Schwarze (eds) *Verfassungsentwicklung in der Europäischen Gemeinschaft* (Baden-Baden, 1984), pp. 95–128 (97).

of use in the construction of a European constitution. This could be related to the necessary transitional phase – one of a two-speed Europe – when a narrower political union of the EC states concerned with creating a single internal market, must coexist with a broader band of states beyond the EC.

It was only as recently as 1989 and early 1990 that such a model of a narrower and a wider federation seemed appropriate to the process of German unification. Now it offers a perspective for a growing together of the various parts of Europe in a fairly smooth fashion. Germany must take on responsibility for such a policy if it is serious about its European calling and wishes to be understood as a European Germany.

The aim of all Germans today must be, precisely because of the historical and European dimensions of the German question, to make the new, democratic and federal Germany into a stabilising element within Europe, positively pursuing first Western European and then pan-European integration and acting as a catalyst for the realisation of the long European dream. This must include a pan-European security order which must reach across the Atlantic and the whole of Europe and bind together the two super-powers of the USA and the USSR.

The Germans must show their European neighbours and partners, through the policies pursued, that the historically understandable fears of a united Germany are groundless, that a democratic Germany does not close itself to its history, but has learnt from that history and renounces that old Germany which still preoccupies others. Only in this way can a new image of Germany and a new understanding of Germany emerge from the shadows of the past. What is also important is the cultivation of a European consciousness.

Salvador de Madariaga noted in 1952 in his portrait of Europe:

> 'Fiat Europe' will not be possible until Europeans cease to trumpet the age-old war cries of their tribes, scantily covered over by nationalist historians with the fig-leaf of academic history. Europe must think its history anew and experience it afresh as what it really is, as European history.[46]

As Europeans we must all take responsibility for the construction of a genuinely European history, for the 'future of history'. Graf Ferraris referred to an important step in this work when he demanded:

> If German history…is once again to be fitted harmoniously into the history of Europe, then Europeans must be conscious of their history and must cease, in common with Germans, to be prisoners of the recent and dramatic past. That past is indeed dramatic, but it is also short.[47]

46. Madariaga, op.cit., p. 9.
47. Ferraris, op.cit., p. 16.

Today the chance is offered to Germans and to all Europeans to seize the opportunity that is offered and to find unity.

SUGGESTIONS FOR FURTHER READING:

Luigi Barzini, *The Europeans* (Harmondsworth, 1983).

David Calleo, *The German Problem Reconsidered. Germany and the World Order, 1870 to the Present* (Cambridge, 1980).

Jean-Baptiste Duroselle, *Europe. A History of its Peoples* (London, 1991).

John Gillingham, *Coal, Steel, and the Rebirth of Europe 1945–1955. The Germans and French from Ruhr Conflict to Economic Community* (Cambridge, 1991).

Wolf D. Gruner, *Die deutsche Frage – ein Problem der europäischen Geschichte seit 1800* (Munich, 1985); new enlarged edition 1992 (Series Piper Aktuell).

Wolf D. Gruner, *Deutschland mitten in Europa* (Hamburg, 1991).

Wolf D. Gruner, 'European Integration and the German Question,' in Brian Nelson, David Roberts, Walter Veit (eds), *The European Community in the 1990s. Economics, Politics, Defence* (Oxford, 1992).

Wolf D. Gruner, 'The Impact of the Reconstruction of Central Europe in 1814–15 on the System of Peace in the 19th Century,' in A.P. van Goudoever (ed.), *The Great Peace Congresses. Proceedings of the Conference. Utrecht August 16–17, 1991* (Utrecht, 1991).

Wolfram Hanrieder, *Germany, America, Europe: Forty Years of German Foreign Policy* (New Haven, 1989).

Olov Riste (ed.), *Western Security, The Formative Years. European and Atlantic Defence 1947–1953* (New York, 1985).

John K. Sowden, *The German Question 1945–1973* (London, 1975).

Richard H. Ullman, *Securing Europe* (Princeton, 1991).

Derek W. Urwin, *The Community of Europe. A History of European Integration since 1945* (London and New York, 1991).

Dirk Verheyen, *The German Question. A Cultural, Historical, and Geopolitical Exploration* (Boulder, 1991).

Dirk Verheyen and Christian Soe (eds), *The Germans and their Neighbors* (Boulder, 1992).

Nils H. Wessell (ed), *The New Europe. Revolution in East-West Relations* (New York, 1991).

CHAPTER TWELVE

Conclusion: nationalism and German reunification

John Breuilly

The historian is no better equipped to predict than anyone else; studying the past only makes one aware of how uncertain is the future. However, it is worth trying to relate the themes of the changes and significance in the role of political nationality in modern German history to the present and immediate future.

What role did nationality play in the 'revolution' of 1989–90? To understand that we need first to remind ourselves of the speed with which changes took place. At the beginning of 1989 Erich Honecker was still in power and insisting that the Berlin Wall would remain 'as long as the conditions leading to its erection have not changed, it will still be standing in 50 and even in 100 years' time'.

The events which developed rapidly from mid-1989 can be broken down into three elements: the impact of changes in Eastern Europe, especially the USSR, upon East Germany; the shifts of political power and mood in East Germany; the policies pursued by the West, especially West Germany, in response to events in East Germany. In turn, political action in East Germany can be divided into those involving the power-holders, the political opposition, and large numbers of previously politically uninvolved who sought to leave East Germany from September 1989 and took to the streets from October.

By mid-1989 the USSR faced many internal problems and it was increasingly clear that it would not intervene in the affairs of Warsaw Pact countries in order to sustain existing Communist regimes. In July at a Warsaw Pact meeting in Bucharest this position was made explicit, and the countries rejected the Brezhnev doctrine which had legitimated such intervention in Czechoslovakia in 1968. The satellite states of Eastern Europe were on their own. Already a number had embarked on major political and economic reforms, leaving East Germany behind in this respect. One reform was to remove border controls between Hungary and Austria. For many East Germans, Hungary had been important as a holiday resort and a place where one could escape some of the rigours of their own situation. Such possibilities had in turn been an important element in the way the East German government had sought to make life more attractive for its own citizens, without abandoning its basic economic and political policies.

Now Hungary came to serve as an escape route to the West as well, and many East Germans flooded into the country, and into the missions of the Federal Republic of Germany in Budapest as well as Prague and East Berlin. By August the situation was sufficiently serious for the West German government to reach agreement with the Hungarian and Austrian governments for tens of thousands of East Germans to cross into the Federal Republic. By early September the Hungarian government had decided it could no longer restrict the exit of East Germans, and announced the complete opening of its borders. Some 50,000 East Germans travelled by this route to West Germany.

This touched off an internal crisis in East Germany. Opposition groups now came into the open politically in early September, with the formation of the New Forum, and within a couple of weeks the first protest demonstrations had started in Leipzig. East Germans continued to vote with their feet, and various agreements were struck to allow them to move from other East European countries to West Germany. The East German government was faced with the dilemma of allowing this to continue or to seal its borders with the rest of Eastern Europe.

The obvious response was to pursue political reform in order to remove the pressure both of political opposition and mass emigration. It was clear that the USSR favoured this course. Gorbachev visited East Germany in early October on the occasion of the fortieth anniversary of the regime. He made this clear and also distanced himself from Honecker, encouraging other elements within the country's political elite to remove Honecker and embark on a reformist course. Within a fortnight Honecker had gone, and was replaced by Egon Krenz.

Political change also continued apace in other Eastern European countries. There were mass demonstrations in Czechoslovakia and on 23 October Hungary declared itself a multi-party republic. In early November the GDR revoked its border controls with Czechoslovakia. Thousands more East Germans escaped to West Germany by this route. Between 8 and 10 November a new Politburo was elected for the GDR. The dramatic change came on 9 November, when the GDR government finally decided it could hold the line no longer against mass pressure to emigrate and declared the Berlin Wall open.

So far in the crisis the West German government had only acted in its role of welcoming anyone who wished to leave East Germany and making arrangements to enable such movement. 'Nationality' played a role only in the sense that it was the 'two states, one nation' doctrine which underpinned that commitment, and also that awareness of this commitment had long encouraged East Germans to compare their situation with that of West Germany and to look to West Germany as a refuge, even as a 'home'.

At this moment, however, Chancellor Kohl moved on the other 'national' element of West German policy, namely the commitment to reunification. On 28 November he presented to the *Bundestag* a ten-point programme for overcoming the division of Germany and of Europe. He placed that programme firmly within a commitment to NATO and the European Community, insisting that it was those alliances whose firmness at times of crisis had helped bring about change in the east. He also argued that good relations with East Germany, especially allowing so many cross-border visits, had helped maintain a sense of national unity. But now was the time to move decisively to end the division in Germany.

First, there needed to be emergency aid to assist the many East Germans coming into West Germany. Also communications with East Germany needed improving. West Germany could help East Germany if she introduced democratic political reforms and economic reforms that would move the country towards a market economy. There could be more treaty arrangements with East Germany, and one could even consider the establishment of confederal relationships, but only once a democratic government had been established in East Germany. Interestingly Kohl appealed here to German history, pointing out that political structures had most usually taken a federal or a confederal form. However, he also insisted that these developments must take place within a European context and Kohl's next points concerned agreements with the USSR, further integration and extension of the European Community, and arms reductions and controls undertaken by the Conference on Security and Cooperation and the various arms limitation talks. Finally, Kohl reiterated the commitment to German reunification.

Kohl had moved the debate from issues of refugees and internal crisis to one of fundamental political and economic reform which would press East Germany towards democracy and a market economy and open up the prospects for reunification, but set within a broader European context. Yet even Kohl had as yet no inkling of the speed with which events would move in East Germany, assuming that there would be for some time a credible government with which to make agreements and exert pressure. For a short period this seemed to be the case as the GDR, with Hans Modrow as prime minister, introduced various reforms and negotiated treaties and agreements with West Germany.

However, these agreements and the reforms undertaken in the GDR actually hastened its demise. Political reform led to the formation of political parties in readiness for elections to the *Volkskammer* which were to be held in March 1990. Bringing down the Berlin Wall reduced the rate of emigration to West Germany, but now allowed a steady loss of population which created severe economic problems. That, along with the exposure of a frail economy to Western competition and the collapse of Comecon trading patterns, meant that the idea of reforming the GDR economy with a gradual move to market economics had to be given up in favour of the idea of West Germany taking responsibility for all of Germany.

In both cases what mattered was in effect a West German intervention. The attractions of her economy and the right of all Germans to move undermined the GDR economy. One can see this at a number of critical points. For example, in the early demonstrations of late September/early October in Leipzig, one of the major slogans had been '*Wir bleiben hier!*' ('We are staying here!'). This was a rejection of emigration as the solution to problems. It was also a commitment to the idea of an internal renewal within the GDR. However, the removal of the Berlin Wall now made emigration easier. What is more, the policy of the West German government to give every East German visitor 100 Marks to spend in the West helped reinforce the sense of common deprivation in the East and the attractions of a rapid integration into West Germany. The size and number of the demonstrations increased (there was now much less danger involved in participation), the social basis extended downwards. Another popular slogan in the early demonstrations had been '*Wir sind das Volk!*' ('We are the people!'). This was not only a commitment to democratic reform but also an indignant repudiation of the governmental propaganda which had presented the demonstrators as an irresponsible and self-interested mob. Now the slogan became '*Wir sind ein Volk!*' ('We are one nation!'). Never have the multiple meanings of the word *Volk*, combined with a shift from the definite to the indefinite article, reflected so profound a change in mood and purpose. What is more, the new GDR government gave some support to this commitment to unification, with Modrow's emotional statement that there was but a single German fatherland.

This rapidly increasing mass commitment to joining the West, along with the sheer political and economic bankruptcy which was made clear in the early months of 1990, pushed events on rapidly. West German political parties, in particular the CDU, effectively took over the campaign of its East German counterpart for the March 1990 elections. The GDR CDU obtained a majority of seats with other conservative political groupings in a coalition calling itself the 'Alliance for Germany'. This led in turn to the formation of a new government with a CDU (East) prime minister, Lothar de Maizière, committed to German unity.

At the same time Kohl was removing the international obstacles to unity. He tied the USA and the European Community into this process by getting their agreement to his unity policy and to measures to integrate the GDR when this was achieved. In February he visited Moscow to agree on the steps to unification with Gorbachev, who made it clear that he did not oppose this in principle and that there would be no Soviet military action to halt such a process. This led on to talks (known as the Four plus Two talks) between the wartime Allies and the two German governments.

By May a treaty between the two Germanies establishing monetary, economic and social union was signed. This came into effect in July. In August treaties on all-German elections and unification were signed, and were ratified by the two German parliaments through September. The old *Länder*, which the GDR had abolished in 1954, were restored. This made possible, on 3 October, the unification of the GDR with the Federal Republic by means of Article 23 of the Basic Law of 1949 which permitted accession by individual *Länder*. In the same period final agreement was reached with the USSR on the united Germany choosing to be a member of NATO and a timetable for the phased withdrawal of Soviet troops from GDR territory. Finally, on 2 December the first all-German elections to the *Bundestag* were held, resulting in a victory for the CDU/CSU/FDP coalition. Interestingly, the electorate did not reward Kohl and his own party for his policies. The arguments of the FDP leader Genscher, who took much credit as foreign minister for the unification process, that it would be dangerous to have a simple CDU/CSU majority were heeded. The FDP did particularly well in GDR territories. By now the SPD reservations about rapid unification, as expressed in the campaign of their Chancellor candidate, Oscar Lafontaine, had become a clear vote loser.

In retrospect one can see that by the end of 1989 the major factors at work were the policy of the West German government and popular opinion in East Germany. Kohl's decisive shift of policy from November 1989 had made it clear to the East German population that rapid change was to be encouraged. For the bulk of East Germans rapid change meant moving closer to West Germany rather than pursuing a course of reform within an independent state. This undercut the position of the existing political opposition as well as the government in East Germany. Lacking any other political elites, the key political forces became in effect subsidiaries of West German parties.

It is clear that in many respects Kohl moved ahead of public opinion in West Germany. Opinion polls in early 1990 point to scepticism about moving too rapidly towards unification, above all for fear of the extra burdens it would place upon West Germany. The SPD built its own political line around those reservations. Its Chancellor candidate, Oscar Lafontaine, identified himself with that policy and went on to contest the December election on that basis. In early 1990, in East Germany as well as West Germany, there had been widespread fear that over-rapid unification could prove painful. In the euphoria created by the collapse of the East German political and economic system and the removal of international obstacles to rapid unification, these doubts and fears were temporarily forgotten.

Three things above all had undermined these doubts in the short-term, or at least prevented them from slowing down the path to re-unification. First, the speed of collapse of the East German political and economic system meant that there was little alternative but for the West German government to make the running. Second, the monetary union of July 1990, on the unrealistic conversion rate of 1:1 (with some exceptions for certain kinds of savings) provided a temporary glow of satisfaction – giving East Germans a sudden surge of purchasing power and increasing demand for goods from West Germany. Coupled with Kohl's assurance that unification would be economically painless, something people were only too anxious to believe, this enabled the third element to play its part. The latent sense of national identity, that it was 'natural' for there to be a single German state, could now come to the surface, unhindered by all the political and economic considerations which had relegated the idea of unification to the realm of fantasy. All this helped Kohl and his coalition to a decisive election victory in December.

In all this, therefore, nationality mattered decisively. It underpinned the West German commitment to accepting citizens of East Germany, and that in turn shaped the way East Germans acted. Emigration to the 'better Germany' rather than political dissent began the internal crisis and the popular vote for the Deutschmark and integration with West Germany brought the crisis to an end. The commitment to unity meant that it was the intervention of West German political forces which resolved that crisis rather than internal political opposition, either from within the SED or from among the emergent opposition movements. In other East European countries change was brought about by shifts within the political elite (Hungary), by the rise in political dissent and opposition (Czechoslovakia), by the development of mass oppositions (Poland), or by some combination of these (Romania). The national dimension to the German situation gave the internal crisis a different character and meant it was very quickly resolved by means of unification. Reformist Communism, political dissent, and mass politicisation were all undercut by a West German takeover before they had been able to become politically significant.

Yet that option of radical change by means of rapid unification emerged as a practical one only some time after the crisis had begun. It was not nationalism as a determined politics of unification which mattered, so much as nationality as a latent sense of identity which underpinned the political obligations of the Federal Republic to GDR citizens and gave focus to a 'fixation' with the West among the population of East Germany. For many years East Germans could be visited by relatives from the West, could watch German television, and in some cases could visit West Germany. In this way the 'national' and the 'West' were fused, as a model and as an objective. This was counterposed to the bankruptcy of the GDR. For example, people watched West German television not only because it revealed to them lives they could only dream of (in a way West Germans watching *Dynasty* and *Dallas* were doing the same), but also because so much of GDR television output had nothing to offer, be it attractive fantasy or an engagement with the real problems of its viewers.[1] It was not only the Deutschmark payments and the lure of Western consumerism that attracted people to the West but also the knowledge of the bankruptcy of their own economy. In this double way, West Germany served as a focus for most people's hopes. Once it became clear that the East German government could no longer maintain control, this fixation swept all before it.

Perhaps the only really puzzling feature of the whole event is why

1. The point has been interestingly made that, where GDR television did engage in that way (and where its successors still do) – in the field of drama rather than news or current affair programmes – then such programmes have secured much larger viewing figures than other programmes. How far this will continue when a greater diet of Western programmes becomes available is another matter. See P. Hoff, 'Continuity and change: television in the GDR from autumn 1989 to summer 1990', *German History: The Journal of the German History Society* 9/2 (1991), pp. 184–96.

the Kohl government decided to exploit this fixation to the maximum when so many in West Germany had been reserved about too precipitous a policy. Partly this seems to be due to the problem of the unexpectedly rapid collapse of control in the GDR: if the Federal Republic had to assume responsibility, better to do so swiftly and completely. Partly it could be seen in terms of electoral calculation: to be able to go into elections as the man who reunified Germany. Kohl had been doing badly in opinion polls and reunification certainly did rejuvenate him and his party. Partly it could be seen as exploiting a brief opportunity. One could never be sure at what point the USSR might harden its position,[2] or indeed whether various of Germany's allies would start indicating serious reservations about the process. Partly it could be seen in terms of economic pressures. At the beginning West German business seems to have been sanguine about the impact of reunification. Few anticipated the subsequent difficulties and many could see rich pickings. But above all I would plump for the simplest explanation. For decades German conservatives had tried to combine the apparently contradictory – full integration into the West with the reunification of the nation-state. Suddenly in late 1989 this appeared possible. They had no desire to see a reformed GDR perhaps insist on different kinds of German–German relations; maybe to try to uncouple the Federal Republic from its strong Western orientation. In this sense, therefore, the specifically conservative view of national unification in the Federal Republic also played a key role in the events of 1989–90. Nevertheless, that particular policy worked only on the basis of a much broader support for unification which flowed from the underlying sense of national identity.

The character of unification and the role of nationality in unification was, therefore, very different from 1871. It was very much *re*-unification, in the sense of a commitment to the idea of a nation-state which had in some sense already existed. Strictly speaking, of course, it was unification because it brought together two states which had never previously been connected to each other, but this sense of a pre-existing nation-state made it appear as reunification. It was also above all a popular idea, and not so much a nationalist idea as a route for East Germans to an imagined world of prosperity and freedom. Obviously there was a good deal of truth in this idea, but there were also unrealistic expectations which actual reunification would be bound to expose.

2. I write these words on 21 August, just after the collapse of the coup against Gorbachev. During the short time of the coup Kohl argued that an event of that kind justified his pursuit of rapid unification.

At first the idea seemed to have few drawbacks. In the euphoria of 1989–90 it was the German component of a dawning of freedom in the Eastern Bloc countries. And in this case it did appear that many of the difficulties of the transition to that freedom would be carried on the strong back of West Germany. Indeed, at first all the talk was of how much stronger the accession of the GDR territories would make Germany. Few critics saw this in territorial terms – the fears associated with the Germany of 1871 or 1914 or 1938–9 – but rather in terms of economic domination. It was only the critical intelligentsia – both of West and East Germany – who condemned this as Deutschmark patriotism. Otherwise, the only reservations concerned the pacing and modalities of the change. The *Bundesbank*, for example, warned against rapid monetary unification on an unrealistic exchange rate.

Events since December 1990 have rather altered this mood. The 1:1 convertibility of the Mark has proved a grave error. Hopes that money wage levels would stay unchanged in the former GDR, thereby compensating for lower productivity rates, proved false. Economists now consider that even the productivity differences understate the relative inefficiency of the GDR economy in relation to the West. Measured in terms of the purchasing power of GDR products to West German products in international markets, a conversion of 4:1 would have been realistic, as a few economists argued at the time. However, the effect on East German living standards made such a rate unacceptable. The 1:1 rate rendered much of GDR economic activity hopelessly uncompetitive at a stroke. Coupled with the loss of Comecon markets, a lack of access to USSR natural resources, and the insistence of the USSR on trading for the hard currency of dollars, the result has been catastrophic.

A few figures tell the grim story more effectively than words. GDR gross national product fell some 20 per cent in 1990, with industrial output down 50 per cent. Comecon trade has been cut to one-third of its earlier level. From an 'official' zero rate of unemployment, by the end of March 1990 there were over 800,000 jobless and some 2 million people working short-time, much of that subsidised by the German government. (This support has now been extended to December 1991.) Some economists think unemployment could go up to 2 million with another 0.5 million on short-time working. Another 2 million people (usually the younger and more energetic and more skilled) have moved west out of former GDR territory, and 20,000 still leave every month. In a total population of around 17 million, these represent serious losses to the total labour force of the former GDR territory and to its economy.

All this reveals just how weak and uncompetitive most of the GDR economy had become, probably weaker relatively in 1990 than it had been ten years earlier, thanks to a precipitate fall in capital investment, itself partly due to an attempt by the GDR regime to legitimise itself by bolstering consumption and social benefits.

The West German economy faces very different problems. There was a huge 'demand shock' as East Germans used their savings to purchase hitherto unavailable goods, especially as such purchasing power was inflated by the favourable convertibility rate. The result was inflationary pressure, over-employment, and a push on wage rates. Another result was a switch away from production for export to production for domestic consumption (though, of course, what had originally been counted as exports to the GDR now became a component of domestic consumption). Germany's traditional balance of payments surplus was wiped out in a single year. There was pressure on public finance – for example paying social security and retraining programmes in the former GDR which also led to government borrowing. The effect was to raise interest rates and to put pressure on the Deutschmark.

The way the contrasting economic difficulties combined has also been unfortunate. German trade unions, concerned about lower wage levels in the East undercutting the rates of most of their members in the West, have pressed for national wage rates with East German earnings rising to that of their West German counterparts. The effect can only be to increase inflationary pressures, reduce resources for capital investment, increase unemployment and closures in East Germany, and sustain or increase the flight to the West. However, that in turn will put pressure on housing and job markets and create further tensions.

The situation has not been helped by the doctrinaire economic policies which at first accompanied the reunification process. The collapse of Communism has been seen as automatically indicating the superiority of the free market system. The German government at first wanted to see as rapid a transition to market economics as possible. The *Treuhand* concern which took over all former state enterprise in the GDR saw its task primarily as one of privatisation. The market would take care of everything and 'intervention' would only slow down and possibly even undermine the rapid transition which was so necessary. This also had the attraction of appearing to avoid the need for higher taxes to finance any interventionist policy.

In recent months the German government appears to have seen the error of its ways. *Treuhand* increasingly sees its role as restructuring as much as of privatisation. The necessity to raise taxes has finally been recognised. Policies to encourage investment in infrastructure (e.g through loans to local government) are being adopted. But much more remains to be done. Perhaps the biggest bullet to bite might be the idea of a labour subsidy to former GDR areas to enable employers to keep their work force but at competitive wages. But a measure of that kind would cost an enormous amount, and meets the problems of unpopularity in western Germany as well as going against the general philosophy of the government.

Indeed it is the immensity of the reconstruction task and its un-popularity in western Germany which now (August 1991) dominates public opinion. It appears that the government has no clear idea any more of just how much reconstruction will cost and how it is to be financed.[3] There is also fear that this might undermine the lead Germany has taken in European affairs. For example, the issue of mon-etary union in the European Community has been tied very firmly to notions of 'economic convergence'. Germany realises more strongly than ever the consequences of monetary union with 'backward' areas. What is more, it will be difficult for the German government to press a policy of monetary restraint upon a future European bank, if it itself is being more spendthrift in terms of borrowing and printing money. The government has made it clear that an early casualty of its over-ex-tension will be aid to Eastern European countries. Yet at the same time, it is the economic weight of the European Community which appears to offer the one slim chance of preventing the break-up of Yugoslavia. It is also argued that only Western aid will prevent even worse crises erupting in the USSR. (This argument will surely increase in weight since the unsuccessful coup in August 1991.) Germany is more acutely aware of the dangers posed to itself by such crises; yet at present seems to be less capable than a year ago of taking the lead in responding in a positive and preventive way.

Pessimism is not confined to the German economy and European developments. East Germans in many walks of life are finding reunifi-cation a bitter experience. In the universities and academies there are closures of politically suspect institutions and a scrutiny of the political and intellectual credentials of those who remain. There is, in my view, no alternative to such a policy – one cannot allow corrupt propagan-dists and party hacks to continue to teach and enjoy academic privi-leges. However, individual cases are never simply black or white; and so far as academic credentials are concerned the blame lies less with the individual than with the limited opportunities and resources avail-

3. *Der Spiegel*, 1 July 1991: feature article 'Steuer-Opfer für den Osten: Wieviel noch?'

able to scientists, social scientists and other academics in the GDR. This problem of accommodating to West German standards is repeated in every sector of skilled employment.

At the same time resentment and a sense of superiority can be discerned among West Germans. There is resentment at having to pay to help East Germans. There is also an increasing awareness that living in two very different societies and states has created very different people. At times East Germans are talked about in ways which in other countries would be regarded as racist. 'Nationality' as a latent sense of identity inherited from the existence of a nation-state between 1871 and 1945, as a commitment of the Federal Republic to the GDR, and as a fixation upon the Federal Republic shared by many GDR citizens is turning out to be something very different from 'nationality' as actual habits and values and ways of living together.

My own feeling, however, is that much of this pessimism is as unrealistic as the optimism was a year ago. Indeed, one exaggerated mood has followed in reaction to the disillusionment of the first. In economic terms surely the most basic point is that the dynamic West German economy which had an ageing population has suddenly acquired access to a younger population. Not only that but also this population is itself German and is well-disciplined and quite well-schooled at least up to secondary level. Indeed it has recently been asserted that young East Germans are better equipped in basic literacy than their West German counterparts. When one considers the problems Germany faced in 1945 and compares them to the problems that it confronts now, and when one thinks that the most basic components of economic success in developed economies are technology and what in economic jargon is known as 'human capital' – then the pessimism appears misplaced. There will be problems in the short term, but provided a sensible policy of infrastructural investment is followed in the GDR areas, I would think these will be overcome within a decade.

The same will then apply to the 'problem' of cultural tensions and 'national identity'. German intellectuals, and less understandably, intellectuals from Britain, constantly agonise over an alleged problem of 'national identity' in Germany. But what the historical evidence suggests, as analysed in this book, is that there is no problem. 'National identity' does not develop as a consequence of deliberate propaganda and governmental policy, or as a product of historians and others who betray their vocation as social scientists to engage in myth-making. National identity develops at two levels – institutional and cultural. Institutionally it develops by people learning the same 'habits' – of voting, joining organisations, using the courts, dealing with the police, paying taxes, etc. Culturally, in modern industrial societies, it develops through the construction of a 'standard national culture'.

So far as the first is concerned, the majority of Germans have now learnt thoroughly the 'habits' of the Federal Republic of Germany. In terms of 'institutional loyalty', in certain respects it might appear that the Federal Republic is more stable than the United Kingdom. In the United Kingdom there is one part of the country – Ulster – where institutional loyalty has not really established itself. Partly as cause, partly as consequence of that, Ulster actually has different institutions from the rest of the UK. If one takes willing tax-paying as a measure of institutional consent, then the poll tax, especially in Scotland and many inner cities, reveals far less institutional loyalty than anything in Germany.

At a cultural level, a recent opinion poll showed that even most whites, let alone non-whites, believed Britain to be a racist society. (It might be said that this also applies to German attitudes towards foreign workers, but unlike the United Kingdom or France, large numbers of these ethnic minorities do not possess citizenship rights in the state so this is politically, although not of course morally, a less important problem.) No doubt there is a difficult learning process to be gone through in Germany – not only by East Germans who must come to terms with living in an 'open society', but also one hopes by West Germans who will see that the optimal solution to problems is not always just to adopt the existing West German approach. But the population is ethnically homogeneous and shares in the major components of a 'standard national culture'. I cannot see that the remaining problems of integrating East and West Germans are somehow more difficult tasks than those faced by other developed industrial societies. In many ways a strong economy and a well-accepted set of economic and political institutions makes the task a lot easier.

The Federal Republic by 1989 had developed into one successful democratic and industrial society among others. Unification – based on the acceptance of the nation-state of 1871–1945 (less certain eastern territories) as the 'normal' political unit – in one sense was not unique either. *Everyone*, German and non-German, sees the nation-state as normal. It is indeed this perception of the nation-state as natural that gives it its power as a political idea. What history should do is make us aware of how novel and in many ways strange is this idea. The assumption that the German nation-state is a natural entity is largely the product of the modern German nation-state, just as French identity and British identity are products of their nation-states. Before that state was created, conceptions of nationality were less central and served many different, often conflicting purposes. After that state was created, internal and external tensions meant that there were competing forms of nationalism, but underlying this there did develop a more latent, 'natural' sense of national identity. The same happened in other countries with stable political institutions, fairly successful economies, and mass cultural institutions. One can assume that such a sense of identity will continue to exist, now modifying itself as it incorporates GDR territory and citizens.

At the same time, the character of recent German history has meant that Germans are less politically committed to the idea of the nation-state as a hard concentration of sovereignty. Federalism has been more important in a much more recently unified country than in the longer-existing unitary nation-states of Britain, France and Spain. At the same time over-assertive nationalism was discredited and destroyed by the Third Reich. Ideas of incorporation into larger international blocs do not disturb Germans in the way they do many British people. I would not see this policy of European integration as some cunning German route to indirect domination (now that the direct route has been discredited). It is not even uniquely German: inhabitants of countries which were occupied by Germany between 1939 and 1945 are also well aware of the limitations and fragility of nation-states. It is not an 'escape' from national identity – with the implication that identity is a matter of deliberate choice rather than a set of habits which develop over time. Rather it is a part of the way German habits have developed since 1945.

That does not mean the Europeanism of Germans is 'right' and the hostility of many British people to such Europeanism is 'wrong'. It may be if Germany does prove economically successful in the medium-term she will dominate integrated European institutions, and that may cause problems in other parts of Europe. But in part the dispute is based upon the way national identity has been developed within different kinds of nation-states. In a way the British state is as many of its politicians see it – very centralised, with inseparable links between executive and legislature, with little idea of the rule of law as entrenched in written constitutions. Equally the German state is not like that, but more federalised, with a written constitution, and a matter of fact acceptance of the idea that different powers can be located in different places. In other words, different kinds of states promote, by the habits their institutions inculcate, different kinds of national identity. To understand Germany today, and to understand its relationship with Europe, requires us to understand how different and changing conceptions of nationality have developed. We need to see national identity neither as a deliberate and special belief nor as part of the natural order of things, but as a central component of modernity, closely bound up with the way modern states have developed. I hope this book has made something of that clear for the case of Germany.

SUGGESTIONS FOR FURTHER READING

The events considered in this conclusion are too recent and unfinished to have yet given rise to much in the way of historical analysis. I have mainly relied on British and German newspapers and periodicals. The German government has published some useful chronologies and collections of documents such as *Umbruch in Europa: Die Ereignisse im 2. Halbjahr 1989. Eine Dokumentation* (Bonn, 1990). There is a large amount of material being published in German but little, if anything, has yet filtered through into English.

Index

Cleo

How a small black cat
helped heal a family

HELEN BROWN

HODDER &
STOUGHTON

First published in Great Britain in 2010 by Hodder & Stoughton
An Hachette UK company

3

Copyright © Helen Brown 2009

The right of Helen Brown to be identified as the Author of the Work has been asserted by
her in accordance with the Copyright, Designs and Patents Act 1988.

A CIP catalogue record for this title is available from the British Library

ISBN 978 1444 70013 8

All photographs courtesy of the author

Typeset in Adobe Jenson by Hewer Text UK Ltd, Edinburgh

Printed and bound by CPI Mackays, Chatham ME5 8TD

Hodder & Stoughton policy is to use papers that are natural, renewable
and recyclable products and made from wood grown in sustainable forests.
The logging and manufacturing processes are expected to conform to the
environmental regulations of the country of origin.

Hodder & Stoughton Ltd
338 Euston Road
London NW1 3BH
www.hodder.co.uk

To those who say
they aren't cat people
but deep down
know they are.

Contents

Choice

A cat chooses its owner, not the other way around

'We're not getting a kitten,' I said, negotiating our stationwagon around a bend the shape of a pretzel. 'We're just going to look at them.'

The road to Lena's house was complicated by its undulations, not to mention the steepness. It snaked over what would qualify as mountains in most parts of the world. There wasn't much beyond Lena's house except a few sheep farms and a stony beach.

'You said we could get a kitten,' Sam whined from the back seat before turning to his younger brother for support. 'Didn't she?'

The back seat was usually the boys' battleground. Between two brothers aged nearly nine and six the dynamic was predictable. Sam would set Rob up with a surreptitious jab that would be rewarded with a kick, demanding retaliation with a thump, escalating into recriminations and tears—'He punched me!' 'That's 'cos he pinched me first.' But this time they were on the same side, and my usual role of judge and relationship counsellor had been supplanted by a simpler one—the Enemy.

'Yeah, it's not fair,' Rob chimed in. 'You said.'

'What I said was we *might* get a kitten one day. One big dog is enough for any family. What would Rata do? She'd hate having a cat in the house.'

'No she wouldn't. Golden retrievers like cats,' Sam replied. 'I read it in my pet book.'

There was no point recalling the number of times we'd seen Rata disappear into undergrowth in pursuit of an unfortunate member of the feline species. Since Sam had given up trying to become a superhero and thrown his Batman mask to the back of his wardrobe, he'd morphed into an obsessive reader brimming with facts to destroy any argument I could dredge up.

I didn't want a cat. I probably wasn't even a cat person. My husband, Steve, certainly wasn't. If only Lena hadn't smiled so brightly that day at our neighbourhood playgroup when she'd asked: 'Would you like a kitten?' If only she hadn't said it so loudly—and in front of the kids.

'Wow! We're getting a kitten!' Sam had yelled before I had a chance to answer.

'Wow! Wow!' Rob had echoed, jumping up and down in his sneakers with the holes I'd been trying to ignore.

Even before we'd met Lena I'd been in awe of her. A willowy beauty with an eclectic fashion style, she'd migrated from Holland in her late teens to become a highly regarded painter. Her portraits invariably contained political comment about race, sex or religion. An artist in the deepest sense, she also chose to live independently from men with her three children. Personally, I wouldn't have been surprised if Lena had summoned her offspring from some parallel universe only she and Pablo Picasso had access codes to. I wasn't about to make a fuss about a kitten in front of her.

+

Raising a pair of boys was proving to be more demanding than I'd imagined back when I was a schoolgirl watching baby-shampoo ads on television. If there'd been an Olympic medal for teenage mother naivety I'd have won gold. Married and pregnant at nineteen, I'd smiled at the notion of babies waking up at night. Those were *other* people's babies. Reality struck with Sam's birth. I'd tried to grow up fast. Midnight phone calls to Mum three hundred kilometres away hadn't always been helpful ('He must be teething, dear'). Fortunately, older, more experienced mothers had taken pity on me. With kindness and great patience they'd guided me through Motherhood 101. I'd eventually learned to accept that sleep is a luxury and a mother is only ever as happy as her saddest child. So in those closing days of 1982 I was doing okay. They were gorgeous boys and put it this way: I hadn't been to the supermarket wearing a nightgown under my coat for several months.

We were living in Wellington, a city famous for two things—bad weather and earthquakes. We'd just managed to purchase a house with the potential to expose us to both: a bungalow halfway down a zigzag on a cliff directly above a major fault line.

Minor earthquakes were so common we hardly noticed when walls trembled and plates rattled. But people said Wellington was overdue for a massive quake, like the one of 1855, when great tracts of land disappeared into the sea and were flung up in other places.

It certainly seemed like our bungalow clung to the hill as if it was prepared for something terrible to happen. There was a faded fairytale appeal to its pitched roof, dark-beamed cladding and shutters. Mock Tudor meets Arts and Crafts, it wasn't shabby chic, it was just plain shabby. My efforts to create a cottage garden had resulted in an apology of forget-me-nots along the front path.

Quaint as it was, clearly the house had been built with a family of alpine goats in mind. There was no garage, not even a street front. The only way to reach it was to park the car up at road level, high above our roof line, and bundle groceries and children's gear into our arms. Gravity would take care of the rest, sucking us down several zigs and zags to our gate.

We were young so it was no problem on sunny days when the harbour was blue and flat as a dinner plate. Whenever a southerly gale roared up from Antarctica, however, tearing at our coat buttons and flinging rain in our faces, we wished we'd bought a more sensible house.

But we loved living a twenty-minute walk from town. Equipped with ropes and rock-climbing shoes we could have made it in five. When we headed into the city, an invisible force would send us plummeting down the lower end of the zigzag. Hurtling through scrub and flax bushes, we'd pause for a glimpse. A circle of amethyst hills, stark and steep, rose above us. I was amazed we could be part of such beauty.

The path then pulled us across an old wooden footbridge spanning the main road. From there we could either take steps down to the bus stop or continue our perpendicular journey to the Houses of Parliament and central railway station. The slog home from the city was another matter. It took twice as long and demanded the lungs of a mountaineer.

The zigzag had a sharply divided social structure. There was a Right Side, on which substantial two-storeyed houses nestled in gardens with aspirations to Tuscany. And the Wrong Side, where bungalows sprinkled themselves like afterthoughts along the edge of the cliff. Wrong Side people tended to have weed collections rather than gardens.

The prestige of jobs declined in direct correlation to the zigzag's slope. On the top right-hand side Mr Butler's house sat like a castle. Grey and two storeyed, it oozed superiority not only over the neighbourhood but the city in general.

Below Mr Butler's, a two-storeyed house opened out over the harbour, looking as if it would hardly be bothered by mere social comparisons. With eaves graceful as seagull's wings, it seemed ready to take off in the next decent gale to a far more glamorous world. Rick Desilva ran a record company. People said that, before they were married, his wife, Ginny, had been a fashion model, New Zealand's answer to Jean Shrimpton. Shielded behind a thicket of vegetation that no doubt could be dried and smoked, they had a reputation for parties.

There was a ridiculous rumour that Elton John had been seen staggering out of their house drunk as a dog, though in reality it was just someone who looked like him. Their son, Jason, was at the same school as our boys. They were perched on the lip of a gully about half a mile further up the hill, but we kept our distance. The Desilvas had a sports car. Steve said they were too racy. I had no energy to argue.

Our side of the zigzag specialised in recluses and people who were renting for a while before moving somewhere less exposed, with better access and not so close to the fault line. Mrs Sommerville, a retired high-school teacher, was one of the few long-time residents of the Wrong Side. She inhabited a tidy weatherboard house one down from us. A lifetime with adolescents had done nothing for her looks. She wore a permanent expression of someone who'd just received an insult.

Mrs Sommerville had already appeared on our doorstep with complaints about our dog terrorising her cat, Tomkin, a large tabby cat with a matching sour face. Even though I tried to avoid her, I bumped into her most days, giving her the opportunity to point out skid marks where boys had been zooming down the zigzag illegally on skateboards, or the latest graffiti on her letterbox. Mrs Sommerville's pathological dislike of boys included our sons, who were suspects of every crime. Steve said I was imagining things. While she loathed boys, Mrs Sommerville knew how to turn the charm on for men.

•

I worked at home, writing a weekly column for Wellington's morning newspaper, *The Dominion*. Steve worked one week home, one week away, as radio officer on one of the ferries that ploughed between the North and South Islands. We'd met at a ship's party when I was fifteen. A grand old man of twenty, he was the most exotic creature I'd ever encountered. Compared to the farmers who steered us around country dance halls near New Plymouth where I grew up, he was from another world.

His face was peachy white and he had baby-soft hands. I'd been mesmerised by his blue eyes, that glowed under their long lashes. Unlike the farmers, he hadn't been frightened of conversation. I'd assumed that, being English, he was probably related to one of The Beatles, if not the Rolling Stones.

I'd loved the way his tawny hair draped across his collar, just like Paul McCartney's. He'd smelt of diesel oil and salt, the perfume of the wider world that was impatient for me to join it.

We'd written to each other for three years. I'd sprinted through school and a journalism course (straight Cs) then flown to England. Steve was literally the man of my dreams—I'd met him in person for only two weeks during the three years we'd been letter writing—and reality had no hope of matching up. His parents were probably unimpressed with his big-boned girlfriend from the colonies.

We'd married in the Guildford registry office a month after my eighteenth birthday. Only five people had been brave enough to turn up for the ceremony. The officiant was so bored he forgot to mention the ring. My new husband slipped it on my finger afterwards outside in the porch. It was raining. Distraught back in New Zealand, my parents investigated the possibilities of annulment, but they were powerless.

About two weeks after the wedding I'd stared at the toilet seat in our rented flat and thought it needed polishing. That was when I knew getting married had been a mistake. Yet we'd upset so many people by insisting on it I couldn't back out. Short of running away and causing more pain, the only solution I could think of was to create a family. Steve reluctantly obliged. Honest from the start, he'd made it clear babies weren't really his thing.

We returned to New Zealand where I'd laboured through a December night, too frightened to ask the nurse to turn the light on in case it was breaking hospital rules. Somewhere through a drug-induced haze I'd heard the doctor singing 'Morning Has Broken'. Minutes later she'd lifted baby Sam from my body.

Before he'd even taken his first breath he turned his head and stared into my face with his huge blue eyes. I thought I'd explode with love. My body ached to hold this brand-new human with his downy hair glowing under the delivery room lights. Sam was wrapped in a blanket—blue in case I forgot what sex he was—and lowered into my arms. Kissing his forehead, I was overcome by a sensation I'd never be safely inside my own skin again. I uncurled his tiny fist. His life line was strong and incredibly long.

Even though it was supposed to be our first meeting, Sam and I recognised each other immediately. It felt like a reunion of ancient souls who'd never spent long apart.

Becoming parents hadn't brought Steve and me closer together. In fact, it had the opposite effect. Two and a half years after Sam's birth Rob slid into the world.

Lack of sleep and jangled nerves had made our differences more apparent. Steve sprouted a beard, a look that was becoming fashionable, and retreated behind it. Returning from a week at sea, he was tired and irritable.

He became annoyed with what he perceived as my extravagance over the boys' clothes and upkeep. I bought a second-hand sewing machine that emitted electric shocks and taught myself to cut their hair. I grew louder, larger and more untidy.

The times we weren't sure how much longer we could stay together were interspersed with phases of holding on and hoping things might improve for the sake of the boys. Even though we were drifting apart like icebergs on opposing ocean currents, there was absolutely no doubt we both loved them.

◆

'Now boys,' I said, pulling up outside Lena's house and heaving the handbrake high as it would go. 'Don't get your hopes up. We're just going to look.'

They scrambled out of the car and were halfway down the path to Lena's house before I'd closed the driver's door. Watching their blond hair catch the sunlight, I sighed and wondered if there'd ever be a time I wouldn't be struggling to catch up with them.

Lena had opened the door by the time I got there, and the boys were already inside. I apologised for their bad manners. Lena smiled and welcomed me into the enviable tranquility of her home, which overlooked the playing field where I often took the boys to run off excess energy.

'We've just come to look at the . . .' I said as she escorted me into her living room. 'Oh, kittens! Aren't they adorable?'

In a corner under some bookshelves a sleek, bronze cat lay on her side. She gazed at me through amber eyes that belonged not to a cat but a member of the aristocracy. Nestled into her abdomen were four appendages. Two were coated with a thin layer of bronze hair. Two were darker. Perhaps once their fur had grown they'd turn out to be black. I'd seen recently born kittens before, but never ones as tiny as these. One of the darker kittens was painfully small.

The boys were on their knees in awe of this nativity scene. They seemed to know to keep a respectful distance.

'They've only just opened their eyes,' Lena said, scooping one of the bronze kittens from the comfort of its twenty-four-hour diner. The creature barely fitted inside her hand. 'They'll be ready to go to new homes in a couple of months.'

The kitten squirmed and emitted a noise that sounded more like a yip than a meow. Its mother glanced up anxiously. Lena returned the infant to the fur-lined warmth of its family to be assiduously licked. The mother used her tongue like a giant mop, swiping parallel lines across her baby's body, then over its head for good measure.

'Can we get one, please, PLEASE?' Sam begged, looking up at me with that expression parents struggle to resist.

'*Please?*' his brother echoed. 'We won't throw mud on Mrs Sommerville's roof anymore.'

'You've been throwing mud on Mrs Sommerville's roof?!'

'Idiot!' Sam said, rolling his eyes and jabbing Rob with his elbow.

But the kittens . . . and there was something about the mother. She was so self-assured and elegant. I'd never seen a cat like her. She was smaller than an average cat but her ears were unusually large. They rose like a pair of matching pyramids from her triangular face. Darker stripes on her forehead whispered of a jungle heritage. Short hair, too. My mother always said short-haired cats were clean.

'She's a wonderful mother, pure Abyssinian,' Lena explained. 'I tried to keep an eye on her, but she escaped into the bamboos for a couple of nights a while back. We don't know who the father is. A wild tom, I guess.'

Abyssinian. I hadn't heard of that breed. Not that my knowledge of pedigree cats was encyclopaedic. I'd once known a Siamese called Lap Chow, the pampered familiar of my ancient piano teacher, Mrs McDonald. Our three-way relationship was doomed from the start. The only thing that hurt more than Mrs McDonald's ruler whacking my fingers as they fumbled over the keys was Lap Chow's hypodermic-needle claws sinking into my ankles. Between the two of them they did a good job creating a lifelong prejudice against music lessons and pedigree cats.

'Some people say Abyssinians are descended from the cats the ancient Egyptians worshipped,' Lena continued.

It certainly wasn't difficult to imagine this feline priestess residing over a temple. The combination of alley cat and royalty had allure. If the kittens manifested the best attributes of both parents (classy yet hardy), they could turn out to be something special. If, on the other hand, less desirable elements of royalty and rough trade (fussy and feral) came to the fore in the off-spring, we could be in for a roller-coaster ride.

'There's only one kitten left,' Lena added. 'The smaller black one.'

Of course people had gone for the larger, healthier-looking kittens first. The bronze ones probably had more appeal, as they had a better chance of turning out looking purebred like their mother. I'd already decided I preferred the black ones, though not necessarily the runt with its bulging eyes and patchy tufts of fur.

'But the little one seems to have a lot of spirit,' Lena said. 'She needs it to survive. We thought we were going to lose her during the first couple of days, but she managed to hold on.'

'It's a girl?' I said, already stupid with infatuation and incap-able of using cat breeder's language.

'Yes. Would you like to hold her?'

Fearing I'd crush the fragile thing, I declined. Lena lowered the tiny bundle of life into Sam's hands instead. He lifted the kitten and stroked his cheek with her fur. He'd always had a thing about fur. I'd never seen him so careful and tender.

'You know it's my birthday soon . . .' he said. I could guess what was coming next. 'Don't give me a party or a big present. There's only one thing I want for my birthday. This kitten.'

'When's your birthday?' Lena asked.

'Sixteenth of December,' said Sam. 'But I can change it to any time.'

'I don't like kittens to leave their mother until they're quite independent,' she said. 'I'm afraid this one won't be ready until mid February.'

'That's okay,' said Sam, gazing into the slits of its eyes. 'I can wait.'

The boys knew the best thing to do now was to shut up and look angelic. Maybe nurturing a kitten would wean them off war games and tune them into feminine sensibilities. As for Rata, we'd do our best to protect the kitten from such a monstrous dog.

Further debate was pointless. How could I turn down a creature so determined to seize life? Besides, she was Sam's birthday present.

'We'll take her,' I said, somehow unable to stop smiling.

A Name

There's only one correct name for a cat – Your Majesty

'It's not fair!' Rob wailed. 'He's getting a kitten *and* a digital Superman watch for his birthday!'

Lifting the banana cake out of the oven, I burnt the side of my hand and suppressed a curse. The pain was searing but there was no point yelling. Not with an electric sander drilling my eardrums and the boys on the brink of World War III. I plonked the cake on a cooling rack and glanced out at the harbour.

The risk of living on the fault line was neutralised by the sea view framed by hills stabbing the sky. Who cared if the bungalow had been 'renovated' twenty years earlier by a madman who used wood one grade up from cardboard? Wandering over its ivory-coloured shag-pile carpet, ignoring the lurid wallpapers, we'd echoed the estate agent's mantra: 'Character . . . Potential.' Besides, Optimist was my middle name. If the town was hit by a serious earthquake the house would almost certainly plummet off the cliff into the sea, but we'd probably be somewhere else that day. Yes, we'd just happen to be inside one of those downtown skyscrapers built on gigantic rollers specifically designed to endure the earth's groans.

Steve and I were both hoping our differences would dissolve in the bungalow's magical outlook. A marriage between

12

two people from opposite sides of the world and whose personalities were as likely to blend as oil and water could surely be crafted into survival here. Besides, Steve was willing to renovate the 1960s renovations, as long as it didn't cost too much. His latest project, to strip back the paint on all the doors and skirting boards to expose the natural wood grain, was deafening.

'Can you turn that noise down, please?' I shouted down the hall.

'I can't turn it down!' Steve yelled back. 'There's only one volume. It's an *electric* sander.'

'Sam has to wait eight more weeks for the kitten,' I explained to Rob, running my hand under the cold tap and wondering why it wasn't doing any good. 'Besides, if you ask nicely I'm sure you can have a digital Superman watch when it's your birthday.'

'Sam doesn't even play Superman anymore,' Rob said. 'He just reads books about history and stuff.'

He was right. Sam's new phase didn't include comic book heroes. A Superman watch wasn't Sam anymore. Nevertheless, when he'd opened the parcel that morning he'd smiled and been gracious.

'I hate my watch,' Rob said. 'It should go in a museum. Nobody has a watch that ticks anymore.'

'That's not true,' I said. 'There's nothing wrong with your watch.'

The sander's shrieking mercifully stopped. Steve appeared coated in paint dust and wearing a mask and a bath cap.

'You look funny, Daddy,' Rob said. 'Like a big white Smurf.'

'It's no good,' Steve sighed. 'That paint's glued to the wood. I'll have to take the doors off. There's a place in town that'll soak them in acid baths. It's the only way we'll get rid of that paint.'

'You're removing all our doors?' I asked. 'Even the bathroom's?'

'Only for a week or two.'

Lured by the smell of banana cake, Sam wandered into the kitchen. Rata trailed behind, clicking her toenails over the vinyl. If boy and dog were ever twin souls those two were it. She'd arrived, a milk-coloured puppy, when Sam was just two years old. They'd grown up together, comrades in arms whenever the fridge needed raiding or Christmas presents unearthing two weeks early from under our bed.

I couldn't remember exactly when Rata decided she was the senior partner and assumed the mantle of guardianship. Perhaps Rob's birth, two and a half years after Sam's, had something to do with it. With Rob's arrival, Rata took on nanny duties. The retriever would stretch in front of the fireplace, her tongue lolling nonchalantly on the carpet; Rob used her as a pillow while he sucked on his bottle of milk. The drawbacks of living with such an animal—layers of silvery hairs over our carpet and furniture, a pervasive doggy smell that I imagined made visitors baulk—were a miniscule price. Rata had a heart bigger than the Pacific Ocean. I hoped that heart could encompass a small furry stranger.

'Have you thought of a name for the kitten yet, Sam?' I asked.

'She could be Sooty or Blackie,' Rob volunteered.

Sam fixed his younger brother with the look of a tiger about to lunge at a chicken.

'I think E.T. would be a good name,' Sam said.

'Noooo!' Rob wailed. 'That's a horrible name!'

Rob hadn't fully recovered from the movie *E.T.* His terror of Steven Spielberg's alien had provided Sam with a wealth of fresh material to freak Rob out. Ever since Sam told him the gas metre on the zigzag was E.T.'s cousin, Rob refused to walk past it without clutching my hand.

'Why not?' Sam said. 'The kitten looks a bit like an E.T. with hardly any hair and those bulging eyes. But not as scary as the E.T. I saw in our bathroom last night. He's still there but don't look at him, Rob. If he sees you looking he'll eat you up and it's worse than being eaten by an alligator because he's got no teeth . . .'

'Sam, stop it,' I warned. But it was too late. Rob was already running out of the kitchen with fingers planted in his ears.

'He makes green slime run out of his nose so he can dissolve your bones and suck you up!' Sam yelled after him.

'Not funny,' I growled.

Sam slid onto a kitchen chair and examined his cake. Apart from the times he was teasing his brother, Sam had transmuted into an introspective soul, so unlike the wild warrior he used to be. I occasionally worried what went on inside his head. Mixing icing in a saucepan, I asked if he'd like to help decorate the cake. He said yes—just a few jellybeans would do.

Sam had kept his word about a modest birthday and invited only one friend, Daniel, from around the corner. He claimed to be sick of 'those big parties where everyone goes crazy'. I had to agree. Those tribes of boys who trashed the house and tied sheets together to leap out of windows surely needed medication, or more of it.

At the last minute I'd felt guilty and tried to persuade him to ask more boys. But he said he was happy with just his best friend, Rob and Rata. The only thing he insisted on was to be allowed to light his own candles. It seemed a small enough request.

I spread newspaper on the kitchen table and spooned the pale icing onto the cake. The texture was about right for once, smooth and easy to shape. To prove I was a half-creative mother, I added cocoa powder to the dregs of the icing in the pot, stirred in some boiling water and trickled a large, wonky '9' on top of the cake. Sam pressed the jellybeans into the sticky surface.

As he glanced up at me his sapphire eyes darkened. He suddenly appeared ancient and wise. I'd seen that look several times recently. It unnerved me, especially when he said things that seemed to emanate from a soul who'd been on earth countless times before and was aware he was merely passing through.

'It's a good time to be alive,' he said, sneaking a black jellybean under the table to Rata.

'It's a *great* time to be alive,' I corrected.

'I'm jealous of Granddad. He was alive when the first cars were made and they started flying planes. He saw towns get electricity and movie theatres. That must've been exciting.'

'Yes, but when you get to be an old man you'll have seen even bigger changes. Things we can't imagine now. You'll be able to say to your grandchildren, "I had one of the first digital Superman watches ever."'

He glanced down at his wrist and arranged his lips in a diplomatic smile. I wanted to take him by the shoulders, hold him close so I could savour the delectable smell of his skin.

'I was just joking about calling the kitten E.T.,' he confided, scraping a teaspoon around the pot to collect what was left of the chocolate icing and shovelling it into his mouth. 'Her mother looks like an Egyptian queen. I think we should call her Cleopatra. Cleo for short.'

'Cleo,' I said, running a hand through his hair and wondering if children ever understand the painful depth of their parents' love. 'That's a great name.'

'I'm giving Rata a lot of attention, so she doesn't get jealous of the kitten. I brushed her coat twice yesterday. We've talked a lot about it. She's going to like Cleo.'

Rata put her head in his lap and gazed up at him with liquid eyes.

'She seems to understand every word you're saying,' I said.

'Animals know a lot more than people do. Dogs can tell when there's going to be an earthquake. Birds can fly halfway around the world to find their nest. If people listened to animals more often they wouldn't make so many mistakes.'

Sam's connection with animals had become apparent when he was a baby. Our outings were devoted to animal spotting more than anything else. Enthroned in his pushchair, he'd wave chubby arms at dogs and cats wherever we went. One day, he pointed at a seagull circling above our heads and said his first word—'Dird!'

Animals were a tactile experience for Sam, too. He adored the feel of fur and feathers. Mum gave him an old goatskin rug that was black and white and shiny with age. Sam had dragged it into his bed to sleep on its comforting smoothness every night.

He was born with a wild sense of humour, a tool to test boundaries. When he was small I feigned shock at his use of rude words. He retaliated by following me around humming 'Bum, bum, bumble bee'. Never afraid of flamboyance, he'd flung himself fully dressed into a bath of water and insisted on wearing a monkey mask with matching feet for the duration of his eighth birthday. Life was too magnificent not to be made fun of. I understood where he was coming from. Teachers were either amused or appalled by him, though none of them complained when, at the age of eight, he scored a reading age of thirteen. While he wasn't disruptive at school, he enjoyed making bold personal statements, like excusing himself from class if he thought I might be in the school grounds, or asking to have his hair cropped close to the scalp when other boys were diligently growing theirs long.

I knew and loved every part of his body, especially the so-called imperfections: the scar above his left eyebrow where as a toddler he'd collided with the edge of the coffee table; his square hands with their chewed fingernails; the wart in the middle of the palm of his right hand. I adored the chip in his front tooth (tricycle accident), the flecks that made his eyes seem so wise sometimes, his feet (often grubby) and his nuggetty legs toasted by the sun. Without these he'd have been a flawless boy, a cherub too perfect for planet Earth. His scratches, bruises and scars formed a secret code only the two of us knew the history and formation of. Knowing Sam the animal lover and clown, I wasn't sure what to make of his serious approach to his ninth birthday. Maybe he wanted to prove how much he'd grown up.

The knocker rapped against the front door. Sam and Rata trotted down the hall to answer it.

Daniel seemed to understand it was an understated birthday. The three boys sat around the kitchen table with Rata strategically positioned underneath to collect her share of the feast. I snapped a few photos while the birthday boy lit his nine candles. The atmosphere was rich with feeling, yet strangely sombre.

Weeks later, when the photos came back from the processor they were so dark it was hard to make out the images. Even though the kitchen had been flooded with sunlight that afternoon, Sam's image was cloaked in shadow, with a halo of gold light around the edges. Maybe I was a lousy photographer. Or perhaps it was one of those supernatural tricks some people believe cameras are capable of performing.

Loss

Unlike humans, cats are accustomed to loss

Most days are so similar they're forgotten almost before the sun sets on them. Thousands of days dissolve into each other, evolving into months and years. We slide through time expecting each day to be as predictable as the one before. Lulled into routines involving the same breakfast cereals, school runs and familiar faces, we're anaesthetised into believing our lives will go on unchanged forever.

The twenty-first of January 1983 started out that way. There were no hints this date would slam down on us and slice our lives permanently in two.

After breakfast the boys wrestled in their pyjamas on the living room floor, with Rata refereeing while Steve unscrewed the bathroom door from its frame. The last door headed for the acid dipper in town, it was also the most political. Nobody wanted to pee in public.

Doors are heavier than they look. It took the four of us, aided by cheerful tripping up from Rata, to carry the thing up the zigzag and stow it in the stationwagon. It was January—summer holiday time on this hemisphere, and the boys were bronzed, their hair almost white from the sun. Unlike me, they were keen to meet the mysterious acid dipper. After Steve had tied the bathroom door to the car, the boys slid into what was left of the back seat.

On the way into town, Steve dropped me at my friend Jessie's place in a suburb wedged between the hills. Climbing out of the car, I turned and invited Sam to take my place in the front passenger seat. Smiling, I told him I'd see him after lunch. His blue eyes beamed into mine as he slid into the front. We had no reason to believe that 'after lunch' would never happen.

Jessie was on the mend after a week in bed with the flu. Like a Victorian heroine in her white nightgown, she stretched on the covers and made the most of her semi-invalid status. We drank soup, talked and laughed about our kids. Her boys were older than ours, well into high school and turning into artistic rebels. I imagined Sam and Rob would be getting up to similar antics in the not-too-distant future.

Somewhere a phone rang. Jessie's husband, Peter, answered. I was vaguely aware of his voice in the background. His tone was clipped, then jagged. He seemed to be receiving some kind of bad news. Wondering if he'd lost an elderly relative, I arranged my face in what I hoped was a sympathetic shape as he entered the bedroom. He looked pale and on edge, like someone being devoured by a drama he wanted no part of. He glanced at Jessie, then at me. His eyes were black as onyx. The phone call, he said, was for me.

There'd obviously been some kind of mistake. Who'd ring me at Jessie's house? Hardly anyone knew I was there in the first place. Confused, I walked into the hallway and lifted the receiver.

'It's terrible,' I heard Steve's voice say. 'Sam's dead.'

His voice reverberated across space into every cell of my body. His tone was measured, almost normal. Sam and dead were words that didn't belong together. I assumed he was talking about some other Sam, an old man, a distant cousin he'd previously forgotten to mention.

I heard myself scream into the telephone receiver. Steve's voice arrived like rounds of artillery fire in my ear. Sam and Rob had found a wounded pigeon under the clothes line. Sam had insisted on taking it to the vet. Having seen the Disney film

The Secret of Nimh the day before, he was feeling even more attuned than usual to the suffering of animals.

Steve had been making a lemon meringue pie in preparation for lunch. He'd told the boys if they wanted to take the bird to the vet, they'd have to do it themselves. They'd lowered the bird into a shoebox and carried it down the zigzag. Lennel Road was a main route into town from the outer suburbs. In a less car-obsessed age, a town planner had decided to wedge in a bus stop for people wanting to travel up the hill out of town. The road narrowed so dramatically at the footbridge that there was only room for a footpath on one side of the road. Any pedestrian wanting to go further down the hill into town had no choice but to cross the road at the bus stop. It was a perilous crossing with no signs to make traffic slow down.

As the boys arrived at the bus stop at the bottom of the steps, a bus pulled in on its way up the hill. Rob told Sam he thought they should wait until the bus had moved on before they tried to cross. But Sam was impatient to save the bird. Determined to reach the vet's rooms down the hill as quickly as possible, he told Rob to be quiet, and ran out from behind the stationary bus. He'd been hit by a car coming down the hill.

The words were like pieces from different jigsaws that didn't fit together. A nightmare voice that wasn't mine yelled down the phone, demanding to know if Rob was okay. Steve said Rob was fine, though he'd seen the accident and was badly shaken. A shudder of relief jolted through me.

When people receive ghastly news, some say a sensation of disbelief sets in. Perhaps it was the simple harshness of Steve's language, but his words hammered through me straight-away. My mind collapsed into different compartments. From a position high on Jessie's hall ceiling I watched myself wailing and screaming below. My head felt about to burst. I wanted to smash it against the glass panels of Jessie's front door to stop the pain.

At the same time, I registered the incongruity of the situation. The purpose of my visit had been to cheer Jessie up. Now here she was, standing in her white nightgown, trying to soothe me. Having trained as a nurse, Jessie switched into practical mode. She rang the hospital's accident and emergency ward. When she asked if Sam was D.O.A. the logical part of my brain deciphered the abbreviation. I'd heard it as a cadet reporter late at night on the police round. Dead On Arrival. Leaden with resignation, she put the phone down.

I wept and raged, but couldn't encompass the grief. No collection of human tissue was resilient enough to endure such pain. My life was over. Time squeezed up like an accordion. We waited for Steve and Rob to arrive. Refusing offers of tea and alcohol I watched light filter through a window and listened to the bellowing from the back of my throat. Part of my mind was curious about the noise my body made, and the way it seemed to go on like a chant, for infinity.

I wanted to compose myself for Rob's arrival. The poor kid had seen enough. But my mind and body refused to obey instructions. I'd become a roaring animal. We waited maybe twenty minutes for Steve and Rob to appear in Jessie's hallway. It felt more like twenty years.

They materialised like a pair of ghosts, a sad man, hunched over as if he'd been shot in the stomach, holding the hand of a traumatised child. I'd seen that body language before in photos of refugees and war victims. Steve's face was blank as a wall, his eyes empty like a marble statue's. Rob seemed to have shrunk into himself. I looked into the boy's face, so passive and contained. Falling to my knees, I wrapped my arms around our surviving son, and wondered what nightmares were whirling inside his head. He'd just seen his brother run over and killed. How could he ever recover?

Clutching my son, I sobbed. My body shook. The intensity of my grip must've been frightening. He wriggled and withdrew from my embrace. Trying to regain composure, I asked Rob what had happened. He explained how he'd tried to stop Sam crossing the road, to wait on the footpath until the bus had gone, but Sam wouldn't listen. His last words to Rob were 'Be quiet'.

Sam had looked like a cowboy lying on the road, Rob said, with red string coming out of his mouth. It took a while for me to understand what he'd meant by red string. His young mind had interpreted the scene as a Western movie. Sam had become John Wayne, flat on his back after a gun fight, with stage makeup trickling down his chin. It was my first glimpse of how differently a child perceives death.

As we staggered numbly towards the car, Rob asked if he could have Sam's Superman watch. I was shocked, but he was only six years old.

The road unfurled beneath us like licorice. Houses peeled away at drunken angles. I hated this town with its hills and twisted streets. Everything about it was harsh and ugly, on the brink of destruction. I didn't want to go back to the house. Couldn't face the zigzag and the sight of Sam's possessions. But there was nowhere else for us to drive to.

When Steve asked if I wanted to see the footbridge I hammered my head against the car window and screamed. I never wanted to go anywhere near that thing. He drove the long way home so we wouldn't have to pass under its shadow. People might still be there, shaking their heads, looking for stains on the tarmac.

Accusations shot like flames from the back of my throat. I yelled at Steve, demanding to know why he hadn't driven the boys to the vet. He'd been busy with the lemon meringue pie, he replied. Wild as a she-wolf, I accused him of caring more about lemon meringue pie than his sons. A cooler part of my mind knew that my behaviour was cruel and irrational.

Absorbing my recriminations without the retaliation they deserved, Steve pointed out that the vet was only a short walk down the hill. He reminded me the boys knew the road rules, and there was no stopping Sam when he got an idea in his head. 'We both know what Sam is like—*was* like—with animals.' Steve's change of tense was an obscenity.

Like an octopus, my mind scrambled for possibilities. Maybe there'd been a mistake and Sam wasn't dead. Steve refused to be dragged into my fantasies. He'd spoken to the ambulance driver, who'd told him he was sorry but our son had passed away.

Passed away? The words unleashed a fresh onslaught of fury. Back in journalism school our tutors had drummed into us that dead meant dead, not passed away, passed over or sleeping in God's arms. How could an ambulance driver who saw death every day use such euphemistic language?

Ignoring my raving, Steve continued to repeat what the ambulance driver had said. If by some miracle Sam had managed to survive such a severe head injury his only triumph would have been to spend the rest of his life a vegetable. My subconscious snared that snippet of information.

Dead. Lifeless. Gone. Such final words. If our son really was dead, then someone had killed him. My mind boiled, desperate for someone to blame. A murderer who deserved punishment. I created a Hollywood villain inside my head, a man full of hate with a history of crime.

'It was a woman,' Steve said, 'a woman in a blue Ford Escort. She'd been driving back to work after lunch. There was hardly any damage to her car. Just a cracked headlight.'

A cracked headlight for my child's life? I'd kill her.

Staggering down the zigzag to the house I couldn't believe I'd never again feel Sam's weight on my lap, his arms around my neck. Never was such a finite word. Rata greeted us at the door, her head to one side, gazing up at us, questioning. I flung myself on her neck and wept. Her head drooped, her tail curved under her hind legs and she tumbled to the floor. Sam's words echoed in my head. Animals understand . . .

Hands trembling on the receiver, I made the worst phone call of my life. Mum's voice sounded nonchalant when she answered. There was no way to soften the news. Her cherished grandson was gone. I was the ultimate failure as a parent. I could hear her intake of breath. Her voice deepened. The tiny part of me that remained an observer was surprised by her calm response. She belonged to a more seasoned, tougher generation that through the horrors of World War II had developed strategies to deal with outrageous loss. She brought my yelps and wails to a halt and said she was on her way.

I fastened the Superman watch around Rob's wrist and flung myself on Sam's unmade bed, its sheets and blankets still in the shape of his living body. I drank the smell of his clothes, heard his voice in my head. Steve led me to the living room and coaxed a glass of brandy between my lips. Hot alcohol shot through my veins.

An hour or so later, two policemen, young and embarrassed, arrived on the doorstep. They said the pigeon was still alive and asked what we wanted done with it. What had gone wrong with life's logic? How could a bird have more right to survival than our boy? Steve told them to take the pigeon to the vet as Sam had wanted. The police also needed someone to go to the morgue and identify the body. Steve steeled himself and went.

He arrived home ashen-faced. Sam still looked the same, he said. Beautiful. Nobody would have known anything had happened, except for the gash in the side of his forehead. Just a tiny gash. He'd meant to cut a lock from Sam's hair, but had forgotten the scissors. I yearned for the lock of hair, anything that was part of Sam, but Steve was stretched like a rubber band about to snap. I could hardly insist he go back to the morgue.

◆

Mum appeared at the door. She seemed weighted with triple quantities of sadness. On top of her own grief I could tell she was carrying concern for the rest of us. She would have been tired, too, after a five-hour drive. I expected her to burst into tears, but she squared her shoulders and raised her head. I'd seen actors do the same thing before stepping on stage.

'I saw the most beautiful sunset just now,' she said. 'Glorious streaks of reds and golds. I thought Sam must be part of it.'

My ravaged mind interpreted her words as callousness. How could she surrender her grandchild to a *sunset?*

A funeral director turned up while she was unpacking. Harbour lights twinkled malevolently behind him as he sat in the corner of the living room asking for Sam's measurements—height and breadth. *Didn't he have a nine-year-old son of his own to go by?* White coffins, he said, were favoured for children. *There were fashion trends in death?* I couldn't face a church service. Not when there was so much business to discuss with God over this. Someone had recommended the new university chaplain. A short ceremony conducted by him at the grave side would do. The funeral director made no effort to hide his disapproval. While I was stunned by his coldness at the time, I now realise he probably had no idea what to say so was clinging to the framework of his professional training.

Soon after the funeral director strode into the night, the university chaplain stepped cautiously over the shag pile. He was young, barely out of school, and nervous. He told us he'd never buried a child before. We said we were in the same position. When he asked what we'd like I wanted to scream: 'Isn't it obvious? We want our son back!' But he was faced with a daunting task. There was enough sanity left in me to feel sorry for him. I offered to write a poem for him to read at the grave side.

Our family doctor arrived and scribbled a prescription for sleeping pills. Over a mug of coffee she mused that maybe it was a good thing from Sam's perspective, because the adult world was so hard to survive in.

Steve mentioned he'd taken the Superman watch away from Rob—he hadn't felt comfortable passing it on so quickly.

I protested but he assured me Rob understood. Steve had put the watch away in a box inside his desk.

Rata collapsed across the boys' bedroom doorway. We tried to coax Rob into his old bed but he refused to sleep in the room he'd shared with Sam. His eyes flashing with terror, he said a dragon lived in there. Steve carried his mattress into our bedroom and placed it in a corner under the window. Like shipwrecked sailors we drifted into our first night without Sam. I thought falling asleep would be impossible, but unconsciousness dropped like the blade of a guillotine, delivering me into merciful nothingness.

Leaving what our world had become was the easy part. Returning to it was almost unbearable. Opening my eyes next morning, I heard a thrush call, its 'took took' echoing across the hills. For an instant I imagined life was normal. I'd just woken from a nightmare of grotesque proportions. With sickening horror, the events of the previous day exploded in my mind and sent me plummeting into despair.

It was no easier for Steve. A few days after the accident I awoke under a waterfall of his tears. He'd never cried in front of me before. I should have reached out and embraced him then, but I was half-awake, unprepared. Distraught, momentarily confused, I simply asked him to stop. I didn't imagine the request would be taken literally and he'd never express sorrow in front of me again.

Our house choked with flowers. As days passed I became weary of their sickening fragility. Water in their vases turned rancid in the summer heat, filling the air with the stench of stagnant ponds. In every room stalks drooped, petals dropped like tears on the floor.

Steve decided flowers upset me. Maybe he was right. He took to hiding freshly delivered sheaths of chrysanthemums, lilies and carnations, deathly in their perfection, under garden shrubs to keep them out of sight. It's impossible to judge whose behaviour was more strange—the grieving woman who went hysterical at the sight of floral deliveries or the husband who hid them under bushes.

The front door stayed permanently open as scores of people, many of them strangers, streamed down the hallway over the carpet I'd never liked. Some oozed platitudes or quotations from the Bible till I wished they'd go away. The only words that resonated with me were Shakespeare's—'time is out of joint'. Other visitors appeared angry—among them a doctor who said he'd seen the accident. It affected him personally, he said. He had two sons of his own. His anger was irrelevant. Doctors seemed to excel at injecting negative interpretations into the atmosphere.

A few (women, mostly) claimed to be suffering similar levels of anguish. Spurting tears and demanding comfort, they thrust their sobbing faces at me. Their words were tactless: 'I wouldn't survive if it happened to me'; 'At least it'll give Rob a chance to flourish. He was always in his big brother's shadow.' I assumed they were self-indulgent, possibly even crazy, though I was no longer capable of judging the dividing line between sanity and madness.

A distorted remnant of what was left of me, a hysterical joker, wanted to screech with laughter at their pale faces and quivering lips. When they said they'd 'felt the same' after their father/dog/grandmother died I wanted to slap them. How could the predictable death of an old person compare with this?

Still others brooded silently out the window over the harbour. Immune to human suffering, the bay sparkled, ridiculously turquoise. I found no comfort in its beauty, loathed its shimmering indifference.

A Maori friend from journalism school, Phil Whaanga, turned up unannounced and simply put his arms around me. We'd never been particularly close, but there was more comfort in his embrace than the thousands of words I'd been forced to listen to. From a culture less afraid of death than our own, Phil didn't feel a need to examine aloud the freakishness of what had happened. I was grateful to him.

Mostly I sat on the sofa, nursing the scar where my hand had been burnt making Sam's birthday cake. It was impossible to accept the scar was still part of the living world while he was not.

Adding to the disjointedness of our situation was the lack of our bathroom door. Our bathroom was like our hearts, torn open for public viewing. Visiting mourners had no way of relieving themselves in private. Neither did we. Steve pinned a shower curtain over the door frame, but its flimsy floralness stopped well above floor level, exposing visitors up to their knees. I hadn't realised what a substantial, noble piece of furniture a door can be. But then there were a lot of things I hadn't thought about before.

+

Several days after the funeral I assured Mum we'd be okay. She nodded uncertainly and climbed into her Japanese hatchback. Steve's mother phoned from England. I sighed when she said she'd been in a theatre audience to see the famous medium Doris Stokes. Apparently Doris had called her up on stage and said she had a message from Sam. Doris told her Sam wanted us to know he was all right. I'd nodded impatiently when Steve passed this on. Every spiritual medium says the same thing. Doris went on to describe a strange new set-up Sam was in. Like boarding school, but more fun. Just as I was about to make derogatory comments about English mediums and their tendency to recreate images involving pubs, tea rooms and scenes that were quintessentially British, there was one more thing. Steve's mother said she had no idea what Doris was talking about, but perhaps it made sense to us. Sam said it was okay. Rob could keep his watch.

The Intruder

A cat doesn't go where it's invited. It appears where it's needed

Forever. Sam was gone forever. How long was that going to be? Was it some kind of infinity? The symbol for infinity is a figure eight. If I waited long enough in some universal bus shelter would Sam spiral back to me?

Never. I'd never see him again. Not unless I believed in heaven, reincarnation or the boarding school of Doris Stokes. I couldn't imagine Sam at boarding school, even one run by angels. He'd find out what the rules were and break them straightaway so he could be expelled and sent home.

If any of those other realities, present or future, existed I had no access to them. Nevertheless, I liked to think I'd inherited some of my dad's connection to the non-physical world. One of his favourite quotes from Shakespeare was: 'There are more things in heaven and earth, Horatio, than are dreamt of in your philosophy.'

Dad often spoke of the near-death experience he'd had as a young man on an operating table. He'd shot up a tunnel of sparkling light to meet some wonderful people at the top. He was overjoyed to be there, but then a voice told him gently, 'I'm sorry. You have to go back.'

Hurtling down that tunnel back to the ordinary world was, he said, the biggest disappointment of his life. The experience left him open-minded about ghosts, nature spirits, Ouija boards, any form of spirituality that wasn't what he called 'churchianity'. He'd met too many people who'd claimed to be Christian while demonstrating none of Jesus' more admirable traits.

Dad certainly was an unusual person. With his delphinium blue eyes he had a habit of looking not so much through people as around them. He often gave the impression of carrying out a conversation simultaneously with the person and their invisible companions.

Some people are happy to die on a golf course. Dad managed his equivalent during the interval of a concert he'd taken Mum and me to when the boys were still small. Having just heard his favourite Bruch violin concerto, he turned to me and said, 'God, the acoustics in here are great'. His head suddenly drooped over his chest and he let out a cry of pain. I put my arm on his shoulder and asked if he was okay. He raised his head, gazed at a point above the stage and smiled ecstastically. This time whoever was at the top of the tunnel was saying, 'Come on up!' and Dad couldn't wait to get there.

While it was a shock for us, it was a perfect death for Dad. He'd been ready and willing. Longing for him to return seemed nothing short of selfish. But Sam was another matter. I searched for signs Sam might still be with us. If a curtain trembled there was always a breeze to account for it. On the wall I saw a shadow that resembled Sam's head, but it was simply the branches of a tree fern waving outside.

The only message we found were the words 'Dumb Bell' scribbled in green felt pen in his handwriting high on a bedroom wall that Steve had started wallpapering. Sam would've had to climb a ladder to get up there to accomplish his graffiti. It was typical of our son to dispel expectations with a joke. If he was telling us anything it was he thought we were idiots for wallowing in our misery.

Never. Sam would never grow up and savour the ecstasy of falling in love, the joy of seeing his own children born. Forever. He was lost to the world forever, remembered as a golden boy who never had the chance to become a man. The only way to stop the words spinning through my head was to go to the picture window—one that couldn't be taken to the paint strippers because it was attached to the house—and attack it with a small crimson paint scraper. *Never, forever, never,* until my wrist ached and my fingers were bleeding and on the brink of bursting into flames. The view through the picture window of city, hills and harbour felt malignant but it was the frame that needed scraping. With each stroke I stripped another layer of pain. Maybe when the wood was finally bare and smooth my heart would be healed. One time (was it daylight or dark?) Steve led me gently away from the window that had no solution. My pointless, obsessive behaviour was disturbing.

On the few occasions I ventured out into the world—the impersonal stage set of shops and offices—I had no qualms burdening strangers with the facts of my recent tragedy. 'My son died,' I'd confided to the woman behind the post office counter. 'Yes, he was run over three weeks ago. He was only nine.' The woman had turned pale all of a sudden, narrower and taller. She seemed to want to dissolve into the poster advertising a new series of pictorial stamps. Collector's items, an excellent gift for friends overseas, convenient to post. Glancing nervously towards the door, she'd said she was sorry. Her tone was flat and quiet. Sorry about what? That I'd used her as a receptacle for shocking information or that I'd walked into her post office in the first place?

A fleeting wave of shame had washed over me. What business had I ruining the day of a normal person who was simply trying to earn a living? She'd had every reason to think I was mad, lying, or both.

I told the bank teller, too. His reaction was similar. What was this need to expose my wounds, so horribly raw, to strangers? The satisfaction of witnessing their shock and discomfort had been minimal. I must have had some kind of need to redefine my place in the world, to wear a label for strangers to read and, ultimately, force myself into accepting the unacceptable. Perhaps there was logic in olden-day mourners wearing black for a year. It would be a signal that the wearer was at best unstable.

While I resented roosting at home to be the target of compassionate visitors, I was in no shape for the outside world, either. Walking down the main street searching for new clothes for our surviving son, children's designer clothes of a quality so fine he'd be protected and sheltered *forever*, I became suddenly lost and disoriented. Awash in a tide of faces, all of them unfamiliar and disengaged, I fought an urge to cry out. Glossy shop windows leaned forward, threatening to crush me on the pavement. My knees weakened. An acquaintance spotted me and guided me back to the car. Humiliated by my need, I thanked her and sent her away.

Gulping breaths in front of the steering wheel, I knew exactly how I must've looked. A human skull with hairs protruding from its scalp. Glancing in the rear-vision mirror, I was astonished to see a twenty-eight-year-old woman, unaccountably young, with red eyes.

We tried to resume normal life, whatever that was. A couple of weeks after the funeral, wearied from my weeping and yelling, on top of the burden of his own secret grief, Steve packed his bag and headed off like a sleepwalker for a week at sea. I hoped he might find serenity in the routines and order of shipboard life.

A few days later I heard the knocker pound against the front door. Sheltering in the shadows at the end of the hallway, I contemplated the figure behind the frosted-glass panel. While the silhouette appeared feminine, its shape wasn't familiar. It seemed tall for a woman, the hair short and shaggy.

Rob glanced up from the kitchen table, where he was building a space station with his new Lego set. In past weeks he'd been showered with toys and clothes, all blindingly bright in their shiny wrapping. Rata, once a reliable guard dog, maintained her prostrate position in the doorway of the boys' old bedroom and pricked an ear. Ever since the accident she'd been immobile, inconsolable, and would barely lift her head. Whenever anyone tried to comfort her, she rolled a mournful eye.

'Let's not answer it,' I said. 'They'll go away in a minute.'

Another visitor was the last thing we needed. Exhausted and numb to the core, I wasn't capable of conversation. The story would have to be told *again*. He—or she—would gaze at me with whirlpool eyes while I explained how our two beloved sons went down the road and only one came home. Retelling the story, reciting it like plainsong in an empty cathedral, wearied me. I didn't want their tears, was tired of their cancer-ward voices.

Alternatively, perhaps our visitor was one of the people who'd brought food. Countless plates laden with sandwiches, muffins, roasted chicken, food for uncertain appetites had appeared on the doorstep over the past three weeks. I was grateful to those cooks for their practicality and restraint. Their anonymous gifts were a welcome relief from emotional confrontation. Even though food was of no interest to me the meals seemed to disappear.

A guilt-inducing pile of empty plates was growing taller on our kitchen bench. I had no idea who had brought them. Perhaps the visitor was one of those benefactors, with sufficient courage to revisit a house of sorrow and reclaim her plate.

No, I wouldn't open the door to whoever was hovering behind the frosted glass. He or she could leave the food, flowers

or sympathy card oozing saccharine prose on the mat and retreat to a life without pain.

As I stepped backwards to the safety of the kitchen, the
figure tapped on the glass. Rata leapt to her feet and let out a
simultaneous bark. It was the first time we'd heard her emit
anything other than a whine since Sam's death.

'Good girl!' I said, stroking the lovable rug of her back as
she lunged towards the front door, her tail wagging.

The head behind the glass shifted expectantly. Whoever
it was had heard both the bark and my response. There was
no choice now. Refusing to open the door would be plain old-
fashioned rudeness.

Looping Rata's collar through my fingers, I turned the latch.
Sunlight stabbed my brain. The graceful figure belonged to
Lena. Attached to her long elegant arm was her son, Jake, who
was the same age as Rob.

Most people had kept their children away. All except one
or two of Rob's closest friends had maintained their distance.
Understandably. The death of a grandparent is enormous
enough for a child to encompass, let alone the annihilation of
someone their own age. Who knows what effect the sudden
departure of someone from their own generation could have on
their unformed nervous systems? And there's no proof tragedy
isn't contagious.

I wasn't confident about my reactions to other people's
children yet, either. When names were mentioned, especially
boys Sam's age, vengeful rage would boil inside. *What right has
your son to be alive when mine is not?*

Lena's son stared up at me unblinkingly, then at Rata joyously
bursting to escape my grip on her collar. Jake peered around
me into the hallway. Perhaps this was going to be a half-normal
visit after all, refreshingly free of the old 'I'm so terribly sorry.
Please let me know if there's *anything* I can do'.

'Would you like to see Rob?' I asked the child, in case Lena wanted to express the platitudes I'd learned to expect. 'He's building a city on the moon.'

Jake stood still, a smile flickering on his lips.

'You could use the toilet if you like,' I blabbered, trying to stop Rata's flailing tongue drowning him in saliva. 'Except it's not very private at the moment, I'm afraid. They said they'd need two weeks to strip the door, but it's taking forever. We're in a bit of a mess . . .'

Lena bent like a willow over her shoulder bag, a huge patchwork sack, flamboyant and colourful enough to have been made by the artist herself. Reaching into the bag, she excavated a small creature with large triangular ears. It was black and not so much furry as sprinkled with occasional hairs. Perhaps she'd stitched together some kind of toy to comfort a boy grieving for his lost brother.

I was alarmed when the tiny thing's head moved. Its eyes bulged like a pair of glass beads. A set of impossibly dainty feet draped themselves through Lena's fingers. I was reminded of those photos of premature babies whose miniature scale is demonstrated alongside an adult human hand. An organism so helpless it would surely have difficulty supporting its own life.

'We've brought the kitten,' said Lena, smiling steadily.

The kitten? What kitten?

'Sam's kitten!' said Rob, running down the hall and squeezing around me.

Rata barked loudly and sprang free of my grip. Jumping on her haunches, she almost knocked Lena over. The kitten recoiled into Lena's breast. Our dog must have seemed a monster to the little thing. The two animals obviously loathed each other.

'Down, girl!' I growled. 'She's not used to cats.' Grabbing the dog firmly by the collar again, I led her inside and back down the hallway.

'Don't worry, old thing,' I said, rubbing a hand through her coat. 'We'll sort this out.'

Rata seemed to understand that being jailed in the kitchen was a temporary inconvenience. The kitten, Sam's kitten, didn't belong in our house. It had arrived like E.T. in a space ship (disguised as Lena's patchwork bag). The kitten was from another time. We were different people when Sam was with us and our lives were whole. Now that we were broken, frayed remnants of our former selves there was no place for a kitten. Not with us.

I couldn't possibly cope with a baby animal and all its needs. Not when I'd already proved myself a failure as a parent of one human child, aged nine. How could I nurture such a tiny, vulnerable creature? Besides, poor Rata had suffered enough. She certainly didn't need her life messed up any more than it was already by a natural born enemy.

Lena would have to take the intruder back. She'd understand. Finding a family better equipped than ours to look after the kitten would be no problem for her. It was a presentable enough animal and she was a brilliant saleswoman. Heading back to the front door, I prepared my speech. Lena would feel let down, but her disappointment would be nothing compared to what we'd been through.

As I reached the front doorstep I saw Lena haloed in sunlight, lowering the kitten into Rob's hands.

'She's yours now,' Lena said softly.

'I'm sorry, Lena . . .' I was about to launch into my speech.

But then I saw Rob's face. As he gazed tenderly down at the kitten, and ran a chubby finger over her back I saw something I thought had vanished from the earth forever. Rob's smile.

'Welcome home, Cleo,' he said.

Trust

A cat is always in the right place at exactly the right time

As Rob disappeared inside with his new kitten, Lena turned to go. Seized with panic, I grabbed her elbow.

'There's something you should know,' I blabbed. 'I'm not really a cat person. I mean our family *had* cats when we were growing up, but they were more like wild cats. They just lived under the house and we fed them occasionally. Mum grew up on a farm, you see, and she never really *got* cats. She let a couple of them come inside and we semi-tamed them, but they weren't friendly . . .'

Lena's face clouded. She needed to hear this. Not telling her would've been worse than filling out a customs form and ticking 'Haven't been on a farm in the past thirty days' when in fact you've been helping cousin Jeff milk his dairy herd for the last two weeks.

'One of them, Sylvester, used to poop in Mum's shoes, which was horrible for her because she sometimes forgot to look before she put her shoes on. She'd scream the house down. She said Sylvester was temperamental because he was part Persian, with the long hair, you know. Black and white, he was. The thing is, Lena, I'm pretty sure we're more dog people.'

Lena turned her head like an exotic lily and surveyed the scrub that was our garden. Casting her eye over the mountainous piles of dung Rata had bombarded the front lawn with, she sighed.

'This is a very special kitten,' Lena said. 'And if you don't like cats . . .'

'It's not that I don't *like* cats,' I continued. 'It's just I don't really know how to look after them. I haven't read any books about kitten rearing or anything.'

'They're very easy to care for,' she said in kindergarten teacher tones. 'Much easier than dogs. She'll be no trouble. Just keep her inside for a day or two to settle. Give me a call if you have any problems. And if you change your mind you can give her back to me.'

'But . . .' Lena didn't seem to realise I'd made my mind up already. I didn't want the kitten.

'All she needs is a little love.'

Love. Such a simple, four-letter word to roll off the tongue. So much easier for the facial muscles to arrange themselves around than 'lasagne', 'leisure suit' or 'leave me alone forever, please'. My heart had been ripped out and pulverised. How could it possibly squeeze out a drip of anything resembling the L word for a creature I'd forgotten we'd ever agreed to own and wasn't in the slightest way equipped to look after?

Besides, a cat, assuming by some miracle it survived long enough in our company to grow into one, is an arduous, practically never-ending responsibility.

I'd gone down enough in Lena's estimation without tactfully asking how long a cat of this breed might live. From what I could remember, the ones I'd grown up with, even the semi-tame ones, were lucky to spend more than six years in our company. Most of them met sudden fates usually described in solemn, no-nonsense terms by our parents: 'poisoned', 'run over' or 'run away'. Further questioning was not encouraged. 'Who did it?' or 'Where?' were invariably answered with: 'Who knows?'

Even if this kitten by some miracle managed to reach the grand old age of nine, that would take Rob through to the age of fifteen, a million years into the future. Considering the battering our endocrine systems were taking, I doubted any of us could realistically expect to survive that long.

Lena smiled thinly and disappeared with Jake down the path. Poor Lena. I should have been more diplomatic. Abandoning her kitten to self-confessed dog people, she must have felt wretched. Nevertheless, she *had* offered to take the kitten back. Maybe I could let Rob play with it for a day or two, then we could return it to the embrace of a cat-loving household.

Rata moaned loudly from behind the kitchen door.

'Don't worry!' I called to the old dog. 'We'll sort this out.'

Rob was curled up in a corner of the living room, cradling the tiny creature in his arms. To have called it beautiful or even pretty would have made Elton John's spectacle frames the understatement of the eighties. It was a scrap of life wrapped in a dishcloth. A toy you'd take back to the department store to exchange for one with more stuffing. I refused to think of it as something with a name, but if it did have one 'Cleopatra' would be far too long and elaborate. Something that miniscule wasn't hefty enough to handle a name with more than one syllable. It wasn't going to be staying with us long, so for now 'it' would suffice.

Sam's observation had been spot on. With the prominent head and neck narrower than a vacuum cleaner hose, the animal was more like E.T. than a kitten. To the non cat person the lack of fur offered too much information about feline anatomy. I tried not to notice the folds of semi translucent skin draped over its ribcage. The skin was a deep charcoal shade, which mercifully concealed some of the detailed rippling of movement under the surface. If I looked any closer it might've been possible to see the throb of a tiny heart. It was safer to avert the eyes.

How anything could be born with so much spare skin was a mystery. The flaps under its arms (front legs?) were generous enough to double as wings. A saggy pouch hung under its abdomen. There was enough spare skin to make at least two other animals the same size. The struggle to survive as the runt had obviously been touch and go. No doubt older brothers and sisters had pushed their puny sibling off their mother in order to fill their own bellies.

The kitten would need to do an awful lot of eating and growing to fill those empty pouches. Even then it stood no chance of looking presentable. A larger, filled-out version of the kitten had freak potential. I took a step backwards. It was definitely one of those things that looked better from a distance. At least the colour was consistent. The kitten couldn't have been blacker. From the claws and pads of its feet to its whiskers it was black. Even the pins of its claws were black. Its eyes were the only things that broke the rule. They were shimmering green mirrors that hardly belonged to a cat. Surely they'd been stolen from a creature from another world. As Rob stroked her forehead with his finger, the kitten gazed adoringly up at him. My heart lurched. All of a sudden the kitten wasn't ugly any more. Sun caught her fur. Affection beamed from her eyes. She radiated a kind of silvery light. The room filled with beauty, the pure essence of all new beings. They looked so perfect together, like a scene from a 1950s advertisement.

'Sam was right,' he said, beckoning me forward and lowering her into my reluctant hands. 'Animals *can* talk. Listen to her. She's growling.'

Maybe it was the warmth of her miniscule weight, the fragility of her limbs or the softness of her fur, but my chest suddenly filled with a fluttery sensation as I lifted her into my hands. 'That's not growling,' I said, running my finger along the delicate beads of her spine. 'It's purring.'

Gazing into the innocent furry face overshadowed by gigantic ears I felt momentarily overwhelmed. Even though we'd lost Sam and I sometimes felt my existence was finished, this scrap of feline life had summoned up the cheek to burst in on our world with no apologies. Not only that, curled in my hands, she was apparently expecting things to turn out perfectly. She was tiny, helpless. And had no choice but to trust us.

Cleo stretched a lazy paw and yawned, revealing a lolly-pink mouth palisaded with dangerous-looking teeth. The astounding eyes gazed into mine with an expression that hardly matched the vulnerability of her size. Her unwavering stare said it all. As far as she was concerned this was a meeting of equals.

'Touch her ears,' Rob said. 'They're soft.'

Cleo didn't object to having her ears rubbed. In fact she dipped her head and nudged firmly into my hand to intensify the contact. Delicate as antique silk, her ears slipped between my fingers.

A reward was the last thing I expected. It was delivered in the form of a sandpapery swipe from her tongue. Cleo's lick on the back of my hand was startling, like a lover's first kiss. Part of me wanted to envelop her and never let go. The other part, so wounded, was wary of the tsunami of affection washing over me. To love is ultimately to lose. The unwritten contract that arrives with every pet is they're probably going to die before you do. The more devoted you are to them the more sorrow their departure will inflict. Opening my heart to Cleo would've been the equivalent of placing an already bruised organ on an airport tarmac and inviting planes to land on it.

'Let's see how she walks,' I said, lowering the kitten to the floor. We watched her paddle like a clockwork toy through the carpet. The shag pile was the equivalent of tall grass for her. Using the worm of her tail as a rudder she paced jerkily towards the rubber plant.

I'd never been a fan of the rubber plant. We'd inherited it from the owners of our previous house. I gradually understood why they'd left it behind. With its big waxy leaves it had an indestructible, vaguely humourless presence. Like an unwelcome guest at a dinner party, it eavesdropped on every conversation and contributed little in return except, perhaps, when it was in the mood, oxygen. We'd been hoping to leave the thing behind when we moved to the zigzag, but the removal men had mistakenly packed it into their truck with our furniture.

When I transplanted the rubber plant into an ugly orange plastic tub its confidence surged. It sprouted dark-green branches the size of frisbees and sent feelers trailing creepily around picture frames and across curtain rails. Technically more a tree these days, the darned thing had ambitions to engulf the entire suburb. I'd tried cutting it back with a pair of hedge clippers, but that only encouraged it to swamp the sideboard.

About a metre away from the plant's orange tub Cleo paused. Her ears and whiskers pointed forwards. Her nose twitched as if she was sampling some dangerous perfume. She crouched and, with the stealthy determination of a lion stalking an antelope, eyed her prey—a pendulous leaf dangling from one of the lower branches. Quivering on her haunches, she waited for the moment the leaf would be least suspecting. Satisfied her prey was foolishly absorbed in leafy thoughts, she attacked furiously, claws exposed, teeth perforating the startled victim's skin.

Then something strange happened. It began with a noise, unfamiliar at first, a soft gurgle followed by vague hiccuping. Our mouths widened, the soft tissue at the back of our throats went into spasm, but not for crying this time. Laughter. Rob and I were *laughing*. For the first time in weeks we revelled in the simplest, most complex healing technique known to humanity. Grief had pulled me so deeply into its dungeon I'd forgotten about laughing. It took a boy, his kitten and a rubber plant to engage me in a function essential to human sanity. The horror of past weeks dissolved, padlocks of pain were unlocked momentarily. We laughed.

In the Cleo versus rubber-plant leaf war, there was no doubt who was winning. The leaf was twice Cleo's size and firmly attached to the plant's trunk. Every time she tried to grip the vegetation between her claws it slipped away and bounced insolently skyward again.

'She's a gutsy little thing,' I said.

The kitten suddenly stopped and collapsed on her haunches. She looked up at us and emitted a dictatorial mew. No interpreter was needed. Cleo was tired of entertaining us. She demanded to be scooped up for more cuddles. A mournful howl from the kitchen reverberated through the wall, reminding us it was time for Cleo to meet the lady of the house.

I instructed Rob to let Rata out of the kitchen while I held on to Cleo. But what if the dog lunged at the kitten and tried to eat it? Adult muscle strength would be needed to restrain the dog. The only option was to instruct Rob to hold the kitten carefully while I brought Rata in.

Overjoyed to be released from kitchen confinement, Rata showered me with saliva. She was seemingly oblivious of my prison-warden's grip on her collar.

'Now girl, there's someone we'd like you to meet,' I said, sounding like a dentist introducing a first timer to the drill. 'There's nothing to worry about, but you'll have to be very gentle.'

The golden retriever knew exactly where we were going. Like a jet boat with a water skier in tow, she dragged me into the living room. Rob stood by the window anxiously clutching Cleo close to his chin. Rata took one glimpse of the kitten and tightened every muscle under her collar. Cleo's eyes widened to become a pair of glittering jewels. The kitten puffed her patchy tufts of fur out to double her size, though she was still hardly big enough to intimidate a chihuahua. She arched her back and flattened her ears. Just when I thought things couldn't get worse, Rata barked, puncturing the air like gun shots. The poor little kitten was going to die of terror.

Any normal animal outclassed in size would have recoiled into Rob's arms, but Cleo was no common beast. Glowering down from her human fortress, she shrank her pupils to pin points and lasered out enough malevolence to intimidate the entire canine empire. She then peeled back her mouth, exposed two parallel rows of fangs—and hissed.

Rob, Rata and I froze. Frighteningly primeval, Cleo's hiss was something a python would emit before swallowing a rabbit, a hiss worthy of Cleopatra herself. It was an imperial hiss, one not to be argued with.

Rata fumbled under her collar and collapsed on her haunches. Shocked at the kitten's ferocity, the retriever hung her head and studied the floor. The old dog seemed disappointed, confused.

Then it struck me. I'd been misreading Rata's signals all along. Her jumping at Lena by the front door had been a welcome, not an attack. The growl just now had been one of friendly excitement, the bark an invitation to play. Rata's feelings had been wounded not only by me misinterpreting her intentions but by a stroppy kitten not much bigger than her front paw.

'It's okay,' I said. 'Bring Cleo over here.'

Nursing Cleo in his arms, Rob walked cautiously to our side of the room. Rata gazed up at the kitten with an expression so soft and kind it could have been stolen from Mother Theresa. Nevertheless, I maintained the grip on her collar.

'See? Rata doesn't hate the kitten. She's just not sure how to make friends. Put Cleo down and see what she thinks. I won't let Rata go.'

Rob took several steps backwards and lowered Cleo to the floor. The kitten stood on all fours and blinked at her monumental housemate. Rata tilted her head, pricked her ears and whined tenderly as Cleo advanced steadily towards her. When the kitten finally reached Rata's front paws, Cleo stopped and glimpsed up at the monstrous dog face towering above her. She then turned around twice, curled up like a caterpillar and snuggled between Rata's giant feet.

Our retriever trembled with delight at being recognised for the super nanny she was. Not since the boys were babies had I seen her so bursting with maternal instinct. In the way she'd been utterly protective with our children, I knew Rata would be equally trustworthy with the kitten.

Ours weren't the only hearts that had been mashed to pulp. Whatever dog-deciphering system Rata had access to, there was no doubt she knew what had happened to Sam. In some ways Rata's grief had been more consummate than ours. Without the release of language and tears, she could only lie on the floor and will the hours away. Pats and tender words from us seemed to provide only momentary comfort. But the kitten had rekindled something in the old dog. Perhaps Rata's heart was resilient enough to open up one last time.

As I let go of her collar her tongue unfurled like a ceremonial flag. Without a twitch of uncertainty, the young intruder succumbed to being lovingly slurped over from tail to nose and back again.

'Where's Cleo sleeping tonight?' Rob asked.

'We'll set up a bed for her in the laundry. I'll fill a hot-water bottle to keep her warm.'

'We can't do that! She'll be missing her brothers and sisters. She'll have nightmares. I want her to sleep with me.'

Rob hadn't mentioned the words 'missing' and 'brother' in the same sentence since 21 January. Nevertheless, the Superman watch stayed glued to his wrist. During daylight hours Rob gave a surprisingly good impression of a child enjoying a trauma-free life. Nights were a different matter. Tortured by dreams of being chased by a monster in a car, he slept fitfully on the mattress in a corner of our bedroom.

'There isn't room for all three of us *and* a kitten in our bedroom,' I said. 'Besides, Cleo's probably going to make a fuss the first few nights while she's settling in.'

'I don't care,' he said. 'She can sleep with me in my old bedroom.'

The bedroom Rob and Sam had shared still sat empty. We'd bundled up Sam's clothes and toys and dumped them in a school charity recycle bin on an afternoon so surreal in its hideousness I'd felt like a figure in a painting by Hieronymous Bosch. After that we'd done the expected thing and set about giving the room a makeover. Steve painted the walls sunshine yellow. I sewed some Smurf curtains and pinned up a Mickey Mouse poster. Steve nailed together a kit-set bed and stained it red. I bought bright new covers. But for all its primary-coloured dazzle the revamp hadn't made a cat's hair of difference to Rob. I'd envisaged him sleeping in the corner of our bedroom until his twenty-first birthday and beyond.

'You're ready to move back into your bedroom, Rob?'

'Somebody has to look after Cleo at night.'

Ensconced in his new/old bedroom that night, Rob looked almost as disoriented as his new kitten. The smell of fresh paint spiked our nostrils. The bed cover had an almost neon glow. The new sheets were crisp and cold.

Adding to the uncomfortable sense of newness was the acid dipped bathroom door that had been delivered and fitted back in its frame that afternoon. Even though the house was piecing itself together around us, we in no way shared its confidence for the future.

Certain favourite bedtime stories had to be avoided these days. *Green Eggs and Ham* was out because of the character Sam I Am. I couldn't face *The Digging-est Dog* because it featured a boy named Sam Brown who was devoted to his dog. With Cleo curled between us we settled for *One Fish Two Fish*, so familiar and comforting in its rhythms I could recite it pretty much from memory.

As we reached the last page, I could sense Rob's anxiety swelling like a wave on the horizon. 'Are you sure there are no monsters in here?' he asked, glancing anxiously under the bed.

'Absolutely.' It didn't seem the right time to tell him where the worst monsters hide. They conceal themselves cleverly inside our heads and wait for the moments we're at our most vulnerable—bedtime, or when we're sick or anxious.

'Will you check for me?'

'I looked under the bed before.'

'Can you look again?'

'Okay,' I said, bending to re-examine the battalion of fluff balls in hiding from the vacuum cleaner.

'What about behind the curtains?'

Picking up Cleo—why did I make excuses to hold her all the time?—I peeled back a corner of the curtains. For the first time I detected a glint of hope in the city's sparkling lights. Or was it? More likely, they were playing a cruel trick, laughing at us for even wondering if tonight might be a little easier.

'No monsters,' I said, tugging the curtains firmly shut. 'Now, goodnight, darling boy.' I stroked his hair and kissed his forehead, savouring the delectable smell of his skin. Strange how every child is born with a distinctive aroma, complex, intoxicating and immediately recognisable to the mother. I wondered if he had any inkling how much my life depended on his at that moment. Without the example of his courage and his need for me the lure of brandy and several bottles of sleeping pills would have been too strong.

'Did you look in the wardrobe?'

'Nothing but soccer balls and raincoats in there.'

'Can I have Cleo now?'

The kitten. Rob's kitten officially. As I lowered the furry bundle into the crook of his left arm Rob sighed and raised his thumb to his lips. He and Cleo had a lot in common. When a wife loses a husband she becomes a widow. Children are called orphans when their parents die. As far as I knew there was no word for someone grieving for a sister or brother. If there was such a word it would have described both boy and kitten. Since birth their lives had overflowed with clumsy hugs, play fights, the noise and physical warmth of their siblings. Now brutally brotherless, they were both lost and frightened. Yet they were so brave and full of life. The only option for them was to snuggle into the night together and trust that tomorrow would sort itself out.

I switched the light out and ran the day's events across a screen of darkness in my mind. The relentless ache of living without Sam permeated everything. Nevertheless, I realised with a sense of guilt, almost, that the past twenty-four hours hadn't been entirely bleak.

Steve would still need to be convinced, of course, but Cleo, as kittens went, was proving remarkably civilised.

Awakening

A kitten knows joy is more important than self-pity

'*Oooow! Help!*'

I woke with my hair pinned painfully to the pillow. A wild beast was attacking my scalp, clawing my hair and making dangerous chomping noises. It had to be a tiger or a lion escaped from a television wildlife show. Whatever it was had mistaken me for an antelope that needed eating. Emitting a stifling odour of fish breath, it obviously had a taste for marine mammals as well.

'It's only Cleo,' Rob giggled.

Cleo? How could a kitten morph into a woman-eating panther in a matter of hours?

'*Get it off!*' I yelled.

'She's not an "it",' he said, disentangling the kitten from my hair and placing her gently on the floor. Her legs barely touched the carpet before she sprang back on the bed for a fresh lunge at my hair. I wailed in agony. The kitten's purr of satisfaction reverberated through my eardrum. Is this the last sound a cat's prey hears?

The moment I disengaged the animal from my head and set her on the floor, she bounced up on the bed again. How anything that small could leap several times her height was beyond me. She was like an Olympic pole vaulter minus the pole.

49

Maybe she'd had springs surgically implanted in her hind legs. I sighed and plonked her back on the floor. Eyes gleaming like neon signs, ears huge as moth wings, she bounced up again. She seemed to think it was a game. The animal had no respect for the fact we were engulfed in a grieving process so overwhelming we had little chance of recovering.

'Noooo!' I whimpered, using the pillow as a shield. Cleo was jubilant and hugely pleased with herself. Anyone would think she was the first creature on earth to invent the hair-attack-jumping-back-on-the-bed game. Come to think of it, she probably was. The pillow offered no protection: Cleo simply burrowed under it. I put her on the floor _again_. She jumped up. Down. Up. Down. Up. This dance routine was going to last all morning if I didn't do something.

If Steve had been home I might've been able to employ him as a human shield. But he hadn't officially agreed to having a kitten in the house, let alone one that ate humans. Cleo was just an _idea_ of a kitten to him. Over the phone I'd described to him her every curve. 'You're going to love her!' I'd said. Even with my best marketing job, he sounded less than keen. I wasn't looking forward to his reaction when he arrived home from sea. He was as likely to warm to Cleo as the Pope was to Buddhism.

Rolling reluctantly out of bed I slid into my dressing-gown. As I stomped semi-conscious towards the kitchen, I experienced a tugging sensation. Looking down I saw Cleo hanging from the belt of my gown like Tarzan from a vine.

'Naughty kitty!' I said, peeling her off my belt and putting her on the floor. The moment I tried to reclaim the belt and loop it around my waist she sprang at my thighs, dug her claws into my flesh and, with her tail swinging wildly, snared the belt between her teeth. I wailed painfully for the second time that morning.

Removing the kitten from my thigh inflicted more pain than the world's worst Brazilian wax. Obviously there was only one way to deal with this young cat: firmness. I wrapped the belt around my waist, tied a knot and proceeded forwards with all the dignity it was possible to muster. Cleo raced ahead and flicked swiftly between my ankles, before suddenly skidding to a halt. In a single slow-motion movement I tripped over the hump of her spine and sailed through the air, only just managing to grab hold of a wall-hanging to stop myself landing on top of her.

Clinging to the macramé tassels, I froze in a position worthy of an advanced yogi and apologised. The kitten rolled on her back, raised a bent paw and fixed me with a wounded expression. I felt terrible for hurting her.

Just as I bent to pick her up, the furry ball exploded to life, sprang to its feet and lunged away from me. Relieved, I followed—until she bounced to a halt and tripped me up again. And *again*!

Cleo seemed to have decided I was a ridiculous animal, with my bird's nest hair and insistence on prancing about on two legs. Her mission was to trim my coat and get me down on all fours so I could savour the exuberance of being a cat.

But I didn't need a crazy kitten. The animal had no right to dance through our grieving chambers as if life was some kind of joke. If Sam were here, I thought, he'd know how to calm her down. I could almost see him bending over her, hand outstretched, lips damp and tender . . .

I hurried to the bathroom, the only place I could weep in private, and closed the door. Rob didn't need to witness any more adult distress than he'd already seen. If only events had unfolded differently that day. If Sam hadn't found the pigeon, if Steve hadn't been making lemon meringue pie, if I hadn't been out for lunch, if that woman hadn't been driving back to work . . . *That woman*. It was all her fault. I wondered if she had children of her own and any idea the anguish we were going through. My mind had turned her into a monster.

A series of jagged sobs erupted. Trying to repress the noise, I leant my forehead against the cool blue tiles and clutched my stomach. My chest muscles ached. The capacity of human tear ducts continued to amaze me. How many buckets could one pair of eyes fill? Just when I thought I'd exceeded the lifetime quota, another tanker load would discharge down my cheeks. Crying had become just another bodily function, like breathing, something that happened without conscious effort.

As I bent over the toilet bowl, part of my consciousness peeled away to float on the bathroom ceiling. It looked down with benevolence at the howling woman doubled over with hurt and hatred. This other me who examined things from a distance didn't take things so personally. It was spooky and detached. Maybe it had been there since birth and I'd spent the rest of my life crowding it out with emotions, obligations and conforming to what was expected.

At the same time it frightened me. What if I was tempted to float away with it for eternity, smiling down on human drama like an amused zoo keeper? The idea of shedding my body and escaping pain was suddenly attractive. I slid the cabinet drawer open and held the bottle of sleeping pills to the light. Each pill glowed like a promise through the brown glass. There were plenty left. They didn't smell too bad. Washed down with enough brandy they'd be tolerable. I unscrewed the lid.

The bathroom door opened a crack. Dammit. I hadn't closed it properly. The shower curtain rippled. Assuming Rob had opened the front door and set a draught going through the house, I leant forwards to shut the door. It continued to nudge itself open. Glancing down I saw a black paw run down the gap. Cleo pushed her way in, padded over the tiles and mewed for me to pick her up. Sighing, I put the pills back in the drawer and closed it quietly. To arrange a permanent exit would be the ultimate act of indulgence. Cleo's impertinent arrival in the bathroom was a reminder of my responsibilities. I had no right to opt out when a boy and a kitten needed continuity in their lives, and someone to nurture them through to adulthood. Gathering Cleo in my hands, I sobbed into her fur. She didn't seem to mind being a handkerchief. Purring, she nuzzled my neck and gazed at me with such affection I was taken aback. Not since the boys were babies had a living creature offered so much undiluted love. Once I'd regained composure I lowered her to the floor. She skipped away and I went to find Rob.

The house had gone through a metamorphosis overnight. The hallway resembled the aftermath of a battle. Empty supermarket bags were scattered over the shag pile. Among them lay a selection of unmatched socks. Rob's blue and white sports sock lay shrivelled alongside one of Steve's. A rainbow-striped bed sock curled around a fallen deodorant bottle. With its cap resembling Napoleon's hat, the deodorant bottle looked like a deceased general who, knowing he'd lost the campaign, had taken a bullet and tumbled on his side.

In the family room rugs were rumpled and mysteriously askew. Lampshades hung crooked like jaunty headwear. Chairs and tables had rearranged themselves at subtly different angles. Photos had toppled on the window ledge. A rubbish basket lay on its side spewing apple cores and chewing gum wrappers.

The kitchen blinds had collapsed at half-mast and wouldn't budge up or down. Closer inspection revealed the curtain cords had been either surgically severed or chomped through.

Assuming we'd been burgled, I hurried to the living room. To my surprise the stereo and its speakers still lurked inside their ugly veneer cabinets. The television hadn't budged either, though the flock of sympathy cards had taken wing during the night and fluttered to the floor.

The rubber plant lay toppled on its side, its pendulous leaves stretching over the sofa and coffee table. Dirt from its tub avalanched over the carpet. The landslide was decorated with three small, bullet-shaped turds.

I'd never been house proud, but this was too much. Our kitten had undergone a personality change after dark. She was nothing short of a feline werewolf.

The day ahead stretched towards a horizon littered with socks, fallen rubber plants, supermarket bags and acupunctured ankles.

'Where's Cleo?' I roared, scooping up a blanket I'd lovingly stitched together for Rob. The blanket had taken months to knit. As I clutched the manifestation of mother's love to my chest, three half-eaten tassels dropped to the floor.

Rata tilted a lazy ear from her sleeping post in the doorway. Rob shrugged. On the tree fern outside a bird was practising scales. A ship's horn moaned out on the harbour. Inside, the house was eerily silent. Except for strange tinkling noises coming from the kitchen.

I marched over the lino to declare war on a creature one-tenth my size. The clock emitted bored ticks from its watch post above the kitchen sink. The tap, like a drummer with no sense of rhythm, wept into the plug hole. Otherwise, silence. Our furry delinquent had gone bush.

For no logical reason, I reached for the oven door. Just as well we weren't expecting a visit from Martha Stewart. Grease stains trickled like frozen tears down its glass front. I'd get around to cleaning them off some day, in the next year or two, or whenever there was a day on the calendar marked 'World Oven-Cleaning Day'. A pair of roasting dishes glowered back at me from the gloom.

I was about to check out the pot cupboard when we heard the unmistakable sound of plates shattering. Rob lowered the dishwasher door. Cleo was having too much fun crashing around last night's dinner plates to take notice of us. She ignored my yells to get out. When Rob reached into the dishwasher Cleo shot out and slithered between his legs, then scampered away before either of us could lay hands on her slippery fur.

I'd heard people say kittens were playful and could be almost as demanding as new babies. *Almost?* Babies stay in their bassinettes, for heaven's sake. They don't go out of their way to attack your hair or send you flying through the air with the prospect of spending the rest of your days in a wheelchair. This kitten's behaviour was beyond any normality curve—human, animal or vegetable. She was uncontrollable, destructive, possibly psychotic and a sock fetishist to boot. In less than twenty-four hours she'd changed from helpless, charming aristocrat to crazed feral.

We chased after her down the hall, leaping over socks and supermarket bags, but Cleo was nowhere to be seen. We stopped and listened. All that could be heard was the sound of our laboured breathing.

I peered through the crack of Rob's door. Curled on his pillow was the personification of kittenly cuteness. She mewed affectionately, stretched, and gave the prettiest yawn. Cleo had morphed back into the creature we'd fallen in love with.

Rob moved towards her. Cleo's eyes snapped wide open. Glaring, she pinned her ears back and lashed the pillowcase with her tail. Before either of us could get any closer she sprang to her feet and flitted mischievously across the room. Rob flung himself to the floor, trying to pin her down in a rugby tackle. She slithered through his grasp, leapt on top of his bookshelf and scrambled out of reach up the Smurf curtains, using her claws for crampons.

Swinging from Smurfland, the kitten was deaf to my concerns for the interior decor. Nevertheless, a glimpse towards the ceiling confirmed she couldn't climb any higher. Descending meekly into our arms, however, wasn't an option. In less than a breath, she dropped onto my shoulder, a mere springboard from which she then plunged to the floor.

Back on the carpet, she leapt in wild circles around the room, bouncing off the window ledge, the bed, the bookshelf. This was not a kitten. It was a dynamo with enough energy to power a discothèque. Even watching her was exhausting.

It wasn't going to last. We weren't cat people. Our house no longer belonged to us. Cleo had invaded and turned us into prisoners. Even though she was tiny, her personality filled every corner of every room. If she wasn't stealing socks from the laundry basket or chewing the covers of precious books she was hiding in a shopping basket waiting to ambush us.

Admittedly, the trouble she was causing had provided diversion from our pain. Every moment spent worrying what part of the house she was destroying was one not steeped in grief. But I was a barely functioning human being and in no condition to deal with the undiluted force of nature that was Cleo.

The only thing more unnerving than her presence was her sudden, inexplicable absence. 'Where's Cleo?' I muttered after resurrecting the rubber plant and disposing of the turds. The house was too quiet. Rob found her eating potato peelings inside the kitchen cupboard that contained our rubbish bin.

I'd once read somewhere that cats sleep seventeen hours a day. Presumably kittens needed more than that. Going by the damage to our surroundings, Cleo must've slept a total of three hours in the past twenty-four. Some other kitten in a blissfully calm household had surely stolen Cleo's designated down time and grabbed it for itself. It'd be pigging out on hours of extra sleep, dozing on a cushion in a patch of sunlight somewhere, not causing any trouble. Its stress-free, thoroughly spoilt owner would look at its plump, snoring form and wonder at its passive nature.

I couldn't stand another minute of that kitten. I persuaded Rob to leave the house with me for an hour or two. The only terms he'd agree to was a visit to a pet shop that sold stuff for kittens.

We crept around the abandoned supermarket bags toward the front door. I turned the lock smoothly to avoid loud clicks that might draw attention to our escape. Just as I shuffled Rob out ahead of me, the supermarket bag closest to the door suddenly inflated to twice its size, exploded to life and emitted a terrifying yowl. A miniature panther pounced from its depths and dug its teeth in my ankles.

I tried to shake her off. The kitten was several notches below us on the Darwinian scale. She had no right—let alone the brains and technology—to detain us. Nevertheless, she was having a damn good try.

Rob picked up a sock and shook it. Cleo was immediately mesmerised. Ferocity: 10. Attention span: 0. She leapt and danced after the hosiery. When Rob threw it to the other end of the hall she scurried after it.

We slid out the front door as Cleo's tail disappeared into the shadows. *She's only a cat, for heaven's sake!* my mother's voice lectured inside my head. But I hadn't felt so guilty since I'd tried leaving the boys at a day-care centre that was clearly run by a direct descendent of Adolf Hitler.

We headed along the path to the zigzag. A force tugged me back towards the house. I turned to see our kitten peering out of Rob's window. If a representative of Hallmark cards had wandered up the zigzag he'd have signed her up for a lifetime of schmaltzy photo shoots. Nestled in a basket or garden pot, dangling from a Christmas stocking, she'd have been irresistible.

Back in the bathroom she'd rescued me from one of my bleakest moments. I was grateful to her for that. She was beautiful, wonderful. And impossible to live with.

Taming the Beast

A cat tames people when they are ready

Cats and people are unlikely allies. If they were logical, humans, with practically the entire animal kingdom to choose from, would opt to tame creatures more like themselves for pets. Monkeys would be an obvious choice. Furry, intelligent and largely vegetarian, monkeys can learn tricks. But people don't warm to primates on the whole. In a monkey's eyes they recognise their own cunning gleaming back.

Instead, humans prefer creatures closely related to their fiercest enemies—lions and tigers and wolves, who'd rather gnaw their bones than sit at their feet and amuse.

The pet shop mostly catered for this preference. Out of habit or instinct, I headed for the dog section. An Aladdin's cave of squeaky balls and rubber bones, it was Rata heaven. Rob steered me to the other side of the shop and pointed out a cushiony thing he thought would be an excellent bed for Cleo. The leopard-skin cover certainly reflected something of Cleo's personality.

A shop assistant homed in on us and recommended a sack of dried kitten food. (*Special food for kittens?* I could almost hear my mother wail. *Has the world gone troppo?! We'll have women running the country next.*) The shop assistant said our kitten would love a soft toy stuffed with cat nip, adding that it made them extra playful. Imagining Cleo on the feline equivalent of LSD, I said no thanks.

On our way to the counter she talked us into buying a bag of kitty litter and a plastic tray to put it in. I didn't want a kitten. Steve was almost certain to spit the dummy when he came home and saw what Cleo was capable of. What were we doing purchasing all these accessories? Rob stood on tiptoes and slid the cat bed across the counter's glass top.

She was a talented saleswoman. Beaming down at him, she asked for his kitten's name. His face turned pink with pride as he said the word. And, he added, she was the best kitten in the whole world.

◆

Life was complicated. I drove the long way home, winding down the gully past the Botanic Gardens, where the boys and I used to feed ducks. Visiting the ducks was always a good way to defuse their energy when they'd been cooped up inside after days of bad weather. Feathered or furred, animals always had a way of reaching into their frazzled, overactive souls and calming them down. The sight of a brown duck gliding over silvery water tuned all three of us into a wider world where problems didn't seem so insurmountable. We invariably left the duck pond feeling calmer. In spring we'd count the ducklings, always one or two fewer than the week before. But it was impossible to mourn for long, not when the tulips were out. The boys would run, their hair fiery gold in the sunlight, through rows of dazzling reds, pinks and yellows.

I asked Rob if he wanted to see the ducks but he was keen to get back to Cleo. I couldn't face them, anyway. And I wouldn't be visiting the tulips this year, either. They would have to flower by themselves. Every corner of Wellington housed gut-wrenching reminders of our previous life. The town was one big mausoleum.

But home was no longer a shabby retreat from the world. Within twenty-four hours the kitten had taken charge and transformed it into The House of Cleo, invading every centimetre of my personal space, coiling between my ankles, scrabbling up the back of my chair if I sat down for a coffee, following me to the bathroom and pouncing on my lap the instant I settled on the toilet seat. Socks, supermarket bags and all the collateral damage from the night before still had to be cleaned up. If I wanted to avoid making explanations to Steve I'd need to find someone in the Yellow Pages to fix the curtain cords. And who knew what additional acts of vandalism she'd pulled off while we were out?

Maybe we didn't need to go home. We could just keep driving till we hit the motorway that slithered around the harbour and headed north. The house, cat, shaky marriage and friends with their harrowing outbursts of sympathy could all be left behind. We'd go and live with Mum in New Plymouth, the provincial town I grew up in—for about two weeks until Mum and I drove each other nuts. The town and I didn't seem to fit together any more, anyway. Whenever I went back for funerals or birthdays, people invariably asked two questions: 'How's the writing?' and 'When are you leaving?' The second was always easier to answer than the first. I never classified what I did as 'writing'. It was more about sharing stories with people whose lives were equally imperfect, and having a few laughs together. Readers of my column were like friends, with the added bonus of almost never turning up in the flesh. They had been amazingly kind lately. I'd grown so accustomed to sharing intimate aspects of our lives with them through my weekly instalments it seemed appropriate to tell them about Sam's death. The only alternatives were to continue writing diverting tales about domestic life as though nothing had happened (impossible), or retire. As I sat in bed, dripping tears into my portable typewriter, and recounted the events of that dreadful day, I had no idea I was tapping into a great source of healing. Letters and cards arrived in the hundreds, demonstrating the enormous generosity of strangers. Their letters, a few from people who'd also lost children, offered more strength than almost anything else. I carried a carefully typed sheet of paper around in my handbag. It was from an Indian couple whose two-year-old had wandered into a national park and was never seen again. Ten years after the event they said they were still sad, but surviving. They were living proof that parents who lose children in dreadful ways—they're *always* dreadful—can survive.

An even bolder option would be to keep heading north till we reached the flashy lights of Auckland, a bigger city, where I'd get a job on a newspaper or magazine. Except only a lunatic would hire a grief-raddled, worn-out solo mum.

I nudged the car against the clay cutting draped with ferns at the top of the zigzag. The city spread below us in cubes of grey, windows glinting in the sun. In one of those office towers would be the woman who'd taken Sam's life on her way back to work from her lunch break. I wondered what she looked like, and what she was doing. Sliding a file out of a cabinet, on the phone to someone? Wellington was such a small place we were bound to have some acquaintances in common. Nobody had given a hint they knew her. Perhaps they sensed her life would be in danger if I set eyes on her. She'd have to appear at the court inquest soon and confess she was drunk or driving too fast. Her punishment would come in good time.

Beyond the office blocks and over the hills past Lena's house was the cemetery where Sam's body lay. Beyond that, on Makara Beach, families would be making the most of what was left of the summer. Mothers would be spreading rugs over the stones, pouring orange cordial and telling their children the waves weren't as cold as they looked. Boys would be charging into the surf, their skin goose-pimpled and gleaming in the waves. Some of them would be Sam's friends. I didn't want to see them or their mothers again.

A southerly breeze spiked my nostrils. Not so long ago I'd relished the thought of living in our house on the fault line, fixing the place up, along with our marriage. Suddenly it seemed too hard.

Rob scrambled out of the car, eager to show Cleo her new bed. Laden with kitty litter and the plastic tray I followed him down towards the house. I tried to prepare mentally for whatever fresh hell the-house-that-now-belonged-to-a-cat had to offer. At least it was still standing, its painted beams peeling in the sun. There was no sign of the kitten.

When I turned the key a tiny panther gambolled down the hall towards us, her tail waving like a banner. She emitted squeaks of welcome, each ending in a higher tone: *Where have you been? Why did you take so long? Did you bring me anything?* She sprang up on her hind legs, plunged her chin into our hands and flossed her teeth on our fingernails. The throb of her purr told us all was forgiven. We'd turned the sky blue again and glued the sun back in the sky simply by returning. I was entranced once more. How could I have considered sending her away? We needed her almost as much as she needed us.

But when Rob thrust the leopard skin bed at her, Cleo arched her back and fluffed her tail out like a bottlebrush. She hissed violently. The cat bed was as threatening as the leopard it imitated. She pounced and savaged it, thumping it with her hind legs before swiftly withdrawing under the sofa. The enemy had no time to retaliate.

Cleo refused to emerge until her foe had retired to the laundry. We didn't realise at the time but it was the beginning of life-long 'issues' with bedding. Once it was gone she shot out from under the sofa to skid on a supermarket bag before climbing inside it. After catching her breath inside its plastic belly she ambushed the phone cord and scuttled to the safety of the kitchen pot cupboard.

Our cat was wired tighter than a violin. Every shadow, ball of dust, shopping list, discarded ribbon and household implement was a potential attacker. Noises alarmed her. She jumped at the squeak of a door. A distant bird's song spiked every hair on her body.

No sock in the house was safe. She abducted them from bedrooms, empty shoes and the laundry basket, carefully separating each one from its twin so it was vulnerable to assault. The sock was then dragged through the house by its toe, tossed in the air, caught between two sets of claws and tortured mercilessly until it feigned death.

I was developing a headache. Cleaning up the day's mess was pointless. It only gave the kitten scope to invent some new form of household devastation.

'Don't you *dare!*' I said when Cleo sprang on the hall table and patted a tall vase of foxgloves with a tentative paw. Looking up at me she shook her whiskers and shrunk into her coat. I was serious. She lowered her paw and jumped obediently back on to the floor. I'm not proud to say I felt a glow of satisfaction. Having a close to wild animal respond to my commands was exhilarating. Megalomaniac teachers must experience similar power surges. Pleased with my venture into authoritarianism I glided into the kitchen to put the kettle on. But like every dictator I was delusional.

The house shook with a resounding thud. I charged back into the hall. Foxglove stems were sailing through the air, closely followed by the vase, from which billowed a spout of water. Surfing the waterfall was a four-legged figure, spread-eagled in an attempt to stay upright.

The vase crashed to the ground. Foxgloves scattered in elegant angles down the hallway. I watched as the kitten was engulfed. Caught in a flower-vase pipeline, she had no choice but to ride it out.

Like most natural disasters, it was over almost as quickly as it started. A house that seconds earlier had resembled a normal, if scruffy, family home was now worthy of relief funds from the UN. Sploshing through the tide, Cleo shook each paw after each step as if the water caused personal offence. Ears flattened, tail drooped, she wouldn't have won first prize in any beauty contest. Or even best and fairest.

I yelled at Rob to get some towels. Together we tried to bring the house back to dry land. I soaked up the carpet damage while Rob towelled the animal dry. It was the first time I'd seen her anything close to humble.

Healer

A cat loves with all its heart, but not so fervently that there's nothing left over for itself

Steve was back from his week at sea just in time to experience the mayhem our new kitten had caused. While he cleaned and tidied the house, I stood at the kitchen bench watching a seagull glide on the updraft from the cliff. The bird and I were at the same eye level. It swivelled the slash of its beak towards me. We exchanged glares.

Not so long ago I'd liked birds, empathised with their struggle. Around the age of eight or nine I'd found a baby thrush on the front lawn. It couldn't fly. Our cat Sylvester was bound to get it if I didn't do something. I scooped the ball of feathers up in my hands. It didn't seem to mind resting its reptilian feet on my fingers. Its beak and claws were too big for its body. It was not yet a functioning bird. I had no choice but to take it inside. A shoebox was lined with cotton wool. Holes were punched in the lid with a knitting needle. The thrush took eager gulps of sugared water from an eye dropper. Certain the bird would die overnight, I closed the lid. The box chirruped. Not a call of alarm. Just a chirrup. The box sat on my dressing table all night. I dreaded what I'd find next morning. But when I scrambled out of bed and opened the lid, the bird was sitting upright. Its eyes shone black and expectant. I closed the lid and took the box outside to the front lawn. When I opened the lid the thrush hopped onto the grass. It wobbled uncertainly, then with a thrilling whirr of wings flew up onto a branch. It perched there for a while, pretending I didn't exist. I called, but it hurtled across the valley to the pines. I thought it might fly back to thank me. Of course it never did.

The seagull peeled away, swooped down over the ferry terminal and across the harbour. Five weeks had passed since our older son, inside his white coffin, had been lowered into the hills behind Lena's house. We'd visited the grave a couple of times. I found no comfort on the windswept summit of Makara Cemetery, with its soldier lines of plaques. The first few times we went it took a while to work out where Sam's grave was in that mosaic of misery. Steve pointed out it was in line with the toilet block. I could almost hear Sam laughing about that. He'd always had a lavatory sense of humour. In typical incongruity he'd been buried between two people who'd lived well into their eighties. Kneeling above him, my tears irrigating the grass, I searched for something of his essence. There was nothing of him in the gnarled bushes bent permanently against the wind. Clouds wrapped themselves in improbable shapes. Sheep bleated. Sam didn't belong in that empty place.

I felt like an actor wearing someone else's clothes. On the outside we resembled the same people we'd been a month or so earlier. I drove the same car, went to the same supermarket, but my internal organs felt like they'd been rearranged and scrubbed with steel wool. Shock, probably. I no longer trusted the goodness of being alive. Hatred and fury flared easily. I was angry at the people who lay alongside Sam. They had no right to live so long.

Even though the new school year had started we'd decided to keep Rob home for a couple of weeks. He hardly ever mentioned Sam but he still wore the Superman watch every day. Maybe he thought the action figure on his wrist was a hotline to his big brother. Rob needed a superhero more than any boy I could think of. If only Superman could jump through his bedroom window with Sam laughing in his arms.

I began to wonder if the point of superheroes isn't so much the extraordinary feats they perform as the fact they have other lives as uncool males struggling for acceptance. Most boys relate to Clark Kent, geeky and rejected by the woman he loves. Like Clark Kent, every boy has an inner hero. His only hope of knowing a real live Superman is to become one, a goal that sets most young men up for disappointment. As they grow older the search for Superman continues. Sports heroes, rock stars, billionaires. Yet the real hero isn't so far away. He lies within.

Reluctant as I was to admit it, I was getting help from Cleo. She seemed to know when I was bottoming out, whatever time of day or night it was. A paw would slide down the crack of a door, she'd leap on our bed or sit nearby, not demanding anything. Purring patiently, she'd simply wait until I surfaced.

Even her destructive behaviour seemed to have purpose. It dragged us into dealing with the here and now. During the few moments I was yelling at her about curtain cords or toppled photo frames, I wasn't eating my insides out over Sam. Infuriating, impish and bursting with affection, Cleo pulsed with exuberance. From the point of her tail to the tips of her whiskers she was one hundred per cent alive. There was more Sam in her than there was under the whistling skies of Makara.

But Steve didn't seem to see it that way. Even though I'd explained how Sam had picked her out, I had the feeling Steve associated the kitten with the life we'd had before Sam died, not this surreal existence we were trying to eke out now. Adopting a pet without his consent was hardly a functional family thing to do. Besides, he came from a long line of dog people.

+

Steve unpacked his sea bag under Cleo's watchful gaze. She appeared to be making an inventory of his clothes, and which might be portable. His eyes slid sideways at her. I could tell he was thinking only one word. Mess.

One of the many differences in our personalities was attitude to mess. I was, and still am, comfortable with quite a lot of disorder. Amazingly creative ideas can spring from piles of old paper and clothes you forgot you ever had. At least, that's what I tell myself when I can't be bothered sifting through them, which is almost always.

Steve, on the other hand, could have been mistaken for a graduate from the Zen school of the obsessively tidy. As a teenage bride, I'd strived to satisfy his craving for immaculate surroundings. Whenever he was due home from a week at sea, I'd rush around the house dusting skirting boards, straightening curtains and arranging rug tassels in parallel lines. I was a slow learner. It took years to realise that no matter how perfect I thought the house looked it made no difference to Steve's perception. Oblivious to my efforts, he moved like a robot through the same routine every time he arrived home from sea: unleash vacuum cleaner, wipe benchtops, even if I'd cleaned them half an hour earlier, and unpack sea bag. Vacuuming had been out of the question today, due to the saturated shag pile. He had to content himself with picking up socks and supermarket bags.

Just as I launched into a spiel about how much Rob adored the kitten, Cleo dived into Steve's bag and emerged with the toe of a black sock between her teeth. Scurrying away, she tossed it above her head and jumped in the air. She caught it between her front paws with panache, before rocketing away full pelt, the sock trailing between her legs. One of her back legs stepped on it, bringing her to such a sudden halt she somersaulted through the air and landed on her back. I sucked a breath. The poor creature had surely damaged her spine. We'd have to take her to the vet's. She'd writhe in agony. There'd be no cure. Unperturbed, Cleo wriggled to her feet, picked up the sock again and sprinted away.

Unimpressed, Steve trudged out of the room in search of his sock. It generally took us two days to adjust to Steve's routine after he'd been away. With the additional tension of an unwelcome kitten, domestic harmony was more problematic.

I'd read somewhere that seventy-five per cent of marriages fail after the death of a child. I wasn't prepared to buy into that. Defying statistics was one of my specialities. But I was beginning to understand why so many relationships crumble.

Steve's pain was no less than mine, but it was different, more internal. I grieved in wild expressionist brushstrokes, sobbing, wailing, accusing, wanting to be held. His sorrow was more orderly and restrained. Words, when he said them, were as carefully considered as dew drops on an orange in a Dutch master's still life.

While Steve had been able to undertake the tasks expected of a man—identifying the body, the police interview and, tomorrow, an appearance at the court inquest—his ability to convey what was going on behind the fortress of his face had shut down. I was to blame for some of that. I should never have asked him to stop crying that morning after the accident. His gaze slithered everywhere these days, from curtains to carpet to rubber plant. Never into my eyes. When he'd asked if I'd go along to the inquest with him I'd refused. The thought of reliving it all in front of strangers was too much. If I'd had the courage to agree I'd have been a better wife. We were both at our most needy, yet neither had reserves to soothe the other.

Rob called us to the living room, where he was crouching over Cleo, dangling Steve's sock. He tossed the sock across the room. Cleo chased it, caught it neatly between her teeth, trotted back to Rob and dropped it at his feet. She then sat neatly beside Rob and waited, staring up at him expectantly.

'See? She can fetch!'

'Only dogs can fetch,' said Steve, swooping his sock off the floor.

'No, you try it,' said Rob.

Hesitantly, Steve flung the sock into the air. Cleo barrelled away and retrieved it, depositing it at my feet this time.

The kitten ensured we were all awarded equal time throwing the sock. She wanted it to be a family game.

'Cleo can play sock-er!' said Rob.

Her enthusiasm was limitless. The three of us were soon mesmerised by the wiry figure dancing to and fro after her sock victim. When it rolled under the sofa's underskirts I was almost relieved. No way would she be able to slide into the two-inch gap between the sofa and the floor.

But I'd underestimated Cleo's yogi-like flexibility. Without hesitation she flattened her haunches and wriggled under the sofa. It was like watching birth in reverse.

The silence that followed was unnerving. She was stuck under there. Seconds later, a single black paw appeared from behind the high back of the sofa. It was swiftly accompanied by another paw. With leverage from two sets of claws a face appeared, much narrower than the last time we'd seen it, the eyes half-closed, the ears reduced to mere flaps flattened against its skull. Clamped victoriously between its thin lips was the sock.

◆

The sun glinted like a giant tiger eye as it sank behind the hills. The sky was turning pink with exhaustion. Slipping on a cashmere cardigan, I chopped chicken breasts. Risotto was bland enough not to offend anyone's tastebuds.

Cleo lifted her nose and, like a connoisseur analysing the aromas of a rare Bordeaux, half-closed her eyes. Following my ankles as I moved about the kitchen, she emitted a series of squeaks. Not the mews of a cat begging for food, but the demands of a priestess impatient to have offerings laid at her feet.

Gathering her up, I snuggled her against my chest and sat down with her on a kitchen chair. She strained wistfully towards the chicken but soon became intrigued by my precious cashmere cardigan. Simple sheep's wool was of no interest to Cleo. Fibre removed from domestic goats and then painstakingly dehaired was another matter. She chomped the wool around the middle button.

I disentangled her and lowered her firmly to the ground. Cleo sprang back on my lap. Like a famished lion she dug her teeth into my cardigan. I tried to dislodge her. A sudden pain in my thumb as she sank a fang through my flesh. Not only had she ruined my cardigan but she'd drilled a hole in me.

Crying out, I stemmed the river of blood with a paper towel. When Steve saw my injury he was unimpressed: Cleo was doing a good job fulfilling his prejudices against kittens.

When we sat down to the meal the furrow between Steve's eyebrows deepened as Cleo demonstrated how unwilling she was to understand the words 'Don't jump on the table'. She attacked all three of our plates, not to mention the tablemats, salt and pepper shakers and cutlery.

Heat pulsed up the back of my neck. My thumb throbbed. The effort of selling a kitten to a reluctant husband was taking its toll. I grabbed her and shut her firmly in the laundry.

'She hates it in there,' Rob whined.

'She can't ruin our lives!' I shouted to drown out the yowls from behind the laundry door. Something about her jagged cries tipped me over a precipice. It wasn't just the kitten, the thumb and the husband. The inquest was the next morning. Steve would come face to face with that woman. Policemen would prove her guilt. She would go to jail. I would finally have to accept Sam was dead.

Cleo's yelps intensified. My body started shaking. Breaths came in shallow gasps. 'I can't stand it anymore! She'll just have to go back to Lena!'

Rob stared into his risotto and swallowed back tears. 'You're. So. Mean.'

Scraping back my chair, I reeled to my feet and ran to the bedroom. Sobbing loudly into the pillow, I knew Rob was right. I *was* mean. And out of control. A bad mother, hopeless wife, a failed human being in general. I longed for sleep to drop its blanket over me.

Instead, a boy's hand touched my shoulder. 'She loves you, Mummy,' he whispered. 'Listen . . .'

A bulk of fur nestled into my neck. The rhythmical growl of her purr roared in my ear. It was the deep primeval sound of waves rolling in on the black sand beaches of my childhood, the noise a baby hears when it's in the womb. Wise and eternal, it could be the earth's lullaby or the voice of God.

A cat's purr is said to have a profound effect on the human body. Tests have proved purring reduces people's stress, lowers blood pressure and helps mend muscles and bones. The healing powers of cats are increasingly acknowledged by the many hospitals and nursing homes that employ resident cat doctors. Regular doses of purring have the potential to repair heart tissue as well. Listening to her throaty melody, my chest filled with liquid honey.

Cleo nudged her head under my chin, stared at me with maternal concern and to my amazement planted her damp nose on my cheek. It was an unmistakable kitten kiss. Nestling into my neck, she stretched a delicate front leg across my face. I took the paw between my fingers, caressed it and watched the claws gently open and close. No threat of attack this time. The pads of her foot were softer than my fingertips, and sensitive enough to feel the earth's subtle tremors (or so I'd heard). As we lay 'holding hands', our souls reached across the divide of species and shared a connection beyond words.

I awoke several hours later with Cleo wedged between the sheets, her head resting on the pillow beside me. She felt entitled to be there. Her motionless form, the peaks of her ears against the white cotton, the restful comfort of her breathing made me wonder if we hadn't slept that way, human and feline, side by side, since Earth's first dawn.

Goddess

A cat is a priestess in a fur coat

'You do like Cleo, don't you?' Rob asked over breakfast next morning.

I opened the kitchen window. Another seagull screeched across the agate blue harbour. The half-eaten curtain cord swayed in the breeze. Steve had already put on his tie and left for the magistrate's court.

'Yes,' I sighed.

'Good, because she likes you.'

'Of course she does,' I said, smiling weakly.

'No, Mummy. She *really* does!' he said. 'She told me last night.'

'That's nice, dear,' I said. 'Finish your toast.'

'She told me other stuff, too.'

Rob was a sensitive boy. He'd suffered more trauma than any young child should endure. We hadn't discussed the inquest with him, but he'd probably picked up on the vibes. Now he was dreaming up ideas of the kitten talking to him.

'She said she comes from a long line of cat healers,' he continued.

The poor kid's imagination was off its leash.

'You mean in a *dream?*' I asked, fearing for his grip on reality.

74

'It didn't feel like a dream. She said she's going to help me find friends.'

There'd always been a psychic streak in the family, but talking to a kitten was too much. If word got out at school that he was having conversations with his kitten he'd be a target for bullies and all sorts of misery.

'I'm sure she is,' I said, putting my arm around his shoulder and kissing his ear. 'But let's keep it a secret for now.'

'You won't give Cleo back to Lena, will you?' he asked.

I crouched beside him, rested my hands on his shoulders and examined his face, so serious. His body was rigid with tension. 'No, Rob. We're keeping her.'

His shoulders dropped. Relief rippled through him. He put his head down. His hair moved like wheat. His arms wriggled in a subtle dance of joy. Even though he wasn't looking at me I could tell he was smiling.

◆

Humans were slow to understand how essential cats were to their survival. One of the attractions of giving up nomadic wandering in favour of farming permanent settlements was the reduced risk of attack from large predators. People spent several generations congratulating themselves on this achievement without realising a more devastating enemy was thriving in their walls, basements and grain stores. The humble rodent was responsible for far greater devastation than its carnivore cousins. A hoard of mice could destroy a year's crop, leaving an entire village diseased and starving.

Wild cats circled the settlements, drooling at the prospect of mousey banquets. Occasionally some were bold or desperate enough to venture into the villages to hunt rats, mice and snakes. People gradually began to realise the cats weren't doing any harm. In fact, they were useful pest controllers.

They started to appreciate the creature's qualities. They noticed its elegance, admired its aloofness and its refusal to submit to human superiority like a cow or dog. The ancient Egyptians were the first to be impressed by the fact that a cat did not necessarily come when it was called.

Felines were decked out in gold jewellery and allowed to share food from their owners' plates. Punishment for killing one of these creatures was death. Cats often had more elaborate funerals than people. When a family feline passed away its body was displayed outside the home and the entire household shaved their eyebrows as a sign of mourning—behaviour that in today's suburban neighbourhood would result in phone calls to local authorities.

As well as saving millions of lives by killing rodents, our soft-footed friends have helped heal countless hearts. Sitting quietly at the ends of beds, they've waited for human tears to ebb. Curled on the laps of the sick and elderly, they've offered comfort impossible to find elsewhere. Having served our physical and emotional health for thousands of years, they deserve recognition. The Egyptians were right. A cat is a sacred being.

◆

The kitchen clock dragged itself through the morning. The hearing was taking longer than expected. I assumed there was time-consuming evidence against the woman, previous convictions for dangerous driving – *anything* to explain what had happened.

A mug of coffee. And another. The harbour was a turquoise Frisbee just as it had been the day Sam died. Malevolent in its perfection. While I willed the second hand to circumnavigate the clock, Cleo introduced Rob to an old paper bag she'd stolen from the cupboard under the kitchen sink. She seemed to love the crackling sound it made as she rolled on it. When Rob held the paper bag open, Cleo bounded away from him across the kitchen and skidded to a halt. Turning, she crouched low and focused on the paper cave Rob had created. With pupils dilated, her eyes were almost entirely black apart from their thin green rims. Shifting her balance, she lifted her right front paw and positioned herself for the assault. The preparation was so painstaking and time consuming her audience was in danger of losing interest. Just as we were about to give up entirely and turn our attention to an unopened packet of chocolate chip biscuits, a black dart flew across the vinyl and shot into the crinkled depths of the paper bag.

'Look, Mummy,' he said, lifting the bag that was now satisfyingly round and weighty.

I moved to rescue the kitten from her paper prison, but the bag emitted happy purrs.

Steve returned close to noon, hollow-eyed and semi-transparent in the hallway. His tie, half-undone, hung limp over his chest.

The pity I felt for him was immediately obliterated by hungry rage. 'What does she look like?' I asked, surprised at the harshness in my voice.

'Why are you angry, Mummy?' I hadn't noticed Rob following me down the hall with the purring paper bag in his hands.

'I'm not angry.' My tone was dry and cold.

'Daddy, look what Cleo can do!' As Rob offered him the paper bag, Cleo's head emerged mischievously from its mouth.

'Not now,' I snapped. 'Take her into the kitchen, will you?'

Sensing the jagged atmosphere, Rob left obediently. If only, I wished, one day there could be a time when our son might be able to understand, and forgive.

'Well?'

'I dunno,' he sighed, rubbing his eyes wearily. 'Ordinary . . .'

I probed as much out of him as I could. Her hair was brown, possibly fair. Her build was on the heavy side. She worked for the Health Department. She was wearing a coat, probably navy blue. He couldn't remember if she wore glasses. They hadn't really looked at each other across the courtroom. She seemed sad, but offered no apology.

I needed more, much more. The shape of her nose, the placement of moles, her smell . . . I wanted to devour every detail about her.

'How old is she?'

'Mid thirties, maybe.'

'Is she going to jail?'

Gazing over my left shoulder, he shook his head slowly.

'They must be prosecuting her for *something*. A fine, at least?'

A fly performed a lazy figure eight above his head.

'They can't.' His voice was calm and kind, as if he was speaking to a lunatic. 'It was an accident.'

What did he mean *accident*?

'There was no way she could've seen him running out from behind the bus. It wasn't her fault. She didn't do anything wrong.'

My brain spun to a halt. He might as well have been saying the sky was green. If Sam's death really had been an accident and the woman wasn't at fault, there was no one to blame. I had no right to hate her. I might even be expected to forgive her.

My heart was tight and hard. Forgiveness was for the gods.

Resuscitation

Cats are willing to take into account the fact that people are slow learners

The moment my old school friend Rosie heard we had a kitten there was no stopping her. I put her off the first time she phoned. That was like a bowl of sardines to a starving stray. A couple of days after the inquest she broke through the invisible barricades around our house. Notorious for her ebullience and lack of tact, Rosie wasn't everyone's favourite person. Steve suddenly remembered an important appointment he had in town.

'Poor itty bitty baby Cleo,' she crooned, examining Cleo through giant red spectacles. 'Fancy having to come and live wid a whole lot of humans who aren't cat people.'

'I didn't say we're not cat people, Rosie.'

'So you can honestly say you *are* a cat person?' she asked, peering at me over her crimson horizons.

'Yes. Maybe . . . I'm not sure.'

'Then you're definitely *not* a cat person,' she said. 'You'd know if you were. It's like being a Christian or a Muslim. You just *know* when you are one.'

Rosie didn't have a Church of England background like mine, where you could mumble the Lord's Prayer, sing 'There

79

Is a Green Hill Far Away' and slurp tepid tea while avoiding conversation with the vicar before going home free from any sense of allegiance.

Rosie was a cat lover extraordinaire. She'd adopted six strays she'd named Scruffy, Ruffy, Beethoven, Sibelius, Madonna and Doris, though it was impossible to guess which one belonged to its name. Adopted wasn't exactly the right word. More accurately, Rosie had invited a sextet of four-legged thugs to invade and decimate her property. Ungrateful to the core, the fur balls shredded her curtains and splintered her furniture while sprinkling her house with the unmistakable stench of ammonia. When they weren't indulging in gang warfare and raiding rubbish tins they were murdering local wildlife. Whenever humans dared venture through Rosie's gate, six sinister shapes skulked under her bed. None of which, she said, stopped them having *fabulous personalities* and being *unbelievably cute* and *adorable*.

There was nothing Rosie didn't know about cats. Her radar was bound to suss out a member of the kittyhood that had been condemned to life with us on the zigzag.

'She's not exactly the *prettiest* kitten, is she?' Rosie continued. 'I've seen more fur on a golf ball. She looks like she's been in prison camp. And those eyes. They're so . . . bulgy.'

'Nobody's perfect,' I said, riding an unexpected surge of loyalty. 'She's a work in progress.'

'Hmmm,' said Rosie doubtfully. 'Part Abyssinian, eh? Famed for their love of water and high places.' Rosie used every opportunity to show off her knowledge. 'Even taking into account that she's related to the short-haired Asian cats that are lightly built and therefore able to tolerate warm climates more easily than their more sturdy European cousins, she's pretty skinny. What are you feeding her?'

'Cat food,' I sighed.

'Yes, but what *sort* of cat food?'

'I don't know. Stuff from the pet shop.'

'Vitamin supplements?' she asked in courtroom tones.

'Of course,' I lied, changing the subject. 'Do you want to see her play sock-er?'

I held a sock above Cleo's nose. Cleo pretended she'd never seen such a thing before.

Rosie shook her head. 'Cats don't play fetch,' she said. Her ginger curls tumbled forwards as she reached into her red handbag. I felt a tinge of remorse. Even though she could be irritating, she deserved a thousand brownie points for turning up. So many of our friends had found excuses to withdraw.

Rosie hadn't changed her manner since Sam's death. Her behaviour was mercifully dictatorial and cheerful as ever. What's more, she wasn't speaking to me in that hushed, now familiar, tone that implied the house had some kind of curse over it.

'You'll need these,' she said, thrusting a pair of dog-eared books at me. *Kittens and How to Raise Them*, and *Your Cat and Its Health*. 'Oh, and I thought this might be helpful.'

Bossy, crazy, sweet Rosie. For all her quirks and her conviction I had Cleo's worst interests at heart, her deep-down goodness was undeniable. Why else would she present me with *On Death and Dying* by Elisabeth Kübler-Ross offhandedly along with the kitten books?

I knew about the five states of grief Kübler-Ross put together to help people deal with grief. There was a lot I recognised.

1. Denial. Definitely during those initial shocking moments after the phone call at Jessie's house. A big chunk of me continued to be in denial. On street corners and in shopping malls, I still saw Sam running and laughing. They were all blond-haired impostors. Something in the dungeon of my subconscious clung to the ambulance man's words that Sam would have been a 'vegetable' if he'd survived. Several nights a week I dreamt everyone had decided to hide from me the fact that Sam was still alive. Suddenly aware of their lies, I'd sprint through a

labyrinth of hospital corridors to find him attached to machines in a darkened room. He'd then turn his head and fix me with those blue eyes, just as he had when he was born. I'd wake up, heart thumping, pillow saturated.

2. Anger. It would've been helpful if, after a few weeks of Denial, I'd faded recognisably into Anger. Every cell in my body raged at pigeons scattered like pieces of torn paper in the sky, women driving Ford Escorts, in fact, women drivers in general, and Sam's school friends who had the effrontery to still be living. If only I could be assured the Anger stage would pass. Trouble was I was angry *and* in denial all at once. And yes, there had been a few pathetic . . .

3. Bargaining sessions. Sometimes, in the bathroom or behind the steering wheel, I conducted one-sided negotiations with God asking Him (or, if Rosie was to be believed, Her) to please wind the clock back, so the events of 21 January would unfold five seconds earlier, so the car rolled down the hill before Sam's foot touched the kerb, the pigeon was delivered safely to the vet and we all sat down around the kitchen table for Steve's lemon meringue pie. What was a little time shuffling for someone (or something) as omnipotent as the Great Creator? In return I'd do anything He (or She) required, including join a nunnery, take up women's rugby and pretend to enjoy sleeping in tents. All of which would save me from . . .

4. Depression. The wardrobe of sorrow houses many outfits. For casual daywear there's plain old self-pity, which sufferers sometimes flippantly refer to as depression. Postnatal depression is slightly dressier. For full-blown formal occasions (complete with attendant psychiatrists and pills) there's clinical depression, suicidal sadness and, ultimately, insanity.

My uncles returning scrambled as eggs from World War I were said to be depressed, possibly crazy. One of them was incarcerated in a mental home. A maiden aunt didn't speak for years after my grandparents insisted she put an end to her affair with the local postmistress. With the compassion and understanding typical of rural 1930s New Zealand, the wider family called her Creeping Jesus. As far as I could understand, my aunt and uncles had logical reasons to be depressed.

Even though all these variations of sorrow are shoved into the same closet, they seem to have as much in common as flax skirts and Dior gowns.

The word depression wasn't big enough to describe the ocean of melancholy I'd slipped into. There was no shoreline. The sea had no floor. Some days I fought to stay afloat. On others I was suspended lifeless, like a broken willow branch, drifting in its infinity. For Kübler-Ross to label this mere 'depression' and a 'stage' was outrageous folly. And then, to imply there would be a final stage of—

5. Acceptance. No way was I *ever* going to say it's okay for a beautiful nine-year-old boy to die. Kübler-Ross missed a few other stages while she was at it, including guilt, self-hatred, hysteria, loss of hope, paranoia, unacceptable confessions in public, a powerful urge to open the car door and hurl oneself onto the motorway.

I thanked Rosie for the books and flicked through *Your Cat and Its Health*.

'You will read it properly, won't you?' she said.

'Look Rosie, we mightn't meet your standards, but we'll do our best. We're not going to kill her, at least I hope not . . .'

'Never mind, baby Cleo,' Rosie said, putting on that silly voice again and burying the kitten between the steamed puddings of her breasts. 'Itty bitty kitty can come and live with Auntie Rosie any time.'

Cleo writhed between Rosie's sweltering mounds. Then, in a split second that seemed to be happening in slow motion, she flattened her ears, rolled back her lips, hissed and swiped a fully armoured claw at Rosie's face.

'Ohmyyyygoooodddd!' wailed Rosie.

'I'm so sorry!' I said, dabbing the blood on her cheek with a paper tissue that had been doubling as a table napkin. 'I'm sure she didn't mean . . .'

Clutching the tissue to her cheek, Rosie glared down at her assailant.

'This kitten . . . *your* kitten . . . has fleas!' declared Rosie, rearranging her spectacles.

'Really?' I said, scratching an ankle. Steve and Rob had complained of being 'itchy' over the past few days. I'd dismissed their complaints as neuroticism. It now dawned on me I was itchy too. An archipelago of miniature volcanoes encircled both ankles and stretched up my legs.

'Yes, look,' she said, parting the sparse forest of Cleo's underbelly. 'Dozens, possibly even hundreds . . .'

The sight resembled one of those shots taken by helicopter over Manhattan. Oblivious to us staring down at them, an entire city of fleas bustled through avenues of Cleo's hair. So engrossed were they in their flea workday, so confident that whatever they were doing was the most important job on earth right now, not one paused to glance up at a pair of horrified human giants.

'That's a serious infestation,' said Rosie, a tinge of awe verging on admiration in her voice.

'How do we get rid of them? Do I get some powder from the pet shop?'

'Too late for that,' pronounced Rosie. 'What this kitten needs is a *bath*.'

When I pointed out cats have a natural loathing of water, and that immersing a kitten would surely be close to animal cruelty, she shrugged. 'Well if you don't want to take responsibility for your kitten's health . . .'

Rosie had me cornered. If I didn't obey her she'd report me to some kind of committee of animal protection feminists.

They'd plant burning crosses on our front lawn and glue posters around the neighbourhood.

'But we don't have a kitten bath,' I said, almost certain I'd never seen such a household item, not even in a pet shop. 'Or kitten shampoo.'

'The bathroom vanity will do,' she said. 'And mild human shampoo is fine. Now, find me a handtowel, please.'

The closest thing we had to a handtowel was a faded blue rag that had enjoyed a previous life as a beach towel until the boys and Rata tore it apart during a tug of war. With the efficiency of an Egyptian embalmer wrapping up a cat mummy, Rosie wound the cloth around Cleo's shoulders. With her legs (and claws) tucked against her body, Cleo was defenceless. Her startled, furry face emerged from one end of the towel. The other end was wedged deep in the folds of Rosie's T-shirt. I desperately wanted to rescue Cleo. But, immune from any more scratch attacks, Rosie had taken control.

She instructed me to fill the basin with warm water, then tested the temperature with her free elbow. When the depth and temperature were ideal, Rosie swiftly unwound the cloth and passed Cleo to me.

'I thought *you* were going to do this?' I said, wrestling with legs and tail, which were moving in opposite directions simultaneously.

'You're the mother,' Rosie replied, taking a step back towards the safely of the towel rail.

Our kitten relaxed in my arms. I took it as a huge compliment. Staring down from her dry vantage point, Cleo was fascinated by the water, and expectantly watched it glistening in the basin, as if it might house a school of goldfish. I unwound too. Maybe Cleo had inherited the famous Abyssinian love of water and was going to enjoy her bath.

Inhaling deeply, I lowered her into the water. Swift handling combined with respect for feline pride would be required. Cleo seemed to understand the procedure. She kept still as a statuette while I massaged baby shampoo into her coat. The kitten was soon wreathed in a cloak of bubbles.

I was proud of her nestled in the basin. Fortunately, Cleo couldn't see what a bath was doing for her looks. With her fur slicked down and whiskers pasted against her cheeks, she could've been mistaken for a rat. Nevertheless, Rosie had to be impressed with Cleo's understanding of hygiene requirements.

'Good girl,' I crooned.

'See? Nothing to it,' Rosie said. 'Every cat needs a bath now and then.'

Cleo suddenly let out a primeval yowl. It was a shocking noise that penetrated my maternal genes as instantly and powerfully as the cry of a child lost in a supermarket. Cleo's little head drooped sideways and, to my profound horror, she went limp as a dishcloth in my hands.

'Get her out! *Get her out!*' Rosie bellowed.

'I *am* getting her out!' I bellowed back. As I lifted the little creature from the water, her head and legs swung lifelessly. 'Oh . . . !'

What was Rob going to say? His heart had already been shattered. He wouldn't be able to take another blow. I'd already proved myself a failure as mother. No way should I have been given command of something as small and helpless as a kitten. I was barely capable of putting my clothes on.

Snatching the towel from Rosie, I engulfed the lifeless form.

'Oh Cleo, I'm so sorry!' I cried, rubbing her with the towel and hurrying her through to the living room. I flicked the gas heater on, held Cleo as close as possible to the flames, and massaged her frantically.

'You were right, Rosie. I'm hopeless with cats. This is terrible!'

Rosie towered over us disapprovingly. 'The water was too cold,' she said.

'Why didn't you *say* something?'

'I thought it would probably be all right. Or it could've been the wrong shampoo . . .'

The tiny body lay lifeless in my hands.

'I've killed her, Rosie!' I sobbed. 'She's the only thing that cheered things up around here. Now I've drowned her! I know you don't think I'm a cat person, but I was starting to love this kitten.'

So this was going to be my life from now on. Everything I touched was destined to shrivel up and drop dead in my hands. For the sake of the world I'd have to climb a mountain at the bottom of the South Island, crawl into a cave and wait for things to end.

Then, to my astonishment, the rag on my lap emitted a single, demure sneeze. A shudder of life rippled through her body. She raised her head, climbed unsteadily onto her paws and shook herself indignantly, showering me with water.

'Oh, Cleo! You're back! I can't believe it!' She hardly needed the additional rinse of my happy tears.

The kitten fixed me with eyes the size of satellite dishes and bestowed a lick on my finger, as if she'd woken from a pleasant dream and was wondering what was for breakfast. Jubilant with relief, I rubbed her precious fur until it was nearly dry. Not since the boys were born had I felt so ecstatic to see a creature alive and functioning.

'Listen, she's purring!' I said to Rosie. 'Do you think she forgives me?'

Rosie didn't look convinced. 'Just as well she has nine lives,' she said. 'One down, eight to go. That poor kitten's going to need every one of them in this house.'

After Rosie left, I kissed Cleo, thanked her for coming back to life, and held her close to my chest to keep her warm.

From that moment on, Cleo and I had an understanding. Baths, as far as she was concerned, were strictly for the birds.

Cleo was turning out to be quite a teacher. Like all good educationalists, she adopted her techniques according to the abilities of her students. Her near-drowning experience demonstrated I wasn't doomed to destroy everything in my path, after all. For the first time in my life I'd actually revived a living creature. And Cleo was giving me a second chance.

Compassion

*Even though the cat is a solitary creature, it is capable of acts of
great kindness*

'Sure you're going to be okay?' I asked, clicking Rob's school
lunch box shut. His sandwiches were made of wholemeal
bread, the healthiest available on supermarket shelves. Rob
would've preferred white fluffy bread, naturally, but I was
determined he'd sprout to a vigorous adulthood. If he couldn't
learn to love broccoli and bean sprouts I was going to stuff
them into him, anyway. No more bad things were allowed to
happen to this boy.

The school had been understanding about us keeping
Rob home for an extra couple of weeks. It was his second
year of school, so he knew most of the kids in his year group.
Nevertheless, his first day back without Sam loomed over us.
Since Rob's education began, Sam had been woven into the
fabric of every day. In playground warfare, the extrovert older
brother provided a protective shield for the younger, quieter
one. Nobody would pick a fight with Rob when they knew
they'd also have to confront Sam (famed for his Superman
kicks). Older and younger brother were Starsky and Hutch,
Batman and Robin, each incomplete without the other.

'Will you drive me?'

'Of course,' I said, fastening the buttons of his new shirt. Western style, it featured winged golden horses flying against a white background. Wings and feathers seemed to haunt every aspect of our lives. The shirt was on the lurid side, but Rob loved it and I was encouraging him to express his individuality.

There were no arguments with Steve about the cost of children's clothes anymore. With Rob's help I'd managed to venture into an impressive range of shops over the past couple of weeks. Like most New Zealand primary schools, Rob's had a no-uniform policy. The intention was to create a laid-back atmosphere. The reality was, children's fashion trends absorbed more time and money than most parents would've liked.

On his first day back, everything about Rob was fresh from the packet, including the shoes with marshmallow-soft soles. ('They squeak,' he said, as we wrangled with the spaghetti of his shoelaces. 'People will laugh at me.' 'They're just jealous,' I assured him.) His clothes and professionally trimmed hair presented a mother's challenge to the world: this boy is precious; damage him at your peril. The only item on him that wasn't new was the Superman watch on his wrist.

'What if bullies get me?' he asked, clutching the stainless steel band of his watch.

My insides melted. If only I could shadow his every step through the day ahead, monitor each breath that filled his six-year-old lungs, and roar at his adversaries.

'They won't,' I said, fiercely hoping I was right. But what if I wasn't? His status as grieving brother had the potential to single him out for special attention from emotionally disturbed retards. 'Tell the teacher to call me if you want to come home any time.'

'Look after Cleo for me,' he said, opening the fridge door and removing a jug of milk, too full for his child's grip. The jug wobbled as he poured the milk into a saucer, slopping a pond on the floor. Cleo arched with delight as the delicious liquid flowed. Her tail uncoiled and her tongue set about its work with crisp strokes.

Rob was sleeping more soundly since he'd moved back to his old room. His nightmares and dreams were less disturbing. No doubt the comfort of a centrally heated kitten had something to do with that.

A sharp tapping on the window jangled my nerves. The unmistakable cheekbones of Ginny Desilva, the most glamorous woman on the zigzag, pressed against the glass. Her perfectly shaped lips were arranged in a magazine smile. She raised three moisturised fingers, waved her glistening talons at us and called, 'Hallooooo!'

Ginny was wearing a gold vinyl jacket, false eyelashes, earrings the size of chandeliers and a ponytail that was perched high on one side of her head. My regulation trackpants and stained T-shirt didn't stand a chance.

A boy about Rob's size was holding Ginny's hand. He had spiky hair and a pixie face.

'That's Jason!' said Rob in awe.

'What's he like?' I hissed through my teeth, while nodding and smiling at Ginny.

'He's one of the Cool Gang.'

Ah yes. The legendary Cool Gang. I'd heard Rob and Sam talk as if they'd rather paint their willies blue than join the Cool Gang. That was only because the Cool Gang hadn't asked for their membership.

The only thing cooler than the Cool Gang was the Cool Gang's parents. They were doctors, lawyers and architects who arranged tennis matches on a rotation basis so they all had a chance to show off the courts in their back gardens. Ginny and her husband, Rick, were Queen and King of the Cool Gang's parents because they transcended the run-of-the-mill professionals. Rick ran a record company. And Ginny, well, all she had to do was drape herself in fake fur and be Ginny.

Journalism had trained me to make snap judgements. Fashion model means way too beautiful *and* skinny plus shallow plus competitive about physical appearances and men plus dim-witted equals an excellent person for me to avoid. Ginny, in the single conversation I'd had with her when we'd bumped into each other on the zigzag, claimed to be a midwife, though this seemed too outlandish to be true. I'd assumed she was on something at the time.

'Hi,' I said, almost blinded by the sheen of her mahogany hair as I opened the back door.

'Wow! A kitten!' her son yelled before any of us had time to exchange formalities. Weaving around my trackpants, Jason burst into the kitchen.

'Rob, you didn't tell me you had a kitten!' said Jason. 'It's so cute! Can I hold it?'

'She's Cleo,' said Rob, proudly presenting his pet to Jason. 'Her dad's a tom cat. He was wild. We're pretty sure he was a panther.'

'Jason adores cats,' Ginny laughed, as we watched Jason burying the kitten in his neck. I was waiting for her eyes to settle critically on my trackpants and the lake of milk on the floor (which Rata was obligingly slurping), but she seemed oblivious to our chaos.

'I heard Rob's going to be in Jason's class this year,' she said. 'Jason was wondering if Rob would like to walk to school with him today, weren't you, darling?'

Jason nodded, though somewhat dutifully. Rob walk to school *with Jason*? But the morning was all planned. I'd played it over in my head so many times—mother and son make tragic appearance at school gates. Mother gives son invisible injection of power and protection before son steps boldly into new school life.

'Thanks but we're driving,' I said, immediately aware how clipped and ungrateful I sounded. What was *wrong* with me?

Not so long ago I'd been considered a warm, friendly person. When I was at primary school the other kids gave me the nickname 'Happy'. There was no danger of a name like that anymore. 'Would Jason like us to give him a lift?'

Of course she was going to say no. She'd do it on the grounds of politeness and respect for the hermit shell of misery I'd retreated into. I'd escape with the appearance of having made the offer. She'd decline, and we'd get on with our appropriately separate lives.

'That would be lovely,' Ginny replied, fixing me with brown eyes conveying unexpected warmth and something else. What was it—a fleeting spark of wisdom? 'Byeeee!'

Byeee? Must be retired fashion model speak. Watching Ginny sauntering away like an apparition from a punk rock magazine, I felt ambushed. With a tap of her fingernails on our kitchen window she'd gazumped our ceremonial drive to school.

Not only that, she and Jason had blustered into our kitchen as if it was the most natural thing to do. Her audacious swoop of neighbourly intimacy was unnerving. She was crazy, obviously. Either that or unbelievably compassionate, with greater depths than I'd assumed she was capable of. Yes, Ginny had to be insane. Or incredibly wonderful. How else would she know that the best way to treat traumatised people is to behave normally (give or take a byee or two)? I hadn't been prepared for a guerilla attack of kindness, not so soon after breakfast.

I couldn't help admiring the woman. A gold vinyl jacket *and* leopard skin tights? What was that perfume trailing behind her—tiger musk? And how come those chandeliers didn't pull her ears apart? I was too thick-headed to realise I'd just made a friend for life.

With his punk hairdo and purple schoolbag covered with rock band stickers, Jason was the personification of

Cool. Yet he was besotted with Cleo in an unselfconsciously
boyish way.

'This is the cutest kitten!' Jason said, rocking the black
bundle in his arms. 'You're so lucky!'

It was the first time in ages that anyone had put the words
luck and our family in the same sentence.

'She likes friends,' Rob replied.

A tingle fizzed down my spine. Rob was remembering
Cleo's so-called promise to help him find new friends in the
talking cat dream.

'Can I come over here and play with her after school?'
Jason asked.

'Course you can!' we answered in unison.

Cleo settled herself in a pool of sunlight on Rob's bed and
we headed out the door. Rata paddled behind us like a steam-
boat. Halfway up the zigzag, the old dog seemed to run out of
puff and plonked herself down. I waited with her a moment.
Even though she was panting, she slapped her tail reassuringly
on the path as if to say, 'Nothing to worry about.'

Once Rata had recovered her breath we climbed the rest
of the hill. The boys watched anxiously as she straggled to
the car. Suddenly aware she was being observed, the dog
rallied, lifted her tail and leapt youthfully into the back of the
stationwagon.

The school gates hadn't changed, which seemed strange
considering so much else had. Those gates were at least seventy
years old. The first children who ran through them were old
men and women now. Their bodies were disintegrating around
them in retirement homes, while the gates had merely gathered
a layer of rust. The deal hardly seemed fair. Yet, given the choice,
I'd still rather come back as human, with a limited quota of
laughter and pain, than gates that lasted one hundred and fifty
unfeeling years.

Kids were pouring through them, still buzzing with stories from the summer holidays. No doubt Sam's demise had been a hot topic around every kitchen table. Were they going to smother Rob with too much attention or, not knowing what to say, simply ignore him? I fought the urge to scramble out from behind the steering wheel and escort him through every nanosecond of the day.

Rob and Jason climbed out of the car.

'I'll pick you up here at three-thirty,' I said.

'S'okay,' Jason said. 'We'll walk home together, won't we, Rob?'

Rob squinted through the sunlight at Jason and smiled. 'Yeah, we'll walk.'

Walk? Meaning *cross roads?* My insides swirled at the thought of Rob's feet going anywhere near roadside tarmac without my protective shadow. But Jason and Ginny were right. The sooner Rob adjusted to a new routine, maybe even created new friendships, the easier his life would become. Their advice had arrived in the most powerful package—generosity wrapped in action, not words.

At the risk of Jason thinking I was deranged, I took an old shopping list from my handbag and scribbled on the back the exact route they needed to take walking home. The pedestrian crossing outside the school was monitored by senior students who presumably had some respect for traffic. Following the footpath along the bend of the gulley, they'd have to cross one quiet street before reaching the busy road Sam had died on. They'd cross not at the bus stop further down the hill but at the zebra crossing several hundred metres higher up, near Dennis's grocery store and the new deli. Pressing the shopping list into Rob's hand I made him promise not to cross until he was certain every car was safely distant. 'And remember to ask the teacher to call me if you want to come home early,' I called, the unmistakable whine of smother love in my voice.

But Rob was already halfway through the school gates, laughing at something Jason had said. Jason strolled alongside him, turned, waved at me and flung an arm across Rob's shoulder.

Huntress

Unlike most humans, a cat embraces the Wild Side

Waiting on the zigzag that afternoon with Cleo in my arms, I listened for children's voices. Rob and Jason should have taken about twenty minutes to walk home if they'd followed my map. They were now seven minutes late.

My head filled with what-ifs. If Jason had persuaded Rob to take a longer, more dangerous route, if he'd forgotten Rob was going to walk home with him and gone off with a bunch of cool boys . . . A river rock sat in my chest. Then boyish laughter echoed up the valley. Some of those whoops, the like of which I'd never imagined hearing again, were unmistakably from our son. His first day back at school must have been more successful than I'd dared hope.

I watched as two heads rounded the corner of the leafy path—not two blonds but one fair-headed, one dark.

'How was it?' I called to Rob.

'Fine,' he said. The sincerity in his voice sounded genuine.

Jason's face lit up when he saw Cleo.

'Let's teach her to hunt!' he said, sliding his schoolbag off his back.

'Isn't she a bit young?' I asked, nursing the black bundle I'd become so protective of since bringing her back to life. 'She's hardly left her mother.'

'No way!' said Jason, dumping his bag in our hallway as if it was already his second home. 'Have you got a piece of old paper and some wool?'

Why hadn't I thought of it before? We'd been so engrossed in our misery I'd forgotten an essential piece of kitten development. Rob, Cleo and I watched as Jason scrunched a rectangle of newsprint and with a string of red wool tied it into a bow.

'Here girl,' Jason whispered, laying the newsprint bow like bait on the floor and twitching his end of the wool. 'It's a mouse! *Catch it!*'

Cleo looked puzzled. Maybe she really was an Egyptian princess trapped in a feline body, and unable to lower herself to playing with scraps of paper.

'C'mon!' he said, trailing the lure across the floor towards the rubber plant. 'It's running away!'

Cleo's ears flicked forwards as she watched the thing skip across the carpet. A paw shot out, almost involuntary in its speed. Paw and paper collided briefly. Jason pulled the string. The kitten tuned into some ancient programming. Crouching on her hind legs, she shimmied her nether regions and tried to hypnotise her target.

Why cats sway like that before they pounce is a mystery. The closest to the cat shimmy I've seen in humans is when professional tennis players propel themselves from side to side as they wait to bash back a one-hundred-miles-per-hour serve. Maybe the shimmy, for cats and tennis players, is a subconscious way for them to prepare muscles on either side of the body for sudden action.

The boys laughed as Cleo pounced on the paper bow and juggled it between her front and back paws.

'Here, you try,' said Jason, handing the string to Rob. Generosity was second nature to that child. 'Hold it higher so she has to jump.'

Cleo hid behind the rubber plant and waited like an assassin.

When the paper bow flew past above her head she grabbed it in midair, between her teeth and front paws. Sailing towards the carpet with her prey locked in a death grip, she looked up at us for the admiration she deserved before crashing in a bundle of legs, fur and paper.

The hapless bow was shredded in minutes.

Jason was even more impressed when Cleo demonstrated her prowess at sock-er. He became a daily visitor to our house after that, while I was gradually introduced to the glittering world of Ginny Desilva. The first time I ventured through the leafy shield up the white gravel path to her place, I felt like a naughty girl escaping from a correctional institution. A hedge of gardenias emitted sensual perfume. A fountain trickled and splashed. With every step I could sense Steve's disapproval. The racy Desilvas weren't our kind of people.

'Come in, darling!' cried Ginny, flinging her front door open. 'You're just in time for bubbles.'

Nobody on our side of the zigzag called anyone darling. Certainly not people they hardly knew. Ginny, with her false eyelashes and cheekbones to die for, was the first person I'd ever met who could make drinking champagne at four in the afternoon seem the most natural thing in the world. I was amazed at her capacity to never wear the same outfit twice. I was in awe of her white leather sofa and the stainless steel sculpture that towered like an electric pylon over a corner of her living room. She couldn't remember the name of the artist, or at least she said she couldn't. With Ginny, it was hard to know if she was genuinely vague or just pretending to be in order to put you at ease.

After an hour or two at Ginny's, the world seemed a softer place. When streetlights sparked to life and windows of the office blocks glowed yellow in the city below, I knew it was time to leave. The gravel path undulated under my feet as I wandered home to cook dinner and deal with a hungry cat.

✦

Like everyone else in our family Cleo had a highly developed interest in food. Being half-aristocrat, she made it clear she considered herself a cut above pet shop rubbish.

Once she'd figured out the fridge was the source of high-class menu items, such as salmon, she spent many hours worshipping its great white door. Occasionally she'd run an exploratory front paw along the plastic seal, but her attempts were fruitless.

When I opened the fridge door one morning, she accelerated like a furry cannon ball across the kitchen floor and jumped right inside the vegetable chiller. When I yelled at her to come out she burrowed further into the carrots. No way was she relinquishing the right to live inside her own five-star restaurant. When I tried to prise her out she batted me with a claw.

I closed the fridge the door to a crack and peeked inside. Eyeing off the ice cliff of the door, with its built-in cartons of milk and juice, Cleo didn't look so confident. When I flung the door open again she pounced from her nest of carrots and shook herself on the kitchen floor, as if to say, 'I was only doing it to keep the vegetables happy.'

Abandoning the idea of fridge habitation, Cleo worked on other ways of adding gourmet flair to her diet. Emptying her litter box one day I discovered two rubber bands and a length of cotton thread had worked their way through her digestive tract.

With newly discovered power in her back legs, she'd spring onto the kitchen bench for a gastronomic preview of whatever we were having for dinner. Chicken breast and fish were favourites, but she developed a taste for mincemeat, cake, raw eggs and, of course, butter.

If I didn't stow the butter safely away in the fridge, suspicious-looking tracks would appear on its surface. It's hard to know if Cleo really liked butter or just pretended to enjoy it to taunt Rata, who was trapped unwillingly down at ground level. Our omnivorous golden retriever was genuinely obsessed with processed animal fats. At Sam's fifth birthday party she had wolfed down an entire slab of butter that had been left inadvertently on the coffee table. We waited for her to turn green around the whiskers, and prepared for an ambulance run to the vet, but Rata remained cheerful as ever. The dog's Teflon-lined stomach could handle anything from shoelaces to picnic lunch leftovers, including (if available) the paper napkins.

As the days shortened Cleo discovered the sort of food she liked best. Thanks to Jason's hunting lessons, she tuned into her wild cat side and learned the thrill of self-service. Prowling through the flowerbeds like a black panther she explored the victim potential of everything that moved, including blades of grass. Even the daisies were in danger. A crack in the path near the front gate revealed an exciting potential prey: ants. Her head would dart from side to side as these corporate workers of the garden went about their business. Cleo would tease them with her paw, only to be disappointed. Instead of playing a game, the ants would simply keep marching ahead, oblivious to fun or danger.

Her first triumph was a praying mantis she discovered on the window ledge in Rob's bedroom. I've always had a soft spot for praying mantises. Their revolving eyes and articulated limbs make them look like visitors from outer space. Geeks of the insect world, they live quietly and are endearingly harmless (except to the occasional fly or grasshopper). Unlike other insects they have no interest in sucking blood, stinging or spreading fatal illness.

Which is why I was upset to find one in Cleo's clutches one sunny afternoon. She was teasing the poor thing, letting it imagine it had escaped and then pouncing on it again. My first instinct was to rescue the insect. But it had already lost a leg. There was no hope.

For the first time I was mildly repelled by our kitten. On the other hand, if I tried to stop her hunting and occasionally killing other creatures I'd be denying her essential catness. Somewhere in the back of my head I could hear Mum saying *You can't interfere with Nature.* Not that her pioneering upbringing mirrored the sentiment. Our ancestors had no qualms reducing huge tracts of land to ash.

Guilty with praying mantis betrayal, I backed out of Rob's room and closed the door. Ten minutes later, I discovered Cleo dozing in the sun on Rob's pillow. She opened a self-satisfied eye at me and closed it. The headless torso of the praying mantis lay on the floor under the window ledge.

Cleo swiftly graduated to mice and birds, much to my horror. Headless corpses were deposited on the front doormat like little gifts. Digging graves for them beside the forget-me-nots was a reminder life has always been a struggle for living creatures. Somewhere along the line, we humans got hung up about death. We invented expressions like 'passed away', and took pains to conceal the process of transforming a cow in a paddock into a hamburger. We hid away the sick, old and disabled, so that suffering was a mystery and death the ultimate abnormality.

People persuade themselves they deserve easy lives, that being human makes us somehow exempt from pain. The theory works fine until we face the inevitable challenges. Our conditioning of denial in no way equips us to deal with the difficult times that not one of us escapes.

Cleo's motto seemed to be: Life's tough and that's okay because life is also fantastic. Love it, live it—but don't be fooled into thinking it's not harsh sometimes. Those who've survived periods of bleakness are often better at savouring good times and wise enough to understand that good times are actually *great*.

I wondered if I'd ever feel strong enough to follow her example.

Letting Go

A touch of a paw can work better than aspirin

Autumn was upon us and the hills around the harbour were burnished gold with gorse flowers. The new season had crept in so gradually I'd hardly noticed the change as it was happening. One moment Cleo was making herself so hot sunbathing on the front path she had to retreat to the shadow of the house to cool off. Next she was jostling for prime position in front of the gas fire with the rest of us, and somehow always getting the best spot. Suddenly there was a bite in the wind and poplar trees were shimmering bronze. My powers of observation had been equally remiss with Cleo. I'd grown so accustomed to telling visitors we shared our house with a cat who looked like an alien I no longer regarded her through accurate lenses. I was taking it for granted that we lived with an ugly cat.

I was out in the garden raking leaves one morning when I noticed an extraordinary cat sitting on Mrs Sommerville's roof. Sleek and elegant, its beauty sucked the breath out of my lungs for a moment. It was an awe-inspiring sight. My semi rural background ensured I wasn't usually affected by animals like that. Mum had raised me to believe anything with four legs that wasn't a table was at best an economic unit, at worst a bloody nuisance. But this being was beyond in-built parental prejudice. Its profile was noble as any lion's. With its head tilted slightly to one side, and tail curved in mathematical perfection around its rump, it was a feline version of a top model posing for a Vanity Fair photo shoot. Except there was no self-consciousness in the cat's pose. It wasn't even interested in me. Ears forwards, nose slightly aloft, its attention was focussed on a potential meal in a nearby tree.

I felt a stab of envy for the human who belonged to such a beast. I could see him sitting smug by his log fire, one hand encircling a decent red wine, the other massaging the handsome cat's fur. Although black from tip to tail like Cleo, it was obviously a pedigree of impressive lineage. It probably had enough papers to set a house on fire. Going by the sheen on its coat, it dined on fresh sardines every night. Next to a cat like that, poor Cleo would resemble something that had just crawled out of the drains of Calcutta. Fortunately, Cleo was nowhere in sight. She was probably inside investigating the fruit bowl, which had recently proved an interesting source of insect life. I put my head down and continued raking. I have yet to discover the Zen approach to raking leaves. Autumn leaves are disobedient at the best of times. Trying to do anything with them on a windy day is physical and emotional torture. The moment I herded them into a satisfactory mound a playful breeze scattered them like kittens and shook another shoal down from the poplars. It was a frustrating job that would've been considerably more pleasant if Rata had been able to understand the intricacies of human plumbing services and why they'd been invented.

Muttering one of Sam's forbidden rude words, I scraped Rata's contribution to global soil fertility off the sole of my sneaker on a stone. The pleasures of autumn gardening, if there were any, were lost on me. I was about to give up and go inside in search of tea, when I heard a familiar meow.

'Cleo!' I called, checking her favourite sunbathing place in the weeds under what once had been a rose bed. The only evidence of her there was a flattened oval of long grass. Scanning the window ledge outside Rob's bedroom, I called again. The black cat on Mrs Somerville's roof stared down at me with steady curiosity.

'It's fine for you, you spoilt snooty thing!' I growled up at it. 'We can't all be best in show.'

The cat yawned and rose effortlessly to its feet. I watched it float along the roof guttering and sail into the branches of a tree. It then slid gracefully down the trunk and skipped toward me, meowing delightedly.

'Cleo?' I said bending to stroke the bridge of her back as she nudged her chin against my calf muscles. I lifted the manifestation of feline perfection into my arms and sank my nose into her fur to make sure it really was her. 'Goodness, when did you become so gorgeous?'

I'd been so absorbed by grief over the summer I hadn't noticed Cleo had undergone a makeover beyond extreme. Over just a few weeks our skinny runt with unnerving eyes and hardly any fur had evolved into a drop dead gorgeous cat. Her fur, jet black, grew thick and glossy in preparation for her first winter. She no longer looked like E.T.'s cousin. Her face had been sculpted into the aristocratic angles of her mother's.

It was time to make up for my shocking lack of observation, haul myself out of distraction and notice Cleo. The changes she had gone through while I wasn't looking were a reminder that life's relentless cycles were rolling on no matter what. Whether I was going to miss out on some magnificent episodes of change and rebirth was largely up to me.

Scooping her up, I carried her to the front porch and sat on the step with her on my knee. Cleo writhed ecstatically and rolled onto her back, her legs paddling the air. This un-catlike position was one of her favourites. She often fell asleep that way draped upside down across someone's knee in front of the television, her head drooping backwards so the underside of her neck and chin were exposed to whomever she was sitting on.

Stroking her was a tactile adventure, a journey of discovery through Cleo's landscape of fur. Her ears were cool and slick the way I'd imagined a seal's skin would be. Their design was vaguely aerodynamic, potentially giving her descendents the option of flight. The velour ridge of her nose was tipped with a patch of damp leather. On the slope descending between her ears and eyes, the fur was sparser, the closest thing Cleo had to a bald patch these days. But it was in no way unattractive. In fact it was intriguing and stylish in the way Yves St Laurent could make tartan a perfect match for polka dots. Taut skin around her eyes was helpful whenever I needed to roll specks of sleep from their corners, which was surprisingly often. Strange there were no eyelashes in this plethora of fur. Two pairs of antennae, a memory of eyebrows, sprouted from her forehead. No doubt they had some stealthy purpose such as measuring rat holes. Her whiskers were like dried grass, her chin a fuzzy beard.

The fur on her torso was fluffy, softer than a rabbit's. Her 'under arms' sprouted longer fringes that seemed vaguely out of place, like human underarm hair, filing cabinets for ancestral memory. A raised ridge of fur ran like a mini mohawk down the centre of her chest. The growth on her lower abodomen was coarser and longer, but still soft. On the inner sides of her legs the fur was silky, the outer thighs slippery and smooth.

Her purr intensified as I rubbed her long back legs with their elongated kangaroo feet. The pads, smoother than vinyl, gleamed purple black in the sun. They were lined with closely cropped hair concealing the sheathed scimitars of her claws.

No decent petting was complete without attention to Cleo's pride and joy, her tail. Smooth and oily, it had sprouted into an elegant accessory. Serpent-like in appearance and flexibility, it had almost as much personality as Cleo herself. It lay in wait beside her when she woke in the mornings, and coiled stealthily around her last thing at night. Every time she looked over her shoulder there it was again, the stalker snake, shadowing her every move.

Most of the time, Cleo regarded her tail as a playmate. They could spend the best part of an afternoon chasing each other in circles around the floor until they collapsed from dizziness. On other occasions, the tail took on a more malevolent mood. When Cleo was dozing on the window ledge the tail would sometimes twitch, disturbing her sleep. She would open one eye to examine the mischievous appendage. Rippling under her gaze, that tail was asking to be taught a lesson. Cleo would attack, tumbling off the window ledge so she could grab the creature with all four sets of claws and sink her teeth into it. Twitching and writhing between her jaws, the snake put up a noble fight, inflicting mysteriously brutal pain on its attacker. Cleo and her tail were like a warring married couple, glued together for reasons they'd long forgotten and fighting several times a day over imagined insults. It took a long time for them to settle their differences and cohabit in peace.

I resisted the temptation to call Rosie and boast how our 'ugly' kitten was transforming into a beauty. Cleo's newfound elegance aroused two hopes in me. One, that she wouldn't realise how gorgeous she was and become vain (few weaknesses are more tiresome to live with than vanity, especially in someone who has suffered the indignity of plain looks in their past). Two, that the theory about dog owners developing a physical likeness to their pets might also apply to cat owners. Neither of these aspirations seemed likely to happen. Cleo was too playful and fascinated with life to start behaving like a movie star. And I continued to resemble a food-addicted golden retriever.

Cleo awakened a depth of tenderness in Rob I hadn't seen before. He'd always been the baby of the household, the one everybody else looked out for. Now, for the first time, he was responsible for something smaller than himself, and a gentle, caring side of him began to emerge. Feeding, combing, cuddling his lovable kitten (often with enthusiastic advice from Jason) was helping him grow stronger and more self-assured. I watched in awe as he carved a fresh identity for himself at school, and a trickle of new friends made their way down the zigzag to our place.

Our affection for Cleo was fiercely returned. As her adopted slaves, we were duty-bound to include her in everything. If she heard a conversation going on in another room she scratched and called at the door until she was part of it. Occasionally she was content to witness goings-on from a vantage point in the sun on the back of the sofa. Mostly, though, she preferred to be wedged into a warm lap, her paws tucked neatly under her body, purring approval.

If someone was reading a book, particularly if the reader was lying comfortably on his back, Cleo knew she was being invited to position herself between him and the pages. Supremely confident that a cat was far more fascinating than any printed word, she'd be astonished when the reader lifted her, evicting her gently to the other side of the book. How could an inferior human be so rude? Once she'd regained her composure, she would examine the outside cover. She could only presume it had been placed there for grooming purposes. Cleo discovered cats don't need toothbrushes when they can run their teeth along the cardboard edge of a paperback cover.

She waited on Rob's window ledge with more than a hint of accusation in her eye whenever we went out. Was time going to limp by while we were away? As if. The moment she'd seen the back of the last raincoat disappear up the zigzag she'd get up to secret cat's business. A pot plant would tumble mysteriously on its side. Telltale paw prints appeared on the kitchen bench. Half-eaten blowflies sprinkled themselves over the carpet. The joint certainly jumped while we were out. When we arrived home Cleo would be waiting in the window again. She seemed to have an inbuilt radar that told her exactly when we'd be back. She would dance down the hall to greet us, her tail raised in an elegant curve of greeting. Anyone who picked her up in their arms would be rewarded with a kiss from her damp, liquorice nose.

If dogs could talk, Rata would have been a reliable inform-ant. Gazing mournfully at a tangle of pulled threads on the sofa she'd sigh as if to say, 'What can you expect from a cat?' But when Cleo snuggled into the dog's belly to be slobbered with giant retriever kisses, all was forgiven. For all her uppity, occasionally murderous, habits, we adored her.

The more we let ourselves love our young cat, the more readily we seemed able to open our hearts and forgive the unfamiliar people we'd become since the loss of Sam. As we turned towards each other and started to rebuild a sense of family, a hopeful warmth resurfaced in our marriage. Steve dismantled the barricade of his newspaper one night, looked me straight in the eye and said: 'You look so terribly sad and beautiful.' His words stretched across the icy distance and enveloped us.

I'd forgotten how amusing his quirky sense of humour could be. That's what had drawn us together in the first place. Both outsiders, we'd been hopelessly uncoordinated at school sports and shared a talent for feeling awkward in groups. Together we'd created a separate universe and tried to persuade ourselves that life as a pair of misfits on the edge of the mainstream was a comfortable place to be.

Vulnerable as a pair of oysters without their shells, we put on our winter coats and went on our first movie 'date' since our lives had changed so drastically. A divinely youthful and sexy Richard Gere in *An Officer and a Gentleman* diverted my attention long enough for me to feel surprised, then guilty, I'd gone for a few minutes not thinking about Sam. When the credits rolled, the lights went up and Joe Cocker launched into the theme song 'Up Where We Belong', reality crashed in again.

Soon after, Steve visited a specialist to investigate the prospect of a vasectomy reversal. Complicated micro-surgery would be involved, and he was warned the chances of success were minimal, as low as ten per cent. Nevertheless, taking our circumstances into account, the surgeon was willing to give it his best shot. Even though we knew our marriage was on a fault line and on the verge of crumbling, we both desperately wanted another child. A date for the surgery was set.

We weren't looking for a replacement for Sam. We both knew that would be impossible. But our house and hearts felt empty. I still set the table for four every night, until a cold gong in my heart reminded me I was living in the past. One set of knives and forks had to be put back in the drawer.

I longed for sorrow to shrivel and sail effortlessly into oblivion. If an autumn leaf could release the memory of summer and float into nothingness, fearless and with such grace, why was it impossible for me?

An inner lioness of motherhood refused to relinquish anything connected to Sam. Alone in the house, I'd carry his blue Boy Scouts jumper around with me like a comfort rug, over my shoulder. His name tag had been hand-sewn clumsily inside the collar. After he'd earned the red patches for Reading, Art, Chess and (laughably) Housework, I'd shared his pride by sewing them on the sleeves with small careful stitches. The garment had shrunk to the shape of his torso. It was redolent of him and now also of my tears.

Mothers are the ultimate power junkies. When we lift a newborn human from our bodies we experience an adrenaline high far headier than anything Bill Gates or Pablo Picasso knows about. Multi-zillion-dollar businesses and the world's greatest art fade to trinkets alongside the miraculous creation of a human being. The reason so few women become great concert masters, politicians and inventors isn't so much because of prejudice (not that there's a shortage) or lack of opportunity (hardly a drought of that, either). Why would anyone bother writing a symphony when she can create a collection of cells that will one day ask to borrow her car?

Our passion for our children springs straight from the jungle. Would Bill Gates lay down his life for Microsoft? Picasso commit murder for one of his paintings?

Mothers have power beyond politics, art and money. We're the people who give life, nurture babies and make them grow. Without us humanity would wither like seaweed on a rock. Knowledge of our power is so deep we don't talk about it often, but we use it all the time.

Ancient mother's power is employed to make our kids eat green vegetables, aim straight at the toilet bowl and grow a few centimetres every year. When we yell *Come back here!* across a supermarket or a playing field, they freeze, turn around and obey—most of the time, anyway. It's magic. It works. Because we say so.

I'd brought Sam to life when he slid out of my body all those years ago. Surely I was strong enough to muster enough mother's power to will him to life again? *Come back here!* I yelled across the universe. The silence was darker than midnight. I longed to see even his ghostly form standing at the end of the bed. But Sam had flown further away than the distance between stars, to the empty nothingness of space.

I dreaded bumping into Sam's old school friends. Their innocent faces still fired me with irrational resentment, then profound shame at my reaction. Rage flared whenever I saw a blue Ford Escort. It had yet to occur to me that the events of 21 January could have ruined the woman's life almost as drastically as ours. I often wondered how events had unfolded that day. After Sam had fallen, Rob had run up the zigzag to find Steve. Had she climbed out of her car to comfort the dying child?

But the sight of our young cat scampering down the hallway invariably lifted my mood. Not so long ago Lena's instruction to simply love our kitten had seemed an impossible ask. Yet Cleo overwhelmed us all with affection so freely, we couldn't help loving her back. The youngest, most joyous member of our family, she had woven herself into our life after Sam. I couldn't believe I'd ever contemplated giving her back to Lena.

✦

Leaves of a birch in our garden transformed themselves into a curtain of gold medallions that shimmered against pewter branches. Oblivious to its chances, a late summer rose unfurled on a bush.

A squall direct from Antarctica pummelled the harbour to stainless steel, scattering birds across the sky. No wonder birds greet a translucent dawn with consummate joy. They don't dwell on the previous night's storm. Their chorus betrays no concern for the winter ahead, either. They simply embrace the miracle of being alive in this instant on one perfect autumn morning. I had so much to learn from them.

If anything, the beauty of these sights was heightened now I understood how achingly brief the lifespan was of any living thing. Maybe the key to healing isn't found in books, tears or religion, but in affection for small things—a flower, the smell of damp grass. Love for a kitten was helping me embrace the world again.

Observer

A wise cat steps back from emotional response and observes without judgement

Our first winter after losing Sam was particularly harsh. Snow draped itself over the hills across the harbour. Giant bruises of clouds rolled up from Antarctica and pushed against our windows. Rain pelted sideways at the glass. Wind tore our coats as we scurried down the zigzag, which had become a waterfall.

I gradually trained myself to drive under the footbridge. The first time I held my breath and focused on a triangle of harbour in the distance as the car hurtled down the hill. Next time, driving slowly up the slope, I allowed my eyes to drift to the bus stop and the kerb Sam's foot had left.

A reluctant spring arrived with spikes of yellow bloom. Reliving Sam's last steps, I forced myself to walk down the zigzag and onto the tired wooden planks of the footbridge. Pausing in the centre, I gazed down at the road. It was an unremarkable strip of tar seal. No stains, no hollows or irregularities. Nothing to indicate a boy had lost his life there. I hoped he hadn't died frightened and alone.

I gave up scouring the streets for mousey-haired, thirty-something largeish women with or without spectacles in navy coats. A Ford Escort parked on the side of the street was no longer an invitation to inspect its headlights. The damage would've been fixed months ago, anyway. It was probably beetling up and down hills, pretending it had never killed.

With warmer weather a gut-wrenching series of firsts had to be endured: what would have been Sam's tenth birthday, closely followed by our first Christmas without him, then the anniversary of the accident. I've never been able to love summer wholeheartedly since.

Sometimes I'd been paralysed with guilt if a few minutes went by without grief for Sam. A moment of laughter or happiness would shame me into thinking I was letting Sam down. But I gradually realised that being locked in a state of misery wasn't helping Rob or honouring the life we'd had with Sam or the fact I was still alive.

With courage worthy of Superman himself, Rob had settled back well into school. Teachers whined about learning difficulties but the main thing was he seemed to have plenty of friends. While Steve and I hadn't fallen in love again, we'd accepted some of our differences and were getting along better. Cleo was constantly springing out at us from behind doorways, reminding us life was too profound to be taken seriously.

I was beginning to relate to Cleo's attraction to high places. Even if it was just a hereditary Abyssinian thing, the notion of taking a step above daily life and gazing down at it from a distance had compelling logic. I'd been doing it myself at night recently, standing at the top of the zigzag, the chill wind slicing my cheeks, and staring down at the glittering city. When observed from a great height, pain sometimes shrinks and subsides into the wider pattern of life. With practice and time I was learning it's possible to disengage emotion occasionally and experience the serenity of a cat observing the world from a rooftop.

Gazing down at the grids of streetlights, I would wonder if a person's life is packaged in a predestined design. When

Sam was just two years old we'd walked through a picturesque old cemetery one morning. He ran ahead and stopped at a gravestone engraved with the name 'Samuel'. Pointing at the headstone, he howled uncontrollably. I'd had to lift him, red-faced and sobbing, in my arms and carry him away from the place. He couldn't even read at the time and had no way to understand the technicalities of death and cemeteries. How could a toddler comprehend so much, let alone experience a terrifying premonition? The memory of that day still makes me shudder.

The night sky that had once seemed so icy and indifferent would draw me into its magnificence. Maybe the cloak of space wasn't empty after all, but full of profound energies humans have yet to perceive. Instead of limitless nothing, that giant bowl of stars could be where we've come from and the place we return to. So far away and yet intimately close. Light that had left those stars years ago travelled across time to enter the retinas of my eyes and become part of my experience. They were as close to me now as darling Sam, distant as the stars and yet an integral part of every breath. The sky, stars, Sam and I were closer than I'd dared imagine. Maybe that's what Mum had been talking about when she'd said Sam was part of the sunset. Perhaps she wasn't insensitive after all, but incredibly wise. When it's my turn, maybe I'll discover death isn't a terrifying full stop but a return to the eternal mystery that is home.

✦

With help from Jason and Ginny we ploughed through another winter into a second spring. As nights grew longer, evenings after school were a favourite time for the four of us to get together. Ginny and I would meet in the garden and soothe the day away with a glass of bubbles while we watched the boys burn off the last of their energy before bedtime.

I'd gone along with Ginny's dizzy act in the beginning. With her whacky earrings and fabulous hairdos, she gave the impression of being a blonde in brunette's clothing. Nothing could've been further from the truth. I was amazed when she confessed to not only being a midwife but studying for a science degree as well. More importantly, she introduced me to fake fur and lent me some of her earrings, including some orange dangling perspex lightening bolts that were beyond electrifying. Ginny taught me how to put false eyelashes on straight and to not be scared of platform shoes. She was becoming the friend I'd always dreamt of—zany, wise, kind and equipped with an almost psychic ability to turn up when needed.

Rob and Jason were bonded by their devotion to Cleo. They thought it was about time she had kittens. They were disgusted when I explained she'd had an operation.

'That's *so-o* mean!' said Jason, shaking his head with bewilderment.

'Yeah,' Rob added. 'Why didn't you let Cleo have babies?'

Standing on the grass against an orange sunset, Ginny and I exchanged smiles. We'd become such close friends it felt as though we were living in an Antipodean version of an African long house. With one short zig of the zigzag between our homes, the boys ran freely from one house to the other. Even though Ginny and Jason lived in two-storied splendour, they seemed oblivious to our shabby kitsch.

'Well,' I said, 'a cat can have babies three or four times a year. And if she had five kittens in each litter that means Cleo would have twenty babies in one year. Imagine twenty kittens running through the house.'

Rob thought that sounded fantastic. When I asked where they'd all sleep, Jason volunteered that at least one kitten could live at his house.

'They'd still have nineteen kittens left,' said Ginny. 'And it wouldn't be long before *they* were able to have kittens. They'd end up with hundreds and thousands of kittens.'

'Wow!' said Rob, turning to me. 'Why *were* you so mean?'

I tried to explain the operation's benefits. Without it Cleo would want to go out on dates. She'd get moody when we kept her inside. The vet had assured me having her spayed protected her from infections and some types of cancer.

'Nobody stopped *you* having babies,' Rob grumbled.

This surgical reproductive talk was reassurance we'd done the right thing in not revealing to Rob details of Steve's vasectomy reversal, which had involved considerably more time under the knife and greater discomfort than Cleo had undergone. The patient hadn't once complained, though his eyes sometimes clouded with pain. The surgeon reported that the operation had gone well, though it would be some time before we knew for certain if it had worked. After a stoic recovery, Steve had packed his suitcase and hobbled off to the ferry for another stint at sea.

Cleo tuned into the boys' disapproval of me. Squirming in my arms, she demanded to be put on the grass. She stalked around the side of the house looking like Naomi Campbell. Watching her disappear I felt a momentary tinge of guilt. Perhaps a creature as graceful as Cleo deserved to populate the world.

'You should've let her have babies!' said Rob, harrumphing off down the path. 'C'mon Jason. Let's dig.'

The boys' shared love of Cleo had expanded to other interests, including a vast excavation they'd undertaken in a corner of our garden so wild and neglected I'd barely noticed it before. Shaded with ferns and an air of forbidden mystery, it was a perfect spot for male bonding over a major dig.

Day after day they dragged Steve's pick axe and shovels out from under our house. The equipment looked huge and dangerous in their hands. Today's parent would probably be sued for letting them loose with such man-sized weaponry. But the hole-digging enterprise really mattered to the boys.

A fireball sun was sinking over the hills. A shawl of frost nestled in the valleys. The city hummed companionably below us. When I asked Ginny if we should call the boys back to get them inside and fed she shrugged. Digging was obviously an important rite in the passage to manhood.

Even though I was tempted to swathe Rob in bubble wrap and protect him from every potential dent, I knew it would be a mistake. I had to ease up and allow him the freedom a boy needs to develop into a confident young male. The hole-digging mission went on week after week, much to Rata's delight (the only expert digger among them). Perched on a branch, Cleo kept lookout for inadvertent bird life while the boys swaggered like cowboys and exchanged grown-up curse words below.

Nobody, including the boys, knew exactly why they were digging the hole. Its purpose changed all the time. They were tunnelling through to the other side of the earth for a while, until they started feeling sweaty and wondered if they were getting too close to the core. Changing strategy a few days later, they decided to search for the chest of gold that Captain Cook had almost certainly buried there on his last voyage. A few days later they discovered an old wire mattress base under the house. They carried it outside and stretched it across the hole and made a lethal-looking trampoline.

I wondered if handling the moist weight of the soil was therapy for Rob. The sight of him spattered with dirt and flushed with satisfaction after a digging session reminded me of my grandmother. Mother of nine children, she'd spent most of her life on the same patch of farmland, and must have faced countless anxieties and disappointments. Whenever worry scratched at her innards she headed down her back steps, past the henhouse to her garden. The cure for every sorrow, she said, could be found on her knees on a patch of earth with a trowel in one hand. The ritualistic comfort of turning the earth was her psychotherapy. Deep engagement with her garden's volcanic loam kept her earthed and connected to the planet's ancient rhythms.

Though she'd long since moved on, I was beginning to understand her better now, especially since I'd spent more time outside while the boys were digging.

In a frivolous act of optimism I planted tulip bulbs for spring. To cover a seed with soil is to demonstrate faith in the future. Tearing out weeds, watering and nurturing the sleeping seed are acts of trust in Nature. When a green shoot appears the gardener experiences a similar rush to someone who has just created a work of art or given birth. Gardening is the closest some people get to feeling like a god. To watch a seedling sprout and unfurl into a flower or vegetable is to take part in a miracle. The gardener also learns acceptance of decay and death, to almost welcome a season of withdrawal as part of the cycle.

Cleo, on the other hand, had another way of dealing with life's hiccups. She headed for high places. As we wandered down the path to inspect the boys' earthworks, Ginny suddenly stopped and pointed a crimson fingernail at our roof. Perched on top of a chimney pot was a familiar silhouette.

'What's Cleo doing up there?' she asked.

'Probably sulking about the operation,' I said. 'She must be feeling pretty fit to get up there. *Cleo!*'

But our cat sat still as a statue against the orange sky, her back to us, her tail in a graceful loop over the chimney.

'Are you sure she's okay?' said Ginny doubtfully.

'It's her way of dealing with things.'

'Do you think she's stuck?' asked Ginny.

'Maybe she's enjoying the view.'

Cleo must've had fun climbing up there, but getting down looked impossible, even for an agile cat.

'Why do these things always happen when Steve's away at sea?' I complained. Trudging around the side of the house to find a ladder, I suddenly thought of a new motto: 'Keep one eye on the stars and the other on the ground to watch out for dog shit.'

Ginny, whose generosity knew no bounds, offered to climb up and get Cleo. But even a circus performer would think twice before scaling a ladder in fish-net stockings, platform shoes and earrings the size of post office clocks.

Thanking her, I leant the ladder against the house and looked skywards.

Two tiny black ears stood out against the sunset. The ladder seemed suddenly frail and rickety—and far taller than I'd remembered.

As I climbed, a wave of nausea washed up from my knees to the top of my neck, threatening to burst out from the back of my throat. Vertigo had never had such a physical effect on me before.

'Shall I call the fire brigade?' Ginny called helpfully. I regretted glancing down. Ginny, her face turned up in concern, had shrunk to the size of a brightly collared beetle.

I reached the top of the ladder and edged onto the roof. Except it wasn't so much a roof as a collection of rusty holes holding hands, hardly ideal support for a not very petite woman.

'Here, kitty!' I called. The shape on top of the chimney remained motionless. The poor feline was frozen with terror. 'Oh Cleo! Don't worry. I'll get you down.'

The roof squeaked and groaned in protest as I crawled toward the chimney, my stomach churning. The thought was just occurring to me that if Cleo, an agile animal equipped with four legs, was having trouble getting off the roof it might be close to impossible for a lumbering vertigo victim.

'Hold on! I'm nearly there,' I called.

A pair of luminous eyes loomed above my head and narrowed to a bad-tempered glower. Cleo shook her head in a bored, dismissive manner. She rose gracefully to her feet on top of the chimney, arched her back and yawned. Without hesitation she sprang nimbly down to the roof, leapt across the rusty tin, jumped onto a nearby tree and slid groundwards, landing inches away from Ginny's platform shoes.

'I think I'm going to throw up!' I wailed down at Ginny.

'You'll be fine. Just take it slowly. Crawl back to the ladder, that's right. Turn around. Watch out for the guttering . . . there you go!'

When I finally reached terra firma I took three steps and threw up in a hydrangea bush.

'Why didn't you say you were scared of heights?' asked Ginny.

'It's not usually this bad. I haven't felt this sick since I was . . . pregnant.'

Indulgence

Stress – a waste of nap time

A cat's lips are arranged in a permanent smile. Even when it's miserable, the edges of its mouth point skywards. This is not the case with humans, whose mouths have a tendency to turn down at the corners, especially as they grow older. A human who wears the effortless smile of cat is in possession of a happy secret.

A smile appeared on Steve's lips when he heard the news. He carried it with him back to sea and was still wearing it a week later. I had a cat's smile too. We agreed not to make it official for a few weeks in case the pregnancy came to nothing.

When we decided it was safe to tell Rob, his smile was an explosion of sunlight.

He immediately put in an order for a baby brother. It had to be a boy, he said, because boys were what we had in our family. I agreed and promised to do my best. Then he ran across the zigzag to tell Jason, who of course told Ginny.

Arriving breathless on the doorstep, she enveloped me in the spicy embrace of her Opium perfume and did an excellent job feigning surprise. 'Congratulations, darling! It's going to be wonderful.' She offered to deliver the baby when the time came. I still had trouble believing my zany friend had another life in sterile gloves. Still, I liked the idea of our baby's first glimpse of humanity including a woman in false eyelashes and a zebra-skin jacket.

I sank into a pregnancy that combined squeamishness with ravenous hunger. It didn't seem so long ago that New Zealanders had survived on a diet of grey mince and mutton. During my teenage years, Mum introduced me to an exotic new food called pizza. We'd grown more sophisticated since then. We'd learnt wine didn't necessarily come out of cardboard boxes, bread could be sold in sticks and there were more than two types of cheese in the world. When a smart new deli opened around the corner we knew we'd arrived.

Profiterole. ProfEETerole, if pronounced correctly, according to the deli man who baked them. Roll your tongue around the word and it sounds almost erotic.

The grumpy profiterole man was Michelangelo in a chef's apron. How he could produce the lightest, puffiest, most delectable pastries on earth was beyond me. But who would guess a beige moth could produce a gorgeous green gum emperor caterpillar?

He laid them out every morning like naked sunbathers in his shop window. Lightly tanned, each oblong encased a glob of cream. Mudslides of chocolate sauce trickled over the cases. The shop window steamed around the edges, inviting—no, *insisting*—I venture inside.

'One profiterole, please,' I asked.

'ProFEETerole!' he snapped.

'Make that two.'

After all, I was eating for two now (three, in fact, counting Cleo).

Profiterole man grunted. Anyone would think I was trying to buy his children.

Waddling back up the zigzag I could feel the pastry crumbling and the cream oozing through the paper bag.

It was tempting to lower my globular body onto the seat halfway up the zigzag and scoff them there. But there was a danger I'd encounter Mrs Sommerville. She'd shoot me that Look of hers. Disapproving as ice cliffs, the Sommerville Look was designed to make boys confess to throwing snails at postmen and grown women suddenly feel as if they'd forgotten to put their underwear on.

I decided to slog on. Besides, I wasn't the only one hanging out for profiteroles. Cleo had developed an obsession with profiterole cream. The day she stole a splodge off my finger was like a heroin addict's first hit. Ever since, she'd taken to licking empty paper bags, the edges of my plate, my sleeve, anywhere trace elements could be found.

Every morning she waited, outlined against a stained-glass panel in the porch and looking like an Art Nouveau poster, for my return. The moment I arrived puffing at our front gate she galloped towards me, tail high, head slightly tilted. Together we'd trudge inside and sink into the recliner rocker, footrest up, headrest down, and rip open the paper bag.

Cleo was changing my attitude to indulgence. Guilt isn't in cat vocabulary. They never suffer remorse for eating too much, sleeping too long or hogging the warmest cushion in the house. They welcome every pleasurable moment as it unravels, and savour it to the full until a butterfly or falling leaf diverts their attention. They don't waste energy counting the number of calories they've consumed or the hours they've frittered away sunbathing.

Cats don't beat themselves up about not working hard enough. They don't get up and go, they sit down and stay. For them, lethargy is an art form. From their vantage points on top of fences and window ledges, they see the treadmills of human obligations for what they are—a meaningless waste of nap time.

I loved lazing around the half-renovated bungalow taking chill-out lessons from a cat. I slowed down, zoned out and tried listening to my body. It was screaming for rest, not just to cope with the demands of pregnancy, but to harvest energy for deeper levels of recovery. We became shameless sleepers, indulging in afternoon naps and morning ones, too. Eventually, after I'd waddled home from an after-school visit to Ginny's, Cleo and I discovered the delights of the early evening snooze.

I was her hot-water bottle. Either Cleo sensed the presence of new life inside me and wanted to be part of it, or she simply enjoyed the extra warmth and curves of the expanding mound. Almost horizontal in our recliner rocker, we had an ideal padded nest in which to laze away the weeks.

During the middle months of my pregnancy Cleo arranged herself around the top of the bulge, her head perfectly positioned for an idle tickle. Cleo adored small circular massages in the dent behind her ears, interspersed with full-length body strokes from her forehead to the tip of her tail. The experience was equally pleasurable for the masseuse, and at night my hands tingled with the memory of her fur.

As weeks progressed and my mound grew, Cleo reverted to snuggling wherever she could, stretching up my side or sometimes around the lower regions of my expanding abdomen. Claws were politely sheathed, until she could bear it no longer. Overcome with pleasure, she would knead them rhythmically into her protesting human heater.

A cat's fur has many textures, from the dense velvety covering on her nose to the silky pads of her paws; the sleek fur on her back to the fluffy undergrowth on her belly. Strange that such softness contrasts with claws and teeth sharp as pins. But every feline is a puzzle of contradictions—adoring one moment, aloof the next; a nurturing parent but also a murderer so cold-blooded it toys with wounded prey.

Sprawled in the armchair with Cleo I had an urge to feel wool nudging through my fingers again. To knit the spiderweb delicacy of baby clothes was beyond my capability so I bought three balls of blue wool (thick), and some chunky needles, and embarked on a plain-stitch scarf for Rob.

The rhythm of needles clicking is soothing, like a heartbeat. How a single thread of wool can be knotted together to create a three-dimensional item of clothing is almost as much a mystery as how a conglomeration of cells multiplies to make a baby.

Every stitch is complete in itself, though attached to stitches past and future. As I wound the wool around the needles to form each stitch, I thought of Sam, and I gently cast off. Cross needles, wind wool, *release* . . . cross needles, wind wool, *release* . . . If I practised this ten thousand times, or a million, perhaps my soul could do the same. *Release, release* . . .

Mesmerised, Cleo's eyes revolved in unison with the needles. With precision timing, she swatted them as they swept past her face and caught them between her teeth. The enemy of the knitting needles made such a nuisance of herself sometimes I'd scrape her off my lap and put her on the floor. Yet that was no punishment—the snake of blue wool unfurling from its ball was a thrilling foe.

Apart from occasional squabbles over wool and needles, our days drifted away companionably eating, dreaming and following patches of sun around the house. Every moment was a stitch in a larger fabric that was gradually becoming a life connected to the one we had before with Sam, yet entirely different. Household rhythms unfurled effortlessly as a ball of wool. Spoons clattered into kitchen drawers only to be taken out, used, washed, dried and put back again. Each morning Rob and Jason trudged through long shadows down the path to school to return at that time in the afternoon when the day is getting tired. Piles of laundry waited to be sorted, washed and pegged on the clothesline overlooking the shipping terminal below. Then taken down, folded, ironed, put in cupboards, worn and dumped in familiar-smelling piles again. Complete in themselves, each with a beginning, middle and end, these comforting cycles interwove into the semblance of a normal life.

Watching sun ripple against the wallpaper I wondered why we'd been in such a rush to fix up the house. What was so offensive about the wallpaper? If it stayed attached to the walls long enough the frenzy of black floral arrangements against a white background might become fashionable again. Even the shaggy carpet didn't get on my nerves much any more. Pregnant euphoria ensured everything could wait.

Steve's reaction was the opposite. Every room reeked of fresh paint. Ladders leant at drunken angles all over the house. Plunging into feverish activity, he finished renovating the bathroom. He hauled out the peeling blue bath with its tasteless gold taps and dumped it on the lawn in front of the house. I was so hormoned-out I wasn't bothered when grass grew tall around its edges.

When I wondered aloud to Ginny if she thought he'd ever take the bath away she suggested we turn it into a lily pond with goldfish. God, I loved that woman.

Cleo and I developed a taste for Mozart, not just because of the theory that babies could hear through the walls of the womb and classical music helped their brain cells grow. Cleo seemed to genuinely appreciate the composer's soothing music, particularly the second movement of the *Clarinet Concerto in A*. As the clarinet pulled notes of liquid gold from the air, Cleo's eyes narrowed to silver slits. Rainbows of sunlight danced across her fur. Nestling snugly around my belly, she purred accompaniment while Mozart resolved life's heartache in one exquisite movement. Listening to that piece I was assured even the most profound sadness can be transformed into beauty.

Replacement

A cat listens carefully to every story, whether she has heard it before or not

'It's a boy!' every cell in my body shouted. There was an unmistakable masculinity in the way his feet ricocheted off my ribs. The tiny fists that pummelled my bladder in the middle of the night had the force of a miniature boxing champion. My feet marched 'boy, boy' down the darkened hall to the bathroom for the third time in as many hours.

I sewed a tiny baby's gown and embroidered the neck with blue daisies. We talked about names. Joshua, maybe. Certainly not Samuel, though perhaps as a middle name.

Not a replacement for Sam, I explained to anyone who was interested. The new baby would have his own personality, with just a touch of Sam's roguish sense of humour, the same shaped eyes, maybe, perhaps even a similar grassy smell to his skin. He wouldn't *be* Sam, of course. I'd respect the baby's individuality. However much he did or didn't resemble Sam, the baby would make us a family of four again. I'd tell Joshua Samuel everything about the brother he never knew. A thread of continuity would be woven into our lives.

Steve allowed himself to smile more often. To think all this hope was blossoming against the odds because of a surgeon with a microscope and clever fingers! For the last two babies

Steve had scrounged a second-hand bassinette from the For Sale columns of the local newspaper. Certain there'd be no more babies, he'd quickly disposed of it after we'd moved Rob to a larger cot.

This time he went out and bought a brand-new bassinette trimmed with yellow satin ribbon, a tactfully asexual colour. Peeling away its shiny wrapping, he assembled it in our bedroom. With a net canopy draped over its sides, the cradle was fit for a prince. I smoothed sheets the size of tea towels over the mattress.

Running my hand over the yellow ribbon, I wondered how people handled raising girls. All that tulle and Barbie doll stuff would be complicated. I knew how boys worked. Looking after them involves a lot of physical energy—chasing, mostly, and yelling. Boys are emotionally straightforward. They have special bonds with their mothers. Sam and I had a Kissing Game, a sort of tag, we used to play. The winner was whoever planted the last kiss on the other's face, and it always ended with both of us purple with laughter.

Yes, I thought, examining the latest styles in blue booties and cuddly rugs, I'd teach the new baby the secret Kissing Game, even though it had belonged exclusively to Sam and me. I wondered if Joshua would like Sam's old wooden train set, and if there was anything else of Sam's he'd like. Not that I was in any way planning to replicate what we had. Was I?

◆

Rata was overjoyed when Mum's Japanese hatchback slowed to a halt at the top of the zigzag. It was a car the retriever associated with jaunts to the beach, farms and other happy places. Mum had come to 'help out' before the baby arrived. The length of her stay was unspecified, but if it was like any other it probably wouldn't be more than a couple of nights. Mum and I loved each other dearly, but we both had strong personalities and were prone to amateur dramatics. We usually rubbed each other up the wrong way after a few nights.

As Mum emerged from the driver's door Rata sprang on her hind legs, plonked a paw on each of the old woman's shoulders and swiped her cheek with a sloppy lick. Staggering slightly under Rata's weight, Mum smiled broadly. She'd always been a dog person and Rata was her favourite dog on earth.

After being showered with saliva, Mum patiently lowered each of Rata's paws. Rob ran forward and wrapped his arms around her waist. Tail waving a welcome banner, Rata led us in procession down the zigzag. Second to Rob, there was no one now who Rata adored more than Mum.

Unpacking her bag in the spare room she presented me with her pièce de résistance—a shawl she'd knitted in wool so fine and needles so tiny the entire thing could be passed through her wedding ring. Dazzling white, with scalloped edges and a web of intricate stitches, it was the Ultimate Baby Shawl.

Since Dad's death, Mum passed her nights in front of a flickering screen with only knitting needles for company. Most of the time she created blankets and big bulky rugs made from carpet wool she bought direct from the factory. This baby shawl was in a different league, knitted with such love and attention to detail it glowed with some sort of energy. It was a shawl that might be filled with protective spells to become a magic cloak.

'It's beautiful!' I said, admiring her handiwork. 'He'll love it.'

'How do you know it's a boy?' she asked.

'I just feel it.' But mum was already onto another topic.

'Well, back in the twenties cousin Eve, that's *my* first cousin, which would make her your second cousin or something along those lines . . . She's the one who went to the Sorbonne and had the fling with the married hairdresser until the family found out and stopped her allowance. She arrived back in New

Zealand wearing a fur coat and lipstick. Everyone thought she'd had her lips tattooed . . .'

Poor Mum. What she missed most these days, she often said, was having someone to talk to. Sadly, this inflicted her with the lonely person's disease—she talked too much. As a result, some of her oldest friends had withdrawn to become occupied with bridge, charity work or grandchildren. I couldn't blame them. Some of her stories were amusing, like this one about cousin Eve (which interested me the first time she told it. I was intrigued a family not known for glamorous and wicked women could have produced someone as wonderful as Eve). But Mum was a heavy-duty talker. It demanded great loyalty and affection to endure a barrage of words with a noticeable absence of polite questions about health and weather offered in return. As Mum launched into yet another monologue, smiles would set like raspberry jam, faces went flat as pie crusts. When the listener retreated into a private world of shopping lists and which underwear really should be thrown out, Mum would suddenly startle them with a loud 'You're not *listening*, are you?'.

Even though we lived four hundred kilometres apart, Mum and I had always been emotionally close. Listening to her on the phone several times a week, I longed to ease her loneliness. She invariably mentioned the other widows in her community of concrete block townhouses and how lucky they were to have regular visits from their families. The guilt missile hit bullseye every time. If we'd lived closer I could have been one of those responsible daughters who, every Sunday, arrived on their ageing mother's doorstep nursing a warm casserole dish.

'Let's see how it looks on the bassinette,' I said, leading her and Rob into our bedroom, where the baby's bed waited, a semi-translucent cocoon.

Flourishing the shawl, I prepared to spread it over the miniscule mattress.

'Wait!' Mum yelled.

I froze mid-swoosh. Curled up inside the bassinette was the unmistakable silhouette of a sleeping cat princess. Cleo flicked an ear, and opened a lazy eye to examine us in a bored way.

Our cat had obviously recognised the bassinette for what it was. Her subjects had finally got around to understanding her regal status and provided the level of comfort she was entitled to.

Mum ran forwards, bent over the bassinette and boomed '*Shooooo!*'. Cleo flattened her ears and hissed back. I watched helpless while two of the most powerful females in my life declared war on each other.

'It's okay, Nana,' Rob said. 'Cleo's just trying out the baby's bed. She wants to make sure it's comfortable.'

'There's only one place cats belong,' Mum proclaimed, grabbing Cleo around the belly and marching her to the front door. 'Outside!'

After her abrupt landing on the verandah Cleo shook herself in disbelief. Why on earth had the giant grandmother woman tossed her out of *her* bed?

Back in the kitchen, Mum filled the electric kettle while Rata sat devotedly at her feet.

'That cat will smother the baby,' she said.

Through the window I saw Cleo licking herself all over with long comforting strokes. No doubt she was hatching a plan.

'Cats and babies don't go together,' Mum continued. 'They drop fur everywhere. Have you seen? It's all over Rob's pillowcase. The whole house is covered in cat fur. It gives babies asthma. And the claws. Cats have no patience. They lash out and scratch babies on the face. Cats aren't like dogs, are they, Rata? They get jealous . . .'

'Cleo's not jealous,' Rob said.

'Just wait till the baby's here,' said Mum.

'Cleo's looking forward to the baby,' said Rob. 'She says it's a blessing.'

Mum's hand froze on the kettle's handle. She shot me a worried look.

'What do you mean *says?*' she asked Rob. 'You think the cat's *talking* to you?'

'No,' I said quickly. 'He just had a couple of dreams about Cleo. I don't think it's anything to worry about. You know what kids are like.'

'He's been through an awful lot,' she said to me under her breath. 'You don't think he's going a bit *strange*, do you?'

'He's fine,' I said firmly, arranging mugs on a tray.

'Frankly, I don't know why you've bothered with a cat when most people would give anything to have a dog like Rata,' she continued. 'Rata's practically . . . a human being. She's like having another person around.'

I'd forgotten what a dyed-in-the-wool dog person Mum was. Rata thumped her tail amiably on the floor. Mum was right: Rata was the most lovable dog in the world.

'Whenever Rata stays with me she keeps me company at night. I never feel scared because she always barks at strangers. She's a wonderful guard dog. Her fur's so silky. Don't you love the way it feels? And the best thing about her is the way she *listens*. Haven't you noticed the way Rata *listens to everything I say?*'

My heart stopped. How had a woman who'd once been so strong and forceful suddenly grown into an old lady with wavy grey hair and bifocals? The once regulation stiletto heels and pointy toes had surrendered to sensible shoes made of soft leather and with toes rounded enough not to trouble her bunions.

But she was giving decrepitude a run for its money. With her fashion flair (vibrant jackets with shoulder pads highlighted with chunky jewellery) and a lifelong commitment to coral lipstick, she was at the stylish end of the late seventies age group. Nevertheless, she looked more fragile than before. And for the first time she was actually *asking* me for something. She wanted company, protection, someone to give and receive love, and most importantly a pair of attentive ears.

As I poured the tea Mum wandered down the hall towards our bedroom with Rata at her heels. Compared to hers, my life was brimming with adults, children and animals. And now there was the baby to look forward to. Mum wanted more than television and knitting needles. She needed healing as much, if not more, than we did. A grandparent's grief is a double dose—grief for the lost grandchild and empathy for the unhappy adult child whose dream of family has unravelled.

'I *don't believe it!*' Mum yelled.

I followed her voice into our bedroom. Cleo had ensconced herself in the bassinette again. She and Mum were locked in a mutual glower.

'How did *you* get back inside?' she growled at the cat.

Cleo raised herself on all fours, curved her tail down to look like an old-fashioned pump handle and growled back.

'Through a window, probably,' I answered.

'That cat's a liability!' Mum snapped, scooping Cleo up and putting her firmly outside again. 'You're going to *have* to keep your bedroom door shut.'

The Battle of the Bassinette went on day after day. Even though I tried to keep our bedroom door shut, it constantly seemed to glide open. Cleo never missed an opportunity to reinstate herself in her new bed, and Mum was constantly at the ready to toss her out.

My attempts to call a truce between two determined females were pointless. Tensions between cat and grandmother were driving me crazy. Unable to sleep one night, I climbed out of bed around midnight, went under the house and fumbled in the dark for the hand-mower. Mowing the lawn by moonlight calmed me down for a bit (and probably provided Mrs Sommerville with entertainment).

'Getting restless are you?' said Mum the next morning. 'It's a sign the baby can't be far away. You'd better get rid of that cat.'

I gave up trying to fix things. Mum announced her departure, early as usual. Goodbyes were always clumsy. Our family wasn't big on displays of affection. As she stowed her bag into her hatchback, she looked suddenly frail again, a lonely old woman in a brown coat. We hugged briefly while Rata looked on, her tail at half-mast.

'Take care,' I whispered.

'You too,' Mum said, her vein-roped hand on the driver's door.

The drive ahead would take her five solitary hours, after which there'd be toast and scrambled eggs in front of the television and more knitting. Around eleven p.m. she'd have a mug of tea and a biscuit or two before heading off to bed— all of which added up to twelve hours of not talking to anyone. For someone who needed to talk, the prospect must've been torture. But Mum never complained.

'Would you like Rata to stay with you for a while?' I asked. 'I've talked with Rob and Steve and they're okay with it.'

Mum suddenly straightened her back and shed 10 years.

'I think we'd get on very well together, wouldn't we girl?' she said without hesitation.

Rata looked adoringly up at her with an expression of absolute devotion and barked happily. It'd been a long time since Mum had been the focus of such adulation.

'Just a minute,' she said, looking young and pretty again. She reached into the back seat and produced one of her green knitted rugs, which she smoothed over the front seat. Tail flying, Rata leapt gleefully onto the seat and waited for the engine to start.

If animals are healers, Mum needed one as much as anyone else. The silver-haired woman and the golden-haired dog looked a perfect match as they drove off up the street.

Raising my arm to wave goodbye, I felt a pang—strange, yet familiar. Exciting and frightening at the same time. A new person was about to arrive on planet Earth.

Rebirth

Love, for cats and people, can be paintful

A mother cat is rightfully called a Queen. Personally, I think it would be great if pregnant women were also called Queens. If the gay community protested too much we might possibly accept Baroness, Duchess or Fairy Princess. Anything instead of those glamour-sapping medical terms Gravida, Multigravida and the dreaded Geriatric Multigravida.

Cats arrange to have four or five babies in one hit. If humans did the same the number of months a woman spends gazing into a toilet bowl would be dramatically reduced. She'd have to buy only one set of hideous maternity clothes in her entire life. Children's clothes would be bought in bulk. Deals could be made with baby gear manufacturers and schools (five educations for the price of four?).

Restlessness is a sure-fire sign that a female cat is going into labour. It's the same with humans. I'd been wrong to assume the Battle of the Bassinette was responsible for my moonlight escapade with the hand-mower. I should have realised it was primal instinct telling my body to rev up for a big one.

'Hello? Is that the hospital? Look, I think I might be going into labour. Contractions? Well, they're not all that strong—maybe five minutes apart . . . What do you *mean* try and get some sleep? How can I go to sleep when I'm having a baby? . . . You want me to calm down and take a pill? Are you joking? So what if your beds are all full? I'll give birth in the broom cupboard.'

'Who does that stupid nurse think she is, turning me away from the hospital like that?'

'Here's the pill,' Steve said. 'Try and get a good night's sleep.'

'I think we should call Ginny. She'll know what to do.'

'I did. The babysitter answered. They're at some rock music awards.'

'*Rock music awards?*'

'It's okay. They'll finish around midnight. Ginny will meet us at the hospital, if we end up going there. Try and get some sleep.'

✦

'What time is it?'

'Haven't you gone to sleep yet? It's ten-thirty.'

'These contractions started seven hours ago. I think we should go to hospital.'

'They don't want you.'

'They're hardly going to turn us away if we arrive on their doorstep, are they?'

As we pulled into the hospital carpark I immediately wanted to go home again. Hospitals creep me out, especially when you're not entirely welcome. Even this one, with its 'homely' new birthing unit, could've doubled as a set for a Frankenstein movie. As if I didn't notice the gleam of the machinery, the holes in the wall expecting tubes and wires to be plugged into them, the nasty implements lurking under green surgical cloth. Frankly, I'd have preferred a cardboard box.

My birthing machinery was proving inefficient. I took a bath, breathed and paced. I crouched like an animal, knelt like a peasant woman from the Amazon and would've willingly hung upside down from one of the bad-taste paintings on the wall if it might've got things going. None of it worked. Even though the contractions were increasingly uncomfortable they refused to get businesslike.

The doctor arrived around midnight and went to sleep in the next room. I was boring everyone, including me. I wanted to burst through the hospital doors and run away into the night.

Even though I was planning a natural birth with no pain killers, I developed an attachment to a mask that exuded sickly-smelling nitrous oxide. Why it's called laughing gas I'll never know. Nothing remotely funny happened, except everyone started talking in Donald Duck voices. They were only doing that to annoy me. Whenever they tried to prise the mask away from me, I clamped it over my face and refused to let go.

The doctor appeared and said she was going to rupture the membranes around the baby's head. Baby? Was there a *baby* involved in all this pain? Suddenly a shimmering white cat glided into the room and stood over me, gazing at me with beautiful glittering eyes. Except it wasn't a cat, it was Ginny!

'You're making great progress,' she purred in my ear. 'We can see the head. The baby has a fine crop of black hair. You can give a push with the next contraction.'

'That's it,' said Ginny. 'One more push . . .'

Just as well there was a spectacular waterfall to look at. A comet of diamonds, it arced toward the ceiling and landed somewhere beyond my right knee.

A loud cry filled the air. Miniature crimson legs and dainty feet were intertwined with red and purple rope thick enough to tie Steve's ferry to the wharf. Umbilical cord. Tiny hands curled like pink camellias. A face wise as a guru, fresh as dawn, peered curiously around the room from under a cap of dark hair. Never had I seen anyone look so confident they were in the right place. The baby. *Our* baby! A tidal wave of love surged out of me and enveloped the child.

'She's absolutely perfect,' Ginny said, lowering her into my arms. 'What are you going to call her?'

A girl was the last thing I'd planned for. My longing for a daughter had been so deep I'd been too scared to admit it to anyone, especially to myself. This child's femaleness was a statement she had no intention of being a replica of Sam. Staring up into my face with short-sighted intensity she exuded such strong individuality I wasn't tempted to mention Samantha, even as a middle name.

'Lydia,' I said. 'After my father's mother. I never met her, but everyone says she was a strong woman.'

'Lydia, little one,' said Ginny tenderly. 'May you journey lightly through life's rain showers.' As she delivered her impromptu blessing I noticed for the first time how Ginny's eyes gleamed with unspoken wisdom, like Cleo's.

Risk

*A cat's movements are fluid as milk and
she always lands on all fours*

Rob was right. Cleo wasn't the slightest bit jealous of the baby. Surrendering the bassinette without complaint, our cat seemed to understand Lydia was a precious addition to our household. Fascinated by the new human, Cleo welcomed Lydia's interest in staying awake most of the night. In fact, Cleo seemed to think Lydia had invented a three-hour feeding schedule specifically to relieve the boredom of long, uneventful darkness. Whatever time the baby stirred, two a.m., three-thirty, or four-fifteen, a four-legged silhouette meowed as if she'd been merely napping in anticipation of this fun event. Cleo would spring onto the rocking chair to snuggle into the warm, damp intimacy of mother and newborn. Sometimes she perched on the chair's headrest and, purring loudly, gazed down at us through huge translucent eyes. Standing sentinel over us, Cleo seemed to gather mystical power from the night and envelop us with love and protection. The spirit of Bastet traversed the centuries and beamed from our small black cat.

I'd never met a baby more comfortable in her own skin. Clasping my finger with her delicate hand, Lydia seemed to know she was where she needed to be. It was incredible to think

142

she would never have existed if Sam hadn't left us two and a half years earlier. I still wept for Sam and searched for him in the shape of her head, her eyes. But Lydia was determined to be accepted on her own terms. Great joy doesn't obliterate grief. Both can be encompassed at the same time.

Winter was underway again. Lashings of rain iced southerly gales as they roared through Cook Strait to harass the city. Umbrellas exploded on street corners. Old women clung to lamp posts. As citizens struggled up hills to their homes, not a single one could be accused of having a good hair day. When the wind finally exhausted itself, the hills wrapped themselves in petticoats of cloud and sulked. The city closed in on itself. And still it rained.

Wellingtonians seldom mentioned these minor irritations. Their reward for living on a series of climactically challenged cliffs staring straight into the jaws of the frozen continent was the knowledge that they inhabited the nation's capital, and were therefore (there was no way to put it tactfully) important. They certainly were a cut above those rough Aucklanders, dreary Christchurch people and (heaven forbid) country bumpkins from the provinces. If the weather made day-to-day survival tough, the capital's inner life was furnished with book clubs, night classes and more theatres per head of population than any other city. A cultured lot, they were.

'You must've brought the weather with you,' they'd say in accusatory tones to drenched and shivering visitors from out of town. 'If only you'd arrived yesterday. We've just had two weeks of glorious sunshine.'

But after the tenth consecutive day of rain and wind, Wellington could do something extraordinary. Shaking off its grey cloak, the city would suddenly emerge in crisp primary colours. A smiling yellow sun would turn the harbour blue. Scarlet roofs would glow against green hills. Wellington looked fresh out of a children's picture book. Once again, locals could congratulate each other for living in what they called a tropical paradise (well, practically).

Six weeks after Lydia's arrival Rob was due to turn nine years old. The prospect of another ninth birthday cast an irrational shadow. Would it be an unlucky number for all our children?

'How do you want to celebrate?' I asked Rob one morning, nervous he might ask for a repeat of Sam's eerie ninth birthday 'party'.

'What I'd really like', he said while I held my breath over the kitchen sink, 'is a pyjama sleep-over party.'

'With Jason?'

'And Simon and Tom and Andrew and Nathan . . .'

'A big party?' I asked, imagining happy noises resounding off the wallpaper. 'Let's do it!'

'Can I ask Daniel and Hugo and Mike, too?'

'Of course! Do you want girls?'

Rob looked at me as if I'd suggested he have broccoli and onions on toast for breakfast.

The morning of Rob's birthday we woke him early and presented him with a small packet wrapped in red tissue with a blue bow. Superman colours.

'Do I open the card first?' he asked breathlessly.

He was delighted to find Cleo had added her signature to his birthday card in the form of a paw print made in blue finger paint. Always a careful child, he coaxed the Sellotape off with his fingernails instead of tearing at the paper the way other boys would have done. Watching his face, so sweet and expectant, I wasn't sure he was ready for the gift, but Steve and I had talked it over countless times and chosen it with care.

'Wow!' he cried, his face blazing with joy. 'A real Casio digital watch!' It was out of its box and on his wrist before anyone could say, 'Multiple Functions'.

'I LOVE it!' he said. 'It's even got a light, see? If you push this button you can tell the time in the dark.'

There was no doubt Rob's ease with technology hadn't come from my side of the family. He pored over the sheet of instructions and told us the watch could do just about anything except fly into space. Flushed with satisfaction, he peeled off the protective seal over its face, folded the instructions and placed them respectfully inside the box the watch had arrived in.

'It's the best present I've ever had,' he sighed, lifting his Superman watch from his bedside table. 'But I can't wear two watches.'

His thumb circled the face of the Superman watch. Something jarred in my throat. How could we have been so insensitive?

'I really love this Superman watch . . .' Of course. It was too soon for him to give up the comfort and connection with Sam it provided.

'Don't worry, Rob,' I said. 'We'll take the Casio back to the shop and change it for something else.'

'No! That's not what I meant!' he said, shaking his head earnestly. 'I mean . . . do you think Sam would mind if I put his watch away in my drawer?'

The sharp lump in my throat dissolved as I drew Rob into my neck and stroked his hair.

'Sam wouldn't mind at all,' I said, swallowing back tears of pride. 'In fact I think he'd say you're ready for a big boy's watch.'

◆

Later that night, boys trooped down the zigzag wearing their pyjamas and smiles bright enough to blind the possum who was busy demolishing the tree by the gate. Rob welcomed them inside, decked out in a bright-red dressing-gown and his brand-new watch, with more digital functions than the Space Shuttle.

The house filled with loud, raucous, running boys. Walls shook. The rubber plant trembled. Potato chips were ground into the shag pile. Sausages were thrown across the kitchen. It was the sort of party that would've set my teeth on edge in the old days. Not anymore. Tie sheets and dangle them out the window? Why not! Cricket in the hall? What's a broken lamp or two? I slid into my blue dressing-gown to match the party theme and prepared for boys to run wild.

I hadn't realised how many friends Rob had made in the two and a half years since Sam's death. They weren't dutiful friends who'd taken him on purely out of sympathy, either. They teased, laughed and treated Rob with genuine affection. He'd journeyed such a long way since 1983. The shy younger brother had transformed into an outgoing friend magnet. I almost wept with gratitude and respect for him.

Cats, babies and parties tend not to mix. I'd arranged for Lydia and Cleo to be tucked away in a room at the quiet end of the house. But they were intrigued rather than spooked by the visitors. I let them out to circulate—Cleo on her own and Lydia in my arms. Cleo swiftly adopted Simon, a red-haired cat lover, and spent most of the night on his lap sampling slivers of ham. Lydia, wearing one of her blue baby suits (bought when she was going to be a boy) greeted our guests with the gracious smile of the Queen Mother on a walkabout.

The boys played Pass the Parcel or, in their case, Throw the Parcel (thankfully neither Cleo nor Lydia played the role of Parcel). Rain flung itself at the windows. A drum roll of thunder rumbled above the roof. A flash of lightning coincided with the front door knocker slamming on its hinges.

An elderly magician stood on the doorstep wearing a false nose and glasses. Holding a large suitcase in one hand, he was oblivious to the storm, as if it was just another theatrical prop that followed him around. He must have been close to eighty years old. Apologising for being late, he removed his raincoat and slapped a fez on his bald head. I feared for him. No audience is harsher than a collection of rowdy boys. The boys sneered when he stepped boldly into the living room. He wasn't going to last thirty seconds in there.

His hands were square, with fingers the size and shape of cigarette stubs. Bricklayer's hands, yet they proved deceptively nimble. The magician made ropes change their lengths inside a plastic bag, and ink-spattered scarves wash themselves clean in the privacy of a cardboard box. Though the boys had no intention of being impressed, they couldn't help themselves.

Towards the end of his act the old man produced a top hat. He asked the birthday boy to tap it three times with a magic wand. To everyone's amazement a pure-white living, breathing dove emerged from the hat.

Cleo, who had been watching the show with detached amusement from Simon's knee, suddenly shot across the floor like a licorice bullet and sprang at the bird. The old man tumbled backwards. Alarmed, the dove squawked and slipped out of his grasp. The boys watched in awe as the bird flapped across the room to perch clumsily in the rubber plant. Steve grabbed Cleo and carried her out of the room while I helped the magician to his feet.

'Wow! This is the best party I've ever been to!' yelled one of the boys, as the magician retrieved his bird and carried it out to the kitchen. The others whooped agreement and sent the old man off with enthusiastic applause.

Later, the magician soothed his dove along with his nerves over a mug of tea. Spacey strains of David Bowie reverberated through the walls.

'They call *that* music?' he sighed, sliding his plastic nose and glasses into his pocket. 'I'm a Bing Crosby man myself.'

The old man drained his tea, packed up his suitcase and headed back to the safety of the thunderstorm. I waved him goodbye and ventured into the party room. The sight of fifteen boys in pyjamas jumping off furniture and leapfrogging over the shag pile would have reduced me to a screaming shrew not so long ago. But I'd wasted too many years trying to yell boys into shape: surrendering to the noise, the untidiness and the celebration of it all was much more fun.

I searched the sea of heads for Rob. He was easy to spot in his red dressing-gown with Cleo in his arms.

'You're going to love this one, guys!' he yelled, turning up the stereo even louder. As Bowie boomed out Rob's favourite song, 'Let's Dance', I had only one choice. Surrender. With Lydia perched on my hip I swayed, twirled and waltzed till my legs ached. The room shimmered with joy. I hadn't partied like this since Sam was alive—no, since *ever*. Along with all the tears, I'd shed ideas about what mattered. I didn't have to be in control all the time anymore. The boys weren't disasters waiting to happen to our furniture. A few extra scratches would improve the coffee table. We laughed. We danced. We were alive.

◆

A few weeks after Rob's birthday, there was a phone call from newspaper editor Jim Tucker. Jim was starting up a national broadsheet, *The Sunday Star*, and wondered if I'd like to join his team as a feature writer. Listening to Jim's energy-charged enthusiasm I had to concentrate on his voice to convince myself I wasn't dreaming. A fresh start in an exciting work environment was something I'd longed for. Up till now, I'd been confident that would never happen. After all, my weekly pieces about family life in the Wellington newspaper were hardly Pulitzer Prize material.

Jim was offering every mother's dream—flexible working hours. But there was one thing he wasn't prepared to negotiate. If I wanted the job we'd have to pack up the family, cat and all, and move six hundred kilometres north to Auckland. Heart throbbing in the back of my throat, I thanked Jim and asked if he could give me some time to think.

Cleo glided into the kitchen and stared up at me through crescent-moon eyes. I lifted her up and ran my fingers through her silky fur. We'd made good friends in Wellington. How could we leave Ginny and Jason? Rob was happy at school. The success of his birthday party proved the great progress he'd made. Lydia was young enough not to notice, but even then I'd have to find quality care for her while I was working. And what about Cleo? Cats are famous for being more attached to places than people.

Then there was the job. Jim was obviously confident that I could write about subjects other than babies, carpet fluff and supermarket trolleys, but what if he was wrong? After a decade languishing in the 'burbs, I'd forgotten most of my journalism training. Parts of my brain had almost certainly shrivelled. Why else would I scribble shopping lists in code I couldn't decipher by the time I reached the supermarket? Failure would be embarrassingly public.

I loved Wellington and had learnt to appreciate the character-building aspects of its weather, hills and earthquakes. On the other hand, the allure of a larger, warmer city was appealing. I sometimes wondered if the zigzag bungalow was built on an unlucky fault line and doomed to bring sorrow to whoever lived within its walls. Even though Steve and I had sailed a cloud of elation around Lydia's conception and birth, we were starting to drift back into old patterns of withdrawal and resentment. Love was on ice again. Maybe the romance of hibiscus flowers and long summer nights would muster our strength for one last try.

Always supportive of my writing 'career', Steve was prepared to put up with the inconvenience of selling the house and commuting to his ship every few weeks. Accepting Jim's job offer was risking a lot. On the other hand, turning him down would be taking other, possibly more dangerous, risks.

I'd seen Cleo in a similar dilemma, with her back legs wedged in the fork of a tree and her front paws stretched down and perched perilously on the top of a fence. She knew she had to get down from the tree, and the fence was the only viable option. Her confidence wavered every so often, and she'd try to twist herself back up into the tree. But it was too late—she'd made the move, stretched her body across the space between the tree and fence and there was only one way to go. She had to use every ounce of concentration to land her back legs accurately on the fence. If not, a humiliating tumble into the garden would be involved. Cleo was a risk expert. She took them every day and they nearly always paid off.

We'd survived two Christmases without Sam, and two of his birthdays. The days when grief was still raw were interspersed with a slowly increasing number of 'good' days. Optimism was fragile, though. Like a shoot forcing itself through the earth after a long winter, I was easily crushed.

Bolstered by Jim's offer, I was walking through the city centre one morning feeling unusually buoyant. Valerie, an acquaintance from Sam's preschool, approached, arranging her face in that funeral-parlour expression that had become so familiar. 'How *are* you?' she asked in the old terminal-diagnosis voice. 'I was thinking of you the other day when my Great Aunt Lucy died . . .'

After listening to Valerie's story (Great Aunt Lucy dropped dead digging potatoes, aged ninety-seven) I hurried home and picked up the phone. 'Jim? I'll take the job.'

Resilience

There are no changes in a cat's life.
Only adventures

The saddest thing about leaving Wellington was saying good-bye to Ginny. She stood at the top of the zigzag, wind blowing her earrings horizontal. But with the house sold and the car packed to the roof, it was too late to change my mind. I sensed we'd always be part of each other's lives.

'You'll be fabulous, darling,' she said, blowing a kiss through the passenger window. 'Byeeee!'

Rosie predicted our cat would be traumatised by the move north. Cleo didn't do predictable. The more we treated Cleo as an honorary human, the more she behaved like one—though she was always angling for goddess status (why sit on someone's lap at the dinner table when you can climb onto the table and graze free range?).

An eight-hour car journey cooped inside a basket was hardly luxury travel for a feline deity, but she didn't complain. She dozed contentedly with a sock for company most of the way.

We'd bought an old tram conductor's cottage in Ponsonby, a scruffy inner suburb. I adored the laid-back atmosphere on Ponsonby Road, where Polynesian women glided alongside street kids and drunks pretending to be artists. Even the graf-fiti was worth reading. I didn't realise it then, but it was just a matter of time before the espresso machines and earnest young couples moved in.

I had fallen in love with the cottage the moment I saw it. Sunny, outward-looking and easy to reach, it was everything our Wellington house wasn't. With big sash windows and woodwork furled like lace around the verandah it smiled out onto the street. Wisteria coiled through the lattice work. Flower baskets swung in the breeze. A white picket fence flashed its teeth at a bottlebrush tree.

The inside layout was pleasantly predictable, with three double bedrooms off a central hallway that led to an open-plan living area. Sometime during the seventies a morose hippy had renovated the place. He must have been depressed. Why else would he have laid dark brown carpet in every room and lined the kitchen with treacle-coloured wood? While character features such as panelled ceilings and brick fireplaces had been kept, there were occasional lapses of taste. I was willing to forgive the penchant for redwood fence stain, but had to seriously avoid dwelling on the Spanish archway between the living room and kitchen.

The backyard was perfect for kids. From a sunroom off the kitchen, French doors opened onto a redwood deck, with built-in benches around the edges. Under a pergola groaning with grapes was, joy of joys, a hot tub. Beyond the deck, a luscious patch of grass, miraculously flat, had enough room for a climbing frame and trampoline. A banana tree waved its glistening fronds from over the back fence. Everything about the place screamed happily ever after. Steve wasn't so sure, but was willing to go along with my enthusiasm.

The basket on the back seat emitted a regal meow. Obeying Rosie's pre-trip instructions, Rob carried Cleo, basket and all, through the gate. He went inside and lowered the basket onto the floor. (I'd known the house was meant to be ours the moment I slapped eyes on the carpet. We were destined to live with offensive floor coverings.) Carefully, slowly, he opened the lid. Rosie had warned us Cleo could be so disoriented from the trip she might cower in her carry case for hours.

A pair of black ears rose from the wicker rim, followed by two eyes, black whiskers and a nose. The eyes rolled sideways to inspect the shabby hallway, then upwards to check all people slaves were present. Cleo then sprang daintily from her bower and, like a sniper sussing out an enemy village, padded through the house, sniffing the carpet and investigating corners in every room.

In the bathroom her search for spiders under the decrepit claw-foot bath was rewarded with a satisfyingly crunchy snack. The kitchen revealed another treasure—a colony of hyperactive ants under the sink. With this much live-in livestock, the house was custom-made for her.

Cleo particularly approved of the French doors' ability to intensify solar rays. Yawning, she stretched across the doorway, her fur shimmering blue-black in the heat. Her eyes shrank to translucent slits while the human slaves heaved boxes and suitcases over the threshold, all the time trying not to trip over our Egyptian princess. No doubt her ancestors had dozed through similar scenes while the pyramids were being built.

Rosie had instructed us to keep Cleo inside for two days in case she panicked and attempted to escape back to Wellington. Basking happily in her personal tanning clinic, our cat showed no interest in cutting loose. The genes that had adapted to cope with the heat of ancient Egypt revelled in Auckland's subtropical climate.

✦

I hoped the rest of us would be able to follow Cleo's example and adjust to all the changes, but the fresh start had no hope in the marriage department. Steve's commute to Wellington was going to mean more time apart. We'd given up trying to reach across the valley of our differences and started having separate social lives. The friends I made he found offensively loud, while I found his friends unnervingly introspective. He set up camp on a sofa bed in the sunroom. We tried to kid ourselves that for the sake of the children we could still be friends, but not in *that* way.

Although Rob had been popular at his old school, its formal approach to learning had proved an uncomfortable match for him. I'd begun to dread perching on dwarf-sized chairs during parent interviews listening to twelve-year-old teachers drone on about Rob being bright but needing to work harder. Having spent most of my school career gazing out classroom windows admiring the quality of sunlight on distant trees (and once a pair of dogs demonstrating something I'd only ever seen in line drawings in a book about teenage health Mum had left on my bed), I sympathised entirely with Rob. The only difference between Rob and me was he *was* working hard at school. He was frustrated his Herculean efforts at reading and arithmetic were acknowledged with Cs and Ds. Even though his teachers were barely old enough to chew solids they had power and (like most dictators and children) knew they were right. I was tired of hearing them imply Rob had 'problems', not the least of which was a dead brother and unhappily married parents. They were unable to appreciate his unconventional methods of absorbing information and were too lazy or unimaginative to go out of their way to help him.

The Auckland move gave him a chance to try a more laid-back school, though I hadn't expected it to be quite so relaxed. Every surface, inside and out, was smothered with children's artwork in violent primary colours. The playground equipment (concrete pipes, giant wooden cable spools) resembled leftovers from major roadworks. His new teacher, Mrs Roberts, had a fuzz of red hair and aquamarine eyes with an other-worldly sparkle. With a tie-dye silk scarf looped over her shoulders she casually mentioned Rob's lovely aura.

'She's Alternative,' I explained to Rob as we scrambled through a giant pipe to get back to the car. 'Everything around here is, a bit.'

'What do you mean?'

'They don't expect you to work too hard. If you don't like pottery classes, you get an alternative, like dance or theatre. Nobody here knew Sam. You don't have to be the boy whose brother died anymore. Just be you.'

It had yet to occur to me that dance, theatre and pottery mightn't be a perfect match for a boy who'd built so many model aeroplanes his bedroom was a miniature version of the Battle of Britain. At the beach while other kids jumped mindlessly in the surf he spent hours constructing cities complete with drainage systems and overhead bridges. I should have realised such a child is unlikely to squeeze himself into tights and beg to play the prince in Swan Lake. Nevertheless, he was willing to give the new school a try.

The next challenge was finding someone trustworthy, lovable and entirely faultless to look after Lydia. Even though Jim had promised flexible hours I knew I'd have to show up at the office most days. My heart ached at the thought of leaving one-year-old Lydia with a stranger.

What I was looking for, I explained to the nanny agency, was a cross between Mary Poppins and the Virgin Mary. The nanny agent laughed, but it wasn't the cynical snort of someone who was about to offer a child molester in nanny's clothing. It was a crystalline laugh of recognition. 'I have that exact person on my books,' she said. 'Her name is Anne Marie, and I can hardly believe this, but she's actually available. She has people lining up asking her to work for them, though. You'll have to find out if she likes you first.'

The *nanny* interviews *us*?

Anne Marie's credentials couldn't have been better. Not only had she trained at the prestigious Norland nanny school in London, she'd raised four children of her own.

I was awestruck when she appeared on our doorstep wearing a combination of pastel pink and white devoid of a single stain. Her shoes glowed like a pair of snowballs. Her brown eyes were warm, though, especially when she saw Lydia (who adored Anne Marie on the spot). When the baby beamed a welcome, raised her chubby arms and wrapped them around Anne Marie's neck I experienced the primitive stab of jealousy every working mother feels when she hands her child over to a care giver.

After a day of anxious waiting the phone rang. Anne Marie said she was willing to take us on.

I could hardly believe my luck to be working on a newspaper again. I'd forgotten how much I'd missed the sad/funny/clever misfits who inhabit newsrooms. Like a lost wanderer returned to her tribe, I finally belonged again—alongside all the other outsiders who'd chosen journalism because no other employer would tolerate their quirky antisocial ways.

I loved Mary, the glamorous, self-doubting Irish fashion writer, and Colin, the rock reporter whose sexy melancholy had women sticking to him like plasters. Tina, the features editor, was highly strung, and could erupt into platinum rages. Yet every now and then her ice-queen mask melted to reveal a heart that was passionately pure.

Nicole, the television writer, was beautiful and blonde, with legs she'd stolen from Marlene Dietrich. I assumed Nicole wouldn't waste her time with mere humans. But she'd been a teenage bride like me, and was wading through a divorce and custody swamp. Nicole was off-beat and wounded like the rest of us, and tough as a terrier when she sunk her teeth into a story. I adored them all.

I also revelled in wearing proper clothes again. For the past decade my wardrobe had consisted of trackpants, maternity clothes and dressing-gowns (in tones of mostly grey, black and brown). It was exhilarating to slip into a fuchsia-coloured suit with a cobalt blue bowtie (in retrospect a crime against fashion). Applying makeup every morning and learning to walk in shoes with heels again was thrilling. I felt like Cinderella, who'd just found out the ball wasn't over after all. The music was louder, the guests were zanier and I was invited back to collect my size 10C glass slipper and get back on the floor.

As a general features writer, I didn't care what stories they were going to assign me. I'd have been grateful if they'd asked me to write about bedbugs. To my astonishment, Jim and Tina trusted my abilities beyond logic. They assigned me interviews with international performers like James Taylor and Michael Crawford, and writers such as Margaret Atwood and Terry Pratchett. Crazier still, they sent me to meet our nation's porcine prime minister and even (for heaven's sake) the President of Ireland, Mary Robinson. I soon learnt that the more elevated on the global stage people are the more humble and approachable they tend to be, despite the bewildering jet lag involved in getting to our agricultural outpost. Mary Robinson was more animated when she talked about helping her kids do homework around their kitchen table than anything else we discussed. (Which was just as well. International politics was hardly my beat.)

Jim also had me writing editorials, where I'd switch into pipe-and-slippers mode and hammer out the paper's views on everything from atomic energy to zoos. Producing one of those within the required forty minutes was the equivalent of being spun inside a microwave oven on high.

Distraught with panic one morning, I wrote an entire leader raging against the perils of 'alcahol'. Either my fingers fumbled on the typewriter keys or all those years gazing out of classroom windows had finally come home to roost. My bizarre spelling slipped through the subeditors (spellcheck was yet to be invented), no doubt lowering the newspaper's status to litter-box liner for several weeks. To my disbelief and eternal gratitude Jim and Tina refrained from throwing me back on the streets. They kept on nodding, smiling and tossing plum stories my way. Maybe all the real journalists had caught some form of plague through drinking too much and sleeping with each other and died off.

But much as I loved the office the best part of the day was when I slid the key in the front door of the old cottage to see Cleo prancing down the hall to greet me with a welcome meow.

I'd started to notice Cleo was developing her language skills. Apart from the charming *hello* meow she gave whenever any of us arrived home, and the polite mew when someone picked her up, there was the assertive *let me come in, you heartless morons!* wail when she was shut out. She had better manners than the four of us put together. Whenever anyone opened a door to let her in she always responded with a clipped and demure *thank you* as she sailed past.

Mealtimes, especially if they were delayed, reduced her to a stream of alley cat language. Standing in front of the fridge she'd yowl, *If you don't feed me right now I'm going to jump on your head and tattoo your eyeballs.*

Cleo moved houses and cities without so much as a twitch of a whisker. I worried that living on a street for the first time she might get run over—especially with her penchant for after-dark expeditions. Who'd see a black cat against a darkened street? Once again I was underestimating her. She had a traffic-smart gene, no doubt inherited from her father.

After a raucous fight with a larger cat under the house one night she appeared at the front door with a torn ear. I tried to keep her inside after that, but every night she wailed until I let her out. Even though the fight had been serious, she must have established her territory with it. We never heard another scrap.

Her bird-hunting skills shifted to new levels. The shoes in my wardrobe were stuffed with tiny corpses and clusters of feathers. After persistent begging from the kids, I dug a hole in the corner of the back garden and fitted it with a fishpond and water plants. The resident goldfish became a voyeuristic fixation for Cleo. I doubted they'd survive past Christmas. Fortunately, they were wily enough to spend most of their waking hours up to no good under the lily pads. They made so many babies I wondered if there was such a thing as goldfish contraception.

Cleo demonstrated how good manners and charm can coexist under one skin, along with back-street resilience. Following her example, I tried to shrug off embarrassing moments at work (for example, when I took too long to realise the man panting on the other end of the phone line hadn't been for a run but was indulging in a less wholesome activity. Or the time I had to field dozens of calls after getting the names of two fashion models confused and captioning a classy one with a slutty one's name.) Like Cleo on the rare occasions she slipped off a fence to tumble into the hydrangeas, I endured the humiliation, shook it off, hoped I wouldn't be stupid enough to repeat the mistake—and prayed lawyers wouldn't be involved.

Over the following year, Steve and I settled into a pattern of avoiding each other when he was at home. According to statistics, women are far more likely to end a relationship than men. I've never been a fan of statistics. Another theory is that men who want to end relationships make themselves impossible to live with, so the woman is forced into ending it.

Our marriage was like a bowl of egg whites. We'd both sweated over it, whipping air through, occasionally working it into peaks. At times it looked like we might make a decent meringue out of it, but as any cook knows, if you whip egg whites too long, if you try too hard, they simply go flat.

Things came to a head one afternoon when I arrived home from work. He was standing in the driveway. I can't remember exactly what the conversation was about, probably something trivial, like who'd left the butter on the bench so Cleo could get it. It escalated into an argument—and we *never* argued. Suddenly we were talking about divorce.

We both knew he couldn't go on sleeping in the sunroom the rest of his days. Nevertheless, it was shocking to finally have the D word out in the open.

Steve looked sideways at a red bottlebrush flower and said he wanted to keep lawyers out of it as much as possible. The flower nodded agreement. A car backfired further down the street. The front garden seemed an unlikely place to be having such a conversation. But where *do* people talk about divorce? Certainly not candle-lit restaurants or incense-scented bedrooms, as far as I knew.

He said he'd move out next week. He wanted to take the painting of yachts that was in the hallway if I didn't mind, and some other things as well. I was shocked at how carefully he'd thought it through, though realistically he'd had years to mull it over. He wanted the kids fifty-fifty and suggested we'd sort the money out later.

Oh, and I could keep the cat.

Openness

The only people less enlightened than those who claim not to be
cat people are those who swear they're strictly dog people

The house was hollow as a cave at night without children sighing and turning in their beds. I worried if Rob needed help with his English homework, if Steve was watching Lydia closely enough. At two and a half years of age, she was all confidence and no sense. Cleo wasn't happy about it, either. She carried their socks around and slept on their beds.

I made excuses to see them during Steve's allocated week, collecting Lydia from daycare, driving Rob to Sea Scouts. I tried to make the most of the empty hours, rearranging the bathroom cupboards, reworking feature articles, but my imagination refused to rest. It hovered like a giant telescope in the sky, trained on their every move—was Rob watching for cars before he climbed on the school bus? Was Lydia catching a virus? I wondered if they sensed my presence.

Sam's photo beamed at me from the mantelpiece. A cheeky smirk. I thought about the Ford Escort woman. Her memory of Sam would be different. I accepted now she wasn't at fault. I wondered what I'd have done in her shoes. Moved to another country, tried to bury myself in a new identity. Out late one night with Rob, collecting him from a Sea Scout meeting, I'd run over a cat. It'd happened so suddenly. A flash of white fur, a thump and a grinding thud as the wheel crunched into bone. There was no way I could've stopped in time. The woman would've felt the same. Shocked, sick with remorse, I stopped the car. The animal was crushed, lifeless. I felt wretched enough running over a cat. Killing a child would be infinitely worse.

Sometimes it seemed I was destined to lose children one way or another. I'd never liked self-pity. Undignified, tiresome. I'd begun to discover ways out of it. One was to accept invitations to meet grieving parents, and interview people experiencing loss. Their trauma was often recent and more raw than my own. On the few occasions I was able to offer reassurance, my pain was replaced with a sense of doing something vaguely worthwhile. The past five years had informed me about human sorrow. While no two griefs are the same, nobody understands suffering like those who've been there.

◆

The shrink had a box of tissues on her table. Tears were her trade. Not wanting to give the impression I was one of her run-of-the-mill weepy clients I was determined to keep my eyes dry.

'What you need,' she said, crossing her legs and gazing through her salmon-pink lenses, 'is a fresh start, something to boost your self-esteem.'

Even though I wasn't crying, my body badly needed to ooze. My nose started streaming uncontrollably. I glanced longingly at the tissues, but reaching for them would be an admission of defeat. The only alternative was to emit loud regular sniffs.

'Do you know what would do you the world of good?' she asked, sinking into a chair carefully positioned under a Rothko print in pastel pinks and yellows. Presumably the painting was intended to soothe anguished clients with its gentle shades. It probably worked for those who didn't realise poor Rothko succumbed to depression and killed himself. 'A one-night stand.'

Her words sailed across the room and exploded in my ears like missiles. Mum (due to a range of sexual hang-ups of her own not worth delving into here) had raised me from the cradle to treat my body as a temple, preferably open to only one dreary but dependable worshipper for my entire life.

'You mean finding a man I have nothing in common with but am mildly attracted to and just sleeping with him for the sake of it?'

She nodded. The shrink was obviously mad. She wanted me to die of guilt.

'It would be a healthy way to start a new phase of life,' she said.

'What about the kids?' I asked.

'They needn't find out,' she said. 'It's nothing to do with them. Arrange it for one of the weekends when your ex-husband has custody.'

Arrange it? People *arrange* one-night stands? She asked me to make up a list of potential victims. The only blokes I met were at work. Male journalists are unbelievably indiscreet. I had no desire to be added to the list of women in the office who 'do it with anyone'. A couple of friends' husbands had dismayed me by turning up at the house and thoughtfully offering their services, but I was in no way willing to betray my women friends. My list was blank.

'Good luck,' said the shrink, smiling as I scribbled a shaky signature on the cheque. 'And remember, be *open*.'

✦

An opportunity to put her advice into practice turned up a few weeks later when Mary the fashion writer set me up on a date to accompany her friend to a fund-raising dinner. Mary assured me I'd love Nigel, who was recently divorced from his second wife, though not for the usual reasons of being disgusting to live with and a total reject. I'd read about Nigel's activities in our business pages. He was the corporate equivalent of a giant with an eating disorder, a compulsive devourer of small companies. He was an unfamiliar type, potentially dull, if all he could talk about was money. But I was used to interviewing people. I assured myself I could draw out the interesting side of a house spider if necessary. Mary said Nigel had ticks in all the right boxes. I wasn't sure what she meant. It was years since I'd been on a date. The rules must've changed. In fact, there was only one rule back in the old days—don't let him go all the way unless he's at least hinted he might want to marry you. During the years I'd spent buried in suburbia, dating seemed to have turned into a clinical cross between supermarket shopping and animal husbandry.

The night of the date arrived. I was so nervous my hands were trembling. Cleo always liked to supervise my clumsy attempts to apply makeup. She sprang up on to the bathroom vanity as I opened the makeup drawer—one of Cleo's favourite places in the entire house. Her passion for makeup must've been a throw back to her Egyptian heritage. Given half a chance, she'd steal a sable brush, run away and de-hair it bristle by bristle under my bed. Cleo jumped into the drawer and patted the shiny pots of eye shadow. She seemed to favour purple tonight. With no other beauty consultant available, it was logical to take her advice. She mewed encouragement as I applied two brooding streaks of shadow to my eyelids. The effect was more post encounter with Muhammad Ali than cocktails with Mark Anthony, but I was running out of time. Cleo toyed idly with my lipstick, a lurid crimson, which I snatched from her paws.

'What do you think?' I asked, applying a final circle of lipstick.

Sitting on her hind legs with her front paws arranged as neatly as a ballet dancer's, Cleo put her head on one side and winked. She approved. I doubted my legs would be able to hold me up long enough for the evening to ever qualify as a one-night stand, if that's what it was going to be.

Sensing my nerves, Cleo took over the meet-and-greet role, her tail curled graciously as she trotted towards Nigel. He was unusually tall and regal, with a sandy moustache. I wasn't confident facial hair was part of my one-night-stand scenario, but inside my head the shrink's voice echoed. 'Be *open!*'

'A cat!' Nigel's eyebrows ricocheted like lines on a stock market chart. 'I'm allergic.'

'Oh,' I said, lowering her to the floor, 'sorry.'

Unphased by Nigel's reaction, Cleo stood on her toes and arched her back prettily. She arranged her tail in a gracious curl as she escorted him to the living room. Trotting ahead of us, Cleo really was the perfect hostess. The back of Nigel's suit, I noticed, was frighteningly free of creases.

I guided him toward the most pristine cushion on the sofa and asked if he'd like a drink.

'Chardonnay would be excellent,' he said, perching on the sofa arm. I couldn't blame the poor man for protecting his Armani threads from our crumbs and cola stains.

While the fridge contained an assortment of drinks ranging from milk to cordial, Chardonnay wasn't among them. The closest on offer was a half empty cardboard box of Riesling. Depressing the plastic plunger, I hoped Nigel wouldn't notice.

He seemed agitated, crossing and uncrossing his long scissor legs. Cleo settled a few inches from his feet and fixed her eyes on him like interrogation lights.

'The problem with cats,' he announced as I handed him a wineglass smudged with fingerprints, 'is they always like me.'

Cleo shuffled closer to him as he spoke and intensified her gaze, then hoisted her back leg aloft and proceeded to lick her most private parts.

'Shoooo, Cleo!' I growled. But Cleo resented being spoken to as if she was a mere animal. She rolled on her back and writhed seductively at Nigel.

'There's a compliment,' I said. 'She wants you to rub her tummy.'

'Oh I couldn't do that,' he said, drawing a green paisley handkerchief from his pocket and dabbing his moustache. 'The allergy, you see. In fact, you know, I think I'm going to . . .'

The curtains trembled in the aftershocks of Nigel's sneeze. Startled, Cleo leapt to her paws, dug her claws dug into the carpet, and bushed out her tail.

'Don't worry, I'll shut her in the back,' I said.

When I bent over to collect the cat she slithered out of my grasp and scrambled up the bookshelves. Confident I couldn't reach her and Nigel wouldn't try, she strutted along the top shelf, tapping a precious Victorian vase with her tail. Cleo was extremely pleased with herself.

'You're not getting away with this!' I muttered, dragging a dining chair toward the shelves. The instant I stood on the chair and reached for her, Cleo bounded down from the shelves on to Nigel's lap. He emitted a boyish yelp and I lunged and got my hands around Cleo's belly. But she wasn't surrendering without a fight. Sinking her claws into the Nigel's thighs for leverage, man and cat emitted a simultaneous yowl.

'I'm so sorry,' I said, unhooking each claw while Nigel focussed valiantly on the ceiling.

I returned from shutting Cleo away to find Nigel sneezing discreetly into his handkerchief.

'The thing is,' he said, pocketing the handkerchief and absentmindedly brushing real and imaginary cat hair off the sofa's arm, 'I'm really a dog person.'

'So am I,' I said, trying to improve the atmosphere. 'At least, technically speaking. We have a beautiful golden retriever, but she's gone to live with my mother. She's pretty old now. The dog, I mean.'

'Dogs are less aggressive,' he added. 'When I was a kid I was attacked by a cat.'

'Really?' I said.

'Yes, I was on my bike on my paper round and this wild cat threw itself at me.'

I tried not to smile at the image of a mini version of Excellent Nigel pedalling the streets of Whakatane, being felled by a murderous tabby. Nevertheless, it was clear Nigel's phobia sprang from deep, Freudian waters. It wasn't a mere quirk Cleo and I would be able to iron out in one night.

'Do you think the experience might've given you the drive and determination to become a successful businessman?' I asked, hating myself for employing pop psychology to make a sarcastic joke, but Nigel seemed to consider the question seriously.

'You know I've never thought of it that way, but you're probably right,' he said, reassembling some of his dignity. 'I wouldn't be where I am today if it hadn't been for that cat attack.'

He was reminding himself aloud to tell the hack ghost currently writing his autobiography *Nigel's Nine Notches to Excellence* to include the cat attack when I noticed the bedroom door glide ajar. A four-legged shadow wafted into view. Cleo could open just about any door that wasn't locked and bolted.

As Nigel warmed to recounting his triumph over childhood trauma, Cleo slithered like a commando along the edge of the skirting board. Invisible to him, she crouched in the shade of the bookshelves, and listened to details of a cat nightmare he'd suffered over two decades ago. She was still as a stone with a Cheshire cat grin settled on her lips.

Suddenly, Cleo darted out of her hiding place and ran at Nigel. In a single movement she sprang on to his lap, sending his wine glass flying through the air. Nigel emitted a roar straight from his primeval core. Horrified, I leapt to try and catch the glass, but everything was happening in slow motion. As my hand swiped at the glass it tumbled toward the carpet, drenching us both in a wine fountain.

Nigel stood up and brushed his trousers with agitated strokes. I grabbed paper towels from the kitchen and dabbed the blotches on his knees, while he attended to the more intimate areas.

'I'm so sorry!' I cried.

'Excellent,' he muttered, sinking back into the sofa and crossing his legs. Before there was time to stop her Cleo climbed on his shoulder and wove herself in a knot around his neck.

'She seems to like you,' I said. 'Sorry—your allergy. Here, let me take her.'

'No, seriously,' Nigel sputtered, disentangling Cleo and arranging her uncomfortably on his knees. 'I'm quite comfortable. She can probably smell Rex on me. He's my Doberman. A very athletic, straightforward dog.'

'Yes,' I said, wondering if we'd ever progress towards anything that could be classified as conversation. 'Dogs are . . . straightforward.'

'Dogs are more like men in that respect,' said Nigel. 'Whereas cats are more like women, don't you think? You could write a book about that.'

Nigel's face suddenly turned the colour of Australian Shiraz. As Cleo dived on the floor and disappeared down the hall Nigel's eyes rolled towards the ceiling. For a dreadful moment he appeared to be having one of those allergic reactions that seize people's throats up.

'Are you okay?' I asked.

He raised his hands and his mouth curled down in disgust. 'Your cat,' he whispered. 'Just. Peed. On. Me.'

Nigel insisted on returning to his apartment to change his suit. While he was gone I searched Cleo's favourite hiding places under the bed and in the wardrobe to punish her, but she'd successfully dematerialised. Satisfied the evening was drained of potential romance, Cleo had melted into the walls.

Later I spotted the silhouette of a cat on the roof. Its eyes shone down at me like lighthouse beams. Even from that distance, I could see a glow of satisfaction in them.

✦

If nothing else, the one-night stand that wasn't made a good story to share with Mum when she phoned. She sounded distracted. Her outings with Rata were getting challenging. When they'd walked down a hill to a beach at the weekend, Rata hadn't been able to get back up the slope. Mum said she'd had to carry Rata up the hill. Rata was no small animal. How Mum had managed to lift her was beyond me. The vet had diagnosed emphysema.

At work on Monday morning Nicole asked if I'd do her a favour. Her flatmate was getting married in a couple of weeks. He and his bride were from the States and didn't know enough people to make up a decent wedding celebration.

'*Please* come along?' she begged. 'You won't have to stay more than an hour. Just long enough to make the room look fuller.'

Her confidence that my presence could overflow an empty room was hardly flattering. I wasn't keen on being a one-woman rent-a-crowd. But we both knew I had nothing else to do on Friday nights, except maybe shovel Lego bricks back in their boxes while the children were at their father's.

'Pleeeeease?'

The couple had arranged to get married at sunset on the steps of the city museum. As the sun hovered like a commitment-phobe on the horizon I locked the car and climbed the hill to the museum. Glancing up, I saw the bridal party. She looked like Barbie. He looked like Ken. But it was the best man who caught my eye. He was stunningly good-looking. Not just handsome in an ordinary aftershave advertisement way, but glowingly breathtaking in the manner of a Greek god. Or gay man.

Gay, of course, I thought, admiring the sweep of well-groomed hair over the wide, tanned forehead, and the broad shoulders accentuated by a well-cut suit. Or married. If not, most definitely girlfriended.

To say it was love at first sight would be exaggerating. Lust at first sight would be more accurate. As the sunset glinted on his aviator glasses and I saw his flashing blue eyes I was overcome by another sensation that was less carnal and even more powerful—a sense of recognition. If we hadn't met before in this life, we'd almost certainly known each other in earlier lifetimes. Even though he was a stranger, I felt I knew him at a deep level.

The wedding reception was held at the home of Sir Edmund Hillary. Apparently the groom worked with someone who was related to the famous mountaineer. Sir Ed, who was away doing something bold and heroic on the other side of the world, had graciously opened his home to the wedding party. It was a modest, understated home, not unlike the man himself. The walls were a soft yellow and the decor extremely tasteful. Every painting, every hand-woven rug, seemed to hold a story of great meaning to its owner.

By the time the gay/married/girlfriended best man walked over and introduced himself as Philip with one 'l' I was over him. He was too good-looking to be real. When I discovered the reason for his athletic profile (freshly honed from eight years in the army) and that he'd just entered the professional arena of banking, it was obvious we had no future. To thrash the final nail on its head, he confessed his age. Twenty-six. Practically a baby, he was eight years younger than me. Unmarried, undivorced and childless, he seemed to spring from a completely different (still possibly gay) world. I was practically his mother. Nevertheless, he seemed a nice young man, devoid of the creepy complexities so many males were burdened with. And I hadn't forgotten the shrink's advice. If I drank a lot of wine and didn't tell a soul, and he was crazy (or desperate) enough to consider it, he had definite one-night-stand potential.

I told him I didn't go out much at night, but I did do lunch. I scribbled my work number on a paper napkin. He seemed startled by my offer. Not that he had any reason to. I was more than happy to take on the role of Mother Confessor and counsel the poor boy on his love life. Or just be friends. I was O-pen.

Next morning at work I studied the phone. No one called, except for a disgruntled reader and the same old Heavy Breather in his phone box. It didn't ring significantly the next day, or the next week either. By the time the third week came around I'd forgotten all about Philip with one 'l'. Which is why, when he eventually *did* call, he had to remind me who he was and how we'd met at the wedding.

'Oh, God, it's that army-banking kid,' I sighed after we'd hung up.

'Maybe he wants instructions on how to find the nearest kindergarten,' Nicole said.

'He's invited me to a play,' I said.

'A play*ground*?'

'No, a proper play. A theatre dinner, or a dinner theatre or something.'

'I have to warn you . . .' Nicole said, pointing her pen at me. 'Apart from the age difference . . .'

'You don't have to warn me. He just wants someone to talk to.'

'He's way too conservative for you.'

Red flags have been waved in my face at several important crossroads, resulting in profoundly unimaginable consequences. One was at primary school, when a bossy art teacher instructed the class that if *any*body dared put their fingers in her wet pottery clay they would be in bigger trouble than anyone in this god-fearing world could imagine. Another was at journalism school, when a tutor said in unequivocal words I had no future whatsoever as a columnist. As I listened to Nicole, a familiar, thistly sensation prickled the base of my spine. Its message was the same as the last two times: *You think so, do you? Well, let's see about that.*

After work that day I flitted through the part of town famed for strip clubs and op shops and picked up the perfect outfit to impress a conservative young banker—a black satin Chinese pant-suit with flamboyantly embroidered trimmings. It was gorgeous.

 The Kiss

Nothing is more damply magical than a kitten's kiss

Cats kiss. Cleo did it all the time. It starts with a gentle head butt, a raising of the chin, a narrowing of the eyes, followed by a fleeting union of lips. Hormones are presumably exchanged. Nothing beyond that is asked, except perhaps a soothing stroke. A cat kiss is complete in itself.

Philip with one 'l' was late. Too late to be even considered half-fashionable. He'd obviously forgotten that he'd asked me out to see some trashy play, or that I'd gone out of my way to arrange it for a weekend the kids were at Steve's. I was *that* forgettable. Hot rashes of emotion prickled up and down the back of my Chinese jacket. My skin stuck to the unbreathable fabric, which was proving itself not even a distant cousin of any upmarket natural fibre. Insult flared to anger. I didn't want to see him, anyway. What on earth would we have to talk about? To think I'd gone to the trouble of buying a new outfit.

If Philip with one 'l' had the nerve to show up now I'd demonstrate Helen could be spelt with two 'll's. Nicole and Mary would have words to say about this at work on Monday. He's not worth it. You're too good for him. What a dick.

Darker thoughts nudged to mind as I sat on the bed and shook off one of the dressy sandals that matched the Chinese outfit perfectly. Maybe he had a genuine excuse for not turning up, like catching a glimpse of his own reflection in a shop window and smashing into a lamp post.

Truth was, I had no reason to like him enough to care. I was content orbiting kids and work every day. They were the centre of my universe. Every week that we survived without sore throats, crises at school or disturbing mail in spidery backhanded writing from a deranged reader was a miracle. It didn't matter if ninety per cent of my remaining world consisted of black holes. The shrink was nuts suggesting all that one-night-stand rubbish. Boy, that woman had issues. I should've been shrinking her, not the other way around.

Cleo sprang onto the bed, made one of her squeaking noises and snuggled into my lap. *I'm here, I'm here,* she purred. Calm washed over me like baby shampoo. Hurt and outrage shrank until they weren't much bigger than a pair of bubbles resting in the bathroom plughole. Kicking off the other sandal, I smiled (partly from relief—they were giving me blisters, anyway). The only damage was to my ego. There was nothing wrong with a night at home in front of the fire with Cleo after a long working week. In fact, it was downright welcome.

I carried Cleo down the hall. She watched expectantly while I crouched at the fireplace and arranged the kindling in an uncertain teepee. We were both startled by urgent hammering on the front door.

'I've been driving around the neighbourhood for ages,' Philip said as soon as I opened the door. 'I knocked on the door of 33 *Albany* Road. It's the street parallel to this one. The woman there was confused. In fact so was I. It took me a while to work out you're *Ardmore* Road . . .'

So. Not only was he too young and conservative—he wasn't in danger of becoming the world's next Mastermind either. Just as I was starting to feel irritated, I noticed his face. His eyes were trailing up and down my Chinese suit with the look of someone witnessing the aftermath of mass terrorism.

'You don't like it?' I said, suddenly. 'I can change into something . . . more conventional, if you like.'

Philip didn't object. I was profoundly, unspeakably insulted. Thrusting Cleo into his arms, I hurried back into the bedroom. On the other hand, I thought, changing into a brown skirt and cream blouse, maybe I should be relieved he was honest enough to imply he'd rather re-enact a scenario from the Vietnam war than appear in public with me wearing the Asian rhapsody.

'Nice cat,' he said, as we headed out the door.

We were late for the play. Sitting in the shadows watching an appallingly amateurish version of *Cat On a Hot Tin Roof* I quietly assembled a list of why this was a ridiculous choice, even for a one-night stand: he was hardly out of high school; he couldn't have made more screwed-up career choices if he'd tried (the army *and* banking?!); he had bad taste in plays; he was unable to appreciate my approach to fashion.

I wasn't that shook on *his* clothes, come to think of it. His shoes were so shiny you could pluck your eyebrows in them. The striped shirt, the corduroy trousers, the carefully chosen leather belt. It was all straight out of some old fogey's catalogue.

Yet there was no doubt he looked good in that stuff. He smelt fresh as an alpine forest, compared to male journalists, who invariably reeked of booze, cigarettes and substances I preferred not to know about. His eyes flared like blue gas flames when he laughed at my jokes (possibly too loudly). One of my jokes was about the inadequate snobs who drive European cars. I'd been too traumatised by our dash to the theatre to notice what sort of car he drove. The satirical twinkle when, after the show, he opened the passenger door of his elderly Audi, was nothing short of admirable.

He was obviously a very pleasant young man who probably wanted to download his love-life woes on a pair of understanding ears. There was no harm offering him friendship. I invited him inside for coffee.

'I'd like to,' he said. 'But I don't generally drink caffeine this late at night. Do you have any herb teas?'

While I knew a few people at work who drank herbal teas, I doubted they were the type he was talking about.

'Sorry, I only have black tea.'

The house was unusually quiet without the children. Even when they were asleep I was aware of their shifting blankets and dream-laden sighs. I kicked my shoes off and clattered through the kitchen cupboards, searching for a pair of cups that matched.

'Interesting cat,' I heard from the other room. 'She's almost like a person.'

Carrying the tray with two tea bags cunningly concealed in a teapot and the cracked cup on my side I was surprised at the vignette in the living room. A purring Cleo wound herself through Philip's legs, leapt onto his knees, climbed his shirt and applied neat licks over his chin. Never before had Cleo warmed so affectionately to a stranger.

'Sorry, I'll put her away,' I said.

'No, she's fine,' he said, tenderly running his hand over the mound of her spine. 'You're a good cat, aren't you? So tell me about the kids.'

I stiffened. He had just blundered into No Go Territory. Of course I'd made no secret of the fact I had kids. They were as much part of me as my hands and feet. I couldn't have hidden their existence even if I'd wanted to. Everything about the house screamed 'Kids!' The living room was ankle deep in Lego bricks. Lydia's fauvist playgroup artwork was cellotaped to the kitchen cupboards. Rob's school bag lay like a drunk on the floor outside his room.

The kids were the core of my life, so precious I'd tear my heart out for them. He had no right to ask about them. They had nothing to do with a potential one-night stand who was rapidly losing any chance of becoming one.

'So tell me about your life,' I replied. 'Ever been married?'

He went blank, as if I was asking if he'd ever dressed up in fish-net stockings and lip-synched to Judy Garland.

'No.'

'Kids?'

He shook his head, his smile vaguely bewildered.

'So you're having girlfriend trouble?'

Cleo, having finished with his chin, moved on to his ears.

'No, apart from the fact I don't have one. How about some music?'

Music? He wanted to be interrogated to *music*? Without waiting for an answer he sifted through my record collection and put on my latest purchase and current favourite, Ella Fitzgerald and Louis Armstrong singing 'Can't We Be Friends?'

Philip obviously had some kind of problem. Why else would he be here? I was going to have to muster all my journalistic skills to get him to unravel his woes, so he could pack up, go home and let us both get some sleep.

'Would you like to dance?' he asked.

'What?! Here?'

'Why not?'

Now it was getting silly. Still, if I danced with him he might be satisfied and go home. Standing up, I put my damp, flustered hand in his cool, dry one and lurched painfully over the Lego bricks. If I'd known the room would be transformed into a ballroom I'd have put the kids' toys away and kept my shoes on.

As Ella's liquid voice wrapped the room in a haze of sensuality I noticed his excellent sense of rhythm (years of marching on parade grounds probably had something to do with it). And his body, as it brushed offhandedly against mine, seemed to be encased in some kind of metal suit. Until I realised the curves were too well formed to be metal. They were made of a material totally unfamiliar to me—lean muscle.

'So how old are the kids?' he asked.

Oh no. What was it with him and the kids?

'Nearly three and twelve.'

Painfully, patiently, he dragged their names out of me, what they liked to do at weekends and how they handled having parents who were separated. I changed the subject, and we danced in silence for a while. He did have an exceptional body—but either he was clumsy, or he was deliberately moving closer. With the shrink's words ringing in my ears, I didn't flinch when he lowered his god-like head and pressed his lips onto mine.

The room whirled in a kaleidoscope of toys, cups and saucers against apricot-coloured walls. Cleo looked on approvingly as I savoured the magical kiss. Soft, damp and luscious. It was perfect, beyond perfect. *Too* perfect!

I stopped swaying to the music and straightened my spine. No, dammit! This wasn't how things were meant to happen. The whole point of the night was that I was supposed to be running the show. This man-boy had no right to schmooze with Cleo and then ask me to dance. As for all that probing about the kids . . .

He froze, too. At least he was sensitive enough to notice my mood had changed.

'Shall we go to the bedroom?' he said softly.

For several moments, possibly six months or twelve hundred years, I couldn't summon up a response. She the unshockable was—there was no other word for it—shocked.

'It's not that I don't *like* you . . .' I said, stepping backwards.

He tensed like a cardboard cut-out doll.

'In fact, I'd probably sleep with you if I *didn't* like you. At least that's what my shrink says I should be doing . . .'

He was starting to look almost as horrified as he'd been at the sight of the Chinese pant-suit.

'The thing is, I like you too much to sleep with you . . .'

He stood stunned, like he'd wandered into a friendly camp and was suddenly under enemy fire. It was beginning to dawn on me that probably no woman in the multi-dimensional universe had ever turned down the opportunity to exchange bodily fluids with such a suntanned Adonis.

'It's getting incredibly . . . late . . . and I don't know about you but I'm bushed by the end of the week.'

'Can I call you sometime?' he asked icily, as he gathered up his jacket and I escorted him to the door with Cleo in our wake.

'No. I mean, yes. Yes. Definitely. Um. Goodnight.'

I closed the door softly but firmly. Cleo flicked her tail at me and stalked down the hall.

Exposure

In the face of real danger a cat freezes.

'He made you change your outfit?!' Nicole was trying to control the volume of her laughter, so only half the newsroom could hear.

'He didn't *make* me,' I said, giggling, yet already regretting the capacity women have to be mercilessly indiscreet about their intimate encounters with men. Especially when somebody makes a fool of himself. Except this time the personal humiliation involved was mine.

If only I'd been wise enough to have said 'fine' when she'd asked how the date went and left it at that. But then she would have suspected serious emotional entanglement, and nothing could be further from the truth. 'He just looked mortified, so I offered to change.'

'*Seriously?* I wouldn't have bothered.'

The annoying thing was, Nicole would never *have* to bother. She could walk down the street in her grandmother's dressing-gown and hair rollers and still turn every male head within a square mile.

'And it was a *terrible* play! There were so many ham actors you could've made a pork roast. Honestly, he has no idea . . .'

'Probably trying to impress you. Did you . . . did he try to . . . take things further?'

'Course not!' I said, my face suddenly feeling like it was in a sauna. The kiss was nothing. An aberration best deleted from conversation and memory. 'I think he's just lonely. I won't be seeing him again, anyway. Too young and boring.'

'Told you so,' said Nicole, her fingers galloping over her keyboard. 'Got to get this story in by eleven o'clock, and I haven't done a word.'

'What would a guy like that want with an old solo mum with two kids, anyway?' I muttered, trying to decipher a notepad of shorthand that had made perfect sense when I'd scribbled down the words of a fading international author the previous week. The jottings now resembled ancient Arabic. 'He must have a screw loose.'

'Who?' said Nicole, her attention focused on finding the home number of an elusive television director she needed to interrogate.

'The boy.'

'Oh, the Toy Boy. Forget him.'

Yes. That's what he was. Toy Boy, an excellent, freshly invented expression with a cleansing ring to it, like mouth-wash. With a label like that he could be sealed in cellophane, put in a box and shut away as one of life's more regrettable experiments.

Tina slid a list of story ideas onto my desk. At the bottom of the list she'd scrawled 'Halloween feature. Find some way to make this interesting. We did pumpkins last year. Awful!'

Work. Where would I be without it? There was no better anaesthetic.

'Phone call for you, Helen,' Mike, one of the nosier political reporters, shouted across the room. 'Some snooty-sounding bloke. It's come through on my line for some reason. I'll transfer it to you.'

There's an artform to how a woman journalist answers her phone. She must sound fresh and approachable, in case the caller has a story that has potential to wind up on the cover of *Newsweek*, which is about as likely as dinosaurs stirring themselves out of their graves and plodding through suburban neighbourhoods. And there must also be a Teflon edge to her tone, in case it is a nutter or the Heavy Breather.

'Thank you for last night,' the voice was measured and formal.

'Oh!' I said, stupidly.

Nicole's fingers froze mid-air over her keyboard. She put her head to one side and whispered, '*Who is it?*' Her instinct for a story was always spot-on.

I nestled the phone under my chin and mimed 'one l' with my fingers.

'I had a great time,' he continued.

Oh God. He was lying. He would've had more fun giving blood.

'So did I.'

Nicole rolled her eyes and shook her head at me slowly.

'Sorry the play wasn't up to scratch,' he said.

'It was fine, honestly . . .'

Nicole took a biro from her desktop and ran it like an imitation scalpel across her neck.

'I was wondering if you'd like to go out for dinner next weekend?' he asked.

Shock rippled through me and settled on my feet like a pair of leaden shoes.

'I've got the kids next weekend,' I said, cool and sensible. Nicole nodded approval and resumed her keyboard tattoo. That was it. Finito. No joy, toy boy.

'What about the following weekend?' he asked.

'Oh!' my lead shoes turned molten hot. 'Well, no. I don't think I'm doing anything.'

Nicole towered over me, the steam from her nostrils almost visible.

'Good. How about seven thirty Saturday?'

'Sounds good.'

'See you then.'

'*Damn!*' I muttered, clattering the receiver down.

'Why didn't you say no?' asked Nicole, my frustrated life coach.

'I don't know. Couldn't think of an excuse.'

'Don't you know "no" is the new "yes"? If you say no to something you don't want to do now it saves you having to go through all sorts of demoralising situations in the future. Do you seriously want to go out with someone who made you change your clothes?'

'What can I do?'

'Call him back a couple of days before the date and say your aunt died and you have to go home to the funeral.'

'Good idea. I'll do it.'

I didn't. For several reasons. It never feels good to lie; saying my aunt had died might tempt fate—I was very fond of Aunt Lila; Cleo approved of him and . . . there wasn't really a fourth reason, apart from the memory of that extraordinary kiss.

Considering how many awkward and embarrassing things had happened on that first so-called date he was fool enough to sign up for more. He had to be mad. Or special. Or mad in a special way, or the other way around.

I often told the kids that anything's worth trying if your chances are better than winning Lotto. Yet the possibility of there being more to the toy boy beyond his perfectly groomed surface was almost zero. On the other hand, he'd called my bluff a couple of times. Maybe I'd underestimated him.

Despite Nicole's assurances there was no future in it, the dinner became the first of many. And I was facing a dilemma. I was beginning to enjoy the company of multi-faceted Philip. If our relationship went any further, it could no longer be classified as a one-night stand, even in the loosest terms. After all, the whole point of a one-night stand is it's impersonal, possibly unsatisfactory, and therefore not worth repeating. Sleeping with him now would be tantamount to disobeying the shrink's instructions.

Besides which, there were other more uncomfortable matters to consider. A woman who has given birth three times is unwilling if not insane to expose her body, especially if she has avoided the rigours of the gym. 'Drop a dress size in one week' diets invariably ended in 'gain two sizes a week later'. After the birth of a child the female form arranges itself in mounds and folds that can charitably be described as 'interesting' to artists such as Renoir and Rubens. After the birth of three, her body is more or less a Henry Moore sculpture carved in sponge rubber. A young man whose greatest physical imperfection was a subtly crooked nose (due to a rugby injury) had every reason to be warned against the dangers of unravelling acres of unruly womanly flesh. Yet, like Livingstone in search of the source of the Nile, he refused to give up.

I gradually began to understand why queen-sized sheets were invented. They're the Western woman's equivalent of the Muslim female's chador. With careful planning, a queen-sized sheet can be arranged to cover the entire body and head with just a slit from which the eyes can peer out. 'Gosh,' she says, trying to sound offhand as she peers through the slit at the impossibly toned male body, 'these sheets have a mind of their own.' The other merciful invention is the light switch. Due to a condition that has afflicted her since childhood, known as Extreme Sensitivity of the Eyes to Artificial Light, it must be switched off. My body was no longer a temple. It was a garden for the blind.

It was during a lull in one of these non-visual encounters that he invited me to spend a weekend at his family's holiday cottage on the shores of Lake Taupo. This was starting to sound scarily on the edge of being beyond a several-night stand to something complicated.

'But I'll have the . . .'

'Make it one of the weekends you don't have the kids.'

He'd finally accepted the kids were sacred turf, part of a separate life he was banned from.

'But . . . there's no one to look after the cat.'

'Cleo can come along with us, if she doesn't get car sick.'

I told him Cleo adored riding in cars. So a couple of weeks later on a Friday night after work she jumped eagerly into the old Audi. Perched on my knee, she watched the country-side spinning past. As we headed towards the lake the hills turned gold, then crimson, before drenching themselves in deepest violet.

We arrived at the cottage after dark. The Taupo night wrapped around us like black velvet, making us blind but heightening our other senses. The air was heavy with piney smells. There was a spike of distant snow on the breeze. I could hear the intimate lap of waves licking the shore. The outline of the wooden house was plain and modest. Even though I couldn't see it properly, the place had unmistakable soul. Like a child on a mystery adventure I followed the thread of Philip's torchlight to a flyscreen door.

'Just a minute,' he said. 'There's a special hiding place for the key.'

He disappeared around the side of the house and emerged with the key soon after. 'Here we go,' he said, sliding it in the lock. 'Damn!'

'What's happened?'

'It's okay,' he said. 'I've just broken the key.'

'Oh. *Is* that okay?'

'It's stuck in the lock.'

'Can't we break a window?'

'That would set the alarm off.'

'Let's do it, then.'

'I can't remember the code.'

We stood for what seemed several minutes in the dark together, Cleo tucked under my arm. Our courtship, if that's what it was, seemed destined to be laced with complications.

'We'll just have to stay in a motel,' he sighed. 'I'll call a locksmith in the morning.'

✦

The sign outside the motel said 'No Pets'. Cleo was smuggled through the lobby inside my handbag, without so much as a mew. Next morning, we met the wry, smiling locksmith at the cottage.

Nestled on the lake's edge, the old house had been in Philip's family for three generations. With French doors opening onto a stretch of grass running down to a pumice-laden beach, the setting was more spectacular than anything I'd imagined the previous night. The lake sparkled blue as a Sri Lankan sapphire. A sage-green island rose like an afterthought in the distance.

Cleo stretched gleefully in front of a driftwood fire while Philip and I walked along the river track. We paused at a bend where the river widened and spilled over rocks. Ferns bent over the water's edge to admire their reflections. A group of midges hung expectantly in the air. If Philip wanted to understand who I was, sooner or later he'd have to know about Sam. There was a possibility the information would destroy our burgeoning romance. To take on an older woman is one thing. Add a couple of readymade kids and the scenario becomes more complicated. If Philip was willing to wade in any deeper, he'd need to try to understand the emotional picture of what it might be like to lose a child. Even if we spent the rest of our lives together and had our own children, there would always be part of me that would remain fenced off from him. The part that loved and grieved for Sam.

'There's something I need to tell you,' I said, concentrating on a powder puff of cloud in the distance. 'Rob and Lydia had an older brother . . .'

The edges of the cloud started peeling away as if it was about to dissolve into the sky. A breeze spiked off the mountains. I shivered inside my city rain jacket. If I'd had more outdoor experience I would've thought to bring gloves to a place like this in the depths of winter.

'I know about Sam,' he replied quietly.

'How?' I asked, surprised.

'I read the articles you wrote around the time it happened.'

'Really? What was an army boy doing reading that sort of thing?'

'Your stories were very moving,' he said, staring up at the same cloud for what seemed a long time. 'Tell me about Sam.' He took my hand and rubbed it warm.

'Are you sure you want to know?'

He kissed my fingers, cocooned them in his and tucked them protectively in the pocket of his Gore-Tex jacket. 'Absolutely.'

As we trudged the rest of the river track with my hand nestled in his pocket he listened to Sam's story, the funny bits, the sad. I told him how losing a child was like having an arm or leg lopped off, except probably worse. That I wasn't sure how profoundly the experience had affected me, that in fact it still did. No matter how logical I tried to be, how squarely I faced the facts Sam no longer existed, I often continued to set an extra place at the table, and would probably do so for the rest of my life. No doubt there were mothers all over the world officially 'recovered' from their grief who did the same thing.

I would have forgiven him if he'd said one of the old clichés like 'I can't imagine what it must've been like' or one of the newer ones like 'you must be so strong'. But he simply listened. For that I was grateful.

Cleo was waiting in the glow of the fire when we returned.

'And this cat, she's part of it all,' Philip said, scooping her into his arms. 'She's your connection to Sam, isn't she?'

Purring loudly, Cleo stretched a lazy paw and patted his neck. She yawned and snuggled into his chest. There was nowhere else she, or I, wanted to be.

Later in the day we went fishing in a dinghy, against a backdrop of mountains tinged candy-floss pink in the sunset. A plump rainbow trout provided dinner for all three of us. We drank red wine and laughed. From a 'ticks in boxes' perspective we had little in common, yet we shared something Philip had recognised from the start. We were both strong individuals, unwilling or unable to belong to an in-crowd. In my case, even the out-crowd wouldn't have me. It seemed incredible that Philip hadn't turned away from Sam's story or the scar of my grief. He'd intuited Cleo's part in it too.

I began to realise I was falling in love.

Respect

*A cat demands to be treated as an equal. She expects nothing
less. Patronise a feline at your peril*

Carrying out a secret affair in a newsroom is like working in a
chocolate factory and trying to stay skinny.

'There's someone called Dustin on the phone for you,' said
Nicole, cool and quizzical.

To make ourselves feel more relaxed about our age difference
I'd summoned up famous historical love affairs in which the
woman was considerably older—Cleopatra and Anthony, Yoko
and John and, of course, Mrs Robinson and Dustin Hoffman
in *The Graduate*.

Philip used the codename Dustin when he called me at
the office. At his work I left messages that Mrs Robinson
had called.

'Who's *Dustin?*' Nicole probed.

'Distant cousin.'

'Oh well, I suppose it's good you've moved on from that
toy boy.'

The times Philip and I spent together were growing more
precious. I looked forward to them the way a child counts the
days till Christmas. After two months of clandestine meetings, I wondered how much longer I'd be able to keep my life

so neatly compartmentalised. Whenever he stayed the night while the kids were in residence, I woke him before dawn and made sure he creaked safely out the front door before an impressionable eye flicked open. The last thing I wanted was for them to have to deal with a transient adult male. Yet on our weekends alone together I'd see him looking so comfortable with Cleo draped over his knee it felt like he'd always been part of my emotional framework. Always—a risky word in anyone's language.

'So when do I get to meet the kids?' he asked. 'You've told me so much about them it's like I know them already.'

'Soon.' Cleo looked up at me from his lap and winked.

'In twenty years' time?'

'Not here at the house. I don't want them thinking you're invading their territory.'

'Okay. Let's get together on neutral ground. There's a new pizza parlour in town.'

He'd obviously thought it through. How could I possibly object to a casual meeting in a pizza parlour? I was in love with Philip, but had ongoing proof that romantic love is like a swimming pool. People fall into it and scramble out of it wet and dishevelled, usually in one piece but damaged, all the time.

The love for my children was a different beast altogether. It was fierce and unfathomable. I'd willingly fight to the death for them. Besides, he had no hope of comprehending the grief I carried for Sam. Not that I wanted him to shoulder my sadness in any way, but if he wanted to be part of our lives he needed to acknowledge its existence.

He had every reason to turn around and run. On the other hand, if he burst into my children's lives and abandoned them broken-hearted I'd tear his limbs off, preferably one at a time, slowly and with no pain relief whatsoever.

◆

Rob slipped into his favourite sweat shirt, several sizes too big for him, with USA emblazoned on the front. I buckled Lydia's red shoes, licked a tissue and wiped mysterious goo off her cheek.

'Try and be well behaved,' I instructed them. 'He's not used to children.'

'What sort of person isn't used to children?' asked Rob. 'Anyway, I'm not a kid anymore.'

The pizza parlour was carved out of the ground under a shopping arcade. Descending a fake marble staircase, complete with wrought-iron railings, the kids seemed impressed. Quiet at least. I was grateful the place hadn't been open long enough to reek of tired fat. Fake ivy clambered over polystyrene columns. Red and white checked tablecloths screamed at the glistening cash register. It felt like a movie set, with us as an unlikely set of actors auditioning for the role of Family Group.

I was relieved when the waiter escorted us to a discreet table under the stairs. Anyone from work could turn up at a joint like this. It would be through the office like chickenpox by Monday morning—'Brown and Toyboy Test Drive Family Outing. Has She Lost Plot?!'

We ordered pizza and coke. Rob was no longer a bubbly kid; he'd elongated into a thirteen-year-old with a tank full of testosterone. He was sullen, silent and determined to show no interest in someone who wasn't used to children. I'd warned Philip it was a difficult age. Lydia, who had insisted on wearing three strands of beads around her neck, vacuumed her glass until it was almost empty. Philip seemed slightly unnerved when her slurping noises echoed against the plastic wall panels.

'Don't do that!' I hissed at the child.

'Why not? It's fun.'

'It's not polite.'

'But this is,' she said, lifting the straw from her glass and tipping the remains of her coke onto her tartan skirt.

'No it's *not!*' I said, dabbing her skirt with a paper napkin.
I glanced at Philip, who was studying the menu as if it was a
legal document. Now he surely understood why I never wanted
this collision of realities to take place.

'Haven't you got a mother?' Lydia asked, kicking the table
leg and making the cutlery hiccough.

'Yes, I do,' he said, lowering the menu to welcome the first
unsolicited contact from the children.

'Why don't you go home and be with her?'

Silence. I waited for Philip to scrape his chair back and run.

'She's busy tonight.'

'Tell her not to be. We've got our mother. You've got yours.
You don't need our mother, too.'

'Strangers In the Night' dribbled out of a nearby speaker.
To the untrained ear the recording had been made inside a
shipping container, with musicians scraping instruments made
of tin cans. Their muzak was a welcome silence filler.

Philip's attention moved to the paper tablemats with games
printed on them. He asked Rob if he'd like to play snakes and
ladders. (*Not snakes and ladders!* I wanted to tell Philip. *Rob
grew out of that years ago. He thinks it's a game for babies!*) But
it wasn't Philip's fault he hadn't kept pace with child development. I held my breath waiting for the inevitable combination
of rejection and scorn to catapult across the table.

'I'd rather play this,' Rob said, indicating a mass of dots
arranged in rectangles. I hadn't seen the game before but it
looked brutally competitive. Each player was allowed one pencil
stroke to join two dots at a time, gradually amassing territories
of fully formed rectangles. Whoever gained the largest number
of completed rectangles won the game. This was the restaurant
tablemat version of war.

The game started casually enough for me to munch through
a triangle of Hawaiian pizza while concentrating on keeping

Lydia's mouth full so no more conversational frogs could leap out of it.

To keep the atmosphere cheerful I read from a section of the menu about the history of pizza, since its humble beginnings when the Greeks first came up with the idea of decorating flat bread.

'The real turning point was in the early nineteenth century, when a Neapolitan baker called Raffaele Esposito decided to make a bread that would stand out from everyone else's. He started by just adding cheese . . .'

I was, of course, reading all this while surreptitiously monitoring the battle taking place between the two men in my life. Rob claimed a cluster of rectangles in the right-hand corner. Philip filled in a strip on the other side. The game was evenly matched.

'After a while he started putting sauce under the cheese. He let the dough fluff out to the shape of a pie . . .'

Rob's territory was spreading across the square. Philip, on the other hand, appeared to be making listless progress on his side. My lips wanted to smile, but I tried to keep them in a straight line. Philip was demonstrating unexpected maturity by letting Rob win. Maybe he was stepfather material after all. He certainly looked the part in his corduroy trousers and fisherman's knit jumper.

'Everyone loved Esposito's pizza so much he was asked to create a special one for the King and Queen of Italy. He made one in the colours of the Italian flag—red sauce, white cheese, green basil . . .'

The two blocks of rectangles moved closer together. Their pencils flashed like swords. It was starting to look like a draw. That would be okay, I thought, as long as Rob's dignity was kept intact. There was hardly any free space left now.

'He named his pizza Margherita, after the queen . . .'

The tension was unbearable.

'The new Margherita pizza was a huge hit.'

I didn't dare watch the last few strokes. I knew it was over when I heard two pencils clatter onto the tabletop.

'You won,' said Rob, with a brave smile.

'You *what?!*' I said, turning to Philip.

'It was a tough game,' he said, shrugging with an unmistakable glint of satisfaction.

A tough game? Didn't he understand there's no such thing as a tough game when children were involved, especially *my* children? My kids' lives were tough enough without some jerk in pseudo stepdad corduroys turning up and knocking their self-esteem around.

I should never have let Philip near them. He was behaving like a child. Worse than a child. And the last thing I needed was another child. The relationship was doomed. Rob would be devastated for days after losing that game.

We drove home in silence and exchanged chaste farewells at the gate.

'It's good he's going home,' said Lydia, echoing my thoughts. 'His mother will be missing him.'

'What did you think?' I asked Rob after I'd fed Cleo and put Lydia to bed.

'He's cool.'

'I don't suppose he comes across as a very warm person.'

'No, I like him.'

'You *like* him? But he beat you at that stupid game.'

'I'm sick of the way grown-ups always go out of their way to let me win,' said Rob. 'They think I don't notice. He treated me as an adult. He's cool. You should see more of him.'

People and Places

*Cats have a reputation for being more attached to places
than people. But some remarkable individuals have
proved the generalisation quite wrong*

Mum's voice was jagged over the phone. She told me not to be
upset. I prepared for bad news. She'd had to take Rata to the
vet again. The old dog hadn't been coping. She couldn't walk.
The vet was wonderful, such a lovely young woman. She'd been
a friend of Rata's. She went red in the face when she and Mum
made the decision. Mum stroked Rata while it was happening.
She went out wagging her tail.

Video footage of Rata rolled through my mind. Sam and
Rata charging through the surf, Rata helping the boys dig holes
in the sand and scuffing it over disgruntled sunbathers, Sam
throwing driftwood for her to rescue. Rata shaking her coat and
showering us all in sea water. Rata galloping down the zigzag.
Cleo curled between Rata's giant paws. Tender, loyal Rata.

Rob didn't say much when I told him. We put our arms
around each other. He was so tall now. With the old dog's
departure another connection with Sam was broken. Mum
was going to feel it too. I invited her to spend a few days with
us, though she never stayed long in our 'busy household'.

Frantic was a better word for it. In the weeks the children
were home it was a kaleidoscope of school runs and homework;

rushing home from work to make spaghetti bolognaise; bedtime stories on the run. Once they were in bed I often worked
on a feature that was due the next day. I was too exhausted to
watch television.

It wouldn't have been possible to hold together without
Anne Marie calmly folding laundry, vacuuming, making
sandwiches, tidying toys and countless other things she said
nannies never do. She'd sometimes stay on for a coffee after I
arrived back from work. We learnt to appreciate each other's
strengths, and tolerate the differences. Sometimes I'd arrive
home so tired I'd collapse on the floor and doze in a patch
of sun—something she said none of her employers had done
before. She once commented she'd never seen anyone so tired.
Yet I always managed to dredge energy up to sew fairy wings
for Lydia or teach Rob how to make sushi. Nothing was perfect,
but somehow things got done. I began to think there was a
goddess of solo mothers who gave strength when it was needed
and arranged for the right people to turn up at the right time.
If there was such a goddess I reckoned she looked like a cat.

Steve was carving a new life for himself in a cottage five
minutes' drive away. I was pleased when the kids mentioned
he had some women friends. He deserved another roll of the
happiness dice.

Even though Philip had won Rob's approval on the pizza
night, I wasn't sure the kids and I had met whatever expectations were floating around inside his head. He'd seen us as a set,
and was no doubt beginning to absorb the enormity of entering
the lives of all three of us (plus cat). The phone stayed quiet for
several days. Then, to my surprise, it rang. He obviously hadn't
had enough punishment. He invited all of us, including Cleo,
for a weekend at the lake.

The drive seemed longer by daylight with two extra passen-
gers, one silent, one whining. The road buckled and bent like a
cobra in its death throes.

'I've got a sore tummy,' moaned Lydia as the car meandered up a hill.

'No you haven't.' Unlike more conscientious mothers, I treated children's health complaints as imaginary until proven otherwise.

'I'm going to frow up.'

'Take some deep breaths,' I said, turning to examine the back-seat patient. Her usually jellybean-pink face had turned the colour of a blueberry.

'I think we'd better stop,' I said to Philip. While I was immune to the potpourri of stale vomit and various other bodily fluids in my own car, I was certain Philip wasn't psychologically equipped to have the ambience of his Audi permanently altered by Eau de Family.

He pulled into a siding near the top of the hill. I concentrated on the spectacular spine of ranges spread out below us while Lydia vomited copiously into a ditch.

✦

Misty haze enveloped the cottage as the car pulled up under a silver birch. Rain was something I hadn't counted on. Philip said it wouldn't matter—there was always something to do at the lake. The leafy smell was intensified in the damp. Cleo recognised the place straightaway and sprang gleefully from the car into a thicket of ferns that was suspect mouse guerrilla territory.

The children were slower to be impressed. Rob gathered his sleeping-bag and trudged inside, the screen door slamming behind him. Philip didn't seem the least fazed. No doubt he'd seen the full spectrum of male behaviour in the army. Alternatively, having endured his own adolescence only a few years earlier, he probably remembered what it was like. Either way, Philip seemed immune to the ogreish male teenage stuff I was at a loss to deal with.

I helped Lydia slide from the back seat onto the moist earth.

'It's a forest,' she said, gazing up at a tree.

We carried our bags inside, where the familiar combination of sea grass and burnt driftwood tweaked my nostrils. I paused at a noticeboard covered with family photos. Wholesome, smiling faces celebrating Christmas at the lake. Every one of Philip's family was handsome and tanned, with teeth so white they surely glowed in the dark. Apparently, there were no fat, scruffy, gay, dark-skinned or emotionally challenged people in their circle. Going by the photos, they were also all Olympic champions. Water skiing, tennis, snow skiing, fishing were activities I'd never had the time or money, let alone the muscular coordination, to learn as a teenage mum.

Young women featured in the photos, too. Sleek, pretty bikini-clad girls, who were probably studying law or dentistry. So these must be the ticks-in-the-right-boxes girls, I thought. The type Philip and his two brothers were expected to marry. And why not? Every one of the smiling young women was prime breeding stock. But when I asked about them, Philip dismissed them as boring.

'Please use only a <u>small</u> piece of toilet paper,' instructed a notice in the loo. I wasn't sure the kids and I could qualify as small toilet paper people.

'How about a swim?' Philip called to Rob.

'It's raining.'

'I could help you get out the kayak if you like.' The man was nothing if not persistent.

'Too cold.'

'Bunks! It's got bunks!' Lydia called. I went into the bunk room, where Rob was roosting inside his sleeping-bag on an upper bunk. Lydia bounced up and down on the lower bunk's mattress, circling her chubby arms in the air.

The lake stretched out like a wrinkled sheet of cooking foil. Drops of condensation raced down the inside of windows. Philip crouched over the fireplace and crunched newspapers into balls. After a few false starts the kindling flared and the room crackled to life. Cleo pounced on a spider in the woodpile and munched on its legs with the thoughtful appreciation of a connoisseur, before taking up her usual position in front of the flames. Gazing up at me through half-closed eyes she yawned and seemed to say, *This is how it's meant to be. Don't worry. Everything will be fine.*

'Back in a minute,' Philip said.

Gathering Lydia onto my lap to read her favourite story about the elephant and the bad baby, I surreptitiously wiped her fingers. Even though the cottage exuded rustic simplicity it obviously hadn't been tainted by preschool fingers for decades. I'd hate us to be accused of leaving sticky fingerprints on the furniture.

Philip tapped on the window and beckoned us outside. The rain had eased. I slid Lydia into her gumboots. She scooped Cleo up and carried her upside down (a position Cleo had become nonchalant about since Lydia learnt to walk). We opened the flyscreen to a gift more magnificent than a room full of diamonds: Philip had latched a rope around one of the higher branches of the silver birch and threaded an old tyre through it.

'Wow! A tree swing!' cried Lydia.

She spent the rest of the day begging to be pushed on the swing—lying on her tummy with her legs flying out the back; sitting with her legs forward through the centre of the tyre; standing inside the rim and clinging to the rope. I'd never seen a man demonstrate so much patience with a child who wasn't his own. Still, something held me back. Even if this wonderful man was everything he seemed, with a soul deeper than the lake itself, the prospect of encompassing all three of us and a cat was surely too much for him.

As night enveloped the cottage, the rain eased enough for Philip to grill sausages on a brick barbecue nestled into a hedge. It was too wet for us to eat outside, so I set the formica table. We shared the meal under the inquisitive glare of a light bulb.

'How would you like to go for a bike ride tomorrow?' Philip asked Rob. 'There are some great tracks up in the hills.'

'No.'

'We could hit a tennis ball around . . .'

Rob studied the tomato sauce on his plate. An experienced parent, worn by countless battles of will, would stop at this inter-section, turn back and opt for a change of subject. I was hoping for all our sakes that Philip would do so now.

'How about taking the kayak out in the morning? I'll put the life jacket out for you.'

'It's all very well for you!' Rob exploded at Philip. 'You didn't see your brother killed on the road!'

The teenager scraped back his chair and stomped off to the bunk room, leaving us in a bubble of stunned silence at the table.

'He does this sometimes,' I said quietly. Yet it was more than a teenage eruption this time. The lake cottage, with its garage choked with skis, boats and canoes, made the contrast between our two families all too evident. Philip appeared to have coasted through endless summers of pretty girls and sailboats. Our life, by comparison, was an endless struggle, overshadowed by death and divorce. How could anyone from Philip's back-ground have the slightest understanding of the grief Rob and I shared—and, more to the point, why should he?

'I'll talk to him,' Philip said, standing up to follow him.

'No, don't,' I said. 'He'll get over it.'

In truth I was frightened by Rob's adolescent outbursts and had no way of handling them, apart from letting them blow over—which sometimes could take days.

Deaf to my instructions, Philip departed swiftly into the bunk room. Through the walls, I could hear him speaking gently to Rob. While it was impossible to hear exact words, the tone was unmistakable. Philip was meeting Rob's pain head-on, accepting their differences and talking him down.

'He's okay,' Philip said when he emerged some time afterwards. 'He says he wants to sleep now.'

*

We woke next morning with rain thrumming on the roof. Lydia, plodding around in her pyjamas, was delighted when she found a box of old building blocks in one of the cupboards.

'There's been kids here!' she called.

Cleo was chomping on the remains of a moth while Lydia set about building an elephant castle with a swing for the baby elephants.

'Where's Rob?' I asked.

'Dunno,' said Lydia.

Philip had no idea either. A lump of fear settled in my stomach. If Rob had taken off during the night he could be anywhere by now. He could have hitched a ride back to Auckland on one of the logging trucks that roared along the main highway. Or maybe just wandered into the bush. Either way, it could be dangerous, especially in this rainstorm. His father would have to be called, possibly the police as well. It was a disaster. Why did I always land the box labelled 'disaster'?

'Look,' said Philip, putting a hand on my shoulder and turning me slowly towards the French doors. Through the rain-spattered glass I could see waves, big as ocean surf, smashing on the beach. Purple clouds smothered the island. In the distance I could just make out a figure in a kayak.

The waves pushed the figure sideways and seemed to engulf him completely. He re-emerged, ploughing the oar into the water and turning the kayak around to surf another wave. The canoeist was fearless, intense in his determination to stay afloat.

'You're all crazy around here,' I said. 'Who'd go out in this weather?'

'Rob,' said Philip, smiling enigmatically. 'And I have to say he's making an impressive job of it.'

Freedom

Human beings strive to claim ownership of everything they love. Yet a cat belongs to nobody, except perhaps the moon

Around the time I became a single mother Cleo stepped up her hunting skills. Maybe she sensed we were down to one provider and thought I was doing a lousy job bringing home the bacon. Not only was I a pathetic, two-legged creature with (from her point of view, anyway) a hideously bald body, I couldn't hunt a mouse if world peace depended on it. Cleo more than compensated for my inadequacies with a stream of furry or feathered corpses scattered from the front doormat, through the bedrooms and down the hall to the kitchen. Our house resembled the workroom of an amateur taxidermist. To stem the tide of destruction I bought Cleo a hot-pink collar with fake diamond studs, and a bell to warn potential victims to scurry back to their nests.

'Cats don't wear collars,' Mum said in a tone implying she'd just delivered the Eleventh Commandment.

While the kids and I always looked forward to Mum's visits, she invariably found something not quite right with our set-up. This time it was the cat collar.

'She's killing too many animals,' I said, tightening the buckle around Cleo's reluctant neck. 'Besides, it looks quite Audrey Hepburn, don't you think?'

'It's hideous,' Mum replied. 'And it's a cat's *job* to kill things.'

For once Cleo agreed with Mum. The cat shook her head vigorously, making herself jingle like a Christmas accessory.

'See? It doesn't like that thing!'

'She's not an 'it'. She's a *she*,' I said. 'And she'll get used to it.'

Cleo and I embarked on a serious battle of wills. She detested that collar with more focus than she'd ever hated anything, including non-cat people. Every waking hour was devoted to scratching and gnawing at it. Three fake diamonds fell out. The sumptuous pink strap faded and was reduced to a stringy neck brace. Cleo fixed me with a hooded look that said it all: *How dare you try and brand me with this degrading object! What makes you assume you have the right? Do you think you own me?*

'Is *that* your new boyfriend?' Mum stage-whispered in the kitchen. 'I thought he was a policeman when I opened the door. His hair's so short and he's so clean cut. Hardly your type, is he?'

I never enjoyed her reviewing my personal affairs. Her observation skills were astringent enough to qualify as an ingredient for aftershave. Philip's appearance in our lives provided her with a wealth of new material.

'Just out of the army, is he? Oh well, you were married to a sailor. I suppose it'll be the air force next.'

Life at work was no easier. When the cat got out of the bag that I was still seeing Philip with one 'l' there were enough arched eyebrows to form a Gothic cathedral. Toy-boy jokes echoed from one end of the newsroom to the other. Journalists pride themselves on being broad-minded, but I was learning they're broad-minded only in certain ways. If I'd taken to booze and boogied till dawn with an elderly drug addict they'd hardly have noticed. Movies were (and still are) full of old men as ugly as bulldogs slurping over models twenty-five years their junior. It hardly seemed fair that a woman going out with a short-haired, younger bloke in a suit was regarded as an act of indecency. I tried to retaliate with quips to assure them it was merely a fling. Except the fling was lasting a month or two longer than expected.

Things weren't straightforward for Philip, either. His circle of bright young things couldn't believe he was in such a whacky relationship. He continued to be inundated with invitations to lunches and parties by ticks-in-the-right-boxes girls. The town was packed with highly qualified wrinkle-free beauties all desperate for a man, and Philip in particular.

Falling in love with my one-night stand was the most pleasant surprise that ever happened to me. Getting to know him was like exploring an underground cave, dark and deceptively shallow at first. Yet dig a little deeper, turn a few corners, and there was a cavern full of rare and magnificent crystals. Not only was he handsome, great company and wonderful to the kids, he had a strong spiritual curiosity. He was the first man I'd ever met who seemed genuinely interested in my weird dreams and occasional off-the-planet psychic experiences. We were destined to be together, I thought, encircling him with an invisible version of Cleo's pink collar (camouflage pattern, perhaps; definitely no bell).

'It doesn't matter what wrapping people are in,' I said to anyone who questioned our unlikely union. 'It's what's inside that counts.'

I even loved the aspects of him that had stopped me taking him seriously at the beginning. The age difference between us was fun and interesting (apart from the time he asked, 'Who's Shirley Bassey?'). His conservative manner wasn't so deep-set that I couldn't joke him out of it sometimes. And I had a lot to learn about military life and banks. Our relationship was astoundingly close to perfect.

One of the many aspects of Philip I adored was the way he kept a perfectly ironed handkerchief in his pocket. The handkerchief was flourished whenever required to wipe a woman's tears or, occasionally by *very* special request, less glamorous outpourings from her nostrils. Even more impressive, he insisted on being on the outside whenever we were walking along a footpath. The only other man I knew who performed this ancient act of chivalry designed to protect a woman from oncoming horses as well as mud flying from carriage wheels was my father. The first time Philip gently took my arm, moved slowly behind me and slid my hand into the crook of his other elbow so I was closest to the shop windows and he was nearest the gutter I knew this was a man I'd willingly spend the rest of my life with.

But then . . . why does there always have to be a 'but then'? Why can't the sad solo mother queen just meet her prince, fall in love, stroll down the aisle in a tactfully off-white suit and live happily ever after? Because life isn't written by Rodgers and Hammerstein. Real people have histories, hang-ups, phobias, anxieties, egos, ambitions, not to mention opinionated friends and family just waiting to pass judgement.

We no longer went to huge lengths not to be seen in public with the children. At least, I didn't think so. So when the four of us drove to town one Saturday morning on a T-shirt shopping mission, we parked on the main street and bundled out of the car. Walking down the footpath, Philip completed one of his elegant mud-protecting moves. The kids galloped ahead into the store. I felt like someone in a movie whose life has turned out wonderfully, when people have finished their popcorn and the credits are about to roll.

'I like this one,' Lydia said, holding up a T-shirt featuring teddy bears dressed as fairies. The colour was predictable.

'She's going through a three-year-old phase pink,' I said to Philip. 'I'm not fighting it. If I do she'll probably end up on a shrink's couch some day, blaming me for denying her an essential part of her development.'

He didn't laugh. In fact, he'd frozen like a cat that has spotted a Rottweiler.

'Sarah!' he said, smiling broadly over my shoulder.

I turned. Standing outside a changing room in a bikini so miniscule it could have doubled as dental floss was a blonde with legs longer than Barbie's. I recognised her from the photo board at the lake, one of the famous 'boring' girls. Ticks in every single box.

'Philip!' she beamed. 'Where *have* you been? We haven't seen you at tennis for ages. I've been missing you.'

I waited for Philip to introduce me, but he snapped himself inside a perspex bubble that denied any connection with me. I was just another shopper he happened to be standing next to, and the kids were invisible.

'Work's been full-on,' he said, moving towards her. 'You know what it's like this time of year.'

'Same at the surgery,' she said, rolling her eyes and flicking her golden mane. 'There's heaps of cosmetic work these days. Everyone wants perfect teeth. You're looking so well!'

'So are you!' His voice ricocheted off the walls into my ears, collided inside my brain, spun down my spinal column and ruptured something in my chest.

'And your parents? How are they?'

As their conversation grew warmer and more intimate I stood like a Charles Dickens character shivering out in the snow and peering through a window at a flickering hearth surrounded by happy faces.

'Let's go!' I said quietly to Rob.

'But I want this pink one,' said Lydia.

'Not now!' I said, thrusting it back on a neatly folded pile.

Grabbing her hand, I swept out of the shop with Rob jogging to catch up with me.

'Shouldn't we wait for him?' Rob asked, as we charged through a sea of faces.

'I don't think he even knows we've gone.'

What a fool I'd been. A consummate moron. Why on earth hadn't I listened to Nicole and Mum and everyone else who'd warned me? They'd been right all along. The boy-man and I had no place in each other's worlds. He was no more capable of fitting in with my journalist crowd than I was of suddenly becoming a twenty-four-year-old Barbie dentist. Let alone the kids. It would take an incredibly special man to encompass my kids in his future.

How wrong of me to expose them to someone so shallow and immature. And yes, conservative. So damned conservative and dull he might as well take up smoking a pipe and marry a dentist.

'Wait!' Philip, panting from running to catch up with us, touched me on the shoulder. 'What's the matter?'

I sent Rob into a McDonald's to buy himself chips and Lydia an ineptly named Happy Meal.

'Ashamed of us, are you?' I yowled.

'What do you mean?' he asked, feigning innocence.

'Why didn't you introduce us?'

'I didn't think you'd be interested.'

'You mean you didn't think *she'd* be interested!'

'Look, I . . .' An inquisitive shopper paused to absorb as much of our argument as was politely possible.

'I thought you said Sarah was boring.' I hated the vindictive quaver in my voice. It was hideously unattractive and about as un-ticks-in-boxes as anyone could get. 'You did a pretty good impression of not being bored.'

'She's . . . just a friend.'

'If that's the case why did you act as if we weren't there?'

Philip stared up at a neon sign above our head. In a merciless act of cruelty it flashed the words 'Engagement Rings'.

'Do you think this is easy for me?' he erupted. 'It's not that I don't like the kids. I think they're wonderful. It's just . . .'

I waited as a thousand shoppers changed colour under the flashing sign.

'I'm not sure I want to be an instant father.'

When he dropped us home and drove off I discovered Cleo's collar was missing. She'd finally chewed it off and claimed her freedom.

Witch's Cat

Sometimes it's easier to love the moon

There aren't many options for a broken-hearted woman with attitude, except perhaps to become a witch. Witches fight off curses. They create their own luck. Witchery had potential. Cleo, with her ability to appear on a rooftop and in front of a fireplace almost simultaneously, was the perfect witch's cat, not to mention the ideal colour.

A room is more beautiful when furnished with a cat. Her silken presence transforms a collection of chairs, discarded toys and crumb-sprinkled plates into a temple to soothe the soul. Poised like a goddess on a window ledge she observes the countless frailties of the humans she has blessed with her presence. The poor creatures make countless mistakes with their neurotic attempts to cling to the past and control the future. They need a cat to remind themselves just to be.

A cat's ears absorb the thump of a school bag hitting the floor or a mother's curse when she finds ants in the sugar bowl yet again. Humans and their tragic overreactions amuse her. Nothing they can do disturbs her composure, except for the young, when they go through that horrifying stage of wanting to dress her in baby clothes and imprison her in a pram.

Her paws absorb the earth's slightest tremor. Ever watchful, her eyes perceive more than humans can. When she sleeps, a cat draws a third eyelid, a translucent screen, over her eyes so no movement escapes her. A cat is always watching, but wise enough to refrain from offering an opinion.

A black cat is lucky, or not, depending on which side of the Atlantic you are born. If a black cat crosses your path in Britain expect good fortune. In North America, a black cat spells danger.

With their shimmering fur and mirror eyes, black cats were once regarded as malevolent spirits. They blended into darkness, which to some ill-informed minds made them the personification of evil—the devil himself stalking the rooftops of innocent peasants. Even in Britain, where black cats are considered lucky, the superstition isn't in the felines' favour. It's only because a person suffers no harm when a black cat crosses his path, and has therefore escaped evil, that he can congratulate himself on his luck.

◆

There was no point seeing the shrink again. She'd only tell me to have another one-night stand. We all knew how that ended up. Anyway, I'd learnt from my mistakes. I withdrew from the dating world and tried to be wise. A scary replica of my mother, I developed the lonely person's syndrome of telling people the same stories over and over again. As their eyes glazed I'd stop and say, 'Have I told you this before?' The polite ones said no.

When they asked, I said I'd never been happier. So what? A cat never loses its smile. I did everything possible to become a self-sufficient witch who didn't need a man. Compromise was no longer part of my vocabulary. The Chinese pant-suit enjoyed regular airings. I nailed kitsch pottery ducks to the wall, drank wine and farted when I felt like it. At night, sometimes, when the kids were at their father's, I turned the stereo up loud enough for the neighbours to notice and danced half-naked to Marvin

Gaye (*never* Ella and Louis!). Women friends approved. They said I was empowered.

Empowerment sounds wonderful but, frankly, it's not everything it's cracked up to be. Although a witch may seem in control of her life, she has a diligent stalker: loneliness. After the kids had gone to bed I'd pour a glass of wine. Cleo would pad across the floor towards me. The shadow of her tail, an eerie serpent six-feet tall, would flicker against the wall. A charge of electricity would shudder up my arm as I ran my hand over her coat. I'd scoop her up and carry her out to the back deck. We'd sit under the stars together, licking our wounds and studying the moon's acne.

'Nobody touches a witch's heart,' I murmured, burying my nose in her velvet fur.

Nevertheless, I leapt at the phone every time it rang. It was never him. Why should it be? He'd made it clear enough when we split up. He said he wasn't 'ready', whatever that meant. If people waited till everything was ready, nothing would ever happen. Life isn't a menu; you can't order courses when you're 'ready' for them. I hadn't been ready to lose Sam. And I didn't feel ready to say goodbye to Philip. His words were surgical but his eyes brimmed with sadness and love. Even though I tried to accept what he said I still believed his eyes. Why had he walked away?

I missed his calm presence, his voice warm as a driftwood fire, his ridiculously conservative clothes, the crooked nose, the hairy groves inside his ears. One of the things I missed most was his smell. Even though he seldom wore aftershave, he always smelt like a grove of cypress trees. How come so few sonnets are written to a lover's smell? Rob was missing him, too. Philip had been a desperately needed role model that had turned out fake, heartless as a shop mannequin. What a fool I'd been. I vowed no man would ever hurt Rob that way again.

I wondered what Philip was up to. Had he shed us like one of his Italian jackets? No doubt he was being devoured by bimbo dentists and lawyers. If our worlds had been closer, a few discreet phone calls would have answered my questions. But we had no friends in common. He might as well have taken off to Pluto. Weeks dissolved into months.

If I was to be a witch then Cleo needed to look the part. I taught her to perch on my shoulder. Our first attempts were dismal and painful to us both. But Cleo was a willing student with a sense of balance worthy of Cirque du Soleil. She was soon able to dig her claws into my clothes deeply enough to secure a platform without piercing my skin. I enjoyed the alarm that flickered across visitors' faces when I opened the door with a black cat glaring down at them from my shoulder. For all their technology and sophistication, people are wired like primitive beings. They still believe in witches. Not so long ago, neighbours would have gathered outside my white picket fence at dusk and dragged me and my cat to the nearest bonfire.

'A woman needs a man like a butterfly needs deep-sea diving gear,' I said to Emma, who'd become a regular visitor. I'd met her at a book launch, where we'd both been hovering by the loo doors. Emma worked in a feminist bookstore. She helped me nurture a herb garden and introduced me to her circle of women friends, who had strong views on the male species. Listening to their wine-fuelled discussions, I nodded fiercely. Men were a lesser species, slaves to the bulge in their pants and overdue for extinction.

Even if I couldn't contemplate cutting my hair short and bleaching it silver the way Emma had, I admired her flair. Turquoise was her colour. Only a woman with no children would have time to sift through what must've amounted to hundreds of shops and market stalls to find so much turquoise junk—bangles, scarves, even a pair of turquoise sunglasses. One of her favourite accessories was a feather-trimmed pendant inlaid with turquoise, a gift from a Hopi Indian chief who had cleansed her aura, smudged evil spirits out of her house with sage smoke and identified her totem animal as a cougar.

Emma often brought over books from her shop—*Why Women Bleed, The Disposable Male*. Free from maternal exhaustion, she was honorary aunt to the kids. I envied the excess energy she had to bounce on the trampoline with Lydia or kick a ball around with Rob. I was grateful for Emma's company.

I was also thankful for the restless, throwaway atmosphere of the newsroom. A combination of deadlines and worldly quips from workmates helped stop up the holes in a shattered heart. I was grateful that nobody, not even Nicole, said 'I told you so'. The toy-boy jokes dried up and gradually stopped. They accepted me back into the fold. I loved them for it.

While I didn't know Tina well, she was showing signs of being an empowerment witch herself. Not so long ago she'd asked me into her office and suggested I apply for a Press Fellowship to Cambridge University in Britain. My chances of being accepted were less than zero, but I filled out the form to practise applying for things. The form invited applicants to nominate an area of interest. Confident I wouldn't get in, I invented a zany topic— Environmental Studies from a Spiritual Perspective.

Another weekend without the children stretched ahead like a desert. I was pleased when Emma offered a Saturday night oasis, asking me over to her place for pasta and salad. Thank God, whoever She may be, for women friends, I thought, pulling up outside Emma's cutesy house nestled in the hills outside town.

'How are you?' she said, opening the door.

Emma was one of the few people I could be honest with.

'Good. Bad . . . Dunno . . . Tired.'

She poured a glass of wine, a soulful Australian red. We dined outside under the hypnotic toll of a wind chime.

'You're a wonderful friend,' I said, scraping the remains of home-baked lemon pudding off my bowl. 'It's such a treat to have a beautiful meal just appear like this. It's magic. I can't get over it. I didn't have to peel a potato.'

'My pleasure,' Emma said, flashing her incisors. The Hopi Indian chief was right. There was something cougarish about her, especially in the evening light.

As I stood to help clear the table, Emma took my hand. 'No. Sit down,' she said. 'Tonight's *your* night. I know how hard you work and how demanding it is raising the kids on your own. Tonight I'm taking care of you.'

Her words made me want to crumble with gratitude. At last someone understood.

'What's that sound?' I asked. 'Do you have an ornamental fountain?'

'I'm running a bath for you,' Emma said.

A bath?! Did I smell that bad? I'd showered before leaving home.

'You said a good bath relaxes you more than anything,' she added, sensing my alarm.

'Yes, but that's when I'm at home on my own,' I muttered.

'This is going to be better than anything you've ever had at home,' said Emma. 'I've been saving some special French bubble bath for you.'

'That's . . . very . . . kind,' I said, wishing she could've just handed over the bottle of bubble bath and let me go home.

'I've put a robe out for you,' she said, looking more cougarish by the second. 'In the bathroom.'

I felt suddenly hot and confused. Over the years I'd known lots of women, strong wonderful people like Ginny, who I'd trust with my life. We'd laughed and cried together, moaned about men and shared intimate details about our bodily functions. Those women had helped me grieve and give birth, let go of my marriage and laugh off life's indignities. So far not one of them had invited me to have a bath. A bubble bath at that.

'Don't worry,' soothed Emma. 'It's your special night.'

Oh well. What was wrong with taking a bath? She might think me unsophisticated if I said no. I liked Emma a lot. She was obviously trying to help. I didn't want to hurt her feelings or seem unappreciative.

The French obviously knew a thing or two about bubble bath. Giant rainbow domes rose from the water. A row of coloured candles blazed on the window ledge. Surely a fire hazard. A robe was folded thoughtfully on the vanity. I instinctively raised a hand to lock the bathroom door. There was no lock.

Sinking into the bubbles, I examined the Women Can Do Anything poster on the wall. Had I sent unusual signals to Emma? I hoped not. She knew my tastes were straightforward. Perhaps I'd been naive to assume hers were too. She certainly hadn't gone out of her way to talk about previous love affairs. I'd respected Emma's need for privacy. Maybe I should have been more curious. She'd mentioned a man once, and women friends. But I'd assumed 'friends' was the operative word. Maybe I'd been loose in my use of language. When I'd told her I loved women I hadn't felt it necessary to add 'but not in that way'. Strange sounds warbled from under the door that I had closed firmly as possible.

'Whale song!' called Emma. 'With subliminal messages.'

'Oh,' I replied nonchalantly. 'What do you mean?'

'They recorded messages you can't quite hear under the whale song,' she said. 'To change your way of thinking.'

Suddenly on edge, I craned my neck out of the water to listen for whatever hidden message there was behind the yodelling whales. Some sort of mumbling was definitely going on. Maybe Emma was trying to brainwash me to join some religious sect.

'What does it say?' I asked, trying to conceal my anxiety.

'Oh, relax, let go, that sort of thing.'

If any whale, white, blue or sperm, tried to audition for a choir I was running I'd turn it down. Those things are tone deaf. I sank back into the bubbles and concentrated on relaxing.

'Is it warm enough for you?' asked Emma, bursting into the room and pressing her face so close to mine I could smell garlic on her breath.

'Yes, thanks,' I said, sinking into the bubbles as deep as possible without drowning. 'It's perfect. I think . . .'

'Yes?' said Emma, whose face rose like the sun over the edge of the bath.

'I'd like to get out now.'

'Oh, but you'll miss the massage!' cried Emma, digging her large, practical fingers into my neck.

The massage?! Crouched unwillingly, I endured her attentions with the stoicism of a dog being forced to have its fur washed. Emma's breaths were hot and increasingly loud in my ear. The masculine tang of her perfume (aftershave?) made me vaguely nauseous.

Images arose of a future sharing a rose-covered cottage with a well-built woman and her turquoise collection. There'd been two women teachers like that when I was at high school. They used to drive to school in separate cars to keep the gossip down, but everyone knew. People said they'd arranged to be buried together.

Technically, I supposed it was an option. A life with Emma would avoid some of the cruelties inflicted by men. Testosterone wouldn't pose much of a problem, competition from blonde dentists would be minimal and there'd be plenty of the affection women enjoy. Cuddles and hugs, not unlike the sort of stuff you get from a cat. I liked Emma. There was only one difficulty. I didn't love her. Not in *that* way.

As Emma turned my face in her hands and planted her damp lips on mine I knew straightaway. I wasn't that kind of girl.

◆

Six months had passed since I'd seen Philip. I was over him, at least I pretended to be. I hardly needed a man when I was flat-out with the kids and work, where I was becoming a minor authority on 'wimmin's issues'. Emma had put me on to a local witch, who'd agreed to visit the office for an interview on women's spirituality. Apparently witches needed publicity as much as anyone else. Apart from a few crystals dangling around her neck and sticking plasters wrapped around several gnarled toes protruding from her Birkenstocks, she resembled any mature woman I might clash supermarket trolleys with. I escorted her into the interview room. We exchanged smiles. I quietly wondered if she recognised my witch potential. She surprised me by asking if I had any pets. When I mentioned Cleo she hunched forwards, causing her crystals to clatter.

'A black cat is a perfect familiar for a witch,' she said. 'A spirit will often manifest in a black cat's body and attach itself to a witch to help her on psychic levels.'

'You mean Cleo could help my dreams come true?' I asked.

The witch laughed, an ordinary old lady's laugh, not a cackle.

'On a simplistic level, I guess you could say so,' she said.

We were interrupted by a tap on the door. It was Tina, casting her quick journalist's eye over the witch. From that one glance I could tell she was soaking up enough raw material to produce a thousand words.

'Sorry to trouble you,' she said. 'But there's someone down-stairs wanting to see you. Says his name is Dustin.'

Absence

A cat seizes opportunities whenever they arise

Cleo was on edge, as if a low grade electric current was running through her fur. Whiskers twitching, she paced the carpet. Up, down, under the table and back again. When a car hummed down the street, she froze and flattened her ears. Once the car had gone she'd regained her composure and resumed her carpet patrol. Our next door neighbour's son shouted to a friend. She arched her back and sank her claws in the rug.

She kept returning to the desk under my bedroom window, which had the best view of the street. Its gravitational force pulled her back, and back again to survey our front garden and the houses across the road. At the sound of a bird's call she sprang up on the desk and wove through the curtains to peer out. She then dropped back to the floor with a disappointed thud. The clatter of a distant rubbish tin and she was back on the desk again, scanning the neighbourhood before jumping down again to resume her restless stride.

Then the sound she'd been waiting for – the click of the front gate. Bounding on the desk and through the curtains, she stared intensely at the figure approaching the house. Her tail unfurled and quivered with delight. She sprang to the floor and sped down the hallway toward the front door squeaking mews of delight.

When I opened the door to Philip, Cleo lunged at him and stretched her front paws up his thighs.

'She's been waiting for you,' I said, as he gathered her in his arms. Cleo clambered up his fisherman's jumper, licked his neck and burrowed under his chin. Not since Cleopatra made up with Mark Anthony had a reunion been so loving.

The children's welcome was more cautious. Lydia glanced up from a wooden jigsaw puzzle she was working on with an expression that implied a certain amount of grovelling would be required if she was ever to take Philip seriously again. Rob emerged from his bedroom door and nodded politely.

As weeks melted into months, warmth and trust gradually returned. The bond we'd had before grew even stronger. Even though I tried to keep part of my heart cordoned off in case it was shattered again there was no doubt I loved—we all loved—Philip.

Late one Sunday afternoon he bundled us all—including Cleo—into his car.

'Where are we going?' I had a long time aversion to secrets and surprises.

'You'll see.'

With Cleo perched on Rob's knee and Lydia beside them, the atmosphere in the back seat was surprisingly genial.

'Are you taking us to a circus?' Lydia asked. Her latest ambition was to become what she called an 'upside down lady' in a pink sequin body suit and matching feathers hanging from the roof of a circus tent.

'Not this time,' Philip replied. I was impressed how quickly he'd learned parents' language i.e. use the word 'no' sparingly.

'What are we going to the museum for?' Rob asked as we turned into the botanic gardens that lead up to the museum.

'You'll find out.'

Philip drew to a halt in the same car park I'd used that evening we'd first met. He asked us to wait in the car for a minute, and disappeared up the steps.

'Are we going to see dinosaurs?' Lydia asked.

'We can't,' Rob replied, 'it's too late. The museum's closed.'

'That's right,' I added. 'It's nearly sunset.'

A gold medallion sun sank in candy floss clouds. Long shadows stretched from the columns in front of the museum. It was a perfect night, an almost exact replica of how it had been when we first set eyes on each other. It didn't take much to envisage the bridal party standing on the steps and that powerful surge of recognition at the sight of my handsome army boy. I still wasn't certain if my physical reaction had been the result of a cosmic explosion of soul mates colliding—or simply undiluted lust.

Philip reappeared and beckoned us to follow him up the steps. We clambered out of the car. Normally, Rob would have left Cleo in the back seat, but he seemed to sense something momentous was about to happen. He carried her up the steps, while I took Lydia's hand.

To my surprise, Philip was standing where I'd first seen him, in a shaft of evening sun slightly to the right of the museum doors.

'There's something I want to you see,' he said, standing aside and holding out his hand. He seemed to be pointing toward a concrete window frame so recessed and steeped in shadow it was difficult to notice anything unusual about it. I was beginning to wonder if Philip wasn't as straightforward as I'd imagined.

'Look closer,' he smiled.

To my astonishment, hidden in the deepest recess of the window was a small navy blue box. Inside the box was a diamond ring. In front of Rob, Lydia and Cleo, he slid it on my finger.

'How did you get the right size?' I asked, appalled at my lack of romance but genuinely impressed.

'Stole a ring from your jewellery box. Hoped you wouldn't notice. Did you?'

I shook my head. It was impossible to answer. I was too busy choking back happy tears.

We agreed a long engagement would suit us all under the circumstances. No date was set, but we thought a year or so would give the family time to become fully integrated. I was only 36 and there was plenty of time if (heaven forbid) Philip felt the need to have a child from his own biological blueprint. Even though I felt sheepish telling crusty journalistic friends I was embarking on an engagement long enough to satisfy Jane Austen, it seemed the best way to go about things. This was no normal marriage. It was a union between one man, three people and a cat. All parties needed to feel comfortable.

I was just getting used to the idea of wearing an engagement ring when an important-looking envelope arrived in the post.

✦

'Cambridge must be crazy!' I said, passing Philip the letter. 'They've accepted me.'

He laughed, folded me in his ridiculously sinewy arms and said he always knew they would. The timing was perfect in many ways. He'd just been accepted into the Swiss business school IMD to study for an MBA (sometimes I wondered if he might be planning to drown in a sea of initials). Once I'd finished the Cambridge Fellowship, the kids and I could join him in Lausanne for the rest of the year . . .

Cambridge. Switzerland. It couldn't possibly work. I'd have to leave Rob and Lydia in New Zealand for three months—and Cleo for an entire year! It was impossible. I'd write back to the university, thank them for their generosity and decline.

But Philip urged me not to turn them down. When would another opportunity like this turn up? Steve and Mum agreed with him. Mum offered to look after the children for the first month I was away, and Steve would have them for the remaining two. Cleo gazed at me steadily. Was she daring me to go or stay?

After Cambridge, Lydia would join us in Switzerland and learn French (people said it would be a breeze). Rob said he'd rather stay in his New Zealand high school and visit us during holidays. It was a wild, unrealistic plan with more hidden potential for disaster than an Angolan minefield. We decided to do it.

Cleo helped us interview people willing to rent the house while we were away. First on the doorstep was Jeff, a clean-cut accountant in a blue and white checked shirt. He seemed charming, but Cleo hissed at him and hid under a chair. An hour later Virginia, an aromatherapist, arrived in a haze of silk scarves and patchouli oil. Cleo eyeballed Virginia from a vantage point on top of the bookshelves. When Cleo insisted on claiming higher ground over someone like that it was never a good sign. Lines would be drawn in the litter box. Threats would be exchanged. A battle of wills was bound to follow. I'd already explained to her over the phone that the cat was part of the deal, in fact probably the more important part.

Virginia glowered back at Cleo and said, 'One of the reasons I was attracted to aromatherapy was that cats make me sneeze. However, I've discovered that if a cat is given weekly baths in lavender oil my sneezing problem practically vanishes. Then I just have to deal with watering eyes, but homeopathy could be . . .' I let Virginia drone on as she drained her cup of peppermint tea, then thanked her for her interest.

Personally I warmed to Audrey, a flamboyantly-dressed woman in search of a setting to begin her new life since her husband had run off with a massage therapist of undetermined gender. She turned pink with pleasure when I admired the magnificent necklace draped in layers over her breasts. It was a cross between one of those ribbons police stretch around crime scenes and something I'd seen hanging in my cousin's cow shed. An Italian designer piece, she said, created by a one-armed artist whose work was gaining value by the day.

Our house, she said, was perfect because there was plenty of room for her to dabble in her weekend hobby, sculpturing massive genitalia out of polystyrene, assuming we didn't mind her transforming Rob's bedroom into a studio. Fortunately, Rob wasn't home to have an opinion. As Audrey stood in Rob's doorway mentally erasing his model aeroplane collection and replacing it with monoliths of passion, a shadow flicked between her ankles. Audrey's reflexes were fast enough for her to snare Cleo and press her to her bosom.

'Oh, a pussy!' she boomed. 'A house isn't a home without a furry friend like you!'

Cleo didn't share Audrey's enthusiasm for a bonding session. In fact, she was more interested in Audrey's necklace than Audrey. She raised a paw and patted a silver bauble inquisitively.

'I think perhaps you should put her back down,' I suggested nervously.

'Nonsense! Pussy knows I adore cats, doesn't he?'

'She's a she, actually . . .'

As I tried to disengage Cleo from the necklace, she caught the bauble between her teeth and crunched. Like the first boulder in an avalanche, it tumbled to the ground. In an unstoppable flow of slow motion the bauble was then followed by a cascade of beads, gems and ribbon. Audrey shrieked. Not even the one-armed master would be capable of restoring the pile of festive rubble that now lay at her feet.

Audrey declined my offer to string the beads together again, or at least find somebody who might be able to. I grabbed an old supermarket bag and shoved what was left of the artwork into it. She was gracious enough to leave without strangling me. Or Cleo.

I was starting to feel desperate. Was nobody right for Cleo? Finally Andrea, a young doctor with green eyes and a froth of dark curls, arrived. She swore she was a cat person and would take good care of Cleo. She didn't try to seduce Cleo as others had and failed. She simply looked around the house and asked questions in an easy going way. As Andrea stood to leave, Cleo arched her back in a sensuous curve and invited Andrea to pat her. With our cat's paw print of approval, we signed Andrea up.

I knew that as well as being capable of great affection Cleo was tough and independent, a survivor. Nevertheless, I worried. Sinking my nose into her fragrant fur, I prayed we'd see her again. The prospect of leaving the kids for three months was like chopping an arm off and putting it in the freezer. I tried to tell myself it wasn't going to be an amputation like losing Sam, but a mere putting on ice. Mum and Steve assured me the children would be fine, especially with Anne Marie's help. I knew all three of them loved Rob and Lydia, but they couldn't provide that unique combination of neuroticism and adoration that is a mother's love. They kept telling me three months would fly. Philip assured me he was going to be engrossed by his pressure-cooker MBA squeezing a two-year course into one.

Cambridge has been home to the best of Britain's grey matter for centuries. Being clever people, the inhabitants have arranged to live in one of the most picturesque towns on earth. Its thirty-one colleges, ancient and modern, are tossed loosely together around the river Cam, which can be sluggish or romantic, depending on its mood. Even on that first day in the knife-like January air, the beauty of Cambridge dragged me out of internal melodrama. The turrets of King's College Chapel pointed skywards with such delicacy they were surely fashioned by bees, not human hands.

'Miss Brown, we're expecting you,' said a voice that sounded as if it came directly from God. It carried knowledge, power, authority—and belonged to the college porter.

Something about the porter reassured me I was part of his scene now and everything would be okay. After he showed me to a large, comfortable room overlooking four fruit trees, I spread photos of the children, Philip and Cleo on every available shelf. And burst into tears.

Everything about Cambridge was unfamiliar. Back home, January is one of the hottest months of the year. Even though I knew England was going to be cold, I hadn't imagined the chill would penetrate every form of clothing and footwear I owned. The English version of the sun dragged itself out of bed at half-past seven and hovered in the air like a reluctant twenty-watt bulb before collapsing into the gloom around three p.m.

Nevertheless, I adored the oldness of Cambridge. The cobblestones, the creaking colleges, the dreaminess of boy soprano voices wafting towards what must surely be heaven at Evensong in King's College Chapel (which, by the way, is nothing short of a cathedral). I loved the quirkiness of Cambridge and its adherence to rules so ancient nobody can remember why they exist. Only college Fellows are allowed to walk on the grass (though I never dared, in case I was the wrong sort of Fellow). Because most of Cambridge's rules serve no apparent practical purpose, there's a pleasant tolerance of odd behaviour. If, for instance, a professor turns up at a formal dinner wearing a diving suit and mask (it was rumoured one had) he was simply adhering to some tradition nobody else could recall.

Everywhere I went in Cambridge there were cats. Being hopelessly cat-sick, I tried to befriend the fat marmalade feline who sat on the brick wall behind the fruit trees. He scurried away at the sight of me.

One day I saw a black tail disappearing around the corner of an ancient church. My heart leapt in recognition. Logically, I knew it wasn't Cleo, but maybe the creature carried some of her spirit. But by the time I'd clambered over the slippery paving down the side of the church the cat had disappeared.

A smug tortoiseshell stretched himself in front of a professor's open fire and yawned. He opened one eye, licked his chops, ran a lazy paw over one ear and fell asleep. His claws snapped open and shut. His tail twitched. No doubt he was dreaming of mice.

Homesickness was such a full-time job during the first few weeks there was hardly time for research. I wrote to Philip, sent postcards and letters on tape to the children every day. Cleo made regular appearances in my dreams. One night I saw her three times the size of the Ardmore Road house. With her head resting on the chimney, she stretched her front paws around the windows and meowed. Her meow was like the roar of the Metro-Goldwyn-Mayer lion. Maybe it was her way of saying she was safe and fulfilling her duty as protector of the home. Unable to sleep, I pulled on two pairs of socks and stumbled down the stairs. The one black phone that house residents shared was mercifully free. I listened for the pulse of the phone ringing at the other end and was about to hang up when someone answered.

'Andrea?' I shouted.

'What time is it?' she mumbled in a voice heavy with sleep.

'Sorry. Have I woken you?'

'It's all right.' Damn. I *had* woken her up. 'I was sleeping in. It's Saturday morning. Where are you?'

'Still in the UK. I was just wondering how Cleo, I mean, *you* are getting on. Any problems with the cat, I mean house?'

'I had a rugged night,' she replied. 'Cleo jumped through the skylight onto my bed when I was fast asleep. It was terrifying. I thought she was a burglar.'

That was the start of a series of phone calls across the globe focussing on the topic of an eccentric black cat. Andrea soon discovered Cleo's three great passions: expensive items, anything made with love, and stolen goods.

'I was heading out to work the other morning when my handbag—not the cheap copy I bought in Bangkok, the genuine Gucci one—anyway, it seemed extra heavy,' she said. 'Lucky I looked inside. Cleo was curled up in there! She looked all expectant, like she was sure I was taking her to work with me. She loves that bag. But honestly, how can she tell the difference between the copy and the genuine article?'

She'd always had a nose for quality. If Cleo was looking for something to sharpen her teeth on she'd favour cashmere over wool, Egyptian cotton over polyester, leather over plastic, even high class expensive plastic.

The next phone call featured the tablecloth Andrea's mother had embroidered for her twenty-first birthday present. Andrea had arrived home one evening to find Cleo had dragged it off the table and was curled up asleep on it.

'She's got this sixth sense,' I explained apologetically. 'She knows when something's been made with love.'

A few weeks later Andrea complained the laces of her running shoes, left and right feet, had disappeared.

'Go into the garden and look in the ferns behind the goldfish pond,' I said.

Following instructions Andrea discovered not only both shoe laces (soggy and frayed) but several socks she'd assumed had been stolen off the clothesline by a neighbourhood foot fetishist.

'I'm so sorry,' I echoed across the oceans. 'I didn't realise she was going to be such a handful.'

Andrea was surprisingly forgiving. In fact, she'd found Cleo so interesting she'd enrolled in night classes in animal behaviour.

'Cleo has classic separation anxiety,' she said. 'She needs lots of activities to make her more independent. I've bought her a few toys to keep her occupied. They seem to be helping, but she still prefers my shoelaces. As for jumping up on the table . . .'

'We've tried to stop her, Andrea, but she thinks she runs the joint.'

'Well, I've developed the perfect solution. A water pistol.'

'You squirt her?'

'Only when she's up on the table. Right up the backside. She's a fast learner.'

I felt like the mother of a delinquent child receiving reports from its correctional institution. Nevertheless, Andrea was obviously fond of Cleo and it sounded like her methods were working. I wasn't going to complain if she ironed out some of our cat's quirks in our absence.

The next time we spoke Andrea told me about the personal trainer she'd hired. Roy visited the house twice a week and, according to Andrea, Cleo always knew when it was Tuesday or Thursday—a Roy Day. She waited in the front window until Apollo in a tracksuit opened the front gate. She then bounced to the front door, eager to find out what he'd brought her to play with this time—stretchy bands, balls? The moment Roy unfurled his exercise mat on the floor Cleo spread herself on it and rolled on her back, stretching her arms and legs, flicking her head side to side, watching for Roy's admiration.

'Anyone would think Roy's been hired for Cleo's fitness training,' Andrea grumbled with (thank heavens) a smile in her voice, but she did confess to feeling resentful at times. Whenever Roy engaged Andrea in a particularly harrowing set of sit ups, Cleo would upstage her by burrowing her head under the exercise mat or engaging Roy in her version of wrestling—wrapping her paws around his ankles and kicking him with her hind legs.

Upside down, her toes clinging to the Swiss ball while she attempted 25 push-ups, Andrea could sense Roy's attention wandering to the feline flirting with him from behind the curtains. Roy was a self-confessed dog person, but he was beginning to change his mind. He asked Andrea where he could get a cat like that. She recommended house sitting for unusual families who'd taken off overseas.

Even though Cambridge opened fascinating new worlds to me, nothing surpassed the joy of reuniting with Lydia and Philip after three months. On the pretext of having important business in Ireland, wonderful Mary, the fashion reporter, accompanied

Lydia from New Zealand. Lydia rewarded her by throwing up orange juice over Mary's jacket as the plane flew out of Auckland.

We met at Heathrow, before flying to Geneva and boarding a train that wove along the lake front. The train stopped briefly at chocolate-box villages on its way to the medieval town of Lausanne.

I promised five-year-old Lydia she'd adore her new school and would be speaking French in no time. Wrong on both counts. Apart from having a regime as rigid as the Swiss Alps, the Swiss school was a nightmare for Lydia. She couldn't understand a word anyone said. As we staggered up the vertical path to the local primary school every morning, I tried to divert her attention to rows of tulips standing to attention alongside the path, or the Alps sprinkled with icing-sugar snow across the lake. She always had a 'sore tummy' by the time we reached the school gates. I hated leaving her red-faced and in tears as I abandoned her to the care of her teacher. Madame Juillard's kindness turned out to be a form of inadvertent cruelty. She spoke to the class in French, then repeated everything in English for Lydia. As a result, Lydia remained unable to communicate with her classmates.

The one subject Lydia excelled in was swimming, due to long summers spent on New Zealand beaches. The Swiss sports teacher was intrigued by the Antipodean tadpole. Despite the humiliation of a preswim shower and the insistence on a bathing cap being worn at all times, Lydia could slap out a length of the indoor pool in her deep-sea overarm. Unable to relate to the wild freedom that creates a young surfer, the teacher amused us by suggesting Lydia had a future as a synchronised swimmer.

While I was flat out failing to meet the standards of Swiss house frau-hood, Philip slogged through punishing hours at business school. On one of his rare days off when we were sailing up a mountain slope in a gondola not much bigger than a vitamin pill, Philip took my hand, and remarked that the skin under my engagement ring was turning a delicate shade of green. I was startled to discover he was right. Our year's betrothal was past its use-by date. He suggested if we were going to tie the knot, Switzerland was as good a place as any to do it. Besides, we both liked the idea of getting married far away from those who regarded our unusual set up as a source of gossip and amusement.

There are the Swiss Alps, chocolates, banks, watches, cheese and cuckoo clocks. While Switzerland is famous for many other things besides (including giant mountain horns and nuclear shelters for every household) it is not widely feted as a wedding destination. We were about to find out why.

+

If there was a competition for the most difficult place on earth to get married in, Switzerland would win the prize. But then, Philip and I had a talent for doing things the hard way. We decided the land of clocks and chocolate was ideal for us to tie the knot. Someone should have warned us. As usual, we were insane.

When he wasn't studying the machinations of international business, Philip was warring with petit officials, who demanded to sight and stamp every document that had our names on it (from birth certificates and proof of my divorce to Girl Guide sock-darning awards). After weeks of phoning and faxing lawyers across the globe, the Swiss officials were finally satisfied. Every scrap of paper was signed, countersigned and delivered in triplicate. But that wasn't enough. They then demanded to know how many facial moles our parents and grandparents had, at what age they had sex for the first time and which side they slept on at night. The truth is, Swiss officials don't want people getting married in their country, and they'll do everything in their power to stop it. They don't approve of holy union. It's too much paperwork. They'd rather people lived in sin.

The best thing about getting married in a foreign country is it's so inconvenient that the few guests who *do* make the effort to turn up sincerely want to be there. We arranged the wedding to take place in the September holidays, so Rob and other family members could share the occasion. I bought a cream suit and matching hat. We took a daytrip across the lake to Evian to buy Lydia a French party frock with a lilac sash and stiff petticoat straight out of *The Sound of Music*.

Around forty guests turned up for the wedding. Most of them wanted to stay in our miniscule apartment. We practically had them sleeping in wardrobes. The living area was set aside for itinerant Romanians. Mum and Rob slept in Lydia's room.

Without being biased I have to say it was the best wedding I've ever been to. It was in an exquisite medieval church on the shores of Lake Geneva. Our weekend honeymoon was friendly, too. Five guests, including the bride's mother and children, accompanied us to the dreamy shores of Lake Maggiore in northern Italy. The only thing missing was a small black cat.

After the guests dispersed, Philip returned to his executive sweat shop. Golden autumn days leaked into sleety grey. Cobbled streets that had been picture-book quaint in summer faded to charcoal drawings. We never adjusted to the ferocity of European cold. No matter how thick our socks, our toes became ice.

At the end of our year in Switzerland I wasn't sad to leave. The feeling appeared to be mutual. Officials at Geneva airport decided we were such an unlikely trio we had to be terrorists. They took us aside to interrogate us. How could we possibly be married? Whose child was she, anyway? When I swore we'd packed no guns, they knew they had us. We were escorted into a room, where I was made to unpack my suitcase to reveal a weapon of minimal destruction—my umbrella.

On the way home we had a few days' stopover in New York with my old friend Lloyd. He knew all the right places to take a girl. What gay man doesn't? I made excuses to take a break from the sight-seeing, sneaked into Kmart and bought a pregnancy testing kit. Back at Lloyd's I hurried upstairs past his African mask collection and shut myself in his bathroom. Holding the test stick to the light, it was hard to stop my hands trembling long enough to read the result. Hallelujah! A little plus sign appeared.

Patience

To wait is merely to consider the clouds for a while

'Cleo is *how* old?' Rosie asked over the phone.

'Ten,' I replied.

'Amazing!' said Rosie. 'I never thought she'd live that long.'

'Living with us, you mean?'

'Well, yes, frankly. You must be doing something right.'

One of the many ways in which cats are superior to humans is their mastery of time. By making no attempt to dissect years into months, days into hours and minutes into seconds, cats avoid much misery. Free from the slavery of measuring every moment, worrying whether they are late or early, young or old, or if Christmas is six weeks away, felines appreciate the present in all its multi-dimensional glory. They never worry about endings or beginnings. From their paradoxical viewpoint an ending is often a beginning. The joy of basking on a window ledge can seem eternal, though if measured in human time it's diminished to a paltry eighteen minutes.

If humans could program themselves to forget time, they would savour a string of pleasures and possibilities. Regrets about the past would dissolve, alongside anxieties for the future. We'd notice the colour of the sky and be liberated to seize the wonder of being alive in this moment. If we could be more like cats our lives would seem eternal.

I wasn't sure what sort of reception we'd get from Cleo. A year is a long time to be away from someone you love. There was a chance she wouldn't recognise us. No doubt she'd shifted loyalties to Andrea. That would be understandable. We'd fled while Andrea fed.

As the cab pulled up outside our front gate in Auckland I was relieved to see the house spread like a familiar smile behind the fence. Shrubs in the front garden were a little taller. Wisteria had increased its stranglehold around the verandah posts. I scanned the windows and the roof for signs of a small black cat. Nothing. Andrea, who'd moved out the day before, had assured us our cat was still alive. Maybe she'd tactfully forgotten to mention that Cleo had gone feral.

With a boulder in my chest I helped Philip and Rob unload our suitcases from the cab. The front gate opened with its familiar complaint. The wind in the bottle brush flowers held its breath.

'Cleo!' Rob called in the man's voice that had croaked its way into his larynx.

A black shape trotted down the side of the house in our direction. I'd forgotten she was so tiny. Her pace was businesslike at first, as if she might be heading out to check for spiders in the letterbox. She hesitated, pricked her ears and scowled at us. For a moment I thought she might drop her tail and scurry under the house.

'We're home, Cleo!' Lydia cried.

The cat meowed gleefully and sprinted towards us. We dropped our bags and ran to her, each of us fighting for turns to hold the purring bundle and smother her with kisses. Even though Rob and Lydia had sprouted over the past year, she remembered all four of us.

Once we were inside, the warmth of her welcome cooled. Cleo decided we needed punishment for our absence. She asked to be let outside and perched on the roof for several hours. After we'd unpacked I lured her down to ground level with a bowl of her old favourite—barbecued chicken. Halfway through her meal she looked up at me and winked as if to say *So, pregnant again? Can't you humans control yourselves? Oh well. Guess I can put up with a few more years being dressed up in baby clothes and wheeled around in a doll's pram.*

Early in the pregnancy I went to a specialist and begged him to anaesthetise me from the neck down for the birth of my fourth child. He agreed. At the age of thirty-eight I even had a medical title—Elderly Multigravida (which, by the way, any aspiring rock band in search of a name is welcome to). To reinforce the notion I had everything to fear he showed me a chart of the increased rate of birth defects as mothers approach forty. I left his offices feeling old. Sick and old. Following his advice I underwent invasive tests, one of which brought on worrying contractions. The tests showed the baby was healthy. And a girl.

With Cleo curled on my lap one afternoon, I phoned Ginny in Wellington. Instead of laughing at my vision of a high-tech birth, all bright lights and scalpels, she put me onto a magnificent midwife, Jilleen.

The moment I opened our door to Jilleen the baby somersaulted inside me. Jilleen had the kindest brown eyes. Her small hands were crossed neatly in front of her body. I knew this was the woman who would deliver our child despite the fact that we'd never thought of ourselves as home birth people.

◆

A smudge of cloud crossed the moon. Schubert's music wrapped itself tenderly around the room. An open fire flickered shadows of Philip, Cleo and Jilleen against the wall. Time dissolved. We welcomed each muscular surge the way a surfer greets a wave, with concentration and respect. As the contraction reached its peak Jilleen taught Philip how to massage the pain away with gentle circular movements around my belly. Katharine tumbled pink and disgruntled into the world around two in the morning in her big brother's bedroom. Our support team (including Anne Marie and a local doctor) glowed with that sense of achievement seen on the faces of people who have plunged off a bridge with elastic bands attached to their ankles. Lucky for Rob, he was staying at his dad's house that night. We weren't even going to tell our sixteen-year-old son exactly where the baby had been born in case he refused to ever sleep there again. Our plans were quashed when he discovered an acupuncture needle on his bed covers and demanded to know the truth. To my surprise he wasn't the slightest bit squeamish that his room had doubled as a delivery suite. In fact, he seemed almost proud of the fact.

Time is said to heal everything. Certainly on the surface our lives were looking good. I no longer dreaded parent–teacher interviews at Rob's school. He'd worked hard. The tone in the teachers' voices had changed. Instead of learning difficulties, they spoke of career options like medicine or engineering. His final-year marks were dazzling enough to earn him a scholarship to embark on an engineering degree at university.

I was happy, too, and grateful for the loving stability Philip brought us. Nevertheless, there was part of our lives that Rob and I tucked away and seldom talked about, certainly not in the company of others.

'Sometimes I feel as if our lives have been split in two,' he said one day when the house was silent except for the mews of Cleo pacing in front of the fridge. 'There was the existence we had with Sam, and the one after he died. It's almost as if we've had two separate lives.'

I had to agree. Few things bridged those two worlds, apart from a handful of friends and relatives, and the small black cat Sam had chosen for us all those years ago. Even though we laughed, worked and played, our grief was still real, unresolved in many ways and buried deep inside. Concerned neither of us had undergone professional grief counselling, I sometimes embarked on 'Remember when Sam . . .' stories to encourage Rob to acknowledge our previous life. We thumbed through photo albums, talked and smiled. But to say time had healed us was a lie. Although we'd encompassed the enormity of losing Sam, we were still emotional amputees. We'd lost a limb when he died. After so many years the stump was invisible to almost everyone, apart from Rob and me.

Rob sprouted into a tall, handsome young man. He was a strong swimmer and, with Philip's encouragement, a triathlete and yachtsman. While I sometimes worried about his emotional wellbeing his physical health was never a concern. He had an enviable ability to shrug off any virus within a day.

Watching him plunge into the surf I sometimes imagined his older brother alongside him. What would Sam look like by now? Probably a little shorter than his younger brother, but even-featured and no doubt handsome in his own way. I wondered what byways that unconventional streak might have taken Sam on. Maybe he'd have turned my hair grey dabbling in drugs and embarking on an uncertain career in film-making. Alternatively, he may have become a mother's dream, sailed through law school and be halfway to owning a house in the suburbs. Time-wasting fantasies were no use.

During the holidays after his first university year Rob, Philip and I were walking to the local shopping centre. Rob suddenly turned pale and said he felt unwell. 'Sick?' I said. 'You're never sick.' Rob was equally bewildered. Such a stranger to illness, he had no idea about the etiquette of throwing up in public. Instead of bending discreetly over the gutter, he spun about, showering us with his breakfast. I assumed he'd eaten a dodgy hamburger and would recover in no time. I assumed wrong.

He took to his bed and was unable to eat or drink for several days. His GP assured us it wasn't serious and wouldn't last long. But by the end of the week he was severely dehydrated and admitted to hospital, where he was diagnosed with ulcerative colitis, an inflammatory bowel condition, cause unknown. Rob's attack was diagnosed as very severe.

I sat helpless at his bedside, watching him grow weaker by the day. Once again I mustered all my life-giving power as his mother and willed him to get better. Yet again it seemed to fail. Several times I excused myself to find an alcove to weep in. The prospect of losing another son was unbearable.

A young surgeon in a green gown fresh from theatre stood over the bed. If Rob didn't respond to the drugs and his already swollen colon expanded another centimetre, he said, the entire lower bowel (more than two metres long) would have to be removed. The surgeon described the operation as Big.

A tower was under construction outside Rob's hospital window. I willed time to pass, so we could move forward to a happier phase, when the building was finished and Rob (please every deity that ever existed) was well again. The more I bullied the minutes to speed into hours, the more begrudgingly they crawled. Sometimes they seemed to stop altogether, like belligerent donkeys on a mountain pass.

Rob and I re-enacted his babyhood. I stroked his hair and helped him sip an unpalatable canned drink that contained essential nutrients. I tried to find ways to help him feel better. Reducing his fear was difficult when I was almost equally terrified. A rose quartz crystal on his stomach seemed to help soothe violent seizures of pain. His face always lit up when he was told someone was praying for him or sending healing energy. Rob welcomed a visit from Patrick, a psychic healer. When Patrick took his hand Rob said he felt an invisible force holding his other hand.

I stuck a photo of a mountain glowing pink in a sunset above his hospital bed. Rob looked up at it and said he'd get there some day. He'd always dreamed of taking time out to work on a ski field.

Fleets of doctors and surgeons visited Rob in the mornings. While they claimed to be using blood tests and X-rays to determine if Rob needed surgery, they seemed to rely more on how he looked and responded to them.

As they drew close to making the grim decision, I urged Rob to drag himself out of bed and walk down the corridor when the doctors were due. The effort of struggling fifty metres to the showers was enormous. Rob could hardly walk, let alone wheel the drip he was attached to. As we glided painfully past the team of doctors, their faces froze with astonishment. Rob's triumph at that moment was up there with winning an Olympic marathon.

The surgery was put on hold. Rob's condition slowly improved. We knew he was on the mend the night we found him sitting in the ward's television room.

'How do I look?' he asked Philip.

Not great, to tell the truth. Rob had lost ten kilos through his ordeal. His skin glowed white against his red bathrobe, and he was still attached to a drip. Nevertheless, the return of masculine vanity was the best sign yet.

He was prescribed hefty doses of steroids for the foreseeable future and warned that his colon might eventually have to be removed. By the time he was allowed home Rob was a skeletal version of his former self. Just weeks earlier he'd been water skiing, rising from the lake like a young Apollo. It was hard to believe all that muscle and tan could evaporate so quickly. He was too weak to walk to the carpark. He waited on a bench outside the hospital doors while I collected the car.

We'd tidied and freshened up his bedroom at home, but more than anything he wanted to be outside. I set up a chair and blanket for him in the garden, where Cleo quickly joined him.

'I never realised the sky was such an intense blue,' he said as the cat nestled into the folds of his trousers that were now several sizes too big for him.

He examined the grass, trees and flowers with the peeled-back clarity of one who has been close to death.

'The colours are so bright,' he said. 'The birds, the insects. I used to take them all for granted. It's a miracle. I hope I always see the world this clearly.'

As soon as he was strong enough, Rob packed his ancient car to the roof and drove south. Miraculously, the car held together long enough to get him to the far end of South Island. He spent the winter skiing and making coffees in a ski field cafe near Queenstown. After that, he was ready to get back to university and finish his degree.

But his health was far from perfect. Although he suffered regular 'flare-ups' the steroids ensured none were as bad as the first attack. With a stony sense of dread I noticed the steroid doses had to be increased every few months to keep his condition under control.

In case we were lapsing into an assumption that life was dull, Philip arrived home from work one evening to announce he'd had a promotion. The only complication was the job was in Melbourne, Australia.

Missing

A cat reserves the right to disappear without explanation

My habitual terror of flying was replaced by a different neurosis—cat-in-the-hold anxiety. What if Cleo was freezing back there? Or if her carry box had been placed alongside a pit bull terrier with anger management issues? My ear was cocked for the sound of muffled meowing from the plane's rear. A pair of stewards performed the flight instructions with the flourish of chorus members from *Priscilla, Queen of the Desert*—'Should an oxygen mask appear, bat your eyelashes, swoosh that plastic tube and gyrate those hips!' Clattering trolleys, yelling babies and pilot's announcements drowned all hopes I had of hearing distress calls from Cleo.

I tried not to worry. There was a chance she wasn't even on our plane. We'd been told she might arrive up to twenty-four hours later than us.

The parched continent spread like a giant poppadum beneath us. Engines whined as we descended into Melbourne. Fear flipped into excitement and back again. As we climbed into a cab I savoured the dry air and the giant blue sky. Everything about Australia was magnified, more confident and outgoing. I hoped we could burrow out a life for ourselves on its sunburnt expanse.

The girls regarded the move with almost as little enthusiasm as the convicts who'd been shipped to the country one hundred and fifty years earlier. Unlike the British penal system, we'd gone out of our way to make their transportation to Australia seem attractive. In short, we'd bribed them. Shamelessly. Katharine, who'd initially insisted on a kangaroo farm, settled for a Barbie house with a motorised elevator. Lydia was still working a deal to be driven to her new school in one of the horse-drawn carriages she'd seen trotting around the central city ('the one with red feathers on the horses' heads').

As the cab pulled up outside our rented villa in the leafy suburb of Malvern, I was still worrying about our cat. Poor old Cleo. She was probably languishing in some horrible transit prison for animals. Maybe I should have accepted Rosie's offer to adopt her. Rosie had pointed out that, at the age of fifteen, Cleo was the human equivalent of seventy-five years old. It was, she hinted, nothing short of a miracle our cat had survived this long, considering her rugged lifestyle with us. She'd implied that Cleo's vital organs mightn't be up to the rigours of jet travel. A short retirement in Rosie's cat menagerie was possibly a more humane option. Nevertheless, Cleo was woven into our family history as firmly as cat fur into a favourite blanket. We weren't perfect cat parents. But leaving her behind was unthinkable.

A lot had changed since our return from Switzerland five years earlier. After leaving school with a scholarship Rob completed his degree and decided to embark on an engineering career in Melbourne. Lydia was on the brink of becoming a teenager. Katharine was about to start school. My ex-husband Steve had married Amanda, and they'd produced a daughter. On a much sadder note, Mum had succumbed to bowel cancer and died after a few weeks of illness. Her suffering in the final days had been terrible to watch, yet she embraced death with great courage. As she'd withered to a shell of her former self, her spirit seemed to distil into dazzling purity, which blazed from every part of her. Harrowing as it was, I'd felt privileged to be alone with her as she heaved her last painful breath. I missed our phone conversations, her ceaseless encouragement, her refusal to regard life in its dimmest light.

Some things had stayed the same, however. Cleo was still undisputed queen of our household.

'There's something on the doorstep,' said Rob.

There was a large box in the shadows of the front porch. I assumed it was a piece of junk the previous tenants had left behind. It had a mesh side. We approached tentatively. A pair of familiar green eyes glowered out from behind the wire.

'Look who's here!' said Philip.

The eyes glared back as if to say, *Well you certainly took your time!*

'Cleo! You're here already!' the girls cried in unison.

Typical of Cleo's style, she'd arrived in our new country hours ahead of the rest of us. Somewhere along the line she'd flashed a look at a quarantine officer. He'd recognised an Egyptian goddess when he saw one and given her first-class treatment.

Cleo devoured her first Australian meal in a matter of minutes. She was adapting faster than the rest of us. My first reaction was to reach for the phone to tell countless people back in New Zealand we'd arrived. They sounded warm and happy to hear from me, but I sensed we were rapidly becoming part of their history.

Calling home was the easy part. The hard bit was finding new everythings—from doctors and hairdressers to shopping centres and playgrounds. The most daunting 'new' was discovering new friends. The importance of an amiable network of people struck home when I had to fill out school forms. For 'Emergency Contact: i.e. friend, neighbour etc.' I had no choice but to leave a blank space. We were stranded on a rock of anonymity. If we couldn't find new friends soon we'd have to invent some. I'd decided to work from home sending columns back to newspapers and *Next* magazine in New Zealand. While I loved staying in touch with loyal readers it was a solitary occupation. Mulling over a computer screen in the suburbs was hardly going to raise my chances of meeting friends.

After keeping Cleo inside for the statutory two days I opened the back door for her. She nudged a tentative nose outside. Her whiskers twitched. She lifted an uncertain paw. Australia, with its concoction of garden smells mingled with possum fur, eucalypt and parrot feathers, smelt different. Before I could stop her she slithered like a trout between my ankles and disappeared into a clump of bird of paradise.

'It's okay,' I said to Katharine. 'She's just exploring. She'll be back for dinner.'

Dinner time came and went. Not a whisker of Cleo. In all her fifteen years she'd never disappeared on us. Dusk faded. The sky turned the colour of a bruise and it started to drizzle. Cleo hated rain. We called for her. No answer.

'She's probably sheltering under the house,' I said, hoping it was true. 'She'll turn up in the morning.'

Rain hammered on the roof all night. It wasn't right. Australia was famous for drought and desert, not downpours. Soon after dawn I hurried out of bed to check doors and windows for a cat asking to be let in. Nothing. Losing our beloved Cleo would be a ghastly omen for our move to Australia. Philip left for his first day at work, a cloud of anxiety in his eyes. After breakfast, the girls and I slid into raincoats and trawled the neighbourhood, calling for her. A grumpy white cat stared at us from a window. Across the road I heard a dog bark. While Cleo wasn't as resilient as she used to be, she was still tough. But what if Australian animals were tougher? If she encountered a rottweiler she mightn't be able to stare him down. Even though she could still run, she wasn't an elite athlete anymore.

Tucking the girls under their blankets that night, I tried to prepare them for heartache. 'Cleo's had a long, exciting life,' I said.

'Do you think she's dead?' Lydia asked.

'No,' I said. 'She doesn't *feel* dead, does she? I think she knows we still need her.'

I couldn't help thinking the odds were against us. An old cat runaway in a new country had a survival chance of a thousand to one. With every hour that passed her chances were surely getting slimmer.

Next day the rain had eased. We searched the neighbourhood again. My throat was sore from calling her name. We trailed through laneways and a builder's yard. We scoured a playground at the end of the street. There seemed no point investigating the busy main road just a couple of houses from our new place. If Cleo had ventured in that direction we wouldn't be seeing her again.

Heavy hearted, we turned into the gate. Now I really wished I'd been sensible enough to accept Rosie's offer to let Cleo spend her sunset years with a certified cat lover. We'd been crazy to move countries. Mentally deranged to think we had sufficient charm and energy to make new friends. Gulping back tears, I draped my arms around the girls' shoulders and croaked out one last hopeless 'Cleeeeeo!' The houses and trees of our new neighbourhood responded with silence.

A shadow flickered in the basement of the house across the road, the one where we'd heard the dog barking. The shape pushed forwards and squeezed between some gardenia bushes. At first I thought it was some strange Australian animal, an urban wombat, perhaps. But it had ears and whiskers . . . and . . . to our great relief, Cleo trotted across the street into our arms. We never found out where she'd been and whether some other family had tried to lure her to their fridge. Whatever she'd been up to, she'd made a decision in our favour.

✦

Everything in Australia was bolder and more luridly coloured—including the bird life. I assumed Cleo would reassert her reign of terror over the feathered species once she knew her way around. But Australian birds aren't to be messed with. Assertive as Dame Edna on HRT, they have no intention of becoming a cat's breakfast.

Cleo was dazzled by the colours of the rainbow lorikeets, who set themselves up in our backyard pear tree. She ran her tongue over her lips, imagining the pretty toothpicks their green and red feathers would make. But they cackled derisively at the elderly black cat. They knew that if she got anywhere near them they'd claw her to pieces and fillet what was left of her with their beaks.

A couple of magpies decided to claim vengeance on behalf of the entire bird species. One afternoon I glanced out the kitchen window to see Cleo, head down, tail tucked under, running as fast as she could up the side of the house. Like a pair of spitfires the magpies were chasing her, swooping and diving and squawking with delight. I ran to the door and opened it just in time for Cleo to sprint inside to safety.

Our four walls couldn't protect us from everything, though. Just when we thought we were adjusting to our new life we struck our first forty-degree day. I'd always claimed to be a warm-weather person. A few extra notches up the thermometer would be nothing short of delightful. Having grown up in a country that welcomes every ray of warmth, I threw the windows and curtains open. Nothing like a good through-draft. Except this 'through-draft' was hurtling straight off the sizzling Red Centre into our living room. Heat lumbered through the house like a monster. Instead of wafting through as heat was supposed to, it plonked itself in every room and expanded like a phantom until it filled every corner and reached the ceiling.

My arms and legs swelled to twice their size. My hair hung in damp streamers. My heart thudded in my ears. Paralysed on the sofa, I could hardly move. I managed to drag a basket of laundry out to the clothes line. Our underwear practically caught fire in the wind.

We were all overwhelmed by the heat. It was worse for Cleo. Her black coat absorbed the warmth and distributed it through her body like a personal central heating system. She who liked nothing more than roasting herself by an open fire lay seemingly lifeless on her side, limbs rigor-mortis rigid, her tongue a rippling flag of surrender.

While hot days came and went, Rob's illness continued to debilitate him. The flare-ups were increasingly frequent and severe. At twenty-four, he was a qualified engineer, yet a normal working life was impossible. The extent of his debilitation struck me the day we took him for a bushwalk, or tried to: he couldn't walk much further than the distance between two lamp posts. His gastroenterologist told him the steroid levels he was taking were unsustainable. Rob agreed to see a colorectal surgeon.

I was concerned for him on many levels, including his social life. Having left his friends from school and university behind in New Zealand, he knew hardly anyone his own age in Australia. When I mentioned this to Trudy, one of the mothers at Katharine's school, she brought her niece, Chantelle, over to meet Rob one day. A beautiful young brunette, Chantelle filled the kitchen with her vibrant personality. Oddly, I felt a similar sense of recognition I'd experienced meeting Philip. I put it down to Chantelle's outgoing nature. She was just one of those people who's easy to warm to. Chantelle took Rob to a football game and introduced him to her younger brother Daniel. I could tell Rob had feelings for her, but hopes of anything other than friendship were futile. Not with massive surgery looming ahead of him.

Anxiety clawed at my insides. I hated the prospect of Rob undergoing such a radical procedure. Nobody wants their child mutilated. What if the surgery went wrong? If, on the other hand, he elected not to have the surgery the future would be even grimmer. One glimpse of his pale face, swollen from steroid intake, was enough to convince me. He was dying in front of our eyes.

♦

One morning I opened the kitchen door to find a plump baby thrush lying stunned on its back on the brick path. Cleo was losing her touch. Not so long ago she would have gone in for the kill by now. The baby thrush's eyes were bright, alarmed. Perched on the fence above, two adult birds, the parents, were creating the mayhem that had drawn me outside.

As Cleo crept forwards for the final lunge, my skin prickled with rage. How could she be so soft and loving one minute and a cold-hearted destroyer of families the next? For once I had the opportunity to stop one of her ritual killings. I grabbed her and swept her into the house, slamming the door behind us.

All afternoon Cleo and I watched the adult birds flit between the fence and an overgrown camellia bush. Their shrieks were fractured with desperation. I understood their anguish as they urged their child to fight for life. At least they'd been spared the horror of seeing their child mutilated, I thought. Then again, those two little words 'at least' always carried a shadow of dread with them.'

Cleo was infuriated by my sentimentality. *It's nature, you fool*, she seemed to say. *You're only making things worse. Let me get it over and done with.*

Next morning, I imprisoned her indoors. The baby bird lay motionless in the same spot on the brick path. Its eyes were blank, its claws curled up in a gesture of astonishment. I gulped back tears. To my surprise the parents were still standing guard in the camellia bush, staring down at their dead child in disbelief. I'd never realised birds could feel grief for their lost children the way people do. As Sam had often said, the world of animals is more complex and beautiful than humans understand.

Witnessing the scene from a nearby window, Cleo licked her paws with regal nonchalance. I struggled to even like her at that moment.

Purr Power

A nurse cat is more devoted than her human counterpart,
though some of her methods may be unconventional

The cause of ulcerative colitis and its terrible cousin Crohn's disease is unknown, though research continues. Why this cruel ulcerating of the bowel should occur mostly in young people aged between fifteen and thirty-five is a mystery, although I couldn't help feeling that, in Rob's case, unresolved grief over Sam had contributed. There is as yet no cure, apart from surgical removal of the bowel.

Rob didn't want a fuss. We drove to the hospital as if it were an ordinary day and we were heading into the city to have lunch. As the car hugged the curve of the river, I thought of the surgeon's hands. Today, I hoped they'd be working well. What can you say to a son who's about to undergo a massive operation that will permanently change (mutilate?) his body?

'Isn't the light beautiful on the water?'

He grunted agreement. If by some miracle the surgery was successful it would give him new life. I tried not to think of the enormity of what was about to happen. Eight feet of colon would be removed, and he'd return home with a colostomy bag. It wasn't supposed to be like this. He was born perfect. I'd used every ounce of my maternal powers to make him stay that way. My determination to heal him through sheer will had failed. If all went well there'd be a second operation two months later to remove the colostomy bag and give at least (*at least, at least*—what loathsome words they were) the appearance of physical normality.

Conversation was minimal. Toothbrush. Check. Razor. Check. Why couldn't he have the one thing that mattered? Good health. Uncheck. We caught the elevator to the eighth floor, where a small grey room was waiting for him. A crucifix on the wall was a reminder of previous young men who'd suffered more than their due. He sat in a chair that had arms but could in no way qualify as an armchair. At least the room had a view over the city.

'Chantelle will be in there,' he said, pointing at a grey cube of a building. 'The university.'

My heart lurched. To have twenty-four-year-old male yearnings inside a body that refused to work properly seemed the ultimate cruelty. All the other patients on his floor were the wrong side of seventy.

Our silence wasn't awkward so much as textured.

'I love you,' I said. The words conveyed a tiny percentage of my feelings for my beautiful, sensitive, cat-loving son.

'You can go now,' he said, not moving his gaze from the window.

'Don't you want me to stay till they settle you in?'

He shook his head. 'Tell Cleo I'll be home soon,' he said.

My last glimpse of him as I left the ward was of a lonely figure sitting in a chair facing a window.

Outside on ground level, I crossed the street to find a small church. Wood-lined and colonial, it reminded me of the one in which I'd struggled so hard as a child to learn God's rules. I tried to pray again, but my conversation with God was one-sided as usual.

There was more solace to be found in the park outside, the giant soothing hands of branches reaching over me. It was easier to imagine God here among leaves and flowers that pulsated with life. Death and decay was woven into the beauty in ways that seemed natural and reassuring.

Gulping the oxygenated air, I thanked the Victorian minds that had decreed hospitals needed parks nearby. Grass and trees absorb human worries and help put them in perspective.

Six long hours later I fumbled in my handbag. My hand trembled and was so slippery I could barely hold the phone to my ear. The surgeon's voice was weary, matter of fact, with an upbeat edge.

'It went well,' he said.

✦

Cleo and I nursed Rob through his recovery from the first operation, and a couple of months later, the second. As he regained strength he often draped Cleo over his stomach to let her throaty song reverberate through his wounds. While scientists have proven pets help people live longer, more research needs to be done on the healing potential of a cat's purr. It's a primeval chant, the rhythm of waves crashing on the shore. There's powerful medicine in it.

Cats are known to purr not only to express pleasure but also when they're in great pain. Some say the feline lullaby is comforting because it reminds them of when they were kittens curled in the warmth of their mother's fur. I wouldn't be surprised if some day the purr is proved to be much more than a lullaby, that the vibrations have potential to heal living tissue.

'Listen to that,' he said one day. 'It's a cross between a gurgle and a roar—a rurgle.'

'Do you remember when you were little you said Cleo was talking to you?' I asked. 'Was that real?'

'It felt real at the time.'

'Does she still talk to you?' I asked, no longer concerned for his sanity. Years ago I'd accepted Rob had a special connection with Cleo that only seemed to bring good.

'In dreams, sometimes.'

'What does she say?'

'She doesn't talk so much these days as show me things. Sometimes we go back to when Sam was alive. We'll run up and down the zigzag with him. It's like she's telling me everything's going to be okay.'

Cleo straightened her front legs, arched her back and opened her mouth in a cavernous yawn. Appearing in Rob's dreams was just a pastime, as far as she was concerned.

I'd have willingly exchanged places with Rob to relieve him of his ordeals. Yet he shrugged when I said such things. In many ways, he said, the illness was a gift. I shivered when he talked that way. He sounded like an old man. Certainly, his experiences gave him a perspective well beyond his years.

'I've been through good times and bad times,' he said. 'Believe me, good's better. When you've tasted stale bread, you really appreciate the fluffy stuff fresh out of the oven.'

Rob's body gradually adjusted to eating and absorbing solid food again, though he still looked like a survivor from a wartime prison camp. If, for some reason, his body refused to heal properly and he had complications I wondered if he'd have any strength left to muster a fight. Fortunately, he was young and he seemed have stores of vigour to draw on from his athletic years.

Cleo, a more conscientious nurse than I, trotted after him around the house, snuggling into his blankets and presenting him with the occasional get-well present in the form of a decapitated lizard.

Through our long days at home together, I had the blessing of getting to know Rob better. It's rare for a young man in his twenties to share his thoughts with his mother. In an unexpected way, his illness brought us closer together.

'I used to wish I had an easier life,' he mused. 'Some families sail through years with nothing touching them. They have no tragedies. They go on about how lucky they are. Yet sometimes it seems to me they're half alive. When something goes wrong for them, and it does for everyone sooner or later, their trauma is much worse. They've had nothing bad happen to them before. In the meantime, they think little problems, like losing a wallet, are big deals. They think it's ruined their day. They have no idea what a hard day's like. It's going to be incredibly tough for them when they find out.'

He'd also developed his own version of making the most of every minute. 'Through Sam I found out how quickly things can change. Because of him I've learnt to appreciate each moment and try not to hold on to things. Life's more exciting and intense that way. It's like the yoghurt that goes off after three days. It tastes so much better than the stuff that lasts three weeks.'

My young philosopher in a dressing-gown had theories to rival an Eastern mystic's. Yet deep down we both knew his dreams were the same as every other young person's. More than anything, he longed for love and happiness.

Connection

*A cat who appears in a dream is no less real than one who
pads a kitchen floor*

The psychic cat is connected to the world in more ways than
we imagine. She can creep into a kitchen or, just as easily, a
dream. Waiting on her favourite window ledge, she knows
when her slaves are on their way home to her. Guardian of
unworldly powers, she beams a shield of protection over the
human household she has blessed with her presence. Sometimes
they are aware of her ability to slide between worlds. Mostly
they are not.

A couple of months later Rob was still as thin as a sapling
in winter and, as far as I could make out from an anxious
mother's perspective, not fully healed. Nevertheless, he insisted
on planning an Outback adventure with a couple of old school
mates—'the boys'. They planned to drive through the desert to
Australia's red heart, Uluru. A journey that would take three
weeks. To say I worried was an understatement. Yet I had to
accept that Rob had no intention of having an 'invalid' sticker
attached to his forehead for the rest of his days. He craved a
normal young man's life brimming with adventure, but the risks
were enough to turn a mother's heart to jelly.

I lectured the boys about the Outback being basically a vast
zoo for creatures armed for attack. From crocodiles and sharks

to snakes, spiders and ants, they're all expert killers devoid of affection for the human species. Even kangaroos can be killers, crashing inadvertently through drivers' windows at sunset.

They listened and nodded sagely. They weren't fools who'd go out of their way to get into trouble.

The only thing that concerned me more than wild animals was the danger of mechanical breakdown. Since his surgery, Rob had been urged to keep hydrated as much as possible. If their vehicle sputtered to a halt in some parched wilderness, lack of water could be a serious problem. The boys assured me they had plenty of spare water on board. Technically, they weren't boys anymore but young men well beyond the age of consent. I was left with no choice but to trust them.

'What are you worrying about?' Philip asked one night when I couldn't get to sleep. 'Rob's mates are fantastic. You saw their loyalty when they visited him in hospital every day. They know what he's been through. They won't let him down.'

Their beat-up Ford hardly looked ideal for journeying across the vast emptiness of central Australia. They insisted they were prepared with the latest snake-proof camping gear. Imagining them inching across barren terrain under a merciless bowl of blue sky, I wanted to beg them to stay home and do something safe and sensible—enrol in cookery classes, take dancing lessons. Anything but this. But I'd learnt enough about parenthood to know there are many times when it's wiser to keep your mouth shut. I was hoping this was one of them.

✦

Three weeks later, when they were due to return, Cleo paced the hallway. She leapt to the window ledge, stared out at the street, then sprang back onto the floor to start pacing again. She was twitchy as a cobra on a desert highway. When I picked her up we exchanged electric shocks. Her ears flattened. She wriggled impatiently. I lowered her to the floor so she could pace some more.

'Don't worry, old girl,' I said, talking to myself as much as the cat. 'He'll be fine.'

A waterfall of relief washed over me as their car, red with dust, turned into our street. With Cleo in my arms I ran outside to meet them. Rob uncoiled his considerable length from the back seat to accept with a dutiful grimace my embrace. Strange how the child who once stood on his toes to kiss his mother now bent and inclined his head to receive hers. Running an anxious eye over his entire six feet and more, I noticed his physical condition had, if anything, improved.

'How was it?' I asked.

'Fantastic!'

We persuaded the boys to stay on for a barbecue before they headed off. Basking in the glow of the coals, we watched the stars sparkle to life.

'Nothing like the night sky,' Rob sighed. 'Whenever things get too much all I have to do is think of the stars and all the things they look down on. Here on earth we think our little lives are so important. Even though we're an integral part of everything we're just tiny specks in the universe.'

Cleo took the opportunity to lick some tomato sauce off his plate.

'I had an amazing experience in the desert,' he continued. 'One night when we were camping in a remote spot near Katherine Gorge I dreamt about a weird white cat. It had seven hearts and it was sitting on the edge of an inland sea.'

'Was it a scary cat?' I asked.

'No. It was wise, like a teacher. And it talked to me.'

'Oh no!' I smiled. 'Not again! What did it say?'

'It told me I'd been protected for many years by a cat, that the cat had guided me to the right people. It said our world would continue to be racked with sadness and pain until we learn the most important lesson. To become everything we're capable of we must replace fear and greed with love—for ourselves, each other and the planet we live on.

'The white cat went on to say my cat guide had helped me find love on many levels. There was only one form of love left for it to teach me, and I was already further along that path than I realised. Once I'd discovered that love, the cat guardian's role on earth would be complete.'

A shooting star scurried across the sky. I was lost for words.

'Funny thing is,' Rob continued. 'It was such an outlandish dream I told the boys about it the next morning. I described the shape of the lagoon and the surrounding hills. They laughed when I told them about the talking cat, of course. But then, a few hours later we visited a place that exactly matched the dream landscape I'd described. The lagoon, the hills. They were all there. If I hadn't told the boys about it in such detail earlier they'd never have believed me. An Aboriginal man introduced himself and told us about the area. He said it was a sacred healing ground. He pointed out seven tall mounds around the edge of the lagoon. For as long as anyone could remember, he said, the local people had called them cats.'

From her vantage point on Rob's shoulder, Cleo surveyed every human face in the shadows of the barbecue flames and winked.

Forgiveness

To forgive is in a cat's nature – eventually

One of the downsides of changing countries was that we no longer had access to reliable friends who thought nothing of looking after Cleo for us when we went away on holiday.

Even though we were getting to know our new neighbours, it seemed too soon to impose cat-minding duties on them. We'd never put Cleo in a cattery before. I was worried how a freedom lover like her would adapt to living in the feline equivalent of Guantanamo Bay for a week. She'd proved herself tough and versatile, though. I assumed she'd cope.

Assumption is a dangerous thing. A couple of days after we'd collected her from the cattery, her eyes streamed with gluey fluid. She went off her food and developed a cough. For the first time in her life Cleo was terribly ill.

Our neighbourhood vet was plump and red-faced with a plume of silver hair. He prodded her with fingers the size of salamis.

'How old is she?' he asked, examining our precious cat as if she was something he'd scraped off his shoe.

'Sixteen.'

He looked at me in disbelief.

'Are you *sure*?'

'I know exactly how old she is. She was given to us just after our older son died.'

'Well, if you're certain she's *that* old . . .' He sighed. 'I wouldn't hold out much hope for her. She should have died six years ago, according to the average life expectancy for a cat.'

He was a tough vet. I hated his cold words. Some time in the distant past he must've had enough compassion for animals to envisage himself spending a lifetime working with them. But whatever sympathy he possessed had either dried up or, for some reason, wasn't directed at us. Maybe he shared Rosie's opinion of my cat-mothering skills. Perhaps his wife had left him for the orthodontist around the corner. I wouldn't have blamed her.

'I can't promise anything but we could try her on a course of antibiotics, if you like.'

If you like? Did the man imagine we were ready to give up on her?

'Yes please. She's part of our family.'

He seemed oblivious to the fact that Cleo had been guardian of our household for so long, she wasn't going anywhere as far as we were concerned.

'In that case, when you go home I'd prepare them for the worst.'

The girls gulped back tears when I repeated what the vet had said. They both had memories of Cleo peering over the edge of their cradles. Cleo was practically a surrogate mother to them.

'It's just nature,' I said, sounding more like Mum than intended. 'We were lucky to have her this long.'

To our delight, Cleo's eyes cleared and her snuffle evaporated a couple of days later. In less than a week she was back to her omnivorous diet. No house fly, rubber band or sock was safe. Her coat regained its sheen. She danced across the kitchen table, climbed the curtains. Cleo was her old perky self. The vet may have considered her the walking dead, but as far as Cleo was concerned, she was still in her prime.

But she'd given us a warning. Even though she was doing a good job hiding it, old age was creaking its way into her joints. She slept more than she used to and seemed to feel the cold more readily.

In fact, she adapted to old age with aplomb worthy of a duchess. The meow that used to be so pretty and accommodating became an authoritative yowl. Cleo had seen every form of human behaviour in her long life. She knew when to take a stand and when to disappear. She'd always known exactly where to find the escape routes. In her younger days, she'd barely twitched a whisker when Lydia had carried her around the house upside down. Not so long ago, she'd allowed Katharine to dress her in a hat and specially knitted gloves for Melbourne Cup Day. It had been an act of patience and affection on Cleo's part.

In acknowledgement of her advanced years we decided to make a few changes. Once past kittenhood, Cleo had always insisted on spending her nights roaming rooftops outside under the moon. Even in cold weather she'd preferred sleeping under the house, curled up around the central heating system. For the sake of her health, the girls and I agreed a change of lifestyle was required. She'd have to be an inside cat from now on. The trick was to find her a bed she approved of enough to sleep in.

Having monopolised and destroyed a dynasty of family beanbags, she was bound to adore the supersized beanbag I bought her from the pet shop. Sure, it was designed for large dogs, but there's no way Cleo would know.

Cleo had a built-in radar screen that could detect anything to do with dogs from a distance of a thousand kennel runs. The beanbag couldn't possibly have smelt doggy. It was brand new. Maybe it carried the thought remnants of its maker, who had mused over her sewing machine what kind of dog might end up sleeping on it—a dalmatian, alsatian or a plain old mutt.

So, despite countless demonstrations from us all showing how luxurious and comfortable the dog beanbag was, Cleo refused to go near it. We repositioned it in alluring sites around the house—in front of the fire, in the patch of sun on the kitchen floor. Our efforts were pointless. As far as Cleo was concerned the dog beanbag was disgusting.

Defeated, I flung it under the house for the rats (or whatever it was that chewed things under there). Maybe one bed wasn't enough. Perhaps Cleo was trying to tell us she needed options—a day bed and a night bed. Back at the pet shop (where the assistant was starting to treat me like an escapee from an asylum) we bought a fluffy pink cushion and a brown padded poof, both designed specifically for cats.

We arranged the pink cushion between the sofas in the family room. It was treated with the disdain it deserved. During the day Cleo preferred perching on a sofa arm or, better still, on the belly of a reclining human who was trying to read. Not only did this position provide warmth and a sense of superiority, it was also an excellent opportunity to floss her teeth along the edges of the book's pages. The only bed she showed anything less than hatred for was the brown poof. We set it up in the laundry where she grudgingly agreed to sleep at night, alongside her bowls and (the ultimate indignity) a kitty litter tray.

Holidays were problematic. We weren't willing to risk a cattery again. A live-in cat nanny was the only solution. Cleo's first cat nanny was our friend Magnolia.

Magnolia is one of the world's great cooks. Having grown up in Samoa, one of the few countries where people appreciate the beauty of bellies the size of hot-air balloons, she understands the meaning of quantity. Not only that, she has a gourmet's flair for quality. She stole her recipe for coconut cake from the angels. Her beef bourguignon would make Julia Child turn spinach-green with envy. So Cleo licked her chops approvingly when Magnolia arrived carrying extra cooking pots and bags of undisclosed ingredients.

'Don't you worry,' Magnolia said, slipping an apron over her head. 'Go and enjoy yourselves. We'll be absolutely fine. And you know I love cats. Not in a culinary sense, of course.'

I kissed Cleo on her tiny forehead, but formal farewells were of no interest. Her focus was on Magnolia clattering a large preserving pan onto our stovetop. We worried about Cleo while we were away.

'She's such a sensitive animal,' I said to Philip. 'She's probably traumatised having a stranger in the house.'

Every time we phoned, Magnolia said our cat was just fine. I didn't know if we should believe her. Just fine can mean anything from 'just fine but she was attacked by magpies and had an eye pecked out' to 'just fine but she hasn't eaten a thing'.

'I can't talk now,' Magnolia added. 'We've got some bouillabaisse on the stove, haven't we, Cleo? Then I'm off to the market to get fresh prawns.'

'Do you think Cleo's all right?' asked the girls.

We told them she probably was, but what would we know?

The girls talked us into going home a day early because Cleo was almost certainly pining for us. When Magnolia answered the door the fragrance of a Michelin-star galaxy wafted through our nostrils—warm and meaty with a hint of wine and truffles. A small plump animal was tucked in the crook of Magnolia's elbow. The creature had the expression of a movie star encountering fans on the way to the academy awards—'I see you, but you're not really there. Collect a signed photograph from my publicity team if you're desperate.'

'Cleo!' we cried, all reaching out to hold her.

She hesitated for longer than was decent before allowing Magnolia to lower her into Katharine's arms.

'She likes her food,' laughed Magnolia.

Cleo wriggled to be put on the floor and waddled away towards the kitchen. Not only had she grown chubby over the past two weeks, she'd become incredibly smug.

'I'm going to miss sleeping with her,' Magnolia added. 'She's so cute the way she snuggles between the sheets and puts her head on the pillow beside me.'

There was still enough country girl left in me not to want to share a pillow with our cat, even our treasured cat goddess. And I couldn't cook like Magnolia.

I don't know if those were good enough reasons to punish us. Maybe Cleo was simply annoyed with us for going away. More likely it was a combination of crimes on our part. But she made her feelings clear enough by depositing a carefully placed turd in the middle of our bedcover.

✦

Live-in cat nannies became the norm every time we went away after that. During one of these sojourns a kitchen chair fell on Cleo's tail, leaving a permanent dent near the tip. The nanny apologised profusely. She said there'd been blood. Katharine shed tears over the damage. While the tip of Cleo's tail remained tender for the rest of her days, she didn't ask for sympathy. She wore her dented tail with the suave pride of a battle-scarred cavalry officer. Forgiveness for permanent injury was a straightforward process for her, simple as breathing.

I wished I shared her expertise in the art of forgiveness. We humans hold on to our hurt and nurse it, often to our own detriment. We're quick to assume the role of victim. Yet cats are and always have been at the receiving end of human maltreatment. During medieval times many thousands of them were hunted out and killed because it was believed they were inhabited by witches. In Paris during the sixteenth century thousands of people looked forward to fun outings witnessing the mass burning of bags full of cats. Even today, kittens are routinely dumped into sacks and drowned. Cats of all ages are tortured in experiments for the so-called advancement of science. In parts of Asia, a serving of cat meat is considered beneficial for women of a certain age.

Humanity has brought such suffering upon the domestic cat it's amazing they still tolerate any contact with us. Felines may not forget our atrocities against them. Yet, generation after generation, they continue to forgive us. Every new litter of kittens born helpless and mewing is an invitation to start again, for humans to lift their game. While our past behaviour reveals the depths of the cruelty we're capable of, cats continue to expect better of us. We won't be worthy of considering ourselves fully evolved until we live up to the shine of trust and expectation in a kitten's eye.

◆

I still thought about the woman driver who'd run over Sam all those years earlier. She used to haunt my mind. My anger towards her had been like fire run rampant. In those early days, whenever I read newspaper stories about parents forgiving the murderers of their children, I could only imagine they were avoiding honesty.

Time may not heal everything, but it gives perspective. Ford Escorts went out of style years before. I hardly saw them anymore, let alone blue ones. The car that killed Sam was probably an ashtray. The streets had given way to four-wheel-drives. I was finally able to accept fully that Sam's tragedy was hers as well. That January day in 1983 would be carved into her heart as deeply as it was on mine. Every time she slid behind a driver's wheel, or saw a blond boy crossing a street, she must have seen his ghost.

I was finally emotionally equipped to meet this woman, if it were ever possible. I'd tried throwing out a few lines. In a magazine interview I'd suggested I was ready. I wanted to put my arms around her, acknowledge the pain she must have endured all these years, and tell her I forgave her. Utterly.

A response arrived in the mail, but not the one I was expecting.

Dear Helen,

My wife showed me the recent article on you and she urged me to write to you as we both felt very sad after reading about the dreadfully difficult time you had following Sam's death.

I'm not sure if it will be of any comfort to you, but I came on the scene of the accident very soon after it had happened. The driver of the car was not there and I assumed she had gone for help. My companion went down the road to stop the traffic and I stayed with Sam—he was deeply unconscious and I am quite sure he did not suffer at all. I also think that he did in fact die while I was with him—before the police and ambulance people, who were, without exception very kind and thoughtful, arrived.

Eventually the police said it would be OK for me and my workmate to leave so we did. I was very distressed at what had happened, so much so that when I got home from work that night I had real difficulty in telling my wife about Sam. It seemed such a dreadful waste of a dear little boy's life—but it was no one's fault.

I thought about calling on you at that time but decided against it as I was a stranger and felt it would be an invasion of your privacy. I still don't know if that was the right thing to do, but I feel now that you would like to know Sam was not alone—hence this letter, and if it is even a small amount of comfort to you then I will be very pleased to have written it to you.

Yours sincerely

Arthur Judson
Christchurch

P.S. Have been enjoying your newspaper column for years.

I read the letter again and again. Shock coursed through me as I relived the events of that day from someone else's perspective, a stranger but a man of great heart. The letter I sent in return had no hope of expressing the depth of my gratitude to him. To have stayed alongside a dying boy would have taken courage, and to have written the letter almost as much. His letter had given me a greater sense of completion than anything I could have hoped from meeting the woman driver.

I kept the letter and treasure it to this day. Knowing Sam hadn't died alone or in great pain has gone a long way to easing my sorrow.

The world must be full of silent heroes like him, people who stay behind at accident scenes when it would be easier to leave. Risking their personal tranquility, they give the greatest solace one person can provide another—the comfort of not dying alone. Then, like angels, they disappear without trace.

Conversion

Beware the passionate convert. She may bore you with cat stories

'Oh, look at the dear little kitten!' a stranger exclaimed when she saw Cleo posed sphinx-like on our front path.

'She's not a kitten,' I explained. 'She's actually very old.'

'Really? She looks so . . . young.'

If we could have bottled whatever gene Cleo had that made her look younger the older she grew, we'd have several beach houses, a yacht and a season pass to the Space Shuttle by now. I put a lot of it down to attitude. Hers, of course. Growing old wasn't a tragedy, as far as Cleo was concerned. She simply despised the whole process.

Menopausal women would have nothing to fear if they could see how willingly Cleo shed slinky youth to become an increasingly authoritative, essential ruler of our household. High priestess of the family, she expressed her views on everything from whether her fish had been properly mashed to how early human slaves should be forced out of bed. Anyone who hadn't risen by dawn could expect a screeching wake-up call from Cleo outside their bedroom door.

I too entered a phase where I was more inclined to air my opinions. Having long given up hope of changing the world, I felt it was still entitled to hear my views on everything from presidential politics to how blondes should never be let loose in four-wheel-drives. The only thing missing was a loudspeaker on top of my car through which I could inform other drivers and pedestrians exactly how they were endangering others, themselves and the planet in general.

Following nature's cycle, our nest was emptying out. Lydia took a year off university studies to teach English in Costa Rica. Rob moved to London for a while, where he was working in a wine shop. If ever Rob and I needed proof of our powerful psychic connection all we have to do is try to call each other. Though we were on opposite sides of the earth, we'd often phone each other at exactly the same time. Even today when I call him his line's often engaged because he's trying to ring me.

'You'll never guess who I caught up with,' he said one day, his voice tinged with excitement over the phone. 'Chantelle. She's over here, teaching in one of those tough inner-city schools.'

I felt a little sad when he mentioned she had a boyfriend. A good guy, Rob assured me, an Australian surfie, though it was hard to imagine what a wave-rider did with himself through the depths of an English winter. Not that Rob was lonely—he was living with a nurse from Queensland. Love's often a matter of timing and coincidence: while I knew Rob would always have special feelings for Chantelle, prospects of them getting together seemed increasingly thin.

Several months later I was devastated to hear that Chantelle's younger brother Daniel had died suddenly, of no apparent cause. While tragedy visits every household sooner or later, this was a terrible one for Chantelle and her family to endure. I hoped Rob might be able to help Chantelle with the overwhelming range of shock and sadness she'd be going through.

✦

As the only one left at home, thirteen-year-old Katharine became Cleo's assistant care giver. 'Look what my friends did last night!' she wailed one morning after having a group of girls over for a sleepover. 'They're so mean! They painted Cleo's chest white!'

Closer inspection of the snowy fur revealed it wasn't painted but was white from natural causes.

Cleo developed a geriatric gait, moving stiffly from the hip joints, a sensation I too was becoming begrudgingly familiar with. Cleo gave up playing sock-er, though she kept an old sports sock of Rob's in her bed. She no longer sprang onto the kitchen bench. Likewise, my joints suffered a shortage of elastin. Creaking ligaments pleaded with me to give stairs a swerve if an elevator opened its tantalising doors.

Our coats were changing, too. Teenage hairdressers felt duty-bound to instruct me how to make my thinning hair thick and glossy. ('Just massage a peanut-sized glob of this mousse into your scalp. I know it may seem expensive at one hundred and twenty-five dollars, but it'll last you a whole year'.) Their older sisters lectured me about skin care. ('A cup of blueberries a day will have your skin looking like mine forever. And you'll never guess how old I am. I'm *really* old. I'm twenty-five.')

Free from the attentions of child hairdressers and beauticians, Cleo sprinkled black exclamation marks of fur over our sheets, our underwear, sometimes even our food.

Her black whiskers turned grey. I discovered an unsightly bristle sprouting from my chin.

Cleo and I had always enjoyed roasting ourselves in front of an open fire. Sitting too close nowadays made my legs resemble the surface of Mars. Cleo was even less fireproof. After ten minutes or so she had to stagger away from the inferno and lean against a cool wall to recover.

Quality was more important than we'd realised. I developed an irrational interest in the thread counts of bed linen and Italian stationery.

Our vision was no longer spectacular. An optometrist recommended reading glasses (who, me?). I chose the funkiest frames in the shop, green and blue metallic.

'What do you think?' I asked, showing them off to Philip and Katharine.

Their response made it clear. They were the type of reading glasses an old lady would choose in order to look funky.

Cleo developed strange blotches in her eyes, enhancing the impression she was in direct contact with other realities. I found a vet who wasn't tough and understood how precious she was. He said Cleo didn't have cataracts. The blotches were just a natural part of the ageing process. Soft Vet wasn't so happy about her kidneys, though. He suggested we could fly her to Queensland for a kidney transplant, though the success rate wasn't high. (*A cat flown thousands of miles for a kidney transplant that will probably fail!* I could practically hear my mother wail from the depths of her plastic urn in the New Plymouth graveyard. *The world must be off its rocker.*)

Unwilling to embrace the less attractive aspects of growing older, I focused on body parts that, with some attention, could still look good. I discovered a nail salon run by a Vietnamese family who, I was thrilled to find out, could hardly speak a word of English. This meant they were mercifully free of small talk and unable to instruct me on methods of maintaining youthful hands and feet. As we got to know each other better, they greeted me with nods and smiles.

Around the same time Cleo's toenails started clicking like tap shoes over the floorboards. They weren't getting as much use as in her assassin days. Her claws had worn thin and were as flaky as miniature croissants. I was flattered when Cleo allowed herself to lie on her back in my lap while I attempted to trim her talons with Philip's nail clippers. Reading glasses perched on the end of my nose, I was terrified of hurting her. I hardly trusted myself with hedge clippers, let alone nail trimmers and her tiny paws. Any clumsy mistakes were corrected with swift gentle bites. After the first few attempts, Cleo trusted me enough to actually purr during the procedure. I was honoured to take on the title of official manicurist and (combing dry cat shampoo through her coat) beauty therapist. In short, personal servant.

We'd spent long enough in each other's company for her to know I had her interests at heart. We'd been through so much together and found a kind of peace, not only with each other, but within ourselves. Together we discovered the well-kept secret that, give or take a few inconveniences, old cats have more fun.

Cleo and I decided to become quirky about our eating habits. I was afflicted with an obsession for chocolate, dark chocolate to be precise, preferably seventy per cent cocoa, made in Switzerland and wrapped in something shiny involving photos of mountains. Try as I might to divert my addiction to Italian writing paper or thousand-thread-count sheets, I could find nothing more mesmerising than chocolate. Cleo, on the other hand, underwent an even more powerful food fixation. The word 'no' had never been of particular interest to our cat. She now obliterated it from her understanding of human vocabulary. In her mature years, however, she learnt exactly what the words 'Chicken Man' meant.

Whenever anyone announced they were off to Chicken Man (to buy a rotisserie takeaway bird from the cheerful Asian man's shop round the corner), Cleo trotted behind them and waited eagerly at the door until they returned with the mouth-watering parcel.

Cleo was circumspect about most food, though on the whole she preferred it murdered or stolen. Chicken Man was in a different league. One whiff of the freshly roasted flesh drove her to salivating insanity. Anyone in charge of an unguarded plate of chicken was at risk. Loyalties and past affections were forgotten as she embarked on chicken jihad.

We developed a routine of shutting her out of the room so we could have first choice of the meat.

'Poor Cleo!' Katharine would say, as an elegant black paw appeared under the door.

There was no 'poor' about it. If the door wasn't closed properly, the paw slid down the side and pushed it open. Bones and paper napkins would fly through the air, plates clattered to the floor. It was chicken season for young and old.

Our food fixations were equally unattractive to outsiders. The only difference was, Cleo's didn't make her any fatter. In fact, she appeared to be shrinking. Her chest bones jutted out, the angles of her skull became even sharper and more prominent. With fur draped over her skeletal form, she resembled an amateur attempt at taxidermy.

That's not saying we didn't enjoy moments of friskiness. If the curtains were pulled tight enough and there was no evidence of human life within a five-hundred-metre radius, a determined anthropologist might still have caught a glimpse of me boogieing alone to the strains of Marvin Gaye.

Likewise, after a shower of rain, Cleo shimmied like a kitten up a tree trunk—until halfway up old age got the better of her and she slid unceremoniously back down.

Cleo's legs, once so tapered and streamlined, became slightly stumpy with lumps where (if she was human) knees and ankles would be. She never grumbled, though. I trudged off to the gym and lifted weights to combat back and neck pain that would never have developed if, like Cleo, I'd spent my life on all fours. The old person's fear of falling over would never have to be considered if we'd stayed firmly planted to the ground on four feet. Once again, our cat was proving herself a higher-level species.

While our bodies may have given the appearance of growing old, inside Cleo and I were growing up and getting stroppy. In the supermarket check-out line, people always used to recognise me as a pushover. Anyone from toddlers to old men knew they could sneak in front of me without consequences. But the new, stroppy me stood my ground when queue jumpers tried to nudge in front of me. I was even capable of an indignant 'Excuse *me!*'. I filled out complaints forms without hesitation and stopped thinking twice about hanging up on telephone marketers calling from Mumbai.

Cleo surpassed me by taking uppity to an artform. When our sight-impaired friend Penny visited with her guide-dog Mishka, I placed two bowls of water on the floor—a small one for Cleo and a large one for Mishka. Cleo eyeballed the yellow labrador and claimed the large bowl for herself. Mishka shrunk to half her giant size and retreated to the small bowl.

Penny laughed and accepted my apologies for our pet's ungracious behaviour. I explained that, as a kitten, Cleo had done the same thing to Rata. Nodding amiably, Penny sat on the floor. Mishka parked her rear end affectionately on her owner's lap. They made a charming vignette, a picture of owner and devoted dog. The image was too much for Cleo. She fixed Mishka with a glower that was so withering the poor animal skulked away into a corner and allowed Cleo to take over prime position on Penny's lap.

'And what happened to poor little Cleo?' Rosie asked when she phoned out of the blue one day.

'Oh, she's fine.'

'In a better place,' she sighed. 'I always say there are sardines every day in Pussy Heaven.'

'No, Rosie. I mean fine fine.'

'She's STILL ALIVE! You're joking! How old is she now?'

I was getting sick and tired of people asking us impertinent questions about age. 'Twenty-three.'

'But that's, let me see . . . something like one hundred and sixty-one in human years. Are you sure it's the same cat?'

'Absolutely.'

'How did you do it? What have you been feeding her? What medication is she on?'

'Nothing special. How are Scruffy, Ruffy, Beethoven and Sibelius?'

An awkward silence. 'Well, Scruffy disappeared, Beethoven had kidney failure. Sibelius and Ruffy went to cat heaven ten years ago. I always made sure they had the best of everything, not like your poor little Cleo. I'm surprised you remember their names. You never were a cat person, were you?'

'But I must be!' I replied. 'I couldn't *not* be. Cleo wouldn't have stayed with us this long if I wasn't. Besides, we're both getting so old Cleo and I are practically the same person. No, dammit, Rosie. You're wrong. *I AM a cat person!*'

Not long after, Philip and I were at a restaurant celebrating our fourteenth wedding anniversary.

'I'll never forget that night you took us to the pizza restaurant and you beat Rob at that game filling in the squares.'

'It was snakes and ladders, wasn't it?' he said, sipping his champagne.

'It was filling in squares. You nearly blew it that night. Not letting a boy win. I was going to send you packing.'

'Were you?' he replied with a twinkle. 'I'll always remember Cleo bouncing around the house like she owned the place.'

'She *did* own it. Not many people would have taken us on the way you did, you know', I said, changing the subject. 'A solo mum eight years older with two kids.'

Rob had once said having Philip in our lives was like winning Lotto. I'd been in awe of Philip's love and commitment to all three of our children, never once making a distinction between Katharine, his biological daughter, and the other two. Their love for him in return was equally deep and seamless. I was fortunate to have spent so many years with such a rare, open-hearted man.

'Not work again, is it?' I said as he took his bleeping mobile phone from his pocket.

'It's Kath,' he replied, his face grave as he listened to her distraught staccato.

'We'd better go. Cleo's having some sort of fit.'

Tough Vet, Soft Vet

Chicken Man each day keeps the vet away

By the time we arrived back home Cleo was her normal self again.

'It was so scary!' said Katharine, still flushed with shock. 'She made a horrible growl, then she fell over and twitched. Her whole body seized up. She must've been in so much pain.'

Listening calmly to the report, Cleo licked her paw. *I don't know what you're making such a fuss about,* she seemed to say. *It was just a little hiccup.*

After breakfast next morning, Cleo succumbed to another dreadful fit. I ran to the phone and called Soft Vet. His honey-voiced receptionist said he wouldn't be available until later in the day.

'But we need to see someone *now!*' I said.

'In that case you'll have to try another vet,' she replied sharply.

For a Soft Vet he had a pretty hard-hearted receptionist. The only other vet who knew anything of Cleo's history was dreaded Tough Vet.

'If you bundle her in a blanket and bring her over he'll see her now,' said Tough Vet's nurse.

As I carried Cleo to the vet's clinic, she revived enough to take an interest in the traffic and the sky. She purred lightly as I clutched her to my chest. Maybe a simple pill would do the trick. On the other hand, I wasn't a fool. She was twenty-three and a half years old.

We loathed everything about Tough Vet's surgery. We didn't like the anaesthetic smell of the waiting room or the bags of pet food piled in the corner like headstones. Cleo particularly disapproved of the big black labrador, its pink tongue dripping obscenely from its mouth. It was impossible to ignore the blue plastic bucket over his head. I knew exactly what Cleo was thinking: *How typical of a dog to allow itself to be shoved into such a demeaning fashion accessory.*

Tough Vet appeared from an operating room and beckoned us in. Cleo stood defiantly on the stainless steel table while he poked and prodded parts no lady likes to share with a stranger. Kidney failure and thyroid malfunction was his diagnosis.

'How long do you want to drag this out for?' he asked, his voice drained of expression.

I heard his words and understood what they meant, but couldn't summon up any kind of answer.

'I can put her down now if you like.'

Now? Immediately? The shock must've shown on my face.

'All right, I'll keep her here a few hours for observation so your family can get used to the idea,' he said. 'Phone me at five o'clock.'

I was about to snatch Cleo back and run home with her. But the prospect of helplessly witnessing her fits all day was unbearable. Heading out his door, I hated Tough Vet with every muscle in my heart—until he called out to me.

'You can leave her blanket with me.'

He'd understood that our ancient animal would be more comfortable with a piece of home to snuggle into. Maybe Tough Vet wasn't such a monster after all.

Back home, I pulled the old towels and rugs off our furniture as a reminder of how much prettier and cleaner life was going to be without a dribbling, fur-shedding old cat. Glancing at Cleo's bed in the laundry, I considered dumping the stinky thing in the outside bin—but couldn't quite do it.

No way was she going to vanish up Tough Vet's chimney. A daphne bush by the front gate would be her gravestone, if she had to have one at all.

Philip arrived home early from work to make the five o'clock call. Tough Vet invited us to pay a visit. Not a good sign. Katharine stayed home resolutely watching TV as we headed out on our morbid mission.

Tough Vet was friendlier this time. I thought it must be his 'putting animals down' mode.

'She hasn't had a fit all day,' he said. 'She hasn't eaten anything but her vital signs are good and her heart's strong. She's in remarkably good condition for her age.'

The light in his eye said it all. Even in her decrepit state, Cleo had charmed him with her determination to defy the feline life expectancy chart on his wall.

Wrapping her in the blue blanket, he handed her back with some pills to stimulate her appetite. 'Oh, and if you really want to get her eating again, there's an excellent takeaway chicken shop across the road,' he added. 'I don't know what he puts in them, but one whiff of that stuff and it drives all the cats crazy.'

I guess a visit to Chicken Man each day keeps the vet away. Cleo purred all the way home.

I draped the old towels and rugs back over the furniture and shook her smelly bed. We were on borrowed time, but one thing Sam's death taught me is time is only ever on loan. Life can change irrevocably for any one of us at any moment. Awareness of that is what made me scan my dressing table every time I went out in case for some reason I never returned. Even though I wasn't a tidy person I didn't want to go down in history as a shockingly messy one.

I phoned Rob in Britain to update him on Cleo's latest drama.

'I've just been trying to call you but the line was busy,' he said.

'That's because *I* was calling *you*,' I said, delaying the Cleo news as long as possible. 'What did you want to talk to me about?'

'I can't face another English winter. People live like moles here, in the dark and underground most of the time. I've been offered an engineering job in Melbourne. It sounds great. I'll be home for Christmas.'

✦

Not long after Rob's return a surprise visitor turned up on the doorstep. He was a tall dark-haired young man, with looks that were a blend of Brad Pitt and Johnny Depp. I scanned the movie-star jawline, the well-defined brow. But it wasn't until I looked into his eyes that I recognised him.

Baby-faced Jason from Rob's boyhood zigzag days had morphed into a fine adult. To receive a visit from Ginny's son was an unexpected compliment. He planted kisses on each of my cheeks, leaving me momentarily dazed. This man Jason was a far cry from the brown-haired boy with almond eyes and an impish smile. Last time I'd seen him he hadn't been much taller than my waist. I was touched his memories had been warm enough for him to turn up in person so many years later.

'Don't tell me Cleo's still alive!' he said.

'Only just,' I replied. I called Rob and arranged to meet him at a cafe near his work with our surprise guest. Rob took less than a second to recognise his old friend. I basked in the glory of dining with two young men with rock-star looks. So this was how it felt to go out with two adult sons. If Sam had lived I wondered how many times we would've got together like this. Would it have felt so warm and tinged with almost unbearable sadness? Maybe there'd be no sorrow at all, just a vague pattern of irritations and assumptions families can grind themselves into.

'Do you know what my strongest memory is?' Jason asked, perusing the wine list.

'Digging that hole!' the boys said in unison.

I must've looked blank.

'Remember that wild bit of land below your front gate? Rob and I decided to dig a hole there. We dug for years, and it never seemed to get any deeper.'

A vision of two small boys hacking into clay under the tree ferns suddenly sharpened.

'That's right,' I said. 'You had spades and a pick axe. You probably shouldn't have been allowed that pick axe. I'd be sued these days.'

'That's the whole point,' Jason said. 'It felt manly and dangerous. Do you remember the day we found a rusty old wire mattress? We spread it over the hole and turned it into a trampoline for a while. Then we got bored with that. We took it away and went back to digging.'

Even now sometimes, Rob said he wondered why the hole never seemed to get any deeper. If his adult self could return to the scene he'd finish the job in an afternoon.

'Maybe you were digging it too wide?' I said. 'How deep did you want it anyway?'

'Decent-sized hole deep,' Jason replied.

I felt vaguely guilty the boys' memories weren't of me teaching them Mandarin or Gregorian chants. If Jason had inherited half of Ginny's brains—she'd just finished a doctorate in midwifery—he'd have been more than capable. On the other hand, maybe letting them dig had a hand in making them into the philosophers they'd grown into.

It was hard to believe that somewhere underneath their easy manners and red-wine-drinking maturity were the same little boys who'd lived on the zigzag. Watching them I was reminded of the miraculous renewal of the Australian bush after a fire. Against the blackened outline of taller trees, banksias and wattles create fresh new undergrowth. Similarly, the boys had sprung into strong, handsome young men. During the devastation of those zigzag days I'd underestimated the resilience of nature.

Renewal

To the paradoxical cat, an ending is sometimes a beginning

It's easy to fall in love with a kitten. Everything about its furry softness says hold me, cuddle me. In its middle years a cat can be admired for its gleaming coat and sleek athleticism. But an old cat is an acquired taste. She dribbles on cushions and uses vomiting as a form of peaceful protest. People who live with old cats make allowances. Even those who have never suffered a moment of house pride are compelled to cover furniture with old towels and blankets.

Cleo's fur thinned and carried the odour of an Egyptian tomb. She had to think several times before forcing her arthritic joints to jump onto a sofa. When strangers visited I occasionally imagined distaste flashing across their faces as she teetered to greet them. Our geriatric feline was no longer a great beauty, yet our love for her grew deeper with the knowledge time was running out.

The right side of her face swelled up so spectacularly she couldn't open one eye. I wrapped her in her blanket and carried her back to Tough Vet. We'd changed our minds about him since our last visit.

'Hmmm,' he said grimly. 'A tooth abscess. I could operate and remove her teeth, but she's so weak I doubt she'd survive the surgery.'

He recommended the obvious, gently this time, while running a hand over her back.

'I know what it's like when an animal's been part of a family for a long time,' he said.

He sent us home to mull it over. If Cleo was a person she would have been forced to have a 'natural' death like the one Mum had endured. I'd seen how, as disease takes hold, the victim enters a grey realm of pain that makes death a welcome visitor. Maybe it's nature's way of making the process ultimately acceptable. Given the choice, I wouldn't want to suffer what Mum went through. Fortunately, Cleo's animal status ensured she wouldn't have to. Death is one of the few areas where animals are granted superior rights.

Katharine, her face a waterfall of tears, readily agreed this was the right thing. Philip helped us wrap Cleo in her blanket for the last time to take her to Tough Vet, whom I'd decided wasn't tough at all.

'It's time, old girl,' he said, slipping a tiny needle into the back of her paw. The movement was so gentle she didn't flinch. As we said our goodbyes, Cleo curled in the shape of a crescent moon. Her head drooped. She was suddenly gone.

The vet put her in an opaque plastic bag and we carried her home inside the blanket.

Philip began to dig a hole under the daphne bush in the front garden. The spade hit the ground with soft, regular thuds. He wasn't in the mood for talking. Reading the back of his head as he swung the spade, I could tell he was upset—not in the tears-on-television way that's become grindingly fashionable for both sexes. His was a restrained, dignified grief, the sort men were famous for until they were told it was bad for their health.

I wanted to make him put down the spade and just hold him for a while, but it would only drag things out. Men are better off doing things. Besides, there were my own useless tears to deal with.

After what seemed a very long time, he stopped and rested on the spade. We both stared down at the hole. It was deeper than it probably needed to be, but this is a man who always went the extra mile for his family. And Cleo was an integral part of that.

'I don't suppose we want to bury her in the blanket,' he said.

Unwrapping the blanket he slid Cleo's lifeless form from the vet's plastic bag onto the soil. He bent and kissed her head before lowering her into the hole.

'She's been with this family longer than I have,' he sighed.

Birds sang a requiem as, spade by spade, the earth covered her body.

◆

Some cultures prefer to bury their relatives in their gardens. I was beginning to understand why. Every morning I said hello to Cleo on my way to the letterbox. The gardener looked alarmed when I told him not to dig too deep around the daphne bush. Our precious cat didn't need disturbing.

Cleo presided over our family through nearly twenty-four years. She helped heal wounds I thought we'd never recover from. Maybe her work was complete now, the healing was done, and we could get along without her. Except she left us with a different kind of sorrow. I suddenly understood the logic of ancient Egyptians shaving their eyebrows when a family cat died.

People asked when we were getting a new cat. They spoke as if one cat would lead to another. A friend took me to a pet shop. We watched a bunch of kittens tumbling about in an enclosure. They were mostly tortoiseshell. Adorable. Some were locked in a play fight, rolling around in a bundle of fur. Others dozed. Cute, so cute. A small grey kitten climbed the wire mesh, hitching himself paw by paw above our heads. A

group of shoppers gathered around the cage, the expressions
on their faces tender as a da Vinci portrait. Among them was
a dishevelled man I'd noticed out on the street earlier. He'd
looked angry and so withdrawn people had stepped sideways to
avoid him. The layers of aggression he'd been carrying around
disintegrated when he saw the kittens. His unshaven jaw soft-
ened into a smile. Leaning against the wire he gazed at them
with pure benevolence. Now he was watching the grey kitten,
who'd suddenly realised he couldn't get back down as easily
as he'd climbed up. He glanced anxiously down at the floor,
then back up at the wire. He couldn't climb any higher. There
was no choice. The kitten performed an impressive backwards
flip and landed safely back on ground level. The man laughed.
Maybe the kitten reminded him of himself, climbing for the
heavens only to land with a thump back on earth.

'Can we take one home?' a teenager asked his mother. He,
too was enthralled. If he persuaded her to take a kitten that
day it had a noble task ahead. The young man was mentally
disabled.

A sad woman pointed at a pretty tortoiseshell. Maybe her
house was empty, just waiting for the pad of velvet paws.

Every kitten in the enclosure had a purpose to fulfil, human
hearts to heal, lessons to teach about the true nature of love.
There wasn't one I didn't want to scoop up and hold warm
and soft against my chest. But I wasn't going to take one home
that day.

Cats aren't something to be 'got'. They turn up in people's
lives when they're needed, and with a purpose that probably
won't be understood to begin with. I certainly hadn't wanted a
kitten so soon after Sam's death. Not consciously, anyway. Life
is a contrary business. Sometimes what you think you don't
want and what you need are the same thing. Cleo's cuddles,
her fun, her uppity behaviour, were exactly what we needed to
take our minds off monumental sadness and remind us what

joy there is in living and breathing. She taught us to loosen up, laugh and toughen up when necessary.

Guardian of our household, Cleo watched over every step of our journey. She stayed with us for as long as we needed her—which turned out a decade or two longer than expected. Whether she'd been sent to us by Sam or the Egyptian cat goddess, she bestowed her healing powers on us with more generosity than could be asked of any creature.

Once we started trusting life again magical things seemed to unfold. Wonderful people like Ginny, Jason, Anne Marie and Philip turned up at exactly the right times. Cleo supervised every encounter, sometimes giving the impression she'd actually arranged them. I'll always be grateful to these people and many more who helped us recover from the loss of Sam. Not that I'll ever confidently say we've recovered. We've changed, grown. Sam, his life and death, will always be part of us.

Anger ultimately gave way to forgiveness and, years later, the enormous relief of learning Sam hadn't died alone and frightened. I discovered Superman is real, after all. He's the hero who stops at accident scenes and does what he can for victims. For us his name was Arthur Judson.

◆

For years I'd avoided returning to the zigzag in Wellington. With typical sensitivity, Ginny understood and never pressed me to visit her. We'd arranged reunions in Australia or other parts of New Zealand, anywhere that served good sauvignon, really. But curiosity eventually got the better of me. As the rental car ground up the hill towards Wadestown I prepared for gut-wrenching replays. Rounding the first hook bend, then the second, I noticed there was still a stretch of public land, a mini park, overlooking the harbour. I'd once dreamt of erecting a sculpture there in Sam's memory, but concrete and stainless steel lack warmth. There are better ways to honour a lost child.

The road straightened, narrowed and became steeper as it rose towards the footbridge, still hanging across the cutting like a gallows. As the car sped underneath, I absorbed a rush of impressions. The steps down from the bridge, the edge of the footpath where Sam had turned to his brother all those years ago and said 'Be quiet'. The harsh surface of the asphalt where his blood had spilt. My chest jarred. What was the point of putting myself through all this?

The houses on our old street seemed more brightly painted, the gardens better maintained since we'd left. At the end of the road I was astonished to find the zigzag had disappeared. Ginny had mentioned the neighbours had clubbed together to pay for a bulldozer to create drive-on access for all the houses, but I hadn't imagined anything this dramatic. The old zigzag with its twists and turns had been replaced by a full-on driveway plunging straight down the hill. I stood at the top of the zigzag that was now a road and looked down on the city. It sprawled further up the hills these days. There were several new high-rise office blocks. Wind jagged up from the south.

'Bubbles, darling?' asked a familiar voice. Ginny and I wrapped arms around each other. Laughter lines and streaks of grey through her hair had only intensified her beauty. Leopard-skin tights and wild earrings had succumbed to a flowing skirt and silk shirt that wouldn't have looked out of place on the streets of Milan.

Together we walked down the driveway over what once would have been one zig and a zag to Ginny's place. I deliberately avoided turning towards our old bungalow. A single glimpse had potential to unleash an army of demons. The jungle that used to surround the Desilva's had gone, but their house sat serene as ever. A champagne cork popped as Ginny explained how she and Rick had looked at apartments in town, but nothing could surpass the convenience and outlook of this house.

Nodding, I took in the surroundings. Ginny's taste in interior design had moved on from 80s chic to European understatement. Having lived there nearly thirty years, Ginny confessed she and Rick were the neighbourhood establishment now. The Butlers had shifted ten years ago. Mrs Sommerville had gone to the great staffroom in the sky.

'And our old house?' I asked tentatively.

'A footballer and his girlfriend lived there for a while,' said Ginny. 'Someone wanted to renovate it, but they gave up. It's been tenanted ever since. There's a good view from upstairs, remember?'

I followed her tentatively up the staircase, safe in the knowledge that if I broke down Ginny of all people would know what to do. She pulled a curtain aside and beckoned me towards the window. Our old bungalow was barely recognisable. The front garden with its path lined with forget-me-nots had been obliterated, along with the boys' digging patch, to make way for a concrete slab wide enough to park two cars alongside each other. Sensible, yes. No more rain-soaked treks carrying groceries to the front door. Not that it resembled our front door anymore. The dark panelling had been painted white, along with the mock-Tudor beams that had once given the place 'character'. Someone had decided to rid the place of its ghosts by throwing buckets of white paint over it. The house seemed narrower, chastened. Rob's bedroom window where Cleo used to sit was the same shape, the roof pitched at the same angle, but it wasn't our house anymore. Like the zigzag and everything else in the neighbourhood, it had moved on.

I'd been steeling myself for flashbacks on this visit. Instead, looking down on the old house with Ginny, I experienced an unexpected sensation of lightness and peace. A circle had completed itself. Our life on the zigzag was faded as an old photograph. Nothing but a memory. The only thing that mattered was the lives we had now.

✦

Even after Cleo died she continued to leave physical reminders of her presence. Unmistakable black hairs were scattered through our sheets and clothes. There was frozen cat food in the back of the freezer. Hauling Cleo's rejected dog bed out from under the house, I had an urge to call Rob. His line was busy of course.

'Were you trying to call me?' I asked when I finally got through.

'No, I was talking to someone.'

'Who?'

'Chantelle. She's back in Australia.'

'Oh, that's lovely! With her boyfriend?'

'She's broken up with him.'

The bond of friendship between Rob and Chantelle had deepened with the death of her brother. Sam's loss was so much a part of him that Rob was able to understand a lot of Chantelle's pain. They both now belonged to the nameless club of people who have lost brothers. Within a year they were living together, engaged to be married and discussing what type of kitten they'd like to add to their household. Intense research was carried out over the internet. A British Blue, perhaps, or maybe even a Siamese.

When they stayed a night at the house of Chantelle's Aunt Trudy, who'd introduced them nearly ten years earlier, the resident Burmese insisted on sleeping on their bed.

'No way am I living with a pedigree kitten,' Rob said next day. 'That cat spent the whole night talking to me, telling me to get out of his bed.'

'What *is* it with you and cats?' I said.

'Dunno. Guess it's a Cleo thing.'

I smiled, remembering six-year-old Rob cradling his brand-new kitten, how she'd helped him sleep alone in his bedroom for the first time without Sam, 'spoken' to him through his dreams and helped him develop friendships. Watching over him for nearly a quarter of a century, Cleo our cat goddess had presided over countless birthday parties and nursed Rob through illness. From her resting place under the daphne bush, she was still exerting her influence.

If and when Rob and Chantelle do acquire a cat, Rob says, it'll have to be an ordinary mog. I wouldn't be surprised if it turns out to be a crossbreed with just a whisker of Abyssinian.

The Beginning

Acknowledgements

Every kitten belongs to a litter. Likewise, Cleo's story would never have been born without help from many wonderful people. I'd like to thank Lisa Highton and her magnificent team at Hodder in London for embracing Cleo with such enthusiasm. Thanks to Heather Rainbow for combing through my prose so carefully. And to Louise Thurtell and Jude McGee in Sydney who believed in our cat story from the start. They provided unwavering support through various forms of self doubt, along with an unexpected health hiccough while I was writing the book.

I'll always be grateful to Cambridge University for offering life-changing glimpses of another world, and to the dedicated people at the British Museum who provided inspiration in their preservation and presentation of the Gayer-Anderson Cat.

Huge thanks to Roderick and Gillian Deane, who encouraged me to write about Cleo in the first place. And to Douglas Drury for soothing lunches during what seemed, to a superficial 500-word-story journalist, long months of writing. Julie Wentworth, the world's best yoga teacher, deserves a salute for her flowers and phone calls that arrived just when they were needed. As does Sarah Wood for regular laughs over cups of coffee, along with Heather and Mano Thevathasan for countless acts of kindness. Big hugs to my sister Mary for her loving care during my recovery. And a purr to Liz Parker, Jenny Wheeler,

Judy McGregor, Lindsey Dawson and other exceptional editors I've known.

Thanks from the depths of my heart to Philip, Rob, Lydia, Katharine, Chantelle and Steve for allowing me to share my version of our story with the world. Given the chance to write from their personal perspectives, there's no doubt each tale would unfold differently. Their trust and generosity is boundless. An extra high five goes to Philip and Katharine for taking over cooking, shopping and laundry duties, and Lydia for her heavenly massages.

The deepest bow is for Cleo who loved us with all her heart for so long.

www.helenbrown.com

rSP	3/10
KE	3/13